ENCOUNTERS
REAL LIFE READING

TODAY'S BEST
NONFICTION

ENCOUNTERS
REAL LIFE READING

Montreal

The Reader's Digest Association (Canada) ULC
1100 René-Lévesque Blvd. West
Montreal, Québec H3B 5H5.

Printed and bound by R.R. Donnelley.

www.readersdigest.ca

CONTENTS

THE WHALE WARRIORS

On board a pirate ship in
the battle to save the
world's largest mammals

PETER HELLER

' The hull was 'ice-reinforced', meaning
strong enough to push through moderately
thick ice, and ideal for ramming.
The *Farley* was a ship of war.
Whatever intentions her owners had
when she was built in Norway in the summer
of 1956, whatever fishing fleet pedigree was
expressed in her stout lines, she had been
transformed by the will of her present captain.
No wonder the Japanese Institute of
Cetacean Research had announced that
they were afraid of an attack
by a Sea Shepherd vessel. '

1

STORM

A T THREE O'CLOCK on Christmas morning, the *Farley Mowat* plunged off a steep wave and smashed into the trough. I woke with a jolt. The hull shuddered like a living animal and when the next roller lifted the stern, I could hear the prop pitching out of water, beating air with a juddering moan that shivered the ribs of the 180-foot converted North Sea trawler.

We were 200 miles off the Adélie Coast, Antarctica, in a force 8 gale. The storm had been building since the morning before. I lay in the dark and breathed. Something was different. I listened to the deep throb of the diesel engine two decks below and the turbulent sloshing against my bolted porthole and felt a quickening in the ship.

Fifteen days before, we had left Melbourne, Australia, and headed due south. The *Farley Mowat* was the flagship of the radical environmental group, the Sea Shepherd Conservation Society. The mission of her captain, Paul Watson, and his forty-three member all-volunteer crew was to hunt down and stop the Japanese fleet engaged in what he considered illegal commercial whaling. He had said before the trip, 'We will non-violently intervene,' but from what I could see of the preparations conducted over the last week, he was readying for a full-scale attack.

I dressed quickly, grabbed a life jacket and ran up three lurching flights of narrow stairs to the bridge. Dawn. Or what passed for it in the Never-Night of the Antarctic summer: a murky gloom of wind-tortured fog and snow and spray—white eruptions that tore off the tops of the waves and streamed long streaks of foam. When I had gone to sleep four hours earlier, the swells were twenty feet high and building. Now monsters over thirty feet high rolled under the stern and pitched the bow wildly into a featureless sky. The timberwork of the bridge groaned and creaked. The wind battered the thick windows and ripped past the superstructure with a buffeted keening.

Watson, fifty-five, with thick, nearly white hair and beard, wide cheekbones, and packing extra weight under his exposure suit, sat in the high captain's chair on the starboard side of the bridge, looking alternately at a radar screen over his head and at the sea. He had a gentle, watchful demeanour. Like a polar bear. Alex Cornelissen, thirty-seven, his Dutch first officer, was at the helm, steering north-north-west to run with the waves. Cornelissen looked too thin to go anyplace cold, and his hair was buzzed to a near stubble.

'Good timing,' he said to me with the tightening of his mouth that was his smile. 'Two ships on the radar. The closest is under two-mile range. If they're icebergs they're doing six knots.'

'Probably the *Nisshin Maru* and the *Esperanza*,' Watson said. He was talking about the 8,000-ton Japanese factory ship that butchered and packed the whales, and Greenpeace's flagship, which had sailed with its companion vessel, the *Arctic Sunrise*, from Cape Town over a month earlier, and had been shadowing and harassing the Japanese for days.

Watson had found his prey. He turned to Cornelissen. 'Wake all hands,' he said.

IN 1986 THE International Whaling Commission (IWC), a group of seventy-seven nations that makes regulations on whaling around the world, enacted a moratorium on open-sea commercial whaling in response to the fast-declining numbers of earth's largest mammals. The Japanese, aggressive whalers since the food shortages following World War II, immediately exploited a loophole that allows signatories to kill a number of whales annually for scientific research. In 2005, Japan, the only nation other than Norway and Iceland with an active whaling fleet, decided to double its 'research' kill from the previous year and allot itself a quota of 935 minke whales and ten endangered fin whales. In the 2007–2008 season it planned to kill fifty fins and fifty endangered humpbacks. Its weapon is a fleet comprising the 427-foot factory ship *Nisshin Maru*; two spotter vessels; and three fast killer, or harpoon, boats, similar in size to the *Farley Mowat*.

Lethal research, the Japanese say, is the only way to accurately measure whale population and health, and is essential for the sustainable management of the world's cetacean stocks. The director general of Japan's Institute of Cetacean Research (ICR), Hiroshi Hatanaka, writes, 'The marine resources in the Southern Ocean must be utilised in a sustainable manner in order to protect and conserve them for future generations.' Though the ICR is a registered non-profit organisation and claims no commercial benefit, critics point out that the meat resulting from this heavily subsidised research ends up in Tokyo's famous Tsukiji fish market, and on the tables at fancy restaurants. By some estimates, one fin whale can bring in $1 million.

Each year the IWC's Scientific Committee votes on whaling proposals, and in 2005 it 'strongly urged' Japanese whalers to obtain their scientific data 'using non-lethal means'. The whalers' response was silence, then business as usual.

Although this resolution is not legally binding, much of the public was outraged that the whalers would openly disregard it. The World Wildlife Fund contended that all the research could be conducted with techniques that do not kill whales. New Zealand's minister of conservation, Chris Carter, among others, described the research as blatant commercial whaling. Even dissenters within Japan protested: Mizuki Takana of Greenpeace Japan pointed to a report issued in 2002 by the influential newspaper *Asahi,* in which only 4 per cent of the Japanese surveyed said they regularly eat whale meat; 53 per cent had not consumed it since childhood. 'It is simply not true that whaling is important to the Japanese public,' Takana said.

To Watson there is no debate. The Japanese whalers are acting commercially in violation of the 1986 moratorium. Even more controversially, the whaling occurs in the Southern Ocean Whale Sanctuary, an internationally ordained preserve that covers the waters surrounding Antarctica and protects eleven of the thirteen species of great whales. And although the killing area in 2006 lay almost entirely within the Australian Antarctic Territory, the Australians seemed to lack the political will to face down a powerful trading partner.

It irks Watson that Australian frigates will eagerly pursue Patagonian toothfish poachers from South America in these waters, but will turn a blind eye to the Japanese whalers. 'It sends a message that if you're rich and powerful you can break the law. If the Australian navy were doing its job,' he said, 'we wouldn't be down here.'

Watson has no such diplomatic compunctions. He said, 'Our intention is to stop the criminal whaling. We are not a protest organisation. We are here to enforce international conservation law. We don't wave banners. We intervene.'

Whaling fleets around the world know he means business. Watson has sunk eight whaling ships. He has rammed numerous illegal fishing vessels on the high seas. By 1980 he had single-handedly shut down pirate whaling in the North Atlantic by sinking the notorious whaler *Sierra* in Portugal and three of Norway's whaling fleet at dockside. He shut down the *Astrid* in the Canary Islands. He sank two of Iceland's whalers in Reykjavik harbour, and half the ships of the Spanish whaling fleet—the *Isba I* and *Isba II.* To his critics he points out that he has never hurt anyone, and that he has never been convicted of a felony in any country.

I HAD FIRST met Watson the May before, at the Telluride Mountain Film Festival. He stood in front of 1,000 people in a large auditorium and told a story.

'In June 1975, sixty-five miles off the coast of Siberia, Bob Hunter and I ran our Zodiac between a Russian whaler and a small pod of panicked, fleeing grey whales. We were the first to use a Zodiac in this way. The whalers fired a harpoon over our heads and hit a female whale in the head. She screamed. There was a fountain of blood. She made a sound like a woman's scream. Just then one of the largest males I've ever seen slapped his tail hard against the water and hurled himself right at the Soviet vessel. Just before he could strike, the whalers harpooned him too. He fell back and swam right at us. He reared out of the water. I thought, this is it, it's all over, he's going to slam down on the boat. But instead, he pulled back. I saw his muscles pull back. It was as if he knew we were trying to save them. As he slid back into the water, drowning in his own blood, I looked into his eye and I saw recognition. Empathy. What I saw in his eye as he looked at me would change my life for ever. He saved my life and I would return the favour.'

Silence. Watson let the image sink in like a rhetorical harpoon.

He then said that the Japanese were still aggressively whaling and that he was going to go after them in his ship. He said the ocean is dying: of seventeen global fishing hot spots like the Grand Banks, sixteen have collapsed beyond repair. He said there are now only 10 per cent of the fish stocks that were in the ocean in 1950. He said we should stop, every one of us, eating all fish. There was an uncomfortable stirring in the crowd.

'I don't give a damn what you think of me,' he thundered. 'If you can find me one whale that disagrees with what we're doing, we might reconsider.'

Watson had been among the founders of Greenpeace in 1972. His encounter with the grey whale off Siberia had been part of Greenpeace's first voyage to protect whales. In 1977 he broke away to form the Sea Shepherd Conservation Society, because he wanted to specialise in direct interventions against illegal exploitation of the ocean.

In the last thirty years, Sea Shepherd has been running

campaigns at sea to stop illegal whaling, drift-netting, long-lining, dolphin slaughter and sealing. The organisation, based in Washington state, gets donations through media attention and word of mouth. Pierce Brosnan, Martin Sheen and Christian Bale are generous supporters. As Watson quipped, 'With James Bond, the president and Batman on my side, how can I lose?'

At the end of his talk Watson invited me to come with him to Antarctica as a journalist, and I accepted.

2

THE *FARLEY MOWAT*

5 DECEMBER 2005

The Australian Customs official at Melbourne airport looked up for the first time since scanning my passport and paperwork.

'You're staying in Australia: "a couple of days—not sure"?'

'Right.'

'What does that mean?'

'Well, several days. Probably.'

'Local address the *Farley Mowat*. Never heard of it.'

'It's a ship.'

'What kind of a ship?'

'It belongs to the Sea Shepherd Conservation Society. It's a conservation ship.'

A flicker of suspicion. 'Like Greenpeace, is it?'

'No, sir, not exactly.' It would not be prudent to tell this official that Sea Shepherd made Greenpeace look like Sunday school. Or that several sovereign nations, including Norway and Japan, as well as the US National Fisheries Institute, had levelled charges of piracy against Sea Shepherd and its officers. The Norwegian navy had depth-charged and badly damaged the society's last ship. The Soviet navy, when there was one, had once come within seconds of machine-gunning a Sea Shepherd crew into the Bering Sea. Only the miraculous appearance of a grey whale surfacing and blowing between the ships had defused the situation.

'What then, exactly?'

'Have you seen Jacques Cousteau?'

The man's eyes did not move. The tip of his tongue touched the corner of his mouth. He was wavering between getting mean and deciding to enjoy himself. He waited. It was a bad analogy anyway. Watson was about as far from the benign, grandfatherly Cousteau as you could get. Cousteau loved people. Watson once said that the life of a human being is worth less than the life of a worm. Time and again he had offered up his own life, and the lives of his crew, in defence of a whale. He had written, 'The pyramids, the Old Masters, the symphonies, sculpture, architecture, film, photography . . . All of these things are worthless to the earth when compared with any one species of bird, or insect, or plant.

The officer waited. 'I'm on assignment for National Geographic *Adventure*,' I said. 'I'm covering the Sea Shepherd campaign against the Japanese whaling fleet in Antarctica.'

Truth has a certain resonance. The man's face softened. 'That sounds pretty interesting.' His right hand went to the stamp.

'Antarctica, eh?' he said, handing me back my passport. 'Be careful.'

THE TAXI TURNED onto the street along the wharf at the foot of Port Melbourne. All around the harbour, skyscraper apartment buildings were going up. There, tied to the dock in the bright sun, between piers covered with the umbrellas of bars and restaurants, was a hulk of a ship with a Jolly Roger flapping lazily from her bow. The skull was inset with a circling whale and dolphin, and instead of crossed bones, there were a shepherd's staff and a triton.

The *Farley Mowat*, while only one-third the length of the factory ship she would be hunting, and one-tenth the tonnage, was still over half a football field long. She radiated both nobility and menace. She was completely black, stem to stern. The only colour was the yellow letters on the side that said 'seashepherd.org'. Forward of the bridge, the main deck held three fast Zodiacs—inflatable outboard-motor boats—and two jet skis in their cradles. The hull was 'ice-reinforced', meaning strong enough to push through moderately thick ice, and ideal for ramming. Water cannons bristled off the bow and the helicopter deck, which was a steel second level over the aft deck. The cannons were there to prevent boarding. When I arrived the ship was crawling with crew, all dressed in black T-shirts. Knots of tourists milled on the pier and stared.

The immediate impression of the *Farley* was a ship of war. Whatever intentions her owners had when she was built in Norway in the summer of 1956, whatever fishing fleet pedigree was expressed in her stout lines, she had been transformed by the will of her present captain. The *Farley* had a maverick, menacing air. No wonder the Japanese Institute of Cetacean Research had announced as the whaling fleet left Shimonoseki harbour on 8 November that they were afraid of an attack by Sea Shepherd.

Two pick-ups with pallets of sacked food pulled up to the gangplank amidships. Another truck backed up and three construction workers in union shirts got out to talk with a skinny crew member on the wharf. He seemed to be the one in charge, so I lugged my duffels over the pavement and waited to introduce myself.

As I stood in the drubbing sun and inhaled the dense, intoxicating smells of harbour—of salt, rot, tar, diesel—my eyes wandered over the ship that would be home for the next month. The long arm of the port davit, or crane, swung over the main deck and was being hooked to a rope harness on the port Zodiac. A young woman with wild, curly blonde hair, who wore tattered khaki shorts, yelled orders from a raised platform that held the davit controls. At the wheel of the Zodiac stood a strong kid with black glasses and red dreadlocks under a tied bandanna. In the centre Zodiac, getting a harness ready, was a guy in a military buzz cut, talking into a radio strapped to his shoulder. He was in full black

SWAT gear: cargo pants, black boots, and a military utility vest that held radio, knife, flashlight and a dozen pockets.

'You the National Geographic guy?' I turned. Another crew member: he had a deep tan, broad shoulders and the grave eyes of a wolf. He had grease smeared on his neck, and another military haircut.

'Yeah. Hi.'

'Let me show you your cabin.'

He hefted the duffels like they were two pillows. I followed him through an open gate in the bulwarks of the main deck. He turned and dropped down steep steps into the bowels of the ship. A narrow companionway lit by fluorescent ceiling lights. Immediate press of close heat and mould, the astringent sweetness of diesel fumes. He pushed through a red curtain and swung the duffels onto the bunk. Someone else's gear was already on it.

'Steve.' He shook my hand with a crushing grip. 'I'll have Geert move his stuff.'

Steve vanished. A moment later a tall, gangly biker with a bushy dark beard tumbled into the tiny cabin. On the official crew manifest Geert Vons was listed as 'Ship's Artist'. Smiling over his beard, he gathered up an armful of battered pack, one dirty blanket and pillow, and a sketch pad, and tumbled out again. A few minutes later I saw him on the dock. He was a tattoo artist in Amsterdam. He worked above the Hell's Angels bar, and drove a motorcycle. He had completed a degree in Chinese and was now doing research with a Chinese scientist on the Baiji dolphins of the Yangtze River. He created illustrated children's books on marine wildlife. He seemed like an unlikely Hell's Angel associate.

This was Geert's third campaign with Sea Shepherd. He had been on the last Antarctica campaign in the winter of 2002, when the *Farley* had patrolled the ice edge for a month and never laid eyes on a Japanese ship.

We watched a knot of Japanese tourists reading the public education placard at the foot of the gangplank and then, remarkably, drop some money into the blue plastic whale. One of the union guys called out to the skinny officer, 'Where you want the welding rod, mate?' I noticed that his shirt said, 'Electrical Trade Union. If You Don't Fight, You Lose.'

I asked Geert about the cannons.

'They can't put too much pressure in them, because the pipes are old. But for effect it's still quite good.'

The pipes wouldn't hold the pressure because they were rusted out—because the ship was fifty years old and was being run by an organisation on a shoestring.

'The hull, the bottom—is that rusty too?'

'Last March, on the seal campaign, the hull had a strong leak. The two bilge pumps couldn't catch up. It was off the ice, Newfoundland. Alex dived down with a wood—like a carrot—and plugged it. They found the bottom was all scattered with rust spots, thin like paper. They patched everything in Jacksonville,' he said benevolently, patting me on the back.

Geert went off to his day job—illustrating the logbook up in the chart room.

THE CREW HAD dropped two of the Zodiacs into the harbour and used the central crane to open the steel doors to the fish hold beneath the deck. Out of the hold they were now hoisting the oddest contraption. The thing looked like a Monty Python creation, two parts engine and fan blade, one part rubber dinghy. A hulking man with grey hair and heavy steel glasses limped around the opening yelling orders in a twangy tenor. He caught his breath.

'What is that?'

'FIB. Flying inflatable boat.'

'It flies?'

The man smiled. 'It has wings. Thirty-six-foot span— hoh!' The blonde pulled back on a lever and the FIB thing dangled. The man squinted at it. 'I'm an ultralight pilot. They sent me down to Florida to get familiarised with it. The hardest part is getting it out of here and on the water.' He talked in a rush and peered up at the machine. 'Theoretically, I should be able to handle bigger seas, and the helicopter can handle a lot more wind. Have to land and take off on the water. When there's enough wind for me to take off from the deck, it's too windy to fly. I'll be limited to ten knots. I'll go up as high as I can. The helicopter can go one direction and I'll go the other.'

I could not imagine getting the Thing out of its cocoon and launched in the rough seas of the Southern Ocean. Much less flying in those winds off Antarctica that sailors call 'sudden busters', gale-force blows that scream out of nowhere.

'Chris Price,' the pilot said, and held out a ham of a hand. 'You can ride with me. That little seat behind the pilot.' He grinned as if he was doing me the biggest favour in the world.

'Thanks.'

I turned to go aft and bumped into a short, broad-shouldered, clean-cut guy in his mid-thirties.

'Crazy dude, huh?' he said. 'Personally, I wouldn't use that thing as a stepladder.'

This was the helicopter pilot, Chris Aultman. Before the trip I had asked Watson how he hoped to avoid the washout of the 2002 campaign. How did he know he would find the Japanese whaling fleet in all that ocean?

Watson had responded almost cryptically, 'Well, we're working on getting a helicopter.' Now, apparently, they had one, though I hadn't seen it anywhere.

The 'research' area the Japanese planned to hunt in the 2005–2006 season spanned 35°E to 175°E, in an arcing swathe from the coast of Antarctica, out to 60°S, some 300 miles off the ice. Approximately 1.4 million square miles. Imagine that you are in a car and your job is to find a convoy of a semi-trailer and five pick-ups in all that area. Which way do you go? You have radar, effective out to about twenty miles. Your jalopy goes only ten miles an hour and you have only fifty days' worth of fuel. And there are no cities or towns in the entire region. No grocery stores, no garages, not even a place to replace a blown tyre. One more thing: among the provisions you brought with you, there is no meat or cheese or eggs. The *Farley Mowat* was a vegan ship. You wouldn't find in her holds even a single preserved fish.

Chris Aultman seemed eager to talk about his craft, a little Hughes 300. He was an instructor and commercial pilot out of John Wayne Airport in Orange County, California. He had seven years' experience in a helicopter, but he'd never flown off a moving deck.

We would be picking up the bird in Hobart, Tasmania, on the way south. He said, 'Due to economic restraints we do not have a mechanic on board. The helicopter just went through an annual mechanical inspection. Made as ready as can be. From that point on—if it breaks, the show's over.'

Of all the jobs on the ship, he had, by far, the most dangerous. Piloting a temperamental whirlybird out of an airport with a full maintenance staff is brave enough. Flying off a spray-lashed deck on a corkscrewing boat in the absolute middle of nowhere is another thing altogether. The *Farley* only went nine or ten knots. If Aultman had to ditch, say, eighty miles from the ship, it would take eight or nine hours for the ship to reach his vicinity—if, that is, the crew knew where the hell that was. Aultman said that the chopper had pontoons, so the protocol in the event was to stay in the aircraft as long as possible.

Just then a kid stepped up—a beanpole, maybe twenty-one years old, with a black ponytail and a near-sighted squint behind little wire-rimmed glasses. He was Peter Hammarstedt, the second officer, a Swede. He said, 'Chris, we've got some solid rubber for you. It's three centimetres.'

The kid left.

'Donated rubber. Unbelievable. That stuff is so expensive.'
'Who donated it?'
'The union guys. A bunch of them were working on that apartment building up there. They saw the ship and got curious. We gave them a tour and ever since they've got about every trade union in Melbourne supporting us.'

He explained that the rubber was for the helipad. 'Pitch is not a problem.' He rocked his hand forward and back. 'It's the roll that's the problem. Side to side. I'm going to plant the helicopter on the deck—no messing around making it pretty.' He slapped his hand down on the rail. 'But it takes a second or two for the full weight to get on the skids. If the ship rolls at that moment it will slide. That's where the rubber will help.'

If Aultman was forced down on one of his sorties, I wondered how the officers of the *Farley* would ever find him. 'They'll know where I'm going to be,' he said. 'I'll call them every five minutes with my position. That keeps the search area narrow, about a five-square-mile grid. I'll also have Epurb on board. If I turn the Epurb [EPIRB] on that'll give a smaller search area.' An Epurb is an emergency signal beacon. None of this seemed very comforting.

'Paul knows their killing fields, so to speak. They are thousands of square miles. Which field they'll be in is anyone's guess. But I can see a lot of ocean. If I can get up to three- to five-thousand feet I should be able to see sixty nautical miles on either side of the helicopter. A lot of ocean.'

But in an area the size of the American West, it was a hair's breadth.

Chris was an ex-marine, a Southern California kid who liked to surf the breaks north of San Diego. He had taken two months off work, left his wife in Long Beach, and volunteered to risk his life along with a bunch of vegans.

'You must love whales,' I said.

'They shouldn't be killing them. It's wrong and they shouldn't be doing it.'

THERE WAS plenty of action on deck. Two of the hands were jumping into a garbage pail barefoot and marching in step. Some good Samaritan had donated a heap of ripe grapes. 'We are making ze wine for ze New Year party!' one announced with glee. Note to self: drink no homemade wine on the *Farley Mowat*. Other crew members had got the FIB Thing out and into the water and Price was tearing up and down the inner harbour, albeit without wings. Red Dreads was doing slow doughnuts in one of the purple jet skis. It died and he hand-paddled it back to the rope ladder.

'Our armada's not looking too good,' he called up. I asked a tall, big-boned woman what was wrong with the jet ski.

'Wrecked it going into Henderson Island. Got caught in a wave.'

She smiled and held out a hand tattooed with a leaf. 'Inde,' she said. 'That's my forest name. My normal name is Julie.'

She said that she and Red Dreads, whose forest name was Gedden, aka Jon, did a lot of forest actions with Earth First! Mostly they set up tree sits, to protect areas of forest slated for logging. Last winter she had sat in a Douglas fir for six weeks.

'On a branch?'

She laughed. 'On a platform suspended from ropes.'

'How do you get the first rope up there?'

'Bow and arrow.'

I SAW WATSON ambling down the dock. He was wearing the khaki belted jacket I had seen when I first met him. The same shaggy grey hair and beard.

He looked jovial, like a man about to embark on a great vacation. In fact, he was about to go and do what he loved most in the world—set off on the high seas to intervene in what he deemed illegal exploitation of marine species. Coming into Melbourne two weeks before, the port control had radioed to ask Watson what class of vessel the *Farley Mowat* was. 'Yacht,' he'd replied. Vessel class is a serious matter: merchant ships incur much higher port costs, from pilot to dock fees, and—perhaps more importantly—they require officer and security certifications. Later, as the pilot brought the ship into the inner harbour, port control said, '*That* is a pleasure craft?'

'Why, sure,' Watson said. 'We enforce international conservation law. I take great pleasure in it.'

If a harbourmaster gave him a hard time, he pointed out that he carried no cargo or paid passengers. 'Tiger Woods's yacht is bigger than we are, and carries more crew,' he would say.

He went up the gangplank without casting more than a glance at the hubbub on the deck. He'd learned long ago to leave the details to his crew. I followed him to the bridge. The bridge was all business: a narrow, wood-lined control room that stretched from one side of the superstructure to the other. Thick Plexiglas windows wrapped the cabin. In front of the high, captain's chair on the starboard side was an inset, revolving pane, which allowed visibility in a lashing storm. At the captain's left hand was a chrome lever that controlled the ship's speed. Sophisticated electronics were arrayed all across the forward bulkhead under the windows: three radar systems, Global Positioning System (GPS) screens, three radios with mics mounted to the ceiling or deck head, gyrocompass with electronic autopilot, a handheld electric control on the end of a thick cord with thumb-button rudder controls. Against the aft bulkhead, or back wall, was a traditional brass spoked wheel for manual control of the rudder should hydraulics fail.

Watson tossed his head to get a thick shock of grey hair out of his eyes. 'Find your cabin okay? It's a bit Spartan around here.' I thought my cabin was deluxe. It had a desk, a sink, a full-size bunk, a locker and a glow-in-the-dark poster of the southern constellations taped to the ceiling. I'd half expected something from *Master and Commander*—a hammock slung among a crowded 'tween decks.

But if Watson was concerned about how I'd like my accommodations, I understood. Media relations were a preoccupation with Watson. He'd written a chapter on it in his book *Earthforce! An Earth Warrior's Guide to Strategy*. He recognised that the only way for an environmental movement to accomplish anything was to get the word out. Ramming one illegal Taiwanese drift-netter wasn't going to save the 300,000 whales and dolphins killed in those nets worldwide every year; or halt the 7 million to 20 million tons of 'bycatch' thrown overboard—animals obscenely killed and wasted—by longliners and trawlers and other fishing boats. Nor would sinking eight whalers stop whaling. But the international attention focused on the issue might bring pressure to bear. 'If you have an action and no one covers it, it didn't happen.'

He'd used the strategy masterfully in stopping the slaughter of baby harp seals on the ice of Newfoundland in 1984. Watson had staged confrontations with sealers that drew media attention. And then he'd brought Brigitte Bardot onto the ice for her famous picture with the baby seal. The starlet on the cold snow holding the defenceless fuzzy white pup, and the pup's huge, trusting, liquid black eyes had iced it. An outcry ensued and sealing was shut down for ten years. But it came back with a vengeance. Since 1994 the Canadians have been killing up to 350,000 young seals annually, and almost every year Watson is there on the ice with his ship to try to intervene. It frustrated Watson that most people knew nothing about it. The press seemed no longer interested. The recent advocacy of Paul McCartney was just beginning to renew public interest.

In Watson's book, in the chapter on 'Preparations' the section headed 'Deception' read like a credo. It was basically Watson's MO.

> All Confrontation is based on deception. This is called the strategy of tactical paradox.
> When you are able to attack, you must seem unable.
> When you are active, you should appear inactive.
> When you are near, you should have the enemy believe you are far. And when far, near.
> Bait the enemy.
> Pretend to be disorganised, then strike.
> If the enemy is secure, then be prepared.
> If the enemy be of superior strength, then evade.
> If your opponent has a weakness of temper, then strive to irritate.
> Make a pretense of being weak and cultivate your opponent's arrogance.
> If your opponent is at ease, then ensure that they are given no rest.
> If the forces of your opponent are united, then seek to divide them.
> Attack when the enemy is unprepared.
> Appear when you are not expected.
> The leader who wins makes careful plans.

This section was immediately followed by one called simply, 'Preparation for Death'. 'The Earth Warrior, like all warriors, must be prepared for death . . . you can expect any direct or indirect strategies from government forces including your own assassination.'

All this seemed a bit grandiose. Watson, after all, was not marshalling an army to attack the Russian White House. But then he had used many of these very tactics to pull off, for instance, the complete blockade of the Canadian sealing fleet at the harbour entrance to the port of St John's in Newfoundland in 1983. He had faced down the Soviet Union's navy, and had made one of the very few known unauthorised incursions onto Soviet soil along the Siberian coast without being molested. That was serious business.

Was he being paranoid about government attack and assassination? Greenpeace, during its campaign against nuclear testing by France in the South Pacific in 1985, had been infiltrated by a French agent who supplied intelligence to a team of French commandos. On 10 July they blew up the Greenpeace ship *Rainbow Warrior* in Auckland harbour, killing a photographer. Sea Shepherd had been infiltrated by a slew of informers including an FBI agent who worked as an engineer, and an agent of the Canadian Surveillance and Intelligence Service. Of the FBI informer, Watson said, 'He did a pretty good job. If the FBI wants to pay people to work in our engine room that's fine with me.'

I asked Watson, with so much at stake for the Japanese, if he ever worried about the kind of sabotage that took place on the *Rainbow Warrior*.

Watson looked out the bridge windows at the deckhands trying to get the second jet ski started. 'Greenpeace is so big today because of the *Rainbow Warrior* sinking. That kind of thing would backfire on them.'

'You said in one of your books that you thought you'd meet your end at the hands of an assassin. Do you still think you're going to die by the sword?'

'Oh, I don't know. It doesn't matter anyway. Better than dying of some debilitating disease.' He chuckled.

'How do you plan on finding the Japanese fleet?'

He glanced at me sideways. 'No guarantees, of course, but I think we have a very good chance. I'll show you.' He swung his feet onto the deck and led me into the chart room just aft of the bridge. A small-scale chart of the whole of Antarctica and the Southern Ocean lay spread on the table. A pencil and a parallel ruler lay on the chart.

'There are certain sectors they're operating in. I'm pretty confident they've got to be one hundred to one hundred and twenty miles off the ice pack. That's where the whales are. This time of year the krill blooms are along the edge of the ice pack, and the whales are after the krill.'

'The minkes, fins and humpbacks are all baleen whales?'

'Yeah, but we call them piked whales; we don't call them minke whales. We try to get around naming whales after their killer. No matter what person you name them after, it's an insult. The right whale was named the "right whale to kill". Cachelot meant "catch a lot".'

He leaned over the chart.

'Here is Area Three. You're really looking at a corridor here. Bring the ship down the corridor and then you have aerial surveillance.' He swept two fingers in an arc along the coast between Commonwealth Bay and the Shackleton Ice Shelf. 'Greenpeace is heading from South Africa, going to Areas Two and Three. That's where the Japanese are supposed to survey for their "research". But we got word that three days ago they were spotted off the Kermadec Islands, which means most likely they're going here.' He moved his fingers much further east, almost to the ice-filled indentation of the Ross Ice Shelf. 'So we're looking at an area between about one hundred and sixty degrees east to one hundred and ten degrees east. From Hobart it's about six days to the Virik Bank.'

'So the helicopter is your most important asset in this regard.'

'Well, we've also got the stations down here, the French and Australian, on the lookout; plus the supply planes will help out. Senator Lynn Allison is going to bring up a motion in the Australian senate to help us with intel.'

'And if you find them, they just run away; they are so much faster.'

'Well, you have to catch them when they're transferring whales to the factory ship. They have to slow down to a speed of five or six knots.'

Later I walked up the hill into the warm bustle of downtown Melbourne. The quixotic nature of the whole enterprise was becoming painfully clear. I sat at an outdoor café and made a list.

One, the *Farley Mowat* was on her last legs.

Two, the crew were very brave or nuts. Half of them had never been to sea. The pilot of the FIB Thing was a hang-glider. The chopper pilot had never flown off a moving deck. The Japanese factory ship the *Nisshin Maru* was ten times larger than the *Farley Mowat* and could go 50 per cent faster. The *Nisshin Maru* also had five other, even faster, ships in escort.

Three, 'Aggression on the high seas', as a thirty-year navy veteran had recently informed me, 'is grounds for immediate and deadly retaliation'.

Four, the odds of finding the fleet were low.

Five, the entire world was against Watson, even if only through inaction. The Japanese were taking endangered whales out of an internationally established whale sanctuary in Antarctic Territory claimed by Australia, and Australia did nothing. Nobody else did anything either. Watson was vastly outnumbered.

Six, nobody on the ship gave a damn about odds or allies or anything else but stopping the whalers from killing.

The killing of a whale by modern methods is cruel beyond description. An exploding harpoon, meant to kill quickly, rarely does more than rupture the whale's organs. It thrashes and gushes blood and begins to drown in its own haemorrhage. It is winched to the side of the kill ship and a probe is jabbed into it and thousands of volts of electricity are run through it in an attempt to kill it faster. The whale screams and cries and thrashes. Often, if it is a mother, her calf swims wildly around her, doomed to its own slow death later on. Again, the electricity fails to kill the whale and it normally takes fifteen to twenty minutes of this torture for the whale to drown and die.

Whatever one thinks of whales' high intelligence, the advanced social structures, the obvious emotions and the still mysterious ability to communicate over long distances, this method of slaughter would not be allowed in any slaughter-house in the world.

For the crew of the *Farley Mowat* that was enough.

I MISSED my first dinner on the ship. Meals, I was told, were served at 0800, noon and 1800. I found Geert outside and we walked up the wharf chatting like old friends about the day. On the front of his T-shirt was a buxom beauty cupping her breasts and underneath: 'Scientific whaling? Right. And these are real.'

'Did you do that?'

'Yah, see, that's my trademark. "Whale Weirdo".' His arms were covered with tribal tattoos, Polynesian and Inuit motifs all having to do with the sea. Over dinner Geert shared some of his thoughts about the Vipassana Buddhism that he practised. It was imperative to him to do no harm to anything. That was the first precept. But he was also an expert in kung fu. Buddhist, biker, vegan, black-belt, children's illustrator, eco-pirate.

At the ship, Watson was hanging out with the crew. A semicircle of Shepherds sat on the dock on overturned crates or in folding chairs, and drank beer in the breezy summer warmth. Watson stood on the main deck and leaned against the rail and told jokes. He told blonde jokes, feminist jokes, Irish jokes . . . If it was politically incorrect he told it.

In a rare silence, someone asked if Greenpeace had encountered the Japanese.

'Not yet. Not according to their website. The crew blog today said it was really difficult making banners in the heavy seas. Yeah, right.' He shook his head. 'I've been asking them for months if we can cooperate. With their speed, their ability to keep up with the fleet, and our intervention we could be twice as effective. I've emailed Shane Rattenbury, who is on the *Esperanza* leading the expedition—either they don't respond, or they're superior and snotty. "Sea Shepherd does not meet our threshold of non-violence." We've never injured or killed anyone. What I want to know is, how is damaging property used in illegal activities violent?' He tipped his head back. He was getting warmed up.

'They've never forgiven me for calling them the Avon ladies of the environmental movement. They called me an ecoterrorist. I tried to shrug it off. I was referring to their armies of door-to-door fund-raisers.'

'They don't believe in the destruction of property,' said Alex, the first mate. He shared a crate with the blonde who had been giving orders all day on the deck. Her name was Kalifi.

'What will they do if they encounter the whalers first?'

'Take pictures. That's all they ever do.' Watson drained a can of Foster's and crushed it in his bear paw. 'If they were really interested in stopping the whaling they'd work with us. They come down here, take a lot of pictures of whales being slaughtered, and use them to raise a pile of money. They don't stop a single whale getting killed.' Watson was almost soft-spoken in his telling, but the heat of his anger radiated from him the way it does from a desert rock at night.

A taxi pulled up. A kid with reddish, gelled hair got out. Freckles. A thick, twisted mouth. Tired circles under his eyes. He sauntered up to the ship. You could see he was a scrapper. 'Captain,' he nodded.

'How'd it go?' asked Gedden. 'You have that winning glow.'

'Up three hundred. Justin and Joel are still at the table.' His name was Jeff Watkins. He had a New York accent. They'd been on the ship a week and every night after dinner he and his two buddies from Syracuse—Justin Pellingra and Joel Capolongo, the 'J. crew'—hit the casino in Melbourne. Back home they were committed animal rights activists and professional gamblers who made a good portion of their income playing poker. They had joined the ship as a squad.

I went to bed. I tumbled down the steep steps and pulled the curtain on my snug cabin. Under a musty flannel sleeping bag I lay in the close dark and looked up at the glow-in-the-dark poster of the southern constellations taped to the deck head.

Somewhere far to the south and west of us the monstrous black *Nisshin Maru* was entering a world of ice, slipping its steel bulk through the drifting icebergs, scattering its catcher and spotter ships to look for prey. They must be very close by now.

From Africa the two Greenpeace ships were sailing east. Soon the *Farley* would be pounding south, as fast as she could. No love lost between the three groups.

Nine ships tugged to the bottom of the world by herds of

warm-blooded creatures that slipped through the same ice and breathed the same air, that spoke to each other in songs we could not decipher—who must have known, after decades of being hunted, that their season was come.

I think it's safe to say that the whales did not want to be found by their hunters. The Japanese did not want to be found by Greenpeace or Sea Shepherd. Greenpeace evidently did not want to be found by the *Farley*. The *Farley*, which could match no one's speed, would not want to be seen, would want to sneak up on her prey and catch it unawares. Everybody, in some way, was running and hiding. Their agendas, however, were written bold in the media and in their own releases. I knew that Greenpeace was doing a good thing, exposing the sham of 'scientific' whaling, and not endangering any lives. Sea Shepherd I wasn't so sure about. Watson was an unknown quantity, and his tactics at times were scary.

In 1979, Watson had found the pirate whaler *Sierra* in the waters off Portugal. The whaler was the worst offender in a dirty business. Barred from ports around the world for violating international conventions on whaling and endangered species, and for not paying bills for fuel and provisions, it roved over the globe taking every whale it came across. It had changed its name and flag numerous times in ten years. It was manned by a crew of alleged criminals: numerous countries had issued warrants for their arrest. It often came into port at night and left in the dark before morning. It sold the meat to Japan. By Watson's estimate, in a decade of poaching whales it had been responsible for the slaughter of 25,000 animals. When Watson caught the ship he rammed it at full speed and tore open the hull to the waterline. The next year, after $1 million in repairs, two unnamed operatives sank it at dockside using limpet mines.

No more whales would be killed by the *Sierra*. Watson got a taste for the immediate, undeniable results of direct 'enforcement'. He and Sea Shepherd moved on to the *Astrid*, another pirate whaler operating in the Atlantic. They put out a $25,000 reward for its sinking. The ship was sold out of whaling, as the owners felt they could no longer trust the crew. In 1986, Watson commissioned two men to sink two Icelandic whalers in Reykjavík harbour. What did he mean when he told the Australian press he wasn't going to ram the Japanese, but he was going to stop them? That's what he did: in port he sank ships, scuttled them, or blew them open; on the high seas he rammed.

Live by the sword, die by the sword. When I woke up the next morning, disoriented in the close dark, I found myself in my clothes and remembered: ship rules required all crew members to sleep in their clothes, even in port, as it can take only forty-five seconds for a ship to sink, and those extra seconds getting dressed could cost you your life. I thought again about the *Rainbow Warrior*, and the risk of being sabotaged in port, and what a close, dark tomb would be my berth beneath decks.

3

FINAL PREPARATIONS

7 DECEMBER 2007

The counter was covered with loaves of fresh bread, jam and oatmeal. Behind the counter a pretty, forty-something blonde in dish gloves scrubbed a stack of bowls and bantered with the crew as they filed past. I introduced myself.

'Allison,' she said, and gave me a level, searching look. No nonsense—everything about her, from the short haircut to the visual pat-down. She held out her hand, still appraising me, then realised it was gloved and soapy, smiled and shrugged.

Allison Watson, wife of the captain. In 2003, she and the first mate, Alex, had jumped with knives into a net-caged bay in Taiji, Japan, and freed dolphins that had been corralled there for slaughter. Every year, the locals slaughtered between 2,000 and 3,000 dolphins and continue to do so. The slaughter is part of the 23,000 permits issued by the Japanese government annually for small cetaceans. Allison and Alex were promptly arrested. In 2003 Allison had been hauled before a grand jury in the United States in connection with Animal Liberation Front (ALF) and Earth Liberation Front (ELF), two groups high on the target list of the FBI's anti-terrorism units. She had refused to testify and been charged, oddly, with perjury. To her, everybody was potentially a fed or a foreign agent, and wariness meant survival. And she was nothing if not straightforward. When she first met Watson, after a talk he had given in southern California, she shook his hand and said, 'My name is Allison Lance and I'm going to marry you.'

The mess had four booth tables. A mural of an underwater scene with whales covered one wall. The opposite, starboard side, had two portholes. Crew members who couldn't fit at the tables spilled into the green room beside it; another cabin with tables and long cushioned banquettes, and the pride of the *Farley Mowat*—a big-screen, surround-sound entertainment centre. One whole wall was taken up by a shelf of DVDs and videos.

I squeezed in next to the first mate, Alex, who ate quickly, barely listening to the conversations around him. Chris Price, the pilot of the FIB Thing, turned out to be a cross-country trucker from Memphis, Arkansas; he was saying, 'Craziest town in the world. In my town they rob the people who buy drugs!'

Alex said, 'We have a lot to do this morning. We are going to move to another dock and refuel. Hopefully the DC motors are done and we can leave tomorrow. Basically, that means everything has to be tied down.'

He had been with Sea Shepherd three and a half years. He admitted that it was a very short time for someone with no previous open-ocean experience to become first officer, but he said that in Sea Shepherd you learn fast. Hair shaved almost to stubble, thin neck and cheeks. The perfect complement to Watson. I sensed the same engine of deep anger humming inside him. Alex said he'd seen Watson lecture in Europe. 'I was so impressed with it all I decided I had to join.

At the time I had a partner and mortgage payments, and a contract—I'm a graphic designer. I planned to join for a year. I came back to Holland and spent two months at home. It drove me nuts, so I came back. Too many campaigns I still want to do.'

The buzz of activity was increasing. Marc Oosterwal, the big welder from Amsterdam, was crouched on the steel heli deck drilling three-inch holes across which he'd later weld rods to make attachment points for hooks to strap down the chopper. A few feet away an assistant in fatigues wire-brushed rust off the edge of the deck so Marc could weld anchors for safety railings. The railings would hinge down when the helicopter came in to land to give it an open deck.

Up on the monkey deck—the flat roof of the bridge at the top of the superstructure, which held the three radar masts and the twenty-foot tower of the crow's nest—a compact worker in a sleeveless flannel shirt and union cap was tying down electrical cables, drilling and screwing fasteners, and moving to the next with professional speed. This was Sparky Dave DeGraaff, one of the construction workers who had seen the ship from the top of a building and come by. He was a master electrician and shop steward for his union, responsible for the safety and well-being of dozens of electricians on his job. He was coming with us.

'I was working on that apartment building. We came over and said, "What you need?" They said, "We need an electrician." I get laid off six weeks at Christmas anyway so it worked out well. I thought, What a great cause. I always wanted to go to see it down there. I thought this is it, I've got to go.'

Most of this diverse crew were here because they'd heard Watson speak. Something in the man and his message compelled people to drop everything—jobs, loves, homes—and follow him to the ends of the earth on missions that offered no guarantee of return. It was the simple moral power of hearing someone say, 'I know whaling is wrong. I know killing every living thing in the crippled, gasping ocean is wrong. I don't give a damn about bogus science and legal considerations. I know stopping the killing is the right thing

to do and I am going to stop it, devil take the consequences.'
Watson did it because he believed it was the right thing to do.
Period.

So they came to the *Farley* from every corner of the globe.
The trouble was that certain persons and governments did
not believe in Watson's initial premise, that what he was
doing was the right thing.

LATE THAT MORNING, the crew moved the ship, slowly, to a
more industrial dock less than a mile across the inner harbour.
A tanker truck backed in and emptied itself into some of the
Farley's seven fuel tanks. The driver left and returned. He
made three trips: 110,000 litres of diesel: US$56,000. Watson
figured that his 130,000-litre total capacity was enough to go
fifty days, if the weather wasn't too bad.

We were getting close. The morning of my third day in
port, the op-ed page of Melbourne's daily, *The Age*, featured
a long letter: 'Australia Must Not Surrender to Japanese
Piracy.' Watson blasted:

> Has the Australian government decided to prostitute its
> sovereignty to grovel at the feet of Japanese business . . . ?
> All it will take to save the whales is for one Australian
> naval vessel to confront the Japanese fleet in the territory
> and simply order it to leave. Or are we afraid that the
> Japanese will simply laugh openly in our face because they
> are certainly laughing behind our back now.

Bold move, especially with the *Farley* still in port and with
one more stop, in Hobart, scheduled on the way south. It was
not inconceivable that a pissed-off Australian government
could find some pretext to detain the ship. But Australians
loved their whales: 1.5 million people went whale watching in
Australia every year. Maybe he was gauging public opinion,
which was overwhelmingly against the Japanese, and applying just the right amount of heat. It seemed he couldn't resist
pricking the authorities wherever he went.

Watson had grown up on the rocky coast of Canada's New
Brunswick in a village with the lyrical name Saint Andrews by

the Sea. It was at the heart of a major lobster fishery. He was one of seven children, the eldest. His father was a cook in local restaurants. He was abusive and beat Watson severely when he was a child. Young Paul was fascinated by the sea, but not by fishing. From an early age he abjured any killing of animals.

The town was on a peninsula surrounded by woods. Watson said he spent his childhood running over the forests and brooks, jumping into swimming holes, raising as much hell as a basically sweet kid could raise in the country. He said he and his friends used to play cowboys and Indians with air rifles and bows and arrows, and once he shot a companion in the butt with an air rifle because the boy was about to shoot a bird. They used to run out and lie on the railroad tracks, squeeze into a low place between the rails and let the trains run over them. They'd crouch just beside the road during a heavy snow and let the fast ploughs bury them. It was a wonder any of them survived. Young Paul was 'an activist member' of the Kindness Club, a local humane society; he ran the trap lines in the woods and rivers around the town and freed the animals.

When Watson was eleven, his father left the family and went to Toronto. Watson's mother died two years later. Watson never forgave his father for leaving his wife alone with all those kids, for not being there when he was needed, for letting her die.

The family moved to Toronto, to the father's home, and Watson proceeded to spend the next few years running away. Once he was sent to a Catholic home for wayward boys, where the nuns punished his irreverence by making him sit in tubs of ice. It's not hard to see where Watson got his contempt of authority: first from his father, then from the church. All pain came from the ones who made the rules.

The last time he left home, he was sixteen. His father began to beat him and Watson decked him, walked out of the house and never looked back. At seventeen he hopped a freight train to Vancouver, where he met up with a group of environmental activists who were protesting the nuclear tests on Amchitka Island, Alaska—the group that would later become Greenpeace. He took classes at the city college and soon began going to sea, working on a Canadian coast guard weather ship, then joining a Norwegian merchant ship that took him to Asia and the Middle East. He continued his education on the decks of ships, and in the stacks of books he took with him. He was an ardent lover of poetry, admiring Spenser, Whitman and Coleridge, and he could not read enough about world history and religion. Later he would write, in a passionate repudiation of the crimes inflicted on the world's creatures: 'To the Earth Warrior, a redwood is more sacred than a religious icon, a species of bird or butterfly is of more value than the crown jewels of a nation, and the survival of a species of cacti is more important than the survival of monuments to human conceit like the pyramids.' He would say that all of the arts—music, poetry, architecture—were as dust when compared with the survival of a single species of bird or insect.

BACK AT THE SHIP they were loading aviation fuel for the chopper. Eighteen fifty-five gallon drums of it. Enough for seventy-five hours in the air. The deckhands wheeled them on a dolly to the port side of the open poop deck and lashed them in with heavy straps. The gasoline was highly combustible. Our little fuel depot was directly under the landing zone of the helicopter . . . in case of an accident, any flying debris . . . I didn't want to think about it.

On the night of 9 December, the cry went through the ship that we were leaving the next morning and that everything had to be 'tied down'. All personal items in the cabins had to be stowed and secured. All supplies, all tools, all utensils—everything, down to the last spoon and coffee cup—had to find its place, and its place had to hold the item securely against a thirty to forty degree roll, perhaps more. Squads went through the ship with rope and carabiners, straps. They went into the fish hold and lashed the FIB Thing into submission on its frame. In the same hold, they cinched and bound the long, heavy beams and rods of steel—twelve-foot lengths of four-inch T-bar and angle iron, rebar—and the stacks of lumber used in framing and repairs. On either side of the poop deck aft, under the heli-deck, they strapped down the rows of steel drums: jet fuel to port, lube oil to starboard. Books and videos snugged into their cabinets. Kitchen knives, into their drawered slots. Navigation rulers onto their racks. Sacks of turnips and potatoes were lowered into dry storage, a hole aft of the mess and down a vertical ladder to the lowest deck. Crates and crates of boxed soy and rice milk squeezed into compartments under every bench seat in the mess and green room. Out on the low open main deck the jet skis were lashed into their frames. Further forward, the Zodiacs were tarped and lashed neatly into their cradles. The efficiency of the old hands, the ones who had been on board for the long crossing from the Galapagos, was impressive. Gedden, Colin, Inde, Ryan, Kalifi and Steve: they tore from one end of the ship to the other and in two hours it was done. You could have picked up the ship and shaken it upside down and the only thing falling out would have been a few Australian coins. Maybe a small poster of the southern constellations.

I went down to my cabin and put boots into the locker and laptop into a drawer that was fitted with a shock cord. Then I met Ron Colby, one of the documentary film-makers, and we strolled down the pier, heading for a last hamburger before the vegan wasteland of Antarctica.

Ron is a veteran Hollywood producer and director, in his sixties but seeming much younger, lean, tough, sardonic, with a resonant voice and a way of observing and listening that disarmed everyone he met. He knew everyone and had done everything, and wouldn't talk about it unless you tortured him into it. He produced *The Outsiders*, among other films.

We walked into the first Greek restaurant at the head of the wharf, and were seated next to three hardened-looking young men in black pirate T-shirts—Ryan, Steve and Colin.

'We will eat all the meat they put in front of us,' Colin smiled. Turned out he was a butcher from the Inter-Lakes district outside Winnipeg.

Steve said, 'On the way from the Galapagos we pulled out an old tin of roast beef to cook and Inde and Laura cried.'

We ordered souvlaki, burgers, steaks.

That night I took welder Marc's four-hour security watch at the gangplank. He was really taken with a local woman; it was their last chance to spend time together.

'You got lucky,' I said.

'Yeah, I don't get lucky like this. Good to have a bit of luck.' His broad face with the lamb-chop sideburns cracked open in a big smile. He picked me up by the shirt like a bag of laundry and set me down. 'T'anks,' he said and jogged down the gangplank to find his girl.

I sat at the top of the gangplank in a chilly onshore wind and watched the harbour's seagulls enact a bizarre feeding adaptation. They flitted in and out of the arc lights along the dock, catching insects. They weren't very good at it. They tried to snap and veer like swallows and overshot and missed. I could see the panicked insects. In swallow country the insects would be already dead, but here their odds looked about fifty-fifty. The gulls swooped and pulled up and fluttered awkwardly. They hadn't evolved for this kind of thing. But there must have been enough food, because they kept at it for hours. They seemed a bit like Sea Shepherd, doing the best they could with what they had and not too worried about how it looked.

The next morning I was woken by the deep throb of the *Farley*'s 1,400-horsepower diesel engine, and within two hours we were casting off ropes and turning south for the bay.

The *Farley*, once out from the mouth of the Yarra River and out into the stiff south-west wind of the open bay, began to roll with a gentle, easy rhythm you knew she was born to. After two years of preparation, after a previous Antarctic campaign that was a bust, after patchwork repairs all over the ship, after reading the Greenpeace blogs from the *Esperanza*, which sailed closer and closer to the whaling fleet while the *Farley* was held in port by one maintenance issue after another, Sea Shepherd had a last loosed her on the tide. She was gaited for the gales and heavy weather of the North Sea; and as old as she was, the *Farley* bore south towards the rip in the South Channel with vigour. She was heading almost due south, towards the Southern Ocean and the worst seas on earth.

We got to the narrow rip between the Victorian headlands just after 1300 (1:00pm). We could see the surf pounding on the outer beaches. A dangerous spot strewn with wrecks. The *Farley* banged through the steep chop of the channel, taking water over the bow and a gush through the main hatch that flooded the long companionway, and nosed out into the Bass Strait and the Tasman Sea.

Watson set a course of 131 degrees, south-east, to Tasmania. That put the south-west swell directly on our starboard beam and the eight-foot seas rocked us like a swinging cradle. Geert and I lashed a couple of beat-up wooden chairs next to the life raft pod on the stern and watched the sun lower behind us. A twenty-knot wind blew the tops off the whitecaps and rained them downwind. The sky was bell clear. A half-moon rose out of the sea.

At dinner, in the mess, a free seat was uncharacteristically easy to find. Hardly anybody was eating. Most of the crew who were there picked gamely at their tofu goulash and stared vacantly at the tabletop or the wall. Seasickness can be completely debilitating. On the aft deck, two-thirds of the J. Crew, Justin and Jeff, sprawled in a row of wrought-iron theatre chairs bolted to the deck just aft of the main stack and facing astern. Others stumbled out of the hatches and went straight for the rails, and if they remembered to go to the downwind side they were lucky.

Side rolls were the worst. Most of the bunks were oriented forward and aft, so even the crew who took to their beds had to brace themselves in and hold on to keep from getting thrown to the deck.

Our registered nurse was philosophical. 'It'll pass, I'm sure,' she said. 'I hope.' She didn't look so good herself. Kristy Whitefield was an emergency room nurse in Melbourne. She was five feet in her bright red socks, maybe ninety pounds. Her wild dreadlocks added another couple of inches. She wore rainbow-striped leg and arm warmers she had made herself. She moved around the ship like a brilliant jungle bird whose nest is on its head. 'I didn't bring motion sickness medicine,' she said. 'You just can't bring enough.' Another animal rights activist, she told me she did 'hunt sabs'— actions sabotaging hunters—during the opening days of Australia's duck season. Before dawn she and her compadres waded into the frigid waters under the loaded guns of the hunters, and banged pots and pans, and yelled. She'd been punched, held underwater, threatened at gunpoint.

On the way forward, I passed a lanky figure leaning against the superstructure smoking a cigarette with the relaxed pose of a man leaning on a lamp-post. There was an easy grace in the way he shifted his weight with the roll. He wore dark blue coveralls and red ear protectors propped on his closely cropped head.

'Nice night,' he said.

'For some of us.'

He laughed softly. 'They'll straighten out.' The way he said 'out' I knew he was Canadian. 'Best weather we may get all trip.'

He introduced himself, Trevor Van Der Gulik, the chief engineer. He was thirty and had been coming on campaigns with Sea Shepherd since he was fourteen; he was Watson's nephew—his mother was Watson's sister. Trevor now lived with his Iranian wife on the same rocky coast of New Brunswick where Watson had spent much of his childhood. He had worked on many ships, and had been a supervising engineer in the largest private shipyard in the world, in Dubai. Often he'd had 500 mechanics under him. They worked on diesel engines three storeys high.

'Good money,' he said. 'I should have stayed, but then I wouldn't get to do this.' He smoked, and we watched the stars swing towards and away from the black horizon. 'I live for this,' he said.

Trevor was one of the three paid officers on the otherwise all-volunteer ship. The others were the second engineer, and the first mate, Alex. Trevor said he went to school for his marine engineering technology degree when he was nineteen. He'd already been at sea on and off for five years, so it was easy—all he had to do was buckle down and learn the maths and thermodynamics.

'It's all about the transfer of heat and energy. Energy cannot be created, which makes sense to me. It's always moving from available energy to unavailable energy. But that doesn't mean it's unavailable to the universe. Entropy is the measurement of unavailable energy. I love entropy.'

Trevor rocked off the bulkhead and stood square on his feet. 'Working in the conservation movement, it's all about how we use energy in society, how much we use per person per day. Back in pre-industrial times, we grew our food—or were hunter-gatherers. We may have used an ounce of coal or two in one day. Now we'll use five litres of gasoline to hop into the car and go get cigarettes. May use five pounds of coal per day. Only so much energy on the planet. More we use, the less there is. Inevitably we will have earth death, because there is no more available energy on the planet. Up to us to make sure it's as slow as possible. Entropy. I've got to go take care of some right now. In my Entropy Room. So we can burn a bunch of available energy to do a good thing.' He went through the hatch that led straight down to the engine room.

At some point in the night we would cross into the 'Roaring Forties'. A year earlier the Bass Strait had turned back 57 out of 116 yachts that attempted the Sydney-to-Hobart race. A dangerous stretch of water.

THE MOUNTAINS of Flinders Island, visible at daybreak off port. Australian gannets following the ship, swooping over the wake. Seas calm as we enter the Roaring Forties, still rolling on the beam. By the doorway to the mess was a cork board. Tacked to the board was the following announcement:

If you are unhappy about the way this ship is run, it is simple . . . get off! Discord usually starts with a couple of people and snowballs. This will be our most aggressive and ambitious campaign ever. Therefore we all need to be in sync. Thanks—Allison.

The Enforcer. Seemed a bit late, the part about getting off, unless people marooned themselves in Tasmania. That was not out of the question. Watson had abandoned crew before, in foreign ports, without hesitation, when he thought they lacked the proper discipline or commitment and jeopardised the mission. The import was clear. Dissension would not be tolerated. Watson liked to quote Captain Kirk of the Starship *Enterprise*: 'When this ship becomes a democracy, you'll be the first to know.' The first whiff of grumbling, like a thread of smoke from the forest duff, had been stomped.

The forty-four-member crew was divided, roughly, into four areas: bridge, deck, engine and galley. The bridge and engine room were the only divisions that had scheduled rotating watches, because someone had to be at the helm and manning the machinery 24/7. For the engine room, this meant that Trevor was down there almost every hour when he wasn't sleeping or eating.

The bridge was served by three four-hour teams that rotated around the clock. Captain Watson took the watch from 8:00am to noon; the second officer, Hammarstedt, took noon to 4:00pm; and Alex, the first officer, took 4:00 to 8:00pm. Then Watson again, 8:00pm to midnight, and the rotation began again. Day in, day out. All ships use twenty-four-hour time, so that meant 0800 to 1200, 1200 to 1600, 1600 to 2000, 2000 to 2400, 2400 to 0400, 0400 to 0800. Each of the officers had two quartermasters on his watch to steer the ship when required—as through ice fields. Often the steering was done by autopilot, while the quartermasters monitored the radar, the radio and the ship's position; plotted the position every hour on the chart and entered it into the ship's log, along with speed, current heading and relevant notes about weather, fuel, etc. And kept a sharp lookout for ice, whales and ships.

Especially ice. The waters of Antarctica are exceptionally treacherous, for not only are the winds pouring off the continent the strongest on earth, and the seas the most volatile—three oceans meet, and there is nothing around the whole girth of the continent for thousands of miles to impede their fury—but in the Antarctic summer the calving glaciers and deteriorating bergs litter the waters with drifting ice of every description. Most perilous for the *Farley* were the 'growlers', large chunks that floated just at the surface and were hard to see until you were right on them, especially in fog, especially in heavy swells. The bridge watch, once we got down to the ice, would have its hands full. A pair of good marine binoculars sat in a small cabinet on the port side of the bridge, and would be used constantly by the quartermasters.

Spotting ships on radar in icy waters was another demanding job. The main radar, set into the bridge console, could be set out to sixty-four miles, but it could discern objects with any usable clarity only out to about twenty miles. Also, it is very difficult to tell an iceberg from a ship.

The engine room was the concern of Trevor, the chief engineer; his assistant, the second engineer, Willie Houtman; and four engineers. This allowed for continuous rotating shifts of two men, as needed. The engine room had two decks, or levels, and was a universe unto itself. The 1,400-horsepower Mann German-made diesel they tended had seven cylinders and was twenty-one feet long. The men who worked on it lived in a cloistered din of exploding pistons, racketing valves, thrumming generators—pumps, hydraulics, cams, gears, all clamouring at once, all the time. All these engines and motors and pumps dripped oil, water and fuel constantly, so one of the engineers was pretty much a dedicated swabber. Trevor could stand nothing less than a spotless Entropy Room: he hated a greasy handrail or metal step.

It was monastic down there and, as with many such fraternities, it fostered in the engineers an esprit de corps unlike any other watch on the ship. On a quiet evening you'd see two or three of them on deck just outside their hatch, ear protectors propped on heads, grease-smeared and pale under the grime, smoking cigarettes. You got a sense that for Willie, a twenty-two-year-old Kiwi who joined the ship when he was eighteen, the engine room was a sanctuary, that he'd rather be there than anywhere else.

Trevor could stand in the middle of the thunderous din, eyes closed, and pick out the smallest tic, a hitch in cadence, or a shift in key, and know where to go and what to tweak. On the bridge, in a storm, in the middle of a raucous conversation, he could go suddenly still. 'Lube oil separator,' he'd say and disappear. In the same way, he could be down in the engine room and have a good idea about decisions being made on the bridge: he'd be working figures with fuel tank tables and look up and say, 'They just changed course, about twenty degrees off the weather.'

All things deckwise were under the command of the bosun. Kalifi Moon Ferretti-Gallon was the young woman I'd seen yelling orders and running the davit crane in port. She had plucked eyebrows and a fine aquiline nose, and was fond of wearing pyjama bottoms and pink thong sandals adorned with sequins. Her curly blonde hair was uncontrollable. She was twenty-two, was part-way through college, and came from Montreal, where she had most recently been working as a barmaid and was not sure what to do with her life. Her father, Gary Gallon, started Greenpeace with Watson in 1972, and was a large presence in the international environmental movement. He had died two years earlier, at fifty-eight, of cancer. Kalifi said, 'If he knew I was bosun, in charge of the deck, saving whales, he'd be really proud.' She had been on the ship for six months—this was one of the longest continuous stints among the present crew—and she had worked her way up swiftly into the cadre of officers. Her current boyfriend was Alex Cornelissen, the first officer.

By a happy coincidence, Kalifi's best friend, Emily Hunter, twenty-one, of Toronto, was also on the ship. Emily's father was also one of the pioneers who started Greenpeace with Watson, and also a major figure in the international environmental movement. He died of cancer too, just six months before the *Farley*'s departure for Antarctica, and Emily had his ashes with her to be spread amid the ice and the whales of the Antarctic seas. She said, 'I know the trip is dangerous. I don't want to die, of course; I'm very young. But if I die helping to save a whale, that would be okay. That would be a good way to go.'

Under Kalifi, in command of the deck, was the bosun's mate, Colin Miller, the very focused former butcher from outside Winnipeg. who never went to work on the ship without his SWAT vest. He carried headlamp, tools, knife, radio. At home, on Sunday nights, Colin does serious Close Quarter Breach tactical training—for fun. 'Sweep and clear kind of thing, two teams.' He also trained in Malaysian knife fighting. ('Did you ever see the movie *The Hunted*?') He uses a curved knife called a Karambit with a finger ring for extending reach. 'There is nothing beautiful about knife fighting,' he said. The style, which uses a lot of hand blocks, originated with slaves fighting in the Philippines. 'Being a butcher—' he said, 'the transition to cutting up a person is not that different.'

Colin was universally respected. He never asked a hand to do something he wouldn't do; he was even-tempered and patient in teaching the greener crew. He never got irritated and he never complained. He was a perfect team player.

There were eight deckhands. Three of them were the J. Crew, the gamblers from Syracuse who were now on the aft deck, retching. The deckhands were responsible for rope handling; docking and casting off; launching and manning the attack Zodiacs; securing the jet skis and inflatables; tying down everything on the decks and in the holds; handling the anchors and chains, davits and knuckle boom; and painting, fibreglassing and maintaining almost everything, including the general cleanliness of the *Farley*. They were the backbone of the crew. Their headquarters was the bosun's locker, an all-purpose workshop just off the main deck at the front of the superstructure. The aft bulkhead or wall of the bosun's locker was solid with shelves of milk crates full of cord, rope, cable, shackles, nuts and bolts and chain.

Laura Bridget Dakin, twenty-two, horse trainer and champion endurance rider, was the chief cook. She had a second and a third cook working beneath her, and a galley assistant, who happened to be Allison. Cooking three vegan meals a day for forty-four people, on surfaces that are often rolling twenty degrees or more, might seem a daunting task, especially for someone who had never done any kind of institutional cooking before embarking on the ship last June in Bermuda. But Laura was not easily ruffled. In Victoria, Australia, where she spent much of her childhood, she regularly rode brutal 100-mile races on horseback, many miles of which covered rough and dangerous terrain in the pre-dawn dark. The reports that the Japanese were beginning to kill whales fired her blue eyes with a ferocity that was unnerving.

Her second cook, Roberta Kleber, was an enigma. She came from Brazil, but her accent was German, as were her name and appearance. Her town in southern Brazil had 6,000 citizens, all of whom spoke German. Four generations. She was very quiet and a hard worker. She was hitched up with Gunter Schwabenland, quartermaster and Sea Shepherd photographer, who came from another town of German-speakers in the south of Brazil.

The third cook was Casson Trenor. He was the only person on the ship who had an iceberg's chance in hell of beating Watson at Trivial Pursuit, or solving one of the captain's arcane riddles. Watson's favourite after-dinner activity was to pull out the battered box from the game shelf in the mess; pluck out a brick of stained Trivia cards; pass them to Hammarstedt, who would read the categories and questions; and then whip the pants off of all comers. Watson had an astounding head for historical, scientific and geographical minutiae. Which was evident when he lectured the young quartermasters of his watch on the taking of Persia by the Mongols, the taxonomic relationships of prehuman primates, or the deficiencies of the medieval pope Boniface VIII.

The only one who sometimes beat Watson was Casson. He was lean, slouching, handsome, twenty-six, recently of Monterey, California. He held a master's degree in international environmental policy, and a chef's certificate from the esteemed Pacific Culinary Institute in Vancouver. He spoke fluent French, Arabic, Spanish and passable Japanese. He also knew Latin. He had worked for the Conservation Strategy Fund advising developing countries in the South Pacific how best to spend their limited conservation funds. For those island nations, because they are so bounded and their natural resources so circumscribed, environmental conservation is more obviously a matter of economic life and death than for almost any place else in the world. Introduce one giant African snail that kills off 70 per cent of your cassava, and your economy is wiped out—and your livelihood, your health, your very lives are in danger. Casson had also worked for Seafood Watch, which puts out the wallet cards that list which fish species are environmentally sound to eat. It's a very short list.

Casson believed, along with many of his marine biologist colleagues, that the oceans are on the verge of total ecosystem collapse. Consider: 90 per cent of the large predatory fish, the tuna, swordfish, marlin, sharks—vital to the health of ocean ecosystems—have vanished since 1950. The World Wildlife Fund recently announced that the world's fish stocks are on the verge of extinction. All the world's fish. Right now, half of the world's coral reefs are dead or dying.

'If the oceans die, we die, too—' Casson, at a table in the mess, chopping turnips, saying that much of the destruction is caused by bottom trawlers, the industrial dragnets that scour wide swathes of sea floor, taking everything—the octopuses, the sea turtles, the mammals, the crabs, the urchins—and damaging the reefs. The weighted nets are dragged in and the target species are thrown into the hold, while all the rest are chucked overboard, dead or dying. Wasted. Casson tells us that bottom trawlers scour an area twice the size of the United States every year. That between the longlines and bottom trawlers 7 million tons of thriving ocean life is tossed as bycatch annually. Hundreds of thousands of sea mammals—seals, dolphins, sea lions—are slaughtered and dumped; 100,000 albatross. So many of the widest-winged pelagic birds that they are now also threatened with extinction.

'Bottom trawling is like bulldozing the forest, killing everything in it, to get at the wild turkeys. That's what it leaves, a smoking waste. Longlining isn't much better. It's indiscriminate. Tens of thousands of sea turtles are killed and thrown overboard as bycatch each year. Seabirds, especially albatross, dive on the baited hooks and get dragged under and drowned. It's insanity. It'd be like going onto the African savannah and shooting every living thing, mammal, bird, that you see.'

Laura got up and retrieved a sheet of paper. 'Here, Peter,' she said in her genteel British accent. It was a printout of a forwarded email:

If you read the front-page story of the *San Francisco Chronicle*, you would have read about a female humpback whale who had become entangled in a spiderweb of crab traps and lines. She was weighted down by hundreds of pounds of traps that caused her to struggle to stay afloat. She also had hundreds of yards of line rope wrapped around her body, her tail, her torso, a line tugging in her mouth. A fisherman spotted her just east of the Farralon Islands (outside the Golden Gate) and radioed an environmental group for help. Within a few hours, the rescue team arrived and determined that she was so bad off, the only way to save her was to dive in and untangle her . . . a very dangerous proposition. One slap of the tail could kill a rescuer. They worked for hours with curved knives and eventually freed her. When she was free, the divers say she swam in what seemed like joyous circles. She then came back to each and every diver, one at a time, and nudged them, pushed them gently around—she thanked them. Some said it was the most incredibly beautiful experience of their lives. The guy who cut the rope out of her mouth says her eye was following him the whole time, and he will never be the same.

'How can they kill these creatures?' she asked. The earth is seventy-five per cent ocean. Why is this the only ship out enforcing environmental laws?'

Recently I had been in correspondence with Dr Sylvia Earle, the legendary oceanographer and marine biologist at the National Geographic Society. Earle wrote:

In half a century, we learned more about the ocean than during all preceding history, but at the same time, we lost more. In fifty years, half of the world's coral reefs have disappeared or are in a state of serious decline, ninety per cent of the large predatory fish have been taken—tuna, swordfish, shark, grouper, snapper, halibut, cod and many others . . . In coastal regions around the world, more than 150 'dead zones' have developed as a consequence of noxious substances we have allowed to flow into the sea . . .

The good news is that . . . people are becoming aware of the significance of the ocean to their health, their prosperity, their security, and most importantly, their survival in a universe where there are no immediate alternatives to sustaining ourselves on this water-blessed planet. With knowing comes caring, and with caring, there is hope that we'll find an enduring place for ourselves within the natural systems that sustain us.

There was cross-pollination between animal rights activists and conservationists on the *Farley*. Between Casson and Laura. They were all here together on this single battering ram of ship, which was hurtling like a very slow arrow towards its target. The marriage of the two groups, who are often seen at cross-purposes politically, was epitomised in the marriage of Watson to Allison Lance, who, together, ran the ship. 'He is a conservationist,' said Allison. 'He thinks seven hundred years in the future. I am concerned with each and every living thing that cannot speak for itself.'

She was a strict vegan. 'He is barely a vegetarian,' said Ron, the producer, who had known Watson for twenty years, since long before Allison came into the picture seven years ago. Watson had adopted the diet and now saw the link between animal rights and conservation. 'I think the consumption of domesticated animals is a major contributor to environmental degradation,' he said. 'And seafood—where there is simply not enough fish in the ocean, demand has exceeded supply.'

There are many ardent conservationists who believe that all whaling should stop, but who also think animal rights people are kooks. Watson said, 'I don't give a damn. Opposing hunting, opposing factory farming, is the right thing to do.' I wonder, though, on the *Farley*, how the groups are apportioned, or if there is any real division, aside from a difference in emphasis. Judging by the surreptitious meat eaters at the Greek restaurant in Melbourne the night before departure, I think there is. How many on the ship are vegan? How many are vegetarian? How many eat almost anything?

And does it matter? They were all on board, heading south to stop the whalers. All risking their lives in this one goal. Did it matter if one chose to eat an egg? Or honey? Or elk tenderloin?

Did it matter that on board Greenpeace's marine conservation ship, the *Esperanza*, the crew ate fish?

BRIDGE, ENGINE ROOM, deck, galley. The fifth division on the ship was the media. Of forty-four people on board, seven were journalists. There was Paul Taggart, the slight, 120-pound, twenty-five-year-old war photographer from Tulsa, Oklahoma. He wore wire-rimmed glasses and was clean-cut, sceptical, kind of quiet—but with nerves of Damask steel. The kid spent 300 days a year on the road in places like Baghdad, Monrovia and Banda Aceh, shooting the most horrific scenes. On the ship, no matter how dire the engagement or how bad the storm, he was unruffled. He climbed into the chopper with his cameras. Into the lead attack Zodiac. He got the shot.

'It's kind of nice,' he said, 'shooting an assignment that is not full of dead people.' He had a quiet, deriding laugh and a way of darting his gimlet blue eyes sideways when he heard something over the top. Which was all the time on the *Farley*.

There were three film-makers on the boat, shooting documentaries. Mathieu Mauvernay, thirty, of Paris, was one of the first crew members I encountered on the *Farley*, barefoot in a bucket, stomping grapes.

In March 2005, he had accompanied Watson onto the ice in Newfoundland in an attempt to stop the Canadian seal hunt, and he shot a powerful documentary that is very difficult to watch. Each year, since 1994, weeks after the harp seals give birth, Canadians stalk the ice with hackepicks, long poles with sharp picks on the end, and beat up to 350,000 six-week-old seals to death. Canadian fisheries claim that the seals are responsible for the decline in the cod fishery. Peter Hammarstedt, the beanpole second officer, said, 'The Canadians can't blame themselves for the decline in fish stocks, so they blame the seals. They claim the harp seal is killing all the cod. Just two hundred years ago there were forty-one million seals, now there are only about two million to four million. They certainly weren't killing all the cod!'

The second videographer, producer Ron, had been shooting a documentary of Watson on and off for years. On most days he parked himself in the one armchair bolted to the port side of the bridge. His video camera was on the deck beside him. He read *Walden*.

Kristian Olsen, the third videographer, was thirty-five, with boyish good looks and shaggy, straight blond hair. He was shooting Sea Shepherd for a Canadian film company.

Pawel Achtel was the other crew member who often had a camera on his shoulder. He landed a deal with the Australian Broadcasting Corporation (ABC) to cover the campaign. In exchange for exclusive use of Pawel's images it supplied the ship with a new satellite transceiver, which not only would transmit video clips and interviews over the internet but would give Watson instantaneous email and web surfing capability. ABC also gave Pawel $30,000, which the Polish-speaking Australian promptly handed on to Watson to help purchase the new helicopter. The twenty-year-old chopper cost $150,000 and was cheap at the price because it might be the key to the campaign's success.

Pawel was the world's leading expert on the filming of sea dragons. A sea dragon is a fish that looks like leaves and branches. Or rather like a sea horse dressed up for a costume ball at which the theme is Your Favourite Flora to Hide In. Sea dragons blend in so well with the weeds and corals of the reef that Pawel has been two feet away, staring straight at one of the creatures, and unable to discern it. He will mark the waypoint on his wristband GPS and return six months later and the fish will not have moved more than ten feet. His films of the sea dragons are magical and beautiful, as are his shots of big rays and sharks. He wanted to dive in the ice with leopard seals, perhaps the fiercest predators Antarctica has to offer.

Pawel brought with him a tall, square-jawed, quiet assistant named George Evatt. They were both forty-two years old; their birthdays a day apart. George was also a prominent underwater film-maker, who shot a lot of Australian footage for National Geographic and Discovery. These guys could suit up and be diving in the ice floes in a matter of minutes.

Emily Hunter, the wholesome, pony-tailed daughter of the recently deceased Greenpeace founder, was also shooting video, on assignment for CityTV in Toronto. So she was shooting video and taking notes as well. There was almost no place one could go on the ship without a camera whirring nearby.

The media on the ship had no assigned duties. You would not see a media person on the *Farley* swabbing the decks or cleaning the heads. Once in a while, Kristian or Mathieu would pitch in to chop a vegetable, but that was the extent of it. While everybody else was working, they could be found in the mess at their laptops, organising their video clips or photos, writing notes, drinking coffee.

Chris Price, the lumbering pilot of the FIB Thing, whose job was so limited by weather he might get to fly only a few times, was usually there too, regaling the impressionable media with stories that usually involved dead bodies and a government conspiracy. He always started out, 'Listen, wanna hear a story?' and ended with 'True, I swear. He's in the phone book, you can look him up.' About his job on board, he said, 'I have another role on the ship, too, but it's secret.'

And yet, like all embedded journalists everywhere, the media had to follow the rules in matters of safety, security, or general protocol. If the signboard outside the mess said, 'No email or phone calls today,' that applied to the press, too. Sort of. And if the captain ordered a media person to do something, like wake up and put on a life jacket, or not to do something, like take pictures of the engine room, he had to do or not do that, too—sort of. There was a kind of a freewheeling attitude in the *Farley*'s press corps. During communications blackouts when Allison forbade all outside contacts, Taggart lurched out onto the aft deck, knelt, as if before an altar, propped his laptop on the row of bolted theatre seats, fished out his personal Iridium satellite phone, waved it around for several minutes trying to get reception, and then conducted his commerce in emails. Some of the crew watched him with a touch of suspicion: could he be relaying the *Farley*'s position to an authority? Apprising someone of the ship's assault capabilities?

It was not too outrageous to believe one of us was a government agent: in June 2004 the FBI declared ecoterrorism to be a greater threat to domestic security than al-Qaeda. This was in response to actions like the Earth Liberation Front's burning of the lodge on Vail Mountain in 1998. It was Allison's connections to ELF, and to the Animal Liberation Front (ALF), that brought her in front of a grand jury. Others on the ship also had connections to ALF. Given the political climate and Sea Shepherd's record of aggression on the high seas, and given the public announcements that Sea Shepherd was going to stop the Japanese whaling fleet in Australian Antarctic Territory, I could think of at least three governments that might have been interested in having eyes on board.

Bridge, engine, deck, galley, media. There were some specialists on the ship, like Marc the welder, Kristy the nurse, and Geert the ship's artist, along with the two pilots, who reported only to the captain or his two mates. But it was all pretty loose and good-natured. The bosun's mate could pass Geert and Marc on the aft deck and say, 'Hey, can you give us a hand with the gangplank?' and they'd be glad to oblige. Usually they didn't have to be asked.

It costs a lot of money to keep a ship the size of the *Farley* afloat. Watson said that it cost $250,000 a month to run Greenpeace's *Esperanza* and *Arctic Sunrise*. Despite the generosity of his donors, Watson often didn't know if he had enough money to fuel up for a campaign until the tank trucks actually showed up at the dock. On at least one occasion, the local fuel company simply gave him tens of thousands of dollars worth of diesel with a smile and a 'Forget it'. Watson depended on the kindness of strangers and on the resourcefulness of his crew to keep the ship going. In port, it was every crew member's responsibility to keep a lookout for anything the ship could use. When possible, the crew scrounged and foraged for spare parts.

AFTER THAT FIRST breakfast at sea I went up to the bridge to check in. The captain was on watch with his quartermasters Lincoln Shaw and Lamya Essemlali. Lamya, whom everybody called Mia, was a biology student from France who got into trouble with her university for refusing to dissect a mouse. Watson was playing his favourite comedian, George Carlin, on the bridge stereo. The sun was on the water and the mountains of Flinders Island were six miles off our port.

Watson was sitting in his captain's chair, feet propped on the windowsill. I asked him what countries still actively whaled.

He said, 'The Inuit kill fifty-plus a year. In Alaska, Siberia. There's the Yupik on Saint Lawrence Island. Whaling nations are Japan, Norway, Denmark, United States (the Inuit), then Canada (Aboriginal), Iceland. There is a Russian hunt. The Faroese of Denmark kill three and a half thousand pilot whales. The Japanese hunt in the North Pacific in summer and Antarctic in their winter.'

Watson talks in bursts, in a persuasive rush of fully formed paragraphs.

'Our biggest problem over the years,' he continued, 'is how to control political correctness. Sometimes it gets out of hand. I had a Newfoundlander call me a racist the other day. The Makah Indians kill whales. If you're anti-whaling, you are anti-Makah, a racist. The one I like is, "You are a privileged white North American male." I was raised in a poor family with a bunch of kids.

'The Native American gets a free pass on environmental destruction. People don't realise that by eighteen-twenty the buffalo herds had been reduced by seventy-five per cent. The horse was displacing the buffalo, and the Indians went after pregnant cows. Estimated they took out four to five million buffalo a year. By eighteen-sixty the great herds were almost gone. By the time of the white hunters.

'Back to the Makah of Neah Bay. I was on the radio with a

Makah; he said, "We lived here from time immemorial, we are the people of the cape." I said, "Yeah, well—you came from Vancouver Island, you massacred the Ozettes, stole their land." Now the Makah said, "Oh, the Ozettes are our ancestors."

'In 1996 when we went into Neah Bay in the *Edward Abbey* [Sea Shepherd's converted Canadian patrol boat, which had since been donated to the rangers of the Galapagos], we met a canoe full of whalers in feathers. The Makah! In feathers! They never wore feathers.

'They said: "White man, you come with evil in your heart to interfere with us killing a whale that the people might live." The news cameras were rolling. I said, "You sell most of that whale meat to Japan."'

Watson was getting angry as he remembered. He shook his shaggy hair out of his eyes. 'I've seen Inuit on the Saint Lawrence Islands shooting walrus with M-16s for their tusks.'

Watson swung his feet to the deck and went into the chart room. Carlin cut off and a second later Wagner's *Ride of the Valkyrie* shook the bridge and blasted from the outside speakers over the decks—the same music that thundered from the squads of attack helicopters in *Apocalypse Now*.

4

HOBART

BY MIDDAY the coast of Tasmania came into view off starboard: low mountains covered with forest—eucalyptus, pine, gum trees—falling to cliffs and the sea. A few farms carved out of the slopes above the beaches. The ship alarm sounded, the crew scrambled for the aft deck, and we had our lifeboat drill.

It was brief.

The second officer, Hammarstedt, told us that if the boat sinks it will be most likely from a hull breach caused by an iceberg or another ship. He said the ship will take from twenty seconds to eight hours to sink.

He pointed to three lifeboat pods on port, starboard and stern. They were white fibreglass barrels, about half the size of a steel drum. Each would be commanded by one of the top three officers: Watson, Cornelissen and himself. He passed around the roster for the boats, and I noticed that I was with Watson. In fact, all the media were with the captain. In case of a sinking and lifeboats adrift, I guess he wanted to give daily press releases.

Hammarstedt said each raft was equipped with a knife, flashlight, enough water for about seven days. He said you just unclip the lashings and two hands throw it overboard, and it will explode open. 'Put on as many clothes as possible and grab water from the galley if you're there. Don't jump into the life rafts. Do not. They will fill up with water.'

The quick way in was to jump overboard and then climb into the raft. And the rafts? Given how the Zodiacs had functioned in Melbourne harbour, and how the jet skis did not function at all, I wasn't giving life raft deployment the best of odds. I could imagine tossing them over the rail and seeing an explosion of confetti and a banner that said 'Surprise!' Then Hammarstedt pointed to three waist-high black lockers on the deck. 'The immersion suits are in this locker, and the life jackets are in these two. There are a bunch of immersion suits. The rest will wear these Mustang suits, which are in the locker in the hallway outside the mess.'

The life jackets were bulky Mae Wests that felt as if they were filled with horsehair and newspapers. The immersion suits were orange neoprene coveralls with attached hoods, gloves and booties. Stiff with age, they did not look as though they would seal very well around the face, and if they did not seal, they would fill with water. Little Kristy, the nurse, stepped into the smallest one and disappeared inside it; her hood flopped empty like the Headless Survivor, only a few strands of dreadlock peaking out. Alex said, 'We'll try and find you a wet suit.'

The mustang suits were insulated nylon coveralls with no

seals at the wrists, ankles or neck. They would fill with water immediately and, without latex closures, the icy current would wash through them. They would be about as good as wearing a snowsuit in the thirty-degree Antarctic water. I was very glad I had my own dry suit. I decided that when we reached Hobart, I would buy my own life vest and a thick neoprene hood. If I was going to be in the water, I wanted some time to think about things.

'Oh,' said Hammarstedt, 'Don't take a leak off the stern. Seventy per cent of the bodies they've found at sea had their flies undone.' Man. Think of it. You make your way to the stern under the stars, the ship lurches, in you go, treading water as the running lights diminish. 'Even if someone saw you,' he added, 'it takes fifteen minutes to turn the ship around. You have less than two, so if you go overboard, you're dead.'

As the crew broke up, Ron approached Laura, who was standing on deck in her flip-flops, hugging herself. He held out a pair of sneakers. 'You'll need these where we're going,' he said. She brightened, then asked, 'Are they vegan?'

THAT EVENING, I climbed to the crow's nest twenty feet off the top of the superstructure and watched the sun set over the hills of Tasmania. A pale violet ringed the horizon just over the sea, scaling into luminous blues. A cry came up from the high forecastle at the bow. A mile off, a white thrashing on the port side. Off starboard, between us and the coast, another commotion. The two disturbances were closing, and then we saw the blue forms leaping. The fins, torpedo-fast, and the arching jumps. Two pods of dolphins, running to meet the ship.

I clambered down and across the main deck and up to the bow and squeezed in with a bunch of others to hang over the rail. They ran under the bow, turning right angles with no drop in speed, with the fluidity of water, catching the bow wake with no effort at all, ranging out in a weaving V of escort, skimming the surface and turning it to a rippled glass that magnified what seemed less form than pure blue motion. Then broke, as they leapt over each other and canted half over to cast one curious eye upward at the heads hanging over the rails. They blew in hollow gusts and kept up a commentary of light squeaks. Often they seemed not to move a muscle but maintained the nine knots by some contract with the sea, as if their whole being were a single thought: water-grey and swift; and a single emotion: breaking white glee. They had come to the ship like two squads of kids running to a big game of kick the can, which is exactly what we were.

Recently scientists have proved that dolphins can not only call each other by specific names, but in communication can refer to a third animal by name. They can form shifting alliances—a very sophisticated form of social interaction—and though they lack the part of the brain that governs self-awareness in humans, in controlled experiments with mirrors and body paint they prove to be extremely self-aware.

They seem fantastically superior beings: they don't spend too much time working for a living, they are social and expressive, they have a highly developed sense of fun—stories abound of dolphins sharing waves with surfers—and they don't trash their nest or decimate other species.

The Japanese issue permits to kill over 22,000 dolphins, porpoises and other small cetaceans every year. In Taiji, in Wakayama Prefecture, they corral the dolphins into a netted-off bay and club them, slit their throats and spear them. That the dolphins exhibit human-like traits of loyalty, valour and grief does not affect the fishermen; the dolphin being killed often cries out in front of his family members, who swim frantically around trying to defend him.

It is this killing that Allison Lance and most of the crew of the *Farley* considered murder, that they could not abide. Most of them, in fact, thought the human species was a terrible aberration on the earth and was senselessly devouring and destroying her.

I asked Allison whether, if she had a button in front of her that would painlessly evaporate all the humans off the face of the earth, she would push it. She said without hesitation that she would. She hoped that some epidemic like AIDS or bird flu would wipe most of us out and bring the population back into balance. The savvy captain, on the other hand, wouldn't give a straight answer.

'The planet's chances of survival without us are greater,' he said. 'Would an elephant press that button? Would a dolphin? Probably. Just out of sheer self-defence.'

'And you?'

'We don't hate anybody,' he said. 'We look upon humanity as a problem as a species. I could press that button in the abstraction, but I have a lot of respect for the people doing this. Consider that there are six point five billion people on the planet; you can count the number of activists on two hands.'

THE NEXT MORNING we rounded the high cliffs of Cathedral Rock guarding the eastern cape and turned north into Storm Bay. Hobart sat at the top of it. Watson said we'd be there by noon. The chopper needed a part that was being flown in on a 6:00pm flight, so we wouldn't leave until 1900 or so.

A lot of people had called Watson an ecoterrorist, including several governments and, in a fit of pique, Greenpeace. One group, the Center for Consumer Freedom, had said on its website that the bow of Watson's ship was reinforced with concrete for ramming and had a steel blade called the 'can opener' for gutting the hulls of ships. It claimed that he had AK-47s on board. I thought I'd better ask him about that. I climbed up to the bridge and found the captain on watch in his chair. He was reading *A Devil's Chaplain*, a book about evolution by Richard Dawkins. He was playing Jimmy Buffett on the stereo, to the horror of everybody under forty.

He closed his book. 'I don't know of any ecoterrorists other than Union Carbide and Exxon,' he said. He meant the environmental catastrophes inflicted by the *Valdez*, and the chemical plant explosion at Bhopal.

He said that a coast guard officer had given a talk in Port Angeles, Washington, and described Sea Shepherd as an ecoterrorist organisation. Watson wrote a letter to the commander of the coast guard in Seattle and got an apology; the officer was reprimanded. He officially asked the FBI if there were any investigations into Sea Shepherd and was told no.

'We got audited by the IRS—didn't lose our 501C3 status for our activities, so—they don't give non-profit status to terrorist organisations. If we were terrorists we couldn't dock in the United States. The trouble is, every right-wing anti-environmental group in the country runs around calling everybody an environmental terrorist.' He added that nobody was doing what Sea Shepherd was doing. 'We're filling up a niche. Intervening against illegal activities. We've been called sea cops, eco-vigilantes.'

When asked if he thought he was putting out little fires in front of a massive conflagration, he said, 'I'm sure that the whale that we save isn't too concerned with being a little fire.'

'Is your bow reinforced with concrete? Do you have a can opener?'

'The bow of the ship is not reinforced with concrete. We had a can opener. It was there once, but we took it off; it was getting rusty.'

About guns, he said, 'Well, we use shotguns to destroy the buoys on longlines. Beats jumping into the water with an ice pick.' He said there were no AK-47s on board, and that he'd never had to use any weapons for self-defence. 'We don't shoot at people.'

'Cannons filled with pie filling,' Allison piped in. She was sitting just behind Watson's chair.

I had wondered about the three-inch cannon lashed on the main deck.

'We fired pie filling,' Watson said. 'That was the Faroese. When they tried to board us, we hit them with forty-five-gallon shots of custard and banana crème.'

Since I was airing all my concerns I asked, 'The action that resulted in, say, the sinking of the Icelandic whalers—how do you make sure nobody's on it? That you don't kill anybody?'

'Search the boat. The watchman, he was sleeping up on the bridge. They cut that boat loose. That boat drifted away from the other two. He was in the middle of the harbour when the other boats sank. He was still sleeping.

'Searching one boat in Norway,' he continued. 'It was total dark; went in the galley and some drunk Norwegian was lying on the mess table, passed out.' They left the boat alone.

Watson added, 'People call us pirates but we don't go robbing anybody, so we're not pirates. Kids just like the romance of it. so we do the T-shirts and stuff. We simply don't break laws. The perception is that we do. If we were pirates we couldn't come into ports like this.'

Sink ships but don't break laws. He said again and again that he was simply destroying property used in criminal activities, upholding international law.

At the chart table, Alex was drawing up a design for a steel frame to hold a wooden barrier to protect the barrels of aviation fuel under the heli deck. He said if there was a crash, he didn't want pieces of rotor blade slicing down into the gas depot and blowing up the ship.

The chart room was, for ship's space, a big open cabin. The chart table with logbook and GPS display was on the port side. At any time, one could look up there and read the ship's position, speed and heading. On the starboard side was a long varnished counter that held the computer monitor that displayed the RayTech navigation system, a sophisticated program that allowed the officers to display the ship's position in relation to any number of waypoints any place in the world. Cabinets stuffed with signal flags, flares, smoke bombs and megaphones ran under the counter.

The rest of the chart room was lined with bookshelves, each with its strip of guarding wood to prevent the volumes from going airborne. One small case held marine animal guidebooks: fish, whales, bird guides. Another held Admiralty Coast Pilots, with detailed information about tides, channels, buoys, hazards, lighthouses and ports for every coast in the world. The bookshelf over the nav computer held the most curious collection of titles.

Moving from the *Navy Seal Combat Manual* to *Black's Law Dictionary*, the titles created a narrative that in some way elucidated Watson's approach to direct action and helped explain why he wasn't behind bars right now. The books went from combat to criminal evidence and on to the broader dictates of international treaties, which, evidently, had checked any local prosecutor's enthusiasm for indicting Watson. A nation like Norway simply did not want to focus world attention on its whaling program by giving someone like Watson a public forum. Such nations were already flying in the face of world opinion and international laws. Putting Watson on trial would be bad PR.

Watson enthusiastically exploited this dynamic. After he had sunk the three Norwegian whalers, he repeatedly offered to return to Norway to stand trial. After he rammed two illegal Japanese drift-netters in the North Pacific in 1990, the Japanese refused to admit that the incident had happened.

In the case of the whaling fleet in Antarctica, circumstances were a bit different. The Japanese didn't seem to care much about PR in this arena, aside from publishing booklets that justified the need to kill whales in great numbers. One chart put out by the Japanese showed how whales were depleting the world's fish stocks.

They were certainly not keeping their activities quiet and they were moving boldly in the IWC to lift the moratorium on commercial whaling completely. They'd been trying for eighteen years.

So why wouldn't the Japanese captain of the fleet just blow us out of the water if Watson tried to ram him? Or seize the ship and lock them—us—up?

I guessed that the answer was that there are degrees of bad international PR.

The chart room—being the locus of much decision making and current information on the ship's whereabouts; being spacious and full of books; having counters on which to drop camera gear and of a perfect height for leaning against; and, not the least, being between the bridge and the radio room— was a natural gathering place. Anybody on board who wanted to snatch a whiff of the latest plan, would climb the steep, narrow stairs and hang out in the chart room. From the bridge, as you moved aft across the chart room, in fifteen feet you had a choice: turn right down the stairway; continue straight into the little radio room; or move left, out the main hatch to the heli deck.

The radio room was a cramped office holding an L-shaped desk, a bench seat and a padded swivel chair in reach of everything in the cabin. The two satellite phones were in here, as well as the ship's main computer and a marine radio. It was also the ship newsroom, press office and PR office. From this creaking seat, Watson conducted interviews with news agencies around the world, and churned out, night and day, a steady stream of press releases, op-ed pieces, emails, essays and diatribes; and from here he published, on a sporadic basis, the ship's newsletter, the *Scuttlebutt*. The radio room had a steel door with a bolt and a reinforced steel bracket for holding a stout bar. Its final function was a safe room in case of boarding. From here, Watson could transmit distress signals or fire off a last volley to the press before being seized.

THE HARBOURMASTER in Hobart had, unfortunately, read the Sea Shepherd website. He mentioned it over the radio. In Melbourne, the port authorities had waived thousands of dollars in docking and piloting fees under a provision for the ships of charitable non-profit organisations. Watson had paid a pilot fee coming in, but no pilot fee going out, and no port fees at all for the nearly three weeks tied up downtown. Captain Mike Bass-Walker didn't see it the same way and would not give Sea Shepherd a freebie. The cost for a pilot and a berth in the dock for a day would be over $2,000, so Watson took his anchorage coordinates in the free zone three miles from the wharves, and at 12:30 the deck crew up on the forecastle head lowered the anchors.

They had meant to lower only one, but in lifting the steel block off the windlass they had released both chains. Alex screamed out the window from the bridge. 'Stop the windlass! Both your chains are going out! Stop the windlass!'

The hands swarmed around, not sure what to do. Alex shot down the outside steps, and ran up and took charge. The port anchor grabbed and the *Farley* swung up into the wind. Watson thought it was funny. With an all-volunteer crew he had to be pretty much immune to that sort of thing.

The boat rode at anchor in the short chop with the undulant

motion of a cantering horse. Nobody was allowed onshore until customs had cleared us, so the jet skis were plucked from their cradles and lowered into the windy bay. Geert and Gedden started them up and began roaring around the ship. Practice for attacking the whalers. Gedden was a wild man. He did doughnuts, aerials, leapt a wave and flipped. By the time Geert could tow him to the ship, the ski was barely floating. The engine, which had just been tuned, was swamped with salt water. Gedden had wrecked the one on Henderson Island as well. Then customs cleared us, and two Zodiacs bounded into the docks to pick up supplies.

One Zodiac was loaded in Hobart with booze. Cases and cases of beer and bottles of rum and whisky. On the way back out, it swamped in the whitecaps. The other Zodiac stalled in the middle of the bay with a blocked fuel line and wallowed dangerously in the swells. In the confusion, someone dropped one of the three handheld VHF radios overboard, and the other got soaked. By the time the liquor boat got near the *Farley*'s side it was full of water. The waterlogged Zodiac was secured, and it was so heavy that it bent a cleat on the ship's rail, and the line caught and wrenched Colin's hand. So now the bosun's mate was partially dismasted.

In the mess, Jeff of the J. Crew was drying off and drinking a cup of tea. He mentioned that one of the radios had been lost. Watson happened to be standing behind him.

'It's *lost*? Who lost it?'

Jeff put his head down. 'Aw, c'mon Captain.'

Watson, steely, overbearing: 'Who lost it? Tell me.'

'Aw, c'mon Captain, you want me to rat?'

'Tell me now.' Direct order.

'It was—' he mouthed the word. The captain stormed out. Jeff put his head down on his arms.

There was a big note scrawled on the message board outside the mess:

Only officers may use the handheld marine radios! Do not take one without asking. We've lost half of our radios in one day and we haven't even got to Antarctica!

ON THE BRIDGE, Hammarstedt's watch was sombre. Too many mess-ups in one day. Hammarstedt didn't seem too discouraged. 'This always happens,' he said, 'at the start of a campaign.'

A few hours later, the flight deck crew had swung down the shiny new rails around the heli deck and readied the tie-downs for the arrival of the chopper. The new rubber was down on the deck and painted with a white centre stripe to help Aultman line up. Aultman had picked his crew to guide him in with hand signals, and as soon as he touched down, their job was to rush forward and hook the pontoons to the welded rings before the chopper could think about sliding off the ship into the sea.

It was nearly 8:00pm and the helicopter part had arrived and been installed. The chopper had been cleared by the mechanics, and though the marine band radio didn't work, they'd have to make do. The previous owner, who had also flown it off the back of an excursion boat in Antarctica, radioed the *Farley* to say that Aultman had taken off and would be arriving within fifteen minutes.

The fire crew took their stations, and all decks aft of the superstructure were cleared. Aultman and his crew on the heli deck would be executing their first landing at sea, a truly dangerous manoeuvre. The way things had gone today with all the other auxiliary craft, everybody was a bit tense.

You might have thought Aultman was Lindbergh, landing at Paris. The entire crew lined the rails. Even Watson lumbered out from the radio room, where he'd been composing a press release blasting the personal character of the director of the Institute of Cetacean Research.

Soon a fast-moving speck appeared over the harbour, and grew, and then we heard the signature throp carried downwind and saw the neat red-and-white whirlybird. It was small, not quite toylike—a Plexiglas bubble; a thin spine of tail, engine, pontoons. It seemed diminutive for the vast, raging landscape of Antarctica, but on the upside, it looked light enough to float for a while.

Aultman buzzed the ship to cheers and circled it twice. He came in over the heli deck and hovered, gave the pitching landing pad a look, then lifted off and circled again. He came in a second time and brought the chopper within feet of the black rubber, yawing slightly, trying to centre the white stripe, the stiff wind and pitch of the boat not helping. We could see him now, right hand on the stick, continually adjusting it. Abruptly he lifted, accelerated, tilted forward, and took a wide sweep of the bay. A third time he came in. Aultman brought the chopper down to within inches of the tossing rubber, levitated, then dropped it down. The slack pontoons gave, pancaked, and rebounded. The chopper stuck. The flight crew was on it in seconds, running on the crouch, securing the machine. The ship cheered. The wind whipped. Three seagulls flew by wondering what all the fuss was about. Aultman had never landed on a ship before, and after all the stuff-ups, it was heartening to see something so beautifully executed.

Within a couple of hours we weighed anchor. The *Farley* swung off the wind and, with dusk drawn down on Storm Bay, melted into the darkness. Watson had told the media and the crew in Melbourne that we would head south and west, towards the Greenpeace ships coming from Africa, to squeeze the whalers in a kind of pincer action. He had told me we would head more eastward. Now we were heading almost due south and I wondered where we were going.

WE WEREN'T AN HOUR out of Hobart. Our life at sea, beyond the reach of port authorities or police, had truly just begun.

'You in, dude?' Justin of the J. Crew shuffled the cards at a booth table in the mess. He had long dark eyelashes, a black beard, big glistening black eyes. He looked innocent, benign. And he could wipe you out of a pay cheque in twenty minutes. In first grade he had won a kid's cat, shooting dice.

'Uh, no,' I said, following Price with my eyes.

The FIB pilot with the secret second job was carrying around the bolt of a high-powered rifle. He stopped by the galley counter and wiped it down, then went around the corner into the main companionway.

My heart raced. There was no mistaking the smooth blued steel, the weight of it in his hands.

It was not so much the gun itself, the piece of it, that shook me. I'd been around guns my whole life. What prompted a wave of anger was betrayal. And fear. I was suddenly afraid that Watson had a deadly agenda of which few others on the ship were informed. We were all in this together. The thing about a ship like this is that there is no getting off.

Price ducked back into the mess and continued on into the green room, where he sprawled on a cushioned bench seat. I followed him.

'Hey, Chris.'

'Hey.'

'You want tea?' I grabbed the electric hot water pot.

'I'm okay. Thanks.'

'Nice bolt you were carrying around. Looked pretty high-calibre.'

Price always seemed a little amused about everything, even his own fate. Must have come from circling the earth for days on end under a few square yards of gossamer nylon. He pushed his steel-framed glasses up on his nose and looked away like a kid who had stolen a candy bar. 'I don't know anything about that,' he said.

'I don't give a sh— what it was,' I said. 'I'm a hunter. Hunt elk every year I can. Savage 99, .308. You know, the one with the safety on the tang?'

The mention of a specific gun—make and model, calibre— was too much for the big trucker from Arkansas. There was not a soul on this ship full of vegan hippies he could talk guns with, except maybe Steve, who wasn't much into idle chat. It was like hitting the On switch.

'That's a lot bigger than a .308,' he said. 'It's a .50-calibre BMG.'

'Oh?' I said, making to head for the clean water jugs with the pot.

'Two thousand pounds of pressure. A guy just set the world record on five shots at a thousand yards. A two-and-a-quarter-inch group! Think about it!' He was beside himself.

I turned. 'Could blow right through about anything.'

'Right through the engine block of a Humvee!'

'Through the hull of a ship, even.'

'Piece of cake!'

'Better keep it oiled good out here.'

'Yeah, the guns got wet in the crossing.'

Guns. How many guns? Fifty-calibre. Serious firepower. What the hell was going on? I took some deep breaths, trying to control my fury and my fear.

The captain's cabin was a sanctum. I lifted the brass whale's tail and hammered.

'Come in!' I turned the ornate handle and pushed, and wasn't at all prepared for the genteel scene within. I had lived for the past week with the cramped quarters of an old trawler, and the spaciousness of the cabin struck me as luxurious in the extreme. It was as big as the bridge and half the chart room above it, and appointed as well as any ship's cabin I'd ever seen. Dark wood panelling, portholes forward, two sumptuous sofas facing each other across a low coffee table. Bookshelves, a chart table, a double bed with headboard and fluffy duvet. A private bath with a Jacuzzi hot tub. Watson later told me that Paul DeJoria of Paul Mitchell hair products had commissioned the cabin for the Watsons as a gift. Watson spent much of his year on the ship and he seemed to work twenty hours a day. If some benefactor wanted to provide decent living quarters, bully for him.

The captain and Allison sat across from each other on the sofas, each holding a drink. 'Oh, hey,' they chimed. 'Come on in. Want a drink?'

They took a look at me and their demeanour changed.

Allison, crisp, no longer pleasant: 'What's up?'

'How many high-calibre rifles do you have on board?'

Silence.

'I just saw the bolt of a .50-calibre BMG. That's a sniper rifle.'

'No, it's not,' Watson said.

'Yes, it is. It fires a two-and-a-quarter-inch group at a thousand yards.' I'd never seen a .50-calibre, but anything that accurate at that distance was a sniper rifle. It was certainly not designed for self-defence.

'It doesn't fire in a group. It's a single-shot recoilless rifle.'

Watson sat on his sofa, drink in one hand. His voice was calm, relaxed, with the almost offhand, confiding tone he used whenever he was mining the narrative field with deadly facts, as he did all day long. He lived in a state of war and acted as if he were sitting on a picnic blanket, handing out fried chicken on little napkins.

Allison, by contrast, sat on the edge of her seat. Her natural tautness was now the stillness of a big cat about to leap. Her mouth was tight and her eyes blazed.

'No,' I said to the captain, 'I mean, you fire one shot, reload, fire another shot. Five shots making a group like this.'

'We've had it onboard for four years. We've never used it. It's missing a part. I don't even know if it works.'

Price had a secret role and he was lovingly oiling the bolt to a junk rifle.

'How many guns do you have?' I said.

Allison cut in. She was leaning forward as if she might spring off the sofa. 'You're a hunter. Why are you upset about guns? You should understand!'

Watson held up one pacifying palm towards his warrior wife.

'We have two shotguns and this rifle,' he said.

I sat against the foot of the double bed.

'Is it part of your plans for the campaign?' Would he tell me if it was?

'No,' he said without hesitation.

'You've never used it? It's backup?'

The captain took a sip, put his glass down on the coffee table. 'Sometimes, in some places, you want a gun. We sail in places where there are real pirates.'

I nodded.

Allison glared. 'Every boat has weapons on board.'

Our eyes locked. We had a long trip ahead of us. I looked back at the captain.

'Okay,' I said. I got up and walked out. My fears about Sea Shepherd seemed to be bearing out. To what lengths would they go to protect the whales?

5

SOUTHERN OCEAN

I WOKE AT 3:00AM, braced against the rails, and was nearly thrown from my bed. The ship groaned and lay over, paused, rolled back hard. I groped for the light and tensed and timed my launch out of the bunk so that I wouldn't be fighting the G forces of the roll. I slipped on a jacket and clambered to the bridge, gripping the handrails. The bridge was dark but for the pulsing green of the radars and the glow of the compass. The ocean heaved darkly, gleaming back the moon from the tops of the swells, then dimming to a vast plain of black motion that seemed to suck the umber from the edges of the sky.

Hammarstedt said we had just cleared the southern cape of Bruny Island, the last sheltering land. 'That's what you're feeling,' he said. 'It's open ocean now, all the way to Antarctica. It's all downhill from here.'

I stood on the dark bridge, braced into the port corner. The ship rolled, pitched and yawed, moving in every direction it could at once, and sawing back. I tried planting my feet and swaying in a fluid circle, leaning into the tilt of the deck—one wave, two—and lost my balance. I crashed halfway across the bridge and stout Gunter caught me.

I waited until the ship canted against me, and pushed through the heavy hatch on the port side. I didn't want to do it on the downslope and go flying through the door and over the rail. The cold air washed over my face. It had been chilled by miles of open ocean. Here was a little covered deck, no bigger than a bathtub, with waist-high bulwarks and a rope safety railing. It was called the bridge wing. It was a great perch, just behind the bridge, outside but sheltered.

For a while I just watched the dark sea and listened to the

hiss and rush as the bow laboured out of the troughs. The wake had a phosphorescent glow, trailing into the hills of water. I could make out the pale forms of birds, probably shearwaters, swooping to circle the bow. Silent ghosts.

I made my way back to my cabin and fell asleep until breakfast.

ONE MILLION, four hundred thousand square miles was too big. Watson said he had sources of intel, but having eyes at a few research stations and on a few supply flights was not enough. After breakfast I asked him if I could email my friends at SpaceImaging, a private satellite imaging company based near Denver. They had proved invaluable in obtaining images for the last expedition I'd been on, in the Tsangpo Gorge in Tibet. Watson said, 'Sure.'

I wrote from the radio room, 'Can you possibly look for a group of four to six 60-metre to 130-metre ships between 30 degrees east and 175 degrees east within 200 miles of the ice?'

The response was almost immediate. My friends said they'd need approximately 800 shots and 100 days to scan that area. They said it was like looking for a needle in 100 haystacks.

Despite the discouraging information, Watson was energetic on the bridge. He tortured his watch with Canadian folk music.

'This is supposed to be the Roaring Forties. The Furious Fifties. The Savage Sixties.' He was talking about degrees of latitude. A degree of latitude consists of sixty minutes, each representing one nautical mile; so with every ten degrees we went south, we were 600 miles further from an inhabited country.

A steep roller lifted the ship and barrelled underneath. Half of us were thrown across the bridge. The *Farley* rolled back just as hard. The little roll gauge over the centre window swung out past thirty degrees. Watson got up from his captain's chair and walked aft. He looked out through the heavy plate window.

'Helicopter's looking pretty secure.' He went to the gyro-compass in the centre of the bridge console and turned the knob that adjusted the autopilot. 'Try that for a while,' he said to his quartermaster. 'One hundred fifty-five degrees. We'll head a little more east, run with the waves a little more.'

Another big swell pitched the ship. We all hung on. Watson said, 'They're called Cape rollers. Can get huge. Yeah, *The Perfect Storm*—we were rooting for the storm. Load of crap. Nobody's going out on a yardarm in those kinds of seas with a welding torch. Those guys died because of their own greed. Sitting there systematically wiping out the swordfish.'

Two royal albatross soared up past the starboard windows. They were huge and white, with black on the upper side of their wings—and their wings were something like ten feet across. Without moving them they dived down past the lunging bow and swept almost straight up like kites on strings. Whereas the *Farley* laboured and rolled, they swooped with exuberant ease, trailing the long extended wing tips an inch, or less, above the tossing water, rising out of a protected trough as if gravity were for other worlds than theirs, canting over with the angle of the swell, stiff-winged, to skim it without touching, to peel off downwind in a sudden capitulation to sheer speed. They widened the arc to swoop down into the ship's wake, to land without a single beat of their wings. They floated there on the foaming track, watching us chug away, bobbing as neat and easy as swans on a millpond. Sometimes they did all this in pairs, as did the shearwaters and fulmars, in perfect, terrifying sync—the terror of sheer, heedless, inhuman beauty. A wandering albatross can cover over 9,000 miles in a single feeding trip and in a lifetime will clock ten times the distance to the moon.

Watson saw them. 'Longlines—that's what they were using in *The Perfect Storm*. The leading cause of the rapid diminishment of albatross numbers worldwide. They dive on the bait as it goes out and get pulled down and drown. Right now, seventeen of twenty-four species face extinction.'

The next two days passed quickly. Marc worked morning to night on the main deck, welding and grinding on some four-inch steel T beams. Shy Willie was often out of the engine room and in the bosun's locker, working on pieces of steel. The two seemed to be working together. The grinder's gritty sear whined late into the nights, which where getting shorter. The sun rose at five and set at nine. The weather held, the seas were ten or twelve feet out of the north-north-west, the racing overcast unremitting. More albatross accompanied us now, black-browed, wandering, royal. According to Dennis Marks, a greying deckhand who was a bird biologist, they had special bones in their wings that locked them stiff and took the stress off their muscles so they could glide for hours, days. They never seemed to tire of following the ship. Why did they do it? It wasn't opportunistic: I never once saw them catch a fish in the wake. I liked to think it was because all sentient beings have a measure of curiosity and enjoy company.

On 15 December Alex announced that we would be in the ice in four days.

After dinner we played poker. The J's, Trevor, Darren, the captain. We sat at the biggest booth table and Watson popped the latches on the ship's poker kit, a little briefcase with chips, cards, markers.

It was agreed: $5, any currency—Aussie, Kiwi, US. No pesos, no euros. No yen.

When I lost all my chips I wandered out onto the stern. Electrician Dave and Wessel were back there smoking. It was 10:00pm, and the sky had cleared enough so that we could see a full blood moon rising. The sun had gone over the horizon and was flaying the grey overcast to the west. Cold wind and cobalt water.

We were back on an unwavering 176-degree course, and the black ship seemed to be driving head down into the south— plunging, pitching, rolling—with a purpose now almost of her own. It was as if the will of the captain ran through the *Farley* like a pulse.

Wessel, in shorts and flip-flops in the raw cold, hand-rolled a cigarette. 'We're in the middle of nowhere. We've been lucky with the weather.'

Dave pried a lighter out of his checked flannel overshirt and lit up. 'Watch the birds, mate; they'll tell you when a storm's coming.'

'How?'

'They'll piss off.'

The two smoked. Night passed over the reefs of cloud to

the west like the shadow of a wing. The clouds lost their colour and deepened to match the sea. The moon brightened.

Dave said, 'Yeah, you can tell everything from the birds, eh?'

THE NEXT MORNING I got a cup of coffee from the big pot in the green room and wandered out onto the main deck before breakfast. The day was cold, solid grey, and it felt somehow as if we were entering a different marine landscape. I glanced at the steel T beams lying on the deck. The steel struts Marc had been working on now formed a blade. A seven-foot triangular cutter, polished and sharpened at one end, exactly like a can opener. It was at that moment that I fully realised this was not a game.

AFTER LUNCH, a dense fog rolled in over the water and the wind and temperature dropped. The mist seemed to settle the swells like a calming hand. The wash of the bow was amplified, as were the hammerings on the deck.

Watson said, 'Some sailors hate fog. I love it.' I thought, Of course you do; you are all about evasion and surprise.

He said, 'A few years ago the USS *Enterprise*, the aircraft carrier, was coming into Puget Sound in heavy fog. They radioed ahead, "This is the USS *Enterprise*. You will change your course." The radio came back: "Be advised that you will change *your* course."

'"This is the warship USS *Enterprise*. You will change *your* course."

'"This is the Puget Sound lighthouse. Please be advised that you will change your course immediately."'

He laughed. He went over to the chart table and moved his plump hand over the small-scale chart that covered all of Antarctica.

'Antarctica is bigger than Australia—like New York to LA, going from here to here.' He pointed to the coast of Wilkes Land and then to the northern end of the Antarctic Peninsula. This is six hundred to seven hundred miles of solid ice.' He spread his fingers across the Ross Ice Shelf, to the east of our present course.

I said, 'You put out a press release in Melbourne saying that you were cooperating with Greenpeace. You told everyone that you were heading south, then west, to converge on their ships. But we're going east of south if anything.'

'That's what we want the Japanese to think. But I think they'll be hunting over here'—he pointed at the Ross Sea, the George V Coast, off to the east—'to avoid Greenpeace.'

It was big, all right. More coastline than the Atlantic and Pacific coasts of the lower forty-eight, plus the entire coast of Alaska. I was beginning to think Watson had no idea where the Japanese were.

The fog rolled across the decks all afternoon like smoke. I thought it was a good metaphor for Watson's strategy of deception. He was turning the *Farley* into a black ghost ship, sailing her into a fog bank and off the map. Nobody would know where we were, not even conventional satellites. How often do you sail to Antarctica with no clue of where you are going? Just southward, latitude by latitude, pulled by the force of a single will. It made me feel uneasy. We were flying under the radar, so far under that we might disappear without a trace. We were all alone. Strike an iceberg, go down in two minutes. I was sure we had an Epurb on board, the emergency radio signal beacon; Aultman said he had one on the chopper. Did it work? On the *Farley*, I gave the odds as fifty-fifty. What good would it do in the empty vastness of these seas?

THE MORNING OF 17 December broke with cold misting rain and following seas. A sense of taut excitement, inexplicable, ran through the ship.

Just after breakfast, Trevor climbed to the monkey deck above the bridge to test the topmost water cannons. A thwomp like a sumo wrestler hitting the mat, and then the windows of the bridge were covered with a deluge of water. Old pipes bursting. A valve shut somewhere, and again only the fine drizzle running down the windows and an empty black sea.

Trevor breezed onto the bridge holding a monkey wrench and said, 'We could hook the diesel pump right to the water cannons. Spray the factory ship down, then toss a couple of Molotov cocktails. That would do it.' He smiled so that I knew he was joking. Maybe.

Marc, Willie and Steve readied the can opener for deployment on the starboard bow. Marc, cheerful in his bright slicker in the near-freezing rain, welded a reinforcement plate on the deck just behind the slot in the bulwarks.

The chopper pilot, Aultman, was in the radio room, bent over the desk, which was covered with pieces of a ham radio. He was so anxious to fly that he had to keep his hands busy with something. He'd been talking with the captain, and the plan now was to stop the ship and launch the chopper for a long sortie ahead, then move. That way they could save fuel and stay out longer.

At 10:40 Lincoln reported five mic keys on channel 13. That's what you hear if there's a radio transmission too far out of range to make out voices. A chirp or cough. Somebody was within 100 miles.

Moods pervade a ship and can change as fast as the weather in the Southern Ocean. Secrets are hard to keep, and if they are kept, an uneasy awareness of an obscure significance, of a withholding, is also universally felt. Most of the crew knew that Allison and Watson had something up their sleeves, though not what.

I asked Watson where he got his authority to weld up can openers and ram ships.

'The UN Charter for Nature,' he said in his offhand, easygoing style. 'Article Twenty-one, under the section for Enforcement.' He got up, went to the international treaty bookshelf, and came back to the bridge. 'Here it is.' He'd opened one of the books to a dog-eared page.

'The United Nations World Charter for Nature, ratified by the UN General Assembly in nineteen-eighty-two, states: "Any non-government organisation, individual, or nation-state is empowered to uphold international law, specifically and especially in international waters."'

'Do you think they actually meant you could go out and damage ships?'

'You know, I was arrested off the Grand Banks in nineteen-ninety-three. Canada arrested me, but not the Cuban trawler that was fishing illegally. They tried me on two counts of mischievous damage to property, two counts of threatening life. I faced two times life plus ten. More than the O.J. trial.' Watson chuckled, but his dark eyes were deadly serious.

'I was the only witness for the defence. The Newfoundlanders hate me for my stance on sealing and other things, but they hate the government more. They were the jury. My lawyer said that I acted in accordance with what I thought was proper and lawful. Our defence was that the UN Charter for Nature gave us the right.' He folded the charter. 'They acquitted me.'

'Why go to such lengths to stop the whalers? The Japanese say there are 760,000 minke whales. They say it's sustainable.

'That's bull. The IWC says it could be 300,000 and they admit they don't know. All great whales are endangered now. The bowhead whale, the Pacific grey whale, would now be extinct except for conservation laws. The remaining whales are threatened by whaling, heavy metals, global warming, pollution, longlines, drift nets, low-frequency sonar, ship strikes; 300,000 whales and small cetaceans are killed every year by getting tangled in fishing gear or as bycatch. They say the great whales need at least fifty more years to recover. The earth's whales simply cannot endure another period of open commercial whaling.'

The bridge was full now—the seats along the back, the places by the windows along the side. For a lot of the crew, listening to Watson was like going to church.

'You know what a Japanese delegate said to me at the nineteen-ninety-seven IWC meeting in Monaco? He said he didn't care if all the whales died. He said his duty was to his family, his company, his country, to harvest all the whales they could before they were all gone. "Realise maximum profit from them before they go extinct" are the words he used.' Watson took a deep breath. He wanted to shift gears. 'Hey, somebody get that kid Watkins.'

A minute later Jeff stood in the doorway, rubbing his cold

hands together—he'd been wire-brushing rust on the aft deck. Watson appraised him.

'I hear you're supposed to be an expert on comics. We'll have to have a debate.

'That's one you'll definitely lose, Captain.'

'What was Spiderman's first girlfriend's name?'

Watkins didn't blink. 'Gwen Stacey. What was her father's name?'

'Captain George Stacey. Who else did he date?'

'He had some run-ins with Betty Brandt at the *Daily Bugle*.'

They were off. I went out the bridge wing and down the outside steps. A wandering albatross glided by in the fog, and I wondered if I were in a weird dream. Watson had talked about the vulnerability of whale populations. There was the question of why the Japanese were whaling at all. From an economic standpoint it made little sense.

One fin whale might bring close to $200,000 on the wholesale market, and much more at retail; but in 2004 the fleet had brought in $78 million, which the Institute of Cetacean Research (ICR) said covered only 90 per cent of its expenses. A large government subsidy helps keep the ICR afloat. Masayuki Komatsu, legal counsellor of the Fisheries Agency of Japan, said at the annual meeting of the International Whaling Commission in 2001, 'It has been ten years since we started scientific whaling. Though the surveillance study has made progress, the ten years has been a dark period on selling the by-product in good quality for reasonable prices.'

The market for whale meat has got dimmer since then. Recently I had read two surveys that found the Japanese appetite for the dense red meat to be at an all-time low. A survey conducted by Britain's leading research company, MORI, in 2000, found that only 1 per cent of the Japanese public eat whale meat once a month, and that only 11 per cent support whaling. The *Sydney Morning Herald* reported a glut of unsold whale meat—a record 4,800 tons stockpiled in freezers at the start of this whaling season. The price had fallen from $15 to $10 per pound. There was such a surplus that it was being used in pet food. The meat was being shunted by the government into school lunch programs in the hope of encouraging consumption. The Japanese government was also spending $5 million a year on programs to boost sales, according to the *Washington Post*. There was even a Whale Cuisine Preservation Association—all this at a time when numerous environmental organisations were reporting that whale meat could be dangerously high in toxins such as mercury and PCBs.

In the face of opposition, the Institute of Cetacean Research pointed to the fact that whaling was an important part of traditional Japanese culture.

But the truth is that only isolated coastal communities such as Ayukawa and Taiji had been hunting whales for centuries. The mainstream Japanese public didn't become acquainted with whale meat until the food shortages just after World War II, when Macarthur encouraged the Japanese to eat it. And according to the MORI poll, 'Virtually nobody fears Japan's cultural identity would suffer greatly were whaling to stop.'

Although the first Japanese whaling fleet went to Antarctica in 1934, it wasn't until 1948, when the whalers became part of the fishing powerhouse Nissui, that the meat was aggressively marketed. Two other large fishing companies, Maruha and Kyokuyo, also whaled in the Southern Ocean through the 1960s; and in 1976 they merged to form one company, Nippon Kydo Hogei. It is estimated that the three companies killed nearly 500,000 whales between 1929 and 1986.

In 1987, with the implementation of the IWC's moratorium on commercial whaling, Japan established the non-profit Institute of Cetacean Research, to conduct its 'research' in the Southern Ocean. Japan's Research Program in the Antarctic (JARPA) was born. To most observers, this was a program designed to circumvent the moratorium and keep the commercial whaling fleet afloat until the moratorium could be overturned. In eighteen years of JARPA, the scientific committee of the IWC had lodged no fewer than twenty objections to Japan's 'lethal research'. (At the meeting of the IWC Scientific Committee in 2001, thirty-two scientists from around the world submitted a paper claiming that JARPA lacked scientific rigour and would not meet the minimum standards of peer review.) Also in 1987, Nippon Kyodo Hogei became Kyodo Senpaku. The three big fishing companies—Nissui, Maruha and Koyokuyo—each owned a one-third share.

The ICR contracted exclusively with this corporate giant to conduct research whaling in Antarctica and the North Pacific. The ICR set the price of the meat, or 'by-product', and consigned the company to sell a portion of the catch to licensed wholesalers for a commission. Nissui and Kyokuyo continued to package and sell the meat. The meat that cannot be sold on the open market continues to be stockpiled, and sold at discounted prices to schools, hospitals and other public institutions, and to local governments to promote the eating of whale meat.

The ICR has never brought in enough revenue with the sale of whale meat to cover its expenses.

So why, if whaling was essentially unprofitable, was the Japanese fleet in Antarctica—and in the face of so much international outcry and pressure?

Some international observers believe it is exactly this pressure that is responsible for Japan's recalcitrance. As quoted by the BBC, Hideki Moro, a top official at the Fisheries Agency, recently said, 'If the current ban on hunting whales is allowed to become permanent, activists may direct their efforts to restricting other types of fishing.'

Japan is the world's largest consumer of seafood. According to a report by the Carnegie Endowment, 40 per cent of the protein in the Japanese diet comes from marine species. And with these sources threatened by shrinking fish stocks worldwide, the Japanese may be sensitive to criticism of any of their harvests. This may be why they are so anxious to blame whales for the decline of fisheries.

'As long as officials present the issue [of whaling] as one of Japan being bullied by the rest of the world,' the BBC quotes Greenpeace's John Frizell as saying, 'they can probably keep the Japanese public behind them.'

All the indicators seemed to suggest that the Japanese people don't particularly like whale meat, that they don't think it's an important cultural value, and that the industry is facing a tough time making money. If, in the end, the Japanese fleet was now gunning for whales because of notions of national pride, it seemed to me that vulnerable species shouldn't be hunted.

NO DARKNESS now at night. The sun set just after midnight but an uncertain twilight lingered until dawn four hours later. Near midnight I took my every-three-days, three-minute shower in the cold stall, then went to the green room to watch a movie. The engineers wanted to watch *Death Race 2000*, and the J. Crew voted for *Jughead*.

Geert stepped forward, gangly, bushy beard, in his biker vest and heavy work boots. He'd spent all day drawing sweet pictures of big-eyed seals.

'How about *Miss Congeniality*?' he said shyly, holding out a DVD.

A shocked silence settled over the cabin. Everybody blinked.

'*Miss Congeniality*? Dude!' Justin blurted.

Marc spoke up for his countryman. 'Geert has got a fat love crush on Sandra Bullock.'

Geert winced. Somebody grabbed the DVD and slid it in. Everybody was fond of the ship's artist.

6

GHOST

THE FOG DESCENDED again on 18 December and the ship moved within it like a scent hound. In this case, her nose was two radars that spun silently on their masts above the bridge. Black swells pushed the *Farley* gently from behind. At breakfast we were at 62°S, now only about 250 miles off the coast of Antarctica. Visibility was less than 300 yards. The quartermasters watched the pulsing green screens with avid attention.

During dinner our first iceberg loomed out of the fog, ghostly, condensed from the same whiteness as the air; then, closer, a solid alabaster wall crazed with blue crevices. It was a cliff 100 feet high, a quarter-mile long, flat-topped like a mesa, and the swells washed against its base with a sound like low laughter. They carved a hollow undercut of a fierce and vivid blue. The colour was almost the blue of shallow reefs seen from the air, but colder, harder.

At 2200 Alex stood over the main radar screen.

Watson was in his chair.

The fog closed around the bridge like a shroud. For the first time I saw chunks of ice floating and heard the grate as the bow sloughed one off.

There were three blips on the radar, two moving. The size of small peas. The closest was 6.4 miles off. It was ahead, off to our starboard, about three o'clock, moving almost due north at eleven knots. I noticed that we had swung around to the north as well and were in pursuit. Another blip was at ten o'clock, moving more slowly. The third was behind us at five o'clock, motionless. On channel 13, the chirps of keying mics were constant. Two or more ships were talking to each other.

Had Watson sailed straight into the middle of the fleet? It was too good.

Alex had slid a cursor over two of the blips and marked them with tracking circles. Around the third—the biggest, the one moving fast—he had a box. The marks gave him the speed, bearing and range, or distance, of the blips. From the box extended a line that projected the ship's path half an hour out.

'I'd say they're not icebergs,' he said to Watson.

'I'd rather go for the one that's moving fast.'

Alex picked up the hydraulic rudder thumb control, and the *Farley* began to swing away from the groundswell to starboard. She rolled as the waves came abeam. The GPS over the console showed the heading at fifty-five degrees. On the radar, a projection line from the centre of a circle, the bull's-eye that was the *Farley*, swung to cross the course line of the other ship.

'Intercept half hour,' Alex said. 'Five-point-two miles.' He handed the helm control to Hammarstedt. 'Keep it there. Fifty-five.'

'Fifty-five.'

'Alert the crew,' Watson was very calm. 'Get someone in the crow's nest.'

Casson said, 'I'll go. Should I bring a radio?'

'No, don't bring a radio.'

'Port five,' Alex said.

'Port five,' Hammarstedt repeated.

'They're moving faster. Port five.' Alex was swinging by degrees to port so they didn't beat us across the bow.

'Hey, Alex,' Kalifi said, 'should I get the Zodiacs ready?'

'Not till we find out what it is.' Watson glanced up at the secondary radar over his head. Moving objects made a smear, so the operator could quickly tell the direction of travel. 'He's moving this way.'

'They haven't changed course at all. Three hundred fifty-three degrees. We are heading twenty-five.'

The radio stuttered with static. More mic keys. The neighbourhood was certainly getting crowded.

'Is it channel thirteen they're coming on? Hammarstedt asked.

'Yes,' Watson said. To Alex, 'How far is it?'

'Four-point-nine miles.'

Silence. The dense fog in no hurry as it rolled across the bow. Light creaking of the bridge timberwork. Something swinging rhythmically against a bulkhead in the chart room. Less than fifteen minutes had passed since I arrived on the bridge. Time was at once compressed and slowed. A lot had happened in a very few minutes, and yet it was all unfolding with the choreographed slowness of a Japanese Noh play. I was not used to the pace of the sea.

I leaned over Alex's shoulder. 'We're trying to intercept this one'—he pointed to the only one presently moving and now at about two o'clock—'and pass this one.' He indicated the blip in the circle at about eleven o'clock. 'Get two for the price of one. We're heading almost towards it. It's about four miles away.'

Visibility was less than 300 yards so I watched the radar. Alex pointed to another blip that had just appeared, also about two o'clock, but further out. Possibly four ships together.

'That's a ship. No doubt.' Skinny Alex had every sinewy ounce focused on the screen.

'Probably a Greenpeace boat trying to figure out if we're a whaling boat, trying to sneak up on us,' Watson said. 'Well, in two and a half miles we'll know if it's an iceberg or a factory ship.'

Watson had been preparing four years for this moment, and he seemed almost too relaxed.

Alex said, 'Could be three icebergs and a boat, of course. Fifteen minutes.'

Allison handed Watson his Mustang suit, which he stepped into. It was orange and black, and it said 'US Coast Guard' on the back. 'Got it on eBay,' he said. He shrugged into the arms and glanced at the radar above him.

'Is the other guy changing? How close can we get?'

'About a mile. He's moving too fast to intercept.'

'If you're absolutely sure that's a ship, maybe we should get a Zodiac in the water.'

Alex sprang. 'Yup,' he said simply. He straightened and twisted away from the screen. 'Okay,' he barked. 'Get a Zodiac in right now!' His hand came down hard on the wood of the console. 'Go! Now!'

Half the bridge emptied. Through the windows we could see crew pouring out onto the deck, whipping the tarp off the port Zodiac. Kalifi clambered to the davit controls and the crane swung over. Mist rolled over them in veils.

'Tell them to bring the radio for emergency,' Watson said. 'Don't use it except in an emergency. How are we going to direct them where to go?'

'In this soup it's hard to find anything—they should be wearing Mustang suits! Lincoln, go down; tell them to put on Mustang suits. Not to launch it till we give them the sign. We'll slow down.' Alex turned to Watson, 'The ship is pretty much on a northbound course. They've got a GPS and a radio.'

'The radios off unless there's an emergency?' Hammarstedt asked.

'No, the radios on. Just don't transmit.'

Watson said, 'That thing in front is definitely an iceberg. Another flat-top, it looks like.' It was. It loomed out of the fog, 30 feet high, maybe 400 long, the same dimensions as a factory ship. But the other blip was moving at eleven knots on a course of 353 degrees, unwavering. Icebergs didn't do that. Of course, whoever it was had radar at least as sophisticated as ours and could see that at our present speed we would not force a collision.

Alex had shoved down the sliding window in front of him and was watching the deck like a fierce hawk.

Colin, Lincoln and Gedden were in their orange suits, ready to go. Colin tossed a small buoy attached to a coil of steel cable into the Zodiac—a tangle line for fouling a ship's prop.

Alex, out the window: 'Get someone to pump that pontoon up!' He pulled his head back in. 'There's, like, six people standing there. They can pump it up right now.' I hadn't noticed, but the right pontoon of the Zodiac was wrinkled and sagged like a flat tyre. I looked out onto the bridge wing and saw the thermometer marking half a degree above freezing. The colder air contracted and it would make the whole Zodiac slack.

Watson said, 'Better take a second radio as a backup.' He was still thinking about the safety of his crew. It would be easy to motor off in this fog, and never be seen again. Beyond about a mile, a Zodiac, even on the primary radar, was lost in swirling wave tops and chunks of ice. The chopper could not take off in this soup. I realised how vulnerable any of our craft would be—Zodiacs and FIB and chopper alike—as soon as they got out of sight of our little mother ship.

Alex said, 'We can follow them.' He craned around to Mathieu, the French film-maker. 'If you're on time you can get in—hey, get them a handheld compass—no, it's pointless. Magnetic south.' Hadn't thought of that. We were within 350 miles of magnetic south and all the magnetic compasses were haywire. The south magnetic pole was about 1,500 miles north of the south pole and shifted year to year. It did not have nearly the force of magnetic north, but it wrought havoc on compasses that were nearby. The ship's binnacle, a big dial compass, was about sixty degrees off at the moment.

The outside hatch swung open, letting in a gust of cold. 'Jeff's ready,' Lincoln said. 'They're ready to go.'

WATSON LEANED out the window and yelled, 'Anybody loses a radio, he'll never get on a boat again!'

Alex: 'Get the ladder ready!'

We passed the iceberg close enough to port to hear the wash of the waves against it through the open windows. The blue at its base was the only colour in a movie that had gone black-and-white. This was a sea story that might have taken place in the early twentieth century, or in the nineteenth. No battles unfolded this slowly any more. No targets were this uncertain, no boats could be lost so easily. *The radio the radio the radio.* Watson kept repeating it. But what good would the radio do if they got out of range? Or if they could not work the GPS and tell the ship where they were?

Almost on cue, Gedden burst onto the bridge. 'The batteries on this GPS are shot.'

That figured. Nobody knew where there were extras. I tore down the three flights to my cabin and retrieved my own GPS. I handed it to Gedden. 'This is the compass screen. Here's your current position. It's waterproof, so don't worry about that.'

He tumbled down the steps.

Watson said, 'How far is this guy now?'

'About two and a half. When we get to one and a half, we'll launch. Tell them ten minutes.'

Hammarstedt called down, 'Zodiac, we're launching in ten minutes!'

Just then Emily rushed in, flushed, her ponytail flying. 'They need a flare. Where's a flare?' She was hyperventilating.

'Over there.'

'Two flares, yeah?'

Alex shrugged.

Watson said, 'There's a French base directly to the south of us. These guys are heading due north. I bet it's a French supply ship. Mia, hail the ship in French on channel sixteen. Say, "French supply vessel". Repeat it. Don't identify us.'

Mia took down the mic and spoke the words, repeating the phrase half a dozen times.

Silence. Watson waited. We could hear the ice chunks thudding off the bow. 'Nope. No answer. If they were a French ship they would have answered us.'

Alex peered ahead through the dense fog. 'It's pretty risky, Paul,' he said.

They couldn't even get a load of beer from the Hobart dock without nearly sinking. We weren't in any harbour now, we were in the remotest waters on earth. Whoever was ahead of us did not want to communicate. In a vast, lonely ocean, where it was a courtesy to hail a fellow ship, they were not answering our call. They were making tracks away from us and were not slowing down to see who we were.

'We can follow them,' Watson said, meaning the Zodiac.

'Okay, they can launch at will. Get it under four knots.'

Watson said, 'Tell them it's at one o'clock right now, two miles . . . Just get going straight ahead! Slightly on starboard side! Let's go!' He pulled back the chrome lever that adjusted the propeller pitch and the *Farley* slowed.

Alex called out, 'Launch at will.'

Kalifi, on the winch, shouted 'Good luck!' and raised the hook. She was wearing her pyjama bottoms in the freezing mist. The harness went taut, and the Zodiac lifted out of its cradle. Colin, Jeff, Gedden and Mathieu were in the boat. Just then, young Luke and Willie rushed across the deck and piled into the Zodiac like a couple of puppies. Kalifi lowered the boat to the water. For a moment they were being dragged, bouncing against the slow-moving hull and then they unhooked, started the outboard and gunned off into the fog. Except that they were gunning very slowly. Even I could see they were overloaded. In less than a minute they were swallowed by the fog.

Watson swore. 'Who's on that boat?'

Lincoln said, 'I told them three, max.'

'They're going the wrong direction!' Alex said. 'Okay, they adjusted; if they keep on going straight they should be all right.'

Watson fumed. 'We're going to have drills on this!'

Alex was watching the radar intently. 'I've got them, barely,' he said. 'Not very good.'

He straightened and looked at Watson. 'Before they intercept they're gonna be four or five miles out, and then . . .' What he meant was that they would be lost to us. Four or five miles in this ocean, blind, could be a few miles over into the Next World. Everybody looked at the captain. The bow struck ice and it scraped along the hull. The low swells rolled and there was the shirring rush as the *Farley* rode over them. Kalifi came through an outside hatch and pulled it shut.

'They should be almost on them,' Watson said. 'It shouldn't take long to do two miles.' He reached up and slid the mic out of its bracket anyway. 'Zodiac, do you copy?' No answer. He looked at Kalifi. 'Did they turn them on?'

'I think they understood not to turn them on unless they saw something.'

'Zodiac, do you copy?'

Nothing.

'Obviously, they don't have them on.'

We all watched the captain. There was ice in the water. The seas were calm now, but in these latitudes the weather could change fast. In the time it took to strip a line of laundry, waves could be washing over the deck. In minutes, in their unsealed Mustang suits, the Zodiac crew would be dead. It wouldn't take much to swamp the little rubber boat, especially as it was overloaded. The helicopter would be useless in low visibility.

'There!' Straight ahead, through a rent in the fog, was the stern of a great ship. It seemed terribly far away. The suggestion of a towering superstructure like an empty gate, whiter than the fog around it. Then it was gone.

'That is a whale ship,' Watson said. 'I think it's the Japanese "researcher".'

The captain keyed the mike again. 'Zodiac, do you copy?'

'Copy.' It was Gedden's voice, out of the static. Relief.

'Is it clearing up where you are?' Watson said. Ahead, the

ship was visible again for a few seconds, more as an absence of miasma, the vague shape of a stern.

'It's clearing up.'

'That is a ship; there is a ship ahead of us. It is a whale ship.'

'Do you want us to proceed in the direction your bow is facing?' Gedden asked.

'Roger.'

That seemed like a strange question. But a minute later the Zodiac appeared. It was coming up behind us. They had done a complete circle in the fog. No wonder they hadn't caught the whaler. I didn't get it. They had a GPS with a satellite-guided compass.

Geert said, 'Do you think they can see us?' The whole bridge erupted in laughter. I guess everybody was relieved.

'Passing on port side now,' Gedden said without irony. 'We can see the ship. I'm heading 030.'

'Yeah, we can see that,' Watson said drily. 'Next time you take a coffee break let us know. Go ahead.'

It was 2323, almost midnight. The pursuit had lasted almost an hour and a half. The target ship was dead ahead of us and gaining. At 2.3 miles we couldn't see it any more. Gedden was motoring off thirty degrees to starboard, heading for empty ocean. The captain got on the radio, frustrated, and reiterated the course: dead ahead, 000 degrees.

'We're not moving very fast,' Gedden answered.

'It would help if you didn't have six people. Return.' That was the final order.

Allison said, 'You don't think it's the mother ship?'

Watson said, 'No, it's a research ship, white.'

'It's going north too.'

'Yeah. It's coming from the French research station. There was a supply ship scheduled to leave this morning. Going back to Hobart.' Watson exhaled. 'We have to have a dedicated crew for each of these boats.'

'We do,' she said. 'Unfortunately they're not in it.'

I thought the ghost ship could have been the *Nisshin Maru*. There was no other reason for its eerie silence. We were two miles away from it. Its officers could see that on their radar.

We had hailed them in French. They maintained their silence and sailed off. Watson first suggested it was a research ship, then a supply ship. It did not look white to me. The superstructure looked white and the rest looked like fog. I thought our captain was in denial.

I could understand it. To prepare for four years for this attempt. To come almost straight south from Hobart and run smack into the factory ship in the middle of a white-out. And then not to be able to do anything about it. Because the *Farley* was too slow. Because the outboards on the Zodiacs were underpowered. Because the crew was incompetent. It was too awful to swallow. Watson had to believe that big ship was somebody else.

What would he be able to do the next time? There was one thing. If they could get the Zodiacs sorted out they should be able to run up on the stern and throw out a prop fouler. That is, if we ever got within a few miles of the factory ship again.

When the Zodiac was at last swung back into its cradle just before midnight, Luke and Willie climbed out of it with less enthusiasm than they'd climbed in. Gedden came onto the bridge, sheepish, still in his Mustang suit, his thick glasses steaming.

'What were six people doing on that boat?' Watson demanded.

'I have no idea. I was with the GPS and the radio.'

'You were right behind us and the boat. What happened?'

'I don't know. My glasses fogged up; I couldn't see anything. I was telling them where to go. I think Colin's understanding was to go out a mile and if we didn't see anything, come back.'

They had been terribly exposed. That made sense.

Mathieu said in his heavy French accent, sheepishly, 'The first one was going great and then we saw the *Farley* from the stern.'

'Well, that does it, I guess. The fog's back.' Watson got up. It was the end of his watch, anyway. 'Turn her around,' he said to Hammarstedt. 'Go one-six-eight.' Twelve degrees east of due south. He was still heading for the Virik Bank.

7

ICE

I WAS GETTING into the habit of waking and climbing to the bridge once during the graveyard shift, Alex's watch, between 0400 and 0800. The ship then was mostly asleep.

Early on the morning of 19 December, I woke just after five and climbed to the bridge. The ship was ploughing due south in the fog, only thirty feet off a towering wall of ice. It was over 100 feet high, pure white but luminous, as if lit from inside. The groundswell washed against its base with an explosion of spray and a hollow boom that repeated with the rote warning of a bell buoy. High up against the smooth face, storm petrels flew and veered like so many cliff swallows.

This was not a cliff, and they were not swallows. It was a great, glacial piece of ice, bigger than Manhattan. The wall ran as far as we could see ahead, and as far behind.

'We've been passing it for over an hour,' Alex said. 'Over ten miles. The radar shows it out ahead at least as far.'

Hard to imagine the catastrophe when this mass of ice broke from its glacier. I went back to sleep. What woke me again, at seven, was a loud thud. I lay for a minute and listened. The porthole was bolted shut, so the cabin was dark except for a trace of fluorescent light bleeding around the red curtain over the doorway. The vibrations of the diesel, usually pitched at full bore, were subdued. The slosh and gurgle of water along the hull inches from my head had changed from boisterous, even violent, to leisurely, if not tentative. Another thud and a long, gritted scrape. I dressed and clambered up the stairs to the main companionway. I shoved open the hatch and stepped onto the main deck.

The *Farley* was moving slowly in a dream of fog and ice. All around the ship, hemming it in, were rafts of broken bergs. Some were the size of dinghies, others like barges. Most were flat to the water, pack-ice platforms of old snow; others gestured out of the mist like abstract sculptures of animals. Some were smooth, old and stained; others were broken into sharp-edged geometric forms. The *Farley* moved gingerly through them, hewing to a narrow, jagged trail of open water that disappeared into the fog. She shouldered the smaller bergs aside. The water, smoothed and protected, was a deep lake blue. All of it, this whole floating world, rose and fell on the easy groundswell.

White, grey, black, and the singular, remarkable blues. These were the only colours. The air coming onto the bow smelled cold and sere, pure—not a trace of smoke, of earth, tree, rock, grass. The place did not seem to belong to earth, and yet there were the birds, veering and circling, to remind you that you had not untethered from the planet. Seven or eight penguins porpoised fast along an edge of ice, flying through the dark water as their forebears once flew through air. Dennis had told me that penguins and albatross were closely related. Some of their common ancestors had made their homes on an island free of predators and no longer needed to fly. Both families had a gland that allowed them to drink seawater and secrete the salt.

'Check it out!' It was Casson, our wonkish cook. He pointed to three little penguins who bellied up onto a flat raft of ice and stood gawking at the high black bow approaching them. They were Adélies. They tottered forward, craned upward, spoke loudly to each other, hustled back a bit. They stood in a ragged line and waved their stubby wings. Just then the bridge cut forward power and the *Farley* ground into the barge of ice and stopped.

I think the penguins thought they had done it. They had evidently never seen such an animal. They rushed, waddling, forward. One tipped over in her excitement and bellied along on the hardened snow and righted herself. They stood together before the bow like emissaries and flapped their flipper arms and squawked at each other and at the ship.

Wessel nudged me. 'Look at that.' He pointed to a huge

brown seal lying on its own raft. Its head looked to be as big as a lion's. 'That's a leopard seal,' he said. 'The fiercest predator out here. It'll shoot upward, break ice, and grab the other seals. A real badass.'

We were about 120 miles from the coast of Antarctica. The Antarctic Circle was about 70 miles to the south, and just 180 miles to the south and west was the Australian station at Commonwealth Bay, the windiest place on earth. Wind speeds of 250 miles per hour had been recorded there.

On the bridge, the officers surveyed the scene. We were hemmed in on all sides by undulating ice. None of them seemed too concerned.

Watson said, 'When the fog clears we can get the helicopter up to tell us the path.'

Chris Aultman brightened. 'We can do it,' he said, and went aft to the heli deck and began slipping the covers off the chopper blades and engine. He moved with a new vigour. This would be the bird's maiden flight off the ship.

The fog didn't clear. We all went down to breakfast.

Alex said, 'This pack ice could be an ice field, or it could go all the way to the coast. I don't think we can go any further south. We are sending the chopper to take a look—though in this fog, it's less than one mile visibility.'

Watson shook his head. 'It doesn't pay to work your way around.' He meant to push further into the pack ice, trying to find a route. 'This is the edge. Next thing you know the wind shifts and you're locked in like Shackleton.'

In the first years of the third millennium we faced the same uncertainties as a ship in the 1800s. The wind could change, and the ice could close in around the ship. Now, this morning, there was almost no wind. The fog drifted without purpose like smoke on a still day. The ice, the chunks and rafts, kept their spacing, a jigsaw puzzle spread out by a madman unwilling to lock the pieces. The black *Farley* sat in the middle of it, tempting capture. In the stillness, even the colours seemed to stay quiet. The one leopard seal hadn't moved.

As breakfast ended Watson said that he had emailed the *Esperanza* two days ago with our position. 'Can't get an answer from them,' he said. 'They said they wanted to co-operate.' He meant certain crew members on their ships.

He showed me the email he'd sent to Shane Rattenbury, the head of Greenpeace's Southern Ocean expedition, who spent time aboard both its ships: the fast flagship, the *Esperanza*, and the slow reconditioned sealer, the *Arctic Sunrise*. It read:

Dear Shane

The *Farley Mowat* is patrolling east of the 130-degree east line. We have reason to believe that the Japanese may be avoiding the area west of the 130-degree line to avoid a confrontation with Greenpeace and Sea Shepherd. We can save you lots of time and money by scouting ahead. What I am trying to find out is how far east are you now and how far east will you be going? There is no need to dupli-cate the area covered. It is a big area and we should be able to cover it all with three ships.

We will go east and then double back west again. If we spot them we will notify you.

We have posted a $10,000 reward for the Japanese coordinates.

Captain Paul Watson

I wondered again about the friction between the two groups, which were ostensibly working towards the same ends. It had the heat of sibling hatred, the kind of animosity that arises from intimate mutual knowledge and betrayal. Hammarstedt, the Swede, who had been a member of Greenpeace between 1999 and 2002, said he had gone on a Greenpeace ship and that the Greenpeacers sat around talking about Sea Shepherd the way the *Farley*'s crew talked about Greenpeace.

Watson often talked about founding Greenpeace in 1972. He said he left in 1977 to found Sea Shepherd because he wanted to physically enforce international laws. The story popular with many Greenpeacers is that he was ejected for grabbing a sealer's club and throwing it into the water. The way Watson tells it, 'I was voted off the board for opposing Patrick Moore as the new president of the board.'

At 0950, Trevor started the engines again. We gave up on

launching the chopper and Watson pushed cautiously into a wide arc through the leads of open water and turned around. We headed back the way we'd come. The fog was still heavy and spumed across the bow.

Watson tried to put the *Farley* east of north at eighteen degrees—why was he so intent on the Virik Bank?—but we quickly ran into more thick ice. He narrowed his course to ten degrees and then eight degrees, forced to port by the thick pack ice.

'Looks like it's opening up now,' he said to Alex. 'You never know.'

'Not really. The radar is still a minefield.' He was right; growlers thumped off the bow.

And then we were up against the great cliff, the sheared continent of ice, and he ran just off it, now on our starboard, and followed the cold wall due north. There were the petrels again, flying along the cliff face as if they were country birds hunting bugs, but there had not been a bug in our world for 1,200 miles.

Before lunch, Kalifi called an all-hands briefing in the mess to discuss yesterday's action.

Alex stood in front of the food counter. With his buzzed head and wasted cheeks, his serious grey eyes, and his scrawny neck sticking out of the black sweatshirt, he looked like a POW. He had told me, 'That's one reason I hate the Japanese whalers—for making me come down here again where I'm always cold.' He wasted no words now.

'Couple of things went wrong yesterday. Especially with the Zodiacs. We've got to get really good at this.' He looked around the room. Kristy, the tiny nurse, plucked at her rainbow arm warmers. Big Marc crossed his arms over his coveralls and pursed his lips. The J. Crew, crammed into the back booth, watched impassively, like kids in a classroom sizing up a new teacher—or like the poker players they are.

Alex continued, 'Too many people in the Zodiac. When the captain says four, he means four, not six. Need somebody to listen to the radio. Communication is essential. Pretty risky—you go out into the fog and we don't see you any more.

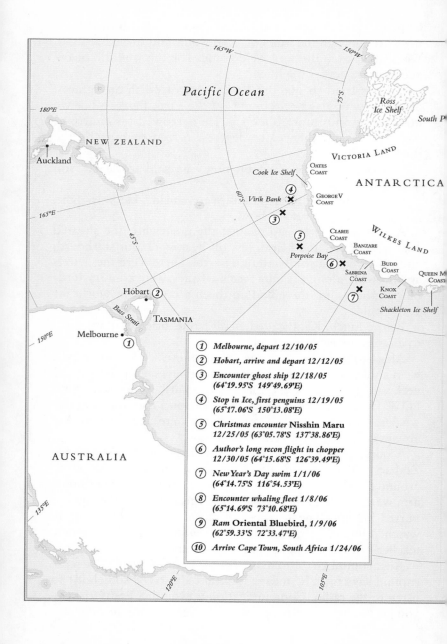

Pacific Ocean

Ross
Ice Shelf

South P

NEW ZEALAND

Auckland

VICTORIA LAND

Cook Ice Shelf

OATES
COAST

ANTARCTICA

④

Virik Bank

GEORGE V
COAST

③

WILKES LAND

⑤

CLARIE
COAST

BANZARE
COAST

Porpoise Bay

⑥

SABRINA
COAST

BUDD
COAST

QUEEN M
COAST

KNOX
COAST

⑦

Shackleton Ice Shelf

Hobart ②

Bass Strait

TASMANIA

Melbourne

①

AUSTRALIA

① *Melbourne, depart 12/10/05*

② *Hobart, arrive and depart 12/12/05*

③ *Encounter ghost ship 12/18/05*
(64°19.95'S 149°49.69'E)

④ *Stop in Ice, first penguins 12/19/05*
(65°17.06'S 150°13.08'E)

⑤ *Christmas encounter* Nisshin Maru
12/25/05 (63°05.78'S 137°38.86'E)

⑥ *Author's long recon flight in chopper*
12/30/05 (64°15.68'S 126°39.49'E)

⑦ *New Year's Day swim 1/1/06*
(64°14.75'S 116°54.53'E)

⑧ *Encounter whaling fleet 1/8/06*
(65°14.69'S 73°10.68'E)

⑨ *Ram* Oriental Bluebird, *1/9/06*
(62°59.33'S 72°33.47'E)

⑩ *Arrive Cape Town, South Africa 1/24/06*

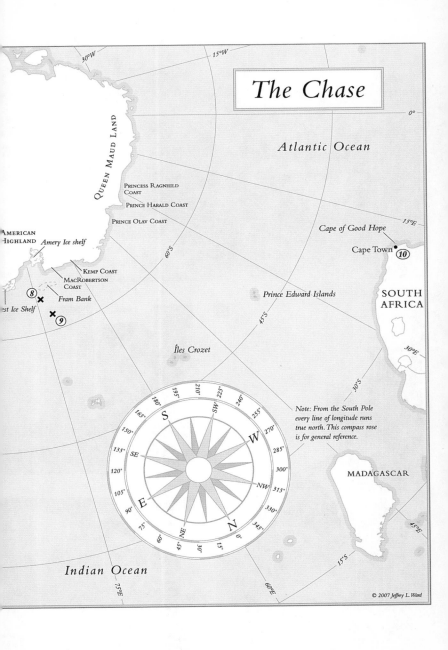

The Chase

Atlantic Ocean

QUEEN MAUD LAND

PRINCESS RAGNHILD
COAST

PRINCE HARALD COAST

PRINCE OLAV COAST

AMERICAN
HIGHLAND Amery Ice shelf

Cape of Good Hope

Cape Town ⑩

KEMP COAST

MACROBERTSON
COAST

⑧ ✕   Fram Bank

Prince Edward Islands

SOUTH
AFRICA

est Ice Shelf ✕
        ⑨

Îles Crozet

Note: From the South Pole
every line of longitude runs
true north. This compass rose
is for general reference.

MADAGASCAR

Indian Ocean

© 2007 Jeffrey L. Ward

1 The crew assembles on the deck of the *Farley Mowat*.

2 The Can Opener: chief engineer Trevor Van Der Gulik preparing a support for the weapon. He is being belayed by engineer Willie Houtman. The can opener is a seven-foot steel blade designed to tear open the hull of another ship.

3 Quartermaster Lamya Essemlali, from France.

4 Second Officer Peter Hammarstedt, from Sweden.

5 Bosun's Mate Colin Miller, left, and deck hand Joel Capolongo, preparing the ship for departure.

6 Left to right, engineer and punk rocker Luke Westhead, and the J. Crew, semi-professional gamblers from Syracuse—Jeff Watkins, Joel Capolongo, and Justin Pellingra.

7 Two Dutchmen: welder Marc Oosterwal (left), and ship's artist Geert Vons.

Ship's Nurse Kristy Whitefield, an emergency room nurse in Melbourne who joined the ship just before departure.

South African Zodiac pilot extraordinaire Wessel Jacobsz.

Quartermaster and Earth First! forest activist Gedden, aka Jon Batchelor.

Quartermaster and news reporter Emily Hunter. She carried her father's ashes to Antarctica and spread them on top of an iceberg.

Chief engineer Trevor Van Der Gulik. Highly trained, he has supervised teams of 500 ships' engineers in Dubai at the largest shipyard in the world. He is Watson's nephew.

Melbourne local electrician and union boss Sparky Dave DeGraaff. Dave saw the *Farley Mowat* from the top of one of the new buildings under construction in the harbour and signed on.

7 Weapon making 101: deck hand Inde—aka Julie Farris—shows another hand, Mande Davis, how to splice an eye into a steel cable. They are making prop foulers, a weapon designed to disable another ship's propeller.

8 J. Crew Jeff with the 'Jellyfish', a prop fouler with multiple cables.

9 The Fourth Estate: videographers Ron Colby (left) and Kristian Olsen.

10 Dutchmen Marc and Geert with a time capsule they built. Inside are letters and messages to future generations. The capsule was left the next year on a tiny rock islet in the Southern Ocean called Scott Island.

11 One of several crew members who went swimming on New Year's Day.

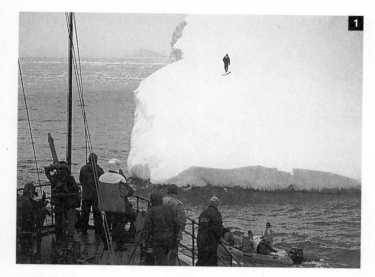

1. Trevor decides to snowboard Antarctica.

2. A dead juvenile sperm whale.

3. The chopper lashed to the heli deck in big seas, Christmas Eve, 2005. The deck is about twenty feet off the water and the waves tower above it.

4. Captain Paul Watson with his wife, and galley assistant, Allison Lance Watson. Allison is a fierce animal rights activist who once leapt with a knife into a net-caged bay in Taiji, Japan, and freed dolphins penned there for slaughter.

5. Giving chase to the *Oriental Bluebird* after the ramming. She fled north, never to rendezvous with the *Nisshin Maru* again. The 'Whale Meat' on her stern was painted by Greenpeace activists during a transfer of whale meat from the factory ship to the *Bluebird*.

'I wanna go ahead with the teams we talked about. I don't wanna see anybody else on deck. The three drivers all have their own teams. Kalifi's launching teams are posted at the bosun's locker.'

The electronic alarm buzzed loudly in the galley. Watson was on the bridge and summoning somebody. Alex exited.

Wessell said, 'Each team must have a boat navigator talking to the skipper.'

Allison nodded. 'When the Zodiacs go out, whoever is captain of the team should take a GPS.' She too was spare, hollow-cheeked, wired hot like Alex. Her baby-blue eyes shone with a warrior's zeal. She and Alex made a good pair of operatives. One could imagine that in a place like Taiji, where they'd freed the dolphins, it would have been next to impossible to stop them.

'And we must know how to use it,' Wessel said. The South African was one of the Zodiac pilots.

Alex slipped back into the mess. He must have run up and down the steps. 'Okay,' he said. 'We'll do a little training, then. There's an instruction book on the GPS.' He looked around the mess. 'I realise we have a very inexperienced crew. You can't expect somebody to do everything right away. The navigator didn't do that well but we've never followed a ship into the mist. Even with experienced people, we've never done that before.'

Kalifi said, 'I think everybody did a good job as far as launching was concerned.'

Grey-haired Dennis, the bird biologist, said, 'I saw some cotton get into the boat. That's bad. Cotton kills.'

Cotton. Good point. It's a basic tenet of outdoor survival that one should never wear cotton in any situation that is likely to get cold and wet. The stuff clings to the skin and stays clammy, and saps the body heat. Wool is warm when wet, as are synthetic undergarments and fleeces. Dennis's comment underscored how green so many of the crew were. Eager and willing and green. Also, how little basic training they were getting.

Alex said, 'Looks like we will be launching the helicopter

today. But it's got to clear up. If not, we're probably going to have to keep on going till we clear up.'

Joel raised his hand in the back. 'I have a question about the mission itself. It seems we're unprepared. We're in the dark as to what we will actually do when we meet them.'

'We're talking about that,' Alex said.

'It seems,' Joel continued, 'like we need to make preparations, so when we do find them—so we're ready.'

Steve said, 'It doesn't seem the toys are being worked on.'

'Basically a steel cable and a couple of floats is something you can put together,' Alex said. What were they talking about?

'Aren't we going to see if we have any stuff left over from the last campaign?' Allison asked, turning to Wessel. 'Get barrels, get the cable. From the meeting last time I thought you would work on it.'

That must have been another meeting many of us weren't privy to. Again there was a sense that a lot more was going on beneath the surface than met the eye.

The smell of baked squash was beginning to smother the mess. Kristian, the boyish videographer from Vancouver, spoke up. 'What is the primary purpose?' he asked. 'Is it to foul the propeller, get between a ship and the whales? What's it going to be?'

'We're still talking about it,' Alex said. 'We don't know if we're going to find a factory ship, killers taking the whale back, or what. We wanna be prepared for different scenarios.'

'Paul does have his own plan,' Allison said. 'All these others are secondary.'

'Maybe the Zodiac needs to carry something that will reflect radar. If I'm going to go in the Zodiac with a camera I'd feel much more safe,' Kristian said.

Allison said, 'Every Zodiac will have a GPS programmed, and you can reverse it. Chris will train them.'

Casson said, 'Little by little we have food going off. Can somebody show me how to prepare the pie cannon?'

'It's more of a gimmick. It's not gonna do much. What we should do is have the water cannons hit them.'

Steve said, 'Yesterday, whatever the battle plan was—'

Alex cut him short. 'There wasn't a battle plan. Just send the Zodiac out.'

Wessel said, 'I think if no media are on board, should only be three people. Those Zodiacs aren't big.'

'Four is good,' Alex said. 'You can have one on communications, two for light handling, and if you lose one you have a spare.'

Laughter.

The meeting broke up. I went out on the main deck to catch some air just before lunch. Prop foulers, can openers and pie cannons. In Monty Python they catapulted a cow over the castle wall. Just as I got to the rail I heard the whale alarm sound. We were still following the ice cliff, maybe 200 feet on our starboard. Up ahead I saw them, two blows, a billow of mist trailing downwind. They swam right at the *Farley* and passed within fifty feet. My God, they were big. The smooth, glossy back, grey-black with one small fin, seemed to go on and on. I heard the gasp of a blowhole, like an air brake. They were two adult fin whales. They might have measured seventy-five feet and weighed eighty tons— the largest mammals on earth aside from the blue whale. They were unconcerned with the ship, perhaps curious, and they glided by like a distillation of wild goodwill.

An eighty-ton, warm-blooded nod in an ice-filled sea. They were endangered. The IWC estimates that there were 85,200 fin whales left in the southern hemisphere in 1979, but other scientists claim that today there could be as few as 2,000 to 5,000. These were the other species the Japanese were hunting this Antarctic summer. They planned to kill ten. Next season they would kill ten more, then fifty every year after that.

By the 1970s, the fin whale had been driven to near extinction. It now numbered about 10 per cent of its pre-whaling population. A recent study, by geneticists from Stanford and Harvard of pre-whaling populations using DNA analysis, published in *Science,* stated, 'In light of our findings, current populations of humpback or fin whales are far from harvestable.' The authors added, 'Minke whales are closer to genetically defined population limits, and hunting decisions regarding them must be based on other data.'

Big Marc was beside me at the rail. He grinned and clapped me on the back. Then he knelt down beside his pride and joy on the deck. The can opener was looking more and more vicious.

'Yah, we make it ready,' he said, picking up his face guard. 'Putting it outside will be difficult. Put it where ship is strongest, facing forward. Two and a half metres it is.'

'You think we'll get that close?'

'Yah, I hope.' He pulled down the face mask and lit his torch with a hiss.

I WENT to the stern. I untied the broken wood chair that I'd lashed to a pipe, and retied it with a longer leash. I sat in the cold breeze and felt the push of the deck surging and yawing, heard the boom as the swells sprayed up against the ice wall and watched two Cape pigeons fly over the wake in a tight pair. They were the size of a laughing gull, black with white markings along the tops of the wings. A little while later a wandering albatross hung right over the stern, balancing on wings eleven feet across. The longest wings of any flying bird on earth. Dennis had told me that some albatross can fly the girth of the earth without rest.

I went up on the bridge. All the officers were there. It was Alex's watch, but Watson sat in the captain's chair.

He was fuming, but nobody who hadn't been observing him for a couple of weeks would know. It was revealed in the energy with which he was telling a story about the Confederate raider, the *Shenandoah*.

'Many of the great whales would be extinct if it wasn't for the *Shenandoah*. She went after and decimated the Yankee whaling fleet in the Pacific. Destroyed forty whaling ships. A good role model, too, because her captain, James Waddell, did it without taking a single life.'

He motioned at the iceberg out the window. 'More damn fresh water in that thing than in Lake Ontario.' He finished his story and swung out of the chair. 'Got an email from

Shane the Rat,' he said to me and went back to the radio room. Shane, the Greenpeace expedition leader. Watson handed me the letter.

Dear Paul,

Thanks for your note. We are also currently patrolling in search of the fleet, but thus far have only been successful in sighting a spotter vessel. When we find the fleet, we will advise the location to all parties through a press release.

He went on to say that Greenpeace did not wish to enter into a formal cooperative relationship with Sea Shepherd.

As you noted . . . there have been differences and disputes between our organisations over the years. I do not wish to comment on those, since there is little value in that at a time when we should be focused on the whalers. However, no relationship can be repaired with a flick of a switch. Building trust takes time.

He concluded by saying that it should be possible for the two organisations to pursue their respective missions without interfering with each other.

That is our preference. If we can find peaceful coexistence on this expedition, that may open further opportunities at a later date, but let's take a single step at a time.

I could see why Watson was livid. He had founded Greenpeace and now, in a bid to cooperate, was being shrugged off by the young sons with a patronising and sanctimonious note.

'Why wouldn't they want to cooperate?' I asked. 'The real reason?'

'Because they know that when we show up we'll actually do something. Stop the killing. Make them look bad.' He let out an exhale of frustration. 'You know, I don't think they want to stop the whaling. They make too much money. They raised one hundred and thirty-five million off this campaign.'

Watson sat down in his swivel chair in the tiny radio room and banged out a response. The boat pitched and his fingers flew over the keyboard without pause:

'. . . I give up, Shane. After decades of trying to work co-operatively with Greenpeace, I give up. You people are just simply unbelievable, so full of yourself and so cocksure and conceited that your way is the only way . . .'

He hit SEND.

IN THE MIDDLE of the afternoon we cleared the end of the ice island and turned due east along its northern edge. Alex said that Watson wanted to check out the area around the Balleny Islands off the Oates Coast of Victoria Land. He felt that the whalers might be working to the east, staying away from Greenpeace.

'Why not further south?'

'The whalers wouldn't be whaling south of where we are. Too much ice. From all the footage I've seen of whalers, they're usually around pancake ice, just frozen ice, not this glacial ice.'

On the main deck, Chris Price and Pawel were teaching the Zodiac crews how to use the GPS-radios. You could not fault the Shepherds for their ardour. The training session broke down when another whale, this time a humpback, blew off port.

After dinner, on the way to my berth, I passed Gedden leaning into Colin's cabin in heated discussion. Colin huddled over a sheet of paper on the workbench.

Colin's voice: '. . . go after the shaft and the rudder and propeller. Like a flail. If you use cable and it gets caught in the propeller it will act like a big wire saw.'

Gedden said, 'My concern is that if you use longline as a feeder line it'll cut right through.'

They went quiet when I stopped. 'Prop foulers?'

They looked at each other. Gedden nodded. 'Ops props.'

'Explain.'

'The best thing we could hope for,' Gedden said, 'is a steel cable wrapped around the propeller shaft, breaking some of their seals so it goes inoperable. Probably the most likely method is coming up on the rear quarter of the vessel and feed-ing a smaller line into the prop wash and having the smaller line suck in the cable. Attach it all to a buoy, so if it kicks free we can pick it up and use it again.'

I asked if it had ever worked before.

He pushed his thick, black-framed glasses up on his nose and laughed. 'Various governments throughout the world have tried it on us—mainly the Norwegian navy, the Faroe Islanders. They were dropping nets in front of the bow in hopes the prop would suck it up and get stuffed by it. Didn't work. We ran right over them, chopped them up. That's why we want to use cable.'

Gedden explained that they might try using oil drums as buoys—the Zodiac could run in front of the ship and drop the line across the bow. He and Colin continued discussing the relative merits of feeding cable into the prop or just chucking the whole thing overboard.

'What if they have prop guards?'

'But what's a prop guard?' Gedden said. 'A tube around the prop. Their actual function is nozzles—sort of like streamlines your propwash or something so you get more pushing power. If you get a mooring line or something caught between the prop and nozzle you can actually jam it, the prop, so if they don't get the engine shut down right away you can do some major damage internally. The propeller's not going to cut the cable. It seems if you're in the rear of the vessel and you drop a lead line in, it should in theory suck it right up.'

I followed Gedden up the stairs to the bosun's locker. Inde was in there, sitting on a low stool, splicing half-inch steel cable into an eye. Gedden began to look around the locker, his design gears turning.

'There's some butyric acid on the ship,' he said finally. 'We need better delivery methods.'

'What's butyric acid?'

'It's not, like, debilitating, it just really stinks.'

'It's derived from rotting cheese milk,' Inde said. 'Think of some cheese like Limburger and magnify it by, like, a hundred.'

'If you break a bottle of it on the deck of a ship they can't be there.'

Much later, after the *Farley* had cleared the north side of the iceberg, which turned out to be over forty miles long, I went into the mess and found Wessel and Casson in intense conversation.

Wessel said, 'How do you know we're not going to sink a ship full of Japanese? Fouling a prop can sink a ship. What if a bad sea comes up? You foul the mother ship's prop, and in five days' time a big storm comes up and that ship is left—' He tipped back his beer. 'Endangers lives,' Wessel said emphatically.

'I don't know,' Casson said. 'It's Paul's call.'

'He would sink every goddam ship.'

'No, Paul would never sink a ship at sea.'

'Yeah, all but one,' interjected Shane, a young hippie from Tasmania who was listening from the next booth. 'So it could rescue the others.'

'That's impossible,' Wessel said. 'There's one hundred and twenty-eight people on the mother ship. Twenty on each of the other ships. It'll even be a squeeze with all the people on the mother ship. All I'm saying is, you're endangering people's lives. Fouling props in Antarctica is no funny business. If we foul one of theirs, what's to keep them from coming to us and fouling ours?'

'Hopefully it would never come to that. We've never harmed anyone,' said Casson gravely.

'You go full steam ahead with that thing sticking out, you can't hurt anyone?' Wessel was talking about the can opener.

Casson cricked his neck, 'That's why I'm not too happy with that.'

'You have no way of knowing whether fouling a prop will kill people as well. All I'm trying to say is that in this kind of action, there's a possibility.' The Zodiac driver was calling it like it was; he wasn't shying away from the action, but he was being realistic about possible consequences.

One night in the green room, I had seen a video of one of Watson's actions in the Pacific, ramming a Japanese drift-netter, and it was hard to believe no one had got hurt. The impact of the two vessels almost tore off the power block at the stern. The Japanese crew—most of them froze and watched the oncoming trawler with shocked disbelief, the way you might react if Godzilla were about to step on your house.

I wandered up to the bridge. Watson was in the radio room, writing some late diatribes. Pawel was in there, too, hunched intently over a laptop, surfing for news of Greenpeace and the Japanese.

'Here's something,' he said. 'One of the Japanese crew has appendicitis and needs a medevac to Hobart. It says that one of the killer boats is bringing him back to Tasmania.'

'Huh,' Watson cocked his head. 'That would put us in the right vicinity. We're almost due south of Tasmania now. You wouldn't think the fleet would want to get too far off. They'd want to rendezvous later.'

He went back to the keyboard. I went down the outside steps off the bridge wing, taking the outdoor route to bed. It was after 1:00am.

The wind was up and so were the swells. It looked as though we were heading for a massive barrier of low ice that completely blocked the horizon. The light was flat, grey, dusky. Small chunks of ice floated by, and off to the south was a small island, a single pointed mountain of white. The iceberg distilled and intensified the low light. The barrier was actually a strip of lighter sky along the horizon. This twilight world was so deceiving. Hammarstedt had told me that the ice sheet at this meridian extends about 150 miles from land. We were about 180 miles off now.

Trevor was at the bottom of the steps in his blue coveralls, jacketless, smoking.

'You think the weather's changing?'

'I never pay attention to the weatherman when I'm on a stinkpot. What are you going to do? You're not fast enough to outrun it. Do the old-fashioned thing and head into it and pray like hell.'

The swells wrinkled in the fresh wind.

'You think we can catch them?'

'We've got the can opener from hell out there. I can do a few things to tweak the engine to get more power. I can get an extra one and a half knots out of her. Probably two. I can get four, but that would be the end of the engine. It's Paul's—it's up to him. I'd gladly destroy the engine to destroy a whaling ship.'

He had a lot of his uncle in him.

THAT NIGHT, or morning, two humpback whales swam directly at the ship while I was sleeping. The crew on watch said they dived and passed under. They surfaced and blew six feet from the low main deck. Justin said they raised their heads out of the water and opened their mouths and made an unearthly sound.

'What kind of sound?' I asked him at breakfast.

'I don't know. Like nothing I ever heard. It raised goose bumps. I'm not a religious kind of guy but it was mystical.'

It gave me a shiver too. Justin thought they were speaking to the *Farley*. Given their proven ability to communicate across thousands of miles in what scientists are beginning to discern as a syntax, maybe it's not too much of a stretch.

Geert had mentioned recent studies showing that humpbacks make 622 social sounds. Research has also found spindle neurons in the brains of humpbacks, fins, orcas and sperm whales. Previously thought to be unique to humans, these specialised cells are located in areas of the human brain associated with social organisation, empathy, speech and intuition. They are thought to process emotion and are the cells responsible for feelings of love, grief and suffering. The researchers found that the whales' spindle neurons reside in the same area of the brain as those in humans, and that they have existed in whales' brains much longer than in ours, and that whales have proportionally three times more of the cells than we do. Not only are whale brains larger than ours, but they have four lobes to our three and more convolutions in the neocortex.

That whales are intelligent, are self-aware, and have a capacity for suffering and grief, was not in doubt. Why wouldn't Justin's humpback call out to the *Farley* in a mystical way?

Humpbacks seemed to be the most charismatic of the great whales, if only because of their exposure to humans. They were the staple of a worldwide whale watching industry that brought in over $1 billion every year. They had the long lateral fins, sometimes as expressive as arms, and a love of the leaping breach. They were also on the Japanese menu. JARPA, the Japanese 'research plan' called for killing fifty of the endangered humpbacks annually. Some estimates put their worldwide population at only 18,000, and some biologists thought that figure much too generous.

The new statistical DNA research on the whales, which can remarkably and accurately assess ancient population numbers and their dispersal patterns, has raised estimates of the humpback's pre-whaling numbers to as many as 1.5 million. Imagine 1.5 million humpbacks patrolling the ancient seas, calling across oceans where only the songs of cetaceans echoed in the deep pelagic blue.

There were no engine sounds then, and the water was as clear as krill and plankton would allow. The whales called over great uninterrupted distances in complex syntax while our human ancestors were still jumping around in trees. This was the magic of whales, that they expressed loyalty, grief, gratitude—all well-documented among present-day humpbacks and other cetaceans. And they had done it all for millions of years and had swum the oceans in peace.

They had left the sea unpolluted, mostly quiet, the reefs teeming; the shores and the mangroves rich, protective; the fish in their schooling numbers as prolific as the stars that wheeled above. They had loved the ocean, if love is a deep attention in which one does no harm. They had perceived it, attended the greens of the reefs and the blues of the deep and all its creatures and passed on, generation to generation. They had not turned on each other with wholesale vengeance and bloodlust, nor massacred another species off the face of the waters because they could.

The ocean they swam in now had changed. Old drift-nets called ghost nets, thousands of miles of them, abandoned, drifted in every sea; the whales could not detect them until it was too late, and then became tangled and died by the thousands. Other fishing gear did the same—lines of lobster traps, longlines, abandoned seines. Ships, the sound of engines and props, turned the great currents into a cacophony through which the old, distant whale songs were mangled and lost. Low-frequency active sonar being used by the US Navy, one of the loudest sound systems devised by man, emitted sonic booms that ruptured delicate hearing mechanisms, caused internal haemorrhage and destroyed cetacean navigation systems so that whole pods washed up disoriented on beaches in the Caribbean and in the Pacific, bleeding from their ears. Overfishing dramatically depleted fish stocks so that for cetaceans, food was harder and harder to find. Pollution concentrated toxins in their flesh to such a degree that many environmental organisations claim that the eating of whale meat is patently unsafe.

WE WERE NOW in a land of ice. Where the Japanese were, where we moved, depended much on what the ice would allow.

After breakfast, just at 0900, we heard the wave-washed silence of the *Farley*'s engines shutting down. We drifted. We were a few hundred yards off a flat-topped iceberg the size of an aircraft carrier. The threatening winds of the night had died down, and the sea was calm, wrinkled with a light breeze that blew snowflakes around. It was time to get the chopper up to scout ahead and find an opening.

Watson said, 'I'm quite confident that if we go all the way to one-seventy-five degrees that way [east], and then come back this way we'll run into them.'

But the last time he was here, in 2002, he had completely missed the six large ships of the whaling fleet.

With the engines off, it was easy to hear all the other activity on the *Farley*. She hummed with a renewed vigour. In the bosun's locker the grinder whined and smoked. Steve was at the vice, hacksawing a piece of four-foot angle iron for a prop fouler. Trevor and Willie were out at the forward end of the main deck, starboard side, helping Marc lower the can opener into position on the outside of the hull. Marc had on a harness and was roped up. Willie belayed him. Trevor worked the knuckle boom crane that lowered the blade slowly. Once in place, Marc dangled and began to weld.

I went up to the bridge. I looked at the GPS over the

charts. We were at 65°41'S, 155°55'E, eighty-five miles east of the Virik Bank and about fifty miles north of the Antarctic Circle. The Krylov Peninsula was 200 miles to the south.

We were facing almost due south. The sun sat in the south-east, about thirty degrees off the horizon.

At 1031 the crew lowered and launched Alex on a jet ski. They also put one Zodiac into the water.

At 1040 I was scanning the horizon from the main deck with my binoculars and my heart began to thud. I saw a distinct black shape like a ship.

'Hey!' I called up to the bridge. 'Is that a ship?'

'It's probably ice,' Watson yelled down from his window, very calm. 'The helicopter's going out in ten minutes; he'll check it out.'

Alex headed in that direction, south, on the jet ski, and halfway to it he stopped. His voice came over the bridge on channel 16. 'Home-base, this is whale party, over.' On the radar I could see that he was only a mile off. Distances were completely deceiving. What I thought was a ship was probably a crooked finger of backlit dark ice about two miles away and the size of a refrigerator.

Alex told Hammarstedt that the engine of the jet ski had failed. Hammarstedt sent the Zodiac to tow him back. Hammarstedt said into the mic, 'Alex, for future reference use only channel ten.' He explained to me that the ship's marine radio carries at least 100 miles.

Lincoln, watching on the bridge, said, 'Whenever we send a jet ski out there's a breakdown.'

Producer Ron, from his armchair, added drily, 'The other thing is, they have no sense of direction. I've seen it on a couple of occasions. They take off and, man—'

It seemed like just another morning of exercises on the *Farley*. Except for the chopper. Aultman had his engine blaring, and his deck crew circled around him while he went over the hand signals. The crew would be crucial to his safety—guiding him in, centring him, grabbing and strapping the pontoons down fast before the bird could pitch off into the sea. All week they'd been training together—tweaking the chopper's tie-down system, repairing a cracked fuel pump, hosing down the machine with precious fresh water when the ship plunged through spray. Theirs seemed to be the one unit on the ship that had been practising constantly.

At 1121 Aultman and Pawel strapped themselves into the two seats. They had taken the doors off the bubble for better filming. Pawel was in his elite night-coloured dry suit, excited, hanging out the door with his video camera. The rotor started turning, and the deck crew crouched and unhooked the tie-downs. In a very light roll the chopper lifted, hovering a foot off the deck. Aultman held it there, getting used to being air-borne. And then patiently, carefully, he backed the bird off the ship as he climbed. Thirty feet up he tilted it forward and accelerated, and then he was circling the ship like a wild hawk, twice, gyring upward, waving, and he broke away off to the south-east and out of sight.

Meanwhile, Alex was lifted back onto the main deck. The jet ski had a hole in it. They went to start the other one and found the electrical box full of soupy water. After Gedden's fiasco in Hobart bay, they'd towed it back and left it as is in its cradle, unrinsed, undrained. They had remembered to hook the bat-tery up to a pulse charger, which, with the water, fried all the electrical parts. Alex, Trevor and Price spent much of the after-noon bent over the engine, replacing the burnt pieces.

The chopper touched back down at 1244, landing flaw-lessly. The news wasn't good for a trip to the islands. To the south and east was ice. Aultman pointed at a dark cloud bank shedding snow. 'About ten miles ahead the clouds closed right down to the water.' That would be his nightmare, being over-come by storm, with no visibility. The ship would prove hard enough to find on a clear day.

He went into the chart room to debrief the captain. The two bent over the chart.

'I'd say we flew twenty miles from the ship. The weather is not really conducive to surveillance. You can see nothing over here. Well there's a lot of ocean over there.' He pointed to the west of us. 'The ceiling is fifteen hundred feet, pretty much steady. I would say at times I was able to see sixty miles from the ship in clear weather—over here, where we made the turn back west, it was particularly clear; could probably see forty miles.'

He went back outside to attend to his steed. Down on the main deck, the can opener was in place and Marc was perched on his baby over the water, welding on more supports.

Watson said, looking down at it from the bridge, 'If you sideswipe something it'll probably crush that thing like a piece of paper.' But it looked vicious. Maybe that was the point.

In the afternoon Pawel and his assistant, George, took a Zodiac and went diving in the ice. The light snow thickened.

After dinner, the J. Crew and Casson, Ron, Watson and I played poker. Price was telling us another grisly story, whether we wanted to hear it or not.

'Want me to tell you a story?' he began.

'Not really,' Jeff said. 'We're trying to have a game here.'

'No, really. Listen—the Mormons massacred all those people in Arkansas. They have a marker in a field, but it's not there.' He nodded, emphatically. 'Go to another field and you could dig up all those bodies! I could show you where . . .'

When Price left, Jeff shook his head over his cards. 'I'll tell you what, if I heard they found forty-eight bodies in that guy's backyard I'd feel a lot of things, but surprise would not be one of them.'

Later that night, I saw an announcement on the eraser board:

Refresher course on CPR and management of critically injured. I need at least five crew for a resuscitation team—Kristy.

By midnight we were heading not far off north at twenty-one degrees. There was ice everywhere, chunks and rafts and growlers littering the water. Watson said, 'We have to head around the ice—can't go through it. At least we know they're not in it.'

IT IS 21 December, summer solstice in Antarctica, the longest day of the year. My GPS claims the sun sets for an hour and a half before it rises at 1:18am, but we have not seen the sun for days. Ominous storm fronts, almost as black as the smoke from forest fires, move along the horizon covering the sea with what must be blizzards, but so far they have left us alone. We are zigzagging north in a Monument Valley of ice trying to get around the frozen edge lying to the south and east. To the north and west is slate-grey open water scattered with great monoliths. They could be stone, these floating islands. Shadowed blue by distance or blazing strangely with a captured light. The sun never breaks through and the cliffs of ice miles away seem to emanate a cold white fire.

Watson wants to send the chopper up again to look for a passage to the Balleny Islands. He has started to call the Japanese ship we seek the *Death Star*.

We cut the engines again and drift. The whole landscape, cliff islands and all, moves with us, two knots westward, on the Antarctic coastal current. Aultman takes off an hour later, with Ron this time. While he is gone, Geert, Marc, I, and a few others who will be on the *Farley* during any action take a refresher course in CPR and critical care with little Kristy in the green room. She shows us how to use the oxygen tank and mask. She straps Mandy into a folding stretcher, and Marc and Geert hoist her out of a simulated sea.

Two hours after the chopper took off, one of the dark cloud banks that veiled down to the water overcame the ship and shrouded us in thick snow. Every ear out on deck was listening for the throp of the helicopter.

The blizzard passed and the lid lifted and we rocked easily. Aultman landed from his second flight at 1340. Low clouds had socked the ship in all around, and it was hairy flying back. His deck crew guided him in perfectly, and Ron climbed out with his big video camera. He said, 'Had a great time. We saw two whales, I think fin whales. Flew 1,400 feet when we could, then came down when the visibility went down. The whale was huge, man.'

Aultman said, 'We were a hundred feet off the water. The whale was blowing. A smaller whale two hundred yards to the north. They were going east, right towards the ice. Visibility was great to the north. We thought we could see sixty miles.'

Ron said. 'You can see quantum leaps more with binoculars than with the naked eye. The ship looks pretty small coming back, pretty alone.'

'As far as I could tell, sixty to seventy miles north of here, to the east, is all ice. And to the south was ice.'

Hammarstedt pulled out the *Sailing Directions*. 'It says that between the islands and the mainland is almost always impenetrable.'

Alex at the chart swept his hand between the coast and the islands. 'Okay, this is basically a no.'

The engines growled to life and we headed east a few miles to the ice edge and then followed it north, looking for a way around.

In the mess the J. Crew were recovering from an hour's hard work with a paint roller. They were capable of extreme concentration at the poker table, but when it came to manual labour they were desultory. The waiting was wearing on everybody, and the crew channelled their energies wherever they could. Most of the ship retired to the green room to watch the movie *Phone Booth*, which is about a man who is also in a terrible limbo, waiting for the call.

Emily burst into the dark cabin and announced, 'Greenpeace found the fleet!'

8

UNINVITED GUEST

WATSON WAS LEANING over the chart table. He had on his reading specs and he was holding a sharpened pencil and the parallel ruler.

'Apparently Greenpeace located them around here. Somebody in Australia tipped us off.' He moved the pencil over an area of sea about fifty miles north of the Mertz Glacier tongue on the George V Coast. Far to the south and west of us—311 nautical miles. At nine knots, that was almost thirty-six hours away. A day and a half away.

The chart room was suddenly full of crew, and Watson cleared it out. But the word went through the ship like an electric current. Everybody knew the coordinates, the distances. I looked out the bridge windows and saw the little nurse Kristy dancing wildly alone up on the forecastle, on the bow, to some music that was in her head, her nest of dreadlocks flying.

Allison said, 'We got a phone call. From somebody in Melbourne.'

Watson said to his second officer, 'Peter, can you set a course for sixty-six degrees south, one hundred forty-six degrees east?'

The beanpole Swede shoved his wire-rimmed glasses up on his nose, smiled his impish smile and nodded. 'Yes, sir.' He took the parallel ruler down from its peg and got to work.

'Two hundred forty-three degrees,' he called out a minute later.

West-south-west. The *Farley* rolled and then settled into the new heading. The waves, which had been on our port bow, were now quartering onto the stern, pushing the *Farley* southwards. The engines seemed to thump with a slightly different tone.

Crew members ebbed back to the ship's nerve centre. Allison said, 'Chris Price, we've got to get our thing up and running.' They had been lovers once, and she called him by his full name. She was referring to the FIB.

'I'm going to have a really great Christmas!' Emily chimed, her ponytail bobbing in her excitement.

Watson said, 'I've got to get more information,' and headed for the radio room.

Aultman turned to me. 'The way it was explained to me, Greenpeace has satellite data that located the fleet. Who else would have six ships grouped within a hundred nautical miles of each other?'

I went over to the chart and found Hammarstedt's little pencil cross and the initials GP, Greenpeace. Every hour, the officer on watch took down the ship's position from the GPS, marked it on the chart, and extended a pencil line from the last position. I followed the ship's track south to the point where we had turned around in the ice pack and fog—where the penguins had stood—and traced the stuttering line back to where it struggled to find a way around the ice. We had been very close to the Japanese without knowing it. From that most southerly point to where they were now, it had been only about 120 miles, a little over twelve hours away. But without intelligence they might have passed us and we would never have known.

It was 2100 hours. Watson was in the radio room firing questions into the Iridium sat phone.

'That's about three hundred miles from where we are now. Have you checked their website? Have you actually nailed the position down? . . . Uh-huh.' (Listens.) '. . . What is that—Is that because they're medevacing this guy? From the Japanese vessel? Okay, who is it that called Paul? Uh-huh. And that came from Greenpeace? How does he know what's going on with the fleet? Well, there's no—thank you. Okay, we'll just have to see. If we get that close, we can use the helicopter. Okay—' He hung up.

'Now I'm really pissed at Greenpeace,' he said. 'They specifically will not put their position on the website, so that Sea Shepherd doesn't get the info. It's the first time in history they haven't posted it.'

He leaned back in the chair, and it squeaked under his weight. 'They're medevacing a Jap guy with appendicitis out to Hobart and this contact in Hobart called—got it from the hospital. Called our guy in Melbourne. They're doing it on Christmas Day. Don't know why they're waiting. This Shane Rattenbury, the Greenpeace expedition leader, is saying that. So they put out their Zodiac today in front of the fleet and displayed a banner that said, "Get Out of the Southern Ocean Sanctuary Now."'

Watson made a face, like 'How lame is that?'

'Paul Martin in Melbourne called Greenpeace to get the position and Shane told him that we couldn't have it.' Watson didn't fume like ordinary people. The only way you could tell was that his voice got softer.

'One of their officers apparently calls a meeting on the

Esperanza, with Shane the Rat. Says he's fed up that they won't cooperate with us, and they're not doing anything. They're taking pictures and hanging banners.' He shook his head. 'By tomorrow afternoon we should be within helicopter range of that position.'

Just then Pawel stepped into the tiny room and hooked his laptop up to his satellite dish. The first thing he did once he got a connection was pull up the Greenpeace website. Pawel turned his screen towards Watson.

Others filed in to look. Alex was the most interested. The serious first officer studied the video clip with an almost salacious intensity. He muttered to himself, and went back to the bridge. He stared out ahead in a kind of reverie. 'That Greenpeace Zodiac is beautiful. Maxed out, it's got a one-forty.' He was talking about their outboard motors. He looked down at his own sad Zodiac fleet lashed to the main deck. The biggest had an old 115-horsepower. Zodiac envy.

I asked Alex if he was excited. He blinked. 'No, I don't get excited. I'm Dutch. We don't have a sense of humour that we know of.' He tightened his mouth into a quick smile. 'Nah, I'm not excited. Waiting three months for this.'

Watson couldn't keep himself away from Greenpeace's website. When I returned to the radio room he was reading its account of the skirmish.

'"We will not harm you or your equipment,"' he read aloud. '"We will use all means necessary to prevent you from killing whales." What the hell does that mean?'

There was a picture of the *Nisshin Maru* looming behind the festively painted *Esperanza*. Watson turned the laptop away in disgust.

An hour later the sat phone rang. Watson listened intently, said, 'Thanks,' and hung up. It was one of the crew members on board the *Esperanza* who was sickened by the savage killing they were witnessing. He was also tired of the bureaucratic stonewalling and knew Watson could stop the whaling. He called in secret, at the risk of losing his position with Greenpeace.

'The position he gave us is thirty miles closer than the one we have,' Watson said, going to the chart. 'He thinks they're heading north but doesn't see them moving around much.' He plotted the new position: 65° 55', 146° 33'.

Watson said, 'I asked him how long they were going to hang around. He said three weeks. I was thinking, "Not if we get there."' He set the parallel ruler between our current position and theirs and drew a fine pencil line along it. 'Two hundred forty-seven degrees,' he said to Hammarstedt.

Allison narrowed her eyes. 'Greenpeace is there; the killers are there—everybody is there but Sea Shepherd. We are the life of the party.'

'We are the uninvited guest,' Hammarstedt said.

Watson leaned against the chart table. 'I went to the IWC meeting in Monaco in nineteen-ninety-seven. I put on the master's uniform. About six hundred people at this reception. Everybody's staring at me. The Japanese, the Icelanders, the Norwegians, three hundred people walk out in protest. McTaggart [then chairman of Greenpeace International] walked out too. John Frizell, the director of Greenpeace UK, comes up, says, "It's not nice to come to places you're not invited." I said, "I thought that's what Greenpeace was all about. Showing up at places you're not invited."'

EARLY THE NEXT morning, Pawel pulled a story off the internet, from *The Age*, Melbourne's daily paper. In the vastness of waves and birds and ice, these missives were a concrete reminder of the other players, and of a world beyond the bounds of the horizon, and we read them avidly.

Greenpeace Clashes with Whalers
22 December 2005

Greenpeace activists have found and tackled the Japanese whaling fleet in Australian Antarctic waters, opening the most extensive campaign yet to halt the 'scientific' hunt.

The fleet was catching and processing minke whales when it was tracked down by Greenpeace ships *Esperanza* and *Arctic Sunrise* yesterday. In an initial skirmish, the *Esperanza* and a catcher ship collided in what Greenpeace expedition leader Shane Rattenbury said was a violation of the rules of the sea by the Japanese.

The encounter opens the first hostilities between the two sides since water cannon aboard the factory ship *Nisshin Maru* forced Greenpeace protesters to retreat in early 2002. It comes as Japan doubles its self-awarded quota of minke whales to 935 and includes 10 fin whales for the first time.

Mr Rattenbury warned that Greenpeace's 61 campaigners, who have strengthened their defence against the water cannon, were there to stay.

'Our small boats will be doing everything they can to get between the harpoons and the whales,' Mr Rattenbury said.

The whaling fleet was located within 160 km off the Antarctic coast near Commonwealth Bay yesterday.

The location puts the fleet deep inside an Australian whale sanctuary, but a Federal Court judge said earlier this year that an attempt to prosecute the whalers was futile, since Japan does not recognise Australia's Antarctic claim.

For the first time, Greenpeace is devoting two ships to the anti-whaling campaign, and the hard-line group Sea Shepherd is also sailing to confront the fleet with its vessel *Farley Mowat*, raising the prospect of the whaling program being severely disrupted.

Yesterday's collision happened when the Greenpeace ships steamed in close behind the *Nisshin Maru*, preventing a capture boat, *Kyo Maru No. 1*, from transferring the minke whales it had caught.

'They started attacking us with water cannon and sounding their horns,' Mr Rattenbury said. 'Then when we didn't move, *Kyo Maru* turned into *Esperanza* and struck it. It was a touch more than a direct ramming, but a touch nevertheless.'

He said that when the *Kyo Maru* turned in towards the *Esperanza* again, the Greenpeace ship backed off.

Federal Environment Minister Ian Campbell last night repeated Australia's call for Japan to respect the International Whaling Commission's condemnation of the hunt. He also confirmed that one of the whaling fleet is due in Hobart on Christmas Eve with a crewman who is understood to have appendicitis.

After breakfast, Watson handed me an email he'd just got from the crew member on the *Esperanza*.

Dear Paul,
     One more thing. The Japanese whalers DO indeed have firearms on board.
     I heard at least 4 shots when they had a whale on the harpoon cable right under their bow . . .

Now everybody was armed. Except Greenpeace, whose people were 'Quakers with attitude', according to Watson. The only actors we hadn't heard from were the Japanese, but word came in a press release a few hours later. It was dated the day before.

For Immediate Release
Safety Fears in the Southern Ocean

The organisation that conducts Japan's research whaling in the Antarctic said tonight it feared for the safety of its crew and scientists after one of two Greenpeace vessels in the Southern Ocean collided with a Japanese vessel.

The Institute of Cetacean Research (ICR), which carries out Japan's research whaling in the Antarctic, said the actions by these environmental groups were putting at risk the crew and scientists of JARPA vessels.

'We have told Greenpeace to keep their distance from our research vessels. They are severely compromising the safety of crew and scientists,' the ICR Director General, Dr Hiroshi Hatanaka, said.

The same thing occurred five years ago when in 1999 another collision occurred between Japan's research vessels and a Greenpeace vessel. 'Greenpeace and any other group in our vicinity now are acting unlawfully, recklessly, and absolutely irresponsibly. This is beyond legitimate protest.'

Japan's research whaling is legal under all relevant

international law and authorised under the International Convention for the Regulation of Whaling.

'Our whale research program provides vital information for the management of Antarctic marine resources, which cannot be gained using only non-lethal methods. The number of whales to be taken in no way threatens these abundant populations,' Dr Hatanaka said.

The International Whaling Commission (IWC) Scientific Committee had sent Japan twenty protests over the eighteen years of JARPA. A review of the Japanese program in 1997 declared that the research failed to meet its stated objectives, and that the data were not required for management. The ICR said that non-lethal means could not 'gain' vital information on marine resources. But the World Wildlife Fund had recently published an extensively supported report showing how non-lethal techniques of gathering skin tissue revealed far more—through DNA and chemical analysis—about population health and stock structure than the decades-old methods the Japanese used.

The Japanese claimed that one crucial data set, however, can never be garnered through non-lethal means: a whale's age. Which they determine by fixing it—the age—with a harpoon and then examining the ear bone. But a recent report in *Science* by a team from Australia claimed that scientists are close to being able to accurately determine a whale's age from DNA analysis of a skin flake sample.

The strongest indication that this was not about research, however, came from the fact that at every IWC meeting the Japanese lobbied to lift the moratorium on commercial whaling. JARPA was set up on the heels of the moratorium in 1987, with the job of keeping the whaling fleet afloat and the market for the meat simmering along until the moratorium could be lifted. In the past eighteen years, Japan had given $160 million in fisheries aid to half a dozen Caribbean nations alone, with the understanding that these countries would participate in the IWC and vote with Japan to legalise commercial whaling. Tens of millions of dollars more went to countries in Africa and the South Pacific. Mongolia had even joined, at the behest of Japan. The whaling nation of land-locked Mongolia.

THE GREAT WHALES underwent roughly three periods of hunting. The first, stretching back thousands of years, involved going after coastal whales in small boats and either herding them into bays for slaughter or spearing them with handheld harpoons. The targets of the herding method were the smaller whales such as the pilot, beluga and narwhal. Hunters with handheld harpoons went after the slower, more docile whales such as the right and bowhead. Cultures around the world, from Japan to Greenland to the Caribbean, practised primitive coastal whaling.

As species were wiped out along the coasts, ships began the second broad era of deepwater, or pelagic, whaling. As early as the fourteenth century, Basque whalers in search of whale oil were hunting off the Grand Banks; and in the sixteenth and seventeenth centuries, Norwegian, Icelandic, Dutch and English whalers were roving across the Atlantic. By the eighteenth century, Americans joined the hunt, and the whaling fleets of many nations were pushing into the North Atlantic and the Arctic. The Pacific Arctic followed. The Yankee whaling fleet at its zenith in 1846, comprised 730 ships that hunted primarily in the Pacific. Sperm whales supplied lamp oil; ambergris for perfumes; and spermaceti, a very fine oil used in lubricants and high-quality candles. The discovery of petroleum in 1859 drove the price of whale oil down and may have saved the sperm whales from extinction. (Today they are listed as endangered.)

The third period of whaling, beginning in the late nineteenth century and continuing today, involved a combination of engine-powered boats and harpoon guns with explosive tips. These allowed whalers to go after the faster baleen whales such as fins, blues, minkes, greys and humpbacks. They were hunted not only for meat, but for, among other things, oil for margarine and special lubrication products, and glycerin for nitroglycerin. Many of these species were driven to the brink of extinction. By the late 1970s, according to some estimates, the humpback population numbered fewer than 5,000. The western Pacific grey whale numbers now only about 100 individuals.

The rest of the great whales are recovering slowly. Experts in marine biology such as Roger Payne and Sylvia Earle believe the great whales should never again be hunted, period.

Earle put it to me eloquently: 'As supposedly intelligent creatures, doesn't it seem odd that humans might think that the best way to engage whales is to eat them? When our numbers were small and whales were numerous, killing a few whales for sustenance for people who had few choices about what to eat was a matter of survival. Today, it is a matter of choice. Can commercial killing of whales be justified? Biologically, ecologically, economically, logically, morally, ethically, realistically it cannot—not now, not in fifty years, not ever. It defies logic to think that mobilising large ships consuming large amounts of fuel with large crews travelling large distances to bring whale meat back over thousands of miles of ocean to satisfy the tastes of a small number of consumers that live half a world away qualifies as a reasonable use of resources, let alone as a "sustainable" enterprise.'

When I asked biologist and famous whale researcher Dr Roger Payne if he thought whaling could ever be sustainable, he said: '. . . I believe that people are educable, and that a society which does not kill the largest, most complex animals around it for the most mundane purposes is likely to have a more luminous future than one for which all animals are but fuel for its meat grinders.

'I believe that if you were betting on which animals' brains were most sophisticated and therefore which animals had the most to teach us and the most to contribute to the joy of our lives, you might select whales, elephants, apes and wolves. I think that the killing of whales for food is no different than the killing of apes, elephants, or wolves for food. Considering how much complexity of structure and behaviour these four species groups have, and therefore how much we could learn from them about living, to kill and eat them is not much different from using the works of Shakespeare to light your fire. The sonnets make good kindling and lots of people have probably used them for such, but such people, I suspect, haven't left much of a mark on history.'

THE WEATHER was changing. By late afternoon we had come up and around the great cliff island and turned almost due south-west, going as fast as we could, making almost ten knots. The sun struggled to break free all day—our first sun in over a week. Once it did, the thermometer read thirty-two degrees, but the day felt much warmer. Deckhands stopped and closed their eyes, letting their bodies sway with the roll, and letting the sun touch bare necks and faces.

We were 130 miles or so from the target. Marc was harnessed up, over the side, welding on more braces so that his can opener might really tear a hole. Trevor burst more rusty pipes trying to feed the water cannons, and finally ran fire hoses to the guns. Colin and Steve worked furiously in the bosun's locker, building a downrigger system for their Zodiac, similar to the rig used in deep-sea fishing, where you trail a weight from which your line extends so that you can troll beneath the surface. They wanted to meet the *Nisshin Maru*'s propeller where it lives. They wanted to make it easy for the prop to grab the steel cable and strangle itself.

Watson and Alex were in the radio room reviewing the posting Greenpeace had put up on its website the day before. It included a video that showed the *Esperanza* positioned to block the slipway, the large ramp cut into the stern of the *Nisshin* up which the whales were hauled. Orange Zodiacs ran up under the looming black sides of the *Nisshin*'s hull and got thrashed by powerful water cannons. One of the Zodiacs had a banner that read, 'Defend the Whales'. The video showed the catcher ship *Kyo Maru* running up alongside the *Esperanza* and brushing it, and the *Esperanza* backing off. There were some aerial shots of the killer boat's aft deck, whales stacked like logs, five across, and of the *Nisshin Maru*—dead minke whales on her deck and blood running from the scuppers and pumping in a crimson gush out of holes above the waterline.

'Their ship is bigger than the whaler,'Alex said. 'Look at that. Greenpeace had a f—ing chance and they left it.'

'It's just a media hoax,' Alex continued, disgusted. 'Do you think they're leaving the area now that they have the footage?'

'That's where they really could have done some damage,' Watson said, pointing to the mild bump of the two ships. 'The can opener would've done some damage.'

'It's the David and Goliath thing,' Alex said. 'They wanna look like victims. They've got to try hard to keep the Zodiac right under the hose, to fill it up. They could pull out of the spray at any time.' The video showed the Zodiac filling, and crew members on the *Nisshin* leaning over the high rails and trying to spear the inflatable's pontoons with long-poled flensing knives. It looked dangerous.

'I got wet defending the whales. We have to make a T-shirt that says that.'

'This is going to work out well,' Watson said. 'Greenpeace gets beaten up by the Japanese, the Sea Shepherd comes in and beats up the whalers. Protects the little kid from the big bully.' More blood running from the scuppers. 'Do you see any place to drop butyric acid?'

'Right on the deck,' Alex said.

'Yeah, but without hitting anyone?'

'Best thing is, aim for them, then you won't hit them.' I had underestimated the dryness of the Dutch first officer's humour.

Now we were running south-west. The seas were on the port quarter, dark walls of water patched with ice that barrelled in towards the high stern. Gunter stood at the bridge windows with binoculars and called out the deadly growlers to Alex, who steered with the manual control.

At 1736 Watson came onto the bridge and said, 'Our Greenpeace friend just called me. They're twenty-five miles south of where they were yesterday. 65° 55', 146° 33'.' He plotted the new course, anticipating we would be near the target in about twelve hours.

On the way down to dinner I noticed Inde on a stool in the

bosun's locker teaching Mandy how to splice and eye the steel cable. They were making more prop foulers. On the corkboard was tacked a new *Scuttlebutt*, Watson's newsletter for the ship, headlined '*Tora! Tora! Tora!*'—the battle cry of Japanese pilots. 'The *Farley Mowat* will ram the whaler with the objective of damaging the harpoon platform. . . . We need to stop one of the harpoon vessels dead in the water. If we do, the other boats will be forced to come to the assistance of the damaged vessel . . .'

Dinner was noisy with expectation, excitement, maybe a little fear. Outside the portholes the sky was darkening.

Kalifi called an all-hands meeting in the green room. They packed onto the bench seats, sat cross-legged on the deck, stood in the doorway to the mess. The only one who didn't attend these meetings was Watson, who kept aloof.

'We are about twelve to fifteen hours from the target,' Alex said. The laughter died fast.

'Tomorrow morning we're going to be there. Greenpeace just pulled away. They chose to do nothing. Obviously, we're going to have a different tack.'

Silence.

'When we get there we'll put three Zodiacs in the water and a helicopter in the air. The attack Zodiacs are gonna be Wessel with Luke, Jeff and Gedden. Colin with Steve, Joel, Pawel. The third will have media.'

He gave orders to use smoke bombs, water cannons, butyric acid. 'Try not to hit anybody with the acid,' he said.

Alex looked as if he hadn't slept in days. His painter's pants and black sweatshirt hung loosely on his frame. His buzz cut emphasised the shape of his pale skull. But his focus outward was fierce. I thought he and big, round Watson fitted together like a bow and arrow.

'If you use a prop fouler,' he said, 'don't get your hand caught.' He looked at Chris Aultman at the near table. 'We're gonna send you off tomorrow around seven a.m. Maybe six. Don't use the radio.'

'If we are in a confrontation, then we can use the radio?'

Alex nodded.

Alex said, 'There's gonna be teams. Watch each other. If

you're in a Zodiac you've gotta pay attention; don't let people stay in the water.'

Jeff said, 'Is the chance of action pretty high?'

'Yes, if they haven't moved. Get the Zodiacs ready at six.' He swayed with the ship and tapped the air with a finger. 'Be *ready* at six a.m.; don't have breakfast at six. Be ready.'

Now Pawel. He was such an odd fish. Impish smile, rapid blinking: 'If we have the opportunity to snatch a sample of a Japanese scientist, should we?'

Alex said, 'I think if it's non-lethal research it'd be okay,' he joked. Then he clarified: 'No, I don't think Paul wants us to board any ships.'

Allison said, 'The paint locker. That will be our brig.' She was serious.

Mandy, always serious, said, 'What is the policy if the Japanese board us?

'Kick them off,' Alex said. 'That goes for Greenpeace too. If we end up with one of their Zodiacs, they have to give us an apology for missing an opportunity yesterday.'

'Okay,' Alex said. 'Try to get some sleep.'

That was it. As soon as the meeting broke up, the frenetic clamour of soldiers preparing for battle took over the ship. All night the smell of burning welding rod, the hammering, and grinding, filled the hallways. We had come 2,000 miles and the target was hours away.

In the chart room to discuss the attack, Watson said to Hammarstedt and Alex, 'It seems to me, if we can ram into the slipway at full speed, come down on that point off a wave, then they have a structural hole. The slipway comes down to the water; if we come down right there it will compromise the integrity of the hull.'

He had talked earlier about the danger of the can opener, saying that above the waterline it posed no danger of sinking the attackee. He had said he would never threaten a ship with sinking on the high seas. But now he was talking about cracking the *Nisshin*'s hull right at the water line. A 'structural hole' at waterline is what a torpedo tried to do. He wanted the ship out of action at all costs.

Watson leaned against the chart table. He was looking dapper in wide-wale corduroys and a fleece sweater, and I noticed that his hair was freshly washed and brushed. Apparently he viewed the coming showdown as a special occasion. He motioned with his beefy hands. 'If they can't bring a whale up the slipway, that's the end of their whaling. Ram that thing so far up the slipway we stick.'

The new intercept point was forty-three miles away.

'We'll launch the chopper in four hours,' he said.

9

FORCE 7

THE SHIP WAS PITCHING more heavily. The wind had swung around to the south-east and increased in speed, and the swells were maybe fifteen feet. Aultman's crew was out on the heli deck struggling to strip the chopper of the blade covers, checking fluid levels. They were harnessed up and tethered to taut lines and the long red covers were whipping wildly.

The ship laboured directly downwind and the big swells pitched her head down, surfing the face, then shoved her nose to the sky and she floundered in the trough. The tops of the waves erupted in white. We were two miles south of the intercept point.

At 0303 Hammarstedt came onto the bridge. Watson had his orange-and-black Mustang suit on, and his feet were propped on the sill.

'We're not going to stop, Paul?'

'No.' Watson glanced at the radar.

'The helicopter crew's getting ready to launch the chopper.'

'Right.' Watson would go back down the fleet's projected course, hoping to run into them head-on. Aultman would hit that line to the south and run back up along it, scouting. Our new course, south-south-west, would put the weather almost square on the beam, where it would roll the *Farley* without mercy.

The snow thickened and flew sideways across the decks. Through the shuddering of the gusts against the superstructure I heard the engine of the chopper start up. On the bridge, Hammarstedt was peering intently at the main radar.

We were about 240 miles due east of the south magnetic pole and about 120 miles west of the Mertz Glacier. Aultman came onto the bridge. 'Paul, we're not going. It's too rough. About a forty-five-knot wind.'

'Okay.' He said it with no emotion.

The *Farley* came down off a steep roller and yawed to port she took the next wave heavily and slammed over. The back sides of the waves under us were strung with foam. Hammarstedt went off watch at 0400 and Alex came on with his crew. Watson went to his cabin to catch a few hours of sleep.

At 0800, refreshed, Watson took his watch. He was still in his Mustang suit, which meant that he still held a reasonable expectation of action. The suit was bulky and hot, and you didn't wear it unless you might end up in the water.

'I guess if it was easy, everybody would be doing it,' he said, lumbering into his chair.

His stony detachment had been transmuted into his usual upbeat playfulness. Allison had said that he had no emotional range. Casson had added, 'He goes from grumpy to surly and back.' Now that I was used to his moods, I thought I had seen him go from fury to euphoria.

The ship continued down the intercept line. Watson emailed his informant on the *Esperanza* that we were in place to intercept but that the fleet must have altered course, slowed down, or stopped, as we hadn't seen it. He pulled a newspaper story off the Melbourne *Age* website and read to us from the article:

> The hard-line group Sea Shepherd likely to arrive off Commonwealth Bay today, saying that unlike Greenpeace it intends to stop the fleet from whaling.
>
> Prime Minister John Howard said that at a recent

meeting with the Japanese Prime Minister Junichiro Koizumi he had raised the whaling issue.

'I did not lose the opportunity of telling him of my continued opposition to Japan's position on whaling,' he said. 'However, I do not support action which endangers lives or breaks the law.'

Watson said, 'If the Australian navy comes down to arrest us for committing a crime in Australian territory, that'd be great. "Gee, well, we're going to arrest you because you recognise our territorial claim, but we're not going to arrest the Japanese because they don't recognise our territorial claims"—'

'I just got a new target,' Lincoln said. He was standing ramrod-straight, hands braced on either side of the main radar hood.

Watson ignored him for the moment. 'There's a whale!'

Half a dozen minke whales were running across our bow from west to east. They blew and breathed about every five seconds, a constant mist of staggered plumes torn away by wind. They looked terrorised, panicked. Their fear hit the bridge like a blow. It must have been like the instantaneous transmission of emotion Watson had described in his encounter with the big grey whale as it died.

Watson said, 'They're running scared. They seem very agitated, moving fast, blowing every few seconds.'

We watched them move off into the waves and fog. All of us were thinking the same thought, that they had been attacked and were fleeing. The catcher or killer boats could go twenty-five knots. A minke whale can swim in bursts of twelve knots, but if the *Kyo Maru* or *Nisshin Maru* saw them and wanted them, there was nothing they could do to stop it.

The groundswell was black walls of water now, looming to the level of the bridge deck. We looked to be sailing directly into a darker cloud front of snow and fog. Whatever this was, it was not abating, but building.

So was the sense of frustration, of fury, on the ship. We had come within hours of the whaling fleet and missed it. We were casting back and forth like a hound that has lost the scent. I thought how completely vulnerable we were to everything: to the caprices of the weather, to our old and fragile equipment, to the inexperience of the crew who would jump into a Zodiac and overload it at a critical moment in the chase, and to the speed and efficiency of the Japanese fleet. Any of a hundred things could imperil the mission or our lives.

Just then Lincoln said, 'Got a target! Two hundred eleven degrees, heading away from us.'

Watson waited.

'Twenty-one miles away. Now six, now back up to thirteen.'

Now the target was just sitting there, looking more and more like an iceberg as we got closer. Again, the lift of adrenaline and the let-down of a sea that was empty of whalers.

Watson wasn't ruffled. 'Listen—' He read from another news report he had pulled off the web earlier:

The Federal Minister for the Environment, Senator Ian Campbell, should put the Japanese whale-killers out of action when the *Kaiko Maru* docks in Hobart tomorrow, Greens Leader Bob Brown said today.

'The ship coming to Hobart is part of a fleet harpooning our whales in our territory off Antarctica. The government should impound the ship as it does Indonesian fishing boats and the pirate Portuguese Patagonian tooth-fish ships.'

Watson continued reading:

Senator Brown went on to say that the Japanese ship was expected to dock at the Self Point Oil Wharf at 8:00am Saturday 24 December, and should not be allowed to return to the kill.

Watson grunted his assent. He was pleased that at least some Australian government officials were showing some spine.

WE CHUGGED ON towards our ship of ice. The seas were approaching twenty feet. Can a ship be glad? Maybe not. The *Farley Mowat* met the side-on waves with a deep-bellied buoyancy. Most of the time. Sometimes she would yaw just wrong when coming down into a trough and the next roller would slam her to starboard and you could hear sundry objects hitting the bulkheads and cabinets and the roll gauge would read thirty degrees or more. Kalifi went onto the fore-castle dressed in light cotton pants and with no foul weather gear, unharnessed, and was trying to fit a fire hose into the shooting end of the centre water cannon; I guessed to back-test the pipes. She could barely stand in the wind. She clutched at the cannon with one white-knuckled hand, then gave up.

On the bridge, Watson said to Lincoln, 'Maybe when we get up to that iceberg we can get around it and get the heli-copter up.'

'Yeah, six and a half miles to the iceberg.'

'Fourteen miles to where they were last seen,' Watson said.

'Visibility is better,' Lincoln said. 'Wind still a bear.'

Now Trevor made his way up on the forecastle. He went from rail to stanchion to guy wire, like a jerky square dancer being passed from hand to hand in a lunatic reel. When he got to the cannon he swivelled it, aimed it over the starboard side, and let loose. A flaccid stream arced over the side and wavered in the gusting wind.

'That'll show them,' Watson said. 'We piss in your general direction.'

The iceberg Lincoln had mistaken for a whaler was a mile long. The floundering *Farley* went for it the way a skier bee-lines for a mountain hut in a storm. We passed two Adélie penguins on a floe the size of a Zodiac. They stood side by side like figures on a wedding cake.

The *Farley* swung up into the lee of the big iceberg, and the bridge went quiet. The wind that had been battering the super-structure was gone. The creaking and whistling. The heavy rolls. The *Farley* nosed up into water that had gentled to near smoothness.

Alex stepped onto the bridge. Watson said, 'They can't be more than fifty miles from here. We're seven miles from where they were yesterday.'

Aultman came up, shrugging into his Mustang suit.

'What's it look like?' Allison asked.

'Looks great; let's do it.' Did he know what the wind would be like as soon as he cleared the top of the ice cliff? Watson asked him to make a sixty-mile-radius arc west and south.

'We're about a hundred and eighty miles from the French station,' Watson said. In case Aultman got into trouble.

'Okay.' Aultman went aft to strip the chopper of its covers. His deck crew, scattered over the ship, put on foul weather gear and gloves and headed for the heli deck.

The chopper wouldn't start. The battery seemed dead. It needed a jump.

At 1230 Dennis blew a gust of cold air into the chart room and reported that the battery was fine, it just wasn't getting any juice to the motor. Half an hour later, George said, 'All fixed. Just a wire that had eroded away.'

Oh, just a wire. Eroded away. I watched George closely. He didn't seem to be muttering prayers under his breath. Aultman was beginning the start-up sequence, so George zipped into his dry suit, picked up his camera, and went aft. Quiet George was scheduled to fly and film today, and I was kind of glad it wasn't me.

They took off at 1330. Aultman cleared the berg and steadied the helicopter, then rose and accelerated downwind like a petrel. Even the two penguins lifted their beaks to watch.

If the Japanese whaling fleet was over the horizon, just beyond the reach of the radar, tracking northward, then we would know in less than an hour. Aultman, eschewing the marine radio so as to keep our presence secret, would call Watson on the Iridium sat phone. The fog had been torn away by the wind and, though there were fast-moving dark snow squalls that came down to the water, the visibility wasn't bad.

The crew became jocular when they had to wait. It was Hammarstedt's watch, and the three Dutchmen joined him on the bridge and began to torment him for being Swedish, recapitulating some ancient lowland enmity which I suspected had something to do with Scandinavian bloodlines being forcibly introduced into their own at some point in the horn-helmeted past.

'If you visualise your language,' Geert said to the second mate, 'it is the colour pink.'

'At least it is not a throat disease,' countered Hammarstedt, holding the *Farley* up under the berg in its sheltered berth.

Watson was in the radio room, keeping up his end of the media war.

This time the target of his scorn was Australia's beleaguered minister for the environment, Ian Campbell. Campbell had been consistently against commercial whaling, as had his government, which for decades had been part of the core anti-whaling group in the IWC, led by the United States, England and Australia. But that wasn't enough for Watson, who knew that Australia was one navy frigate ship away from shutting down the entire Japanese operation in the Australian Antarctic Territory.

Watson's fingers flew over the keys as he composed a press release taunting Campbell, egging him on to send a navy ship to intervene against Sea Shepherd. That would be a public relations coup Watson could milk for months.

A force 7 gale was raging on the other side of this cliff of ice, two little Adélies were squawking at each other in envy of our helicopter, there was a big blade welded to the bow and the ship was hiding in the radar shadow of the berg, waiting to pounce on a whaling ship. Meanwhile, Watson was in the cramped radio room firing off one media salvo after another—to Greenpeace; to his website; to newspapers in Australia, New Zealand, England and the United States.

He came out of the radio room shaking his head. 'Did you see the new stuff on the Greenpeace website? Some Japanese guy hit one of them over the head with a pike yesterday—with the end of one of their own banners.' He looked out at the storm beyond our wind shadow. 'Still no coordinates, but they do say they're not far from Commonwealth Bay, which is 120 miles from here. They are trying to root out the leak on their boat.' For some reason the Dutchmen laughed heartily. Maybe it was the word 'leak'—they came from a country of dykes.

'They haven't figured out it's him. Keep your fingers crossed.'

AT 1420 THE LEAK emailed Watson to say that the Japanese were now at 63°44' S, 146°31' E—120 miles due north of us.

'That means they would have passed us in the night over the horizon,' Watson said. 'Too bad we couldn't get the helicopter up this morning.' If we had got the helicopter off at 0245, we would have seen them.

Hammarstedt went to the chart and, after a minute of figuring with ruler and pencil, said, 'We passed within about twenty-two miles of each other at seven this morning.'

In the storm, with the heavy seas and fog and all the ice around, the watch hadn't been able to see them on radar. We were chasing shadows and reflections.

Watson got on the sat phone and called the helicopter back. As was typical, he registered no disappointment. Rather, he turned to the ice cliff face of the berg, which was crazed with a diagonal blue fracture. 'I bet if you put a shot right there, that big piece is going to come down.' He was still in his Mustang suit, ready for action—unwilling, I guess, to let the moment pass without some sort of rough fun.

'You got your gun,' I reminded him.

'Never fired it—I wonder if a parachute flare would bring that down.' He disappeared into the radio room and we heard drawers and cabinets opening. He came back clutching a couple of signal flare tubes. 'We got so many of these things,' he muttered. He went onto the port bridge wing, aimed one and fired. It went straight into the water with a sizzle. 'I'll try again.'

The berg was 100 yards away. He pulled the string. The flare arced up, maybe eighty feet, and floated down on its little parachute, a red phosphorus flame trailing white smoke.

'Hmph,' Watson said. 'Not very accurate. It'll be interesting if the helicopter saw that—might come in handy.' He looked again at the cracked wall. 'Wonder if the fifty-calibre would take that down.'

I wondered myself if all this was just a way of easing the big gun out of its hiding place without alarming the crew, and of getting some practice before any encounter with the whalers. Or was it just Watson's inability to resist fun?

'Go for it. It'd be cool. Let's go,' I said.

'It's Chris Price's call; I've never fired it.'

I thought it was missing a part and wouldn't fire.

AULTMAN TOOK the chopper in over the stern just as a snow squall overtook our haven in the lee of the iceberg. He was pushing his edge. He hovered, unsteady in the new gusts, watching his timing, and then dropped the chopper onto the deck. As soon as the heli crew had the pontoons strapped down, Hammarstedt engaged the propeller and manoeuvred the *Farley* back out into the waves.

The first waves caught the *Farley* on the starboard stern quarter and rolled her hard. They were often up to the bridge deck now, over twenty feet, and sometimes a backwater wall obscured the horizon as the *Farley* dropped into the trough. In this weather, everything was a challenge. The galley crew kneaded bread and chopped turnips while bracing themselves into a corner between counter and bulkhead. Dishes clattered in the drying boxes, and Allison attacked them with a gymnast's athleticism. Walking down the long companionway, you could lean at a cartoon angle from side to side while the boat rotated around you and never miss a step. Even going to the head was an adventure. You hoped the seawater wouldn't slop out of the bowl, and you held tight to whatever you could. And sleep—forget it. Every muscle in your body went taut, pressing the sides of the bunk in an effort not to go airborne.

At 1510 Watson was in the mess having a cup of tea. He had pulled out the little poker case, hoping to catch some suckers in a game of Texas Hold'em. When he shuffled the cards the J. Crew glanced over and licked their chops. The captain cocked his head. 'We're not allowed to play cards during the day, captain,' Joel said with his best soft-spoken gunfighter's civility.

'Captain's exemption; get your money.'

AT 2130 THE WHALE alarm sounded. Three humpbacks—two adults and a calf—swam across the bow, breached one after another, did a slow lap of the ship and moved off. The calf didn't really breach, just lifted its head to take a look at us. I hoped that in 2007, when the Japanese had humpbacks on their kill permit, these whales would be more circumspect about approaching a boat like us—we were just about the size of the catcher ships. Or maybe they knew. I thought they probably did. Not that they were safe this season: a sampling of whale meat at the Tsukiji and other markets between 1993 and 1999 found blue, sei, humpback, fin and the critically endangered Western Pacific grey whale, of which only 100 remain. With whale meat at $10 or $15 a pound, I wasn't sure what kept the Japanese from taking any whale that crossed their path.

When I went to bed just before 2000 we were at south 64°50'.

CHRISTMAS EVE, 0500: we had halved the distance to the fleet's last position since last night. Sixty to a hundred miles to go, depending on how fast they were moving and if they held their course.

On the bridge, Alex maintained a silent vigil. The radar was set out to thirty miles.

Trevor came up after 0700, clean-shaven and fresh in clean blue coveralls. He told Alex that he'd just sounded the tanks and we had thirty-one days of continuous motoring left. There were seventy-nine to eighty tons of diesel fuel in the tanks, and we used about two and a half tons per day.

'In thirty-one days we'd better be in port,' Trevor said.

Watson came up for his watch at 0800.

'Our spy says the fleet is moving south, moving west; doesn't make any sense what they're doing. They are not whaling. They haven't whaled since they started running.'

He checked our position, then told Lincoln to change course to 300 degrees. He wanted to come across, west, at a shallower angle, staying south of the fleet in case it should head back for the ice where the whales were. So now we would head almost directly with the storm and the seas, which would make the ride a lot more comfortable.

Alex and Trevor retired to the chart table.

'Be nice to have an hourly update,' Alex said.

'Yeah, that'd be pretty good. I like the idea of working together. Most of the crew are on that boat because they can't get on this one.'

Alex smiled. I wondered how the Greenpeace crew really saw Sea Shepherd. They were getting $17 an hour to crew, so they were paid to be loyal. Undoubtedly they had the integrity of their own pacifist mission, because they took great risks pounding their Zodiacs up alongside the whalers who were flailing down at them with flensing knives on poles and shooting harpoons close over their heads.

They studied the chart. Alex said he liked the idea of moving south and waiting for the fleet to come back to a good whaling ground. But nobody knew in which bay the Japanese would decide to hunt. And anyway, Watson was heading west-north-west. He had his own ideas.

WATSON TOOK his captain's chair and gave all of us on the bridge an update on the media war. There were new articles in the *Age* and the *Sydney Morning Herald*, which he flourished. The *Herald* story opened with this lead:

The hardline anti-whaling group Sea Shepherd yesterday raised the stakes in the Antarctic whaling crisis, saying it was about to attack the Japanese whaling fleet and could lose its own ship . . .'

Watson cracked his knuckles. 'I never said we would attack them!' Incredulous. Then: 'Of course we will attack them, but they don't know that! Oh, listen to this:

Federal Environment Minister Ian Campbell said the statement was 'quite scary'.

'There appears to be a prima facie case that they may be setting out to break the law,' Senator Campbell said. 'I think there is a very good distance between this and the generally positive approach by Greenpeace. I think what Greenpeace has been doing is a service to the cause,' he said. 'But if Captain Watson does what he says he's going to do, it will set the cause of whale conservation back for decades.'

Watson was disgusted and energised. He lived for this. It was 1010 on Christmas Eve, the *Farley* was being battered by a building Antarctic storm, and it was time to fire off some squibs and see whom he could piss off more. He lumbered back to his radio room, hardly noticing the hard rolls, sat down at the keyboard and composed a rebuttal to Campbell, saying that the Australian navy is a dog being kept on a chain while the government helps the burglars. 'The [Australian] government says that the Japanese do not recognise the Australian claim to the Antarctic Treaty,' he wrote. 'In 1942 they did not recognise Australia's claim to Australia.'

In 1988, Watson flew back to Iceland to face charges for the sinking of the two whaling ships. He egged the prosecutors on, then practically ordered them to charge him. The poor, dour, polite Icelanders—they had no idea how to deal with this cagey bear. The lead prosecutor, growing ever more suspicious of being led by the nose into some trap, finally flashed, 'You can't make us prosecute you! This is our case! You said you weren't actually at the sinkings? Well, then! You are not guilty.' Watson was released the next day. According to Watson, the Icelandic minister of justice said, 'Who does he think he is, coming to Iceland and demanding to be arrested? Get him out of here.' The Icelanders breathed a sigh of relief when they got Paul Watson out of the country.

'Here's the other thing,' he said, looking up from his keyboard, 'This is a Canadian ship. The Australians have already said they're not going to enforce international laws in their territory. So this is between the Canadian authorities and Sea Shepherd.'

The last section of the article Watson had just read from said that the Japanese crew member with appendicitis had been winched aboard a helicopter from the spotter vessel *Kaiko Maru* about fifty nautical miles south of Tasman Island. Plans for the ship to refuel in Hobart had been scrapped in the face of demands that the ship be restrained to keep it from returning to the whaling grounds. After delivering the sick man, the ship had sailed south again.

Watson's media campaign was having some effect. He

and Greenpeace had focused so much negative attention on the Japanese fleet that they could no longer safely enter an Australian port.

AT 1145 WATSON told Mia to change the course to 280 degrees. This would set us directly downwind, running with the seas, and eliminate much of the hard roll. The new course would also send the *Farley* safely south of the last known Japanese position. Watson knew that the whaling fleet would head south again at some point, and there would be less risk of missing it again if we were ahead of it and waiting.

At 1200 we all went to lunch. Running with the seas was theoretically the least jarring ride. Try telling that to your pea soup. Every fourth mouthful, the ship would surf down the front of one of the waves and cant over, and eighty-eight hands from one end of the mess to the other, in the engine room and cabins, would find themselves in a sudden dilemma: grasp for the tabletop, bulkhead, or bunk edge and save themselves, or steady and cover the soup, the spanner wrench, the pen and journal. The results of many of these choices were revealed in the next instant when a coffee mug, a plate of pasta, and George the videographer went flying across the mess.

The barometer on my altimeter watch was dropping like a stone. Generally, the lower the pressure, the stronger the storm. There was a little graph, courtesy of Casio, that showed the barometric pressure in three-hour increments; it looked like a staircase to hell. The wind in the last twelve hours had also swung around more to the east from the south-east. When it had howled from a more southerly direction, it had essentially poured off the continent of Antarctica. There were mountains, jutting peninsulas, and lots of big ice—all sorts of obstacles to obstruct and break up the wind. But look due east of the *Farley* and all you saw was ocean. Unobstructed Southern Ocean girdling the naked globe. The two variables that govern the wind's effect on water are wind speed and reach, reach being the distance the wind travels unobstructed. Here, around the disc of Antarctica, for something like 10,000 miles, there was nothing but reach.

The *Farley* pitched forward, yawed to port and gouged a white tear out of the trough. Down in the bottom, we were surrounded by walls of water. The backside of the wave ahead was monstrous and easily blocked our view of the horizon, putting it at about twenty-five feet. I went to the port bridge window, looked aft through the thick window, and saw that the next wave barrelling in behind us rose black and ominous over the level of the high heli deck.

The whole bridge shuddered in heavier gusts.

Many of the crew were lying low, trying to catch up on sleep. The frenetic preparations had ceased. The pressure drop of the storm mirrored the mood, the depressing suspicion that we might be on a wild goose chase.

The ship was quiet, if a ship in a gale can be said to be quiet: the hull sloshed and boomed; the engine throbbed and growled; provisions and anchor chain clattered and thumped in the holds; the steel bones of the *Farley* groaned. Anything slung on a hook knocked against the bulkheads. And wind. It drove the ocean westward like a herd of terrified cattle in which the *Farley* floundered like a blinded horse. The ship was concentrating all of her energy outward, trying to keep her balance and her speed, and inside a stillness took hold. Nobody ran the grinder over newly-fashioned weapons or bragged about prop foulers. The companionways were empty.

Alex should have been asleep, but he came onto the bridge with Aultman. Hammarstedt was already there, as it was his watch. It seemed that in a storm this big, none of the officers wanted to be too far from the bridge. Watson said to his first mate, 'I did get a message from M——. They're zigzagging all over the place, tending south.'

He nodded to Aultman. 'I think, once we get down there where it's nice and calm, we'll be sending the helicopter up to find them along the coast. I think they're just trying to shake everybody off. Maybe they're just waiting for the other boat to rejoin them. They've got to start whaling sometime. The other boat didn't refuel in Hobart. So they might be waiting for them to refuel at sea.'

The captain finally retired for a while. We fell into a

trough, and the world was suddenly circumscribed by two walls of dark water—one forward, one aft. They must have been thirty feet. The top of the one ahead of us blew off white like a spuming snow cornice. I looked off to starboard and a wandering albatross, nearly as white as the froth, slipped down the face astern and glided up the face ahead, just as we began our own floundering rise. To me, she was a visitation. A simple reminder of a world that worked, that was at home with itself and friends with the storm.

Hammarstedt said that late last night, on his previous watch, eight humpbacks swam by and surrounded the ship.

The barometer was still in a nosedive. At 1600, when Alex came back up for his watch, it read 29.05 and dropping. He immediately told Gunter to swing the ship around to 234 degrees, and he showed me the chart.

'We can either mess around here or head here'—sixty miles north of the Dibble Ice Tongue, on the coast—'which is what the captain decided to do, and I'm glad. We'll arrive there in twenty-two hours. Sit next to the ice and wait for them. If they go east we can move east; if they go to Porpoise Bay we can trap them in the bay. Going up here, it's just getting rougher and rougher. Can't launch the helicopter, can't do nothing.'

That would put us there at 1400 on Christmas Day.

As Gunter swung her to the new course, the *Farley* was slamming head-on into the waves cresting at thirty feet. They broke over the bow and washed the main deck, and there was no horizon; there was only the deep trough, and black and white water, no longer tossing but heaving with a monolithic power, a three-storey wall held up against the sky by an accumulation of violent forces—days and days of them, thousands of miles.

That's what met the *Farley*'s bow, and washed over it with a flood of green water, and then the ship reared like a terrified horse. The wild launching into a fog-spumed featureless sky—that was the place where time stopped. Where we were held weightless, not of water or earth or air, and the longer the moment, the more likely the sawing descent would be a jarring slam, an explosion of white out of the next trough.

Any big chunk of ice could have torn her open. I knew, watching the ship taking wave after wave, that in this water, a man overboard or ship damage necessitating the launching of lifeboats. Well … The lifeboat would never get launched; the man would never be recovered. If something bad happened out here there would be no rescue. The safety gear we had on board wouldn't do a bit of good.

At 1130 Aultman staggered up to the bridge in his Mustang suit and went out through the aft hatch. He took Casson as a spotter and they were harnessed and tethered. When he came back ten minutes later, he told the captain to turn the ship around. Running into the wind was shaking the rotors of the helicopter apart, bending them nearly to the deck as they pulled against the tethers at their tips. Along that axis, the composite blades had very little strength and could snap. The wind might have been sixty knots. Turn it around, he begged, or we'll lose the bird. Watson said okay. He ran west with the storm. It was a significant decision.

10

FORCE 8

IT WAS THREE o'clock on Christmas morning. What woke me was the sudden drop of the bow and the impact of my right shoulder hitting the locker at the head of my bunk. The *Farley* shivered. Then the wave pitched the stern out of water and the prop howled, beating air. Water gurgled along and sloshed at the bolted porthole. I lay for a moment and breathed, and listened. Something was different in the pulse of the ship; a quickening. I swung out of the bunk, grabbed my dry suit and life jacket, and ran up the stairs to the bridge.

The sea was a frenzy. The waves were now over thirty feet, and snow blew by in the tortured fog and mixed with the plumes of exploding spray. It was now a full force 8 gale. The timbers of the bridge creaked and groaned and the wind battered against the half-inch Plexiglas windows with a pitched moan like an animal.

Watson sat up in the high captain's chair in his Mustang suit, focused and calm. Alex was at the helm, trying to keep the *Farley* running straight on the waves. Hammarstedt was at the main radar to his left.

Alex said, 'Good timing.' His eyes were red-rimmed. 'Two ships on the radar. The closest is under the two-mile range. If they're icebergs they're doing six knots.'

'Probably the *Nisshin Maru* and the *Esperanza*,' Watson said. 'They're riding out the storm.' Where the *Arctic Sunrise* and the five other boats of the whaling fleet had scattered in the gale, no one could say.

I stared at the throbbing green blips on the main radar screen. Was it possible? Had Watson found, in hundreds of thousands of square miles of Southern Ocean, his prey? It was against all odds. Even with the informer on board the *Esperanza*. Even with the storm that could now be veiling his approach from the unwary Japanese. Watson turned to Cornelissen. 'Wake all hands,' he said.

We were 220 miles north-north-west of Antarctica's Commonwealth Bay, about twenty miles west of where we'd been when I went to sleep a few hours before. The gale howled out of the east-south-east. We had not got an update from the mole on the *Esperanza* since yesterday afternoon, so if this really was the *Nisshin*, we had been brought directly to it by the storm.

At 0350, maybe three miles ahead and a little off to port, I saw a shadow that was not mist or wave. It was a ship.

Alex said, looking over Hammarstedt's shoulder, 'We got three targets. The second ship is two miles ahead of this one.'

Watson said, 'Don't know what we can do here, but we can do something. Get Price up in the ultralight.' He was joking.

'Looks like the *Esperanza*,' I said. 'The bigger one beyond must be the *Nisshin Maru*.'

Silence. Everybody was straining to see through the snow and fog and blowing water. Watson said, 'We've got the advantage because the ship was built for this weather. How far to the nearest Japanese boat?'

'Two point seventy-five miles,' Alex said. 'The *Esperanza* is half a mile. The big ship is moving about seven knots.'

We were running ten knots, going with the storm. The *Esperanza* took shape out of the mist. It was much bigger than the *Farley*, painted blue-and-white with a big rainbow arcing across its side. It had white satellite and radar spheres stuck to the top of the superstructure, an enclosed crow's nest with canted windows, and an open heli deck with an enclosed hangar that must have made Aultman green. The *Farley* came up on its stern, a black apparition, and passed it.

'A thirty-million-dollar boat,' Watson said. 'Just the retrofit.'

'Always wanted to overtake a Greenpeace vessel,' Alex said.

'We could do so much with a ship like that,' Hammarstedt murmured.

And then we noticed something astounding. Its starboard bridge wing was crowded with people, and they were waving wildly and pumping their fists, and one was swinging a big Canadian flag back and forth. I blinked. They were saying, Thank God you're here—stop the bastards.

We *were* all in this together. They had been harassing the whaling fleet for days now, watching whales harpooned and electrocuted and drowned. They had been doing what they were mandated to do—letting the world know it was going on. They waved us on. A minute more and the Greenpeacers were swallowed in mist and spray. And then we were thrown over to port and two bodies went flying across the bridge, and the rest scrabbled to hold on to something.

'That's a forty-degree roll,' Alex said.

The *Farley* seemed to shake herself off and resumed her patient climb and plunge.

'The *Nisshin Maru* is increasing speed—*Nisshin Maru* six point eight knots, we're doing nine point four.'

All eyes ahead. From the top of the next wave, I made out a thickening of mist, monstrous in size.

'There it is!' Hammarstedt cried. 'That's definitely it!'

A terrible suggestion of a ship. Straining, as if the eyes

themselves could clarify the image. Then the fog did it for us, rending like ripped gauze, and there for a second was the giant stern, the slipway, the white block letters that read *NISSHIN MARU*, TOKYO.

Trevor, with his engineer's telepathy, down in the engine room, must have known. The *Farley* was taking the waves at what for her was a dead run.

Alex said, 'We're doing eleven knots. They're doing six.'

'I have tweaked the engine.' Trevor was in the doorway, ear protectors propped on his head, an elusive smile just slipping away.

Allison said, 'The captain says we're severely limited with what we can do in this weather. Don't want anybody out there—hell!' She pointed out the forward windows. 'Look at Gedden!'

Gedden, the tree climber, was crouching on the forecastle like a man in battle under fire. He had something black clutched against his right side, and he scrambled forward now on hands and knees. An explosion of spray covered him. When he got to the bow rail he whipped a carabiner from his harness and clipped it to the rail. Tethered in, holding the thing against him with his elbow, he went for the flag mast at the bow. He was going to hoist the Jolly Roger. In sixty-knot gusts. He did. He got the flag clipped on somehow and hoisted it and cleated it off. Then he waited for the first climb out of a plunge and unclipped himself and scrambled aft.

This was a psychological war as much as anything. The Japanese had said in their press when they left on 7 November from Shinoseki harbour that they were afraid of an attack by Sea Shepherd. Fear would make them run. When they ran, they did not kill whales.

I didn't think fog happened in near-hurricane winds, but there it was. Shrouding the *Nisshin Maru* after the first glimpse. The ship might have seen us, but probably it hadn't. It was maintaining its speed, just under seven knots. Nobody bothered to step out on its bridge wing to look back and check. I could only imagine what we would look like ourselves, appearing out of the ragged fog, black and battered, the gale-stiffened Jolly Roger flying, with an avowed mission to cripple or destroy.

Alex kept one eye on the radar now and one eye on the sea ahead. He had the ship targeted on the screen, in a small white box, which gave him a continual read-out of its speed, direction, range, and time to contact.

'Seventeen minutes,' he said. 'Twelve knots.'

Gedden stepped dripping onto the bridge. 'Kind of limited with the Zodiacs,' he said, catching his breath.

'We're pretty much the can opener right now,' Trevor said.

We took another wave over the bow, green water, and I thought that if Gedden had been out there it would have knocked him over the rail. Another wave flew up hard against the windows, and then it was as if we had come through a curtain. The fog ripped away and just ahead was the slipway ramp cut into the stern where they winched up the dead whales, and the tall cranes. A banner over the slipway read, 'Greenpeace Misleads You'. Running down the length of the hull, visible when it corkscrewed on a swell, was the large block-lettered word RESEARCH. We were 1.2 miles away.

Watson said, 'I think the best tactic here, Alex, is the prop foulers. Bring it as close to the bow as possible. Low profile.'

Alex was leaning forward into the window like a cat watching a mouse, except that the mouse was the size of a city block. 'Do we want to ram them? Punch a few holes in their ship?'

I thought it was a rhetorical question.

'No. Prop fouler's the best thing right now.' He seemed to be protecting his crew. No sane person wanted a collision in these seas. Watson turned to Trevor. 'Tell them to get the prop foulers ready on the stern. Tell them to stay down, stay hidden. Don't deploy them until I blow the horn.' Trevor nodded, exited.

'I can't believe they're going so slow,' Watson said. We were coming right up on their stern, half a mile now and closing. 'How far is the *Esperanza* behind us?' The proximity of a potential rescue ship might determine Watson's level of aggression. Though I didn't think a rescue boat could even spot swimmers in the violent waves.

'One point two miles,' Alex said. 'We've got a third ship straight to port, six miles. They're doing only five knots.'

The *Nisshin* was very close. It was like sneaking up on a browsing deer, holding your breath, praying a twig wouldn't snap. Maybe somebody on the *Nisshin* finally saw us. The pace with which we closed the gap slowed a little.

'The factory ship is increasing speed to eight knots now!' Alex said. 'Increasing speed again, nine knots. Nine point four.'

Watson watched his prey. Not excited, not angry, just focused. He did look like a polar bear, with the same pitiless detachment, the sense one got of icy calculation, weighing distances, speed, odds. It was easy to see that this was not his first rodeo.

Alex said, 'Our speed is eleven. Their speed is nine and a half.'

We were off to its starboard, coming up on its stern. It was monstrous. Even so, the bigger waves were throwing its prop out of water. Some of them were over forty feet. Trevor shoved open the bridge wing door and entered. He had on his Mustang suit now, and he was wet.

'They have the trail line ready.' The trail line was three-quarter-inch thick longline on a spool on the stern. There was half a mile of the stuff. Watson would try to push across the *Nisshin*'s bow while Trevor and his team unleashed the floating line. The bigger ship would have to plough over it. The line would work its way down the hull and, Watson hoped, get sucked up in the *Nisshin*'s prop. But I didn't see how that would not be dangerous to the Japanese crew in this kind of storm. If the prop did jam, the *Nisshin* would broach sideways to the seas and wallow. They'd have to launch life boats in seas like this, in water that was at or below freezing.

Watson said again, 'As soon as I hit the horn, then deploy it. We have to get far enough ahead so we don't hit them.'

'Nine point six.'

'Keep pulling alongside.'

Watson said, 'I hope we can disable those bastards. They're not going to let us have a second chance. The bag with the passports, get someone to find it.'

Kalifi went out. Watson was making preparations to abandon ship if necessary.

Alex, his voice rising, called out, 'We're getting pretty close here. Point four miles.'

'I'll hit the horn when I want Trevor to deploy.'

'I found the passports.'

'Just put it by the safe so it's ready to go.'

'Greenpeace is speeding up too,' Alex said. They had to be glued to their radar, watching the signal blips of the two ships starting to overlap.

'We could ram her up the slipstream if you want,' Alex said. 'What do you say, Paul?'

'Yes, the swells are good,' piped up Hammarstedt, who was again at the main radar; it was the first thing he'd said in a while. He meant that we had following waves of great size, so it would be easy to come down off the top of one and crack down with force into the opening of their slipway.

'No, we're going to do this,' Watson said. 'Is he picking up speed at all?'

'Nine point nine knots.'

'He can't go any faster. He's going to cut the swell as soon as we go by him, too.' Meaning Watson thought he would turn.

'Towards us?' Alex asked.

'Yes.' Watson was thinking they might try to ram us. 'I think just past the "Research" thing is the best time. You feel safe enough?'

'We've got a knot,' Alex said.

The *Farley*, to everyone's astonishment, overtook the *Nisshin*'s stern and began to move up alongside. It was about 300 feet to port. Black hull, white superstructure, four storeys high, with three massive crane gantries. RESEARCH. Clean, innocent block letters. We were edging up along the word. When the bridge reached the H, Alex would swing in towards the ship. He would count on our extra speed to angle us in front of the bow and get us clear across it before a collision.

'There's nobody there, nobody even looking at us,' Watson said. 'I think we caught them unawares!'

Just then it was as if the *Nisshin Maru* jumped in surprise.

Someone put the hammer down and it began to pull away.

'He's turning away,' Alex said.

Watson, curt: 'Turn with him—is he speeding up?'

'Turning—not very smart, they're going to take the waves on the beam—Yes, they're getting away! Ten point seven— matching speed—they're faster, eleven point five, eleven point seven.'

'Go right on their ass, then—'

As Alex began the turn to follow, a hard wave hit the *Farley* on her port quarter and she slammed over. We were falling back along *Nisshin*'s endless aft deck. And taking the seas, like it, on our port stern. It was not a good angle to the storm.

'Go for it if you can. Straight into the slipway.'

It was too late. The *Farley* was straining with all she had, eleven, eleven point six, twelve knots. But the *Nisshin* was too powerful. She came up to speed and fled at sixteen knots.

And then it was as if the *Nisshin*'s skipper snapped. Captain Toyama had been harassed for days by Greenpeace; their Zodiacs swarmed his killer boats, his harpooners had shot whales right over their heads. And here, out of the fog, was a ship willing to disable his own. The *Nisshin* was a quarter-mile away when it turned to starboard, slowing down. Toyama seemed to be saying, 'Okay, you want to mess with me? Come ahead.'

Alex matched the turn, all but thirty degrees of it, and set a collision course. He too was completely calm. Watson, out of his chair now, stood with a hand on the lever that controlled our speed. We caught the crossing seas and the *Farley* slammed over to port in a forty-degree roll that sent Kristian crashing across the bridge. The *Farley* righted. Alex turned to Kalifi and said, 'Tell the crew, collision in two minutes.'

Most of the crew were gathered in the mess in their exposure suits, aft of amidships, and a long companionway away from the main hatch exit. One of the officers—it wasn't clear who— had ordered them there. Not a good place to be. If the *Farley* broke apart they wouldn't have a chance of getting out.

The two ships approached each other at an acute angle. By the law of the sea, we had the right of way, as we were on his starboard. The *Nisshin*'s bow lunged off a thirty-five-foot wave, airborne, and crashed down like a giant axe. Now we could hear the blare of their horn through the tearing wind. Repeated blasts, short and long, enraged.

'Collision one minute.'

I tugged on the zipper of my dry suit and had one thought: you're going to be wet and cold in about twenty seconds. The bow loomed, 200 feet away, aimed at our belly, amidships.

Alex glanced at the radar, at the juggernaut, held his course. He was focused, intent. A deadly game of Antarctic chicken: 150 feet away. Alex blew the horn, which was the order to unleash the prop fouler. A squad on the stern stood, braced themselves, and whipped several hundred feet of the mooring line off a big spool, enough to tangle any propeller.

And then the *Nisshin* blinked. Whoever was at the helm threw it over to port. For an agonising second the two ships ran parallel, and then they were pulling away into the fog. As they ran, Watson pulled down the mike on maritime channel 16, and barked, '*Nisshin Maru, Nisshin Maru*, this is the *Farley Mowat*. You are in violation of an international whale sanctuary. Time to go now, you murdering scumbags. Now move it! And run like the cowards you are.'

Watson handed the mic to Casson, who spoke rudimentary Japanese. '*Nisshin Maru*,' he said. '*Nisshin Maru*, you are murderers. You are dishonourable.'

Alex lifted his watery blue eyes from the radar and smiled. The first one I'd seen in days. 'They actually increased speed when you said that.'

Everybody breathed.

I asked Alex if we would have sustained damage at those speeds. 'They would have sunk us,' he said. 'A ship that's ten times as heavy as your own ship—it's gonna basically slice your ship in half.'

I nodded. 'There was a point there, where it was up to him whether we were T-boned or not.'

'Yes, he definitely had that choice.'

The captain said, 'If they had sunk us, there'd be such bad PR for them. They'd be hauled in for investigations. Australia would have to intervene. We have Australian citizens on board.'

'But no one would have seen,' I said.

'The *Esperanza* was close behind. Close enough to see. Legally, the *Nisshin Maru* had to give way. I think he might have hit us, but he could have shut himself down. If he hit us he would sustain so much damage he'd have to go home.'

Watson looked doggedly out from under his shag. 'We've always won every game of chicken we've played,' he said. 'We did it with the Spanish navy, bow to bow. Same with the Russians. I told them, "Your ship is worth a hell of a lot more than ours is, so you'd better get out of the way—" and they did. Well, we're chasing after them. I wonder where the harpoon vessels are?'

Watson ducked into the radio room. By 0605 he had his first press release posted. It began: 'No whale will be killed this Christmas Day . . .'

I peeled off the dry suit and let the adrenaline wash through me. I thought, No doubt, now—Watson is terrifying in his fearlessness, and in his willingness to sacrifice everything, including our lives—to save the whale.

A certain sombreness took over the ship. The storm raged. Watson showed me the weather fax. 'Looks like a freight train,' he chuckled. A line of five Ls for 'Low'—tightly packed storm systems—marched one after another east to west across the sixty-second parallel. We were in the middle of the track. We couldn't turn south, because we'd take the waves on the beam or the quarter, and two forty-degree rolls had been violent enough. Minutes or hours of them would shake the ship apart. We had to run with the storm.

Alex set the *Farley* down the waves with a heading of 290 degrees west-north-west, the exact bearing of the *Nisshin*, which evidently didn't wish to challenge the gale either. It had settled back to a more reasonable fourteen knots and was patiently opening the gap. The *Esperanza* was moving up on us and would soon pass. Alex tracked them both on the radar.

I went down to the mess. Wessel and Geert were there in a booth. Wessel had been out on the stern, exposed in the storm, one of the handful of crew who had run out the fouling line. He looked a bit dazed. I slid into the seat opposite.

'I thought, this is it,' Wessel said. 'I was ready to die there. But I had a good feeling in my heart. I was watching some of the guys on their ship. I was holding on for dear life. When we turned just a little off the waves, the wind tore into the aft deck and me and Luke went flying. Wind and rain, so slippery—I thought, Jeez, I'm going overboard. Just then Luke grabbed my headgear and held me. And I looked up and saw the *Nisshin Maru* and saw four or five people looking down at us with arms crossed—quite detached. And we got ready to launch a prop fouler—as soon as we were ready to drop it in the water, their ship turned. I think they saw the blue line—now they're running with their tails between their legs.'

Wessel took a deep breath and put his back against the bulkhead. 'That was a defining moment in my life, I reckon. From now on I'm devoting my life to saving the whales, direct action. That sort of settled it for me.' He shook his head. The images of his near demise kept intruding. 'Things happen so fast—one little shift of the boat and you're sliding.'

I climbed back up to the bridge in time to see the *Esperanza* passing us with its festive rainbow paint job, and to hear channel 16 crackle with the voice of its captain.

'*Esperanza* to *Farley Mowat*: the captain of the *Nisshin Maru* will ram you if he gets the chance. Good luck.'

Gee, thanks, I thought. The warning's a bit late. Toyama had demurred at the last second. Or maybe one of his officers grabbed the helm. Though, at the speed the *Nisshin* was travelling, one small miscalculation would have sent its bow ripping into the *Farley*.

I was amused to see camera flashes popping from the *Esperanza*'s bridge wing. Its crew were taking pictures of us. The Jolly Roger was flying, stiff as a board, frayed in the punishing wind. The *Farley* tore white out of the ocean with every plunge of her bow. She must have looked mean.

It was 0748. Twelve more minutes of Alex's eventful watch. He was still mulling how close he had come to cracking open the *Nisshin* like a fat nut. 'If we could have got closer I would've rammed up their spillway, absolutely. It's a matter of aiming. It's a bit rough in this sea.'

'Do you think the Japanese are raising alarms now with the Australians, with their own government?'

He flicked his eyes to the radar, and pointed at the blip that was the *Nisshin*, ten miles away now. 'I wouldn't be surprised if they already called the environment minister, Ian Campbell.' Very matter-of-fact: 'I was surprised they didn't ram us.'

It was like saying he had actually expected most of us to die.

'But if they had, you said we would have sunk.'

He smiled. 'Oh, definitely. Did you see the size of that thing? In sea like this I'd prefer to keep her afloat—'

No kidding.

Alex glanced at the clock on the GPS screen. 'Hope that storm dies out in the next twelve hours so we can send out the helicopter, keep track of them. Greenpeace is keeping up with them. Seems to me we are tossing the ball here.'

The watches changed. Mia and Lincoln took over while Watson hammered out more PR in the radio room. The sultry French girl sat up in the captain's chair, cupping a lidded mug of coffee while Lincoln steered, her dark hair spilling onto her delicate shoulders. 'I want to die with a harpoon in my chest at eighty-six,' she said as spray hit the windows. 'That would be a beautiful way to die. Of course I hope there is no whaling by then.'

Watson entered the bridge, plucked the mic out of its cradle and hailed the captain of the *Esperanza*. 'Captain Boyer, you're doing a good job. I don't think they'll be killing whales today,' he said.

All very cordial. Watson's beef was not with the crew, but with the brass.

Then more crackling and another voice from the *Esperanza*. 'It's Paul.'

Watson smiled broadly. 'Ruzycki? I was wondering when you'd say hi.' Paul Ruzycki was first mate of the *Esperanza* and an old friend of Watson's.

'Glad to see you guys,' the disembodied voice said. 'Merry Christmas. Wishing you and the crew the best.'

In fact, Greenpeace did mention Sea Shepherd on its website: a single line in a crew member's blog about the *Farley* appearing in the area on Christmas Day, along with a link to Sea Shepherd's website. But that was it. The website editor had probably been reprimanded.

BY NOON the barometer had plummeted to 28.80. Everybody—the *Esperanza*, the *Farley*, the *Nisshin Maru*—went with the gale because it was the only place to go. West-north-west. At 1100, the *Farley* skewed and caught the wrong looming forty-footer and rolled harder than she had yet. The port bulkheads for a moment became the deck—in laymen's terms, the wall became the floor. There was an ominous thud from up forward. Chris Price came into the green room looking as though he were about to cry. The flying inflatable boat had busted loose from its cradle and cracked itself against a stack of strapped-down steel. It was a broken bird.

The ship was weirdly quiet. Quieter even than after the last let-down. Mandy, an animal rehabilitator and kayak guide, said that just before the near-impact the green room was a scene. Some were running around yelling that we were all going to die. Others were sitting cross-legged staring into space as if they suddenly got it—understood that dying was definitely one likely option.

Just before lunch the Associated Press called Watson for an interview, which he gave with relish on the sat phone. By that night the story was picked up by *Newsday*, the *Washington Post*, the *Mercury News*, China Broadcast.

Watson issued another press release: 'Sea Shepherd Requests the Australian Navy to Keep Peace in Antarctica.' I laughed. If he had his way he'd have every warship in the hemisphere down here.

THE OLD *Farley* strained and groaned as the walls of erupting water surged beneath her. Watson didn't want to keep trending north. He was being taken further and further from anywhere he was likely to intercept the whaling fleet again, which was down near the ice edge.

When he came on watch after dinner he ordered the course changed to south-east, directly into the seas. The pounding was immediate. Wave after wave like that. The storm was still building. Some of the waves were easily four or five storeys.

Chris Aultman rushed onto the bridge, dripping wet. He said the rotors of the helicopter couldn't take the stress of the head-on wind and asked the captain to turn the ship around again. Watson did. Before I left the chart room I checked the barometer there: 28.75. Still dropping.

That night in my bunk I lay in the dark and thought that to much of the world, Watson would be deemed insane. Maybe he was. Certainly, from the bridge of the *Nisshin Maru*, watching the much smaller ship hold its course to the brink of destruction must have sent cold horror through the officers. Honour was one thing, murder and suicide on the high seas another. But I also thought about the whales, swimming tonight in their herds and pods through the islands of ice.

I did not think he was exactly insane. Countries around the world pledged to protect the whales in treaties and laws, and yet in reality the whales were as vulnerable as if there had been no treaties at all. Japan's fleet allotted itself whatever number it wished to kill, endangered and non-endangered species alike, and came down and took them. It shot them right over Greenpeace's head. The whales could not advocate for themselves. They had no allies on the entire planet who were willing to intervene at all costs—except Watson and Sea Shepherd. What was insane about that? Human beings lay down their lives for territory, resources, national honour, religion. What was more insane about being willing to lay down your life for another species? Whatever one said about Watson's methods, they were relatively effective. His campaigns against the English, Irish and Scottish seal hunts in the early 1980s shut them down for good. His battle against the Canadian seal hunt had halted the slaughter in 1984—for ten years.

WHEN I WOKE on 26 December, we were still in the teeth of the gale. Soon after, Watson got sick of being pushed west and north where he didn't want to be, and wheeled the Farley around again, this time to the south-east. He had a hunch that the Japanese would resume whaling in Porpoise Bay—whose mouth was 270 miles to the south of us.

Aultman had been out early, tending to his helicopter. He'd fashioned some wood props for the rotors, to hold them stiff and high in the relentless wind. With the chopper exposed on the heli deck as it was, having been shaken to its bones and washed with seawater, with the rotors bending against their tethers—given all that, all he wanted to do was fly.

Aultman gave Watson the nod, and the captain turned the ship back up into the hammering waves, heading south-east. The *Farley* was still ghostly, seemingly devoid of people. Half seemed to be seasick and the other half suffering from some sort of flu. Even stout Marc, who'd had a lot of time at sea in rough weather, was overtaken with exhaustion and nausea.

I went out into the whistling relative shelter of the bridge wing and held tight to the rope rail and watched the snow and spray fly by. I loved this. The raw beauty of storm. I'm not sure why, but our close encounter had not scared me. I had spent half my life kayaking whitewater rivers, and the power of the ocean whipped to such a frenzy filled me not with fear but with a profound and grateful awe. I did not want to die out here but I could not, honestly, think of a better place to be.

The WATCHES on the bridge changed quietly, with Mia clinging to the radar hood and wishing to God that her stomach would not revolt again; with Emily clutching her water bottle, and responding to orders from the officer with fluttering eyelids and an unconscious touch of the Dramamine patch behind her ear. The ashes of her father—the Robert Hunter who started Greenpeace and committed his life to trying to get humans to care for the planet—were under her bunk in a box, waiting to be scattered in one of the last truly wild places. The J. Crew crawled out of their berths only to watch a DVD of the TV show *Lost*. Even forest wildman Gedden didn't look well. He sat on the bridge on his watch with a sullen determination not to get seasick.

In the radio room, Watson was playing solitaire on the laptop on his left, while he sat at the main keyboard and pounded out more correspondence and invective. He had international media on the hook with the dramatic Christmas encounter, and he was going to play that fish for all it was worth.

'There's a rumour,' he said with glee as I leaned into the room, 'that the Japanese are sending down a warship.'

Good God. He wouldn't make that up—or would he?

'Are you winning?'

'Huh?—oh, that. You know, Al Johnson, one of the first Greenpeacers, once said if you're ever lost, really lost in the wilderness, just start playing solitaire.'

'Why?'

'Start playing, and before you know it someone will be looking over your shoulder telling you how to play the next card.' He laughed.

I asked Watson for an update on his plan.

'The way I figure it, they've got to come into the ice again. Once we get down to the ice edge, we can send out the helicopter.' He watched the bow gash into the trough and take a wave over the rounded whaleback. 'Doesn't make any sense why they'd be out there—the storm isn't even down in the ice edge. Maybe they thought they'd lose us in the storm. Our mole won't tell me where they are. Sometimes he does, sometimes he doesn't.'

All day the waves and wind seemed to be backing off a little. We were heading as due south as the *Farley* could withstand. At 2200 Watson got a new fleet position from his source on the *Esperanza*. Fearing discovery, the source had called a brother in North America who had just called Watson on the sat phone.

The *Nisshin Maru* was almost 200 miles east-south-east of us, and not far from the south magnetic pole. The report said the factory ship was generally going in circles.

Watson didn't understand it. 'Maybe they're waiting for the killer ship to come back from Hobart,' he said.

He would hold his course to the south-east, aiming for the east side of the long cold protrusion of the Dibble Glacier Tongue. Then he would work along the ice edge to where he thought they would have to return.

11

THE LAW OF THE SEA

ON 27 DECEMBER Alex came onto the bridge muttering, 'This is insane. What is this, a party cruise? Everybody is in their berths.'

Watson barely noticed. He was talking about his only child, his daughter Lani. He said, 'When Lani was in sixth grade the teacher asked the class what was the function of government. Lani said, "The government is a bunch of people who get together and plan how to kill people and animals." That raised a few eyebrows.'

He went to the radio room to scan his morning's emails. He came back flourishing an open letter from the director general of Japan's Institute of Cetacean Research, Hiroshi Hatanaka, to Junichi Sato, the campaigns director of Greenpeace Japan. Accusing Greenpeace and Sea Shepherd of piracy and terrorism, the letter set the legal stage for severe counter-measure. Under the law of the sea, acts of piracy constitute grounds for arrest, seizure of the perpetrating ship, and even deadly retaliation. It was a warning shot across the bows: we are defining your activities as piracy, and we will respond.

Things were heating up on the diplomatic and media fronts, which is exactly what Watson was trying to do. No wonder he looked so happy, humming away on the bridge, while his ship got pummelled by icy seas and his traumatised crew hibernated.

The weather changed on the morning of 28 December. From the deck it was a different world: an innocent, seven-foot swell, light fog, fulmars and petrels circling the ship. The rhythmic thresh of the bow wave.

On my way back down the hall, I saw Mandy corner Electrician Dave outside the bosun's locker.

'You're a hunter, right?'

Dave looked up at her. Mandy is formidable: tall, broad-shouldered, with a hawk's beak of a nose and dark eyes. She towered over the little Australian. Dave knew she had spent a considerable amount of time doing 'hunt sabs'—trying to sabotage hunters in California and Colorado.

Dave cocked his head. 'Aw, yeah. Well—the only thing I hunt is introduced non-native feral species.' Wow, I didn't know he had it in him; I'd never heard him so eloquent. 'Foxes and pigs. They're doing terrible damage. Terrible.' He shook his head morosely. 'Nobody's doing anything about it, you know, so we do.'

He looked up at his adversary, measuring the effect, and he grinned, showing his missing tooth. As I passed, I thought he knew he'd escaped this time, barely.

By noon we were forty-eight miles from the Dibble Glacier Tongue, and the mood of the crew was getting better all the time. At four in the afternoon we were sailing slowly into a luminous, fog-shrouded snowfall. The seas were maybe eight feet. The dark water was peppered with growlers, and Alex's watch steered through them carefully. We were forty miles south of the south magnetic pole, and the compass in the binnacle was skewed to the north-west, 180 degrees wrong. Amazing that anybody could have navigated down here before satellites. We were 100 miles from the whaling fleet's last communicated position.

Watson came onto the bridge and told Alex to slow and just head into the waves.

'We'll wait here for a while. I haven't heard anything from the Greenpeace ship for two days. They were probably given new orders.'

By nine, the *Farley* was pushing slowly into a dense fog. The bent and rusted thermometer on the bridge wing was still pegged at thirty-two degrees, and the fog verged—half a degree colder and it would shiver into a veil of ice. Visibility was under 100 yards. I went to bed.

At 0400, Hammarstedt and his quartermasters handed over the bridge to Alex, Gedden and Gunter.

Watson was already there. 'Okay,' he said, his focus on the whalers. 'M— contacted me at midnight. M— says they're not making any sense. Going this way, that way, not hunting. No sign of the killer ships. He gave me the position at midnight. He had a friend call from Toronto. The friend said he can't call directly or email. They're starting to suspect. He said to keep a position to the south. Now they're directly north of Porpoise Bay.'

So Watson, it seemed, had a good instinct in wanting to follow the ice to Porpoise Bay. If we kept steadily cruising west, and the weather held out, we could be there in twenty-four hours.

MID-MORNING, the ice continent was less than 100 yards off to port—an undulating false coast of broken, floating ice that stretched south to the real shoreline. Other than an occasional fat seal dozing away the summer morning, everything was unrelieved greyish-white as far as one could see. The dark blue water of the Southern Ocean met the ice edge in a sharply defined, wavy line. We followed the seam westward.

It began to snow, and the fog thickened with it. We slowed, paralleling the ice edge, very close, perhaps thirty yards off, like a blind man holding on to a rail. A large leopard seal lifted his broad head and then put it back on his ice pillow.

Trevor appeared on the bridge. The captain had asked him how much fuel we had left and he'd been sounding the *Farley*'s seven tanks. Watson didn't want to get so far along the coast that he would pass the point of no return and be unable to get back to Australia. If the whalers continued west of Porpoise Bay, he might try instead for Cape Town, South Africa.

'Seventy-eight-thousand-plus litres, which translates into twenty-eight days. We're going back to Australia.' He twisted his mouth into a wry smile. 'It just means we have to stay in this area. South Africa is five thousand nautical miles further.'

For the rest of the morning we churned west. Watson wanted badly to send up the chopper to look for killer ships along the ice edge. He looked out into the mist that kept the helicopter decked. 'All we need is one more whack at them.'

Mia steered now, and Lincoln looked ahead with binoculars for growlers. We were cruising at a steady nine knots, the fastest we'd gone in days. Aultman came through the port bridge wing door.

'Thirty-four degrees. Woo-hoo! Heatwave! I want to give her a bath.'

'Don't you wish you had a mechanic to check her over after all that storm?'

'Tell you the truth, I'd be happy to have someone who'd even seen a helicopter before.' The former marine continued on through, going to look for Casson or Dennis to help wash the chopper.

If it didn't feel exactly like a heatwave, it felt like a reprieve. The *Farley* seemed to loll on the little swell. There were more birds now than there had been at any time before, and the sea seemed devoid of menace. In the bosun's locker, Geert hummed while he cut a sea turtle out of scrap plywood. He was beginning to populate the wainscoting of the bridge with cameos of wildlife, all painted with swirling designs. He took the job of ship's artist very seriously. The rest of the crew was recovering and back at work.

Kalifi called a meeting of the deckhands and sat in the bosun's locker on a folding chair with her legs crossed, sequin sandals winking, sunglasses propped fashionably in her unruly blonde hair—though there hadn't been any sun for two weeks. The oil drums had shifted in their straps. The FIB wing had been lashed to the starboard rail and needed to be broken down and stored. There were piles of longline on the main deck, which Inde would supervise in coiling. And the old ship would get a scrub-down, stem to stern.

The *Farley* pushed a quarter-mile in, straight into the broken sea ice, opening a black curving swath behind her. Alex shut down the engines and she ground to a halt.

A little while later Aultman started the chopper and did a careful half hour run-up of his engine, and then he lifted off with Kristian and took off to the north-west, heading towards the *Nisshin*'s last position. He had been gone about an hour when Watson got a communiqué from the *Esperanza*.

The fleet had broken its pattern of indirection and was running almost due west. It was about 350 miles west-north-west of us. The *Nisshin* was going fourteen to fifteen knots, about as fast as it could go. Still no sign of the killer ships. The message also said that the *Arctic Sunrise* was 100 miles behind the *Nisshin Maru* and the *Esperanza* and losing ground.

We were getting low on fuel. If we went further to the west we wouldn't have enough to get back to Australia, and Trevor didn't think we'd make it to the southern tip of Africa. In a few days we'd be past the point of no return. The seas were calm now, but if we hit more bad weather, we'd use our remaining diesel at an even faster rate.

Watson was unfazed. He patiently waited for the helicopter to return; then the *Farley* nosed a slow circle out of the ice and followed her own trail, now loosely filled in, back out to open water. We followed the ice edge north-north-west into the stubborn twilight. Watson would round this pack and continue west in chase.

FRIDAY 30 DECEMBER. First sun in two weeks. The pale blue directly overhead is so novel, I go out on deck and lift my face and let the colour soak like rain. Today is my day to go up in the chopper. Watson wants Aultman to take a particularly long scout out ahead of us. We have rounded the corner of ice extending from the Dibble Glacier, and the *Farley* is now chugging due west in an open cobalt sea.

I still don't see what Watson wants to accomplish with his recon flight, or even with this chase.

'The *Nisshin Maru* is now four hundred miles away and increasing the gap,' I say, pointing to the chart.

'Those guys—Greenpeace—don't know where the harpoon vessels are; they haven't seen them for days. So if we stay down to the south we may run into them. Really a flanking motion: the *Arctic Sunrise* is on one side, the north, we're on the other. We're sweeping a good bit of area.'

That still didn't answer my question. The harpoon vessels could easily go twenty-five knots—take one look at us, put the pedal to the metal and be gone.

But I was glad to be going up with Aultman. We'd been on the ship a long time, and any opportunity to get off, short of swimming, was a welcome diversion. I put on my dry suit and a life jacket as well. Aultman smiled when I climbed in.

'You're certainly not going to drown,' he said over the blast of the engine.

'That's the plan.'

We put on our headsets. The roar muffled; Aultman spoke through his mic. 'If something goes wrong and we have to ditch in the water, out here we stay in the chopper. In these seas she'll bob like a cork. If she starts to turn over and we have to bail, I climb out, I throw out the life raft.' He pointed his thumb to a compartment outside and behind him. I gave him the thumbs-up. Everybody knew that something had better not go wrong out here.

The *Farley* was pitching hard and Chris waited for the right timing and lifted off abruptly. Immediately we were buffeted by a twenty-five knot headwind. He rolled away from the ship and then we tipped forward and he accelerated into the weather, which was coming now from the west. We climbed fast to 5,000 feet.

The sea was a black floor, rippled in long stripes by the swell and flecked with whitecaps that sparked and disappeared in a vast and silent propagation. We angled for the blinding-white coast of the ice edge, which lay taut as a skin over the curve of the earth.

The chopper rattled along at seventy-five knots. It was exhilarating to be airborne, to be free of the waves, and to cover so much territory so fast. We saw big solitary vessels we thought might be ships, but when we flew over them they were islands of chisel-cut ice, cupping lagoons of electric blue. Nothing. No Japanese, no harpoon boats. At eighty miles from the ship, we ran into menacing dark squall lines and decided to turn around.

Eighty miles. The expanse of empty ice and sea around us was almost overwhelming. We were thousands of miles from nowhere. Should we have to ditch, we were at least nine hours from a lumbering ship, a speck as small as the whitecaps. We headed for the ice to see what wildlife we might find and ran back along it.

The false coast was a tiling of tightly packed, geometric ice cobbles that merged in the distance ahead to solid white. The dark sea pressed it into a mimicry of coves and bays. Spires stood to the south like bone cities. Not a whale breaking the surface, nor a seal to relieve the relentless mosaic.

The world below was black and white. Pure and lonely. That's what it was about Antarctica: you are either hot-blooded and hungry or you are a cold element. You are water or ice. There is no middle ground here, no compromise. It seemed apt. In Watson's war on whalers, there were no conditions for truce.

Aultman spiralled the chopper to 600 feet and we raced over the puzzled, frozen plain. With no references, it seemed the pack ice was just below our boots. We climbed and broke north over open water. We ran straight into the gleam of low sun. And then I saw the ship, a black shadow on the dark blue sea, pitching into the swell.

Conditions had worsened since we left. We had been gone over three hours, the longest flight he'd yet taken, and I suppose we were lucky that the seas hadn't become even more raucous. Had the *Farley* been rolling this hard before, Aultman would never have taken off. He lowered the helicopter to the tossing deck twice, hovered, then baulked and jammed the throttle and lifted again for a go-around. He got on the radio. 'Hey, Alex, how fast are you going?'

'Two knots.'

'Could you increase it to four? And keep her as straight as you can into the waves.'

'Sure thing.'

The ship smoothed out a little. Aultman brought the chopper down to within four feet of the deck and hovered like a bee for a full minute, gauging the wind and the motion of his landing surface, which was rolling and yawing and pitching all at once. His right hand on the stick was adjusting, adjusting. And then he dropped it. Suddenly. Fast, but not hard. The deck crew rushed forward and ratcheted the chopper down to keep it from sliding into the water. They took only seconds. Pretty good for vegans with advanced degrees. Alex called Trevor for full power and we were under way again, as fast as the *Farley* could go, due west. Away from Australia, away from a return route we could make with the fuel we had left.

At midnight, Watson got a report from his mole on the *Esperanza*: the *Nisshin Maru* and one harpoon vessel were now 650 miles to the west of us. They were staying just outside the 200-mile limit of the Australian Antarctic Territory and continuing west at fifteen knots. No sign of the spotter vessel or the three other killer ships.

THE LAST DAY of 2005 was unfolding without incident. Sometime in the night we had passed north of Porpoise Bay and left the Clarie Coast behind. We were heading west. That was all anyone knew. Trevor kept sounding the fuel tanks, and he looked less and less happy. Were we to run out of diesel, we would be no better off than a ship with a tangled prop. Should a big gale come up, like the one from which we had just emerged, we would flounder and beat against the floating ice and sink.

The *Nisshin Maru* and the one harpoon boat with it were continuing west at fifteen knots. It seemed we had no hope of catching up unless the *Nisshin Maru* reversed direction or stopped dead in the water. Nor could Watson be hopeful of contacting a harpoon vessel even if we saw one, as they go something like twenty to twenty-five knots. Was Watson waiting for the possible arrival of a Japanese warship?

The ship was Watson's primary weapon—that and the blitz of press releases—and we all wondered what he intended to do with it. Hatanaka's talk of piracy was disturbing. On a website posting yesterday, Watson said:

> The Institute of Cetacean Research has made an open accusation of piracy and ecoterrorism against the Greenpeace Foundation and the Sea Shepherd Conservation Society. If Japan adopts the false accusations that acts of piracy have

been committed against their ships, they can use the accusa-
tions as an excuse under international law to attack and
seize the ships they accuse . . .

You didn't have to be a lawyer to make a case against Sea
Shepherd. Welding a seven-foot blade onto the bow for the
express purpose of damaging the hull of another ship, and
then ramming—or attempting to ram—that weapon into
said hull, clearly could be construed as an act of violence. As
could running out a line to foul the prop of another ship in a
storm. The *Farley*, it seemed, under the Law of the Sea, could
rightly be said to be a pirate ship, subject to attack and
seizure. She didn't even need to fly her Jolly Roger.

The leaden sky closed in around us again; the wind died;
we cruised west. Flurries of snow came and went, as did pairs
of storm petrels, the small black birds with the white rumps. I
went to the green room in the afternoon, and Allison put on a
video made by Mark Votier, who had been hired in 1996 by
the Institute of Cetacean Research to make a documentary
about Japanese whaling. Votier was so disgusted by what he
filmed, that he released the footage. The video was not long,
maybe twenty minutes, all taken from the deck of a harpoon
boat, or from the *Nisshin Maru*. It had a jerky, home-movie
quality, the handheld effect of a cameraman trying to stay on
his feet in heavy seas, trying to stay out of the way of flying
flensing knives on long poles.

Here was a heavily dressed hand loading the harpoon gun
with the explosive-tipped harpoon. Here was the ship moving
fast in the swell. There were the blows of a pod of minke
whales ahead, fleeing for all they were worth, blowing every
few seconds, clearly panicked. *Fire*. The flight of the harpoon,
the arrow-straight line of cable following. Miss. Fleeing
whales. Now the camera focused on a whale in the rear of the
pack. Good size. The harpooner focused on her too. *Fire*.
Miss again. And another. Fourth shot hits her in the flank.
Explosion and fountain of blood. Whale thrashing. Cable
winch engaged, thrashing, screaming whale reeled in, gushing
blood, turning the sea red. Hauled to the side. Still convulsing,

haemorrhaging everywhere. Another spear, probe, on long pole with cable attached thrust into her side. Whale writhing. Electrocution current now coursing through the spear. Whale in bloody agony. Not even close to dead. Finally hauled, tail up, suspended so they can hold her breathing hole under.

She drowns after fifteen more minutes in a sea of her own blood.

I wanted to vomit.

Transfer to mother ship. Two whales being winched by the tail up the slipway. The banner on the stern, 'Greenpeace is a sham.' A hard-hatted crew stepping forward with the long flensing knives and slicing the first whale open. Three-foot-long foetus removed. Still alive. Tiny scale model of a whale. The pregnant mother was not as fast as the rest of the pod. Foetus carried to a bench with scale, measured and weighed by the scientist. Guts spilled on deck by the long hooks and knives.

The choppy film ended. Silence, but for the reassuring vibration and throb of the diesel engine and chortle of the sea along the hull.

There is no more barbaric method of slaughter in any meat industry. The prolonged butchery and torture are reserved for the most intelligent, most social order of beings. The fact that the Japanese thought that filming this would be good PR seemed to point to an almost insane departure from reality.

I went out to the main deck to digest what I'd seen. I leaned against the rail and listened to the soothing rhythm of the bow wave. When I needed to get my physical bearings, I pulled out my GPS, got a fix on three satellites and knew in a moment my exact latitude and longitude. I knew, within a few metres, where I stood. But where did I stand with whaling and Watson's aggressive methods of protection? Out here, my moral bearings were less easy to find. Many people, and nations, were calling Watson a pirate. But was he? Pirates tended to kill people. Watson, on the other hand, was trying to preserve all life, human and animal alike. He said again and again that he wished no one harm. He would damage property alone. And yet his tactics, especially as executed by his freewheeling and inexperienced crew, put people at grave risk.

I thought about something Watson had said earlier. He quoted Jacques Cousteau as saying that the oceans are dying in our lifetime. I watched the wind spray the whitecaps downwind and thought about the first time I had seen beneath the surface of the sea. I was twenty-three, just out of college and travelling in the Pacific Rim. In Fiji I signed up to go snorkelling off a barrier reef. On a sunny morning we anchored in twenty feet of glass-clear water. I went over the side and kicked towards a ridge of coral. For a few moments I forgot to breathe. Orange and purple coral fans waved with the passing swell, black urchins bristled out of pockets in green and red coral heads, branched plants swayed like forest leaves. And the fish. I swam into schools of brilliant fish and divided them like a ship pushing through currents of colour. Yellow fish, speckles of electric cerulean blue, greens and vivid indigos I had never seen. And through it all the sunlight sprayed and the shadows shifted with a rhythm that was wholly strange to me, and magical. I marvelled that the smaller fish did not seem alarmed when a bigger, blunt-headed hunter, half as large as me, drifted among them. Could anything in the entire universe be this unabashedly beautiful?

The other time I had forgotten to breathe was when I was in the Sea of Cortez, crewing on a sailboat. We had anchored off some rocky islets that were occupied by an active and voluble sea lion rookery. You could hear the barks and roars of the bulls for a mile. I put on a shortie wet suit and jumped in wearing mask, snorkel and flippers. People had told me that the sea lions here were fairly used to snorkellers and, though they would never let you touch them, they would swim by very close. They did. Adult females swam straight at me and twirled as they passed, keeping their eyes locked on mine as they whizzed by. Big bulls ignored me. Curious youngsters jetted by like fast planes. Then I saw two adolescents playing nearby. I wanted to play too.

I took a big breath and dived to the bottom and as I did, I

executed an upside-down triple lutz, somersault, jackknife thing. Very awkward. Their heads turned. They looked incredulous. What the hell was that? they seemed to say. They rushed over, and as they did, they each performed a twisting barrel-roll figure eight. Oh, yeah? I responded, Watch this. I dived again, somersaulting and somersaulting, then twisting and fully extending. They were astounded. They sped up, jetted around me like the Blue Angels—loop the loops, flips, twists, rolls. I doubled my efforts. They seemed to think it was hilarious. Then I felt a hard tugging on my flipper. I twisted around to look and one was pulling at my fin and watching me with bright, liquid black eyes. Slowly I arched myself into a half circle and grabbed her two little black back flippers. Ever so slowly we turned in the water in a circular doughnut. Then she released and broke away. But she swung around and came back and I reached out my arms and she swam up to my extended hands and took my left fist in her teeth. She had pulled hard on the flipper, but her needle teeth held my fist gently and her black eyes, a foot away, looked directly into mine.

The surge of warmth and glee that went through me—I'd never experienced anything like it. We played and played. I held her torso and she pulled me through the water. We hung upside down a few feet apart and just looked at each other. I forgot my name. I forgot to breathe and came to the surface gasping.

When finally I was blue with cold and the crew was calling me and I swam back towards the boat, she swam around and around me in fast figure eights.

If the oceans are dying in our time and we kill them, which is what we are doing, we shall have committed a crime so heinous that we shall not ever be redeemed.

THAT NIGHT we had a New Year's party. Mathieu produced the stomped grape juice that had been fermenting in the aft hold. iPods with attached speakers came out, and Emily Hunter danced up and down the narrow aisle while Mandy relinquished herself to embrace-the-universe twirls. Stashed beers and wine came out. In the end, we all counted down the life of the old year and sent it packing with a yell. New Year's is always a funeral and a birthday at the same time.

I went down to my cabin and crawled under the old flannel sleeping bag. I lay in the dark and felt so lucky that I had grown up in a time when nature had seemed mostly untroubled. Few were worried then about global warming, or the death of most of the earth's coral reefs and thus perhaps the death of the million-plus species they shelter. Nobody saw then the death of the earth as we knew it. Of course, we should have known.

12

AMONG THE PENGUINS

I WAS UP EARLY on the first day of the year and saw no one as I took a cup of steaming coffee out onto the main deck. The first beings I greeted in 2006 were an impossibly wide-winged sooty albatross and a little snowy petrel, who circled and circled and crossed each other. The albatross was dark brown and came over the deck like the shadow of a flying dinosaur. The petrel was pure white and small, his wings also straight and still.

Watson was on the bridge, uncharacteristically reflective. We were making a steady nine knots west in the calm sea. Finally he spoke up.

'It's just strange. The Japanese have not been seen whaling since December twenty-four. They were idling in the storm when Sea Shepherd showed up, then ran west and haven't stopped. I can only conclude that they are being chased out of whaling and are either, one, waiting for a Japanese warship; two, waiting to run us out of fuel; or, three, whaling with the three missing harpoon boats and the spotting vessel.'

We were now off the Sabrina Coast. He said we would head for the old Wilkes Station, established by the United

States in 1957, later abandoned. Maybe we would wait there, in the bay, to see what the Japanese had planned.

A few hours after lunch, the *Farley* approached a cleanly sculptured iceberg the size of a house. Icicles fringed every overhang, and several outriding, smaller floes cupped a lagoon in which two large humpbacks idled and blew. Hammarstedt throttled back the engines and we could hear the whales, perhaps fifty yards away.

Trevor announced that the water was thirty degrees Fahrenheit. Crew began to strip on deck, down to their skivvies. They climbed up on the rail and dived in. The penguins sensed the splashes and looked over as one. What the hell? Happy New Year. I stripped to shorts and dived in, too.

The cold was more like an iron club than enveloping water. Is that pain or just the pressure of imminent death? I flailed for the rope ladder and climbed out like a sodden cat.

Darren, shoulders hunched against the faint breeze, handed somebody his glasses and said with resignation, 'Well, it's the New Year.' He went overboard. Gedden, dressed in a full wet suit, jumped off the crow's nest, about fifty feet off the water. Quiet J. Crew Joel went unadorned off the bridge wing. Aultman took the chopper up for a short recon flight and returned with no news.

Happy, invigorated, we left the lolling whales and continued towards whatever the captain had in mind. Watson went to the radio room and printed out scroll-edged Penguin Certificates for the dozen who went into the water.

The elevated mood didn't last long. There was a cry from the crow's nest. Luke and Simeon had gone up there to take in the view.

'Dead whale!' they cried. 'Dead whale! One o'clock!'

The *Farley* slowed. A shape floated ahead, marked by a flock of birds as if by buoys. In life, in the water, unless it leaps a full-body breach, one never sees the whole body, head to tail, of a whale. Now, in death, he was perfect, except for the raw gouges where the birds had begun to feed. It was a juvenile sperm whale, perhaps twenty feet long. He floated in perfect profile on the night blue water. On his flank were half a dozen giant petrels. Fifty more bobbed in the water beside him, along with a few Cape pigeons and snowy petrels. As we closed the gap, the alpha birds dropped off into the water— all but one, which hopped up to the whale's square head and glared at the ship that was now abreast and looming. This is mine, he seemed to say. Back off.

The young whale showed no signs of injury. He was surely still of nursing age. What had probably happened involved the death of the mother and the slow, stricken dying of the dependent son. The crew, of course, thought immediately of the Japanese. The missing harpoon vessels had probably come along the coast, shadowing the *Nisshin Maru*. Sperm whales were not on their permit, but that didn't seem to stop the whalers, judging by spot tests of whale meat at the Tsukiji market in recent years.

The crew lined the rails in silent homage to the young whale. Then the *Farley* gathered speed towards the smudge of sun low over the horizon.

TREVOR CAME onto the bridge. It was the second day of the new year. The *Farley* had been pushing deeper and deeper into a maze of ice, trying to get south to Wilkes Station. The fog had rolled in again. Dense, wet fog that beaded every surface, dripped off the safety lines and rails. You couldn't see more than a few hundred yards. Aultman stood with binoculars peering ahead and gave Lincoln directions at the helm. Darren called out growlers. The black leads of open water snaked and forked and forked again and then closed down. Watson, watching from his chair, turned to his nephew. He'd asked him to sound the tanks one more time.

'Well?'

'Eighteen to twenty-one days of fuel left. Down to fumes.'

'South Africa, which is about nineteen days—Lincoln, shut her down. We might as well wait until we can get a helicopter up and see where we're going.'

He turned back to Trevor. 'Okay, thanks. We'll be okay, unless we get a storm or something. Then we'll be hitchhiking in the middle of the Indian Ocean.'

The engine shut down. The sudden silence hammered the point home. We drifted. Our breaths on deck trailed northwest. We were the loneliest ship on earth. The latest communiqué put Greenpeace and the two Japanese ships 650 miles to the west. We were as far as we could get from any inhabited continent, almost equidistant between Australia and South Africa. There was ice closing in on every side.

At lunch, Wessel, who had just called home and talked to his mum, said that Sea Shepherd and the Japanese were all over the news in South Africa. Watson had heard again from the *Esperanza* and the fleet was in the east nineties, not whaling.

We lowered the ship's sea kayak into the water. There were enough cracks in the ice pack to manoeuvre the narrow boat. Emily borrowed my dry suit and went for a short paddle in the mist. I saw her just sitting for a long time, a quarter of a mile from the ship, looking off into the fog. Six months was not very much time since losing a father. I wondered when she would spread his ashes.

That evening the fog lifted. Watson sent Aultman up to search out a route. He came back two hours later and said there was ice to the south, as we knew, and a big peninsula of ice to the west. He said that to get to Wilkes, or west at all, the route was north-west, up and around it, then back south.

Watson waited. Every hour he ran the engines was an hour closer to empty fuel tanks. He didn't want to waste a minute.

Trevor, without much to do for once, fished out a hunk of growler, broke it up, and poured himself a rum and Coke on the rocks. He stood at the stern rail in his coveralls, watching the world go by—ever so slowly. The ship nudged up against a small iceberg, about the size of a boxing ring. Its top was about five feet below the level of the deck Trevor stood on.

'Do me a favour,' he said, turning to Dennis. 'Hold this for a second. Drink it, you die.'

He handed the deckhand his drink, then vaulted over the side. He stood on the berg and waved as the ship edged forward. Lincoln thought that was cool. He jumped over, too. The ship slipped further ahead. Trevor took a run, jumped, grabbed a bottom rail and hauled himself aboard. Lincoln judged the distance, but too late. A four-foot gap had opened between the two platforms. Lincoln stood alone on his little berg looking like the Little Prince as the ship began to leave him behind. Trevor and Wessel, acting fast, went to the big spool of longline on the stern. They ran off 100 feet and tossed Lincoln the coil. Just in time, he tied a bowline around his waist, leapt and dangled two feet above the water, and five of us hauled him aboard.

That night I stayed up late watching a DVD in the green room. Mathieu and Kristian dug out some rusted old cans of meat ravioli they'd found in the bottom of the aft pantry, and they heated them up with gusto, to the profound disgust of Mandy and Inde and Laura. I tried a forkful, but it tasted like chunks of mildewed leather.

We began moving just before noon on 3 January. Watson had just got word from the *Esperanza* that the fleet had refuelled at longitude eighty-five degrees east—far to the west of us, over 700 miles; and 240 miles to the north. It was also just inside the treaty zone, which was explicitly illegal.

Alex took the helm, muttering about how the Japanese refuel wherever the hell they want, twenty-six miles inside the treaty zone. The quiet first mate was seeing red.

'How do I get out of here?' he said, scanning the ice-choked sea and looking back east towards the only open water. He pushed the *Farley* around. 'You know, the probability is that the Japanese fleet is much further north than we thought. If we go to the abandoned station, it's further south. So if they come back and we're stuck south and get iced in, then what?'

He gave the helm to Gedden and went to the charts with Watson. Watson pointed to two features on the chart, due west of us on the sixty-fourth parallel, about 270 miles, called the Ice Domes.

'Yeah, we'll head in that direction, and hopefully by then we'll know more from our contacts. If they return east, we can hide there and wait for them, or—whatever.'

Gedden zigzagged back the way we had come, then turned north, hunting open water.

We were now roughly eighteen days' steady sailing from

Perth, if we turned back to Australia. Cape Town was a bit further. That was the very limit of our fuel, should we not encounter any big storms. Heading further west along the coast was stepping into the void. Alex, Watson and the other officers were very quiet this morning.

The rest of the crew seemed intent on keeping up morale and passing time. In the afternoon we came upon a magnificent island of ice weathered into shapes of swooping hills. A bunch of hands put on wet suits with Mustang suits over them and headed off in a Zodiac for the edge of the island. The inflatable buzzed along the bank of ice and pulled up close enough for Trevor to leap off. He had on crampons and he used a claw hammer and a hatchet for ice tools. I noticed, through binoculars, that he had a snowboard slung across his back. He hit the steep bank spread-eagled, like Spiderman. He began to climb slowly. Fifty feet up, he threw down the board and rode it straight down the berg.

I HAD TOLD my fiancée, Kim, that I would be home in the first week of January. Which was now. I missed her badly. I longed for home. We were way down in the southern Indian Ocean halfway between two continents on a ship that could go no faster than a man could run. We weren't going to be anywhere near an airport for weeks—if we got there.

Maybe the most dangerous enemy out here was not a monstrous factory ship, but the monotony of vast expanses of water. The frustrating lack of action. As the gap between the fleet and the *Farley* increased, the sense of our effectiveness was slipping away.

Yet the whaling fleet had not killed a whale for nine days. It was not hunting but running. However fruitless the chase at the moment, Sea Shepherd seemed to be having an effect.

SOMETIME IN THE NIGHT there was a muscular new swell out of the east. 4 January. The barometer was dropping. No telling if this was a freshening breeze or the beginning of a new storm.

I wondered if Watson was getting frustrated. He didn't show it. The day passed quietly and the crew kept busy.

At 2220 Watson said, 'I just got a new position on the Japanese. They've gone almost to the opposite side of their area—seven hundred miles west of us. Haven't killed any whales yet. I think they've probably done this on purpose to get as far away from us as possible. And Greenpeace doesn't seem to know where the *Arctic Sunrise* is.'

Alex went to the computer nav station and typed in co-ordinates. He then quickly plotted a course to the Japanese fleet and back to Perth.

'Three thousand, two hundred miles.'

'Same as going to Cape Town, isn't it?' Watson said.

'Pretty much. Eighteen days. One extra day to Cape Town, actually.'

'Keep going,' Watson said. 'We need one more hit at them.'

Dawn on 5 January was dark and windy, with the cloud-banks thickening. We were far enough from the ice edge now that the only ice we saw were lone drifting islands that thundered and boomed with the swells. On the black water, the snowy bow wake of the *Farley* and the ripped combers of the whitecaps were a relief to the eye. We had been trailed all night by two black-browed albatross that seemed still to consider us worthy company. I went to the chart and figured they had been following us for 110 miles.

The latest idea was to make a beeline for the Kerguelen Islands, a lonely group on the forty-ninth parallel and not too far off the route to Cape Town. Watson said there was a French base there—maybe we could buy fuel from them. Or call a barge to meet us 1,000 miles out of Cape Town. Trevor said he thought we could make it. 'I can crawl into the tanks and extend the suction lines, get three days more fuel. I'll stand by whatever decision the captain makes.'

The wind and the waves pushed us all day long. The sun must have made its low half-circuit, but we never saw it. Watson distracted himself on the bridge by reading aloud from one of his favourite books, *The Darwin Awards*, true accounts of the most idiotic ways people die.

'Tell them the one about the ice,' Allison said.

'Oh, this guy threw some dynamite out to make a hole in

the ice for ice fishing and his dog fetches it, runs under the truck. All died.'

There was a reverent silence, for the dog.

Again, at 2200, Watson received a report from his mole on the *Esperanza*. Now he didn't look so pleased.

'We've got a new position. They're killing today.'

They were 510 miles due west. The gap was shrinking.

'At seventy-three degrees east. They've gone from one extreme edge of the boundary to the other: three thousand miles. They're running from something. I have to put on the website that we're going back to Perth. Surprise them. We don't have to hang around, we just have to get them.'

'Do we have enough fuel?' Lincoln asked. Good question.

'Two and a half more days and we'll get them. Maybe we can talk Greenpeace into giving us some fuel. Probably not. I think we'll probably go to Cape Town. They can't go much further. They're at the edge of their boundary.'

The weather held and the *Farley* made good time through the night. Whatever desultory mood had gripped the crew was gone. The word had passed that we were two days away and that the captain meant to engage at all costs. Out came the grinders, the steel cable, the buoys and line weights. This was their last shot.

On 6 January, we woke to discover that the US Office of Naval Intelligence (ONI) had placed the *Farley Mowat* on its piracy watch. The news was on the international wire services. Online, I found the ONI report listing Sea Shepherd in a communiqué titled 'Worldwide Threat to Shipping Mariner Warning Information'. The ONI would continue to monitor the situation.

Watson's mole on the *Esperanza* reported thirteen minke whales and one endangered fin whale killed yesterday. The Japanese had killed an endangered whale in a whale sanctuary in contravention of at least half a dozen international laws, and the United States was responding by putting the screws to Sea Shepherd. In New Zealand, the whaling controversy was the top story on television news, and its minister of conservation,

Chris Carter, said, 'The program the Japanese are undertaking in the Southern Ocean is not about science, it's about hunting and killing whales to supply meat markets.' He added that New Zealand would be upping the pressure on Japan to stop whaling, and that the New Zealand air force would be sending Orion surveillance aircraft to monitor Japan's activities. Everybody was being monitored by somebody.

I went out onto the main deck to clear my head. The skies had lifted and the seas had calmed to a gentle roll out of the south-west. Then I saw it: a plume of mist just off the starboard bow, and another, smaller. A white-mottled long fin gestured out of the water and the two glossy dark backs, mother and calf, dived under the boat, the mother's articulated, graceful fluke disappearing last. Further off starboard were three more blows, the hot mist trailing gently downwind. Behind them were more and more. Spouts of steam rising and drifting.

I stared, almost stricken. All the way to the horizon, where two flat-top icebergs marked the edge of the world, were humpback whales, swimming slowly east. Pairs and small groups rolled around each other, showing fins, flukes, eyes, and then moved on. They swam past the boat on both sides. Hundreds of whales. Could they be swimming away from their hunters in the quadrant to the west? They were not on the Japanese quotas until next season, but no sizable whale was safe down here. They were not concerned with us at all. I tried to imagine the migration generations earlier, when they weren't a fragmented, isolated population, when they numbered fifty times what they do today.

Alex called a crew meeting. He said we were a day and a half from the whalers and that we would engage them. The new Zodiac crews would be posted on the board. He would also post battle stations for every crew member. He told everybody to grab a Mustang suit, label it, and stash it in the green room for fast access.

Within minutes the *Farley* was a hive of activity again. The sweet, burnt smell of grinding metal wafted out of the bosun's locker where more prop foulers were being hastily manufactured. Others carried them out and stashed them in the inflatables. Crews cleared the decks for fast access to the lifeboats, the water cannons. Marc installed his shiny new lifeboat cradle on the aft deck port side, centring the pod between two stanchions where it could be quickly shoved over the side.

The companionway to the mess was crowded with crew carrying exposure suits into the green room. The vomit-like reek of butyric acid from the old suits polluted the room. Trevor dogged down the forepeak, sealing all hatches and bulkheads forward of the fish hold. People were now taking very seriously the possibility of a sinking, of being dumped into the Antarctic drink.

That evening Aultman lifted off with Watson and Emily as passengers, the first time he'd ventured with three in the chopper. They were going back to a large flat-top we'd seen on the southern horizon. Emily carried the box of her father's ashes. She told me later that they landed right on top of the berg, got out onto the packed snow, and performed an appropriate last goodbye.

Hunter had been Watson's first comrade in arms protecting whales; they had been together in the Zodiac the first time anyone had ever run an inflatable between a harpoon and a whale; and they had both looked into the eye of the big male grey whale that had pulled away from crushing them as he died. Emily commended her father to the ice.

On the way back to the ship they saw a long fin whale swimming with her calf. The pair surfaced and spouted, one after another, the larger cloud of mist followed by the smaller.

Before dinner the sun broke through the cloud and silvered a great swath of sea to the south. And the seas were perfectly calm. It seemed an omen. Only the second time we'd seen the sun in a month. In the packed mess, just as the crew was digging into chocolate cake, Chris Price announced that Sonny Bono had been killed by the CIA. Forks and spoons stopped.

'That's ridiculous,' Watson said, chowing down on his second dessert. 'Sonny Bono hit a tree. He died skiing.'

'That's what they tell you,' Price said.

'That's absurd. He was one of them—a conservative Republican.'

'That's what they tell you.'

The crew started lobbing crumpled napkins at the big trucker. It looked like a hailstorm.

THE EIGHTH OF JANUARY was a good day to die. For the crew of the pirate ship *Farley Mowat* that was the consensus. Before midnight the *Esperanza* had sent another email saying that the fleet had moved to about 65° 20' S, 72° 40' E, so we turned south-west and kept her steady at nine knots and I think everybody held their collective breath. The morning brightened over a sea of silk and glass. The port and starboard Zodiacs looked clean and ready, the tarps off. The Jolly Roger was raised over the bow.

Aultman had got off at 0600 and returned two hours later. He jumped out onto the heli deck and went straight to Watson and the chart table.

'Here was when we first saw them, twenty miles off. Four ships. The factory ship stands out like a sore thumb. They're sitting dead in the water. No wake. No lights. I didn't see any activity at all. There's no wind.' He glanced up at the GPS. 'The course you're on should put you right on them. Paul, you would not believe the krill blooms. Like a pink chequerboard.'

At 10:59am, the factory ship was visible, long and dark, lying across the mirrorlike water. The *Esperanza* was there to the south of it, hanging some distance away. We came out of the east at 9.5 knots, heading straight for the target. With the gap narrowed to under four miles, an irate Scandinavian-accented voice exploded out of channel 16: 'You idiot! Get out of the f—ing way!' It was the usually courtly Arne Sorensen, captain of Greenpeace's *Arctic Sunrise*. Then we saw a curious thing. From behind the huge factory ship appeared another ship, also black-hulled and just as big. It moved away to the south, to our left. Two harpoon vessels, on their way in when the *Farley* showed up, slipped out of radar range.

What we found out later was that the big tanker-freighter

was the cargo ship *Oriental Bluebird*. It had been tied up to the *Nisshin Maru*, and they were transferring whale meat from the factory ship for transport back to Japan. Since the Japanese had doubled their quota from the year before, they did not have enough room—even on the vast *Nisshin*—to store the tons of meat they were harvesting. It was a startling testament to the scale of the hunt.

Greenpeace was bearing witness to the transfer, and manoeuvring the *Arctic Sunrise* near the *Bluebird* and sending in Zodiacs to paint its side with long-handled brushes— 'Whale Meat from Whale Sanctuary' in big white letters. The Japanese ignored them. Until Sea Shepherd came into visual range. Then they panicked. They dropped the lines, and in the rush to disengage and run, they rammed *Arctic Sunrise* twice. An email to Watson from the cooperating Greenpeace crew member on the *Esperanza* said, 'All of this right under our noses, because they know we will not ram or endanger them. . . . At least when you show up, they run like cowards!'

They did. They ran. From the bridge, Watson watched the *Nisshin* gather speed and charge north; the *Oriental Bluebird* fled east. From a window on the bridge he yelled, 'Okay! Get moving!' He slowed the *Farley* long enough to lower the Zodiacs into the sea, then throttled ahead as the eighteen-foot rubber boats were unhooked and sped away.

Two minutes later the helicopter lifted off the heli deck, tilted hard forward and accelerated towards the fray. Up ahead we could see Greenpeace's two orange Zodiacs in the water and its orange Hughes 500 chopper circling overhead. It was a mêlée. All the *Farley* could do now was follow and watch as the fastest Zodiac ate up the distance. The *Nisshin* was clearly expecting a fight—its water cannons were blasting steadily over the stern and sides.

'Our Zodiac is going thirty knots,' Alex said from the main radar screen.

The first Zodiac caught the *Nisshin* and skirted the veil of blasting water. The second reached the side of the ship. Its crew threw two prop foulers against the hull, and then the temperamental old outboard began to baulk.

Everybody knew that for a ship the size of the *Nisshin*, there is no way to replace a fouled prop with a spare; the parts are too massive. If one of the prop foulers caught and got tangled, the crew would have to abandon ship to the killer or spotter boats, and the fleet would return home. Wessel was going to do whatever he could to make that happen. Through binoculars, I watched as he ran the Zodiac up under the bow of the ship. The prow towered over the little boat, pushing up a bow wave that the Zodiac rode. The Japanese tried to reach them with flensing knives on long poles, but couldn't—they were under the overhang of the bow. At times, Wessel was no more than a man's length from the *Nisshin*'s nose. Joel and Steve deployed the prop foulers. When they'd used them all, they tied a piece of scrap steel to a buoy with a long cable and threw that over. Then Wessel slid the Zodiac away in a swooping arc and circled to the stern where they picked up the buoy and sped forward to deploy it again. A false move and they'd be flattened under the *Nisshin Maru* like so much roadkill.

Two hours later, lagging further behind, Watson called the Zodiacs back. None of the prop foulers had engaged. By 3:30pm, the *Nisshin* was sixteen miles away and fleeing at fourteen knots. The fleet had vanished in all directions.

That night, steep swells churned in from the east. They were the outriders of another storm. Wholewheat chapatis and poker chips slid off the tables. Sleepers were thrown from their bunks. Hammarstedt, commanding his watch at 0300, went below and woke up Watson, requesting a course change to the east, directly into the seas. Watson approved it, and for a few hours the violent roll shifted to a steady, hard pitch. It didn't last long. When Alex took his watch at 0400, he kept going to the chart, getting more and more frustrated that the *Farley* was getting further from her prey, which had gone north. At 0600 he ordered a course change back north.

Watson came on watch at 0800. The *Farley* moved gingerly into a sea of scattered icebergs and fog.

When Darren reported a new blip on the screen, Watson swivelled in his chair.

'Range?'

'Sixteen miles, sir.'

'Speed?'

'Ten knots.'

The fog was so dense, it wasn't until we were 1.6 miles away that we could see the black shape. I took out binoculars and made out the white letters that said 'Whale Meat from Whale Sanctuary' along the starboard side. The *Oriental Bluebird*.

It never moved. The crew was ordered to the higher decks and armed with smoke bombs and bottles of butyric acid, the mega stink bombs. Sea Shepherd actions always seemed like a strange mix of an attack out of *Master and Commander* and *Animal House*.

A few hundred yards from the freighter, Watson took the helm. He aimed for midships and charged at full speed. Just before contact he threw the wheel over to port so the can opener's seven feet of steel blade on the starboard bow raked the freighter's side. The *Farley* lurched with the impact. There was an agonising claw-scrape of steel and then the can opener crumpled, leaving a long scratch in the *Bluebird*'s thick hull like a key on a car. Watson picked up the mike: '*Oriental Bluebird*, or should I say the SS *Whale Meat*, please remove yourself from these waters. You are in a whale sanctuary, and you are assisting an illegal activity. Remove yourself from these waters immediately.'

At the same time he swung to port in a tight arc and came back across its bow. The prop-fouling squad was ready to run out a mooring line and lay a tangler across the freighter's path. By now the *Bluebird* was fleeing. Watson drove the *Farley* within twenty yards of their high hammering bow. It was like running a red light in front of a moving semi-trailer. Had the *Bluebird* kept up its speed, they would have T-boned and sunk us. It was as if that's what Watson was tempting them to do.

The *Bluebird*'s skipper, in all prudence, jammed his engines into reverse and groaned past our stern. The deckhands released the fouling line, but it did not get sucked up.

By the time Watson could get around again, they were running due north at sixteen knots. They ran all the way back to Japan, and never met up again with the *Nisshin Maru* to finish off-loading the whale meat.

The international reaction was immediate. The Japan Whaling Association, Keiichi Nakajima, accused Sea Shepherd of being 'circus performers' and 'dangerous vegans'. The *Age* newspaper in Melbourne reported that Japan was considering scrambling police aircraft to the Antarctic to defend its whaling fleet, and might ask Australia for protection. The Australian environment minister, Ian Campbell, called Watson a 'lunatic'. The Maritime Union of New Zealand announced that it would not service any Japanese ships having anything to do with whaling.

Watson despatched a press release saying that he would stop his attacks if the governments of New Zealand and Australia would initiate legal action to stop the whaling.

But the truth was that Watson had no more attacks to launch. The old *Farley* was nearly out of fuel. Trevor came onto the bridge in his blue coveralls, hearing protectors propped on his head, and said, 'We might make it to Cape Town on fumes if we don't encounter too much bad weather.' He ordered the heat turned off to save energy. The cabins went cold.

On 10 January, the *Farley Mowat* turned away from the whales and limped northwards into another gale. There was nothing more she could do. The Japanese could hunt again without intervention. I spent days by the stern chains, watching the acrobatics of the petrels and albatross. The rougher the weather got, the more fun they seemed to have. I thought they were like Watson.

One image from the trip kept coming back to me. It was when Aultman took me up in the chopper and we ran along the desolate false coast of the ice edge. Coming back to the ship, we climbed to 4,000 feet and ran across open water into a sheen of low sun. Then I saw the ship, a jaunty, compact, black shadow on the blue sea that curved to the horizon. It looked completely self-sufficient and alone.

EPILOGUE

THE WHALING FLEET returned to Japan on 14 April, with ten fin whales killed and 853 minkes.

Three weeks before, on 24 March, under international pressure, Nissui and the four other fishing companies that owned Kyodo Senpaku divested themselves of their shares and got out of whaling, citing declining profits. They gave their assets, including the whaling fleet, to public interest corporations, including the Institute of Cetacean Research.

The government and the Institute of Cetacean Research vowed to continue the Antarctic hunt in December 2006.

On 16–20 June, the International Whaling Commission held its annual meeting in Saint Kitts in the West Indies. Led by the United States, Britain, Australia and New Zealand, the strong contingent opposed to commercial whaling accused the Japanese of buying votes from small, poor countries. It was observed that, the year before, Japan had given $5.9 million to Saint Kitts–Nevis, $11.5 million to Nicaragua, and $5.5 million to the Pacific island nation of Palau. All voted with Japan on all votes that came up.

With its allies, Japan launched a frontal attack against the moratorium on commercial whaling. Overturning the moratorium requires a three-quarters' majority, but Japan, with a simple majority, succeeded in passing a non-binding resolution that declared the moratorium 'no longer necessary' and attributed the declining of the world's fish stocks to whales. The vote passed, thirty-three to thirty-two.

In the November 2006 issue of *Science*, a report by an international team of scientists declared that if current trends of fishing and pollution continue, every fishery in the world's oceans will collapse by 2048. No more fish sticks. No more snorkelling along reefs with schools of fish. No more fish cat food. No more fish. The oceans as an ecosystem would completely collapse.

A report published by a coalition of scientists a few months earlier warned that the oceans are now more acidic than they have been for the last 650,000 years, owing to greenhouse gases and the sequestration in the sea of carbon from the atmosphere. By 2100 the oceans could be more acidic than they have been in millions of years, leading to the death of creatures that secrete skeletal structures like coral, shellfish and calciferous phytoplankton.

On 17 October, Iceland announced that it would resume commercial whaling, in defiance of the IWC. The quotas for the first year would be nine fin whales and thirty minkes.

Also, in October 2006, Canada pulled its registry from the *Farley Mowat*. On 19 December, now under a Belizean flag, the *Farley* again sailed for Antarctica to hunt down the Japanese whaling fleet. This time, she was fitted with a can opener made from a bulldozer-strength blade. Watson also dispatched from Scotland the newly purchased *Robert Hunter*, a 195-foot former Scottish Fisheries enforcement vessel. The ship could cruise at sixteen knots, one knot faster than the *Nisshin Maru*.

The *Farley* was only hours out of Hobart, when Belize, under pressure from Japan, stripped her registry, making her officially a stateless ship. Any naval vessel of any nation could now attack her at will, seize the ship and detain her crew.

On 9 February, after nearly two months of searching in the Ross Sea, Sea Shepherd found the *Nisshin Maru*. Bottles of butyric acid were tossed onto her decks from the *Robert Hunter*; the *Farley Mowat*, about three miles behind, sent out two attack Zodiacs. As they sped to catch up to the fleeing factory ship, one Zodiac began taking on water, a thick fog set in, and the little boat became lost. Watson was forced to abort his attacks and send out an international distress signal reporting missing crew. The *Nisshin Maru* responded and joined the search. Eight hours later, the *Farley* found the Zodiac with its two crew members unharmed.

Three days later, the *Robert Hunter* ran down the spotter

vessel *Kaiko Maru* in waters beset with ice. Sea Shepherd Zodiacs managed to foul the prop of the killer ship. The *Kaiko Maru* limped back to Japan with a damaged propeller.

Shortly thereafter, the Sea Shepherd ships, running low on fuel, turned back towards Australia. On 15 February, when the *Farley* and the *Robert Hunter* were 1,100 miles away from the Japanese fleet, the *Nisshin Maru* suffered an explosion and fire below decks. One sailor died. For ten days, the disabled ship, laden with 343,000 gallons of fuel oil, floated dangerously close to the pristine coast of Antarctica and the largest Adélie penguin rookery in the world. Japan refused repeated appeals from New Zealand and other governments to avert a potential environmental disaster and have the ship towed out of the area. On 28 February, the Japanese fleet aborted its whaling season, and headed home with 508 whales.

On 13 February, Japan hosted a three-day conference to push for the lifting of the moratorium on commercial whaling. All seventy-two member nations of the IWC were invited. Thirty-four nations boycotted the meeting.

In the 2007–2008 whaling season in Antarctica, the Japanese will begin taking fifty endangered humpback whales, along with fifty endangered fin whales and 935 minke whales.

PETER HELLER

Peter Heller is the author of *Hell or High Water: Surviving Tibet's Tsangpo River* and an award-winning adventure writer and longtime contributor to NPR (National Public Radio) in North America. He is a contributing editor at *Outside* magazine and *National Geographic Adventure*. He lives in Denver, Colorado.

AN
ORDINARY
MAN

The true story behind
Hotel Rwanda

PAUL RUSESABAGINA

WITH TOM ZOELLNER

' My family and I could easily have been dead. All it would have taken was a slip of my luck, the wrong word to a general, a whim of a militia chief.

I hadn't really grasped the true scale of the disaster and how that membrane of protection around our hotel had been so fragile. With the rest of the country looking like a giant cemetery, there was nothing that should have stopped those killers from wiping us out as well. '

INTRODUCTION

M Y NAME is Paul Rusesabagina. I am a hotel manager. In April 1994, when a wave of mass murder broke out in my country, I was able to hide 1,268 people inside the hotel where I worked.

When the militia and the Army came with orders to kill my guests, I took them into my office, offered them beer and cognac, and then persuaded them to neglect their task that day. And when they came back, I poured more drinks and kept telling them they should leave in peace once again. It went on like this for 76 days. I was not particularly eloquent in these conversations. They were no different from the words I would have used in saner times to order a shipment of pillowcases, for example, or tell the shuttle van driver to pick up a guest at the airport. I still don't understand why those men in the militias didn't just put a bullet in my head and execute every last person in the rooms upstairs, but they didn't. None of the refugees in my hotel were killed. Nobody was beaten. Nobody was taken away and made to disappear. People were being hacked to death with machetes all over Rwanda, but that five-storey building became a refuge for anyone who could make it to our doors. The hotel could offer only an illusion of safety, but for whatever reason, the illusion prevailed and I survived to tell the story, along with those I sheltered. There was nothing particularly heroic about it. My only pride in the matter is that I stayed at my post and kept the Hotel Mille Collines open, even as the nation descended into chaos.

It happened because of racial hatred. Most of the people hiding in my hotel were Tutsis, descendants of what had once been the ruling class of Rwanda. The people who wanted to kill them were mostly Hutus, who were traditionally farmers. This divide is mostly artificial, a leftover from history, but people take it very seriously, and the two groups have been living uneasily alongside each other for more than 500 years. In the late spring and early summer of 1994 it meant the difference between life and death.

Between 6 April, when the plane of President Juvenal Habyarimana was shot down with a missile, and 4 July, when the Tutsi rebel army captured the capital of Kigali, approximately 800,000 Rwandans were slaughtered. This is a number that cannot be grasped with the rational mind. Just try! Eight hundred thousand lives snuffed out in 100 days. That's 8,000 lives a day. More than 5 lives per *minute*. Each one of those lives was like a little world in itself. Some person who laughed and cried and ate and thought and felt and hurt just like any other person, just like you and me. A mother's child, every one irreplaceable.

At the end, the best you can say is that my hotel saved about 4 hours' worth of people. Take 4 hours away from 100 days and you have an idea of just how little I was able to accomplish against the grand design.

What did I have to work with? I had a five-storey building. I had a fridge full of drinks. I had a small stack of cash in the safe. And I had a working telephone and I had my tongue. It wasn't much. Anybody with a gun or a machete could have taken these things away from me quite easily. My disappearance—and that of my family—would have barely been noticed in the torrents of blood coursing through Rwanda in those months.

I wonder today what exactly it was that allowed me to stop the killing clock for four hours. There were a few things in my favour, but they do not explain everything. Let me tell you, however, what I think was the most important thing of all.

I will never forget walking out of my house the first day of the killings. There were people in the streets whom I had known for seven years, neighbours of mine who had come over to our place for our regular Sunday cookouts. These people were wearing military uniforms that had been handed out by the militia. They were holding machetes and were trying to get inside the houses of those they knew to be Tutsi, those who had Tutsi relatives, or those who refused to go along with the murders. Watching this happen in my own neighbourhood was like looking up at a blue summer sky and seeing it suddenly turning to purple. The entire world had gone mad around me.

What had caused this to happen? Very simple: words.

The parents of these people had been told over and over again that they were uglier and stupider than the Tutsis. They were told they would never be as physically attractive or as capable of running the affairs of the country. It was a poisonous stream of rhetoric designed to reinforce the power of the elite. When the Hutus came to power they spoke evil words of their own, fanning the old resentments, exciting the hysterical dark places in the heart.

The words put out by radio station announcers were a major cause of the violence. There were explicit exhortations for ordinary citizens to break into the homes of their neighbours and kill them where they stood. Those commands that weren't direct were phrased in code language that everybody understood: 'Cut the tall trees. Clean your neighbourhood. Do your duty.' The names and addresses of targets were read over the air. If a person was able to run away his position and direction of travel were broadcast and the crowd followed the chase over the radio like a sports event.

The avalanche of words celebrating racial supremacy and encouraging people to do their duty created an alternate reality in Rwanda for those three months. It was an atmosphere where the insane was made to seem normal and disagreement with the mob was fatal.

Rwanda was a failure on so many levels. It started as a failure of the European colonists who had exploited trivial differences for the sake of a divide-and-rule strategy. It was the failure of Africa to get beyond its ethnic divisions and form true coalition governments. It was a failure of Western democracies to step in and avert the catastrophe when abundant evidence was available. It was a failure of the United States for not calling a genocide by its right name. It was the failure of the United Nations to live up to its commitments as a peacemaking body.

All of these come down to a failure of words. And this is what I want to tell you: words are the most effective weapons of death in man's arsenal. But they can also be powerful tools of life. They may be the only ones.

Today, I am convinced that the only thing that saved those 1,268 people in my hotel was words. Not the alcohol, not money, not the UN. Just ordinary words directed against the darkness. They are so important. I used words in many ways during the genocide—to plead, intimidate, coax, cajole, and negotiate. I was slippery and evasive when I needed to be. I acted friendly towards despicable people. I put cartons of champagne into their car trunks. I flattered them shamelessly. I said whatever I thought it would take to keep the people in my hotel from being killed. I had no cause to advance, no ideology to promote beyond that one simple goal. Those words were my connection to a saner world, to life as it ought to be lived.

I am not a politician or a poet. I built my career on words that are plain and ordinary and concerned with everyday details. I am nothing more or less than a hotel manager, trained to negotiate contracts and charged to give shelter to those who need it. My job did not change in the genocide, even though I was thrust into a sea of fire. I only spoke the words that seemed normal and sane to me. I did what I believed to be the ordinary things that an ordinary man would do. I said no to outrageous actions the way I thought that anybody would, and it still mystifies me that so many others could say yes.

ONE

I WAS BORN on the side of a steep hill in the summer of 1954. My father was a farmer, my mother his helper. Our house was made of mud and sticks. We were about a kilometre away from the nearest village. The first world I can remember was green and bright, full of cooking fires and sisters murmuring and drying sorghum and corn leaves in the wind and the warm arms of my mother.

Our house had three rooms. There were small windows with pieces of hinged wood to keep out the sun and rain. The house was built on an incline of terraced farms, but the small yard outside was flat. My mother kept it swept clean of seed pods and leaves with a homemade broom made out of bundled twigs. When I grew old enough she would let me help her. I still remember the happiness I felt on the day when she trusted me to do it by myself.

From the courtyard you could look south across the winding Ruvayaga Valley to the opposite hill. It seemed an awesome distance, like looking into another country. The hill was laced, as ours was, with houses made out of mud and stucco and baked red tiles, dots of cattle grazing, the groves of avocado plants, and the broad leaves of the banana trees that practically sparkled in the sun. On a perfect day you could lie in the grass near our home and see people at work in the fields on the next hill. They looked like ants. Every now and then, somebody's machete would catch the angle of the sun and you'd see the winking of metal across the valley. And far, far in the distance you could make out the clustered roofs of the village called Gitwe, where my parents told me I would one day learn how to read and write, which neither of them could do.

We spoke the beautiful language of Kinyarwanda, in which I first learned the names of the world's many things in rich,

deep vowels made in the back of the mouth. Bird, *inyoni*.
Mud, *urwoondo*. Stones, *amabuye*. Milk, *amata*.

To enter our house through the front door you had to
step up on a stoop made of grey rocks. To the side of the
door was a flat stone used for sharpening machetes. There
was a shallow depression in the middle where rainwater
would collect. When the storms came in September the light-
ning and thunder scared me. My three younger brothers and
I would sometimes huddle together during the worst ones.
And then we would laugh at each other for our cowardice.
Thunder, *inkuba*.

My parents raised nine children altogether, and I was an
island in time's river, separated by six years from my older
sister and five years from my younger brother. I got a lot of
attention from my mother as a result, and trailed her around
the house hoping she would reward me with a chore. The
firmament of our relationship was work; we expressed love to
one another in the thousands of little daily actions that kept
a rural African family together. She showed me how to take
care of the baby goats and cows, and how to grind cassava
into flour. Even when I came back to visit my parents when I
was grown it would be only minutes before I would find
myself holding an empty can and going to fetch well water for
my mother.

There was a narrow path from the main road that twisted
up the side of the ridge and passed through groves of banana
trees. It was our connection with a small village called
Nkomero, which occupies the top of one of the hundreds of
thousands of hills in Rwanda. The nickname for my country
is 'the land of thousands of hills', or *le pays des mille
collines*, but this signifies a gross miscount. There are at least
half a million hills, maybe more. If geography creates culture, then the Rwandan mind is shaped like solid green
waves. We are the children of the hills, the grassy slopes, the
valley roads, the spider patterns of rivers, and the millions of
rivulets and crevasses and buckles of earth that ripple across
this part of Central Africa like the lines on the tired face of
an elder. If you ironed Rwanda flat, goes the joke, it would

be ten times as big. In this country we don't talk about coming from a particular *village*, but a particular *hill*. We had to learn the hard way how to arrange our plots of corn and cabbage into flat terraces on the sloping ground so as not to turn a farm into an avalanche. Every millimetre of arable land is used this way. The daily walk up to a family grove can be an exercise in calf-straining misery going up, and in thigh-wracking caution going down. I think our legs must be the most muscular on the African continent.

Our family had rows of sorghum and bananas planted on the slopes of two hills, which made us solidly middle class by the standards of rural Africa in the 1950s. We would have been considered quite poor, of course, when viewed through the lens of a European nation, but it was all we knew and there was always plenty to eat. We worked hard and I grew up without shoes. But we laughed a lot. And I knew there was love in my family before I knew the word for it.

I think the greatest hero in my life was my father, Thomas Rupfure. He was already an old man, well into his sixties, when I was a child, and he seemed impossibly tall and strong. I could not comprehend that I could one day be his age, or that he was once mine.

I never once heard him raise his voice. He didn't need to. He always spoke without apology or flourish and with a calm self-possession. If he and my mother ever fought I never knew it. On special days he would fold my hand into his and take me up the winding path to the top of the hill, and then down the rutted road that led to the village, where we would go to buy sweet potatoes or bags of corn. We walked past the houses of our neighbours, and he would greet each one with a gentle nod. Anyone who engaged my father in conversation was likely in for a long story. He loved to talk in proverbs. It was the way he understood the world and his favourite way of dispensing wisdom.

Here's an example: somebody might tell him a story about being taxed at too high a rate by the mayor, and he would start talking about a lamb and a dog drinking out of the same river. The dog accused the lamb of dirtying his water, but the lamb pointed out that that was impossible, since the dog was upstream. The dog then said that the lamb must have dirtied the water yesterday, and the lamb pointed out that that was also impossible, because he had not been in the meadows yesterday. Then it must have been your *brother!*, said the dog, and he proceeded to devour the lamb. The moral of the story was that any excuse will serve a tyrant. I would have cause to remember that tale much later in life.

There was not much to our village of Nkomero, then or today. There is a commune house, which is synonymous with a town hall. There is a small Roman Catholic church. There are a few stores that sell bags of sugar, salt, and soft drinks. There is a tavern where men lounge and drink the potent beer made from bananas. A car or a truck coming through was a big event. Behind the wheel, very often, was a white man— a European missionary or a doctor. *Muzungu!* the children would call, a word that means 'white man', and they would say it with relish. It was not meant as an insulting word, just a descriptive one, and the white people would smile back at us. We were always hoping for a toss of candy or a ballpoint pen, which would sometimes come and sometimes not.

The road wound past the church and the tavern, and on along the ridgetop through a grove of eucalyptus trees on the other side of the Ruvayaga Valley, tracing a long horseshoe shape all the way to the next village, Gitwe. I would walk these three kilometres literally thousands of times while growing up, so many times that I could practically do it blindfolded. It was an important symbol in my life, this rutted track that connected my home with my school. It was where I first understood that in order to make progress as a man you had to take a journey. There was only so much you could learn at home before you had to get out in the world and prove what you could do.

It was my father who first took me down this road to the school at Gitwe when I was eight years old, and I still remember him handing me over to the assistant principal and saying goodbye. I suppose it should have been a troubling moment for me—it was the first time I left my parents' care—but I was eager to begin the adventure of learning. My father had told me over and over again: 'If you are willing to do it, you will be successful.' I was experiencing a privilege he had never had and I know now that he was sending a little piece of himself with me that day.

Perhaps it had something to do with growing up with such a large family, but I found that I could get on well with the new kids in my school. We played soccer, of course, and racing games to see who could run the fastest.

When I went home from school in the evenings I would help my mother cook supper. My brothers and I used hoes to carve out brick-shaped pieces of dirt and we built a kind of domed oven out of them. We stuffed a bunch of sweet potatoes inside and then lit a small fire underneath them. They came out charred and delicious. Every oven was used only once. We kicked it back into the ground, so as to bury the ashes, and then built a new one the next night.

Our suppers always came with small tastes of a bitter and delicious beer made out of the juice of bananas. Let me tell you about this drink, which we call *urwagwa*. Visitors to Rwanda always complain that it tastes like spoiled butter-milk, but I think it is tasty. It plays a central role in Rwandan social life, and is also an important symbol of the good-heartedness and generosity that I think represents the best side of my country. There is a saying: 'You never invite a man without a beer.' It is the symbol of hospitality, a way of saying without words, 'You are my friend and I can relax in your presence.'

Brewing banana beer is like the art of friendship: simple and very complicated at once. First you dig a pit in the earth. Because Rwanda is just a few kilometres below the equator, the ground temperature is always warm. It acts like a very slow, gentle oven for the fermentation. You take a bunch of ripe bananas and bury them about 100 millimetres deep. You make a lid for the pit out of the broad leaves of the banana tree. Come back in three days and dig them up. They should be very overripe. You transfer the mushy fruit to a basin made out of a hollowed tree trunk and then press down on them using handfuls of tough grass as your gloves. You drain out the juice into a clay pot, strain out the chunks, mix it with sorghum flour as a fermenting agent, let it sit for about a month, and then you have your banana beer.

It is a simple recipe, but it takes years of practice to get it right. Almost every house in Rwanda has a yellow plastic jug of banana beer tucked somewhere on the premises.

The beer is not really the important part; it is the friendship that it cements. Everywhere in my country you see people talking and laughing over bottles of banana beer. It most often happens at what we call *cabarets*, which are an indispensable part of life in rural Africa. They are like a bar and a convenience store combined, sometimes made of nothing but a few planks of wood. You see them on the sides of roads, in the suburbs, and even in the smallest little villages. Here you can buy canned goods, soap, soft drinks, batteries, toys, and all kinds of other things. The most important part of the *cabaret* is the front, where the owner has set out chairs, benches, and maybe even an old, ratty couch. This is where the local people, no matter what their station in life, will come together for a round of banana beer, often sipped through the same red straw. It is very hard to hate someone with whom you have shared a beer.

Perhaps this simple act taps into something in our national memory. Banana beer is known as 'the drink of reconciliation'. It plays an important role in our traditional local court system, known in the Kinyarwandan language as *gacaca*, or as it is loosely translated, 'justice on the grass'. If somebody had a problem with a neighbour he would not seek revenge. He instead brought it to the attention of a group of men whom we called elders. They were not elected in the classical sense of ballots, but they were put in a position of leadership by a kind of unspoken common assent. To be an elder you had to have a reputation for fairness and sober judgement. Hardliners and loudmouths did not get to be elders.

The elders would invite the village to come sit under the shade of a tree and hear the opposing sides tell their stories. Almost all of the disputes concerned property. A stolen goat, for instance, or somebody trying to grow crops on a hill that belonged to another family. More serious cases—such as those involving violence—were always referred to the courts, but village elders were given wide latitude to help solve local problems.

After the two enemies had finished speaking, the elders would give their opinions, one by one, on what should be done to remedy the problem. It usually involved compensation. A typical punishment for a stolen goat would be to repay the man a goat—and then give him another as a fine. Somebody bringing a charge thought to be false would be ordered to pay the man he had slandered. Confession was always the key. The village put a high value on the act of admitting culpability, even if you were the one bringing the case. It was viewed as a necessary step in the process of absolution. A man who lied before the entire village knew that he would have to wear that lie for years to come. There was an enormous incentive to come clean, and very little penalty was meted out for being honest with the public, and with yourself.

Then came the most important part of justice on the grass: the two aggrieved men were required to share a gourd of banana beer as a sign of renewed friendship. There were usually no lasting scars because it was hard to stay angry at someone who had humbled himself before you. I am convinced the adversarial system of justice practised in the West often fails to satisfy us because it does not offer warring parties the opportunity to be human with each other at the end. Whether you were the victim or the aggressor you had to strip yourself of pride and recognise the basic humanity of the fellow with whom you were now sharing a banana beer. There was public shame in this system, true, but also a display of mutual respect that closed the circle. Everyone who showed up to hear the case was invited to sip the banana beer too, as a symbol of the accused man's reconciliation with the entire people. The lasting message for all who gathered there was that solutions could always be found inside— inside communities and inside people.

I am proud to say that my father was a respected voice in

these sessions. He was usually the elder who spoke last, and his words therefore carried a great deal of weight. One case in particular stands out in my memory. The dispute was fairly typical—one man had planted a crop on a piece of ground that another family had claimed. A *gacaca* was called and the usual grievances were aired. Even a child like me could see that this was a case of a small misunderstanding that had blossomed into a full-scale war of pride. When two people dig in their heels against one another like that it takes quite a bit of mutual humbling for things to be put right again.

For whatever reason, my usually imperturbable father was a bit out of patience that day. Perhaps the silliness of the case or the small-mindedness of the people concerned had finally got to him. When it came his turn to talk he stood up and motioned for the two warring neighbours to join him. They all walked out, with me trailing quietly behind, to the place on that particular hill where the disputed crop was planted. He saw at once that the crop had indeed spilled over onto the neighbour's land, but also that the majority of the field was where it should have been. There was no clear villain or victim.

'Listen, you two,' he said, motioning with his hand. '*This* is where the line is. Respect it from now on, and respect each other as well. I don't want to hear about this again.'

This was a vivid lesson for me.

My father spoke with the same kind of gravitas each New Year's Day, when relatives from all over Rwanda were invited to a feast at our home on the hill. This is probably the most important day in the entire Rwandan calendar, even bigger than Christmas. Most people here identify themselves as Roman Catholic or Protestant, but we tend to emphasise New Year's Day as the time for extended families to come together and give each other presents and wish one another *bonne année*. It is also a holiday to reflect on the events of the past and one's hopes for the future. The meal served is always a belly buster. We would slaughter a bull for a feast of beef, and there were side dishes of beans and corn and peas and bananas, and, of course, banana beer.

After the meal was over, my father would call me and my brothers and sisters to sit around him. He would give us all a verbal report card on our progress throughout the year of becoming good men and women. 'You need to work harder in the fields,' he would say to one. 'You are doing well in school, but you must show more respect to your older brothers,' he might say to another. As a good helper to my mother, and a quiet kid in general, my assessment was usually a kind one. Some parents might disagree with this discussion of a child's failures and accomplishments before the entire family, and I would agree that in the wrong hands it can be hurtful. But my father showed us the same compassion on these occasions as he showed in justice on the grass. His aim was never to embarrass us but to encourage us to do the right thing. Looking back on it I can say that I grew up knowing where the lines of good behaviour were drawn.

My father had a favourite saying: 'Whoever does not talk to his father never knows what his grandfather said.' He was trying to express the linear quality of wisdom. His morality was not something that he made up on his own; it had been given to him by his own father and his grandfather before that, a mixture of Hutus and Tutsis stretching back hundreds of years to the time out of memory when our people had migrated to this hilly triangle between lakes. My father's sense of justice and kindness did not know ethnicity.

He often told us stories to make his thoughts clear, and one of my favourites was about the Rwandan concept of hospitality. We are a nation that loves to take people into our homes. I suppose our values are very much like those of the Bedouin, for whom sheltering and defending strangers is not just a nice thing to do but a spiritual imperative. Rwanda never had a hotel until the European colonists arrived. We never needed one, because a traveller between towns could count on having a network of people—friends of family, family of friends—with whom he could stay.

Rwandans are expected to offer shelter to the distressed, no matter what the circumstances. I took this lesson as gospel, and I grew up believing that everybody felt this way.

TWO

WHEN I WAS FIVE years old, there was an afternoon when people came to our house carrying spare clothes in their bags. My father seemed to know some of them, but not all. There must have been a dozen strangers of all ages in our courtyard. They were frightened and apologetic. 'Don't worry, you're safe here,' I heard my father say. 'Relax and have a drink.'

I asked my mother what was happening, and she told me that there was trouble in the capital city. Some bad things had happened, and these people who had come to visit us were trying to get away from bad men. They would be staying awhile.

We all slept outside that first night, and it was a bit of an adventure to be under the open sky. The adults smoked tobacco and talked in low voices.

On the second night I asked my father why we were sleeping outside and he told me the truth: 'Because if somebody comes to burn the house down we will not cook to death inside it.' The people who had come to stay with us were known as 'Tutsis', he said, and there were people roaming about who hated them. It was hard for me to understand because they looked just like us.

I understood years later that our guests that November week had been fleeing widespread massacres in the wake of what was called the 'Hutu Revolution of 1959'. It was also when the tactic of burning down the enemy's houses was pioneered. Those who tried to protect the Tutsi were considered targets as well. To shelter the enemy was to become the enemy.

HISTORY IS SERIOUS business in my country. You might say that it is a matter of life and death.

It is a rare person here, even the poorest grower of bananas, who cannot rattle off a string of significant dates in

Rwanda's past and tell you exactly what they mean to him and his family. They are like beads on our national necklace: 1885, 1959, 1973, 1990, 1994. Even though this nation is dirt poor and our school system does not match the standards of the West, we might be the most knowledgeable people on the globe when it comes to analysing our own history. We are obsessed with the past. And everyone here tries to make it fit his own ends.

Rwanda is sometimes called the 'Switzerland of Africa', and with good reason. Not only do people here tend to be quiet and reserved, like the Swiss, but our country is also a mountainous jewel tucked into some of the loveliest real estate on its continent. It is an aerie of high hills and grassy meadows and river valleys tucked between Lake Kivu to the west and the plains of Tanzania to the east. The entire region is so small there is usually no room for the name 'Rwanda' on most maps of Africa and the word must be printed off to one side, sometimes with an arrow pointing to the pebble that is my country. But there is abundant rainfall and mild weather and black loamy soil that made it one of the richest spots in Central Africa for the growing of food and the herding of livestock. The good returns on small-scale agriculture there-fore made it an attractive place to settle. And near the year 1500, at the same time that the arts and sciences were begin-ning to flower in Renaissance Europe, a distinct nation of people began to emerge in Rwanda under the banner of a dynastic king that everybody called the *mwami*.

According to tribal lore the bloodline of the *mwami* had a heavenly origin. If there was a dispute over succession the true king was supposed to be known by being born with the seeds of a squash plant clutched in his tiny fist. A court of royal advisers known as the *abiru* would reveal the successor when the current king died. They were also the guardians of the obscure poems, songs, and stories that comprised a kind of underground national history.

Kings were the ultimate guardians of the past and of power, and they were supposed to watch over everybody with equal favour. They fielded extremely tough armies with excellent archers. As a result, we were one of the only regions in Africa where Arab and European slave traders were never able to conduct raids, and so almost none of our people were sold into bondage. It is important to know that the early kings and all the advisers that surrounded them were generally the taller people in the tribe. This established a legend just as colourful as the squash seeds I mentioned, but one that would be infinitely more damaging.

It is well known that the main ethnic groups in modern Rwanda are the Hutu and the Tutsi, but it remains a matter of controversy whether these are indeed two separate races or if that is just an artificial political distinction created in a relatively short period of time. Evidence points to the latter. We share a common language—Kinyarwanda—the same religions, the same children's games, the same storytelling traditions, the same government, even, in most cases, the same outward appearance. There was never any 'Hutu homeland' or 'Tutsi homeland'.

What divided us was an invented history.

The false—but common—explanation for our origins is that the Hutus are a wandering offshoot of the huge group of Bantu-speaking people who have occupied Central Africa for thousands of years. They were said to have come into the country from the west. The Tutsis, on the other hand, are supposed to be descendants of the taller peoples of the Ethiopian highlands near the headwaters of the Blue Nile. They are supposed to have invaded Rwanda from the north about 500 years ago and established the *mwamis* government. Or so the story went. But there is no real evidence for it, and most scholars now think that it is pure invention. Africa's traditional history is one passed down through poems and genealogies and heroic ballads in which details about geography and migration patterns are lost in the fog of time.

One influential man who helped create the 'Tutsis from the Nile' theory was British explorer John Hanning Speke, who is given credit for being the first white man to lay eyes on Lake Victoria. He made some superficial observations in Central

Africa and connected them with stories in the Bible. In his 1863 book, *Journal of the Discovery of the Source of the Nile*, Speke showed a strange fixation with an extended clan of leaders in what is now present-day Rwanda. These people—they called themselves Tutsis—measured their wealth in cows, drank milk, ate beef, and seemed to be taller and have slightly more angular noses than their subjects, who fed their families by growing cassavas, sweet potatoes, and other vegetables. Speke theorised that they were actually a lost tribe of Christians who had migrated from the deserts of the Middle East and were therefore the carriers of a noble line of blood.

The Hutu—whom Speke called the 'curly-head, flab-nosed, pouch-mouthed negro'—was a different story. The name itself means 'one who works', and Speke thought there was a divine purpose behind the differences in lifestyle. Those who grew crops, he said, were probably the distant descendants of Noah's son Ham, who, according to the ninth chapter of Genesis, had committed the sin of looking at his father lying naked in a tent when he, Noah, was drunk on homemade wine. For this transgression Noah cursed his son Ham's descendants for all time: 'The lowest of slaves will he be to his brothers.' And, to Speke's way of thinking, these poor low-borns had found their way to exile in Central Africa and had reproduced themselves by the millions. The Hutus were part of that accursed lot, and this explained their generally subservient role to the cattle-owning Tutsis, even though the two groups of people looked quite similar on the surface.

What seems to have happened was that the ministers and priests closest to the Rwandan king started to conceive of themselves as being a special class of people, in much the same way that large landowners in what is now Great Britain or France began to call themselves lords and dukes and earls. In precolonial Rwanda, however, it wasn't land that was used to reckon a person's wealth. It was cows. Those who didn't have cattle were forced to turn to growing crops for sustenance and took on the identity of Hutu, or 'followers'. Many acquired cows by applying to a local strongman and agreeing to pay an annual tribute of grain and honey beer and pledging to defend him in times of war. These client relationships were known as the code of *ubuhake* and became the glue of the Rwandan social hierarchy.

Intermarriage between the Tutsi and the Hutu was not unheard of, but it was also not the norm. Those taller frames and aquiline noses that John Hanning Speke had fallen in love with were probably the result of just a few hundred years of sexual selection within that particular caste group. This deluded love affair, as you might guess, was soon to become the cause of great misery. I experienced it for the first time when I was nineteen years old.

MY BEST FRIEND, Gerard, was expelled from school in February 1973. This was one of the saddest days I had ever known, not just because I was losing my friend, but because it was my first real taste of the poison in the soil of my country.

I had known Gerard almost as long as I could remember. We had both come from mixed families and we had a lot in common in the way we viewed the world. We had grown up together—played soccer together, talked about girls, made fun of each other, wondered together about our future careers, speculated about who we would marry—all the normal things that make up a friendship between boys. He was as smart a kid as I ever met. Our daily walk to school together had been a constant feature of my mornings ever since we were eight years old. Our footprints grew larger, but our friendship remained.

The year before Gerard was expelled there had been chaos and death in the neighbouring country of Burundi, a nation with an ethnic composition very similar to Rwanda. The president, Michel Micombero, had ordered his armed forces to crack down on a Hutu uprising, and these soldiers took their mission beyond the bounds of rationality. Nearly 200,000 people were slaughtered and even more fled their homes for the relative safety of my country. We have a saying: 'Whatever happens in Burundi eventually spills over into Rwanda, and whatever happens in Rwanda will also spill into Burundi.' And that was certainly the case in 1973.

The government in Rwanda was sympathetic and began taking reprisals against Tutsis as a kind of revenge. Several dozen were massacred with knives and machetes in villages near the border. Others lost their houses and their businesses. The younger ones were kicked out of the schools. One of them was my friend Gerard.

I will never forget the last time we walked to school together. When we arrived there were lists of names tacked to the bulletin boards outside the classrooms. Gerard's name was there. He was told to take his things and go—he was not wanted at the school any longer. A group of Hutu students stood in front of the classroom door as a human wall to block the undesirables from going inside. These were the same children who had laughed, played, and gossiped together just 24 hours before. Now they were being divided in a way that was not fully comprehensible, but I will never forget the look of determination—even glee—on the part of some of my classmates who were accepting their new superior role all too readily.

I stood alone on the grassy quadrangle and watched Gerard walk back down the lane towards his home. That was the last I saw of him for a very long time.

His name was on the list because his mother was a Hutu and his father was a Tutsi. My name was *not* on the list because my mother was Tutsi and my father was a Hutu. Since ethnicity passes through the father's loins in Rwanda, according to this idiotic logic Gerard was considered a despicable Tutsi and I was considered a privileged Hutu. Had the parentage been reversed it would have been me walking down that lane of guava trees with my head down.

I cannot tell you how much I loathed myself that day for having been lucky. It was the first time I became aware of myself not as 'Paul' but as a 'Hutu'. I suppose this dark epiphany is an essential rite of passage for anyone who grew up in my country, one of the most physically lovely places on the globe, but one with poison sown in its heart.

I have to tell you more.

THE FAMOUS Conference of Berlin in 1885 put the seal on what was to become nearly seven decades of colonial government in Africa. This was also where Rwanda's fate was to be determined.

Representatives from Austria-Hungary, Denmark, France, Great Britain, Spain, the United States, Portugal, Holland, Sweden, and Norway met to sort out the conflicting claims their agents had made to vast pieces of real estate in Africa—most particularly, the forests of the Congo that had been turned into a private reserve for King Leopold II of Belgium.

The Berlin conference was remarkable not just for the lack of African participation, but also for laying out a few key principles. The first was that a European nation couldn't just draw lines on a map and claim that area as a protectorate. They had to prove they could 'effectively occupy' and defend that territory. The second was that if a navy could seize a piece of coastline it would also have the rights to whatever lay inland for a virtually unlimited distance.

The African continent was then sliced up with borders that frequently had no logical relation to watersheds, trade patterns, linguistic groups, or geography. Remarked the British prime minister: 'We have been giving away mountains and rivers and lakes to each other, only hindered by the small impediment that we never knew exactly where they were.'

Rwanda fared well in some ways—at least, better than most of our neighbours. The borders shaved some corners from the rugged area claimed by the *mwami*, but we retained a certain amount of territorial integrity. Our colonising power would be Germany, a nation that generally did not share the worst rapacious tendencies of some of the other conquerors of Africa.

The Germans looked on their new possession with indifference. It was a country far from the ocean. The most important provision of the Berlin Conference—the one that required 'effective occupation'—was also a problem. The government of Otto von Bismarck simply did not see the value in sending a large portion of its army and civil service to rule a poor chunk of landlocked farmland. What this meant, in effect, was that the Kaiser's flag flew over our country as a matter of appearance, but the real power continued to be the top-down apparatus run by the Tutsi royalty. After the Germans' catastrophic loss in World War I we were handed over as a spoil of war to Belgium. That was the beginning of real change, for the Belgians showed more of an interest in us.

Belgium wanted to get the most profit out of Rwanda while expending the least amount of men and effort. The new colonisers looked at the social rift between our leaders and farmers and saw an easy way to rule by proxy. It was a version of the old divide-and-conquer tactics used so effectively by colonisers throughout history. The Aztec empire in Mexico was finished the moment that Hernán Cortés realised he could exploit minor resentments between tribes to his own advantage, making friends with one tribe to beat the more powerful rival and thus subdue the entire region for the Spanish Crown. And so the Belgians adopted the bizarre race theories of John Hanning Speke to turn the Tutsi aristocracy into something like junior managers. It was no longer enough to simply co-opt the royal court as the Germans had. There was now an explicitly racial way of separating the haves from the have-nots.

Here's how crazy it became. Belgian scientists were sent down to Rwanda with little measuring tapes. They determined that a typical Tutsi nose was at least two and a half millimetres longer than a Hutu nose. This brand of 'scientific' race theory led to all people in Rwanda receiving in 1933 identity cards known as *books* that specified their ethnic class. Years later these cards would become virtual death warrants for thousands of people; but the immediate effect of these cards was to crystallise the racism into a sanctioned form of segregation.

The doctrine of Tutsi superiority was taught in schools, preached in churches, and reinforced in thousands of invisible ways in daily Rwandan life. The Tutsi were told over and over that they were aristocratic and physically attractive, while the Hutu were told they were ugly and stupid and worthy only of working in the fields. Almost all the colonial administrative jobs were reserved for Tutsis. Professor Alison Des Forges, one of the most distinguished scholars on the history of

Rwanda, has described the net effect this way: 'People of both groups learned to think of the Tutsi as the winners and the Hutu as the losers in every great contest in Rwandan history.'

Rwanda's apartheid system began to fall apart in the 1950s, when it was becoming increasingly clear that the European powers could no longer hold on to their colonies in Africa. Independence movements were sweeping the continent— violently in some places, such as Kenya, Algeria, and the Belgian Congo. Nearly every nation that had participated in the Berlin Conference had been shell-shocked by World War II and no longer had a taste for empire. Under pressure from the United Nations and the world community, Belgium was getting ready to let go of its claim on Rwanda. But one last surprise was in store.

The Tutsi aristocracy had, not surprisingly, been generally supportive of their Belgian patrons through the years. But it was a devil's bargain. The Tutsis received a limited amount of power and a condescending recognition of the *mwami* in exchange for their ultimate loyalty to Brussels. They also cooperated in the oppression of the Hutu, who were forced to harvest timber and crops in crews of road gangs, with Tutsi bosses.

As any social scientist can tell you, any system of organised hatred also damages the oppressor, if in less obvious ways. Tutsi were forced to punish their Hutu neighbours for misdeeds or face punishment themselves. And Belgium left no doubt who was in charge in 1931 when they deposed the *mwami* Musinga, who had resisted all the arguments of all the Catholic priests sent from Europe to convert the natives. The colonisers ignored the squash seeds and handpicked a successor, King Rudahigwa, a man considered sufficiently pliable. He was also an ardent Roman Catholic. His example led Tutsis and Hutus alike to convert to the new faith. Almost overnight Rwanda became one of the most Christian nations on the globe, albeit with a strong flavour of the old mysticism.

A well of sympathy for the Hutu underclass had been building throughout the late 1950s. The key role was played by the Roman Catholic Church. Perhaps it was the words of Jesus'

Sermon on the Mount: 'Blessed are the poor in spirit for theirs is the kingdom of heaven . . . blessed are the meek, for they will inherit the earth.' Perhaps there was finally a sense that too much was too much. Either way, the authorities took steps to empower the people who had been suffering for so long.

The Hutus had always had superior numbers, and official policy began to reflect that mathematical reality. The Hutu slowly assumed power as the ruling class. One administrator in Kigali issued the following secret order: 'I deem it necessary to rapidly put into place a local military force officially composed of 14 per cent Tutsi and 86 per cent Hutu but in effect and for practical purposes, 100 per cent Hutu.' Fearful of losing their longstanding grip on power—and perhaps also fearful of retributive violence—the Tutsi commenced a period of sharp opposition to Belgium's continuing hold on Rwanda. This course would prove disastrous for them, as it finalised the shift in Belgium's favour over to the Hutu they had mistreated for 60 years.

On 27 July 1959, our king died of a cerebral haemorrhage, and speculation ran wild that he had been secretly assassinated by the Belgians. Belgium called for the first free elections in Rwanda's history, but soon found itself trying to put down a rebellion of Hutu insurgents, who had set about murdering Tutsis and setting fire to their houses. Despite the centuries of coexistence, this marked the very first outbreak of systematic ethnic murders in Rwanda. The killers were rewarded with some of the first prosperity they had ever tasted. The homes, fields, and stores of the Tutsis often went into the hands of those who had hacked them apart, establishing a link between patriotism and money. I'll never forget sleeping outside at night during that time, wondering if somebody was going to burn our house down for harbouring Tutsis.

The national elections were held in a climate of fear and— not surprisingly—the Hutus won 90 per cent of the open seats. Suddenly it became desirable, even necessary, to have an identity card that called you a Hutu. Public schools were soon open to the majority, and children who had been denied education for years began learning to read and write and add figures just as adeptly as the Tutsi. This should have given the lie once and for all to Speke's idiotic racial ideas—as if they had not been discredited already. Belgium and the United Nations handed the nation over to a Hutu government and left the nation after a brief ceremony on 1 July 1962, at ten o'clock in the morning. A new flag was hastily designed and raised: a tricolour banner with a plain letter R in the middle. These events, taken as a whole, came to be called the 'Hutu Revolution'. And there was to be no sharing of power.

Tens of thousands of persecuted Tutsis fled the country to the safety of Uganda and other neighbouring nations. One of the refugees was a small child named Paul Kagame, who was said to have been carried on his mother's back.

Rwanda had not seen the last of him.

THE EXILED Tutsis would eventually number more than a quarter of a million. The angriest young men among them began launching guerrilla raids into Rwanda from their hiding places across the border. They were called 'cockroaches' because they came out at night and were hard to kill. This military slang would soon be applied to the Tutsi people as a whole, a term as pernicious and dehumanising as the word *nigger*.

The raids were mostly amateur affairs, but they gave a pretext for the new government of President Grégoire Kayibanda to wrap itself in the flag of the Hutu Revolution and begin a purge of the Tutsis who remained inside Rwanda. There is no greater gift to an insecure leader than a vague 'enemy' who can be used to whip up fear and hatred among the population.

The persecution was made all the easier because Rwanda is a meticulously organised country. The nation is arranged into a series of twelve prefectures; within every prefecture are several communes. The head of the commune is known as the *bourgmeister*, or mayor, and he usually gets his job through a personal friendship with the president. This is the real seat of power in tiny Rwanda, which is like one giant village. Four out of five of us live in the rural areas and nine out of every ten people here draws some income from farming the hills. Even the most urbanised among us has a close connection with the backcountry. Orders came down to the commune: it was the duty of every good and patriotic Hutu to join 'public safety committees' to periodically help 'clear the brush'. Everyone understood this to mean slaughtering Tutsi peasants whenever there was a raid from the exiles across the border. In 1963 thousands of Tutsis were chopped apart in the southern prefecture of Gikongoro. These countryside massacres continued off and on throughout the decade and flared up again after the trouble in Burundi in 1972 that caused the education of my best friend, Gerard, to be stolen.

He never quite recovered. Though he had the skills and the ambition to become an engineer, the only job he could get was selling banana beer in a stand by the side of the road. He later moved to Kigali, where he landed a clerical job in a bank. But he was always plagued by the image of what he might have become had he been allowed to continue his education. When we were both much older I tried to get together with him from time to time, but there was a taint of sadness, and even anger, that always hung over our friendship. He was a Tutsi by accident and he had to live the rest of his life under that taint, occasionally in fear for his life from the public safety committees and destined to work in dead-end jobs. It was an appalling waste—not just of a man but of a potential asset to Rwanda and the rest of the world. Gerard had something to give. It was not wanted.

THREE

ALL THE IMPOVERISHED nations on earth have these few basic things: a flag, an army, borders, something resembling a government, and at least one luxury hotel where the rich foreign visitors and aid workers can stay. When operatives from the Red Cross in Geneva or researchers from Amnesty International in London come here on their missions, they

stay where they are treated to high standards of comfort—
even though they've come to work on uncomfortable problems like AIDS, deforestation, torture, and starvation. So
there is always a demand for a spot of opulence in a nation
of mud houses. It is not all bad. A few hundred locals get
decent jobs as chambermaids, waiters, and receptionists.
Some elite suppliers get food and beverage contracts. Most
of the profits, however, are shuttled back to whatever multi-
national company owns the property. The cost for a room is
usually equal to the yearly income of an average person in
that country. The reality of modern Africa is that in every
impoverished nation on the continent, from Burkina Faso to
the Central African Republic, you can inevitably find that
one hotel a short walk away from the embassies, where
fresh laundry and gin and tonics are taken for granted and
where there is an aura around the place that prevents any
peasant from ever thinking of going inside.

In Rwanda, that place is the Hotel Mille Collines.

The Mille Collines was built in 1973 by the Sabena Corporation, which was the national airline of Belgium until it went
bankrupt a few years ago. The executives foresaw the demand
for an island of stateless luxury in the dirt streets of Kigali, and
so they built the Hotel Mille Collines, aimed primarily at the
diplomatic and humanitarian trade but with an eye towards
snaring the occasional adventurous tourist on his way to see
the gorillas in the north.

It is a modernist building of five storeys, with a façade
of stucco and smoked glass. From the outside it would look
perfectly at home near any large Western airport.

There is only one way in or out of the Hotel Mille
Collines: a two-lane driveway leading to and from the gate
inside and the paved street outside. The gate leads into a
parking lot landscaped with colourful African plants and
shrubs and surrounded from the outside world with a fence
of bamboo poles. The lobby is tiled with sand-coloured flag-
stones and decorated with potted plants and wicker couches.
The staff behind the reception desk has been trained to greet
all visitors cordially in French and English. There are a few

shops that sell all the things a tourist might want. Off to one side is a small suite of offices for the general manager, the assistant general manager, and an agent of the airline.

Upstairs are 112 guest rooms, each one furnished according to the standards of upscale Western lodging. There are televisions with hundreds of satellite channels in multiple languages, beds with firm mattresses, shaving kits wrapped in protective plastic, circular cakes of soap. There are bedside phones, a shower with safe water, a small strongbox with an electronic combination for your passport and money. The rooms smell like lavender cleaning solution.

On the top floor is a small cocktail bar and also a set of conference rooms for visiting corporations or aid groups to hold their presentations. There used to be an unwritten rule in the elite circles that if your meeting wasn't held at the Mille Collines it wouldn't be taken seriously.

Down the hall from the bar and the conference rooms is the Panorama Restaurant. Here you can get escargots or chateaubriand or crab soup of a quality—and at prices—that match what you'd find in Brussels, Paris, or New York. Every morning there is an extensive breakfast buffet with good strong Rwandan coffee and five kinds of juices and a staff of waiters lurking discreetly in the background, watching for an empty cup or a dropped fork. The restaurant has no north wall—it opens up to a striking al fresco view of the Nyabugogo valley.

The most important place in the Hotel Mille Collines is on the lowest level. This is the rear courtyard, where there is a tidy lawn, a huge fig tree, and a small swimming pool without a diving board. There is also an open-air bar with about twenty tables and a few ceiling fans to push the air around.

Around the pool's small square of water is where the real business of the Mille Collines is conducted. What takes place here far surpasses the day-to-day management worries of the hotel. Some people have even called it the shadow capital of Rwanda. It is *the* spot where the local power brokers come to share beer and ham sandwiches with aid donors, arms dealers, World Bank staffers, and various other foreigners who have some kind of stake in our country's future.

Worlds intersect here. Whites and blacks mingle comfortably here inside a thin cloud of cigarette smoke and laughter. I have seen cabinet ministers dispense appointments here, Army generals buying Russian rifles, ambassadors telling casual lies to presidential flunkies. The poolside is a place to advertise that you are a man with contacts and friendships.

I first laid eyes on the Mille Collines when I was nineteen years old. As a typical bored young man on my hill I hitched rides to Kigali whenever I could to wander the streets, browse through the markets, gawk at girls, and drink in the bars, all the typical idle pastimes of youth. The hotel had just been constructed and everybody was coming by for a look. It was then the tallest building in Rwanda and the first with an elevator. Few people had seen such a thing before. The big coup was to sneak inside and see if you could ride the elevator to the roof, where you could get a truly marvellous view of the valley below. Much to the envy of my friends back at home, I was able to charm my way past the bellboy and take that elevator ride up to the forbidden roof, where I savoured a few stolen minutes of beauty. I remember feeling impressed with the hotel and proud of my country, thinking this place represented progress, and that a better way of life was on the way for all of us.

I had no idea just how large a role this strange new place was going to play in my life—or in the life of Rwanda.

I AM A HOTEL manager by accident. The idea of having a career in the luxury hospitality business is certainly a laughable one for the son of a banana farmer from an impoverished African village.

I was supposed to have been a church pastor. This was a path that seemed pre-ordained for me from a very young age. Everybody said I was suited for it because of my willingness to work hard, but even more because of my temperament. My peers in school—even those I wasn't close friends with—seemed to trust me with their secrets, and I always gave them advice that seemed practical to them. The teachers were also impressed with my ability to memorise sections of the Bible and rephrase them in plain language. They encouraged me to become a man of the church. It was always seen as the way up, at least to the people who ran my school. They belonged to the Seventh-Day Adventist Church, a very distinctive branch of Christianity.

I began learning French at age eight, English at thirteen. I still remember the cover of the first book I ever owned, a textbook called *Je Commence*, or *I Begin*. I struggled the first year and resolved to do better. The next year my scores were among the highest in my grade and I saw my father's pride when my name was called during the honours assembly on the grassy quadrangle.

Though I seemed headed for a life of Christian modesty, there was always a streak of the entrepreneur in me. Even as a ten-year-old I was gathering up peanuts and reselling them for a profit. Hard work appealed to me. Where other teenage boys liked soccer and girls, my hobby was painting houses for people in the village. This was where I first learned the art of negotiation. I would start my price far above what I expected to receive and coyly ratchet it down according to what I saw in the face of the man who wanted his house painted. I earned a reputation as a tough bargainer but a conscientious painter. There was never any spot uncovered, and I used attractive shades of blue and indigo. I would get up very early in the morning to start a job, eat something small for lunch, and keep working through the fading light, until I could hear the gasoline generators in town start up.

Though I earned good money I was never prey to bullies or to jealous thugs. If anybody tried to threaten me I would simply look him in the eye and ask him in a firm but friendly voice, 'Why?' The bully would have no choice but to engage me verbally, and this made violence next to impossible. I learned that it is very difficult to fight someone with whom you are already talking.

On 13 September 1967, at the age of thirteen, I was baptised in the waters of the Rubayi River and was allowed to choose a new first name for myself. This is a ritual that merges a bit of traditional Rwandan culture with the Christian rite. To the endless confusion of outsiders, members of a single family here do not usually share the same last name.

My surname, Rusesabagina, was chosen especially for me by my father when I was born. In our language it means 'warrior that disperses the enemies'. I was allowed to choose a new first name on the day of my baptism and I chose 'Paul', after the great communicator of the New Testament, the man who described himself in one of his letters as 'all things to all people'.

WHILE I SEEMED to have a natural gift for languages and banter, I was unfortunately not gifted in the art of making conversation with girls. They had a powerful fascination for me from the time I was about twelve or so, but I think I would have rather had a burning ember pressed into my tongue than talk to a pretty girl. But around the time that I was leaving my teenage years behind me and becoming a man, one young woman in particular started to develop an interest in me. Her name was Esther and she was the daughter of Reverend Sembeba, one of the African pastors of the Seventh-Day Adventist Church and a very powerful man in the region. I fell in love with Esther and we made plans to get married. Our plan was for me to attend seminary and become a minister and she would come with me wherever I was posted. Then we would start having children.

My good behaviour and my interest in religion earned me a scholarship to attend a school called the Faculty of Theology in the nation of Cameroon. It was more than 1,500 kilometres from the hillside where I had grown up, but it would be a free education, and a good one at that. So on 8 September 1976, Esther and I were married in the baby blue church at the top of the hill. It was one of the happiest days of my life up until that point. I had presented her father with a cow, as is the Rwandan custom, and my friends brought in more cows to the reception as a symbol of the prosperity that the marriage was going to bring us. Milk from the cows was passed around and we held up the cups to one another. A few days later we said goodbye to everything that was familiar, caught a ride to

Kigali, and boarded a flight to the city of Yaoundé. Neither of us had been on an aeroplane before.

I cannot say I have very fond memories of my time studying to be a pastor. The instructors taught us Greek so that we could read the New Testament in the original language. I cannot speak a word of this ancient tongue today, but I do remember the thrill of reading Christ's words. But it became apparent to me that this was not a line of work I was suited for. For one thing, it seemed that the life of a pastor was going to be a dull one. I had tasted enough of the modern world to be enchanted with it—the aeroplanes, the elevators, the azure swimming pools—and the job of African gospel preaching did not go hand-in-hand with that kind of lifestyle. If I was going to lead a Seventh-Day Adventist flock, I wanted it to be in Kigali at the very least, where I could live an urban life. But only a very few senior men, five at most, were privileged enough to have such a posting. I looked into the future and did not like what I saw: a long sedentary life spent in a backwater village, getting older and hoping for a promotion that would never come.

This anxiety about my future got me thinking. It was supposed to be the duty of every Christian to put aside his own earthly desires for the sake of heaven. What did it say about my fitness for the pulpit if I was so disheartened about the road opening up in front of me?

It was in this unhappy state of mind that my wife and I moved to Kigali in December 1978. And it was there I found the place where I truly was meant to be. Or rather, it found me.

Kigali sprawls over more than a dozen steep hills near the geographical centre of Rwanda. It is one of Africa's more relaxed capital cities, with a modern airport, a pleasantly unrushed market district, wide avenues shaded with jacaranda trees, and a notable lack of the desperate slum quarters that tarnish so many other African capitals. The main roads are well paved and free of potholes. Most of the architecture is of the late-1960s institutional style and the majority of houses are made of the same adobe bricks and corrugated metal roofs you see in the backcountry. But on clear evenings you can climb to the top of Mount Kigali and look out over the chain of valleys and the soft twinkling lights on the hillsides and think that the old proverb is true, that God wanders the world during the daytime, but comes home to Rwanda at night.

When Esther and I moved into a rented house with our two young children in 1978 I resolved that I would stay here no matter what happened. I had found my place.

Fate had intervened, as it so often does, in the form of a friendship. I had a playmate from childhood named Isaac Mulihano who worked behind the front desk at the Mille Collines. He had heard through the gossip mill that I had dropped out of the seminary and so he sent a message to me back on the hill where I was staying for a few weeks. 'Come work with me in the hotel,' he said. 'We have an opening and you would be perfect.'

The hotel already occupied an exalted spot in my mind—it was the symbol of urbanity I had been craving—and I seized the chance to be a part of it. So I put on a white shirt and a tie and learned the art of how to put people in the right rooms, how to arrange for fresh flowers and taxi rides, and how to handle complaints with a smile and quick action. I seemed to excel at this last skill. If you show the guest you really care about his problem and make him feel as though he is getting his way (even when he isn't) it will give him a positive feeling about the hotel and the staff and make him inclined to come back for a repeat visit. I learned that most people just want to feel as though they are being heard and understood. It is a simple lesson, but one that so many seem to forget. I learned that I could usually make even the most irate guests leave the front desk at least a little mollified if I showed them I was listening.

Month followed month. I worked hard at my job. My managers were impressed with my command of French and English, as well as with the cheerful attitude I tried to bring to work every day. At that time, a Swiss company named Tourist Consult had a contract to train all the new employees, and they put me through the program. While I was busy trying to make sure I was doing everything right, the training director,

Gerard Rossier, came up to me and asked, 'Why are you working at the front desk?'

The question surprised me.

'This is the job that I enjoy,' I told him.

'You are not in the right place,' he told me, and explained that Tourist Consult was offering ten free scholarships to the hospitality program at a college in Nairobi. Would I be interested in applying for one?

I thought that over for about half a second before saying yes.

The application process was only a formality. The only thing I needed was a signature from a government minister, who had to personally approve all the scholarship recipients. And this was where I got my first real taste of the patronage system.

I was a desk clerk, the son of a banana farmer. Nobody with any political connections, either. That made me a nobody in the eyes of the minister and he refused to sign my application.

'Has he had a chance to sign my application?' I asked the secretaries.

'He is still reviewing your application. You should have an answer soon.'

I went back every day for a week and got the same answer. All the other scholarship recipients received their signatures, but mine was in an endless state of review. It became clear that more was holding up my application than just the usual molasses of bureaucracy. It was not as if the minister had anything against me personally. It was that the hotel scholarship was now a commodity—no different from a case of beer or a Honda motorcycle. If I took that last slot, it would be one less favour he could do for a hometown relative or a political acquaintance. Giving his signature to me would have been giving it for free, because I had nothing to offer in return.

It was a dismal lesson in politics. But I will never forget the lesson I learned from Rossier when I told him I couldn't go to the college after all.

'Oh, really?' he said. 'Why not?'

'The minister will not sign my application.'

'I see,' said Rossier. 'Let me take care of things.'

My signature came that very afternoon. I found out later

that a simple message had been conveyed: either Paul gets your signature today or we will never offer hotel scholarships to anyone in Rwanda again.

It seemed that there were multiple ways to solve a problem. And I was a fast learner.

IN NAIROBI I learned many more things. I learned about the various wine-growing regions in France, and how to tell Bordeaux from Burgundy. I learned what separates a good Scotch from an excellent one. They sent me to Switzerland, where I learned even more about fine wine and food. I learned how to do bookkeeping, write a budget, manage a payroll, hire and fire, plan institutional goals. And I learned the art of performing courtesies without making a show of it. The idea is to not be noticed in the act of doing something nice for somebody, but, of course, people will notice. People *always* notice.

I grew in confidence as a manager, but my personal life was not so happy when I was at college. Time and distance took a toll on my marriage. Esther and I grew further apart, and we separated in 1981. I was granted legal custody of our three children, our daughters Diane and Lys, and our son Roger. It was a wrenching experience, one of the saddest periods in my life, but I was sure of at least one thing when I came back home to Rwanda. My career path was at last known to me. I would be a hotel man, not a preacher. My troubles in marriage had made me bitter and hurt, but I threw myself back into my work with vigour and not a little bit of relief. The Hotel Mille Collines became my solace.

I have since come to realise that those years, studying to be a churchman were not wasted at all. It was where I gained an even greater understanding of human beings—what motivates them, where their failings are, where the good might be found that can trump the bad inside. Another thing the ministry teaches you is how to present a forceful case in language that everyone can understand. Learning to be a preacher makes you a better talker. That was one skill that would certainly come in handy in my personal life. And

I also discovered that I had lost my shyness around girls.

One day in 1987 I was invited to a wedding. I have never been a good dancer and so I sat on the edge of the crowd, nursing a beer and watching people dance. I could not take my eyes off a particular woman in a white dress. She was the maid of honour and had a shy smile. I cannot remember what we talked about, but I remember thinking that her ideas were as fresh as her appearance. We exchanged phone numbers and said goodbye, but I did not forget her. I learned that Tatiana worked as a nurse in the town of Ruhengeri in the north. She happened to be a Tutsi. I could not have cared less about that, but other people certainly did. She was suffering a huge amount of prejudice at her workplace and she wanted to leave.

At last, a matter of the heart where I knew what to do! I went straight to work. The minister of health was a frequent guest at the poolside of the Mille Collines and I arranged a favour. Tatiana soon received a transfer to Central Hospital in Kigali. By that time my divorce was final and I was a free man. I courted my new girlfriend assiduously and we married after two years. Diane, Lys, and Roger accepted Tatiana as their new stepmother almost immediately. Tatiana conceived and gave birth to a daughter, who perished before she could be given a name on the eighth day, according to the Rwandan custom. It made us all grieve. But before long, my wife was pregnant again and we brought our son Tresor into the world. And I settled into a loving family life, feeling like a complete husband and father once more.

My stock continued to rise at the Mille Collines, where I was made an assistant general manager. They gave me an office of my own, as well as the authority to dispense little perks here and there to favoured guests. An Army general who came in frequently would get a free cognac, or perhaps a lobster dinner. It made them feel appreciated, which is a universal hunger among all human beings. The gifts were also an indication of their status in front of whatever companion they had brought in. This helped to not only cement their fidelity to the hotel, but to make them appreciative to me personally.

I learned to take my morning coffee not in my office but

down at the poolside bar. At 10:00am some of the capital's big shots would start to drift in. Some of them came in alone with reams of paperwork. Others brought their friends and co-workers. Most had the thick Rwandan coffee, some breakfasted on beer. The talk was a stew of personal chitchat and government business. I don't know why so many of them thought of the Mille Collines as an office out of the office. Perhaps the walls had ears at their ministries. Perhaps it just felt more relaxed here. Whatever the case, an astonishing number of decisions were made next to the pool, and I watched it all happen from my perch at the bar. I learned to tell from subtle body language whether I should approach a table for some welcoming banter or whether it was best to remain invisible.

I know that my promotion was resented among some of the people I had worked with at the front desk. Some of them started to call me a certain name behind my back: *muzungu*, the Kinyarwandan word for 'white man'. We used to yell it out gleefully to European aid workers and missionaries when we were kids. It is not insulting in that context. But applied to me it was meant to be insulting. I suppose this should have got under my skin, but it did not. Never once did I feel as though I was being untrue to the life my father had wanted for me since the first day he took me to school at Gitwe and told me that if I was willing to do the work I would be successful in the world.

Year followed year. I kept climbing. In 1992, I was made the general manager of the Hotel Diplomates, the other capital city luxury hotel owned by Sabena. It was a smaller property, barely a kilometre up the hill from the Mille Collines, but no less prestigious. The Diplomates catered mainly to ambassadors, presidents, prime ministers, and other dignitaries visiting Rwanda from other parts of Africa and the world. I was no longer working in my beloved Mille Collines, but this was a huge step up the ladder. I had become the first black general manager in the company's history.

It was a small distinction, I suppose, but I only wish my father could have seen it. He had died the year before, at the age of 93 in a hospital in the town of Kibuye, where he had gone for surgery. The light was still in his eyes the last time I saw him. He said a curious thing. 'Listen, my son. You might meet hyenas on their way to hunt. Be careful.' It was very typical of him to talk in these kinds of parables, but I have wondered many times about what he meant. Perhaps he was just telling me to be careful that day on the drive back to Kigali. Perhaps it was meant to be a caution for the years to come. I'll never know because my father died later that day. He was so important to me, a man who taught me most of what I know about patience, tolerance, and bravery. He had always wanted me to come back to my home to be the mayor, and I suppose on this count, I hadn't quite lived up to his expectations. But I knew that he had been terribly proud of the work I was doing in Kigali and that he loved me. I could not ask for too much more than that.

I regret immensely not being able to do something important for my parents before they left the world. They had given me their best when I was a child and, now that I was a grown man, I wanted to build them a new house on the hill or do something else to make sure they were comfortable. This is the Rwandan way. But shortly before my father died, my mother had gone in for a routine doctor's visit and they found a cancer inside her. This strong and lively woman quickly grew frail and the last words she ever said to me were spoken from her hospital bed. 'Son, I am going to my house now,' she told me. I can only hope that, wherever she is today, her house is more splendid than anything I could have ever imagined for her.

As THE GENERAL MANAGER of the Diplomates I had to do a lot of negotiating. There were food contracts to be signed, employee grievances to be addressed, conference rooms to be booked, wedding receptions to accommodate. I had learned how friendship and business can be artfully juxtaposed without corrupting each other.

Let me explain. We have a saying in Rwanda, a leftover from the brief time when we were a colony of the Germans: '*Dienst ist Dienst, und Schnapps ist Schnapps.*' It means 'work is work and booze is booze'. There were often sticky issues to work through in my new job, but I discovered that you could never let your opinion of a person interfere with the business between you. He may be your best friend or somebody you detest, but the conversation should not change. *Dienst ist Dienst.*

I met many people in Rwanda whose racial ideology I couldn't stand, but I was unfailingly polite to them, and they learned to respect me even though our disagreements were obvious. This led to a priceless realisation for me. The very act of negotiation makes it difficult, if not impossible, to dehumanise the person across the table from you. Because in negotiation you will never get 100 per cent of what you want. You are forced to make a compromise, and by doing this you are forced to understand, and even sympathise with, the other person's position. And if cups of good African coffee, some wine, a cognac, or all of the above could help lubricate this understanding, it was all to the good.

So I spent as little time as possible shut up inside the walls of my office. I took my morning coffee at the bar, watched the comings and goings, made careful note of who the regulars were, followed the gossip about their careers, and saved up that knowledge for the frequent times when I would find myself clinking glasses of complimentary merlot with a man whose friendship was another link to the power web of the capital and whose favour I could count on in the future.

FOUR

ON 8 AUGUST 1993, a new radio station went on the air. It called itself Radio-Télévision Libre des Mille Collines. I would come to wish that the name of this station wasn't so similar to that of my beloved hotel.

The station called itself by the call letters RTLM. It billed itself as the very first private radio station in the country, and it was an immediate sensation. It started by playing Congolese music virtually nonstop. RTLM then started to broadcast a few human voices, like a shy child finding its courage. The disc jockeys began to talk more. Then they started telling mildly dirty jokes. Then they started a call-in format in which ordinary Rwandans could hear their own voices broadcast over the air. People began calling in with road information, song dedications, complaints about local politicians, rumours, opinions, chatter. We have a phrase here about the nature of neighbourhood gossip. We call it *radio trottoir*—or, the 'radio of the sidewalk'. RTLM was the radio of the sidewalk suddenly blasted out to the whole country.

I can't begin to tell you how revolutionary this was. Unlike the dull government marginalia you usually heard on the official Radio Rwanda, RTLM was fresh. It was irreverent. It was *fun*. It constantly surprised you. It was giving us what we wanted but in a way that was lively and modern. Even those who were offended were hooked.

Just as Rwandans are serious about history, we are also serious about news. You see small battery-powered radios everywhere in our country. They are playing on the edges of cornfields, inside taxicabs, in restaurants and internet cafés, balanced on the shoulders of young men and old women and on the kitchen tables inside mud-and-pole houses on distant hills.

RTLM pulled off another feat. It convinced ordinary citizens that it could be trusted to give a truthful account of what was really going on inside the nation. And it did this by taking a sceptical attitude towards the current president, Juvenal Habyarimana. For a people who had been raised on a diet of official propaganda, this was something new indeed. Any voice that was less than worshipful towards the president *had* to be independent.

As the winter faded into the new year of 1994, the talk on the radio grew bolder and louder. Listeners couldn't help but notice that almost every broadcast seemed to feature an over-arching narrative. And that story was that the country was in danger from an internal threat and the only solution was to fight that threat with any means necessary. There were daily on-air debates that represented two sides—the extremist and the even more extremist. The station had helped gain credibility by shaming lazy government officials. Now it started to name ordinary citizens. And the tone began to change. A typical broadcast:

> Jeanne is a sixth-form teacher at Muramba in Muyaga commune. Jeanne is not doing good things in this school. Indeed, it has been noted that she's the cause of the bad atmosphere in the classes she teaches. She urges her students to hate the Hutus. These children spend the entire day at that, and it corrupts their minds. We hereby warn this woman named Jeanne, and indeed, the people of Muyaga, who are well known for their courage, should warn her. She is a security threat for the commune.

I wanted to stop listening to RTLM, but I couldn't. It was like one of those movies where you watch a car speeding in slow motion towards a child in the middle of the road. You want to scream, but you cannot look away.

In fact, when I think back on what we all heard on RTLM in those strange slow-motion months before April 1994, it seems impossible that we could not have known what was coming.

IT ALWAYS BOTHERS me when I hear Rwanda's genocide described as the product of 'ancient tribal hatreds'. I think this is an easy way for Westerners to dismiss the whole thing as a regrettable but pointless bloodbath that happens to primitive brown people. And not just that, but that the killing was random and chaotic and fuelled only by brute anger. Nothing could be further from the truth.

There is a reason why Rwanda's genocide was the quickest one in recorded history. It may have been accomplished with crude agricultural tools instead of gas chambers, but 800,000 people were killed in 100 days with a calculated efficiency that would have impressed the most rigorous accountant.

Make no mistake: there was a method to the madness. And it was about power. What scared our leaders most was the idea that Rwanda might be invaded and their power taken away. And in the early part of the 1990s that threat was very real.

The Tutsis who had fled the mobs years earlier for the safety of neighbouring countries had always dreamed of returning home. Under the leadership of General Fred Rwigema, and subsequently of Paul Kagame (the same child who had fled the country on his mother's back in 1959) they organised themselves into a military force called the Rwandan Patriotic Front (RPF). These soldiers were far outnumbered by the Rwandan Army, but they still constituted an impressively disciplined and effective band of fighters. On 1 October 1990, they crossed the border and started moving towards the capital. This was not the amateurish vandalism of 30 years earlier. This was a real invasion.

Three nights later, when the RPF was still a long way from Kigali, there was a clatter of gunfire all around the capital, including some mortar shelling. The next morning the government made a stunning announcement: some rebels had managed to infiltrate their way into the heart of the nation and had staged a sneak attack. Only the bravery and talent of the Rwandan Army had saved the country from disaster, and only the deceit and cunning of traitors within the neighbourhoods had made the attack possible.

It was all a charade. What really happened is that some trusted Army soldiers were dispatched to various neighbourhoods and told to fire their weapons in the air and in the dirt. The effect of the 'surprise attack', as you might guess, was to spread fear that an enemy was hiding among the population.

It was a cheap but effective way for President Juvenal Habyarimana to rally the people to his side and shore up his weakening hold on power. A curfew went into effect on the streets of the capital. Thousands of innocent people, mostly Tutsis and those perceived to be their sympathisers, were rounded up and thrown in jail on trumped-up charges. There was suddenly no distinction between Tutsi and exiled RPF rebels; they were lumped into the same category of rhetoric. The war itself was cast as an explicitly racial conflict and ordinary Rwandans started to arrange their lives around this idea.

MY TROUBLES with President Juvenal Habyarimana began when I refused to wear his picture on my suit jacket.

Like many African 'big men', Habyarimana had a penchant for plastering his face on billboards and public spaces everywhere throughout the nation. I suppose it is a combination of vanity, insecurity, and old-fashioned advertising strategy that makes leaders do this. Suffice it to say, Habyarimana loved his own face so much that he eventually decided that his subjects should display it on their breasts. He designed medallions with his own photograph in the middle. Various people—commune administrators, priests, wealthy businessmen—were instructed to wear them while acting in their official capacities. The Roman Catholic archbishop of Kigali helped set the tone by wearing the portrait pin on his cassock while saying mass.

On the 25th anniversary of Rwanda's independence, a big state dinner was held at the Hotel Mille Collines. All the national big shots were there, as well as foreign dignitaries, including the king and prime minister of Belgium. I wore my best white suit for the occasion. But, of course, I had no portrait pin in my lapel.

One of the president's thugs came over to me just before the ceremony was to begin.

'You are not wearing your portrait of the president,' he told me.

I agreed with him that this was the case.

He grabbed me by the collar, yanked me out of the receiving line, and told me that I would not be greeting the president that night. It took the well-timed intervention of my boss, the chairman of Sabena Hotels, to make things right. Either I would be restored to my place in the receiving line or the hotel would refuse right then to be the host of the Independence Day dinner. It was probably a bluff, but it worked. I went back into the line and shook the president's hand without his face grinning up from my lapel.

The very next morning another of his goons showed up at the front desk of the Mille Collines and asked for me. When I didn't appear he handed the headwaiter a brown envelope and told him to deliver it to me. It was stuffed full of Habyarimana medals.

'From now on,' he told the headwaiter, 'your manager will wear one of these every time he comes to work. We will be watching. The rest of these medals are to be given to the employees.'

The next morning I showed up to work without wearing a medal. A black car arrived at the front door roundabout and I was escorted over. They told me I now had earned 'an appointment' at the office of the president. I followed them there in a hotel car and allowed myself to be led into a side office, where I was screamed at for several hours.

'You do not respect the boss, our father!' they screamed at me.

'What did I do wrong?' I asked, although I knew.

'You stupid man, you did not wear your medals! Why not?'

'I don't see the benefit in doing that,' I said.

It went around and around like this before they kicked me out of the office—with a literal foot planted on my butt—and a command to be back the next morning. And the next day, they screamed at me for hours and gave me another kick in the butt before they let me go.

It went on like this every day for a month. I was no longer working at the hotel, just reporting to the office of the president. His thugs became my daily escorts. We started to get used to each other and exchanged morning pleasantries before the daily screaming began. And I would always tell them the same thing: 'I really don't see why I should wear the medal.'

The irony of this show of muscle was that the president was not really in control of his own power base. Everybody who was well informed in Rwanda knew that he was essentially a hollow man, largely the pawn of his own advisers. He had risen up through the defence ministry and was put in charge of the purge against the Tutsis in 1973 that had been responsible for the deaths of dozens and wasted the futures of thousands more, including my friend Gerard. In the midst of all the chaos, Habyarimana launched a coup and took over the presidency of Rwanda, promising to bring an end to the violence. His real talent was squeezing money out of international aid organisations and Western governments while at the same time shutting down any internal opposition. The people who benefited most were Habyarimana's friends from the north-west part of the country. We called these people the *akazu*, or 'little house'.

Empty suit that he was, Habyarimana had managed to stay in power through the depression with the help of the government of France, and particularly because of the French president, François Mitterrand. These two presidents got along famously and shared many dinners. Mitterrand even gave our president his own jet aeroplane. Loads of development money and military assistance flowed to us from Paris throughout the years. When the RPF launched its attack in 1990 and the Rwandan Army exploded in size from 5,000 soldiers to 30,000 to counter the threat, France was there to help train the new recruits. As much as twenty tonnes of armaments a day were airlifted into Kigali, courtesy of Habyarimana's friends in Paris.

The French love affair with Rwanda was, you might say, also a product of a pervasive national mythology. 'France is not France without greatness,' Charles de Gaulle had said, and maintaining a strong web of economic and diplomatic interests in their former African colonies is seen as a key part of that strategy. And so, in places like the Ivory Coast, the Central African Republic, and Chad, where the French tricolour flew until the 1960s, France has provided monetary support, trade links, and frequent military intervention almost from the day that these countries gained their independence. Its eagerness to play such a father-figure role earned it the nickname 'the policeman of Africa'. France never was much of a player in Rwanda during colonial times, but they now considered us worthy of attention for their own psychologically complicated reasons.

If Rwandans are obsessed with height, then the French are obsessed with language. A large part of that mystical *greatness* in the French mentality is centred on the preservation of the pure French language and the repelling of all attempts to marginalise it in favour of English, the international language of commerce, aviation and diplomacy. President Habyarimana and the Hutu elite were considered exemplary guardians of the French language and the kind of cultural values that it represented.

The RPF invaders, by contrast, had spent most of their lives exiled in the former British colony of Uganda and were therefore English speakers. So at France's Foreign Ministry the logic went like this: if the RPF rebels should become strong enough to overthrow Habyarimana it will spell the loss of a small, but important Francophone ally in Central Africa, which could soon be speaking English as the official language. While the French publicly supported peace talks, they were, in reality, working behind the scenes to preserve Habyarimana's shaky hold on power.

So when I decided not to wear the president's portrait on my lapel I was putting my thumb in the eye of a very insecure man. My friends told me later that I had been taking a stupid chance. But it would have cost me a huge amount of self-respect to have worn that dictator's face on my jacket. If this was a risk, it was a calculated one.

I never told my father about my run-in with the president. I didn't want him to worry about my job—or my life. But if I had told him, I like to think it would have made him laugh.

WHILE PEACE TALKS with the rebels dragged on, the programs on RTLM got worse and worse. I do not know how I managed to keep listening to it. Perhaps it was out of a need to understand exactly where popular opinion was heading. Or perhaps it was just morbid fascination. Either way, I began to hear the racial slur 'cockroach' so frequently that it lost whatever power it had to shock.

The anger on the airwaves became so common that it didn't seem particularly out of line when RTLM broadcast the tape of an address made at a political rally in the north-west town of Gisenyi. The speaker was a government official named Leon Mugesera and, I have to say, he knew how to whip up a crowd. Copies of this speech had already been circulating around the country like bootleg treasures, with people commenting favourably that here was a man who really understood the threat to Rwanda. 'Do not let yourselves be invaded,' he kept exhorting the crowd, and it gradually became clear he was making an allusion to the ruling party being 'invaded' by moderates who wanted to engage in peace negotiations with the predominately Tutsi rebels. In words that would become widely repeated throughout Rwanda, he also recounted a story of saying to a Tutsi, 'I am telling you that your home is in Ethiopia, that we are going to send you back there quickly, by the Nyabarongo.' Nobody in Rwanda could have missed what he was really saying: the Tutsis were going to be slaughtered and their bodies thrown into the north-flowing watercourse.

His final exhortation to the crowd could have served as a summary of the simple-minded philosophy of those who were screaming for Hutu Power the loudest: 'Know that the person whose throat you do not cut will be the one who cuts yours.' He was preaching an ideology—and an identity—based on nothing more than a belief in the murderous intentions of the enemy.

I think that was the most seductive part of the movement. There is something living deep within us all that welcomes, even relishes, the role of victimhood for ourselves. There is no cause in the world more righteously embraced than our own when we feel someone has wronged us. Whatever its allure, this primitive ideology of Hutu Power swept through Rwanda in 1993 and early 1994 with the speed of flame through dry grass.

The true purpose of all the revolutionary rhetoric was all about Habyarimana and the rest of the elite trying to keep a grip on the reins of government. It seemed almost irrelevant to point out that Hutus had been in a position of undisturbed power for 35 years and that the Tutsi were in a position to affect very little of Rwanda's current miserable situation—even if they had wanted to. It was a revolution, all right, but there was nobody to overthrow.

The Hutu government wanted all the anger in Rwanda pointed towards any target but itself. RTLM was officially a private venture with an independent editorial voice, but the extent to which it was an arm of the government was kept a secret from most Rwandans. Few people knew, for example, that the station's largest shareholder was actually President Habyarimana himself. The other financiers had close ties to the *akazu*. They included hundreds of people, including two cabinet ministers and two bank presidents.

You might wonder how any audience—let alone the Tutsis and those who loved them—could not have made a protest or at least fled the country when they heard such irrational anger growing stronger and stronger. Could they have not read the signs and understood that hateful words would soon turn into knives?

Two factors must be taken into account. The first is the great respect we Rwandans have for formal education. If a man here has an advanced degree he is automatically treated as an authority on his subject. RTLM understood this and hired many professors and other 'experts' to help spread the hate.

The other thing you have to understand was that the message crept into our national consciousness very slowly. We did not wake up one morning to hear it pouring out of the radio at full strength. It started with a sneering comment, the casual use of the term 'cockroach', the almost humorous suggestion that Tutsis should be airmailed back to Ethiopia. Stripping the humanity from an entire group takes time. It is an attitude that requires cultivation, a series of small steps, daily tending. I suppose it is like the famous example of the frog who will immediately leap out of a pot of boiling water if you toss him into it, but put it in cold water and turn up the heat gradually, and he will die in boiling water without being aware of what happened.

RTLM was not the only media outlet turning up the heat while the rebel army inched across the countryside. Mugesera's throat-cutting speech was played on Radio Rwanda. And in 1990 a new newspaper called *Kangura* (*Wake It Up*) started publishing. It was essentially RTLM in print—populist, funny, and completely obsessed with 'the Tutsi question'. Its publisher, Hassan Ngeze, had an amazing talent for crystallising people's dark thoughts and splashing them on the pages in an entertaining way. And just as RTLM was bankrolled by wealthy people close to the president, this rag was secretly funded by members of the *akazu*.

In a February 1994 article headlined 'Final Attack', Ngeze wrote: 'We know where the cockroaches are. If they look for us, they had better watch out.' Other articles were not as subtle. 'What weapons shall we use to conquer the cockroaches once and for all?' queried the caption of one illustration. The answer was pictured to the side: a wood-handled machete. Children were clearly enemies, too. 'A cockroach cannot give birth to a butterfly,' proclaimed one story.

This farce of a paper had a small circulation but an enormous reach. Copies were sent out to the villages and passed around gleefully. It seemed a welcome break from the usual tired and boring news out of the capital. Here, at last, said many people, is a paper that really says the ugly truth—that the Tutsis are going to kill us when they invade.

Before it stopped publishing two months before the genocide *Kangura* editorialised: 'We must remark to the cockroaches that if they do not change their attitude and if they persevere in their arrogance, the majority people will establish a force composed of young Hutu. This force will be charged with breaking the resistance of the Tutsi children.'

What the newspaper did not say was that just such a force had already been put into place and was busily preparing itself to murder children throughout Rwanda.

IN EARLY NOVEMBER 1993, a shipment of cargo was trucked into Kigali. The wooden crates bore papers announcing that they had been received from China at the seaport of Mombasa in Kenya. Inside were 987 cartons of inexpensive machetes. This was not enough to cause alarm by itself. The machete is a common household tool in Rwanda, used for all manner of jobs—slicing mangoes, mowing grass, harvesting bananas, cutting paths through heavy brush, butchering animals.

If anybody had been paying attention, however, the shipment might have seemed curious when matched with other facts. The recipient, for example, was one of the primary financial backers of the hate-mongering radio station RTLM. Those cartons from China, too, were but a small part of what amounted to a mysterious wave. Between January 1993 and March 1994, a total of half a million machetes were imported into my country from various overseas suppliers. This was a number wildly out of line with ordinary demands. Somebody obviously wanted a lot of sharp objects in the hands of ordinary Rwandans.

If those imports were quiet, the formation of the youth militias was obvious. It was hard to miss those roving bands of young men wearing colourful neckerchiefs, blowing whistles, singing patriotic songs, and screaming insults against the Tutsis, their sympathisers and members of the opposition. They conducted military drills with fake guns carved from wood because the government could not afford to give them real rifles. They were known as the *Interahamwe*, which means either 'those who stand together' or 'those who attack together', depending on who is doing the translating.

Habyarimana's government formed them into 'self-defence militias' that operated as a parallel to the regular Rwandan army and were used to threaten the president's political enemies. They were also a tool for building popular support for the ruling regime under the all-embracing cloak of Hutu Power. The ongoing civil war brought a whole new flock of members. Most of the new recruits came from the squalid refugee camps that formed a ring around Kigali. It is difficult for me to describe just how terrible the conditions were inside these camps: no decent food, no sanitation, no jobs, no hope. There were several hundred thousand people crammed into these tumbledown wastelands, most of them chased away from their homes in the countryside by the advancing RPF army. Kigali itself held about 350,000 people at the time and the strain on the infrastructure was very great. These refugees saw plenty of reasons to be angry at the rebels—and, by unfair extension, angry at each individual Tutsi. Plus, the militias were *fun*. They brought a sense of purpose and cohesion to an otherwise dreary life. It was like being in the Boy Scouts or a soccer club, only there was a popular enemy to hate and a lot of built-up frustration to vent. The boys were also hungry and full of the restlessness of youth. It was easy to get them to follow any orders imaginable.

The groundwork for the genocide went even deeper. In the fall of 1992 mayors in each of Rwanda's little communes were asked by the president's political party to compile lists of people—understood to be Tutsis and people who were threatening to Habyarimana—who had left the country recently or who had children who had left. The implication was that these people had joined the ranks of the RPF. Tutsis throughout the country suspected their names were being entered into secret ledgers. Many tried without success to have their identity cards relabelled so that they would appear to be Hutu.

One afternoon a man wearing the uniform of a soldier tossed a grenade through the door of a bar and sped off on a motorcycle. The bar was destroyed. The minister of public works, Félicien Gatabazi, was gunned down by thugs as he was entering his house. A taxi driver witnessed the assassination; she was shot as a precaution the next day. At least 100 other innocent people would be killed in this fashion by the increasingly violent teenagers of the *Interahamwe* and also rebel soldiers who had infiltrated Kigali. People didn't want to stand at bus stops or taxi stations any more because the crowds were targets for grenade throwers.

A scary incident happened on the road. My wife, Tatiana, was driving our son to school when she was forced off the road by a man in a military jeep. He walked over to her door, took off his sunglasses, and bid her to roll down her window.

'Do you know me?' he asked.

'No,' said my wife.

'My name is Étincelles,' he said. It was the French word for 'explosions', apparently his *nom de guerre*.

He went on: 'Madam, we know your home. We know you have three big German shepherds in the yard for protection, as well as two gate guards. The Youth of the Democratic Republic Movement has said they plan to kidnap you. They will be trying to get ransom money from your husband. So I am telling you, if anybody should try to pull you over, don't stop. Keep driving, even if you have to run somebody over. Do it for your own safety. I am telling you all of this because I come from the same part of the country as your husband and I don't want to see any harm come to you.'

When my wife told me about this I searched my memory for anyone from my village who might be calling himself Étincelles. I couldn't think of who it might be. To this day I have no idea if this was an actual kidnap plot or just an attempt to scare us. Regardless, we no longer felt comfortable living at home after that, and so I moved us all into a guest suite at the Diplomates. It felt awful to be governed by fear, but these were very dangerous times.

Life went on, even in the surreal twilight of that spring. At nights on the terrace I would share beers with the leaders of the militia movement, trying to keep quiet as I heard them talking of events in the neighbouring country of Burundi. The president there, Melchior Ndadaye, had been assassinated by Tutsi officers in his own army. A series of reprisal killings followed. The international community had little to say about these massacres. Was it true the Tutsi were planning to do a similar thing here: take power and then start a campaign of genocide against the Hutu? I heard it said more than a few times over glasses of Carlsberg beer: 'It may come down to kill or be killed.'

During that dangerous time I did something that had the potential to be my death warrant. The RPF leadership was looking for a place to give a press conference and every public venue in town had rejected them. When they approached me about a room at the Diplomates, I agreed to host them, and I charged them the standard rate. It wasn't the profits I cared about. I really believed they deserved to have equal access like anybody else. But I heard later that the government was unhappy with me. I suppose, in retrospect, it was like the incident with Habyarimana's silly medals. These were symbolic stands, probably foolish, but they were ones I thought were worth the risk.

Having said that, those first months of 1994 were like watching a speeding car in slow motion heading towards a child. There was a thickness in the air. You could buy Chinese-made grenades on the street for three dollars each and machetes for just one dollar and nobody thought to ask why. Many of my friends purchased guns for themselves in the name of home protection. This was something I refused to do, despite the urging of my wife.

In one tense conversation she told me I was acting like a coward for not acquiring a firearm. 'You know that I have always said I fight with words, not with guns,' I told her. 'If you want to call me a coward for this, then I guess that is what I am.' She stared back at me, hurt and silent.

A few days later, I took her and our little son, Tresor, along with me to a manager's meeting in Brussels that I had been scheduled to attend. With the other children at boarding school in Rwanda, it was just the three of us, and we made a little vacation out of it. We travelled by train through Luxembourg, Switzerland, and France. Walking amid the grey monuments and plazas, drinking the yeasty beer, and eating the starchy tourist food made it possible—almost—to forget the slow boil back at home.

After three weeks, I had to return to my job, and we arrived in Kigali on the morning of 31 March. At that hour the city was quiet, the militias were mostly asleep and the tension that I had come to associate with Rwanda was at low ebb. The rolling green hills had never looked so good or so welcoming. Perhaps things were finally calming down. The United Nations had sent 2,700 troops to Rwanda a few months earlier to enforce the Arusha peace agreement, and it seemed the visible presence of the blue helmets was finally making a difference in keeping the militias contained. The UN seemed capable of keeping the peace. They had given us hope.

It had been so long since we had been to our house that we decided to go straight there instead of to our suite at the Diplomates. For the first time in almost two years we felt good about the future.

FIVE

I STILL REMEMBER the sunset on that night of 6 April 1994. There was no rain. The sky was hazy with spring moisture and dust and the slanted dying light made the bottoms of the clouds turn blood orange. The colours deepened and darkened as the sun went lower, reaching for the hillcrest in a nimbus of purples, violets, and indigos, the colours of oncoming night. Around town some people paused to watch, cocking their heads to the west. It was a moment of beautiful stillness.

I HAVE BEEN TOLD that it is common for people to mark exactly where they are when they learn of death on a grand scale. I have met Americans, for example, who can tell me in detail which suit they were putting on or what highway they were driving down at the time of the jet attacks on the World Trade Center. Perhaps it is a way to link our own small presence to the great blood-stained currents of history for just a moment.

I know with certainty that you will find nobody living in Rwanda today who does not remember what they were doing in the early evening hours of 6 April 1994, when the private jet of president Juvenal Habyarimana was shot down with a portable missile as it approached for landing at Kigali Airport.

As it happened, I was in my usual place for that time of day. I was eating a dinner of pan-fried fish on the terrace of the Diplomates Hotel. Sitting next to me was my brother-in-law. We were celebrating a small victory—I had helped his wife get a job as a saleswoman for a Dutch car dealer named NAHV.

The airport is about fifteen kilometres away and so we heard nothing out of the ordinary. Less than a minute after the crash, however, the waiter came over with a house telephone. It was my wife on the line.

'I have heard a sound I have never heard before,' she told me. 'Get home as fast as you are able.'

I couldn't have known it then, but phones were ringing all over the city and would continue to ring all night long.

On the way out to the parking lot we talked to an Army major who had been listening to his radio. Roadblocks were going up all over town, he told us, though he could not explain why. Don't take the Gikondo road, he said. Take the one that leads past the Parliament. Oddly, this was where the rebel army had its local stronghold. My brother-in-law shook hands in the parking lot and we urged each other to be careful. I could not have known it then, but I was shaking his hand for the last time.

I drove on the Boulevard of the Organization of African Unity through Kigali, which was unnaturally deserted. The power had been cut off and all the street lamps were off. There was virtually nobody on the streets. It occurred to me that a coup d'état might be taking place, or perhaps the long-awaited RPF invasion. For some reason it did not occur to me to be frightened.

I drove slowly and carefully, but passed no other drivers. Kigali was like a city battening down before the arrival of a hurricane. It was 8:35pm.

THE KILLING could have ended right there. It all could have been stopped quite easily at this early stage with just a small fraction of the police department of any Australian city. Rwandans have always shown respect to authority figures—it is part of our national personality—and a brigade of international soldiers would have found it surprisingly easy to keep order on the streets of Kigali if they had had the guts to show they meant business about saving lives. But they didn't.

A force of 2,700 United Nations peacekeeping soldiers was already inside the country. But they were ill equipped and under strict orders from UN headquarters not to fire their weapons except in defence of themselves. 'Do not fire unless fired upon' was the mantra. The recent US disaster in Somalia, in which eighteen Army Rangers had been killed by street mobs, had made the idea of 'African peacekeeping' a poisonous concept in the minds of many diplomats in the American State Department and the UN Security Council. They saw nothing to gain from it and everything to lose.

The leader of the UN troops in Rwanda was a lantern-jawed general from Canada named Romeo Dallaire. None of us knew it at the time, but he was handcuffed by a lack of resolve from his bosses in New York. He and his troops also had no idea what they had got themselves into. In terms of background intelligence, Dallaire had only a map of Rwanda ripped out of a tourist guide and an encyclopaedia entry hastily photocopied from the Montreal Public Library. But he got a quick and nasty education about Rwanda after an informant from a high level of the Hutu Power movement sneaked over to the UN compound one night, that winter. This man, later nicknamed 'Jean-Pierre', came with a story that would have seemed incredible to anyone who hadn't been watching the frog slowly boiling for the last year.

Up to 1,700 *Interahamwe* members had apparently been trained to act as an extermination squad against civilians. There were secret caches of arms scattered all around Kigali—stores of Kalashnikovs, ammunition, and many more of those damnably cheap grenades—to supplement the militia's arsenal, which consisted largely of traditional Rwandan weapons like spears and clubs. Jean-Pierre himself had been ordered to regis-ter all Tutsis and opposition elements living in a certain area, and he strongly suspected it was being prepared as a death list.

Those who were planning the genocide expected there to be some half-hearted resistance from the UN at the beginning, said Jean-Pierre. And there was a strategy to cope with this—a brutal attack aimed at Belgian soldiers serving with the UN mission. It was thought that the Europeans would have no stomach for taking casualties and quickly withdraw their troops, leaving Rwandans to shape their own destiny.

In disregard of his UN superior in Rwanda, Jacques-Roger Booh-Booh, Dallaire had not sat on this news. On 11 January 1994, he had sent a cable to his superiors in New York informing them of his intention to raid the arms caches. It would have put only the tiniest dent in the amount of sharp-edged killing weapons being stockpiled around Rwanda, but I believe that the architects of the genocide would have seen that somebody was paying attention and that genocidal actions would be met with reprisals. But the response Dallaire received from his UN bosses nicely summarised just about every cowardly, bureaucratic and incompetent step this organisation was to make in a nation on the brink of mass murder. Stockpiling of weapons may have violated the peace accords, Dallaire was told, but going after them was 'beyond the mandate' of the United Nations. He was instead encouraged to take his concerns to a man who surely would be the last one in the world to care: President Habyarimana.

The UN official who directed General Dallaire to take this deferential action was the chief of peacekeeping, Kofi Annan, who would one day serve as secretary-general.

Jean-Pierre's warnings were effectively brushed off. Nobody from the UN ever heard from him again.

SO IT DID not stop.

The guards opened the gate for me at my house, and I walked through my front door to the sound of a ringing telephone. It was Bik Cornelis, the general manager of the Hotel Mille Collines—my counterpart at Sabena's other luxury hotel. He was a colleague as well as a friend.

'Paul,' he said, 'your president and the president of Burundi have been murdered. Their plane was shot down with a rocket just a few minutes ago and they are both dead.'

My wife and I stared at one another from across the living room. The only clear thought I could manage was that Tatiana must have heard the sounds of a plane exploding. I had no idea what that must have sounded like.

'All right,' I said to Bik. 'What does this mean?'

'I don't know,' he said. 'But I think you'd better go back to the Diplomates. We don't know what will follow this.'

'All right,' I said. 'But I don't think I should go alone. I'm going to call for a UN escort.'

We hung up and I told my wife the news while I dug in my

pants pocket for a phone number. Tatiana looked as if she might faint. There was no need for us to discuss the gravity of the situation. Since I was such a political moderate and she was a Tutsi we were both in trouble. How much time would we have before there was a knock at the door?

I picked up the phone.

The leaders of the UN troops had always been cordial to me on their frequent visits to the hotel, and they often said things like, 'If there's anything you need, please call the compound and we'll see what we can do for you.' This seemed like a good time to play that card. I was put on the line to the commander of the Bangladeshi troops that made up the largest contingent of the United Nations' mission in Rwanda. I had heard rumours about their poor training and lack of equipment, but they were wearing the uniform of the UN, which carried a kind of magical protection for them. Unlike nearly everybody else, they could pass roadblocks without harassment by the militia.

'I need a military escort to the Diplomates Hotel,' I told him. 'Can you help me?'

His voice sounded very far away, as if he was speaking from down a long hallway.

'They are stopping people at roadblocks and asking them for identification,' the commander told me. 'Tutsis and those in the opposition are being killed with knives. It is very dangerous to go outside. I don't think I can help you.'

'Well, what am I supposed to do if they come here looking for me?' I asked.

'Does your house have more than one way to get inside?'

'Yes, of course. There is a front door and a back door. Why?'

'It is very simple. If the killers come looking for you through the front door, just leave through the back door.'

It seemed that this was going to be all the help we would get from the United Nations tonight. I resigned myself to staying at home that night and hoping that nobody would come through either door.

My next phone call was to my friend John Bosco Karangwa, who was someone I could always count on for a good laugh. I knew he would be at home alone—his wife was in Europe having medical treatment. John and I had both been in the the Democratic Republican Movement, or MDR—a moderate political party—and we shared a mutual dislike for Habyarimana.

'Habyarimana has been killed,' I told John Bosco.

'What?' he said. 'Are you sure?'

'Yes. They shot down his plane about an hour ago.'

'Let me confirm this before I start celebrating,' he said.

We shared a little laugh, and then I got serious with him. John Bosco was in the political opposition party and the assassination could spell only very bad things for him.

'Bosco, you could be killed tonight,' I told him. 'I want you to stay inside, keep your lights off, and let nobody inside your door.'

I am happy to tell you that I received John several days later as a refugee inside my hotel. He had been hiding in his house as he had promised. A friend had delivered his younger brother's three children into his care because the brother and his wife had been murdered. When I finally saw John Bosco, he hadn't spoken above a whisper for days. We made no more jokes about the death of the president.

Pieces of the story started filtering in from the radio that night. President Habyarimana had been flying back from Tanzania. On the plane with him was the new president of Burundi, Cyprien Ntaryamira; the chief of staff of the Rwandan Army; and nine other staff members and crew. At approximately 8:30 in the evening, as the plane was approaching the airport, two shoulder-launched missiles were fired from near a grove of banana trees in the Masaka neighbourhood. There were no survivors.

It remains a mystery to this day who fired these missiles. But whoever did it must have known that the immediate effect on Rwanda would be catastrophic.

With the death of its president the nation of Rwanda was officially decapitated. Members of the *akazu* gathered around a conference table at Army headquarters and allowed Colonel Théoneste Bagosora—the father of the *Interahamwe*—to effectively take charge of the country. Romeo Dallaire was at this meeting and he urged the new crisis committee to allow the moderate prime minister, Agathe Uwilingiyimana, to take power, as she should have. They refused, calling her a traitor.

Later that night Agathe called the UN detachment and asked for more security. She wanted to go to Radio Rwanda in the morning to tell the nation not to panic, that a civilian government was still in charge. But Rwandan Army soldiers were already surrounding her home in the dark shadows of the jacaranda trees. When fifteen UN soldiers arrived in the hour just before dawn they were welcomed with a burst of gunfire that shredded the tyres and wrecked the engines of two of their jeeps. The prime minister, frightened and screaming, climbed over her back wall into the house of a neighbour.

Agathe's hiding place was discovered and she was led outside in the midst of a cheering mob. There was a brief argument among the Rwandan soldiers over whether she should be taken prisoner or executed on the spot. The squabble ended when a police officer stepped forward and shot the prime minister in the head at close range. She bled to death right there on the terrace in front of her house.

The UN soldiers, meanwhile, were persuaded to give up their weapons and led to Army headquarters near the heart of downtown, right across the street from the Hotel Diplomates, as it happened. Five of the soldiers were from Ghana and they were allowed to go free. Ten of them had the misfortune of being from Belgium—the colonial master country, the ones who had glorified the Tutsis and made them like kings.

A crowd of excited Rwandan soldiers set upon the Belgians and began clubbing them, some of them to death. A few of them managed to grab a loaded rifle and take refuge in a small concrete building near the camp entrance. They managed to fend off their attackers for a terrified hour before their holdout was stormed. They were tortured and mutilated horribly, their tendons sliced so they could not walk.

The secret plan to get the peacekeepers to leave—the one the UN knew about four months in advance—was being carried out according to the letter.

I TRIED NOT TO listen to RTLM in those first hours, but it could not be avoided. Given the choice between listening to filth and missing potentially crucial information, I will choose the filth every single time.

But it was even worse than I could have imagined. The radio was instructing all its listeners to murder their neighbours.

'Do your work,' I heard the announcers say. 'Clean your neighbourhood of brush. Cut the tall trees.'

I would hear variations on these phrases echoing countless times over the next three months. The 'tall trees' was an unmistakable reference to the Tutsis. 'Clean your neighbourhood of brush' meant that rebel army sympathisers might be hiding among Tutsi families and so the entire family should be 'cleaned' to be on the safe side. But somehow the worst phrase of all to me was 'Do your work'. It made killing sound like a responsibility. Like it was the normal thing to do.

The mass murders were under way in Kigali. The *Interahamwe* militias started setting up some roadblocks, which were often no more than a few bamboo poles set on milk cartons in the road, or sometimes the burned-out hulk of an automobile. Eventually, the roadblocks would be made of human corpses. Every carload of people that came by was subject to a search and a check of those identity papers that listed ethnicity. Those who were found to be Tutsis were dragged to one side and chopped apart with machetes. The Presidential Guard paid visits to the homes of prominent Tutsis, opposition people and wealthy citizens. Doctors were pulled out of their homes and shot in the head. Old women were stabbed in the throat. Schoolchildren were hit on the head with wooden planks and their skulls cracked open on the concrete with the blow of a boot heel. The elderly were thrown down the waste holes of outhouses and buried underneath a cascade of rocks.

Thousands would die that day, the first citizens of what would become a nation of the murdered.

I LOOKED OUT the next morning at a street that had been transformed.

There was the usual smoky tang of morning mist in the air,

the usual dirt street and adobe walls and grey April sky, but it was a scene I could barely recognise. People whom I had known for several years were wearing military uniforms and several were carrying machetes dripping with blood. Quite a few had guns.

There was one in particular whom I will call Marcel, though that is not his real name. He worked in a bank. His specialty was helping uneducated people work their way through complicated financial transactions, and I never once knew him to lose his temper. He seemed to be a gentleman who respected himself. But here he was, wearing a military uniform and apparently ready to kill—if he hadn't already.

'Marcel,' I remember saying, 'I didn't know you were a soldier.'

I was trying to keep the irony out of my voice, but he gave me a blank look through his banker's spectacles.

'The enemy is among us,' he told me. 'Many of the people we have been mixing with *are traitors*.'

I thought it best to end the conversation there and went back into my house. Marcel watched me go. I could hear gunfire all around us, though not a heavy concentration from one place, as from a military battle. The rounds were cracking all around periodically, almost lazily, in every direction.

What I did not tell Marcel—what I was not about to tell anybody—was that there were up to 32 of the enemy already packed inside my house. These were neighbours who knew they were on the lists of the *Interahamwe*. Why they thought I might be able to protect them was beyond me, but it was my house they flocked to. We put the visitors up in the living room and the kitchen and tried to stay quiet.

It occurred to me later: I had seen this before. My father had opened our tiny hillside home to refugees during the Hutu Revolution of 1959. I had been a young boy then, a little older than my son Tresor. My father's favourite proverb came back to me: 'If a man can keep a fierce lion under his roof, why can he not shelter a fellow human being?'

Earlier on that endless morning we had lost track of our son Roger. In the chaos of getting all our frightened visitors comfortable my wife and I had failed to keep a vigilant eye on the children. At the time, Lys was sixteen, Roger was fifteen, Diane was thirteen, and little Tresor was not even two years old. We had instructed them all quite sternly not to go outside under any circumstances, but in the early morning Roger could not resist a check on the welfare of our neighbours. He had gone over the wall, as he would in normal times, to see his next-door friend, a boy called Rukujuju.

Rukujuju had been hacked apart with a machete. He lay facedown in the back yard in a small pool of his own blood. Nearby lay the bodies of his mother, his six sisters, and two neighbours. Some of them were not yet dead and were moving around slowly. Roger blundered back over the wall and went immediately into his room. He did not speak for the next several days.

These neighbours had joined others who had been slaughtered around us. The woman who lived in the house behind ours was named Leocadia. She was an elderly widow who used to totter over to my house to gossip with Tatiana. She was a Tutsi, but it didn't matter to any of us. Not until today.

I heard the sounds of a commotion at her front door and peered over the wall. There was a band of hyped-up *Interahamwe* there, holding guns and machetes. There was no time to think through my decision. I leaped over the wall and dashed to get help from my neighbour who I knew was a soldier in the Rwandan Army, but not a hardliner.

'Please,' I told the soldier who opened the door to me. 'They are going to kill this old woman. Come over and save her.' By the time we arrived with his colleague, it was already too late. Leocadia was dead, but without any apparent wounds. She died of a heart attack. I do not want to know what the last thing she saw might have been.

WHAT WAS I going to do? It seemed terribly strange to be thinking about work, but my mind kept drifting back to my responsibilities as the general manager of the Hotel Diplomates. It has since been suggested to me that this is one of the ways that people cope with things too horrible to understand—they gladly throw themselves into the little tasks of normal life as a way to distract themselves from the abyss.

Bik Cornelis, the manager of the nearby Hotel Mille Collines, was a white man and a citizen of the Netherlands. He had told me he would almost certainly be evacuated on the first available flight. This would leave not one but two hotels without any leadership during the bloodshed. I had promised the Sabena Corporation that I would do my best to look after both properties when he left. It seemed vital that I live up to my word on this matter.

In the middle of the day on 7 April, I finally succeeded in getting through on the telephone to Michel Houtard, the director of the hotels division of the Sabena Corporation. He was a European gentleman of the old school, courtly and generous. He came on the line and I could hear genuine concern in his voice. We had a conversation in French.

'Paul, we are hearing very bad reports of violence breaking out all over Kigali. Are you in any danger?'

'Not at the moment, but I am trapped in my house. Some of my neighbours have been killed. The roads are too dangerous to travel and I have not been able to arrange a military escort to the hotel.'

'Can we help in any way?'

'I'm not sure. If I can get to the hotel I will contact you from there and let you know the situation. The radio news has been sketchy. I have to tell you that I am not very well informed about what is going on.'

'Well, I want to let you know that we will be trying to do all we can from here to ensure the safety of you and all the employees.'

It was strange: I could not help but think of the city of Brussels, where Tatiana and I had been just the week before. I pictured flocks of pigeons bobbing their heads in parks, grey mansard roofs, statues of dead aristocrats on horseback, chocolates under glass, pastel-painted town houses, bars full of carefree young people drinking Jupiler pilsner. It had been spring there and the trees were just coming into bud. It seemed like another existence altogether.

1 A panoramic view of Rwanda's capital, Kigali.

2 A truck carrying Belgian evacuees drives past murdered Tutsis as Rwanda descends into genocidal civil war.

3 Hutus with machetes man the roadside as civilians evacuate.

4 Government soldiers stand by as UN troops help Tutsi refugees flee the Hotel Mille Collines on 18 June 1994.

I REALLY SHOULD have been dead. In retrospect it is a miracle that my name was not on the lists of the undesirables that the Presidential Guard were sent out to eliminate in the first two days. I had been an irritant to Habyarimana and a member of the moderate party. I had been the one who hosted that conference at the Diplomates called by the hated RPF. Furthermore, I was married to a Tutsi 'cockroach' and had fathered a baby—my son Tresor—of mixed descent. They had every reason to behead me. Somebody had recently scrawled a number in charcoal on the outer wall of my house—it was 531. I could only guess that it was a code, and an easy way for the death squads to find me.

My plan was to keep working the phones and hope that the military or the UN could find time to get me and my family an escort to the Diplomates. But the radio made it sound as if all hell was breaking loose in Kigali and it was not clear when the troubles would ebb.

On the morning of 9 April, they finally came for me. Two Army jeeps tore into my front yard and a squad of soldiers piled out. The captain walked up to me and poked a finger in my face. He was sweating heavily and had angry eyes. I saw immediately that this conversation could very well end with him shooting me in the face. I looked at him with the calmest expression I could manage.

'I hear you are the manager of the Hotel Diplomates,' he told me. 'We need you to open up the hotel. We want you to come with us.'

Here was my chance. I told him I would be happy to accompany him to the hotel, if only my family could come. This was my opportunity to load my neighbours and family into the hotel van and my neighbour's car. I would call them my 'uncles', 'aunts', 'nephews', and 'nieces' if challenged. I gave my own car keys to another neighbour named Ngarambe.

'This car could save your life,' I told him quietly.

We followed the Army caravan on the road out of Kabeza but went only a kilometre before the captain waved me to pull over at a spot on the road where dead bodies were piled on both sides. It was a scene of a slaughter.

The captain came over to me with a rifle.

'Do you know that all the managers in this country have already been killed?'

'No,' I said.

'You, traitor, are lucky we aren't killing you. We have guns and we're going to kill all the cockroaches in the hotel bar and in your house. You are going to help us.'

The captain held out the rifle and nodded towards the people huddled in the cars. His message was clear: these people were to be killed right now. And I was chosen to be their killer. It would be my rite of passage.

But I noticed something. *He would not look me in the eye.*

In that one small turn of the face, I saw that there might be some room for me to manoeuvre. I saw that I had a small chance to save the lives of my family and neighbours. All I needed to do was find the right words.

I looked at the Kalashnikov rifle this army captain was offering me—bidding me to wipe out the cockroaches like a good patriotic Hutu—and then I began to talk.

'Listen, my friend, I do not know how to handle a gun,' I told him. 'And even if I did, I do not see what would be accomplished by killing these people.'

Surrounding us on every side were the bodies of people who had been freshly murdered. They had been pushed out of the roadway. A few of the lucky ones had been shot, but most had been hacked apart by machetes. Some were missing their heads. This captain had taken me to this spot on the road on purpose and was counting on all the bodies and the blood to send a clear message. You will join these corpses if you don't follow our orders, he wanted me to understand. But he would not look me in the eye when he asked me to kill and that's how I understood—somehow—there was a crack in his resolve that I could exploit.

I went over to one of the cars where my neighbours were huddled. I purposely selected the frailest old man I could find and asked the captain: 'Look, is *this* really the enemy you are fighting?' I pointed out a baby in a mother's arms, and said it again, trying to push all the panic out of my voice: 'Is this baby your enemy? I don't think this is what you want to do. You are what? Twenty-five years old? You are young. Do you want to spend the rest of your life with blood on your hands?'

When I saw this argument wasn't going anywhere, I switched tactics. I aimed lower this time. Morality wasn't working; maybe greed would.

'My friends,' I said, 'you cannot be blamed for this mistake. I understand you perfectly. You are tired. You are hungry. You are thirsty. This war has stressed you.'

Everything now came down to how well I was reading this man—if the promise of money would be enough to tempt him away from the murders he had been ordered to commit. I was like a Mephistopheles trying to corrupt him.

'I know how to solve this problem,' I told him.

We began to talk in terms of cash. It seems strange to say, but putting a price on lives was like a kind of sanity compared to the murders he had been suggesting. At first the captain demanded that each Tutsi cockroach pay every one of his soldiers 200,000 Rwandan francs in exchange for their lives. This was roughly the equivalent of $1,500 per person—many times more cash than an average Rwandan will ever see in their lifetime. But this was negotiation. You always start with the crazy price and then work downward.

'My friends,' I said, 'even you do not have this much money. You cannot expect these people to be carrying that kind of sum. But I can get it for you. I am the only person who can do this here. It is in the safe of the hotel and you will never be able to open it without me. Drive me to the hotel and I will pay you the money.'

I hustled the refugees into the Diplomates' manager's house. In a way, we were going straight into the dragon's den—here were the men who were ordering Hutu citizens to kill anybody in Rwanda suspected of being a descendant of the Tutsi clans or one of their allies. But I knew I would be safe here. Despite the captain's bluster, I knew he would not kill me in the presence of his superiors.

I told the captain to stay where he was—I now felt confident enough to command *him*—and got his money out of the safe. It was the price we had finally agreed on: a million Rwandan francs for everyone. It was the end of the week when we always had a stockpile of ready cash. It was supposed to have been converted into foreign currency and wired to the corporate office in Belgium. Now it was going into the pockets of killers, but I think it was the best use of that cash anybody could have imagined.

I went and paid off the captain. He drove away with his death squad and I never saw him again.

It was later suggested to me that I could have broken my agreement with this killer, simply refusing to pay the money once I and my neighbours and family were safely inside the Diplomates. But this was inconceivable. He would have remembered me and surely taken revenge, for one thing. And I had given him my word. I never make promises I cannot keep. It is bad policy. There is a saying in Rwanda: with a lie you can eat once, but never twice.

He left me with something valuable, too. He told me that I was not powerless in the face of the murderous insanity that seemed to have descended over my country in the last 72 hours.

With that brief refusal to meet my eyes, he told me that I might be able to negotiate with evil.

I SOON DISCOVERED the true reason why I had been brought to the Diplomates and not killed. The interim government of Rwanda—a rump committee of the very same men who had organised the militias—had taken over the hotel as a temporary headquarters of the new government. But they needed the keys. Once I had opened the suites and the bar, my life was expendable. I tried my best to keep myself and my family out of sight and they seemed to forget about me in the chaos, for which I was deeply grateful.

The rebels soon learned what was happening at the Diplomates and started firing mortar shells at the hotel, which was all too exposed on the hillside. They had an easy shot from their stronghold near the Parliament building. Bullets started whizzing through the windows and I couldn't go into my office because it faced the direction of fire. The crisis government hastily started packing supplies and papers into boxes and prepared to decamp to the city of Gitarama, about 50 kilometres south-west. They also looted bedspreads, pillows, television sets, and other items from their rooms. I made a show of preparing to evacuate with them as I had a secret plan in mind.

My family and I would pretend to follow the military train, but then split off almost immediately. We would use the cover of the government convoy as a safe way to get to the Hotel Mille Collines. I had heard that there were 400 refugees who had taken shelter there. Barely a kilometre of hillside separated the two properties; I could have walked it in ten minutes during peaceful times. But it would have been inviting death by machete to do it now while the *Interahamwe* were running about.

We would have to leave my neighbours hidden inside the cottage—it was too dangerous to try to move them out now—but I resolved not to forget them. I would simply have to come back later and rescue them by other means. But I wasn't sure I could even save my family, or myself. I would be leaving the Diplomates, where I was technically still the manager, and going over to the Mille Collines, where I had plenty of friends and a long work history but was technically not the boss. What kind of reception was I going to get over there? I had no idea what would happen.

On the morning of 12 April, the government leaders started their trip to the emergency capital and I rolled out with them behind the wheel of a Suzuki jeep. On that brief five-minute trip I kept seeing patches of red on the dirt of the shoulder. Days later I would see trucks that would normally have been used to haul concrete blocks or other construction material. They would be stacked high with dead bodies—women, men, children, many of them with stumps where their arms and legs had been—for burial in mass graves all over Kigali.

For now, though, there were only the bloodstains on the side of the road. 'Don't look,' I said to my children and my wife. But I had to keep my eyes open to drive.

SIX

I PEELED AWAY from the killers and turned the car towards my beloved Hotel Mille Collines.

A squad of militia had set up a roadblock right in front of the entrance. I had come to dread them on sight—young boys, many no older than fourteen, dressed in ragged clothes with red, green, and yellow stripes and carrying spears and machetes and a few battered rifles. These boys had liberated some beer from somewhere and were guzzling it down, though it was early in the morning. They were checking the identification papers of everyone attempting to get inside the Mille Collines.

I got out of the car to talk to them. It is always better to be face-to-face with the man you intend to deal with rather than have him standing over you. To be on the same physical plane changes the tone of the conversation.

'I'm the manager of both the Diplomates and the Mille Collines,' I told them. 'I'm coming to see what is going on.'

To my surprise they did not ask me for my identification book. They glanced briefly at my family in the car before waving us through. I thought I saw them smirk to each other. If I had to guess what they were thinking, it would be this: 'Oh, why not let six more cockroaches inside? It will make it easier to find them when the time comes.'

ALL OVER RWANDA people were leaving their homes and running to places where they thought they might be spared.

Churches were favourite hiding places. In the village of Ntarama just south of the capital the mayor told the local population of Tutsis to go inside the rectangular brick Catholic church to wait out the violence instead of trying to hide in the nearby swamps. The church had been a safe refuge during the troubles in 1959 and nobody had forgotten the seemingly magical role that it had played. More than 5,000 frightened people crammed inside. But here, as well as every-where in Rwanda, the sanctuaries of Christ were a cruel trap; they only made easy places for the mobs to herd the fugitives.

Four busloads of cheerful Army soldiers and militiamen arrived to do the job at Ntarama. A man named Aphrodise Nsengiyumva was at the altar leading prayers and trying to keep everyone cheerful when those outside started breaking holes through the walls with sledgehammers and grenades. Light streamed into the darkened room. Grenades were tossed in through the holes, blasting some of the refugees into bits, splashing blood and muscle tissue all over the compound. Other militiamen broke down the doors and waded into the crowd with spears, clubs, and machetes.

It happened at secular buildings as well, and there, too, death was usually preceded by a betrayal.

A rumour went around in the suburb of Kicukiro, for example, that the UN troops stationed at a technical school would offer protection from the mobs. There were indeed 90 commandos at the school, but they were less than eager to offer any protection. Nonetheless, about 2,000 of the hunted took shelter in the classroom buildings behind the very thin layer of safety afforded by the blue helmets and their weapons.

On 12 April, the same day my family and I reached the Mille Collines, the order was given for the UN troops to abandon the school and help make sure that foreigners got out of Rwanda safely. The mission had changed. As the country slid further and further into mass murder, the Security Council, Kofi Annan, and the United States decided that the mandate of the UN troops was not to halt the killings but to ensure an orderly evacuation of all non-Rwandans. Everyone else was to be left behind. Anyone with white skin or a foreign passport was given a free trip out. Even their pet dogs were evacuated.

The 90 UN troops at the vocational school were native Belgians. They must have heard the stories of the militia at the roadblocks making sawing motions across their throats with machetes whenever they spotted a Belgian uniform.

Most of the *Interahamwe*, in fact, would be given standing orders to kill any person found carrying a Belgian passport. The militias surrounding the school did not have the firepower to take on the UN soldiers, so they lay on the grass drinking beer and chanting slogans and making threatening gestures. It must have been something of a relief for those Belgian soldiers to move out, knowing they would be killed cheerfully if they ran out of ammunition in a firefight. This was the clearest signal yet that the world was preparing to close its eyes, close its ears, and turn its back on what was happening.

The refugees knew what lay in store. Some begged the departing soldiers to shoot them in the head so they would not have to face slow dismemberment. Others tried to lie down in front of the Belgians' jeeps so they could not leave. Still others chased after the vehicles screaming, 'Do not abandon us!' The soldiers responded by shooing the refugees out of the way and firing warning shots to keep them from mobbing the departing convoy.

The massacre of 2,000 people began immediately after the last UN jeep had disappeared down the street.

I DECIDED TO get rid of that roadblock outside the hotel.

After I made sure that my wife and children were safely behind the doors of Room 126 I retreated into the manager's office with what would turn out to be one of the most formidable weapons I had in my possession. Its existence was kept secret from just about everybody I knew. It was taken out only in moments of complete privacy.

It was a black leather binder that I had purchased many years ago on a trip to Belgium. Inside were about 100 pages of closely written script, arranged in three columns on each page. There were entries for name, for title, and for phone number.

This was my personal directory of numbers for the elite circle of government and commerce in Rwanda. For years I had made a habit of collecting the business cards of local people who passed through the Diplomates or the Mille Collines and then entering their information in pencil in my binder at the end of the day. If they came into the hotel often enough, and if I liked them, I made sure that they occasionally received little gifts from me. Almost everyone in this book had a favourite drink and I tried to keep that information memorised. If I heard gossip that a particular person had been demoted, promoted, transferred, fired, or jailed I made a change to their title. Army officers, managers, doctors, ministers, professors—they were all listed in neat phalanxes, and the eraser marks and crossed-out titles next to their names were a rough map of the shifting sands of Rwandan politics. Now, of course, I had no idea who in this book was still in power—or even alive.

Many of the lines rang without anybody picking up. But then I found myself talking to a young military camp chief named, as it happened, Commander Habyarimana, though he was not related to the assassinated president. After a few minutes of conversation, I began to recall what I had heard about him, and I realised that I had come to the right place. The commander was an angry young man, but not for the same reasons that the *Interahamwe* were angry. His fury was directed at the presidential cronies, who he felt were responsible for turning Rwanda into an armed hothouse of people who hated one another for no good reason. Commander Habyarimana was just as disgusted as I was at the recent outbreaks of murder, and he promised to send me five of his men to help protect the hotel from invasion.

It was a good start, but I still wanted that roadblock gone.

I made a few more calls and finally got on the line with General Augustin Ndindiliyimana, a man whom I had known for several years. He was the commander of the National Police. I did not envy him his position. The army had drafted thousands of his best officers and appropriated a large part of the police arsenal, leaving him with a squad of, at most, 1,000 poorly trained and unequipped recruits to get control of the violent capital streets. Whatever he could do for me was going to be a major gift.

'Now, General,' I said quietly, in the voice of a man calling in a chip. 'We have some refugees over here, as you know, and that militia outside can come inside here any time they want.'

I knew that he was afraid of the *Interahamwe* himself, and perhaps also of being accused of not supporting the pogroms that had recently become the law of the land. But I kept at him.

'General, we are friends and will always be friends. You know that I would not ask this if I weren't in great danger. Something must be done about that roadblock. You could send some officers to encourage those boys to move elsewhere. There doesn't need to be bloodshed in front of my hotel.'

It continued on like this for a while, and he agreed he would help me. I wasn't certain if he was going to come through. But within a few hours the roadblock had disappeared.

THERE WERE TWO main reasons why the Hotel Mille Collines was left alone in those early days even while churches and schools became abattoirs.

The first was the initial confusion—and even timidity—of the militias. Raiding the hotel would have been a fairly high-profile operation and one that surely would have angered a lot of people in power. The Mille Collines had an image of being linked with the ruling elite and was viewed as something not to be tampered with. This mindset was not set in stone, however, and I'm sure it would have changed as the genocide wore on and the killers grew bolder.

The second reason we were able to get some breathing room is one I have already mentioned. We had five policemen standing outside thanks to my new friend, Commander Habyarimana. As fragile as this protection was, it was still much better than what we got from the UN, which amounted to just about nothing. They had a force of 2,700 troops stationed in Rwanda when the president was assassinated, and the majority of them had been evacuated along with all the foreigners. But about 500 peacekeepers were to be left in the country—God knows why—and 4 of them were staying as guests at the Mille Collines. They were well meaning but useless.

In fact, in my opinion the UN was *worse* than useless during the genocide. It would have been better for us if they did not exist at all, because it allowed the world to think that something was being done, that some parental figure was minding the store. Rwanda was left with a little more than 500 poorly trained UN soldiers who weren't even authorised to draw their weapons to stop a child from being sacrificed right in front of them. A total withdrawal would have been preferable to this farce.

On 16 April, I sent General Dallaire a letter informing him of our situation and asking him for some additional soldiers to safeguard our refugees. I heard later that he ordered the Bangladeshis to come help us but that their commander flat-out refused. Dallaire then rescinded his order. This was appalling to me. This incident underlined what a later United Nations report termed 'grave problems of command and control' within the mission and heightened my feeling that Dallaire could have and should have done more to put his men in between the killers and their victims.

This is not a condemnation of Romeo Dallaire as a person. I always liked him and felt he had a compassionate heart and a strong sense of morality. He had acted with honour and determination under extremely difficult circumstances—and with a shameful lack of support from his bosses on the UN staff and on the Security Council.

Early in the genocide he had insisted that with just 5,000 well-equipped soldiers he could have stopped the killings, and nobody has ever doubted his judgement. Dallaire had also proved himself to be a shrewd commander of the media during the crisis, granting multiple radio interviews in an attempt to get the world to pay attention to what was happening here. But I still feel he should have disobeyed his foolish orders from New York and acted more aggressively to stop street murders from taking place. There is no doubt he would have taken more casualties and turned the UN into a third belligerent in the civil war, but I am convinced this action would have slapped the world in the face and forced it to do something about the unspeakable carnage here.

If he did not have the stomach to do this then I think he should have made a spectacle out of resigning in protest over his hopeless job description. This, too, would have drawn some outrage to what was shaping up to be the most rapid genocide in world history. That he stayed in his job like a good soldier was a signal of a trust that the UN strategy of non-engagement was going to be a workable policy even though it appears despicable in retrospect.

THE GROUNDS of the Mille Collines were surrounded by a fence of bamboo and wire. It was about two metres high and intended by the architect to provide a visual sense of a snug compound, all the better for nervous foreign visitors to feel like their hotel was an island of safety embedded in the street grid of Kigali. If you pushed on the fence hard enough it would fall over. It provided an illusion of protection, nothing more.

From the corridor windows of the west wing, and from some of the room balconies, you could see over the top of this fence and also through the gaps. There were figures passing back and forth all day long on the other side, like backstage players making shadows on a curtain. Most were carrying spears and machetes. Some stopped to peer at us through the fence before moving on.

All the refugees, including my wife and children, were terrified of these shadows behind the bamboo. Tatiana's family was living in a small town near the city of Butare, where the killings had not yet started but were imminent. She was terrified for them, terrified for herself and our children and me. Everyone in the hotel felt a similar sense of dread. I felt terribly exposed here, but if we left it would be a sign to the killers that the Mille Collines was being surrendered. Besides, where else could we go? Nowhere in Rwanda was safe.

This belief of mine was the subject of a bitter fight between us. My wife confronted me in the parking lot and insisted we drive to safety in my home area of Murama. To back up her argument she enlisted my friend Aloise Karasankwavu, an executive with the Commercial Bank who was also in fear of his life. He was a persuasive speaker, and we jousted.

'In all of history there has never been a war brought to

that little town,' he told me. And in a sense he was right—at least in my own memory. The uprisings of 1959 and 1973 had created a lot of prejudice in my hometown, but they had never resulted in massacres. But there was no guarantee that blood wasn't being spilled there right now, without our knowledge.

'My friend, the whole country has gone mad,' I told him. 'Do you think Murama will be spared?'

'You are being misled by the Europeans, Paul. Even the *mwami* used to bring his cows there for safekeeping during times of trouble. Throughout history it has always been a refuge.'

'Aloise, even if that were true, how do you think you are going to get there? By flying? There are hundreds of roadblocks out there. You will be stopped and possibly killed.'

I looked at my wife, whose eyes were red and miserable. I only wished we had stayed in Brussels a week ago. I wanted to go to Murama as badly as she did—I still had brothers and sisters living there and I was tremendously worried for them—but I knew it would be risking death to go out on to the roads.

I am not necessarily proud of what I did next, but it happened. I lost my temper.

'Listen,' I told her, 'you have a driver's licence. You know how to drive.'

I held out the keys to the Suzuki jeep.

'Take these,' I told her. '*You* go to Murama.'

She looked back at me with furious eyes. We loved each other fiercely, but she was a Tutsi and I was a Hutu. This trivia of ancestry had never mattered the slightest bit in our marriage, but it mattered to the killers around us, and I loathed Rwanda more than I ever had before because of it. Once again I hated myself for being a lucky Hutu.

I was, of course, not going to surrender the keys to my wife under any circumstances. I only wanted to make a point. But it was a harsh one, and perhaps too harsh. I was trying to highlight our need to stay where we were and wait for the bloodletting to stop. But my wife was hurt by my words.

Aloise later took his wife and children and hitched a ride out of town, trying to get to Murama. He did not make five kilometres. The militia forced them all out of the car and separated him from his family. Amazingly, nobody was killed. Aloise went on foot to the village of Nyanza, and later on to Murama.

Later I would learn it was extremely fortunate that we decided not to leave the capital.

THE MILLE COLLINES grew more and more crowded. The rumour had spread throughout the town that the hotel was a safe haven from the killers. This was far from the truth, but hope becomes a kind of insanity in times of trouble. Those cunning or lucky enough to dodge the roadblocks were welcomed inside, even though the hotel stood every chance of becoming a killing zone without warning.

We charged no money for rooms. All the usual rules were irrelevant; we were now more of a refugee camp than a hotel. To take cash away from anyone would also be to strip them of money they might need to bribe their way out of being murdered.

One exception to this rule was alcohol. Those who could afford it were allowed to buy cocktails and bottles of beer and I used the proceeds to help buy food. It was one way of passing the hat. I also asked my bosses at Sabena to send me more cash and they were able to smuggle 200,000 Rwandan francs to me with the help of a humanitarian organisation that I should not name here.

Room, however, was our greatest asset, and one that could not have a price tag attached. I guarded it closely and had to fight for it on one occasion. One of my employees, Jacques, had taken it upon himself to live in the manager's apartment with his girlfriend. They were in there alone, and wasting crucial space. Other recalcitrant employees had followed his example and were claiming the choicest suites for themselves. In my mind, nobody had this prerogative. We needed to conserve and share everything we had, and that included the most precious thing we had to offer.

So I went to their room and knocked. 'I have two choices for you,' I said. 'Either you can move to smaller rooms or you can have some new neighbours.' After that I felt free to assign other refugees to sleep in the rooms they had been hogging for themselves. It also freed up yet more accommodations for those people who kept finding their way to the Mille Collines from the mayhem outside the fence. I resolved that nobody who could make it here would be turned away.

I CANNOT SAY that life was normal inside that crowded building, but what I saw in there convinced me that ordinary human beings are born with an extraordinary ability to fight evil with decency. We had Hutu and Tutsi sleeping beside each other. Strangers on the floor, many of whom had witnessed their families being butchered, would sometimes sleep spoon style just to feel the touch of another.

We struggled to preserve routines. It helped keep us sane. The bishop from St Michael's parish, a man named Father Nicodem, was one of our guests and he started holding regular masses in the ballroom. There was no such thing as privacy, but occasionally the occupants of a room would clear out to give a husband and a wife some time alone to make love. Several women became pregnant during the genocide—a way of fighting death with life, I suppose.

There was even a wedding. A seventeen-year-old girl was pregnant and her father was a very traditional Muslim who wanted to see her married so the child would not be born outside wedlock. The bishop agreed to perform the sacrament in the ballroom. She was married right there to her boyfriend, and nobody thought to question the difference in faiths.

I suppose it is natural to want a form of government, even in times of chaos (perhaps *especially* in times of chaos), and so five of the guests agreed to serve as a kind of high council to mediate disputes between the residents. I met regularly with them as a sort of chairman. You might have called the Hotel Mille Collines a kind of constitutional monarchy in those days, because I reserved the right to make all the final judgements on matters of day-to-day living. My kingship came not from a heavenly birthright but from the personnel department of the Sabena Corporation who'd appointed me interim manager via fax from Brussels on my first day here during the genocide.

In mid-April we lost our water and electricity. The killers had cut all of our utility lines in an attempt to make us uncomfortable. Perhaps they thought we would all drift away and then they could finish us off outside. It confirmed for me what I already knew—that they had designs to murder us—but it also gave me a bit of hope. The militia still did not want to risk an overt massacre at the hotel. We ran our emergency generator for a while with smuggled gasoline, but it eventually broke down, and so most of our time was spent in darkness.

Life immediately became even harder. The absence of electric lights created a mood I can only describe as disintegrating. How secure those lights had somehow made us feel! Everybody knew the killers liked to do their work in the dark, and the darkness inside the hotel made it feel like a permanent midnight.

Each room held, on average, eight frightened and brutalised people. They slept fitfully in the humid dark and often awoke to the sounds of a neighbour shouting or whimpering in a dream. There were mothers who cried out for sons who they would never see again, husbands who wept in secret for their disappeared wives. And though few people wanted to say it out loud, I think most shared my belief that we would all wind up dead ourselves when the militias outside finally decided to raid the Mille Collines. Those hotel rooms were like death-row prison cells, but we knew they were all that kept us from joining the ranks of the murdered for one more day. I worried there would be no more space, but we kept finding ways to fit more people inside our walls.

That these people crammed together in the rancid half light, each nursing their own horrors, could endure such conditions and keep on fighting on the side of life is proof to me not just of the human capacity for endurance but also of the basic decency inside all people that comes out when death appears imminent. To me, that old saying about one's life flashing before one's eyes is really a love for *all* life in those final moments, and not merely one's own; a primal empathy for *all* people who are born and must taste death. We clung to one another while the violence escalated, and most of us did not lose faith that order would be restored. Whether we would be there to see it was a separate question. All we could do was wait in the dark, with militia spies coming in and going out at all hours, even sleeping among us like fellow refugees. Cats and mice were in the same cage.

The loss of our utilities created another problem. Without water we would all start to dehydrate, forcing people to go out onto the streets rather than die of thirst. We had only a few days to figure out a solution. Every large compound in Rwanda—embassies, restaurants, and hotels—must have its own set of reserve water tanks built on the property as an emergency supply. Ours were located directly under the basement. I went to check their levels several times a day and watched them steadily dropping. There was no way to get a fresh delivery.

The solution came to me: we *did* have a reserve supply of water. In the swimming pool.

The pool was, in some ways, the most important part of the Mille Collines. Built in 1973 when the hotel was still new, it was smaller than Olympic size, but it got a lot of use from our European guests who brought children. A very ordinary looking pool altogether, but it held approximately 300,000 litres. At the time, we had nearly 800 guests. If we limited each person to six litres a day for their washing and drinking needs we could last for a little longer than two months. A rationing system would have to be devised so that each person could be insured of receiving a fair share. So we began a twice-daily ritual: every morning at 8:30 and every afternoon at 5:00 everyone was told to come down with the small plastic wastepaper bin from their room. They were allowed to dip it once into the pool water, which was already turning slightly yellow. In order to keep the water as clean as possible, we did not permit anyone to swim in it.

The room toilets no longer flushed, and so we had to devise a method to get rid of waste. If you poured the pool water into the commode it would still wash the waste down the pipes. The rooms began to smell a little worse, but at least there was no imminent sanitary emergency.

As for food, we were well stocked at first. Before the massacres started, Sabena had a limited partnership with its rival Air France to provide catering for their planes and their ready-to-eat meals for passengers were stored in the basement of the hotel. We did a count: there were approximately 2,000 trays. Those would be a limited luxury that we parcelled out stingily. It was very strange, of course, to be dining on rosemary chicken and potatoes au gratin during such a time.

When the airline meals ran low we had to come up with an alternative plan. Even though there were senseless murders happening all over the country—more than five every minute—the marketplaces were still open. People still had to shop, even in the middle of a genocide. I sent the hotel accountant, a man named Belliad, out with a truck and some cash to get us sacks of corn and beans and bundles of firewood. We tried to acquire rice and potatoes, but they were unavailable. I then asked the kitchen staff to cook up the food. Since they had no electricity to run the stoves and ovens we had to build a fire underneath the giant ficus tree on the lawn. Large pots of food were set in the blaze. We then served up this vegetable gruel in the large metal trays we had used for buffet-style meals on the lawn. We ate as a group twice a day, the hotel's fine china balanced on our laps. If the pool was now a village well, the lawn was now our cookhouse.

Now that was a sight! It used to be that we would use the back lawn to host weddings, conferences, and diplomatic receptions. Now our party was one of exhausted refugees in dirty clothes, some with machete wounds, many who had seen their friends turn into killers and their family turned into corpses, all lined up under the ficus tree for that simple act of eating that unconsciously signifies a small piece of hope, the willingness to store up fuel and keep living for another day.

SEVEN

WE LOST our phone service near the end of April. This was potentially disastrous: without a phone my black binder would be nearly useless. I could no longer call in favours with the Army brass or the government.

But then came a surprise. In 1987, when I was the assistant general manager, the Mille Collines received its first fax machine. We had to request an auxiliary phone line to support it, one that was not routed through the main switchboard. We had asked the technician to feed the fax line directly into the telephone grid of Kigali. This was a glitch I recalled when I was in the darkness of the secretary's office on the day the phones were cut. I was moved to pick up the handset attached to the side of the fax. There was a dial tone humming back at me, as beautiful a sound as I could have imagined.

I guarded this secret carefully. If the hardliners in the military found out that I had a phone, they would send in their thugs to find it and rip it out. So I let only the refugee committee use it and instructed them to keep quiet. The news could reach the ears of any renegade employees, which would be just like telling the *Interahamwe* themselves. I took to locking the door of the secretary's office whenever I was away so that unauthorised people could not wander in and discover my secret weapon. That phone was a lifeline.

I started staying up late at night, often until 4:00am, sending faxes to the Belgian and French Foreign Ministries, the White House, the United Nations, the Peace Corps—whoever I thought might be able to help stop an attack against the hotel. I tried to make the faxes brief and direct and forceful. I described the lack of food, the militia roaming outside, the desperate struggle of refugees to get into the hotel, the constant rumours that we were about to be invaded. I pleaded with these governments and agencies for some kind of assistance and protection. These letters were usually followed by a direct appeal via the little phone handset on the side. But I often felt as though I was a man shouting into an empty room.

One follow-up call to a White House staffer was typical. It was very late at night in Rwanda and the conversation went approximately like this:

'Yes, hello, my name is Paul Rusesabagina. I am the manager of the Hotel Mille Collines in the capital of Rwanda. I sent a fax today to the number your secretary gave me. I was calling to see if you received it.'

'Ah, yes, Mr Roos . . . Roossuhbaggian. How did you get this number?'

'I asked for you at the switchboard.'

'I see. You're calling from Rwanda?'

'Yes, Rwanda.'

'Yes, I remember the fax. I passed it along to a colleague of mine who handles foreign policy details. He will review it and get back to you.'

'So you didn't have a chance to read it? I was told you were the one to handle this matter.'

'No, that wouldn't be me. This has to be routed through proper channels. Have you also contacted the State Department or the embassy of the United States in Rwanda?'

'Your embassy left the country on the ninth of April.'

'Yes, that's right. I see.'

'I was really hoping you could bring this up with President Clinton directly. The situation here is very bad.'

'Well, as I have said, this has to be handled by the foreign policy staff. All I can say is that they will review the document and get back to you.'

'Who on that staff has been given my letter?'

'I can't really say for sure. I've got another call coming in and I have to let you go.'

To all the faxes and phone calls I made to the United States in those weeks, I never once received a reply.

ON 26 APRIL Thomas Kamilindi, who was one of the city's best journalists, gave a telephone interview to Radio France International in which he described the living conditions at the hotel, the lack of water, and the state of the ongoing genocide and civil war. He also described the rebel advance on the capital. The interview was intended for listeners in Paris and all over the French-speaking world, but it was also broadcast in Kigali.

Apparently some of the *génocidaires* had torn themselves away from RTLM long enough to listen, because there was a death order out for Thomas within half an hour.

Friends in the military urged him to sneak out of the hotel and find another place to hide, but I urged him not to leave. I had been in touch with General Bizimungu and General Dallaire about his situation. We had him switch rooms to fool any spies who might have known where he was staying. Some of the refugees were terribly unhappy with Thomas for focusing attention on the Mille Collines—they thought he only reminded the militia thugs that we were here, dancing just out of their reach. Some of the guests wanted to hand Thomas over as a kind of peace offering to the militia.

A friend of Thomas's was sent to the hotel that day to assassinate him. His name was Jean-Baptiste Iradukunda and he was with an Army intelligence unit. They had known each other since they were children. Thomas was smart enough to boldly step out into the corridor and meet his would-be killer face-to-face. They started to talk. I am convinced that had Thomas tried to cower—or worse, to run— he would have been shot. It is so much harder to kill someone after you have talked as one human being to another.

'Listen, Thomas,' said the soldier after a while. 'I have been sent to kill you. But I cannot. I am going to leave now. But somebody else will be coming later and they will not be as hesitant.'

Immediately after Thomas gave the interview, an Army colonel called from the hotel entrance. He was a man I had known for a long time. I went out to say hello, and he wasted no time telling me what he was there to do.

'Paul, I am here to pick up that dog!'

'You are fighting against a dog, colonel?' I asked him with a small laugh. 'Let's go talk about this.'

We went back to my office and I asked a chambermaid to bring us drinks. Sitting in the quiet, and without an audience to encourage him, I could already see that some of the rage had leaked away from his countenance. But he remained adamant: he was going to have the head of Thomas Kamilindi. The interview he had given was an act of treason against the government of Rwanda and the Army. The execution order against Thomas was real and I resolved to save his life by any means I could.

I tried flattery first.

'Colonel,' I began, 'you are too high ranking an officer to be concerned with such a small matter. Thomas is a small man.'

'I have orders, Paul.'

'You have orders to kill a dog? That is an insulting job. Don't you have boys in the militia who are supposed to do that kind of work?'

'It is not a small matter. He is a traitor and must pay.'

I could see that I was getting somewhere, but I switched my argument.

'Listen, Colonel. Let's say you take that dog out with your own hands and kill him. You will have to live with that for the rest of your life. You did not hear this radio interview. You do not know what was said. You are proposing to take a man's life without a trial.'

'Paul, I have my orders. Where is he?'

'Even if you were to order it done instead of doing it yourself, it would be the same blood on your hands.'

It went on like this for quite some time. I don't know why he kept talking to me. But the longer he sat there and sipped his Carlsberg the greater the odds were that Thomas was going to survive to see the sun go down.

'Listen,' I finally told him, after more than two hours had gone by, 'this war has made everyone a little bit crazy. It is understandable. You are tired. You need to relax. I have some good red wine in the cellar. Let me bring you a carton. I will

have it loaded into your jeep. Go home tonight and have a
drink and we will talk more about this tomorrow, when we
can come to a compromise.'

Everything I suggested came to pass—almost. I did find
some red wine from the cellar to spare. I had it loaded into his
military jeep. So far as I know, he did go home and enjoy some
of it that night. But the compromise never happened. The
colonel did not come back and Thomas was not executed.

I HAD DOZENS of conversations like this throughout the genocide, surreal exchanges in which I would find myself sitting
across a desk or a cocktail table with a man who might have
committed dozens of killings that day. In several cases I saw
flecks of blood on their uniforms or work shirts. Human lives
almost always hung in the balance during these talks. But
they were always lubricated with beer or cognac, and usually
ended with my gifting that day's murderer with a bottle of
French champagne or whatever else I could dig out of my
dwindling drinks cabinet.

I have since thought a great deal about how people are able
to maintain two attitudes in their minds at once. Take the
colonel: he had come fresh from a world of machetes, road
gangs, and random death and yet was able to have a civilised
conversation with a hotel manager over a glass of beer and let
himself be talked out of committing another murder. He had a
soft side and a hard side and neither was in absolute control of
his actions. It was like those Nazi concentration camp guards
who could come home from a day manning the gas chambers
and be able to play games with their children, put a Bach
record on the turntable, and make love to their wives before
getting up to kill more innocents. The cousin of brutality is a
terrifying normalcy. So I tried never to see these men in terms
of black or white. I saw them instead in degrees of *soft* and
hard. It was the soft that I was trying to locate inside them. If
sitting down with abhorrent people and treating them as
friends is what it took to get through to that soft place, then I
was more than happy to pour the Scotch.

Another principle helped me in these conversations, and it

is this: facts are almost irrelevant to most people. We make decisions based on emotion and then justify them later with whatever facts we can scrounge up in our defence.

When we shop for a car we make sure to investigate the gas mileage, look at the leg room, peer at the engine, and evaluate the cost, but the decision to buy it always comes down to your gut feelings about the car. How will I look behind the wheel? Will it be fun to drive? What will my friends think? 'Reason' is usually an afterthought, nothing more than a cover story for the feelings inside.

The same is true in politics. Let me give you a rather pertinent example. I seriously doubt the leadership of Rwanda really *believed* that average Tutsis were spies who had melted into the general population. I think they whipped up the flames of fear to create that belief. They were appealing to a dark place in the heart—that unreconstructed part of us that comes down from our ancestors, who lived in constant fear of beasts in the night. There was an emotional reason for people to hate and fear the Tutsi, and nonsense 'facts' were invented to justify the violence. The ethnic violence was only a tool for a set of cynical men to hold on to their power— which is perhaps man's ultimate emotional craving.

It is a dismal principle. But I could use it to save lives.

When I took that colonel into my office, poured him some beer, and puffed up his ego it was not about the facts of the matter at all. It was about his insecurity in his position and his need to feel like an important person. I created a web of words in which the choice I did not want to see him make— killing Thomas—was running counter to his emotional needs. I made him believe that such a loutish task was beneath him. It was not that the colonel was a stupid man. Even the best of us can be slaves to our self-regard.

THEY KEPT coming and coming. From houses in Kabeza to besieged churches in Nyamirambo, they heard about the safe haven at the Mille Collines.

One of them was a man named Augustin Hategeka, who had run from his home with his pregnant wife when the killings broke out. They had taken refuge in a patch of forest and eaten scavenged food for several days. Augustin had stood guard, watching for killers as she gave birth to their new son in the shade of a bush. With the help of some Hutu friends, the family found temporary refuge in St Paul's pastoral centre and I sent Army soldiers to fetch them to the Mille Collines.

Over the next several days Augustin and I talked about the things we had witnessed. Our conversation went something like this:

'My neighbours started killing my neighbours,' he told me. 'I saw people I have known for years taking out machetes and screaming orders. Old people were murdered. Children were murdered. I heard screams.'

'I know,' I told him. 'The same thing happened in Kabeza.'

'They chopped innocent people to pieces in the street. They cut the tendons in their legs so they could not run away. I thought I knew these neighbours of mine,' he told me.

'I don't think anybody knows anybody any more,' I told him.

I remember another guest, whom I will here call Jane, who had worked as a nurse alongside my wife. Her story was not out of the ordinary for Rwanda that spring. Jane was of mixed race and the family had been marked for elimination. A squad of *Interahamwe* broke into their house and began to do their work. Jane managed to scramble into the kitchen and hide underneath a few sacks of charcoal. She stayed there while her husband and two children were cut into pieces in the other room. How she managed to remain quiet I will never know. She stayed under the coal for several hours and then crawled out to see the bodies of her family strewn about the front room. She fled from the house and, with the help of a neighbour, found her way to St Paul's Church. We sent a car with policemen to pick her up. Her eyes were completely empty. I recognised the look. It was all over the hotel.

IN ALL OF this, I was fortunate to have a handful of soldiers who wore the blue helmet of the United Nations. I have previously expressed my disgust with the UN as a collective body, but those individuals serving in its name were capable of bravery. The men in my hotel displayed courage in going out on to the streets of Kigali to fetch the condemned. They were chauffeurs through hell. Two in particular, a captain from Senegal named Mbaye Daigne and his companion, Captain Senyo of Ghana, became legendary for their ability to dodge the *Interahamwe* and plucking refugees from their houses. It was a task that probably violated the ridiculous mission parameters handed down from New York, but these rules deserved to be broken.

These soldiers never used the hotel van; that would have been inviting death, because everybody in town knew that we were a haven for refugees. They used instead a white jeep with the UN logo. Rwandan soldiers also helped rescue people. One day they went out to find a prominent politician who had been hiding in a private house. On the way to the hotel they were stopped at a roadblock manned by an especially savage bunch of militia. There were corpses stacked up on either side, the hacked-up remains of people who had produced the wrong kind of identity card. The car got an unusually thorough search and they discovered the refugee hiding in the back.

'Where are you bringing this cockroach?' they demanded.

The soldier thought quickly. 'We are taking him to the ministry of defence,' he said. 'Now let us pass before the Army starts to wonder where we are.'

That was good enough for the militia and our refugee made it inside the Mille Collines without further incident. I suppose it was fortunate for us there were no mobile phones in Rwanda in 1994, before the widespread use of mobile phones. As we have seen, the violence was inherently full of chaos and mistakes. In such an environment it was possible to make a convincing bluff that you were working for somebody in authority without anyone able to check your story. I have said before that tools of murder can be turned into tools of life. If we had had mobile phones in Rwanda, the *Interahamwe* would have been more efficient, but we also would have been able to coordinate more rescues right under their noses.

I used my secret fax phone many times to get a lead on

where a particular refugee might be hiding. One of them was my friend Odette Nyiramilimo, and her husband, Jean-Baptiste Gasasira, and their children, who I hoped were still in their house. In the first days of the genocide they had traded their family car, stereo, television, and other goods to some policemen in exchange for a ride south of Kigali, to where they thought they might be safe. But the policemen reneged, leaving my friends to try and flee through the marshes on their own. They were captured by *Interahamwe* and led in for interrogation, which they managed to escape. But in the chaos of war somebody made a mistake and put their names on the list of people who had been eliminated. Odette and Jean-Baptiste heard their own names being read on the rebel army's radio station as among those who had been killed. This took the heat away temporarily and, not knowing where else to go, they went back to their house and stayed out of sight, afraid even to answer the telephone. I rang and rang again. But one day when their food was almost gone, the phone started ringing.

'Don't pick it up!' ordered Jean-Baptiste.

'It's all the same,' said Odette. 'We are going to die of hunger here anyway.' She answered the phone and it was me on the other end.

She could not have been more surprised. 'We thought you were dead!' she said.

'I thought you were dead, too,' I answered. 'But don't go anywhere. I'm going to organise a rescue.'

I negotiated again with Commander Habyarimana for the services of a Lieutenant named Nzaramba. His uniform and vehicle would give him partial, but not total, protection against the militias, and so it was going to be a risky operation. Not wanting to risk having the whole family in his jeep, Nzaramba made three separate trips. Odette came first with her son Patrick, and they were stopped at a roadblock close to the hotel.

'Where are you going?' they demanded.

She pulled out a supply of malaria pills and showed them to her would-be killer.

'I am coming to take care of the manager's children inside the Mille Collines,' she said. 'They are sick.'

It worked. When she came in her eyes were glassy and faraway. I had not seen her since the killing had started.

Once she came out of her daze Odette told me that being inside the Mille Collines was like being in a land of the resurrected dead; she was seeing many people who she had heard had been killed.

The next time Nzaramba went out he came back with Odette's children in the back of his jeep, and they too were stopped at a roadblock. This one happened to be right in front of the warehouse of an old friend of mine named Georges Rutaganda.

'Where are you going?' asked the man who leaned in their window. 'Where are your parents?'

'My father is manning a roadblock and my mother is at the hospital,' said Odette's son. The killers did not buy the story and withdrew to discuss what should be done. The machetes were just coming out when a car pulled up. Inside was Georges Rutaganda.

Let me pause here a minute and tell you about this man. We grew up together. He went on to become the vice president of the *Interahamwe* and a man very close to the party of President Juvenal Habyarimana. I tried not to let this get in the way of our friendship. I did tell him several times before the killing started, 'Listen, Georges. What you are doing is wrong. You are going down the wrong path.' But he never got angry with me for my opinions. This absence of acrimony was a key element of our relationship. We both knew where the other stood politically, but our professional dealings continued, as did the presence of good feelings. It was like that German expression I mentioned earlier: *Dienst ist Dienst und Schnapps ist Schnapps*. We continued to do business together even during the genocide. In fact, he was the main supplier of beer, toilet paper, and other necessities to the Mille Collines. Yet another irony of Rwanda: the man near the heart of the militia movement was making cash on the side by helping the refugees. I used these deal-making sessions to take him into my office and speak to him, as only one friend from the hills can do to another. 'Listen, Georges,' I would tell him, 'I would like you to be very careful with my hotel. It would be very bad for me if any of your *Interahamwe* came inside. Please do me a favour and tell them it is off-limits.'

Several people have criticised me for staying close to such a bad man, but I have never apologised for it. People are never completely good or completely evil. And in order to fight evil you sometimes have to keep evil people in your orbit. Even the worst among them have their soft side, and if you can find that part of them, you can accomplish a great deal of good.

So at the roadblock Georges looked inside the car and saw children he thought he recognised.

'Aren't you the kids of Jean-Baptiste Gasasira?' he asked, and they nodded, frightened, not knowing what else to say. Now it was clear: they were cockroaches. They would be killed without further delay.

Georges then stepped in. Perhaps he had a soft spot for Odette and Jean-Baptiste, who had gone to the same university as he had in the 1970s. Perhaps he recalled that Jean-Baptiste had been his parents' personal physician. Perhaps this bankroller of the militias never agreed with the genocide that unfolded from his actions. I cannot say. But he turned to the captain of the roadblock and berated him.

'Let them go right now,' he demanded. And one of the top officials of the murderous *Interahamwe* waved the lieutenant and the jeep and the children on towards the Mille Collines.

JUST AS I DEALT with some questionable people during the genocide, I also sheltered some questionable guests. Several times in those days I drank cognac with a man named Father Wenceslas Munyegeshaka, who was the priest at the Sainte Famille church just down the hill from my hotel. He had abandoned the black robes of a priest and was wearing jeans and a T-shirt and carrying a pistol in his belt.

His church had been turned into a refuge for Tutsis, but the militias felt a lot more comfortable going inside it than they did the Mille Collines. Hundreds of people were taken from their refuge inside its red-brick walls and murdered elsewhere. And Father Wenceslas showed no interest in stopping it from happening. I knew that he even had a working telephone in the sacristy and I don't think he made phone calls to save anybody from execution, even though he also had political contacts.

It turned out that he had more reasons to be afraid than just his job. One day he came to the hotel with an elderly woman in tow. 'Paul,' he said, 'I am bringing you my cockroach.'

It was his own mother, a Tutsi. I assigned her to live in Room 237 without saying anything further.

Another person who found his way to us was a man I will call Fred, though that is not his real name. He was one of my neighbours from Kabeza, but not a very popular person. He had beaten an old man to death several years before and had been released from prison just before the genocide. He was a Tutsi, which made him an automatic target, but he was also a wanted man because he had three sons serving in the RPF. In the opening days of the genocide he was one of the neighbours who took shelter in my house. On that day, 9 April, when the Army had come to take me to the Diplomates, he made several desperate comments, shaking as he spoke. 'I know these people are looking for me. Let me go out there so they can kill me before they kill everyone here.' Fred was not my best friend, but when he showed up later at the Mille Collines I was happy to see him alive and made sure that he got a place in a room and was protected from harassment by those who knew his story. There is no sin so great that somebody should die for it. When you start thinking like that you become an animal yourself.

I suppose Fred was another one of those wounded lions that my father had been so fond of talking about. There was a whole pack of them living in my hotel. By the end of May we had 1,268 people crammed into space that had been designed for 300 at most. There were up to 40 people living inside my own room. They were in the corridors, in the ballroom, on bathroom floors, and inside pantries. I had never planned for it to get this big. But I had made a promise to myself at some point that I would never turn anybody away.

Nobody was killed. Nobody was wounded or beaten in the Mille Collines. That was an extraordinary piece of luck for us, but I do not think there is anything extraordinary about what I did for them with a cooler of beer, a leather binder, and a hidden telephone. I was doing the job that I had been entrusted to do by the Sabena Corporation—that was my greatest and only pride in the matter.

I am a hotel manager.

EIGHT

WAKING UP before the sunrise has been my habit ever since I was a boy. Before the killing started that pre-dawn quiet was one of my favourite times of the day. I would slip out of bed gently, so as not to wake Tatiana, and go out into the yard and potter about at various tasks. There was a radio on the outside ledge and I would listen to the news. This was one of the only times in the day I would have all to myself.

During the genocide I yearned to have one of those quiet mornings in the yard, when the news was just soccer scores and road closings instead of incitements to murder and lists of the dead. I still woke up in the hour before dawn, in a room jammed with people, and I craved that time when I could be all alone. So I developed an early-morning ritual of visiting my favourite spot in the whole hotel: the roof. Here, the whole of the city of Kigali spread out before you.

The hotel was built on the slope of Kiyovu Hill and the panorama is gorgeous. Even in the midst of war and death this eyrie of mine had a peaceful aspect if you didn't look at any spot too closely and focused just on the hills and the sky. To look at the streets for longer than a few seconds was to see homes with broken windows, wrecked vehicles, roadblocks, and corpses everywhere.

To the west, along the line of the far mountain ridge, you

could see the road that snaked away down the valley. It led eventually to the city of Gitarama, where the crisis government held its seat. To the north was the area held by the rebel army. In the middle was Amahoro Stadium, where I knew there were over 10,000 Hutu refugees crammed inside, sleeping on the soccer field. It was a larger version of the Mille Collines, only with a different ethnic majority and living conditions that were far worse than what we had. There was nothing to cover anybody from the rain. Those who were wounded had no real medical care and their cuts grew infected and gangrenous. There was nowhere for people to relieve themselves and so the field became a stinking heath.

These mornings on my roof, with the sky melting to blue from purple, I took the time to prepare myself for what I knew was coming. I was going to die. I had done far too much to cross the architects of the genocide. The only question would be the exact time, and the method of my death, and that of my wife and our children.

I dreaded machetes. The *Interahamwe* were known to be extremely cruel with the people they chopped apart; first cutting tendons so the victims could not run away, then removing limbs so that a person could see their body coming apart slowly. Family members were often forced to watch, knowing they were next. Their wives and their children were often raped in front of them while this was happening. Priests helped kill their congregations. In some cases, the congregations helped kill their priests. Tutsi wives went to sleep next to their Hutu husbands and awoke to find the blade of a machete sawing into their neck, and above them, the grimacing face of the man who had sworn to love and cherish them for life. Children threw their grandparents down pit toilets and heaved rocks on top of them until the cries stopped. Unborn babies were sliced from their mothers' wombs and tossed about like soccer balls. Severed heads and genitals were on display.

The dark lust unleashed in Rwanda went beyond friendships and beyond politics and beyond even hate itself—it had become killing for killing's sake, killing for sport, killing for nothing. It raged on, all around the hotel, on the capital's streets and in the communes and in the hills and in every little spidery valley.

There was a stash of money in the hotel safe. The money was for a last bribe, something to pay the militia to let me and my family be shot rather than face a machete.

SEVEN TIME ZONES away, in the United States, the diplomatic establishment was tying itself up in knots avoiding saying a certain word. A Pentagon study paper dated 1 May 1994, sums up the prevailing attitude. The author was suggesting a way for the US to take limited action in Rwanda without getting in too deep. 'Genocide investigation: language that calls for an international investigation of human rights abuses and possible violations of the genocide convention—*Be Careful. Legal at State was worried about this yesterday—Genocide finding could commit [the US government] to actually "do something".* ' So the pressure was on. There had to be a way to call what was happening by something other than its rightful name.

It is not as though there was an information blackout. The US government—and, in fact, most of its citizens who watched the news—knew what was taking place in Rwanda. Romeo Dallaire had made himself available to anyone who wanted to interview him by telephone, and had taken to calling the slaughter 'ethnic cleansing'. The BBC's courageous reporter Mark Doyle was granted access to the hopeless UN mission and filed a story every day about the ongoing slaughter. Journalists slowly realised this was more than just another African civil war.

By the end of May the broadcasts of the nightly television news and the newspapers in America were full of accounts of mass murders and bodies floating down Akagera River towards Lake Victoria. But even with this incontrovertible evidence the US government would not let itself admit that what was happening was a genocide. This played right into the official lies of the *génocidaires*: the killings were a spontaneous uprising of grief among the villagers at the assassination of the president and not something that had been carefully planned.

The peculiar avoidance of the word *genocide* was for a reason. The word was coined by a Polish-born lawyer named Raphael Lemkin who then helped persuade the United Nations to pass a resolution, in 1948, expressly forbidding the destruction of a group of people because of their religion, nationality, or ethnicity. Lemkin had been horrified by the Turkish slaughter of the Armenians during World War I, but was even more appalled that it seemed to be no crime in the conventional sense. Nations could not be held accountable for murder in the same way people could. Furthermore, there was nothing legal or otherwise that separated the random killing of civilians from the attempt to eliminate an entire race.

Grappling for a way to express the magnitude of the Nazis' plans for and actions against the Jews during World War II, Lemkin decided that we needed a new word to embody the concept. It had to be short and easy to pronounce and convey a certain horror. After some experimentation he chose *genocide*, blending the Greek word for 'race' (*genus*) with the Latin word for 'kill' (*cide*). The word caught on and was quickly added to *Webster's New International Dictionary*.

UN member states signed a treaty in 1948 threatening criminal penalties for the leaders of any regime found to have conducted an extermination campaign against a particular religious or racial group. But the United States dragged its feet and it was not until 1986 that the US Senate finally ratified the agreement. By then genocides had been carried out in Cambodia, in Nigeria, in Pakistan, in Burundi, and in many other places on the globe.

In the case of Rwanda, if US officials actually said the word 'genocide' out loud, they might have been morally and legally compelled to act under the terms of the 1948 treaty. Few officials in Washington wanted that with a mid-term congressional election around the corner. Everyone in the Clinton administration was mindful of the disaster in Somalia that had occurred the previous October, when eighteen Army Rangers were killed in the *Black Hawk Down* incident that seemed to symbolise everything that could go wrong with peacekeeping missions. Even though our situation was radically different in origin and nature, anything that called for a commitment of American troops to Africa was anathema in the halls of the US State Department. And, of course, there was no natural resource in Rwanda that anybody cared about either—only human beings in danger.

BEFORE THE KILLING in the hotel could start they would have to get rid of me. I was standing between them and the prize targets inside. We had senators, doctors, ministers, priests, maids, peasants, housewives, intellectuals. Inside the Mille Collines was the remnant of what might be called the 'Tutsi aristocracy'—the living embodiment of the phantom enemy that the hate radio was preaching against—as well as a good contingent of moderate Hutus who did not agree with the genocide. The hotel was becoming a holy grail for the killers, a giant resting place of cockroaches they were eager to wipe out for good. I was worried we would be invaded by the militia any day. I also knew that that would mark the day of my death. We were all condemned prisoners, but we did not know the date of our execution, and we woke up every morning wondering if we were in our last few hours of consciousness.

In the early morning of 23 April I went to bed at around 4:00am. I had spent several hours on the phone in the office, getting nowhere, as usual. I quietly unlocked the door of the suite so as not to wake up the other occupants, and fell into the spot that Tatiana had saved for me on the bed. I knew nothing but blackness for two hours and then I felt my wife pushing me. 'Reception says there is someone on the phone that wants you,' she said.

A man whom I'll call Lieutenant Mageza came on the line. I knew him, but his voice sounded like cold marble. 'Are you the manager?' he asked.

I was still fighting my way out of a deep sleep and my answer was thick. 'Yes. What is it?'

'I have an order from the Ministry of Defence for you to evacuate the hotel within thirty minutes,' he said. 'If you do not I will do it for you.'

'What do you want me to tell the guests? Where are they

going to go? Who is taking them? What security has been organised?'

The lieutenant was having none of it. 'Do you not understand what I am saying? This hotel must be evacuated within thirty minutes. Tell the people here to "go as they came".' He used an expression in Kinyarwanda that means, in effect, if they came by car, they will leave by car. If they came on foot, they will leave by foot. The vehicles that had brought most of the guests were long gone, of course, and so most would have to simply walk away. This spelled certain death for nearly everybody in the hotel.

I had to take action. And my suspicion was that this lieutenant had not been ordered to do the killing himself. The idea was to shoo us out and let the street militia do the actual murdering. It would be less systematic, and many would surely get away, but it would eliminate the government's long-standing problem of the Mille Collines.

I decided then that the best course of action would be to—as the American phrase goes—'kiss his butt'.

'Yes, I understand what you are saying. I appreciate you informing me of the situation. I will comply with what you say. But can I please just have half an hour to get myself awake and get showered before I do what you want? Then I will begin the evacuation.'

'Thirty minutes,' he said, and hung up.

I did not wash. I did not even put my pants on. I ran five flights up to the roof and looked down at the street. What I saw opened a hole in my stomach. The militia had the place completely surrounded. There were hundreds of them holding spears, machetes, and rifles. It would be a killing zone here in an hour.

I raced down the stairs and back into my room, where I quickly calculated global time. It was early to be calling Europe, but far too late to be calling the United States, which had been worthless anyway. There was only one thing I could think to do: get on the phone with somebody in the Rwandan Army who outranked the lieutenant and could order him to rescind his evacuation order. I pulled out the black binder and started calling all my generals. Though it was early in the morning I was able to reach several, and I described the threat with what I hoped was the right amount of urgency. Those that I reached knew that the Mille Collines was being set up and were not willing to say who had given the order. I was still phoning for help when a knock came at the door from a reception clerk. Somebody wanted to see me out front, he said. I started to dress, thinking it was probably the last time I would ever put on a pair of pants or button a shirt.

I went down to the reception area to meet Lieutenant Mageza. I was surprised instead to see a very short man wearing the insignia of a colonel on his shoulder and assorted colourful medals on his chest. I recognised him as a high-ranking police officer named Ntiwiragabo.

'What is the situation here?' he asked.

'I have been asked to evacuate the hotel,' I told him.

'The plan has been changed and this is why I'm here,' he said.

I knew then that one of my phone calls had worked. This colonel had been sent over to help me. I told him that the order had been given by a lieutenant and that it was a very bad order that could have terrible repercussions for the Rwandan government. There would be killing outside that would shock the conscience of the world community.

The short colonel nodded, with an unfocused look in his eyes, and said that he would take care of the situation. I found out later that he had been sent over by the chief of the police, General Ndindiliyimana. His rank carried the day. The militia and the soldiers were immediately dispersed and the evacuation order was called off.

I thanked the colonel profusely.

'Sir, you have saved lives today,' I told him.

'I am only doing my job,' he told me curtly, and walked away.

I KNEW THIS PEACE was fragile, and so I decided to switch from butt kissing to bluster. What I was about to try was a serious risk, but I saw it as the only way to ensure that an invasion could be prevented for at least the next few days. I paced around for a few minutes, took a deep breath, and then telephoned the Diplomates Hotel and asked for Colonel Théoneste Bagosora, one of the leaders of the genocide, who was staying in Room 205.

'Colonel,' I said in my most officious voice, 'I am sorry to disturb you. I have received an order from the Ministry of Defence to close down the Mille Collines, and as the general manager of all Sabena properties in Rwanda, I must therefore also close the Diplomates.'

I could practically hear his veins bulging on the other end of the phone.

'*Who* has given such orders?!' he screamed at me.

'I do not know; they were relayed through a lieutenant. He said his name was Mageza.'

'If you try to close this hotel, we will break down the doors and get back inside.'

'If you want, you can do that, but it is my duty and obligation to close down all the Sabena hotels in Rwanda,' I told him. 'I didn't want to take you by surprise. I only want you to have enough time to pack your things.'

He was silent for a minute.

'Well, that order has now changed.'

This is what I was waiting to hear. But I decided to press my advantage even further.

'Colonel, we can come to a compromise,' I told him, as if *I* was the one who had the power to dictate terms. 'I will not close the Diplomates. But I need water over here. Can you please send us back the water truck you took away from the Mille Collines?'

'Yes, yes,' he said impatiently.

'There is another thing,' I told him. 'There are a group of people staying in the manager's house of the Diplomates. They are valuable employees. We need them over here. Can you please see that they arrive at the Mille Collines safely?'

I think this was the first he knew that there even *was* a manager's cottage, let alone that a group of my neighbours had been staying there this whole time, right under the noses of the *génocidaires*. They had been kept fed by a courageous bellboy.

Bagosora didn't waste any more time. 'Yes, fine, goodbye,' he said, and hung up.

Within the hour a red Toyota pickup pulled up to the Mille Collines. Inside were the neighbours I had not seen since the day their lives were purchased with francs from the hotel safe. A truck also arrived to refill our swimming pool and we had fresh water to drink for the first time in weeks. It was courtesy of one of the vilest proponents of genocide that Central Africa has ever seen. Somewhere I could hear my father laughing.

NINE

ONE OF THE MOST honest conversations I had during the genocide happened near the end of it.

General Augustin Bizimungu, the Army chief of staff, came to see me in my room. It was one of the few times in those few months that I didn't need anything from him. Neither did he want anything from me. We drank and talked for several hours.

He looked awful. There were folds of darkened skin hanging under his eyes. He seemed to have aged twenty years since the time before the killing started. We talked about the rebel army advancing from the east. They had been making slow but steady progress towards Kigali, aiming to link up with their detachment dug in at the parliament building. RPF leader Paul Kagame had fewer troops, but while in exile he had instilled an impressive level of discipline and commitment into his army.

There was now some talk of a swap between the warring armies: the rebels would release the Hutu refugees in Amahoro Stadium if the Rwandan Army would let the people inside the hotel go over to the rebel side. These discussions filled me with hope, but they also terrified me. Being freed from the constant threat of slaughter seemed like a kind of heaven, but to be labelled a rebel prize seemed incredibly dangerous. I was afraid it would only boost our attractiveness as a target for the doped-up militias, who were a law unto themselves.

Bizimungu slumped in his chair as we talked, his drink barely touched beside him.

'Listen, General,' I finally said. 'You are now the leader of a bunch of killers and looters and rapists. Are you sure you can win?'

His reply astonished me.

'Paul, I am a soldier,' he said. 'We lost this war a long time ago.'

Perhaps he had an inkling of what would be in store for him: a human rights tribunal and lifetime imprisonment in a jail cell. Or perhaps he had grown tired of all the murders around him. I am not certain what he was thinking then, but I saw that he could no longer hide the aura of defeat around him and his soldiers. I also knew that we were drawing near to the end of the war.

ON 3 MAY, the United Nations attempted to evacuate the Hotel Mille Collines.

The Army and the rebels had struck a deal: a few dozen refugees from the stadium would be swapped for an equal number of refugees from the hotel. They would be taken to the airport and whisked out of the country.

There was a terrible catch for us, though. Only those refugees who could secure invitations from people living abroad would be allowed to leave the hotel. This seemed very unfair to me. Those people most likely to have overseas contacts were the rich and the powerful. The Tutsi and moderate Hutu peasants we had with us had virtually no chance of leaving. But these were the conditions that had been negotiated by the armies and I had to accept them.

This put me in an awkward position, for I happened to be one of those privileged few who could legitimately arrange for transport out of the country for me and my family. *Out.* There seemed to be no more seductive concept: out of this phantasmagoria of knives and blood, out of the dark rooms that smelled like faeces and sweat, out of this entire pointless conflict and the idiotic life-or-death ethnic definitions and away from the power-drunk fools with their empty smiles and machetes and into a safe place of clean sheets and air-conditioning and warm baths and no worry about anything at all that mattered. Out.

I could have it. I could have it *tomorrow*.

But I could not. I really could not. I knew that if I took this opportunity to leave I would be removing one of the only remaining barriers in between the militias and the guests. Nobody here would be left to act as a middleman between the killers and the refugees. Nobody else had those years of favours and free drinks to cash in. I could donate my black binder to somebody else, but it would be useless to them. If I left and people were killed, I would never be at peace. Food would never taste good again; I could never enjoy my freedom. It would be as though I had killed those people myself. The refugees had even come to me and said, 'Listen, Paul. We are told you are leaving tomorrow. Please let us know so that we can go to the roof of the hotel and jump because we cannot bear to be tortured with machetes.'

But one thing I did for myself: I used my contacts with the Sabena Corporation to secure invitations out for my whole family. I was not so courageous a man that I could bear to see my family in danger any longer. I sincerely hoped that I would not be depriving anybody more needy through this action, but if I saw my wife or children murdered when I *knew* I once had the chance to see them to safety, my life would be ruined. This was the most painful decision I have ever made in my life. I had decided to stay and face whatever would come.

Beyond this I had no control over who would be staying or leaving. This was a profound relief, because I did not want to have that decision over life or possible death. On 2 May, I, together with the refugee committee, presented a list to the United Nations soldiers of all those refugees who had obtained invitations via my fax telephone. Handing over that list made me extremely uncomfortable, as it spelt out who was leaving and who was staying. This could have put lives in danger. But I had no choice. All I could do was hope that the UN would not let it leak to the killers.

Around midnight, I found my wife and children awake in our room. I previously had not had the courage to tell them I would not be going with them in the evacuation, but the time had arrived. I told them, 'I have made a different decision. I am remaining with the refugees. You are leaving.'

Everyone raised their voices and talked as if they were one person.

'But how can you stay?'

'Listen. I am the only person here who can negotiate with these killers outside. If people inside this hotel are killed, I will never be able to sleep again. I'll be a prisoner of my own conscience.

'Please,' I told them. 'Please accept and go.'

The next day, at approximately 5:30pm, I saw my wife and children off at the roundabout in front of the hotel. They and the other fortunate guests were loaded into UN trucks. While I helped them climb inside, I tried to be almost casual about it, telling them I would see them soon, as if they were off to the grocery store, but inside my heart was breaking. I said nothing special, nothing *climactic*, because that would have upset everybody, me most of all.

I watched the first truck go by, and then the second. In Rwandan culture it is never acceptable for a man to cry, but I came very close that evening. I made it through those awful minutes the same way I made it through the entire genocide: by losing myself in the details of work.

I was then 40 years old. Everything I had in life was pulling away in those trucks, and it was my decision to stay and face probable execution. I knew that I was taking all the responsibility now. That gave me some peace.

OUT IN THE front courtyard, many people had their radios turned on RTLM, and I heard the names of my wife and children being read aloud, along with the other refugees who had just pulled away. 'The cockroaches are escaping,' said the announcer. 'Stop all the cockroaches from leaving the Mille Collines. Put up roadblocks. Do your work. Do not leave the grave half full.'

The list had leaked. Somebody from the hate radio had apparently stolen it or bought it from the United Nations or the Rwandan Army. I even saw a correspondent from RTLM standing in the parking lot.

There are no words to describe what it is like to hear an execution order broadcast for your own family, and to know that you played a role in putting them in death's hands. Their beautiful names—Tatiana, Tresor, Roger, Lys, Diane—were a profanity in that announcer's mouth. I felt as if he was raping them with his voice. I hated that I was utterly powerless to save my family. I wanted to follow the jeeps in my own car, but the roadblocks would surely catch me alone and I would die like the other 800,000. All I could do was frantically work the phones.

WHEN SHE WAS able to speak again, Tatiana told me what had happened.

The first convoy of 63 refugees was escorted by eight soldiers wearing the blue helmets of the UN. They were stopped at a roadblock two kilometres away from the hotel, at a place called Cyimicanga, where some men from the *Interahamwe* were standing alongside a few observers from the Rwandan Army. All the evacuees in the trucks were ordered out onto the roadside dirt. The street boys at the barricades had been given Kalashnikovs, and one of them fired an opening shot into the dirt near the feet of a refugee named Immaculate. It also happened to come perilously close to a soldier. A second shot struck and killed a member of the Presidential Guard.

'They are going to kill us!' somebody screamed, and that caused the militia to get even angrier. They used their rifle butts to start beating the refugees. Men were slugged in the gut, women were slapped across the face, children were kicked. A few used their machetes to cut open the skin on the forearms of some of the captives: it was the usual sick prelude to a total dismemberment. My wife was worked over particularly hard; she was thrown into a truck which so twisted her back that she could barely move.

The UN soldiers, meanwhile, were disorganised. Some were bravely trying to insert themselves between the militia and their intended victims while some others put their hands in the air like stick-up victims.

My son Roger was approached by a boy he had known from school, a former classmate and friend. 'Give me your shoes, you cockroach,' said the boy.

Roger obeyed without protest and gave over his tennis shoes to his old friend, who was now a killer with a machete. They had once played soccer together. I suppose it was an echo of the meaningless gulf that had opened that day in 1973 between myself and my best friend, Gerard. My son was now experiencing much the same thing, only now he was the unlucky one.

Ah Rwanda, why?

The only thing that saved the caravan was the bitter argument between the Army and the militia. They were beginning to open fire on each other. Some of the UN soldiers saw their chance. They picked up the refugees in the dirt, threw them into the trucks like lumber, and roared off back towards the Mille Collines before the militia could regroup.

I ran out to the roundabout to meet them coming back and found my wife lying in a puddle of blood on the floor of one of the trucks. She was moaning slightly.

'Can you move?' I asked. She shook her head.

I was nearly blind with a red whirling of fury and relief and fright, but I had a job to do and I forced myself to stay in control. We took the wounded off the trucks and led them back into the hotel they had thought they were escaping. We called for Dr Gasasira and another doctor named Josue, who began to bandage up the cuts immediately. The Mille Collines was full of people screaming and crying and hugging one another. I took Tatiana up to our room, 126, and made sure she was resting on the bed. Her eyes were blank with shock. The children were unhurt but completely quiet.

Once I was sure that our wounded were all being tended to, I rushed to my office. There was no time to spare. We needed more protection immediately. It was now clear that the government and the militias knew the identities of many of the high-profile refugees we were hiding. They might not chance an all-out invasion of the Mille Collines, but they might begin a series of individual assassinations. I was terrified that their bloodlust had been aroused beyond the point of control. I had already taken the precaution of finding an outdated guest list to give to any killer who might come asking for it at the reception desk. I had also ordered the room numbers pried off the doors to further confuse anyone who came in here looking for a specific target. But more protection was crucial. I called everyone I knew who was still alive. And then I called them again, insisting we have more policemen posted outside.

It seems strange to say, but it was a relief to be *doing* something, even if it seemed like I was getting nowhere with all my military friends and, of course, the UN.

WE DID NOT have long to rest. On the morning of 13 May, at 10:00am. I was visited by a Rwandan Army intelligence agent, named Lieutenant Iradakunda. I had known him only slightly, but my impression had been that he was a less than loyal supporter of the ongoing genocide. My suspicions were confirmed when he took me aside to a quiet area.

'Listen, Paul,' he said. 'We are going to attack you today at four pm.'

'Who?' I asked. 'How many?'

'I do not know details.'

'Are they coming to kill or are they coming to clear it out?'

'I do not know details. Don't ask me for a solution. But I am telling you this as a friend: four pm.' And with that he turned and left.

I had only a few hours. I went straight to my office and began calling names in my book, pleading with them to lobby the *Interahamwe* to call off the raid. If that was impossible, could I at least get some more protection from policemen or the military? It was clear that I would have to invoke some international pressure to stop the raid, and so I started pestering the White House, the French Foreign Ministry, the Belgian government—anybody I could think of.

One of the calls I made, of course, was to my bosses at Sabena, who shared my panic and pledged to raise hell with the French government. This 'French connection' was a key pressure point that already had saved us from disaster many times. I was going to press on it once more—hard. Let me explain.

The Hutu Power government maintained close ties to France throughout the genocide. It was the French who had provided military training and armaments to most of the Rwandan Army and smuggled French guns kept flowing in through neighbouring countries even after Habyarimana's plane was shot down. Even the *Interahamwe* were under strict instructions not to harm or harass any French nationals who came through their roadblocks. Belgians, meanwhile, were supposed to be murdered on sight.

A general panic in the hotel would have been disastrous, so I told only a few refugees of the upcoming deadline. I dialled the world, with the clock ticking down. We had a few weapons in the hands of our policemen. We had some cash. Some drinks. But all this would hardly be enough to bribe our way out of a wholesale raid. When four o'clock arrived I stood near the entrance and waited. And nothing happened. No mobs had gathered behind the bamboo fence. Five o'clock ticked by. And then six. The sun went down and there was nothing but quiet. I did not relax. It seemed that one of my telephone pleas had got through—I could not be sure which one—but it may have only purchased a temporary stay.

At about 10:00pm, a rocket-propelled grenade smashed into the south wall just above the second floor. It tore a hole in a staircase wall and blew out the glass in Rooms 102, 104, and 106, but nobody was injured. I braced for an invasion, but that single shot was all that came. I immediately got on the secret phone with General Dallaire and told him we were being attacked. But no further rounds were fired. Dallaire showed up about half an hour later with a squad of subordinates and looked at the damage.

They tried to decide where the missile had come from. One pointed to the headquarters of the gendarmerie down the valley. Another pointed off towards the RPF lines.

About half an hour later they left with a shrug. Would there be more rockets fired at us? There was no way to tell. All I could do was try to keep my cool when and if it happened. Nearly delirious with fatigue after what had been one of the longest days of my life, I crawled into bed beside my wounded wife and fell into a dark unconsciousness.

TO MY HUGE surprise things became quiet for a few weeks after that. No more missiles were fired. We counted down the days until 26 May, when the United Nations, the Army and the rebels wanted to make a second try at an evacuation. This time they would send us not to the airport but to a hill behind the rebel lines.

My friends made several attempts to convince me to sign up for it. No way, I said. There were hundreds of refugees who would not be evacuated and they still needed my protection, for the same reasons I had cited when I refused to go along with the first evacuation. And this time I would not allow Tatiana and the kids to go either. I did not trust the UN. My wife was now able to sit up in bed, and even walk around a bit, but she was shaken and frail and frightened of every bump in the hallway.

The night before the evacuation, four families gathered in Room 126. We were all old friends. In the room were: Odette and Jean-Baptiste and their four children; John Bosco Karangwa and his three children; journalist Edward Mutsinzi and his wife and child; and Tatiana and me and our four children.

We were going to do a *pacte de sang*—a blood oath. It is one of the most powerful bonds you can form with someone in Rwanda.

'Listen to me,' said Jean-Baptiste. 'Listen to me, all the children here. Look around. You see all the adults in here. We have decided from here onward to become brothers and sisters. If your parents should be killed, then the adults in the room tonight become your parents. Get away from danger and find them if you can. Everyone in here has promised to raise the orphans as their own children. And if all the adults should be killed, then the oldest child will take care of everyone.'

We all sipped from a glass of red wine as a symbol of the promise we had made. We all stood up, many of us crying, and shook hands. There were bitter tears in the room that night, but also love. We had been through a sea of fire and we clung to one another, not knowing if we would ever see one another again or even be breathing after the next twelve hours.

THE EVACUATION started much like the first, with stony goodbyes that did not match the emotion of the previous night. I watched my friends pull away and went back inside. This convoy was much better organised than the first, and the militias had been ordered to keep their distance. Several hundred were moved out that day, leaving the Mille Collines still jammed with people, but feeling oddly empty.

Not long after, I had a meeting with General Bizimungu, who was at the Diplomates. It was one of the few times I ventured outside the grounds of the Mille Collines since I had arrived there nearly 70 days earlier. The trip was only ten minutes long but it wound past the heaps of corpses and bloodstains on the road that seemed like natural parts of the scenery now. I met the general in the lobby and took him immediately down to the wine cellar, where I knew there would be some remaining stocks of Bordeaux and Côtes du Rhône or something else I could give him.

We talked about the war and he repeated the mournful prediction that he had made in my hotel room. The government was losing. They could hold the lines temporarily, but their supplies were running low. The rebels had too much momentum and superior military. They would be flooding into Kigali before long and would perhaps put all the leadership on trial for war crimes.

As we talked amid the dusty bottles of wine, I wondered how much longer he was going to be able to hang on.

Suddenly, our conversation was interrupted by the arrival of one of the general's staff who came with an urgent message: 'The militia has entered the Mille Collines.'

So this was it. My worst nightmare was coming true and I wasn't even there to see it happen. My children. My wife. My friends. All those people.

'General, let's go back to the Mille Collines,' I said, and he did not hesitate to come with me. It seemed that he was just as eager to be there as I was. On that drive through downtown Kigali it came to me quite calmly that this was almost surely the end of my life, the last day I would ever exist. I had contemplated my own death so many times in the last two and a half months that it had lost whatever power it had once had to upset me. All I wanted to do any more was the work in front of me; I had lost the desire for everything else. Death no longer frightened me.

When we passed the roadblock near the front of the hotel I saw that none of the killers was there—a very bad sign. The driver sped us to the front entrance. I heard General Bizimungu deliver an order to the sergeant with us. I'll never forget what he said:

'You go up there and tell those boys that if one person kills anyone I will kill them! If anybody beats anyone I will kill them! If they do not leave in five minutes I will kill *all* of them!'

I ran inside the hotel, feeling as though I were underwater, and discovered the reception desk unmanned. But I heard shouting and crashing upstairs. One of the *Interahamwe* was in the corridor. He was dressed in ragged clothes and holding on to a rifle. He stared at me. I was wearing a plain white T-shirt and black pants.

'Where is the manager?' he demanded of me.

'I think he went that way,' I said, pointing down a corridor. And then I strode off in the opposite direction.

Once I was out of his sight I slipped upstairs. The militia had broken down several room doors, to make sure they had discovered everyone. The door to 126 had also been smashed open. So they had found my family.

I went inside the room, wondering if I would see their corpses. But the room was untouched. There did not appear to be any signs of a struggle. I went inside the bathroom and something motivated me to peek behind the shower curtain. There they all were, clustered in the arms of my wife, staring back at me.

Relief flooded over me, but I had to see what was happening to the others. I told them to stay put without making a peep, dashed down the stairs, and ran down that spiral staircase near the bar and out to the back lawn, where I saw all my guests on their knees near the swimming pool. This quiet square of water appeared to be the site of an imminent massacre. The militia was strutting around, demanding that everybody put their hands in the air. One of the men waved his machete in the air. I saw one of my receptionists among the militia—I had always suspected him of being a spy.

They had herded everyone to the swimming pool. But why had they not just started the killing machine? The only thing I could imagine was that they were aiming to shove the dead bodies into the swimming pool to foul the water for any refugee who might have escaped their notice.

Whatever the reason, the delay in rounding everyone up saved us all.

Bizimungu emerged onto the pool deck now, enraged, his pistol drawn, his face taut with anger. Bizimungu was known as a quiet man, but his temper was volcanic. He roared out his order again: 'If one person kills anyone I will kill them! If anybody beats anyone I will kill them! If you do not leave in five minutes I will kill *all* of you!'

There was a moment of surprise. The militiamen looked at one another, as if seeking the approval of the group for whatever actions would follow. The lives of hundreds hung in their uncertainty. They could easily have disobeyed him. Bizimungu was a powerful man with powerful allies, but there had been hundreds of mutinies against Army officers during the genocide—thousands of unapproved murders. And this was the Hotel Mille Collines: the citadel of Belgian arrogance, the luxurious island of privilege, the best redoubt of cockroaches anywhere in Rwanda. Didn't the general see what kind of prize he was giving up?

I saw surly looks on the faces of several of those boys. Their lust had been rising and now it had been denied. They were primed to kill and this traitor general had put a stop to it. I could tell they now wanted to turn their fury on to him. But they didn't. They lowered their machetes and began to file out.

GENERAL AUGUSTIN Bizimungu now sits in a jail cell. He will probably be there the rest of his life.

After the genocide he fled to Zaire, and then into far-away Angola. He was captured by local police there and brought before the International Criminal Tribunal that was organised to prosecute war crimes committed during the genocide of 1994. Bizimungu was charged with supervising the arming and training of the militias. As I write this, he has not yet been convicted and is being held in Arusha in Tanzania.

I have been criticised for my friendship with him during the genocide, but I have never apologised for it. 'How could you have stayed close to such a vile man?' I am asked, and my answer is this: I do not excuse whatever he may have done to promote the genocide, but I never heard him agree with any of the bloodshed when he was in my presence. I had to stay close to him because he could help me save lives. I would have stayed close with anyone who could help me do that.

There is a saying in Rwanda: 'Every man has a secret corner of his mind that nobody will ever know.' And I do not think I know enough about Bizimungu's secret corner to judge him. He may well have done terrible things in Rwanda before and during the genocide, but I know that he stepped in for me at crucial moments to save the lives of innocent people when it was of no conceivable benefit to him.

THE ABORTED SLAUGHTER at the Mille Collines was what it took to convince all parties that the hotel must be cleared out without further dithering. The United Nations, the rebels, and the Rwandan Army conferred and decided to do it that very day. They assigned us five Tunisian soldiers to guard the parking lot for the last night. It made me furious that they were given to us long after we needed them. On that afternoon I busied myself with making sure everybody was out of their rooms safely. There was a line of jeeps and trucks outside, the third such time that an evacuation convoy had been assembled there, but I had a feeling this would truly be the last one.

I made a last check of the hotel where I had spent 76 of the longest days of my life. Though I had been convinced I would die inside it, I felt affection for the place. When I was a young man it was where I had found my true occupation. I had met some of the most generous people in my life within its walls. Sabena gave me a job when I needed one and taught me things I never would have learned otherwise. They showed me how to respect myself by respecting others. When the killing started the hotel had saved people. It had projected the image of an ultimately sane world that kept the murderers at bay. I am not a particularly sentimental man, but I felt the odd urge to stroke it like a pet dog.

I made sure that the hotel was empty of everybody who wanted to go. Some employees had asked to stay, and I let them. I couldn't tell how many had been spies for the militia all along. By that point I was beyond caring. It was time to leave. When the UN convoy pulled away I was in the back seat of the last jeep. I hid under a plastic tarp for fear that the militias would recognise me and shoot at me as we drove by the roadblocks.

TEN

IN THE TIME BEFORE the genocide it had been fashionable for the elite to buy country estates near a region named Kabuga just outside the capital. The area is attractive, with low hills and unusually large plantations full of grazing livestock.

We were hustled to Kabuga by the RWF, which had turned it into a kind of refugee holding area. But it was no camp in the conventional sense. It was a looting zone.

Soldiers from the rebel army had stolen food from all the shops. Potatoes had been dug out of the fields. Goats had been captured and slaughtered. This made me furious. It was the same kind of impunity we had seen in 1959 during the Hutu Revolution, only this time it was yesterday's victims who were helping themselves to the spoils. War is hell, and ugly things happen in its midst—I know this. But they always create permanent resentments that have a way of erupting later in history. The casual disrespect for other people and their property was what helped create the genocide we had just lived through. I was afraid I was watching the conception of another. It made me feel as though Rwandans had learned nothing at all.

It therefore does not make me proud to tell you this: I, too, was among those who had to forage for food. I can only say that it was a choice between that or going hungry. My family and I also slept in the house of an unknown family who had fled the advancing rebel army. I can only hope these strangers would forgive us today. I never knew who they were, but it made me terribly uncomfortable to be using their property.

There was a surprise in the camp. We spotted the children of my wife's brother—the man with whom I had been dining on the terrace of the Diplomates on the night Habyarimana's plane had been shot down. Anaise was two and a half and Izere was barely a year old. They were being taken care of by our housemaid, who had managed to struggle into the camp. Both of the children were covered in dirt and appeared to be starving and barely alive. They had been living for months on ground-up chicken feed. Where were their parents? Tatiana was frantic to know. But the maid could only hold up her hands. My brother-in-law and his wife had both disappeared shortly after the genocide broke out.

There were stories like that all over the camp: unexpected reunions and revelations of awful news from the past two and a half months. Nights were the hardest for us. Weeping filled the air. I found it hard to find even the mindless release of sleep. Wives came to understand that they would never see their missing husbands again. Parents had to force themselves to stop imagining how their irreplaceable children had died at the hands of strangers. And that emptiness in their lives would go on and on. It took a tremendous force of will to keep your own heart together in this unending grief.

The rebel soldiers were hardly welcoming. They treated us like prisoners of war. Some of the stronger men among us were offered the chance to take a few days of military training to fight against the Rwandan Army, but I refused. 'I always fight with words,' I told them. 'Not with guns.'

What I really wanted was to get the hell out of Rwanda. I had had enough. We were away from the militias but still in danger of being killed any time by the rebels. We were also filthy and exhausted and needing a break. I told my new hosts that I and my family wanted either to be driven to the Ugandan border or flown to Belgium. What I got in reply was: 'We will look into it for you, Mr Manager.' Nothing happened, of course. Day followed day. All we could do was eat more purloined bananas and wait for the war to be over, or to be killed ourselves.

MEANWHILE, ONE of the largest mass migrations of people in African history was under way.

The government of France had been in continual contact with its allies at the top of the Hutu government and was growing increasingly alarmed at the likelihood of their neo-colony falling to English-speaking rebels. In mid-June, just as my hotel was being evacuated, the French announced plans to send a peacekeeping mission to the western part of Rwanda for 'humanitarian' reasons. This gave the *génocidaires* the chance to look like victims instead of aggressors, and they started to pack up and leave for the protected area that became known as 'the Turquoise Zone'.

RTLM radio then performed its final disservice to the nation by scaring the living daylights out of the people remaining in Rwanda, a considerable number of whom had just spent two months murdering their neighbours and chasing the less compliant ones through swamps. The radio told them that the RPF would kill any Hutus they found in their path and encouraged all its listeners to pack up their belongings and head either to Tanzania or the western part of the country and the borders of the Democratic Republic of Congo (what used to be called Zaire), where the French soldiers awaited.

Nearly 1.7 million people heeded the call. Entire hills and cities mobilised into caravans: men carrying sacks of bananas, some with bloody machetes in their belt loops; women with baskets of grain on their heads; children hugging photo albums to their chests. They wound their way past corpses piled at the side of the road and the smouldering cooking fires in front of looted houses. I am sorry to say that the dire predictions of the radio were not rooted in fantasy, as the rebels did conduct crimes against humanity in revenge for the genocide and to make people fear them. In any case, what was left of Rwanda emptied out within days.

The UN Security Council, so ineffective in the face of the genocide, lent its sponsorship to the camps the French set up to protect the 'refugees'. The main place of comfort to the killers was at a town called Goma, just over the border into the Democratic Republic of Congo. It is in a bleak area at the foot of a chain of volcanoes and the town is set in a plain of hardened black lava. Into this hellish landscape, the French airlifted 2,500 well-equipped paratroopers, Foreign Legionnaires, helicopters, fighter jets, tents, water supplies, food, jeeps—everything, in short, that the pathetic UN force could have used when the murders were at their height in April. Now all of these assets were being used to feed and shelter some of the very people who carried out the slaughter.

In a surprise for all of us, the US finally was persuaded to act. When cholera and other diseases broke out the Clinton administration announced it would seek $320 million in aid for the camps at Goma and announced a public health initiative to clean up the water-bloated corpses that had floated over into Uganda. This US aid package totalled more than sixteen times what it would have taken to electronically jam the hate radio, which would have stopped many of those people from becoming corpses.

On 4 July, with much of the civilian population in flight, the

RPF captured the capital of Kigali after a brief battle. They had conquered a ruined city and caused further destruction. Houses were knocked over. Churches were covered in blood. Hospitals were empty shells, looted of supplies. Land mines and live mortar rounds were lying everywhere. Wrecked vehicles blocked the roads.

And the corpses were stuffed everywhere: inside closets, underneath desks, and down water wells, and shoved casually to the edge of the sidewalks. The stench of decaying flesh choked the air. Barely 30,000 people remained, a tenth of Kigali's population before the genocide began.

Rwanda's other major cities toppled swiftly from there and the country was all but conquered. On 14 July, the plug was pulled on RTLM for good. Less than a week later the rebel army swore in a new government. It marked the official end of the genocide, but not the end of the killings. The aftermath would be long and dirty.

I was informed that my request to travel to Belgium had been approved on one condition: that I travel alone, leaving my wife and children behind. 'Forget it,' I told them.

The rebel army took us back to the Mille Collines, which was in wretched shape. After I had left, some people had taken it upon themselves to start cooking fires on the lobby tiles and ash was everywhere. The hallway carpets were covered in a disgusting glaze of grease and human waste. Doors were broken from their hinges. The RPF had looted the remaining supply of drinks and alcohol that I had used to keep so many people alive. The kitchen was a disaster. Almost everything of value had been stolen or damaged beyond repair.

I cleared the squatters out, rallied what staff I could find, and got to work. We obtained some cleaning solution and carpentry equipment to make the place semi-presentable again. My colleague Bik Cornelis had arrived back in the country from the Netherlands and was working side by side with me. The hotel had to start functioning again. Rwanda was about to be besieged with journalists, humanitarian workers, peace-keeping soldiers, and more than 150 NGOs (non-governmental organisations). All those people who had abandoned us during the slaughter were coming and they needed a place to stay. The irony was too bitter to think of for long.

We reopened on 15 July, having been closed a little less than a month.

MY FAMILY settled back into the manager's house at the Hotel Diplomates, where some of our friends had hidden under the noses of the *génocidaires*. It was where we felt the safest. We did not dare to go back to our family house in Kabeza, and I had no particular desire to see those neighbours of mine who had transformed themselves into lunatics during those first days in April.

My wife and I had been continually worried about our families in the south and I was able to take a day off so we could go and check on them. My friend John Bosco hot-wired an abandoned car, as was the custom in those days immediately after the genocide. When the road opened up into the lush hills that I loved, we found ourselves in a twilight country we did not recognise. The silence was near complete. Everybody was either dead or exiled. The only thing I heard was dogs barking and snarling as they fought each other to feast on human remains. Crowds of people normally line the sides of the roads in Rwanda: boys driving herds of goats; women in colourful shifts balancing baskets on their heads; elderly men carrying sticks and wearing donated T-shirts; merchants hawking batteries and leaves of tobacco on blankets spread on the ground. They were nowhere to be seen. The life of the country had been sucked away.

'I don't know this place,' said my wife. 'I'm scared.'

I found myself scanning the brush on the side of the road for the flash of a machete or a grinning killer. We saw so many dead bodies scattered on the side of the road that we began not to see them any more. Yet, each of these dead shells represented someone who was irreplaceable, as irreplaceable to the people they loved as I was to my wife, or she was to me, or we to our children. Their uniqueness was gone for ever, their stories, their experiences, their loves—erased with a few swings of a cheap machete.

Ah, Rwanda. Why?

My family and I could easily have been a part of that caravan of the dead. All it would have taken was a slip of my luck,
the wrong word to a general, a whim of a militia chief. Even
after everything I had seen in the previous three months I felt as
though I had been terribly naive. I hadn't really grasped the true
scale of the disaster, how deep it had gone, and how that membrane of protection around our hotel had been so fragile. That
it had held up for 76 days was a miracle. With the rest of the
country looking like a giant cemetery there was nothing that
should have stopped those killers from wiping us out as well.

We arrived in my hometown after a few hours. It was as
deserted as the roads had been. The genocide had come here,
too. More than 150 people connected to the Seventh-Day
Adventist Church had come here thinking they would be
protected at the college at Gitwe where I had attended
school. They had all been slaughtered.

Things were no better in the neighbouring town where my
family had lived. I went to the home of my elder brother
Munyakayanza and found him sitting quietly in the front
room with his wife. Seeing him alive made me want to cry
with gratitude. We embraced, but I could feel that his muscles
were tense. His eyes darted from my eyes to the places behind
my shoulder. The area around his house was usually full of
life, but now there was nobody. It was totally quiet.

'Our neighbours have been killed by the militia,' he told me.
He and his wife survived because they were Hutus. Now that
the rebel army had driven out the militia it was not safe any
more to be of this class. In fact, it could be a death sentence.
Some rogue members of the RPF had begun to conduct
reprisal killings in several parts of Rwanda. Around me I could
see burned-out houses where people had been roasted alive
within their own walls.

'Listen, brother,' Munyakayanza told me. 'Please leave this
place. The houses, they have eyes. The trees have ears.'

I decoded his message. My presence here would be noticed
and was a danger to both his family and mine. I quickly hugged
him again and left. My wife started to cry, and I tried my best to

comfort her, but it was impossible. We now headed towards my wife's hometown, the old Tutsi capital of Nyanza. Tatiana was so frightened she could barely speak, but we had to go there, even though we already knew in our hearts what we would find.

Most of her family had been slain by their neighbours. Several of them had been buried in a shallow pit used for maturing bananas. Tatiana's mother had been one of the sweetest, kindest women I'd ever met. She had always shared food with her neighbours in times of trouble and was always available to help look after children in their parents' absence. She had been murdered along with her daughter-in-law and six grandchildren. The walls of her house had been knocked down. I could see some of its distinctive tiles already plastered into the walls of nearby houses. The looting had been quick and efficient.

I felt bright hatred surging up in my throat for the bastards that had done this. I am not a violent man, but if I had had a gun in that moment, and if somebody had pointed me to a convincing scapegoat, I would have murdered him without hesitation. I had saved more than 1,000 people in the capital, but I could not save my own family. What a stupid and useless man I was!

I tasted, in that moment, the poison and self-hatred in my country's bloodstream, that irresistible fury against a ghost, the quenchless desire to make someone pay for an unrightable wrong. My father would have said that I had drunk from the water that was upstream from the lamb.

My wife and I crouched there in the remains of her mother's house, holding on to each other, and for the first time in many years, I wept.

NOTHING COULD ever be the same for us again.

My family and I stayed in the manager's cottage at the Diplomates while Rwanda went about the slow process of trying to rebuild itself. Work is an excellent place to lose yourself, and I proceeded to do just that. My bosses at Sabena had been satisfied with my performance during the genocide, and

I was allowed to keep my job as the general manager of the Hotel Diplomates. Business was booming, of course. Rwanda's expatriate class had swelled once again now that the terror was over.

There was a change in my employment in February 1995. The Sabena Corporation was planning to merge with Swissair, but a condition of the deal was that Sabena would renovate all its existing hotels. They were forced to break their management contract with the new government of Rwanda, which was the legal owner of the Diplomates.

This put me in a difficult spot. I thought about asking for another job in the corporation, but I enjoyed the demands of day-to-day management too much, attending to the thousand little details that make a hotel the welcoming place that it is. This was my deepest image of myself. I was born to be a site manager, not a suit in a conference room. And so Sabena and I parted on friendly terms.

With the Belgian corporation now gone, the government needed someone experienced to run the hotel and I brought them a proposal that allowed me to stay on as manager while still living on the property. My wife opened a pharmacy downtown and we managed to make a decent living together while Rwanda tried to reinvent itself as a new nation.

The government got rid of those wretched ID books and made it taboo for anyone to be officially labelled as a Hutu or a Tutsi—a change that I and millions of others applauded. Informal 'orphanages' spontaneously opened up all over the country, often run by teenagers; few adults were left to take charge. An entire generation of young people was told never to mention their ethnicity to anyone because it could mark them for death in the changing currents of history. Rwandan exiles from all over the world, some of whom hadn't seen their country for 30 years, flooded back inside. There were more than three-quarters of a million of them, which meant there were roughly three new settlers for every four people who had been killed in the genocide. The exiles were mostly from Uganda, Burundi and the Congo, but they came from the United States and Canada and Belgium and Switzerland as well. Prisons, meanwhile, were jammed full of people suspected of having killed their neighbours.

The economy, like the infrastructure, was in a shambles. An entire year's coffee crop had been lost. What little industry there was had been destroyed. But international aid helped get the power back on, and Rwandans have always been creative when it comes to making money. There was a brief period of Wild West capitalism, in which it became possible to grow very rich transporting foodstuffs and goods from Uganda. Anybody with a working truck could make fantastic profits hauling bananas and beans.

My own life, meanwhile, became complicated and a little frightening. It was with profoundly mixed feelings that I returned to the streets where I had seen the bodies of my friends and neighbours stacked up like garbage. Their blood-stains had washed away in the autumn rains, but I always took note of the spots where I had seen them lying. The Mille Collines no longer smelled like a refugee camp, but it was hard to walk its halls without feeling that palpable sense of impending murder. The role I had played in saving those people had not been forgotten, and it was not appreciated in many quarters. I had seen too much and knew too many names. There were many people in the new government who had been complicit in the genocide and who feared any surviving witnesses from that time.

Others had it in for me for economic reasons. The hotel management contract I had received was seen as a cash cow by some of the thugs close to the new government.

One day a friend high up in the government, whom I should not identify, came to my house and made plain what I already knew to be true.

'Paul, I have heard they want to kill you so that other business interests can take over the management of the Hotel Diplomates,' he said. 'But the object now is not to kill you out in the open. It is too dangerous politically. They will pretend they are arresting you and taking you to prison, but you will disappear and your body will never be found.'

The choice now seemed clear to me. I could open my black

binder once again and start dialling all my Army friends for protection. But it would be like living the genocide all over. I imagined my future as a Rwandan hotel manager and saw nothing but constant fear and an eventual knock on the door after midnight. I loved my job and I loved my country, but not enough to die for them and leave my children without a father. My family and I quickly flew to Belgium and applied for political asylum. We had remained in our own country slightly more than two years after the genocide.

We may have left Rwanda, but Rwanda will never leave us. Those thousand hills were imprinted inside us for ever. There are times today when I will be in some public place, in a small crowd at a bus station, for example, and I suddenly cannot bear the presence of the other people because I see them holding machetes. They are always grinning at me.

Tatiana and my children have similar troubles and it is not uncommon for one of us to awake screaming in the middle of the night. When this happens I always come in and hold whoever it is, and we talk in quiet voices, in Kinyarwanda, until calm comes once more. It is the best therapy, I think, to simply talk, and we have talked hundreds of times together about the dreadful things we have lived through. We will probably be talking about them together as long as we are alive, a conversation that will never end.

IT IS NOT SUCH a bad thing to start one's life afresh. I was 42 years old. We had a lot of bad memories, but we were all in good physical health and we all had hope for a better life in our new country. As a twentieth-century colonial power, Belgium had done wretched things to Rwanda, and its conduct during the recent genocide was not honourable, but I never held the actions of its government against the people at large, who were generally very likable and decent to me.

Belgium has a very generous social service net for its citizens, and even for the recent immigrants, but I felt very strongly that I did not want to live on public assistance. I was restless and eager to go to work. I had a little cash saved up from the Diplomates contract and I used $20,000 of it to buy a Nissan car and a permit to run a taxi company. The city of Brussels requires you to take an exam to be a taxi driver and I passed on the first try. I was now a company with one employee: myself. So I started going to work at 5:00am and coming home at 7:00pm. The streets in Brussels are tangled like spaghetti, and many switch their names after only a few blocks, but I quickly learned the major arteries and then started to master the side streets. I cruised all over the city dozens of times in a day, usually with a stranger in the back seat.

Most of the people who were in my cab for more than half an hour became my friends. Quite a few were talkative people and would want to know the name of my home country. When I told them 'Rwanda' it usually led into conversations about the genocide, which almost everyone had heard about. I was occasionally not in the mood to talk about it, but on most days I was, and I would answer their questions as best I could. There were just a handful of passengers, on very long rides, who got to hear me tell the story of the Hotel Mille Collines, and they always left my cab in silence.

THERE IS NOT MUCH left to tell about my new life in Belgium. My wife and I made some friends from Rwanda—fellow post-genocide immigrants like us—and they have their own stories to tell. When the evening is late and the empty glasses multiply on the coffee table, we will sometimes talk about what we have seen with each other, and there will be crying and gentle embraces.

About 15,000 of us now make the old colonial capital our home, and there are a few specialty stores where expatriates can buy goods that remind us of where we came from. We go to each other's baptisms, marriages, and funerals and it is enormously good for us to hear Kinyarwanda and drink beer with others who understand us in a way that the Belgians never can.

But as Rwanda will always be with me, so too will the genocide. It is as much a part of me as the colour of my eyes or the names of my children; it is never far from my thoughts and I cannot talk for more than one hour with a fellow

Rwandan before one or both of us will begin to tell a story or make a reference to what happened during those three months of bloodshed in 1994.

Some of the people who lived through the genocide with me have gone on to what might be called happiness, or at least a future without too much pain or fear. Odette Nyiramilimo became close to the new government and was appointed to secretary of state for the Department of Social Affairs. She is now a senator in the Parliament of Rwanda. Her husband, Jean-Baptiste, reopened his clinic in the heart of Kigali and continues to see patients every day. My journalist friend Thomas Kamilindi took a job with the BBC as a correspondent in Rwanda, where his honest and unflinching news reports continued to irritate those in power. He recently accepted a fellowship at the University of Michigan.

For others, the future was bleak. My other journalist friend Edward Mutsinzi, who swore a blood oath in Room 126 to protect my children, was captured and tortured by RPF soldiers shortly after the liberation of Kigali. For some reason, they thought he had useful information. They beat him to a pulp and left him for dead. A squad of Australian soldiers attached to the United Nations found him lying in the dirt and helped save his life. He lives today in Belgium, blind and unable to work. Another man who swore that oath with me, John Bosco Karangwa, grew sick and died in 2001. His wife and children live nearby and I visit them when I can.

Aloise Karasankwavu, the bank executive who tried to persuade me to flee with him to Murama, wanted to help rebuild my country at the end of the civil war. He had just passed an exam to be the director of one of the nation's largest banks, BCDI, when he was thrown in jail on bogus charges of helping carry out the genocide. He died in his cell one night of suspicious causes. No autopsy was performed.

The architects of the genocide have mostly been rounded up and taken before the International Criminal Tribunal in Tanzania. The colonel accused of planning the genocide, Théoneste Bagosora, is still on trial as I write this. So is the head of the national police, Augustin Ndindiliyimana.

My friend Georges Rutaganda, the vice president of the *Interahamwe* and the main supplier of beer and toilet paper to the Mille Collines, was sentenced to life imprisonment for crimes against humanity in 1999. He was specifically charged, among other things, with organising the massacre at the Official Technical School where the killings began minutes after the UN jeeps disappeared down the road. As for the priest who wore a gun instead of his robes, Father Wenceslas Munyegeshaka, he now lives in exile in France. A judge there brought charges against him in 1995 for the crime of genocide. His case is still caught in the slow gears of the French judicial system and may never be resolved.

I have no idea what happened to that neighbour of mine I called Marcel, the clerk I saw wearing a military uniform and carrying a machete on the morning of 7 April 1994. As far as I know, he has melted back into a normal life and is now going to work, paying his taxes, and raising his children.

General Romeo Dallaire suffered emotional stress and was voluntarily relieved of his command the month after the end of the war. Back in Canada, he wrestled with post-traumatic stress disorder and was found one night in 1997 curled in a foetal position under a park bench, drunk and incoherent. Dallaire has since found a new life as an author and a lecturer and is now a fellow at the John F. Kennedy School of Government at Harvard University. His old boss, Kofi Annan, became the secretary-general of the United Nations.

President Bill Clinton stopped over in Rwanda on 25 March 1998, and offered an apology for America's failure to intervene. He stayed for approximately three hours and did not leave the airport.

The daughters of Tatiana's brother now live in our home in Brussels. We raised them as our own children and they are both healthy and doing well in school. They have no memories of the violence and the awful ordeal they have been through, for which I am grateful. But they will never know their parents. My brother-in-law and his wife vanished without a trace after that first night when the president was assassinated. We can only assume they were slaughtered and their bodies are now in an anonymous mass grave somewhere. I hope their ending came without much suffering, and I also hope that wherever they are they might know what lovely girls their babies have become.

Our relatives in Rwanda tried the best they could to begin life anew. They still raise cows and bananas in the hills near Nyanza. We decided not to remove the bodies of my mother-in-law and her grandchildren from the banana pit where they had been buried, but placed a memorial stone on top of it instead. The house knocked over by the militia was never rebuilt. A pile of rubble stands there today and weeds grow over it. As for my own family, I have lost four of my eight siblings. One died of illness, one died in a car accident, and two were killed by the rebel army. For a Rwandan family, this is a comparatively lucky outcome.

My children sometimes ask me why it all happened and I don't have any final answers for them. The only thing I am able to do is to keep talking to them about what they have seen and how they feel about it. I will listen to them for hours and hours into the night, and sometimes they listen to me and my own bad memories. I did not grow up with any understanding of modern psychology, but I do feel the best way to get rid of bad memories is to speak them out loud and not keep them fermenting inside. It is the best therapy. Words can be instruments of evil, but they can also be powerful tools of life. If you say the right ones they can save the whole world.

WITH HARD WORK and a lot of early mornings I earned enough money to buy a second taxi and hire another driver. The cash flow was slow but steady, and I eventually accumulated enough capital to branch out. I felt strongly that I wanted to invest in Africa. But Rwanda was not a possibility because I could not travel freely there. Through some friends I learned of an opportunity to buy into a trucking company in the nation of Zambia, a former British colony many kilometres south of Rwanda. It is an English-speaking country, so I am able to do business there easily. We now have a fleet of four trucks that haul canned goods, beer, soda, and clothing to rural villages from the capital city of Lusaka. Our trucks can haul most anything imaginable, and it always makes me happy to sign a contract with an international aid organisation bringing something to a needy area.

My income was good enough for us to buy a slim post-war town house just 50 metres outside the city limits of Brussels proper. After so much angst as a young man over the idea of living in a city I have finally come to rest in suburbia. Diane married a man who works for a company that manufactures hospital equipment and Lys married a self-employed business-man. Roger has gone to work for Accor hotels and may one day become a manager like his father. Tresor is still in school. In the afternoons I drive him to his soccer games and we practise his English in the car.

All in all it is a contented life, and I want no more adventure in it. I would have been happy to have lived out my remaining time as a good husband to my wife, a decent father to my children, and a safety-conscious driver for my passengers, with what happened at the Hotel Mille Collines only a private memory, a forgotten episode in history. I went through hell and lived to tell the story, but I never expected to tell my story to you quite like this. The way it happened is a brief footnote.

One day in 1999 the telephone rang. On the line was a young man from New York named Keir Pearson who said he was researching a screenplay on the Rwandan genocide. A friend of his had been travelling in Africa at the time and had heard the dramatic radio interview given by my friend Thomas Kamilindi. The young man from New York had borrowed money from his girlfriend to buy an air ticket to Rwanda and wanted to talk to me. I said, sure. He organised a stopover in Brussels on his way to Kigali. The story of the Mille Collines was already well known. It had been told on the BBC and the Voice of America and other radio programs. But nobody had put it on film.

I spent an hour with Keir Pearson in my town house and was impressed with his sincerity, as well as with his desire to get the story correct. His business partner was an Irish film director named Terry George and together they made the movie *Hotel Rwanda* about my experience. There were a few dramatic embellishments, but the story was very close to the truth. The movie earned Academy Award nominations for Pearson and George as well as for the two main actors, Sophie Okonedo and Don Cheadle, whom I later befriended. I was happy he was chosen, for he is a fine actor and much better looking than I.

It was very strange for me to be called a 'hero' the way that I was when the movie was released in Europe and America. I was invited to the White House to meet President George W. Bush, who told me he saw the movie twice. I started giving lectures about the current state of affairs in Africa today and the importance of truth and reconciliation in the aftermath of genocide.

With the help of some friends I started the Hotel Rwanda Rusesabagina Foundation to provide education and health care to the thousands of orphans and homeless children who live in Rwanda today. Nearly half a million children were left parentless by the murders. The others, the younger ones, are known as *enfants du mauvais souvenir*, or 'children of bad memories'. They are the ones whose mothers were raped, impregnated and left to survive. Quite a few are HIV-positive from birth. Most of them never knew a mother's unconditional love because of the terrible way in which they came into the world. My foundation is dedicated to funding orphanages and medical treatment and to providing education for these lost children so that they may know some hope and not become a part of a future surge of evil in Rwanda. We cannot change the past, but we can improve the future with the limited tools and words that we have been given.

Words are the most powerful tools of all, and especially the words that we pass to those who come after us. I will never forget that favourite saying of my father's: 'Whoever does not talk to his father never knows what his grandfather said.' So I decided to write this book for the sake of the historic record.

I am a Rwandan, after all, and I know that all things pass away except history. History never dies. It is what defines us as a civilisation, and we live out our collective histories every day, in ways both good and evil. Over and over people kept telling me that what I did at the Mille Collines was heroic, but I never saw it that way, and I still don't. I was providing shelter. I was a hotel manager doing his job. This is the best thing anyone can say about me, and all I ever wanted. And that's really the best I have to give.

ELEVEN

I WAS NOT the only one who said no. There were thousands of other people in Rwanda who were also unimpressed by the propaganda and put their lives in jeopardy to shelter fugitives. Individual acts of courage happened every single day of the genocide. Some were partial killers, it is true, showing compassion to some and murdering others. But there were many who refused completely, and there would have been almost no survivors of the genocide without the thousands of secret kindnesses dispensed under the cover of night. We will never know the names of all those who opened their homes to hide would-be victims. Rwanda was full of ordinary killers, it is true, but it was also full of ordinary heroes.

There was a Muslim man, for example, who concealed up to 30 people in his sheds and outhouses. One of his guests reported the following: 'The *Interahamwe* killer was chasing me down the alley. I was going to die any second. I banged on the door of the yard. It opened almost immediately. He took me by the hand and stood in his doorway and told the killer to leave. He said the Koran says if you save one life it is like saving the whole world. He did not know it is a Jewish text as well.'

There was also Father Célestin Hakizimana, who presided over St Paul's Pastoral Centre in Kigali. He stood in contrast to those other priests and ministers who either condoned the genocide or slunk away when danger came. Father Hakizimana turned his church into a shelter for over 2,000 people and refused to budge to the demands of the militia.

There was Damas Mutezintare Gisimba, who received 400 hunted children into his orphanage. Many of them were hidden in chambers in the ceiling, along with prominent politicians. Gisimba also roamed around Kigali poking through the stacks of dead bodies piling up all around. He found several people not yet dead and took them into his care.

There were so many others. A farmer saved people by hiding them in trenches on his land and covering them up with plants and banana leaves to make it look like an ordinary field. An elderly woman pretended to be a sorceress and threatened to call down the power of the gods on any killers who tried to harm the people in her protection. A mayor used his own police force to fight the *Interahamwe* and was killed for his actions. Schoolteachers hid their hunted students in sheds and empty classrooms. Some of the names of these heroes are known, but most are not. Their good deeds are lost to history. The murders were anonymous and irrational, but the kindness and the bravery were there in scattered places too, and that is a big part of what gives me hope for the future.

What did these people have in common? I believe they all shared the long vision. They had an ability to see through the passing moment and to understand that the frenzy that had gripped Rwanda was a temporary condition at best. They acted decently, as was appropriate for decent times, and did not believe the world to be anything less than an essentially decent place, despite the onset of a collective insanity.

This is why I say that the individual's most potent weapon is a stubborn belief in the triumph of common decency. It is a simple belief, but it is not at all naive. It is, in fact, the shrewdest attitude possible. It is the best way to sabotage evil.

I remember reading this in the Bible when I was a young man: 'What is your life? You are a mist that appears for a little while and then vanishes.' Our time here on the earth is short, and our chance to make a difference is tiny. For me the grinding blocks of history came together in such a way that I was able to take what fragile defence I had and hold it in place for 76 days. If I was able to give much it was only because I had some useful things from my life to give. I am a hotel manager, trained to negotiate contracts and provide shelter for those who need it. My job never changed, even in a sea of fire.

Wherever the killing season should next begin and people should become strangers to their neighbours and themselves, my hope is that there will still be those ordinary men who say a quiet no and open the rooms upstairs.

PAUL RUSESABAGINA

Paul Rusesabagina was the manager of the Hotel des Diplomates and later of the Hotel des Mille Collines in Kigali, Rwanda, during the Rwandan genocide. He is a recipient of the US Presidential Medal of Freedom and the National Civil Rights Museum's 2005 Freedom Medal. He left Rwanda for Belgium in 1995. Rusesabagina now owns a trucking company operating in Zambia, and lives with his wife Tatiana and their four children in a suburb of Brussels.

Tom Zoellner is a freelance journalist and writer, who has worked as a reporter for the *San Francisco Chronicle*. He lives in New York City.

DEWEY

The small-town library cat
who touched the world

VICKI MYRON

❛I'd hurry out of my office to find Dewey hunched on the back edge of Kim's big, white daisy-wheel typewriter.

His head would be jerking from side to side as the disk moved left to right, then back again, until finally he couldn't take it any more and lunged at the clacker thingies, which were nothing more than the keys rising up to strike the paper.

The whole staff would be there, watching and laughing. Dewey's antics always drew a crowd.❜

INTRODUCTION

Welcome to Iowa

THERE IS A thousand-mile table of land in the middle of the United States, between the Mississippi River on the east and the deserts on the west. Out here, there are rolling hills, but no mountains. There are rivers and creeks, but few large lakes. The wind has worn down the rock outcroppings, turning them first to dust, then dirt, then soil, and finally to fine black farmland. Out here, the roads are straight, stretching to the horizon in long, unbroken lines. There are no corners, only occasional, almost imperceptible, bends. Exactly every mile, every road is intersected by another almost perfectly straight road. Inside is a square mile of farmland. Take a million of those square miles, lace them together, and you have one of the most important agricultural regions in the world. The Great Plains. The Bread Basket. The Heartland. Or, as many people think of it, the place you fly over on your way to somewhere else. Let them have the oceans and mountains, their beaches and their ski resorts. I'll take Iowa.

In north-west Iowa, in winter, the sky swallows the farmhouses. On a cold day, the dark clouds that blow in across the plains seem to churn the land under like a plow. In the spring, the world is flat and empty, full of brown dirt and hacked-off cornstalks waiting to be ploughed under, the sky and land perfectly balanced like a plate on a stick. But if you come in the late summer, the corn is nine feet high, bright green leaves topped with brilliant gold tassels. Most of the time you are buried in it, lost in the walls of corn, but top a small rise in the road and you can see endless fields of gold atop green, silken threads sparkling in the sun. Those silks are the sex organs of the corn, trapping pollen, flying golden yellow for a month and then slowly drying up and browning out under the stiff summer heat.

That's what I love about north-west Iowa: it is always changing. Not in the way cities change as buildings crowd each other ever higher, but in the way the country changes, slowly back and forth in a gentle motion that is always sliding forward, but never very fast. There aren't many roadside businesses out here. The farmhouses, which are fewer every year, hug the road. The towns pop up suddenly, bearing signs announcing THE JEWEL IN THE CROWN OF IOWA or THE GOLD BUCKLE ON THE CORN BELT, and disappear just as quickly. Every ten miles or so, there's a roadside cemetery, small plain markers behind low stone walls. These are pioneer plots that grew into extended family plots and eventually into town cemeteries. Nobody wants to be buried far from home, and nobody wants to waste much land. Use what you have. Make it simple. Keep it local.

Then, just when you're sliding away, when you're drifting into complacency like a corn row down the back side of a rise, the road widens and you pass a strip of stores: Matt Furniture, the Iron Horse Hotel, the Prime Rib restaurant, but also a Wal-Mart, a McDonald's, a Motel 6. Turn north at the stop light, the first turn in fifty miles no matter which direction you've been driving, not to mention the first stop light, and within a minute you've left the chains behind and you're driving the beautiful low bridge over the Little Sioux River right into the heart of Spencer, Iowa, a town that hasn't changed much since 1931.

Downtown Spencer is picture postcard small-town America: rows of storefronts in connecting two-and-three-storey buildings where people pull their cars to the kerb, get out and walk.

White Drug, Steffen Furniture and Eddie Quinn's Men's Clothing have been in business for decades. The Hen House sells decorating items to farmwives and the occasional tourist on her way to the Iowa lake country twenty miles north. There's a hobby shop specialising in model aeroplanes, a card shop and a store that rents oxygen tanks and wheelchairs. The old movie theatre is still in business, although it shows only second-run movies since a seven-screen cineplex opened south of the bridge.

The downtown ends at The Hotel, eight blocks from the bridge. The Hotel. That's the actual name. It was known as the Tagney in the late 1920s when it was the area's best accommodation, bus depot, train station and only sit-down restaurant. By the end of the Great Depression, it had become a flophouse and, according to legend, the town bordello. The five-storey building, plain red brick and built to last, was eventually abandoned, then rehabilitated in the 1970s, but by then the real action had moved five blocks down Grand Avenue to Sister's Main Street Café, a no-frills diner with Formica tables, drip coffee and smoky booths. Three groups of men congregate every morning at Sister's: the old guys, the older guys, and the really old guys. Together, they have run Spencer for the past sixty years.

Around the corner from Sister's Café, across a small parking lot and just half a block off Grand Avenue, is a low, grey concrete building: the Spencer Public Library. My name is Vicki Myron and I've been working in that library for twenty-five years, the last twenty as director. I've overseen the arrival of the first computer and the addition of the reading room. I've watched children grow up and leave, only to walk back through the doors ten years later with their own children. The Spencer Public Library may not look like much, at least not at first, but it is the centrepiece, the middle ground, the heart of this heartland story. Everything I'm going to tell you about Spencer all flows back eventually to this small grey building and to the cat who lived here for more than nineteen years.

How much of an impact can an animal have? How many lives can one cat touch? How is it possible for an abandoned kitten to transform a small library into a meeting place and tourist attraction, inspire a classic American town, bind together an entire region and, eventually, become famous around the world? You can't even begin to answer those questions until you hear the story of Dewey Readmore Books, the beloved library cat of Spencer, Iowa.

CHAPTER 1

IT WAS 18 JANUARY 1988, a bitterly cold Iowa Monday. The night before, the temperature had reached minus fifteen degrees, and that didn't take into account the wind, which cut under your coat and squeezed your bones. It was a killing freeze, the kind that made it almost painful to breathe. The problem with flat land, as all of Iowa knows, is that there's nothing to stop the weather. It blows out of Canada, across the Dakotas and straight into town. The first bridge in Spencer across the Little Sioux, built in the late 1800s, had to be taken down because the river became so jammed with ice, everyone worried the pylons would collapse. That's winter in Spencer for you.

I have never been a morning person, especially on a dark and cloudy January day, but I have always been dedicated. There were a few cars on the road at seven thirty, when I drove to work, but as usual mine was the first car in the parking lot. Across the street, the Spencer Public Library was dead—no lights, no movement, no sound until I flipped a switch and brought it to life. The heater switched on automatically during the night, but the library was still a freezer first thing in the morning.

I went immediately to the library staff room—nothing more than a kitchenette with a microwave and a sink, a refrigerator too messy for most people's taste, a few chairs and a phone for personal calls—hung up my coat and started the coffee. Then I scanned the Saturday newspaper. Most local issues could affect, or could be affected by, the library. The local newspaper, the *Spencer Daily Reporter*, didn't publish on Sunday or Monday, so Monday was catch-up morning from the weekend.

'Good morning, Vicki,' said Jean Hollis Clark, the assistant library director, taking off her scarf and mittens. 'It's a mean one out there.'

'Good morning, Jean,' I said, putting aside the paper.

In the centre of the staff room, against the back wall, was a large metal box with a hinged lid. The box was two feet high and four feet square. A metal chute rose out of the top of the box, then disappeared into the wall. At the other end, in the alley behind the building, was a metal slot: the library's after-hours book return.

You find all kinds of things in a library drop box— garbage, rocks, snowballs, soda cans. Stick a slot in a wall and you're asking for trouble, especially if, as it did at the Spencer Public Library, the slot opened on to a back alley across the street from the town's middle school. Several times we had been startled in the middle of the afternoon by a loud pop from the drop box. Inside, we'd find a firecracker.

After the weekend, the drop box would also be full of books, so every Monday I loaded them onto one of our book carts so the clerks could process and shelve them later in the day. When I came back with the cart on this particular Monday morning, Jean was standing quietly in the middle of the room.

'I heard a noise.'

'What kind of noise?'

'From the drop box. I think it's an animal.'

'A what?'

'An animal. I think there's an animal in the drop box.'

That was when I heard it, a low rumble from under the metal cover. It didn't sound like an animal. It sounded more like an old man struggling to clear his throat. But I doubted it was an old man. The opening at the top of the chute was only a few inches wide, so that would have been quite a squeeze. It was an animal, I had little doubt of that, but what kind? I got down on my knees, reached over to the lid, and hoped for a chipmunk.

The first thing I felt was a blast of freezing air. Someone had jammed a book into the return slot, wedging it open. It was as cold in the box as it was outside; maybe colder, since the box was lined with metal. I was still catching my breath when I saw the kitten.

It was huddled in the front left corner of the box, its head down, its legs tucked underneath it, trying to appear as small as possible. Books, piled haphazardly to the top of the box, partially hid it from view. I lifted one gingerly. The kitten looked up at me, slowly and sadly. Then it lowered its head and sank down into its hole. It wasn't trying to hide. It was just hoping to be saved.

I know melting can be a cliché, but I think that's what actually happened to me at that moment: I lost every bone in my body. I am not a mushy person. I'm a single mother and a farm girl who has steered her life through hard times, but this was so, so . . . unexpected.

I lifted the kitten out of the box. My hands nearly swallowed it. We found out later it was eight weeks old, but it looked no more than eight days old, if that. It was so thin, I could see every rib. I could feel its heart beating, its lungs pumping. The poor kitten was so weak, it could barely hold up its head, and it was shaking uncontrollably. It opened its mouth, but the sound, which came two seconds later, was weak and ragged.

And cold. That's what I remember most, because I couldn't believe a living animal could be so cold. It felt like there was no warmth at all. So I cradled the kitten in my arms to share my heat. It didn't fight. Instead, it snuggled into my chest, then laid its head against my heart.

'Oh, my golly,' said Jean.

'The poor baby,' I said, squeezing tighter.

'It's adorable.'

Neither of us said anything for a while. We were just staring at the kitten. Finally Jean said, 'How do you think it got in there?'

I wasn't thinking about last night. I was only thinking

about right now. It was too early to call the veterinarian, who wouldn't be in for an hour. But the kitten was so cold. Even in the warmth of my arms, I could feel it shaking.

'We've got to do something,' I said.

Jean grabbed a towel, and we wrapped the little fellow up until only its nose was sticking out, its huge eyes staring from the shadows in disbelief.

'Let's give it a warm bath,' I said. 'Maybe that will stop the shivering.'

I filled the staff room sink with warm water, testing it with my elbow as I clutched the kitten in my arms. It slid into the sink like a block of ice. Jean found some shampoo in the art closest and I rubbed the kitten slowly and lovingly. As the water turned greyer and greyer, the kitten's wild shivering turned to soft purring. I smiled. This kitten was tough. But it was so very young. When I finally lifted it out of the sink, it looked like a newborn: huge lidded eyes and big ears sticking out from a tiny head and an even smaller body. Wet, defenceless and mewing quietly for its mother.

We dried it with the blow dryer we used for drying glue at craft time. Within thirty seconds, I was holding a beautiful, long-haired orange tabby. The kitten had been so filthy, I had thought it was grey.

By this time Doris and Kim had arrived, and there were four people in the staff room, each cooing over the kitten. Eight hands touched him, seemingly at once. The other three staffers talked over one another while I stood silently cradling the kitten like a baby and rocking back and forth from foot to foot.

'Where did it come from?'

'The drop box.'

'No!'

'Is it a boy or a girl?'

I glanced up. They were all looking at me. 'A boy,' I said. 'He's beautiful.'

'How old is he?'

'How did he get in the box?'

I wasn't listening. I only had eyes for the kitten.

'It's so cold.'

'Bitterly cold.'

'The coldest morning of the year.'

A pause, then: 'Someone must have put him in the box.'

'That's awful.'

'Maybe they were trying to save him. From the cold.'

'I don't know . . . he's so helpless.'

'He's so young.'

'He's so beautiful! Oh, he's breaking my heart.'

I put him down on the table. The poor kitten could barely stand. The pads on all four of his paws were frostbitten and over the next week they would turn white and peel off. And yet the kitten managed to do something truly amazing. He steadied himself on the table and slowly looked up into each face. Then he began to hobble. As each person reached to pet him, he rubbed his tiny head against her hand and purred. Forget the horrible events in his young life. Forget the cruel person who shoved him down that library drop box. It was as if, from that moment on, he wanted to personally thank every person he ever met for saving his life.

By now it had been twenty minutes since I pulled the kitten out of the drop box and I'd had plenty of time to think through a few things—the once common practice of keeping library cats, my ongoing plan to make the library more friendly and appealing, the logistics of bowls and food and cat litter, the trusting expression on the kitten's face when he burrowed into my chest and looked up into my eyes. So I was more than prepared when someone finally asked, 'What should we do with him?'

'Well,' I said, 'maybe we can keep him.'

THE MOST AMAZING thing about the kitten was how happy he was that first day. Here he was, in a new environment, surrounded by eager strangers who wanted nothing more than to squeeze him, fondle him and coo over him, and he was perfectly calm. No matter how many times we passed him from hand to hand and no matter what position we held him in, he was never jumpy or fidgety. He never tried to bite or get away. Instead, he just melted into each person's arms and stared up into her eyes.

And that was no small feat, because we didn't leave him alone for a second. If someone had to set him down—for instance, because there was actual work to do—there were always at least five sets of hands ready to grab him, hold him and love him. In fact, when I let go of him at closing time that first night, I had to watch him for five minutes to make sure he could totter all the way to his food dish and litter box. I don't think his poor frostbitten feet had touched the ground all day.

The next morning, Doris Armstrong brought in a warm pink blanket. We all watched as she bent down and scratched the kitten under the chin, then folded the blanket and put it in a cardboard box. The kitten stepped gingerly into the box and curled his legs underneath his body for warmth. His eyes closed in blissful contentment, but he only had a few seconds to rest before someone snatched him up and wrapped him in their arms. A few seconds, but it was enough. The staff had been polarised for years. Now we were all making accommodations, coming together as a family, and the kitten was clearly happy to call the library home.

It wasn't until late the second morning that we finally shared our little guy with someone outside the staff. That person was Mary Houston, Spencer's local historian and a member of the library board. The staff may already have accepted the kitten, but keeping him wasn't our decision. The previous day I had called the mayor, Squeege Johnson, who was in his last month in office. As I suspected, he didn't care. The city attorney, my second call, didn't know of any statutes barring animals from the library and didn't feel compelled to spend time looking for one. Good enough for me. The library board, a panel of citizens appointed by the mayor to oversee the library, had the final say. They didn't object to the idea of a library cat, but I can't say they were enthusiastic.

That's why meeting a board member like Mary was so important. Agreeing to have an animal in the library was one thing; agreeing on *this* animal was another thing entirely. You can't just put any cute cat in a library. If he's not friendly, he's going to make enemies. If he's too shy or scared, nobody will stand up for him. If he's not patient, he's going to bite. If he's too rambunctious, he's going to make a mess. And above all, he has to love being around people, and he has to make those people love him back. In short, it has to be the right cat.

I had no doubt about our boy. From the moment he looked up into my eyes that first morning, so calm and content, I knew he was right for the library. There wasn't a flutter in his heart as I held him in my arms; there wasn't a moment of panic in his eyes. He trusted me completely. He trusted everyone on staff completely. That's what made him so special: his complete and unabashed trust. And because of it, I trusted him, too.

But that doesn't mean I wasn't a little apprehensive when I motioned Mary into the staff area. As I took the kitten in my arms and turned to face her, I felt a flutter in my heart, a moment of doubt. When the kitten had looked into my eyes, something else had happened, too; we had made a connection. He was more than just a cat to me. It had only been a day, but already I couldn't stand the thought of being without him.

'There he is,' Mary exclaimed with a smile. I held him a little more tightly as she reached out to pet him on the top of the head, but Dewey didn't even stiffen. Instead, he stretched out his neck to sniff her hand.

'Oh, my,' Mary said. 'He's handsome.'

Handsome. I heard it over and over again the next few days because there was no other way to describe him. This was a handsome cat. His coat was a mix of vibrant orange and white with subtle darker stripes. It grew longer as he got older, but as a kitten it was thick and stylishly long only around his neck. This kitten face was perfectly proportioned. And his eyes, those huge golden eyes.

But it wasn't just his looks that made him beautiful; it was also his personality. If you cared at all about cats, you just had to hold him. There was something in his face, in the way he looked at you, that called out for love.

'He likes to be cradled,' I said, gently sliding him into Mary's arms. 'No, on his back. Like a baby.'

The kitten shook his tail and nestled down into Mary's arms. He didn't just trust the library staff instinctively, it turned out; he trusted everyone.

'Oh, Vicki,' Mary said. 'He's adorable. What's his name?'

'We're calling him Dewey. After the Dewey decimal system. But we haven't really decided on a name yet.'

'Hi, Dewey. Do you like the library?' Dewey stared into Mary's face, then pushed his head against her arm. Mary looked up with a smile. 'I could hold him all day.'

But, of course, she didn't. She put Dewey back into my arms and I took him around the corner. The entire staff was waiting for us.

'That went well,' I said. 'One down, ten thousand to go.'

Slowly we introduced Dewey to a few regulars known to love cats. He was still weak, so we passed him directly into their arms. Marcie Muckey came in that second day. Instantly smitten. Mike Baehr and his wife, Peg, loved him—which was nice, since Mike was on the library board. Pat Jones and Judy Johnson thought him adorable.

A week later, Dewey's story ran on the front page of the *Spencer Daily Reporter* under the headline 'Purr-fect Addition Made to Spencer Library'. The half-page article told the story of Dewey's miraculous rescue and was accompanied by a colour photograph of a tiny orange kitten staring shyly but confidently into the camera from atop an old-fashioned pull-drawer card catalogue.

Publicity is a dangerous thing. For a week, Dewey had been a secret between the library staff and a few select patrons. If you didn't come into the library, you didn't know about him. Now everyone in town knew. Most people, even library regulars, didn't give Dewey a second thought. There were two groups, though, that were thrilled by his arrival: the cat lovers and the children. Just the smiles on the faces of the children, their excitement and laughter, were enough to convince me Dewey should stay.

Then there were the complainers. I was a little disappointed,

I must admit, but not surprised. One woman took particular offence. Her letter, sent to me and every member of the city council, was pure fire and brimstone, full of images of children keeling over from sudden asthma attacks, and pregnant women spontaneously miscarrying when exposed to kitty litter.

According to the letter, I was destroying the social fabric of the community. An animal! In a library! If we let that stand, what was to stop people from walking a cow down Grand Avenue? In fact, she threatened to show up in the library one morning very soon with her cow in tow. Fortunately nobody took her seriously. I have no doubt she spoke for others in the community, but general anger wasn't my concern. None of those people, as far as I could tell, ever visited the library.

Far more important to me, though, were the worried phone calls. 'My child has allergies. What am I going to do? He loves the library.' I knew that would be the most common concern, so I was prepared. A year earlier, Muffin, the beloved cat in residence at the Putnam Valley Library in upstate New York, had been banished after a library board member developed a severe cat allergy. As a consequence, the library lost $80,000 in promised donations, mostly from the estates of local citizens. I had no intention of letting my cat, or my library, go the way of Muffin.

I solicited the advice of two general-practice doctors. The Spencer Public Library, they noted, was a large, open space sectioned off by rows of four-foot-high shelves. The staff area, my office and the supply closets were enclosed by a temporary wall, leaving six feet open to the ceiling. There were two door-size openings in that wall, and since neither has a door, they are always accessible. Even the staff area was an open space, with desks pushed back to back or separated by bookshelves.

Not only did this layout allow Dewey easy access to the safety of the staff area at all times, but the doctors assured me it would also prevent the build-up of dander and hair. The library, apparently, was perfectly designed to prevent allergies. If anyone on staff had been allergic it might have been a problem, but a few hours of exposure every couple of days? The doctors agreed there was nothing to worry about.

I spoke personally with each concerned caller and passed on this professional assessment. The parents were sceptical, of course, but most brought their children to the library for a trial run. I held Dewey in my arms for each visit. I not only didn't know how the parents would react, I didn't know how Dewey would react because the children were so excited to see him.

Their mothers would tell them to be quiet, be gentle. The children would approach slowly, tentatively, and whisper, 'Hi, Dewey,' and then explode with squeals as their mothers ushered them away with a quick, 'That's enough.' Dewey didn't mind the noise; he was the calmest kitten I'd ever seen. He did mind, I think, that these children weren't allowed to pet him.

But a few days later, one family was back; this time with a camera. And this time the allergic little boy, the object of such concern for the mother, was sitting beside Dewey, petting him, while his mother took pictures.

'Justin can't have pets,' she told me. 'I never knew how much he missed them. He loves Dewey already.'

I loved Dewey already, too. We all loved Dewey. How could you resist his charm? He was beautiful, loving, social—and still limping on his tiny frostbitten feet. What I couldn't believe was how much Dewey loved us. How comfortable he seemed around strangers. His attitude seemed to be, how can anyone not love a cat? Or more simply, how can anyone resist me?

CHAPTER 2

DEWEY WAS a fortunate cat. He not only survived the freezing library drop box, but also fell into the arms of a staff that loved him and a library perfectly designed to care for him. There were no two ways about it, Dewey led a charmed life. But Spencer was also lucky, because Dewey couldn't have fallen into our lives at a better time. That winter wasn't just bitterly cold; it was one of the worst times in Spencer's history.

Some of you may not remember the farm crisis we had here in the US in the 1980s. Maybe you remember reading about Farm Aid and the collapse of family farming, about the nation moving from small growers to large factory farms that stretch for miles without a farmhouse, or even a farm worker, in sight. For most people in the US, it was just a story, not something that affected them directly. In Spencer, you could feel it: in the air, in the ground, in every spoken word. We had a solid manufacturing base, but we were still a farm town. We supported, and were supported by, farmers. And on the farms, things were falling apart. These were families we knew, families that had lived in the area for generations, and we could see the strain. First they stopped coming in for new parts and machinery, making do with bootstrap repairs. Then they cut back on supplies. Finally they stopped making mortgage payments, hoping for a booming harvest to set the account books right. When a miracle didn't come, the banks foreclosed. The price of land began to drop and credit dried up. The farmers couldn't borrow against their land to buy new machinery, or even new seed for the planting season. Crop prices weren't high enough to pay the interest on the old loans, many of which had rates of more than 20 per cent a year. It took four or five years to reach bottom, but economic forces were pulling our farmers steadily down.

In 1985, Land O'Lakes, the *giant* butter and margarine manufacturer, pulled out of the plant on the north edge of town. Soon after, unemployment reached 10 per cent. The value of houses dropped 25 per cent, seemingly overnight. People were leaving the county, even the state of Iowa, looking for jobs.

The price of farmland plummeted further, forcing more farmers into foreclosure. But selling the land at auction couldn't cover the loans; the banks were stuck with the loss. In towns all across Iowa, banks failed. Banks were failing across the entire Midwest. The savings and loan bank in Spencer was sold to outsiders for pennies on the dollar, and the new owners didn't want to make new loans. Economic development stalled. As late as 1989, there wasn't a single housing permit issued in the city of Spencer. Nobody wanted to put money into a dying town.

Every Christmas, Spencer had a Santa Claus. The retailers sponsored a raffle and gave away a trip to Hawaii. In 1979, there wasn't a vacant storefront in town for Santa to set up shop in. In 1985, there were twenty-five empty storefronts downtown, a 30 per cent vacancy rate. No trip to Hawaii was offered.

The library did what it could. When Land O'Lakes skipped town, we set up a job bank that contained all our job listings and books on job skills, job descriptions and technical training. We set up a computer so local men and women could create résumés and cover letters. This was the first computer most of these people had ever seen. It was almost depressing how many people used the job bank. And if it was depressing for an employed librarian, just think how depressing it was for a laid-off factory worker, bankrupt small business owner, or out-of-work farmhand.

Then into our laps fell Dewey. I don't want to make too much of this one turn of events, because Dewey didn't put food on anyone's table. He didn't create jobs. He didn't turn our economy around. But one of the worst things about bad times is the effect on your mind. Bad times drain you of energy. They occupy your thoughts. They taint everything in your life. Bad news is as poisonous as bad bread. At the very least, Dewey was a distraction.

But he was so much more. Dewey's story resonated with the people of Spencer. We identified with it. Hadn't we all been shoved down the library drop box by the banks? By outside economic forces? By the rest of America, which ate our food but didn't care about the people who grew it?

Here was an alley cat, left for dead in a freezing drop box, terrified, alone, and clinging to life. He made it through that dark night, and that terrible event turned out to be the best thing that ever happened to him. He never lost his trust, no matter what the circumstances, or his appreciation for life. He was humble. Maybe *humble* isn't the right word—he was a cat, after all—but he wasn't arrogant. He was confident.

Maybe it was the confidence of the near-death survivor, the serenity you find when you've been to the end, beyond hope, and made it back.

It took Dewey ten days to get healthy enough to explore the library on his own, and once he did, it was clear he had no interest in books, shelves and other inanimate objects. His interest was people. If there was a patron in the library, he'd walk straight up to him—still slow on his sore feet but no longer hobbling—and jump into his lap. More often than not he was pushed away, but rejection never deterred him. Dewey kept jumping, kept looking for laps to lie in and hands to pet him, and things started to change.

I noticed it first with the older patrons, who often came to the library to flip through magazines or browse for books. Once Dewey started spending time with them, they showed up more frequently and stayed longer. They had always given the staff a friendly wave or good morning, but now they engaged us in conversation, usually about Dewey. They weren't just killing time, now; they were visiting friends.

One older man, in particular, came in at the same time every morning, sat in the same big, comfortable chair, and read the newspaper. His wife had recently died, and I knew he was lonely. From the first moment Dewey climbed into his lap, the man was beaming. Suddenly he wasn't reading the newspaper alone. 'Are you happy here, Dewey?' the man would ask every morning as he petted his new friend. Dewey would shut his eyes and, more often than not, drop off to sleep.

And then there was the man at the job bank. I didn't know him personally, but I knew his type—proud, hardworking, resilient—and I knew he was suffering. He was from Spencer, like most of the men who used the job bank, a labourer, not a farmer. His job-hunting outfit, like his former work outfit, was jeans and a standard issue shirt, and he never used the computer. He studied the résumé books; he looked through our job listings; he never asked for help. He was quiet, steady, unflappable, but as the weeks passed I could see the strain in the hunch of his back and the deepening lines on his always clean-shaven face.

Every morning, Dewey approached him, but the man always pushed him away. Then one day I saw Dewey sitting on his lap, and for the first time in weeks, the man was smiling. He was still bent and there was still sadness in his eyes, but he was smiling. Maybe Dewey couldn't give much, but in the winter of 1988 he gave exactly what Spencer needed.

So I gave our kitten to the community. The staff understood. He wasn't our cat, he belonged to the patrons of the Spencer Public Library. I put a box by the front door, right next to the job bank, and told people, 'You know the cat who sits on your lap and helps with your résumé? The one who reads the newspaper with you? Well, he's your cat, and I want you to help name him.'

I had only been library director for six months, so I was still enthusiastic about contests. Every few weeks we put a box in the lobby, made an announcement on the local radio station, offered a prize for the winning entry, and tried to stoke interest in the latest bit of library news. A good contest with a good prize might draw fifty entries. If the prize was expensive, like a television set, we might scrape up seventy. Usually we got about twenty-five. Our Name the Kitty contest, which wasn't mentioned on the radio because I wanted only regular patrons to participate, and which didn't even offer a prize, received 397 entries. That's when I realised the library had stumbled on to something important.

By far the most entries, more than fifty, were for Dewey. The patrons had already grown attached to this kitten, and they didn't want him to change his name. And to be honest, the staff didn't, either. We, too, had grown attached to Dewey just the way he was.

Still, the name needed something. Our best option, we decided, was to think of a last name. Mary Walk, our children's librarian, suggested Readmore. Dewey Readmore. I suggested the last name Books.

Dewey Readmore Books. Do We Read More Books? A challenge. A name to put us all in the mood to learn.

Dewey Readmore Books. Three names for our regal, confident, beautiful cat.

CATS ARE CREATURES of habit, and it didn't take long for Dewey to develop a routine. When I arrived at the library every morning, he was waiting for me at the front door. He would take a few bites of his food while I hung up my jacket and bag, and then we would walk the library together, making sure everything was in place and discussing our evenings. Dewey was more a sniffer than a talker, but I didn't mind. The library, once so cold and dead first thing in the morning, was alive and well.

After our walk, Dewey would visit the staff. If someone was having a bad morning, he'd spend extra time with her. Jean Hollis Clark had recently married and commuted forty-five minutes from Estherville to the library. You'd think that would frazzle her, but Jean was the calmest person you've ever met. The only thing that bothered her was the friction between a couple of people on staff. She'd still be carrying the tension when she arrived the next morning, and Dewey was always there to comfort her. He had an amazing sense of who needed him, and he was always willing to give his time. But never for too long. At two minutes to nine, Dewey would drop whatever he was doing and race for the front door.

A patron was always waiting outside at nine o'clock when we opened the doors, and she would usually enter with a warm, 'Hi, Dewey. How are you this morning?'

It wouldn't take long for him to find a lap, and since he'd been up for two hours that usually meant it was time for a quick nap. Dewey was already so comfortable in the library, he had no problem falling asleep in public places. He preferred laps, of course, but if they weren't available he would curl up in a box. The cards for the catalogue came in small boxes about the size of a pair of baby shoes. Dewey liked to cram all four feet inside, sit down, and let his sides ooze over the edge. If the box was a little bigger, he buried his head and tail in the bottom. The only thing you could see was a big blob of back fur sticking out of the top. One morning I found Dewey sleeping beside a box full of cards, with one paw resting inside. It probably took him hours to reluctantly admit there wasn't room for anything else.

Soon after, I watched him slowly wind his way into a half-empty tissue box. He put his two front feet through the slit on top, then delicately stepped in with the other two. Slowly, he sat down on his hind legs and rolled his back end until it was wedged into the box. Then he started bending his front legs and working the front of his body into the crease. The operation took four or five minutes, but finally there was nothing left but his head sticking out in one direction and his tail sticking out in the other. I watched as he stared half-lidded into the distance, pretending the rest of the world didn't exist.

Dewey's other favourite resting spot was the back of the copier. 'Don't worry,' I told the confused patrons, 'you can't disturb him. He sleeps there because it's warm. The more copies you make, the more heat the machine produces, the happier he'll be.'

If the patrons weren't quite sure what to do with Dewey yet, the staff had no such hesitation. One of my first decisions was that no library funds would ever be spent on Dewey's care. Instead, we kept a Dewey Box in the back room. Everyone on staff tossed in their loose change. Most of us also brought in soda cans from home. Recycling soda cans was all the rage, and one of the clerks, Cynthia Behrends, would take the cans to a drop-off point every week. The whole staff was 'feeding the kitty' to feed the kitty.

In return for these small contributions, we'd get endless hours of pleasure. Dewey loved drawers, and he developed a habit of popping out of them when you least expected. If you were shelving books, he'd jump onto the cart and demand a trip around the library. And when Kim Peterson, the library secretary, started typing, you knew a show was about to begin. As soon as I heard those keys, I'd put down my work and wait for the signal.

'Dewey's after the clacker thingies again!' Kim would call out to me.

I'd hurry out of my office to find Dewey hunched on the back edge of Kim's big, white daisy-wheel typewriter. His head would be jerking from side to side as the disk moved left to right, then back again, until finally he couldn't take it any more and lunged at the clacker thingies, which were nothing more than the keys rising up to strike the paper. The whole staff would be there, watching and laughing. Dewey's antics always drew a crowd.

This was no small feat. Everyone at the library was well-intentioned, but over the years the staff had become splintered and cliquish. Only Doris Armstrong, who was older and possibly wiser than the rest of us, had managed to stay friends with everyone. She had a large desk in the middle of the staff area where she covered each new book with a plastic protective sleeve, and her humour and good cheer held us together. She was also our biggest cat lover, and soon her desk was one of Dewey's favourite spots. He would sprawl there in the late morning, batting at her big sheets of plastic, the new centre of attention and the mutual friend of everyone on staff. Here, finally, was something we could share.

Just as important, he was a friend to all our children, too. Nothing concrete happened—no one apologised or discussed their issues, for instance—but once Dewey arrived the tension began to lift. We were laughing; we were happier; Dewey had brought us together.

But no matter how much fun Dewey was having, he never forgot his routine. At exactly ten thirty, he would hop up and head for the staff room. Jean Hollis Clark ate yoghurt on her break, and if he hung around long enough, she'd let him lick the lid. Jean always found ways to accommodate Dewey. If Dewey wanted down time, he would lie limply over Jean's left shoulder—and only her left shoulder, never her right—while she filed papers. After a few months, Dewey wouldn't let us hold him cradled in our arms any more, so the whole staff adopted Jean's over-the-shoulder technique. We called it the Dewey Carry.

Dewey helped me with down time, too, which was nice, since I had a tendency to work too hard. Many days I'd be hunched over my desk for hours, so intent on budget numbers or progress reports that I wouldn't even realise Dewey was there until he sprang into my lap.

'How you doing, baby boy?' I'd say with a smile. 'So nice

to see you.' I'd pet him a few times before turning back to my work. Unsatisfied, he'd climb on my desk and start sniffing. 'Oh, you just happened to sit on the paper I'm working on, didn't you? Purely a coincidence.'

I put him on the floor. He hopped back up. 'Not now, Dewey. I'm busy.' I put him back down. He hopped back up. Maybe if I ignored him . . .

He pushed his head against my pencil. I pushed him aside. *Fine*, he thought, *knock these pens to the ground*. Which he proceeded to do, one pen at a time, watching each one fall. I couldn't help but laugh.

'Okay, Dewey, you win.' I wadded up a piece of paper and threw it to him. He ran after it, sniffed it, then came back. Typical cat. Always one to play, never one to fetch. I walked over, picked up the paper, tossed it a few more times. 'What am I going to do with you?'

But it wasn't all jokes and games. I was the boss, and I had responsibilities—like giving the cat a bath. The first time I bathed Dewey, I was confident things would go well. He loved the bath that first morning, right? This time, Dewey slid into the sink like a block of ice dropped into a vat of acid. He thrashed. He screamed. He put his feet on the edge of the sink and tried to throw his body over the side. I held him down with both arms. Twenty minutes later, I was covered with water. My hair looked like I had stuck my tongue in a light socket. Everybody laughed, including, eventually, me.

The third bath was just as bad. I managed to get Dewey scrubbed, but I didn't have the patience for towelling and blow-drying. Not this crazy kitten.

'Fine,' I told him. 'If you hate it that much, just go.'

Dewey was a vain cat. He would spend an hour washing his face until he got it just right. The funniest part was the way he would ball up his fist, lick it, and shove it into his ears. He would work those ears until they were sparkling white. Now, soaking wet, he looked like a Chihuahua crushed by a wave of toupees. It was pathetic. The staff was laughing and taking pictures, but Dewey looked so genuinely upset that after a few minutes the pictures stopped.

'Have a sense of humour, Dew,' I teased him. 'You brought this on yourself.' He curled up behind a shelf of books and didn't come out for hours. After that, Dewey and I agreed that two baths a year were plenty.

'The bath is nothing,' I told Dewey a few months into his stay at the library, wrapping him up in his green towel. 'You're not going to like this at all.' Dewey never rode in a cage; it was too much like that night in the box. Whenever I took him out of the library, I just wrapped him up in his green towel.

Five minutes later, we arrived at Dr Esterly's office at the other end of town. He was a quiet, self-effacing man with an extremely deliberate way of speaking. His voice was deep and slow like a lazy river. He didn't rush. He was always tidy. He was a big man but his hands were gentle. He was conscientious and efficient. He knew his job. He loved animals. His authority came from his lack of words, not his use of them.

'Hi, Dewey,' he said, checking him over.

'Do you think this is absolutely necessary, Doctor?'

'Cats need to be neutered.'

I looked down at Dewey's tiny paws, which had finally healed. There were tufts of fur sticking out from between his toes. 'Do you think he's part Persian?'

Dr Esterly looked at Dewey. 'No. He's just a good-looking alley cat.'

I didn't believe it for a second.

'Dewey is a product of survival of the fittest,' Dr Esterly continued. 'His ancestors have probably lived in that alley for generations.'

'So he's one of us.'

Dr Esterly smiled. 'I suppose so.' He picked Dewey up and held him under his arm. Dewey was relaxed and purring. The last thing Dr Esterly said before they disappeared around the corner was, 'Dewey is one fine cat.'

He sure was. And I missed him already.

When I picked Dewey up the next morning, my heart almost broke in two. He had a faraway look in his eyes, and a little shaved belly. I took him in my arms. He pushed his head against my arm and started purring. He was so happy to see his old pal Vicki.

Back at the library, the staff dropped everything. 'Poor baby. Poor baby.' I gave him over to their care—he was our mutual friend, after all—and went back to work. The trip to the vet's office had put me behind, and I had a mountain of work. I needed two of me to do this job right, but the city would never have paid for it.

But I wasn't alone. An hour later, as I was hanging up the phone, I looked up to see Dewey hobbling through my office door. I knew he'd been getting love and attention from the rest of the staff, but I could tell from his determined wobbling that he needed something more.

Sure, cats can be fun, but my relationship with Dewey was already far more complex and intimate. He was so intelligent. He was so playful. He treated people so well. I didn't yet have a deep bond with him, but even now, near the beginning, I loved him.

And he loved me back. Not like he loved everyone else, but in a special and deeper way. The look he gave me that first morning meant something. It really did. Never was that more clear than now, as he pushed towards me with such determination. I reached down, scooped him up, and cradled him against my chest. Dewey put his head on my shoulder, right up against my neck, and purred.

CHAPTER 3

DON'T GET ME wrong, everything wasn't perfect with the Dew. Yes, he was a sweet and beautiful cat, and yes, he was extraordinarily trusting and generous, but he was still a kitten. He'd streak maniacally through the staff room. He'd knock your work to the floor out of pure playfulness. He was too immature to know who really needed him, and he sometimes wouldn't take no for an answer when a patron wanted to be left alone. At Story Hour, his presence made the children so rambunctious and unpredictable that Mary Walk, our children's librarian, banned him from the room.

But nothing compared to his behaviour around catnip. Doris Armstrong was always bringing Dewey presents. One day near the end of Dewey's first summer, she quite innocently brought in a bag of fresh catnip. Dewey was so excited by the smell, I thought he was going to climb her leg. For the first time in his life, the cat actually begged.

When Doris finally crumbled a few leaves on the floor, Dewey started smelling them so hard, I thought he was going to inhale the floor. After a few sniffs, he started sneezing, but he didn't slow down. Instead, he started chewing the leaves, then alternating sniffing, chewing, sniffing. His muscles started to ripple, a slow cascade of tension flowing out of his bones and down his back. When he finally shook that tension out the end of his tail, he flopped over on the ground and rolled back and forth in the catnip until he lost every bone in his body. Unable to walk, he slithered on the floor, undulating as he rubbed his chin along the carpet. Then, gradually, his spine bent backwards, in slow motion, until his head was resting on his behind. I swear the front half of his body wasn't even connected to the back half. When he finally, and accidentally, ended up flat on his tummy, he rippled his way back to the catnip and started rolling in it again. Most of the leaves were by now stuck in his fur, but he kept sniffing and chewing. Finally he stretched out on his back and started kicking his chin with his back legs. This lasted until, with a few flailing kicks hanging feebly in the air, Dewey passed out right on top of the last of the catnip. Doris and I looked at each other in amazement, then burst out laughing.

Dewey never tired of catnip. He would often sniff half-heartedly at old, worn-out leaves, but if there were fresh leaves in the library, Dewey knew it. And every time he got hold of catnip, it was the same thing: the undulating back, the rolling, the slithering, the bending, the kicking, and finally one very tired, very comatose cat. We called it the Dewey Mambo.

Dewey's other interest—besides drawers, boxes, copiers, typewriters and catnip—was rubber bands. Dewey was absolutely fanatical about rubber bands. He didn't even need to see them; he could smell them across the library. As soon as you put a box of rubber bands on your desk, he was there.

'Here you go, Dewey,' I would say as I opened a new bag. 'One for you and one for me.' He would take his rubber band in his mouth and happily skip away.

I would find it the next morning . . . in his litter box. I thought, 'That can't be good.'

Dewey always attended staff meetings, but fortunately he wasn't yet able to understand what we were talking about: it was easy to wrap up the meeting with a simple reminder. 'Don't give Dewey any more rubber bands. I don't care how much he begs. He's been eating them, and I have a feeling rubber isn't the healthiest food for a growing kitten.'

The next day, there were more rubber band worms in Dewey's litter. At the next staff meeting, I was more direct. 'Is anyone giving Dewey rubber bands?'

No. No. No. No. No.

'Then he must be stealing them. From now on, don't leave rubber bands lying out on your desk.'

Easier said than done. Much, much easier said than done. You would be amazed how many rubber bands there are in a library. We all put our rubber band holders away, but that didn't even dent the problem. Rubber bands slide under computer keyboards and crawl into your pencil holder. They fall under your desk and hide in the wires. One evening I caught Dewey rummaging through a stack of work on someone's desk. There was a rubber band lurking every time he pushed a piece of paper aside.

'Even the hidden ones need to go,' I said at the next staff meeting. 'Let's clean up those desks and put them away. Remember, Dewey can smell rubber.' In a few days, the staff area looked neater than it had in years.

So Dewey started raiding the rubber bands left out on the circulation desk for patrons. We stashed them in a drawer. He found the rubber bands by the copier, too. The patrons were just going to have to ask for rubber bands. A small price to pay, I thought, in exchange for a cat who spent most of his day trying to make them happy.

Soon, our counter-operation was showing signs of success. But Dewey became more subtle. He waited for you to turn your back, then pounced on the rubber band left innocently lying on your desk. It had been there five minutes. Humans forget. Not cats. Dewey remembered every drawer left open a crack, then came back that night to wiggle his way inside. He never messed up the contents of the drawer. The next morning, the rubber bands were simply gone.

One afternoon I was walking past our big floor-to-ceiling supply cabinet. I was focused on something else, probably budget numbers, and only noticed the open door out of the corner of my eye. 'Did I just see . . .'

I turned around and walked back to the cabinet. Sure enough, there was Dewey, sitting on a shelf at eye level, a huge rubber band hanging out of his mouth.

I had to laugh. In general, Dewey was the best-behaved kitten I had ever seen. He never knocked books or displays off shelves. If I told him not to do something, he usually stopped. He was unfailingly kind to stranger and staffer alike. For a kitten, he was downright mellow. But he was absolutely incorrigible when it came to rubber bands. The cat would go anywhere and do anything to sink his teeth into a rubber band.

A few mornings later, I found file cards sitting suspiciously unbound on the front desk. Dewey had never gone for tight rubber bands before; now, he was biting them off every night. As always, he was delicate even in defiance. He left perfectly neat stacks, not a card out of place. The cards went into the drawers; the drawers were shut tight.

We never completely succeeded in wiping out Dewey's rubber band fixation. He'd lose interest, only to go back on the prowl a few months or even a few years later. In the end, it was more a game than a battle.

But let's not make too much of it all. Rubber bands were a hobby. Catnip and boxes were mere distractions. Dewey's true love was people, and there was nothing he wouldn't do for his adoring public. I remember standing at the circulation desk one morning, talking with Doris. when we noticed a toddler wobbling by. She must have recently learned to walk, because her balance was shaky and her steps uneven. It wasn't helping that her arms were wrapped tightly across her chest, clutching Dewey in a bear hug. His rear and tail were sticking up in her face, and his head was hanging down towards the floor. Doris and I stopped talking and watched in amazement as the little girl toddled in slow motion across the library, a very big smile on her face and a very resigned cat hanging upside down from her arms.

'Incredible,' Doris said.

'I should do something about that,' I said. But I didn't. I knew that, despite appearances, Dewey was completely in control of the situation. He knew what he was doing and, no matter what happened, he could take care of himself.

We think of a library, or any single building, really, as a small place. How can you spend all day, every day, in a 13,000-square-foot room and not get bored? But to Dewey, the Spencer Public Library was a huge world, full of drawers, cabinets, bookshelves, display cases, tables, chairs, copiers, typewriters, rubber bands, backpacks, purses and a steady stream of hands to pet him, legs to rub against and mouths to sing his praises. And laps. The library was always gorgeously full of laps.

By the autumn of 1988, Dewey considered all of it his.

SIZE IS A MATTER of perspective. For an insect, one stalk of corn, or even one ear of corn, can be the whole world. For Dewey, the Spencer Public Library was a labyrinth that kept him endlessly fascinated—at least until he started to wonder what was outside the front door. For most of the people in north-west Iowa, Spencer is the big city. In fact, we are the biggest city for a hundred miles in any direction. People from nine counties funnel into Spencer for entertainment and shopping. We have stores, services, live music, local theatre and, of course, the county fair. What more do you need?

Spencer started as a sham town. In the 1850s, a developer

sold numbered lots on a large parcel near a bend in the Little Sioux River. The settlers expected a prosperous town in a fertile river valley, but they never found it. There was nothing but a lazy river and a single cabin—four miles away. The only place a town existed was on paper.

The homesteaders decided to stay. Instead of coming to an established town, they scratched a community out of the dirt. Spencer incorporated in 1871 and immediately petitioned the government for a railroad depot, which it wouldn't get for almost fifty years. Later that year, it wrested the seat of Clay County away from Petersen, a larger town thirty miles to the south. Spencer was a blue-collar town. It didn't have pretensions, but it knew that, out here on the Plains, you have to keep moving, modernising and growing.

When the first generation of homesteaders became too old to farm, they moved in to Spencer. They built small craftsman's bungalows north of the river, mixing with the merchants and hired hands. When the railroad finally arrived, local farmers no longer had to drive a horse and buggy fifty miles to market. Now other farmers drove twenty miles to Spencer. The town celebrated by widening the road from the river to the train depot. Those eight blocks, christened Grand Avenue, became the main retail corridor for the entire region. There was a savings and loan bank downtown, a popcorn factory on the north side near the fairgrounds, a concrete block factory, a brick works and a lumberyard. But Spencer was not an industrial town. There were the fields, the farmers and the eight blocks of businesses under our enormous blue Iowa sky.

And then came 27 June 1931.

The temperature was 103 degrees when, at 1:36pm, an eight-year-old boy lit a sparkler outside Otto Bjornstad's drugstore at Main and West Fourth Street. Someone screamed, and the startled boy dropped the sparkler into a large display of fireworks. The display exploded and the fire, whipped by a hot wind, spread across the street. Within minutes, the blaze was burning down both sides of Grand Avenue, completely beyond the control of Spencer's small fire department. Fourteen surrounding towns sent equipment and men, but water pressure was so low, river water had to be pumped into the mains. At the height of the blaze, the pavement on Grand Avenue caught fire. By the end of the day, thirty-six buildings housing seventy-two businesses, well more than half the businesses in town, were destroyed. The cost, just over two million in Depression-era dollars, is still the most expensive man-made disaster in the history of Iowa.

Two days after the fire, a commission was meeting to make the new downtown as modern and accident-proof as possible, even as stores reopened out of houses and out-buildings. Nobody quit. Nobody said, 'Let's just put it back the way it was.' Our community leaders had travelled to the large cities of the Midwest, like Chicago and Minneapolis. They had seen the cohesive planning and sleek style of places like Kansas City. Within a month, a master plan was created for a modern Art Deco downtown in the style of the most prosperous cities of the day. Each destroyed building was individually owned, but each was also part of a town. The owners bought into the plan. They understood that they lived, worked and survived together.

If you visit downtown Spencer today, you might not think Art Deco. Most of the architects were from Des Moines and Sioux City, and they built in a style called Prairie Deco. The buildings are low to the ground. They are mostly brick. Prairie Deco is a practical style. It's quiet but elegant. We like to be modern in Spencer, but we don't like to draw attention to ourselves.

Our downtown is the legacy of the fire of 1931, but it is also the legacy of the farm crisis of the 1980s. When times are tough, you either pull together or fall apart. That's true of families, towns, even people. In the late 1980s, Spencer once again pulled together. And once again, the transformation occurred from the inside out, when the merchants on Grand Avenue, many in stores run by their grandparents in 1931, decided they could make the city better. They hired a business manager for the entire downtown retail corridor, they made infrastructure improvements, they spent heavily on advertising even when there seemed to be no money left in the community to spend.

Slowly, the wheels of progress began to turn. A local couple bought and began to restore The Hotel, the largest and most historic building in town. The run-down building had been an eyesore. Now it became a source of pride, a promise of better days to come. Along the commercial section of Grand Avenue, the shopkeepers paid for new windows, better sidewalks, and summer evening entertainment. They clearly believed the best days of Spencer were ahead, and when people came downtown, heard the music and walked the new sidewalks, they believed it, too. And if that wasn't enough, at the south end of downtown, just around the corner on Third Street, was a clean, welcoming, newly remodelled library.

At least, that was my plan. As soon as I was made director in 1987, I started pressing for money to remodel the library. There was no city manager, and even mayor was a part-time, largely ceremonial position. The city council made all the decisions. So that's where I went, again and again and again.

The Spencer city council was a classic old boy network, an extension of the power-brokers who met at Sister's Café. Sister's was only twenty feet from the library, but I don't think a single member of that crowd had ever stepped foot in our building. Of course, I never frequented Sister's Café, so the problem cut both ways.

After almost a year of being put on the shelf, I was frustrated, but not defeated. Then a funny thing happened: Dewey started to make my argument for me. By the late summer of 1988, there was a noticeable change at the Spencer Public Library. Our visitor numbers were up. People were staying longer. They were leaving happy, and that happiness was being carried to their homes, their schools and their places of employment. Even better, people were talking.

'I was down at the library,' someone would comment while window-shopping on the new, improved Grand Avenue.

'Was Dewey there?'

'Of course.'

'Did he sit in your lap? He always sits on my daughter's lap.'

'Actually, I was reaching for a book on a high shelf, not

really paying attention, and instead of a book, I grabbed a handful of Dewey. I was so startled, I dropped a book right on my toe.'

'What did Dewey do?'

'He laughed.'

'Really?'

'No, but I sure did.'

The conversations must have reached Sister's Café, because eventually even the city council started to notice. Slowly, their attitude shifted. First they stopped laughing at me. Then they started listening.

'Vicki,' the city council finally said, 'maybe the library does make a difference. There's a financial crunch right now, as you know, and we don't have any money. But if you have the funds, you have our support.' It wasn't much, I admit, but it was the most the library had got from the city in a long, long time.

CHAPTER 4

WHAT THE CITY council heard in the autumn of 1988 was the voices of the people that were usually never heard: those of the older residents, the mothers, the children. Some patrons came to the library for a purpose—to check out a book, to read the newspaper, to find a magazine. Others patrons considered the library a destination. They enjoyed spending time there; they were sustained and strengthened. Every month there were more of these people. Dewey wasn't just a novelty; he was a fixture in the community. People came to the library to see him.

Not that Dewey was an especially fawning animal. He didn't just rush up to each person who came through the door. He made himself available at the front door if people wanted him; if they didn't, they could step around and be on their way.

When regular patrons came in and Dewey wasn't there to greet them, they often walked the library looking for him. First they searched the floor, figuring Dewey was hiding behind a corner. Then they checked the top of the bookshelves.

'Oh, how are you, Dewey? I didn't see you there,' they would say, reaching up to pet him. Dewey would give them the top of his head to pet, but he wouldn't follow them. The patrons always looked disappointed.

But as soon as they forgot about him, Dewey jumped into their laps. That's when I saw the smiles. It wasn't just that Dewey sat with them for ten or fifteen minutes; it was that he had singled them out for special attention. By the end of his first year, dozens of patrons were telling me, 'I know Dewey likes everyone, but I have a special relationship with him.'

I smiled and nodded. Of course, if any of Dewey's fans hung around long enough, they were sure to be disappointed. Many times I'd see the smile drop half an hour later when, leaving the library, they happened to notice Dewey sitting on someone else's lap.

Then there were the children. If you wanted to understand the effect Dewey had on Spencer, all you had to do was look at the children. The smiles when they came into the library, the joy as they searched and called for him, the excitement when they found him. Behind them, their mothers were smiling, too.

I knew families were suffering, and that for many of these children times were hard. The parents never discussed their problems with me or anyone on staff. They probably didn't discuss them with their closest friends. That's not the way we are around here; we don't talk about our personal circumstances, be they good, bad, or indifferent. But you could tell. One boy wore his old coat from the previous winter. His mother stopped wearing her make-up and, eventually, her jewellery. The boy clung to Dewey like a true friend; and his mother never stopped smiling when she saw them together.

That wasn't the only boy who wore an old coat that autumn, and he certainly wasn't the only child who loved Dewey. They all wanted, even craved, his attention, so much so that they learned enough control to spend Story Hour with him. Every Tuesday morning, the murmur of excited children in the Round Room, where Story Hour was held, would be suddenly punctuated by a cry of 'Dewey's here!' A mad rush would ensue as every child in the room tried to pet Dewey at the same time.

'If you don't settle down,' our children's librarian, Mary Walk, would tell them, 'Dewey has to go.'

A barely contained hush would fall over the room as the children took their seats, trying their best to contain their excitement. When they were relatively calm, Dewey would begin sliding between them, rubbing against each child and making them giggle. Soon kids were grabbing at him and whispering, 'Sit with me, Dewey. Sit with me.'

'Children, don't make me warn you again.'

'Yes, Mary.'

Dewey, knowing he had pushed the limit, would stop wandering and curl up in the lap of one lucky child. He didn't let a child grab him and hold him in her lap; he *chose* to spend time with her. And every week it was a different child.

Once he had chosen a lap, Dewey usually sat quietly for the whole hour. Unless a movie was being shown. Then he would jump on a table, curl his legs under his body and watch the screen intently. When the credits rolled he feigned boredom and jumped down. Before the children could ask, 'Where's Dewey?' he was gone.

There was only one child Dewey couldn't win over. She was four years old when Dewey arrived, and she came to the library every week with her mother and older brother. Her brother loved Dewey. The girl hung back as far as possible, looking tense and nervous. Her mother eventually confided in me that the girl was afraid of four-legged animals, especially cats and dogs.

What an opportunity! I knew Dewey could do for this girl what he had done for the children with cat allergies, who finally had a cat to spend time with. I suggested exposing her gently to Dewey, first by looking through the window at him and then with supervised meetings.

'This is an ideal job for our gentle, loving Dewey,' I told her mother. I was so enthusiastic, I even researched the best books to help the girl overcome her fear.

Her mother didn't want to go that route, so instead of trying to change the girl's feelings about cats, I accommodated her. When the girl came to the door and waved at the clerk on the front desk, we found Dewey and locked him in my office. Dewey hated being locked in my office, especially when patrons were in the library.

I hated to lock him away, and I hated to miss the opportunity for Dewey to make this little girl's life better, but what could I do? 'Don't force it, Vicki,' I told myself. 'It will come.'

With that in mind, I planned a low-key celebration for Dewey's first birthday: just a cake made out of cat food for Dewey and a normal one for the patrons. We didn't know exactly when he was born, but Dr Esterly had estimated he was eight weeks old when we found him, so we counted back to late November and chose the eighteenth. We found Dewey on 18 January, so we figured that was his lucky day.

A week before the celebration, we put out a card for signatures. Within days there were more than a hundred. At the next Story Hour, the children coloured pictures of birthday cakes. Four days before the party, we strung the pictures on a clothesline behind the circulation desk. Then the newspaper ran a story, and we started receiving birthday cards in the mail. I couldn't believe it; people were sending birthday cards to a cat!

By the time the party rolled around, the kids were jumping up and down with excitement. Another cat would have been frightened, no doubt, but Dewey took it all in with his usual calm. Instead of interacting with the kids, though, he kept his eyes on the prize: his cat-food cake in the shape of a mouse, covered with Jean Hollis Clark's brand of full-fat yoghurt (Dewey hated the diet stuff). As the kids smiled and giggled, I looked out at the adults gathered at the back of the crowd, most of them parents. They were smiling as much as the children. Once again, I realised how special Dewey was. Not just any cat would have this kind of fan club. And I realised a few other things, too: that Dewey was having an impact; that he had been accepted as part of the community; and that, although I spent all day with him, I would never know all the relationships he developed and all the people he touched. Dewey didn't play favourites; he loved everyone equally.

But even as I say that, I know it wasn't true. Dewey did have special relationships, and one I'll always remember was with Crystal. For decades, the library had hosted a special Story Hour every week for local elementary and middle school special education classes. Before Dewey, the kids were poorly behaved. This was their big outing for the week and they were excited: screaming, yelling, jumping up and down. But Dewey changed that. As they got to know him, the children learned that if they were too noisy or erratic, Dewey left. They would do anything to keep Dewey with them; after a few months, they became so calm, you couldn't believe it was the same group of kids.

The children couldn't pet very well, since most were physically disabled. Dewey didn't care. As long as the children were somewhat quiet, Dewey spent the hour with them. He walked around the room and rubbed their legs. He jumped in their laps. The children became so fixated on him, they didn't notice anything else. If we had read them the phone book, they couldn't have cared less.

Crystal was one of the more disabled members of the group. She was a beautiful girl of about eleven, but she had no speech and very little control of her limbs. She was in a wheelchair with a wooden tray on the front. When she came into the library, her head was always down and her eyes were staring at that tray. The teacher took off her coat or opened her jacket, and she didn't move. It was like she wasn't even there.

Dewey noticed Crystal right away, but they didn't form an immediate bond. She didn't seem interested in him, and there were plenty of children who desperately wanted his attention. Then one week Dewey jumped onto Crystal's wheelchair tray. Crystal squealed. She had been coming to the library for years, and that squeal was the first sound I ever heard her make.

Dewey started visiting Crystal every week. Every time he jumped onto her tray, Crystal squealed with delight. It was a loud, high-pitched squeal, but it never scared Dewey. He knew what it meant. He could feel her excitement, or maybe he could see the change in her face. Whenever she saw Dewey, Crystal glowed. Her eyes had always been blank. Now they were on fire.

Soon, it wasn't just seeing Dewey on her tray. The moment the teacher pushed her into the library, Crystal was alive. When she saw Dewey, who waited for her at the front door, she immediately started to vocalise. I believed she was calling to Dewey. Dewey must have thought so, too, because as soon as he heard it, he was at her side. Once her wheelchair was parked, he jumped onto her tray, and happiness exploded from within her. She started to squeal, and her smile, you couldn't believe how big and bright it was. Crystal had the best smile in the world.

Usually Crystal's teacher picked up her hand and helped her pet Dewey. That touch, the feel of his fur on her skin, always brought on a round of louder and more delighted squeals. I swear, one day she looked up and made eye contact with me. She was overcome with joy, and she wanted to share the moment with someone, with everyone. This from a girl who, for years, never lifted her eyes from the floor.

One week I picked Dewey off Crystal's tray and put him inside her coat. She didn't even squeal. She just stared down at him in awe. She was so happy. Dewey was so happy. He had a chest to lean on, and it was warm, and he was with somebody he loved. He wouldn't come out of her coat. He stayed in there for twenty minutes, maybe more. The other children checked out books. Dewey and Crystal sat together in front of the circulation desk. The bus was idling in front of the library, and all the other children were on it, but Dewey and Crystal were still sitting where we had left them, alone together. That smile, that moment, was worth the world.

The relationship between Dewey and Crystal is important not just because it changed her life but because it illustrates Dewey's effect on people. His love. His understanding. The extent to which he cared. Take this one person, I'm saying every time I tell that story, multiply it by a thousand, and you'll begin to see how much Dewey meant to the town of Spencer. It wasn't everybody, but it was another person every day, one heart at a time. And one of those people, one very close to my own heart, was my daughter, Jodi.

I was a single mother, so when she was young, Jodi and I were inseparable. We lived in Mankato, Minnesota, in those days, but we spent a lot of time at my parents' house in Hartley, Iowa.

At thirteen, after we had moved to Spencer, Jodi stopped letting me kiss her good night. 'I'm too old for that, Mommy,' she said.

'I know,' I told her. 'You're a big girl, now.' But it broke my heart.

I walked out into the living room of our two-bedroom bungalow, which was only a mile from the library. Of course, half of Spencer was only a mile from the library.

Brandy tottered up and nuzzled my hand. Brandy had been with me since I was pregnant with Jodi, and the dog was clearly feeling her age. She was lethargic, and for the first time in her life she was having accidents on the floor. Poor Brandy. I held out as long as I could, but eventually I took her to see Dr Esterly, who diagnosed an advanced stage of kidney failure.

'Vicki, there's no hope for recovery.'

I didn't tell Jodi, at least not everything. Partly to protect her. Partly because I didn't want to acknowledge it myself. I loved Brandy; I needed her. I couldn't bring myself to put her down.

I called my sister, Val, and told her husband, Don, 'Please come by the house and pick her up. Don't tell me when, just do it.'

A few days later, I came home for lunch and Brandy wasn't there. I knew what that meant. I called Val and asked her to pick Jodi up from school and take her to dinner. I needed time to compose myself. At dinner, Jodi could tell something was wrong. Eventually Val broke down and told her Brandy had been put to sleep.

I had done so many things wrong by this point. I had left

Brandy to die with my brother-in-law. I hadn't been completely honest with Jodi. And I had allowed my sister to tell my daughter about the death of the dog she loved. But my biggest mistake was what I did when Jodi came home. I didn't cry. I didn't show any emotion. I told myself that I needed to be strong for her. I didn't want her to see how much I hurt. When Jodi went to school the next day, I broke down. I was so distraught, I couldn't even drive to work until the afternoon. But Jodi didn't see that. To her thirteen-year-old mind, I was the woman who killed her dog and didn't even care.

Brandy's death wasn't a turning point in our relationship. It was more a symptom of the gulf developing between us. Jodi wasn't a little child any more, but part of me still treated her like one. She also wasn't an adult, but part of her thought she was all grown up and didn't need me any longer. Even as I realised, for the first time, the distance between us, Brandy's death pushed us further apart.

By the time Dewey arrived, Jodi was sixteen, and like many mothers of girls that age, I felt we were living separate lives. I was working very hard, planning the library remodelling I had finally pushed through the city council, and I didn't have much time to spend at home. Jodi spent most of her time out with friends or locked in her room. Most of the week, we interacted only at dinner. Even then, we rarely had much to talk about.

Until Dewey. With Dewey, I had something to talk about that Jodi wanted to hear. I'd tell her what he did; who came to see him; whom he played with; what local newspaper or radio station called for an interview. A few staff members alternated feeding Dewey on Sunday mornings. Although I was never able to get Jodi out of bed for those Sunday morning visits, we'd often drop by the library Sunday night on our way back from dinner at Mom and Dad's house.

You wouldn't believe Dewey's excitement when Jodi walked in that library door. The cat pranced. He would literally do flips off bookshelves just to impress her. While I was alone in the back room cleaning his litter and refilling his food dish, Dewey and Jodi played. She wasn't just another person spending time with him; Dewey was absolutely crazy for Jodi.

I've said Dewey never followed anyone around, that his style was to retain some distance, at least for a while. That wasn't true with Jodi. Dewey followed her like a dog. She was the only person in the world from whom he wanted and needed affection. Even when Jodi came to the library during work hours, Dewey sprinted to her side. He had no pride around that girl. As soon as she sat down, Dewey was in her lap.

On holidays, when the library was closed for a few days, I brought Dewey home with me. He didn't like the car ride— he always assumed it meant Dr Esterly, so he spent the first couple of minutes in the back seat on the floor—but as soon as he felt me turn off Grand Avenue onto Eleventh Street, he bounced up to stare out the window. As soon as I opened the door, he rushed into my house to give everything a nice long sniff. Then he ran up and down the basement stairs. He lived in a one-floor world at the library, so he couldn't get enough of stairs.

Once he ran his excitement out on the stairs, Dewey would often settle in beside me on the sofa. Just as often, though, he sat on the back of the sofa and stared out the window. He was watching for Jodi. When she came home, he jumped right up and ran to the door. As soon as she walked in, Dewey was like Velcro. He never left Jodi's side. When Jodi took her shower, Dewey waited in the bathroom with her, staring at the curtain. If she closed the door, he sat right outside. If the shower stopped and she didn't come out quickly enough, he cried. As soon as she sat down, he was on her lap, and he purred, purred, purred.

Jodi's room was an absolute mess. When it came to her appearance, the girl was immaculate. Not a hair out of place, not a speck of dirt anywhere. Put it this way: she ironed her socks. So who would believe she could live in a room where you couldn't see the floor or close the closet door, where crusty plates and glasses were buried under dirty clothes for weeks. I refused to clean it up, but I also refused to stop nagging her about it. A typical mother-daughter relationship, I know, but that's only easy to say after the fact. It's never easy when you're going through it.

But everything was easy for Dewey. Dirty room? Nagging mother? What did he care?

Sometimes, just before turning in for the night, Jodi would call me to her room. I'd walk in and find Dewey guarding Jodi's pillow or lying over the top half of her face. I'd look at him for a second, so desperate for her touch, and then we'd both start laughing. Jodi was silly and funny around her friends, but for all those high school years she was so serious with me. Dewey was the only thing that made our relationship light-hearted and playful. With Dewey around, we laughed together, almost like we had when Jodi was a child.

Jodi and I weren't the only ones Dewey was helping. Spencer Middle School was across the street from the library, and about fifty students were regularly staying with us after school. On days when they blew in like a hurricane, Dewey avoided them, especially the rowdy ones, but usually he was out mingling. He had many friends among the students, both boys and girls.

They petted him and played games with him, like rolling pencils off the table and watching his surprise when they disappeared. One girl would wiggle a pen out the end of her coat sleeve. Dewey would chase the pen up the sleeve and then, deciding he liked that warm, dark place, he'd sometimes lie down for a nap.

Most of the kids left just after five when their parents got off work. A few stayed as late as eight—children of parents who had to work extra jobs or extra shifts to make ends meet.

These parents, who came in for only a moment, rarely had time to pet Dewey. But their children spent hours with Dewey; he entertained and loved them. I never realised how much that meant, or how deep those bonds were, until I saw the mother of one of our boys bend down and whisper, 'Thank you, Dewey,' as she tenderly stroked his head.

She stood up and put her arm around her son. Then, as they were walking out the door, I heard her ask him, 'How was Dewey today?' Suddenly, I knew exactly how she felt. Dewey had turned a difficult time apart into common ground;

he was her road back to so much of what she had left behind. I never considered this boy one of Dewey's close companions—he spent most of his time goofing off with friends or playing games on the computer—but clearly Dewey was having an impact on his life beyond the library walls. And it wasn't just this boy. The more I looked, the more I noticed that the ember which had ignited my relationship with Jodi was felt by other families, too. Like me, parents all over Spencer were spending time with their teenagers, talking about Dewey.

The staff saw Jodi and Dewey together and thought I'd be offended that Dewey loved someone more than me. After Jodi left, someone would usually say, 'Her voice sounds just like yours. That's why he loves her so much.'

But I didn't feel jealous at all. Dewey and I had a complex relationship, one that involved baths, brushings, veterinary visits and other unpleasant experiences. Dewey's relationship with Jodi was pure and innocent. It was fun and good times, uncomplicated by responsibility. Dewey loved Jodi because she was Jodi—warm, friendly, wonderful Jodi. And I loved him for loving my daughter.

CHAPTER 5

IN HARTLEY, Iowa, where my family moved when I was fourteen, I was a straight arrow, the head student librarian, and the second smartest girl in my grade, after Karen Watts. My older brother was considered one of the smartest kids ever to attend Hartley High School. Everyone called him the professor. David graduated a year ahead of me and went to college a hundred miles away in Mankato, Minnesota. I figured I'd follow him there.

When I mentioned my plans to my guidance counsellor, he said, 'You don't need to worry about college. You're just going to get married, have kids, and let a man take care of you.' It was 1966. This was rural Iowa. I didn't get any other advice.

After graduation from high school, I moved to Mankato with my best friend, Sharon. While David went to college on the other side of town, Sharon and I worked at the Mankato Box Company. If I wasn't out, dancing, I was usually out with my brother David and his friends. David was more than my brother, he was my best friend.

I met Wally Myron at a dance club. He was very smart and very well-read, which impressed me immediately. And he had personality. Wally was always smiling, and everyone with him was always smiling, too.

We dated for a year and a half before getting married in July 1970. I was twenty-two and I got pregnant right away. It was a tough pregnancy, with sickness morning, noon and night. Wally spent evenings after work out with his friends, usually riding motorcycles, but he was always home by seven thirty. He wanted a social wife, but he would take a sick wife if that meant a baby on the way.

When I went into labour, the doctor decided to speed up the process with two massive doses of Pitocin. I found out later he had a party to attend and he wanted to get this darn procedure over with. I went from three centimetres dilated to crowning in two hours. The shock broke the placenta, so they put me back into labour. They didn't get all the pieces. Six weeks later I haemorrhaged, and they rushed me back to the hospital for emergency surgery.

I had always wanted a daughter named Jodi Marie. Now I had that daughter, and I was dying to spend time with her, to hug her and talk to her and look into her eyes. But the surgery knocked me flat on my back. My hormones went haywire and I was racked with headaches, insomnia and cold sweats. Two years and six operations later my health hadn't improved, so my doctor suggested exploratory surgery. I woke up in the hospital bed to discover he'd taken both ovaries and my uterus. The physical pain was intense, but worse was the knowledge that I couldn't have any more children. And I wasn't prepared to enter sudden and severe menopause. I was twenty-four going on sixty, with scarring through my gut, regret in my heart, and a daughter I couldn't hold. The curtain came down and everything went black.

When I came around a few months later, Wally wasn't there. Not like he used to be, anyway. That's when I noticed, suddenly, that everything meant drinking to Wally.

I finally admitted to myself that Wally had a problem: he was coming home less and less. I almost never saw him sober. He wasn't a mean drunk, but he wasn't a functioning drunk, either. And yet he ran our lives. He drove our only car. I had to take the bus or ride with a friend to buy groceries. He cashed the pay cheques. He paid the bills. Often I was too sick to follow the finances, much less raise a child on my own. My parents didn't have money, but they took Jodi in, two weeks at a time, and raised her like their daughter. Whenever life smothered me, they gave me room to breathe.

My real motivation, my real reason for picking myself up every morning and struggling on, was my daughter, Jodi. She needed me to be her mother, to teach by example. We didn't have money, but we had each other. When I was confined to my bed, Jodi and I spent hours talking. When I was physically able, we walked in the park with the real third member of our family, Brandy. Brandy and Jodi looked up to me; they adored me without question or doubt; they gave me unconditional love, which is the secret power of children and dogs. Every night when I put Jodi to bed, I kissed her, and that touch, that skin on my skin, sustained me.

But I was worn out. I was emotionally drained. My confidence was crippled. I was physically weak from the surgeries. And I was scared. But I eventually went to a lawyer and started divorce proceedings. That's when I discovered we were six months behind on house payments, six months behind on car payments and $6,000 in debt. Wally had even taken out a home improvement loan, but, of course, no work had been done.

Grandma Stephenson—Mom's mother, who had divorced her own alcoholic husband—gave me the money to save the house. We let the bank repossess the car. It wasn't worth saving. My dad passed the hat in Hartley and came up with

$800 to buy me a 1962 Chevy an old lady didn't even drive in the rain. I had never driven a car in my life. I took driving lessons for a month and passed my driver's test. I was twenty-eight years old.

The first place I drove that car was to the welfare office. I had a six-year-old daughter, a high school diploma, a medical history that can only be called a disaster and a pile of debt. I didn't have a choice. I told them, 'I need help, but I'm only going to take it if you let me go to college.'

Thank God, welfare was different in those days. They agreed. I went straight to Mankato State and registered for the upcoming semester. Four years later, in 1981, I graduated summa cum laude, the highest level of honours, with a general studies degree, double majors in psychology and women's studies, and minors in anthropology and library studies. Welfare paid for the whole thing: classes, housing, living expenses.

But I found out it takes more than a college degree to become a psychologist. My sister, Val, who lived in Spencer, mentioned an opening at the local library. At that moment I had no intention of returning home. Despite my minor in library science, I had never really considered working in a library. But I took the interview, and I loved the people. A week later, I was on my way back to north-west Iowa, the new assistant director of the Spencer Public Library.

I wasn't expecting to love the job. Like most people, I thought being a librarian meant stamping due dates in the back of books. But it was so much more. Within months, I was neck-deep in marketing campaigns and graphic design. I started a homebound program, which took books to people unable to visit the library, and developed a major initiative to interest teens in reading. I developed programs for nursing homes and schools; I started answering questions on the radio and speaking to social clubs and community organisations. I was a big-picture person, and I was beginning to see the difference a strong library made in a community.

Then I got involved in the business side of running a library—the budgeting and long-range planning—and I was hooked. This was a job, I realised, that I could love for the rest of my life.

In 1987, my friend and boss, Bonnie Pluemer, was promoted to a regional library management position. I spoke confidentially to several members of the library board and told them I wanted to be the new director. I wasn't qualified. The job required a master's degree in library science and I didn't have one. The board was willing to overlook this fact as long as I started a master's program within two years. That seemed more than fair, so I accepted the offer. Then I found out the nearest American Library Association–accredited master's program was five hours away in Iowa City. I was a single mother. I had a full-time job. That wasn't going to work.

Today you can earn an accredited master's degree in library science on the internet. But in 1987 I couldn't even find a long-distance learning program. And believe me, I looked. Finally, at the urging of my regional administrator, John Houlahan, Emporia State University in Kansas took the plunge. The first American Library Association–accredited long-distance master's program in the nation met in Sioux City, Iowa, in the autumn of 1988. And I was the first student in the door.

I loved the classes. The material was complex, the homework brutal. All the students were working librarians, and there were several other single mothers. This program wasn't a casual decision; it was a last chance, and we were willing to work for it. In addition to attending class from five thirty on Friday to noon on Sunday—after a two-hour drive to Sioux City, no less—we were researching and writing two papers a week, sometimes more. I didn't have a typewriter at home, much less a computer, so I would leave work at five, cook dinner for myself and Jodi, then head back to the library, where I worked until midnight or later.

At the same time, I threw myself into the library remodelling. I wanted to complete it by the summer of 1989, and I had months of work to do before we could even begin. I learned space planning, section organisation, disability compliance. I chose colours, mapped furniture arrangements, and decided whether there was enough money for new tables and chairs (there wasn't, so we refurbished the old ones). Jean Hollis Clark and I made exact scale models of the old library and the new library to display on the circulation desk. It wasn't enough to plan a great remodel; the public had to be enthusiastic and informed. Dewey helped out by sleeping every day inside one of the models.

Once a design was determined, I moved on to the next step: planning how to move more than 30,000 objects out of the building, then put them all back into their correct places. I found warehouse space. I found moving equipment. I organised and scheduled volunteers. And every plan, every penny, had to be tallied and earmarked and justified to the library board.

A library after closing is a lonely place. It is heart-poundingly silent, and the rows of shelves create an almost unfathomable number of dark and creepy corners. Most of the librarians I know won't stay alone in a library after closing, especially after dark, but I was never nervous or scared. I was strong. I was stubborn. And most of all, I was never alone. I had Dewey. Every night, he sat on top of the computer screen as I worked, lazily swiping his tail back and forth. When I hit a wall, either from writer's block, fatigue, or stress, he jumped down into my lap or onto the keyboard. No more, he told me. *Let's play*. Dewey had an amazing sense of timing.

'All right, Dewey,' I told him. 'You go first.'

Dewey's game was hide-and-seek, so as soon as I gave the word he would take off around the corner into the main part of the library. Half the time I immediately spotted the back half of a long-haired orange cat. For Dewey, hiding meant sticking your head in a bookshelf; he seemed to forget he had a tail.

'I wonder where Dewey is?' I said out loud as I snuck up on him. 'Boo!' I yelled when I got within a few feet, sending Dewey running.

Occasionally, he curled up in a tight spot and stayed put. I'd look for five minutes, then start calling his name. 'Dewey! Dewey!' A dark library can feel empty when you're bending over between the stacks and looking through rows of books, but I always imagined Dewey somewhere, just a few feet away, laughing at me.

'All right, Dewey, that's enough. You win!' Nothing. Where could that cat be? I'd turn around and there he was, standing in the middle of the aisle, staring at me.

'Oh, Dewey, you clever boy. Now it's my turn.'

I'd run and hide behind a bookshelf, and invariably one of two things happened. I'd get to my hiding place, turn around, and Dewey would be standing right there. He had followed me.

His other favourite thing to do was run around the other side of the shelf and beat me to my hiding spot.

I'd laugh and pet him behind the ears. 'Fine, Dewey. Let's just run for a while.'

We'd run between the shelves, meeting at the end of the aisles, nobody quite hiding and no one really seeking. After fifteen minutes I would completely forget my research paper, or the most recent budget meeting for the remodelling project, or some unfortunate conversation with Jodi. Whatever had been bothering me, it was gone. The weight, as they say, was lifted.

'Okay, Dewey. Let's get back to work.'

Dewey never complained. I'd climb back onto my chair, and he'd climb back to his perch on top of the computer and start waving his tail in front of the screen. The next time I needed him, he'd be there.

It's not a stretch to say those games of hide-and-seek with Dewey, that time spent together, got me through. Maybe it would be easier, right now, to tell you Dewey put his head on my lap and whimpered while I cried or that he licked the tears from my face. Anyone can relate to that. And it is almost true, because sometimes when the ceiling started falling in on me and I found myself staring blankly at my lap, tears in my eyes, Dewey was there, right where I needed him to be.

But life isn't neat and tidy. Our relationship can't be tied up with a few tears. I'm not much of a crier, for one thing. And while Dewey was demonstrative with his love—he was always a soft touch for a late-night cuddle—he didn't bathe me with affection. Somehow, Dewey knew when I needed a little nudge or a warm body, and he knew when the best thing for me was a stupid, mindless game of hide-and-seek. And whatever I needed, he'd give me, without thought, without wanting something in return, and without my asking. It wasn't just love. It was more than that. It was respect. It was empathy. And it went both ways. That spark Dewey and I had felt when we met? Those nights alone together in the library turned it into a fire.

I guess . . . when everything in my life was so complex, when things were sliding in so many directions at once and it seemed at times the centre wouldn't hold, my relationship with Dewey was so simple and so natural, and that's what made it so right.

CHAPTER 6

CHRISTMAS IS a holiday the town of Spencer celebrates together. It's the slow season for the farmers and manufacturers, a time to relax and spread our collected coins around to the merchants. The activity of the season is the Grand Meander, a walking tour of Grand Avenue that begins the first weekend in December. The whole street is strung with white lights, a co-ordinated display that shows off the fine lines of our buildings. Christmas music is piped in; Santa Claus comes out to receive wish lists from the children. His elves, also in Santa suits, ring bells on corners and collect coins for charities. The whole town is out, laughing, talking, clutching one another to share the warmth. The stores stay open late, showing off their holiday selections and offering cookies and hot chocolate to fight off the biting cold.

Every storefront window is decorated. We call them Living Windows, because in each one local residents act out holiday scenes. The Parker Museum, which houses a collection of

Clay County artefacts, including a fire truck that battled the great fire of 1931, always creates a variation on the pioneers' Christmases. Other windows offer interpretations of Christmas not quite so long past, with Radio Flyers and porcelain dolls. Some have mangers. Others feature toy tractors and cars, a boy's view of Christmas morning. This, the windows all say, is Spencer.

The Festival of Trees, a Christmas-tree decorating contest, is held on the corner of First Avenue and Fifth Street, inside what used to be the Spencer Convention centre but is now the Eagles Club, a military-related social club that holds dances and dinners to raise money for charity. Since 1988 was Dewey's first Christmas, the library entered a tree under the title Do-We Love Christmas? The tree was decorated with— what else?—pictures of Dewey. It also featured puffy kitten ornaments and garlands of red yarn. The presents under the tree were appropriate books, like *The Cat-a-log* and *The Cat in the Hat*, tied in neat red bows. Visitors wandered through the trees for a small charitable donation. There was no official judging, but I don't think it's a stretch to say Do-We Love Christmas? was the winner, hands down.

Christmas at the library, like Christmas on Grand Avenue, was a time to put away other concerns and focus on the here and now. After a stressful autumn, I was happy to stop thinking about school and remodelling and, for a change, focus on decorations. The Monday after the Grand Meander, we took the boxes down from the top shelves of the storage room to prepare for the holiday season. The centrepiece was our big artificial Christmas tree next to the circulation desk. The first Monday in December, Cynthia Behrends and I always arrived early to set up and decorate the tree. Cynthia was the hardest worker on staff and eagerly volunteered for every job. But she didn't know what she was getting into because this year, when we slid the long, thin Christmas tree box off its high shelf, we had company.

When we pulled the Christmas tree out of the box, I could almost see Dewey's jaw drop.

As we pulled each branch out of the box, Dewey lunged at

it. He wanted to sniff and chew every green piece of plastic sticking out of every green wire branch. He pulled a few plastic needles off the tree and started working them around in his mouth.

'Give me those, Dewey!'

He coughed a few pieces of plastic onto the floor.

As Cynthia pulled the last branches out of the box, I started to assemble the tree. Dewey was watching my every move. He came in for a sniff and a taste, then bounced back a few feet for perspective. The poor cat looked like he was about to explode with excitement. This was the happiest I'd seen him all year.

'Oh, no, Dewey, not again.'

I looked over to find Dewey buried in the Christmas tree box, no doubt sniffing and pawing at the scents clinging to the cardboard. He disappeared completely inside, and a few seconds later, the box was rolling back and forth across the floor. He stopped, poked his head out and looked around. He spotted the half-assembled tree and bolted back to chew on the lower branches.

'I think he's found a new toy.'

'I think he's found a new love,' I said as I put the top branches into the notches on the green pole that comprised the trunk of our tree.

It was true. Dewey loved the Christmas tree. He loved the smell of it. The feel of it. The taste of it. Once I had it assembled and set up next to the circulation desk, he loved to sit under it.

Out came the ornaments, the new tinsel in this year's colour, the pictures and special embellishments for this year's theme. Angels on strings. Santa Clauses. Shiny balls with glitter all over them. Ribbons, ornaments, cards and dolls. Dewey rushed up to each box, but he had little interest in cloth and metal, hooks and lights. He was distracted by our wreath, which I had made out of worn-out pieces of the library's previous Christmas tree, but old plastic was no match for the new, shiny stuff. Soon it was back to his spot under the tree.

We started hanging ornaments. One minute Dewey was in

the boxes, finding out which ornaments came next. The next minute he was at our feet, playing with our shoelaces. Then he was stretching into the tree for another whiff of plastic. A few seconds later, he was gone.

'What's that rustling sound?'

Suddenly, Dewey came tearing by us with his head through the strap of one of the plastic grocery bags we used for storage. He ran all the way to the far side of the library, then came careering back towards us.

'Catch him!'

Dewey dodged and kept running. Soon he was on his way back again. Cynthia blocked the area near the front door. I took the circulation desk. Dewey sprinted right between us. I could see from the look in his eyes, he was in a frenzy. He had no idea how to get the plastic bag from around his neck.

Soon there were four or five of us chasing him, but he wouldn't stop dodging and sprinting away. It didn't help that we were all laughing at him.

'Sorry, Dewey, but you've got to admit this is funny.'

I finally cornered him and, despite his terrified squirming, managed to free him from the bag. Dewey immediately went over to his new best friend, the Christmas tree, and lay down under the branches for a nice, comforting tongue bath, complete with his customary fist in the ears. There would be a hair ball, no doubt, either later today or tomorrow morning. But at least one lesson had been learned. From then on, Dewey hated plastic bags.

That first day with the library Christmas tree was one of our best. The staff spent the entire day laughing, and Dewey spent the entire day—plastic bag run excluded, of course—in a state of gooey, romantic bliss. His love for the Christmas tree never diminished. Every year when the box came off the shelf, he pranced.

The librarians usually received a few gifts from grateful patrons, but that year, our small trove of chocolates and cookies was dwarfed by Dewey's enormous stack of balls, treats and toy mice. It seemed that everyone in town wanted Dewey—and us—to know just how much he meant to them.

There were some fancy toys in that stash, even some nice homemade items, but Dewey's favourite toy from that holiday season wasn't a gift at all; it was a skein of red yarn he found in a decorating box. That yarn skein was Dewey's constant companion, not just for the holiday season but for years to come. He batted it around the library until a few feet of yarn stuck out, which he then pounced on, wrestled, and, very soon, got wrapped around his body. More than once, I was almost run down by an orange cat streaking across the staff area, red yarn in mouth, dragging the bundle behind him. An hour later he'd be sacked out under the Christmas tree, all four feet clutching his red buddy.

The library was closed for a few days at Christmas, so Dewey came home with me. After Midnight Mass on Christmas Eve, Jodi and I headed home to Dewey, who, as always, was eager to see us. We spent Christmas morning together in Spencer, just the three of us.

A GREAT LIBRARY doesn't have to be big or beautiful. It doesn't have to have the best facilities or the most efficient staff or the most users. A great library is enmeshed in the life of a community in a way that makes it indispensable. One nobody notices because it is always there, and it always has what they need.

The Spencer Public Library was founded in 1883 in Mrs H.C. Crary's parlour. In 1890 the library moved to a small frame building on Grand Avenue. In 1902, Andrew Carnegie granted the town $10,000 for a new library. Carnegie was a product of the industrial revolution that had turned a nation of farmers into factory workers, oilmen, and iron smelters. He was a ruthless corporate capitalist who built his United States Steel into the nation's most successful business. He was also a Baptist, and by 1902 he was deep into the pursuit of giving away his money to worthwhile causes. One cause was providing grants to small towns for libraries.

The Spencer Public Library opened on 6 March 1905, on East Third Street, half a block off Grand Avenue. It was typical of Carnegie libraries, since Carnegie had mandated a classical style and symmetry of design. There were three stained-glass windows in the entrance hall, two with flowers and one with the word *library*. The librarian perched behind a large central desk, surrounded by drawers of cards. The side rooms were small and cloistered, with bookshelves to the ceiling. In an era when public buildings were segregated by sex, men and women were free to enter any room. Carnegie libraries were also among the first to let patrons choose books off the shelves instead of making requests to the librarian.

By the time I was hired in 1982, the old Carnegie library was gone. It had been beautiful, but too small for a growing town. The land deed specified the town must use it for a library or return it to the owner, so in 1971, the town tore down the old Carnegie building to build a bigger, more modern, more efficient library.

The new Spencer Public Library was modern, but with a brutish efficiency. And it was flat-out cold. A glass wall faced north, with a lovely view of the alley. In the winter, you couldn't keep the back of the library warm. The floor plan was open, leaving no space for storage. There was no designated staff area. There were only five electric outlets. The furniture, made by local craftsmen, was beautiful but impractical. The tables had prominent support bars, so you couldn't pull up additional chairs, and they were solid oak with black laminate tops, so they were too heavy to move. The carpet was orange, a Halloween nightmare.

Or to put it more simply, the building wasn't right for a town like Spencer. The library had always been well run. The collection of books was exceptional, especially for a town the size of Spencer, and the directors had always been early adopters of new technologies and ideas. For enthusiasm, professionalism and expertise, the library was top-notch. But after 1971, it was all squeezed into the wrong building. The exterior didn't fit the surrounding area. The interior wasn't practical or friendly. It didn't make you want to sit down and relax. It was cold in every sense of the word.

We started the remodel—let's call it the warming process— in May 1989. The first stage was painting the bare concrete walls. We decided to leave the nine-foot bookshelves bolted to the walls, so Tony Joy, our painter and the husband of staff member Sharon, simply had to throw on some drop cloths and lean his ladder against the shelves. But as soon as he did, Dewey climbed up.

'All right, Dewey, down we go.'

Dewey wasn't paying attention. He'd been in the library more than a year, but he'd never seen it from nine feet up. It was a revelation. Dewey stepped off the ladder and onto the top of the wall shelf. With a few steps, he was out of reach.

Tony moved the ladder. Dewey moved again. Tony climbed to the top, propped his elbow on the bookshelf, and looked at this stubborn cat.

'This is a bad idea, Dewey. I'm going to paint this wall, then you're going to rub against it. Vicki's going to see a blue cat, and then you know what's going to happen? I'm going to get fired.' Dewey just stared down at the library. 'You don't care, do you? Well, I warned you. Vicki!'

'Right here.'

'You've been watching?'

'It's a fair warning. I won't hold you responsible.'

I wasn't worried about Dewey. He was the most conscientious cat I'd ever known. He raced down bookshelves without a misstep. He intentionally brushed displays with his side, as cats do, without knocking them over. I knew he could not only walk a shelf without touching wet paint, but also tiptoe up a ladder without knocking off the can of paint at the top. I was more worried about Tony. It's not easy sharing a ladder with the king of the library.

'I'm fine with the arrangement if you are,' I called up to him.

'I'll take my chances,' Tony joked.

Within a few days, Tony and Dewey were fast friends. Or maybe I should say Tony and Dewkster, because that's what Tony always called him. Tony felt Dewey was too soft a name for such a macho cat. He worried that the local alley cats were congregating outside the children's library window at night to make fun of his name. So Tony decided his real name wasn't Dewey, it was the Duke, like John Wayne. 'Only his close friends, call him Dewkster,' Tony explained.

One day Tony looked across the library and saw Dewey on top of the wall shelves at the opposite end of the building. That was when Dewey realised he could climb to the top of the wall shelves whenever he wanted. He had the run of the library up there, and some days he never wanted to come down.

When Tony finished the painting three weeks later, Dewey was a changed cat. Maybe he thought he really was Duke, because suddenly he wasn't content with just naps and laps. He wanted to explore. And climb. And most important, explore new places to climb. We called this Dewey's Edmund Hillary phase, after the famous mountain climber. Dewey didn't want to stop climbing until he'd reached the top of his personal Mount Everest, which he managed to do not more than a month later.

'Any sign of Dewey this morning?' I asked Audrey Wheeler, who was working at the circulation desk. 'He didn't come for breakfast.'

'I haven't seen him.'

Five minutes later, I heard Audrey utter what around here was a surprising profanity: 'Oh, my goodness!'

She was standing in the middle of the library, looking straight up. And there, on top of the lights, looking straight down, was Dewey. When he saw us looking, Dewey pulled his head back. He was instantly invisible. As we watched, Dewey's head reappeared a few feet down the light. Then it disappeared again, only to appear a few feet farther on. The lights run in hundred-foot strips, and he had clearly been up there for hours, watching us.

'How are we going to get him down?'

'Let's just wait him out,' I said. 'He's not doing any harm up there, and he'll have to come down for food eventually.'

An hour later, Dewey trotted into my office, licking his lips from a late breakfast, and jumped into my lap.

I asked around, but nobody had seen him come down. It took us a few weeks of constant surveillance to figure out his method. First Dewey jumped onto the empty desk in the staff room. Then he jumped onto a filing cabinet, which gave him a long jump to the top of the temporary wall around the staff area, where he could hide behind a huge quilt of Spencer history. From there, it was only four feet to the light.

Sure, we could have rearranged the furniture, but once he became ceiling fixated, we knew there wasn't much, except old age and creaky bones, that could stop Dewey from walking the lights. When cats don't know something exists, it's easy to keep them away. If they can't get to something and it's something they've made up their minds they want, it's almost impossible.

Besides, Dewey loved being up on the lights. He loved walking back and forth from end to end until he found an interesting spot. Then he would lie down, drape his head over the side, and watch. The patrons loved it, too. Sometimes, when Dewey was pacing, you could see them craning up at the ceiling, their heads going back and forth like the pendulum on a clock. They talked to him. When Dewey was pointed out to the children, his head just peaking over the edge of the lights, they screamed with excitement.

When they found out they couldn't join him on the ceiling, they begged him to come down. Eventually, even the children understood that when Dewey was on the lights, he was only coming down on his terms. He had discovered his own little seventh heaven up there.

THE OFFICIAL remodelling took place in July 1989, because July was the library's slow month. The children were on holidays, which meant no class trips and no unofficial after-school child care. A local tax firm donated warehouse space across the street. Everything in the library was given a number. The number corresponded to a colour-coordinated grid, which showed both its place in the warehouse and its new place in the library.

The move was truly a community effort. The Rotary Club helped move the books out; the Golden Kiwanis helped move them back. Our downtown development manager, Bob Rose, moved shelving. Doris Armstrong's husband, Jerry, spent more than a week bolting 110 new steel plates on to the ends of our shelving units, at least six bolts per plate, and never complained. Everybody volunteered: the genealogy club, the library board, teachers, parents, the nine-member board of Spencer's Friends of the Library. The downtown merchants pitched in, too, and there were free drinks and snacks for everyone.

The remodelling went like clockwork. In exactly three weeks, our Halloween horror was replaced with a neutral blue carpet and colourful reupholstered furniture. We added two-person gliders to the children's library so mothers could rock and read to their kids. In a closet, I found eighteen Grosvenor prints, along with seven old pen-and-ink sketches. The library didn't have enough money to frame them, so a member of the community adopted each print and paid for the framing. The newly arranged, angled shelves led the eye back into the books, where thousands of colourful spines invited patrons to browse, read, relax.

We unveiled the new library with a cookies and tea open house. Nobody was more excited that day than Dewey. He had been locked away at my house for three weeks, and during that time his whole world had changed. The walls were different; the carpet was different; all the chairs and tables and bookshelves were out of place. The books even smelled different after a trip to the warehouse across the street.

But as soon as people started arriving, Dewey dashed back to the refreshment table to be front and centre again. Yes, the library had changed, but what he missed most after three weeks away was people. He hated being away from his friends at the library. And they had missed him, too. As they went for their cookies, they all stopped to pet Dewey. Some lifted him onto their shoulders for a tour through the newly arranged shelving units. Others just watched him, talked about him, and smiled. The library may have changed, but Dewey was still the king.

Between 1987, the year before Dewey fell into our arms, and 1989, the year of the remodel, visits to the Spencer Public Library increased from 63,000 a year to more than 100,000. Clearly. something had changed.

the companion

on display

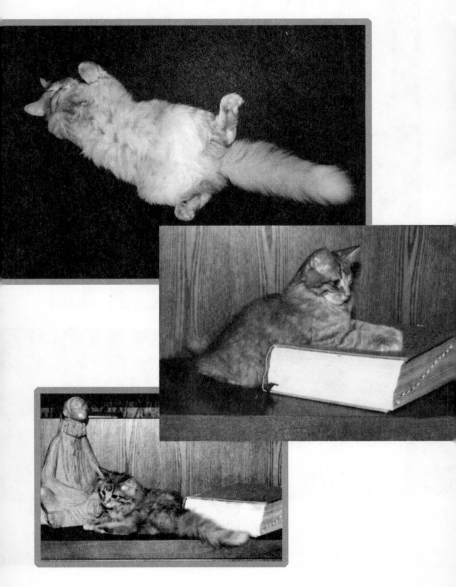

the librarian

TAX FORM
INCLUDED
IN BOOKLET

good times

People were thinking differently about their library, appreciating it more. And not just the citizens of Spencer. That year, 19.4 per cent of our visitors were from rural Clay County. Another 18 per cent came from the surrounding counties. No one could argue, seeing those numbers, that the library wasn't a regional centre.

The remodelling helped; there's no doubt about that. So did the revitalisation of Grand Avenue; and the economy, which was picking up; and the energised staff; and our new outreach and entertainment programs. But most of the change, most of what brought the new people in and finally made the Spencer Public Library a meeting house, not a warehouse, was Dewey.

CHAPTER 7

BY AUGUST of 1989, everything was going perfectly—except for Dewey. My contented baby boy, our library hero, was a changed cat: distracted, jumpy and, most of all, trouble.

The problem was the three weeks Dewey had spent at my house during the remodelling, staring through my window screens at the world outside. He couldn't see the corn from my house, but he could hear the birds. He could feel the breeze. He could smell whatever cats smell when they direct their noses to the great outdoors. Now he missed those screens. There were windows in the library, but they didn't open. You could smell the new carpet but not the outdoors. You could hear trucks, but you couldn't make out the birds.

Between the two sets of front doors at the Spencer Public Library was a tiny glass lobby that helped keep out the cold in the winter, since at least one set of doors was usually closed. For two years, Dewey hated that lobby; when he returned from his three weeks at my house, he adored it. From the lobby, he could hear the birds. When the outer doors were

open, he could smell fresh air. For a few hours in the afternoon, there was even a patch of sunlight. He pretended that
was all he wanted, to sit in that patch of sunlight and listen to
the birds. But we knew if he spent enough time in the lobby,
Dewey would become curious about going through that
second set of doors into the outside world.

'Dewey, get back in here!' the front desk clerk would yell
every time he followed a patron out the first set of doors.
The poor cat had no chance. The circulation desk faced into
the lobby, and the desk clerk always spotted him immediately. So Dewey stopped listening, especially if the clerk was
Joy DeWall, the newest and youngest member of the staff.
So Joy started coming back to get me. I was the Mom voice.
Dewey always listened to me, although, in this case, he was
so intent on disobeying I was forced to back up my threat.

'Dewey, do you want me to get the squirt bottle?'

He just stared at me.

I brought the squirt bottle out from behind my back. With
the other arm, I held open the door to the library. Dewey
slunk back inside.

Ten minutes later, I heard: 'Vicki, Dewey's in the lobby
again.'

That was it. Three times in one day. It was time to put my
foot down. I stormed out of my office, screwed up my best
Mom voice, threw open the lobby door, and demanded, 'You
get in here right now, young man.'

A man in his early twenties almost jumped out of his skin.
Talk about embarrassing. I was holding the door open in
stunned silence, unable to believe I hadn't seen this kid right
in front of my face, when Dewey came trotting past like
nothing out of the ordinary had happened. I could almost see
him smiling.

A week later, Dewey didn't come for his morning meal, and
I couldn't find him anywhere. Nothing unusual there; Dewey
had plenty of places to hide. There was a cubbyhole behind
the display case by the front door that I swear was the size of
a box of crayons. There was the brown lounge chair in the
children's area, although his tail usually stuck out of that one.

One afternoon, Joy was shelving the bottom row of books in the Westerns section when, to her amazement, Dewey popped out. In a library, books fit on both sides of a shelf. Between the rows is four inches of space. Between the books was Dewey's ultimate hiding place: quick, handy and secure. The only way to find him was to lift books at random and look behind them. That doesn't sound so difficult until you consider that the Spencer Public Library contained more than 400 shelves of books. Between those books was an enormous labyrinth, a long, narrow world all Dewey's own.

Fortunately, he almost always stuck to his favourite place in the bottom rows of Westerns. Not this time. He wasn't under the brown lounger, either, or in his cubbyhole. I didn't notice him peeking down from the lights. I opened the doors to the bathrooms to see if he had been locked inside. Not this morning.

'Has anyone seen Dewey?'

No. No. No. No.

'Who locked up last night?'

'I did,' Joy said, 'and he was definitely here.' I knew Joy would never have forgotten to look for Dewey. She was the only staffer, besides me, who would stay late with him to play hide-and-seek.

'Good. He must be in the building. Looks like he's found a new hiding place.'

But when I returned from lunch, Dewey was still missing. And he hadn't touched his food. That's when I began to worry.

'Where's Dewey?' a patron asked.

We had already heard that question twenty times, and it was only early afternoon. I told the staff, 'Tell them Dewey's not feeling well. No need to alarm anyone.' He'd show up. I knew it.

That night, I drove around for half an hour instead of heading straight home. I wasn't expecting to see a fluffy orange cat prowling the neighbourhood, but you never know. The thought going through my mind was, 'What if he's hurt? What if he needs me and I can't find him? I'm letting him down.' I knew he wasn't dead. He was so healthy. And I knew he hadn't run away. But the thought kept creeping up . . .

He wasn't waiting for me at the front door the next day. I stepped inside and the place felt dead. A cold dread walked up my spine, even though it was ninety degrees outside. I knew something was wrong.

I told the staff, 'Look everywhere.'

We checked every corner. We opened every cabinet and drawer. We pulled books off the shelves, hoping to find him in his crawl space. We shone a flashlight behind the wall shelves. Some of them had pulled an inch or two away from the wall; Dewey could have fallen in and got stuck. Clumsiness wasn't like him, but in an emergency you check every possibility.

The night janitor! The thought hit me like a rock, and I picked up the phone. 'Hi, Virgil, it's Vicki at the library. Did you see Dewey last night?'

'Who?'

'Dewey. The cat.'

'Nope. Didn't see him.'

'Is there anything he could have got into that made him sick? Cleaning solution, maybe?'

He hesitated. 'Don't think so.'

I didn't want to ask, but I had to. 'Do you ever leave any doors open?'

He really hesitated this time. 'I prop open the back door when I take the garbage to the dumpster.'

'How long?'

'Maybe five minutes.'

'Did you prop it open two nights ago?'

'I prop it every night.'

My heart sank. That was it. Dewey would never just run out an open door, but if he had a few weeks to think about it, peek around the corner, sniff the air . . .

I told the staff the news. Any information was good for our spirits. We set up shifts so that two people could cover the library while the rest looked for Dewey. The regular patrons could tell something was wrong. We took them aside and told them Dewey was missing. Soon, a dozen people were walking the sidewalks. 'Look at all these people. Look at all this love. We'll find him now,' I told myself again and again.

I was wrong.

I spent my lunch hour walking the streets, looking for my baby boy. He was so sheltered in the library. He wasn't a fighter. He was a finicky eater. How was he going to survive?

I called all the veterinarians in town. We didn't have an animal shelter, so a vet's office was the place someone would take him. If they didn't recognise him, that is. I told the vets, 'If someone brings in a cat who looks like Dewey, it probably is Dewey. We think he's escaped.'

I told myself, 'Everyone knows Dewey. Everyone loves Dewey. If someone finds him, they'll bring him back to the library.'

I didn't want to spread the news that he was missing. Dewey had so many children who loved him, not to mention the special needs students. Oh, my goodness, what about Crystal? I didn't want to scare them. I knew Dewey was coming back.

When Dewey wasn't waiting for me at the front door on the third morning, my stomach plummeted. I realised that, in my heart, I had been expecting to see him sitting there. When he wasn't, I was devastated. That's when it hit me: Dewey was gone. He might be dead. He probably wasn't coming back. I knew Dewey was important, but only at that moment did I realise how big a hole he would leave. To the town of Spencer, Dewey was the library. How could we go on without him?

The mood in the library was black. Yesterday we had hope. We believed it was only a matter of time. Now we believed he was gone.

We continued to search, but we had looked everywhere. We were out of options. I sat down and thought about what I was going to tell the community. I would call the radio station, which was the information nexus of Spencer. They would immediately make an announcement. They could mention an orange cat without saying his name. The adults would understand, but maybe that would buy time with the children . . .

'Vicki! Guess who's home!'

I stuck my head out of the office and there he was, my big orange buddy, wrapped in the arms of Jean Hollis Clark. I rushed over and hugged him tight. He laid his head on my chest.

'Oh, baby boy, baby boy. Don't ever do that again.'

Dewey was purring like he had on our first morning. He was so happy to see me, so thankful to be in my arms. He seemed happy. But I knew him so well. Underneath, in his bones, he was still shaking.

'I found him under a car on Grand Avenue,' Jean was saying. 'I was going over to White Drug, and I happened to catch a glimpse of orange out of the corner of my eye.'

I wasn't listening. I would hear the story many times over the next few days, but at that moment, I wasn't listening. I only had eyes and ears for Dewey.

'He was hunched against the wheel on the far side of the car. I called to him, but he didn't come. He looked like he wanted to run, but he was too afraid. He must have been right there, all along. Can you believe that? All those people looking for him, and he was right there, all along.'

The rest of the staff was crowding around us now. I could tell they wanted to hold him, to cuddle him, but I didn't want to let him go.

'He needs to eat,' I told them. Someone put out a fresh can of food, and we all watched while Dewey sucked it down. I doubt the cat had eaten in days.

Once he had done his business—food, water, litter box—I let the staff hold him. He was passed from hand to hand like a hero in a victory parade. When everyone had welcomed him home, we took him out to show the public. Most of them didn't know anything had happened, but there were a few wet eyes. Dewey, our prodigal son, gone but now returned to us. You really do love something more when it's been lost.

That afternoon, I gave Dewey a bath, which he tolerated for the first time since that cold January morning so long ago. He was covered in motor oil, which took months to work out of his long fur. He had a tear in one ear and a scratch on his nose. I cleaned them gently and lovingly. Was it another cat? A loose wire? The undercarriage of a car? I rubbed his cut ear between my fingers, and Dewey didn't even flinch.

Years later, I would make it a habit to prop open a side door during library board meetings. Cathy Greiner, a board member, asked me every time, 'Aren't you worried Dewey will run out?'

I looked down at Dewey, who was there, as usual, to attend the meeting, and he looked up at me. That look told me, as clearly as if he'd crossed his heart and hoped to die, that he wasn't going to run.

'He's not going anywhere,' I told her. 'He's committed to the library.'

And he was. For sixteen years, Dewey never went into the lobby again. He lounged by the front door, especially in the morning, but he never followed patrons out. If the doors opened and he heard trucks, he sprinted to the staff area. He didn't want to be anywhere near a passing truck. Dewey was completely done with the outdoors.

About a month after Dewey's escape, Jodi left Spencer. I wasn't sure I could afford to send her to college, and she didn't want to stay home. Jodi wanted to travel, so she took a job as a nanny in California and saved money for college. I'm sure it didn't hurt that California was a long way from Mom.

I brought Dewey home for her last weekend. As always, he was stuck to Jodi's side like a flesh-hugging magnet. I think he loved night-time with her most of all. He slept by her side, locked on to her hip. She could breathe, but she couldn't turn over. Did he know our girl was leaving, maybe for good? Jodi didn't get any sleep that night.

The next time Dewey came to my house, Jodi was gone. He found a way to stay close to her, though, by spending the night in Jodi's room, curled up on the floor next to her heater, no doubt dreaming of those warm summer nights spent snuggled up to Jodi's side.

A month later, I took Dewey for his first official photograph: Rick Krebsbach, the town photographer, was offering pet photographs for ten dollars.

Dewey was such an easygoing cat that I convinced myself getting a professional portrait of him, in a studio, would be easy. But Dewey hated the studio. As soon as we walked in, his head was swivelling, his eyes looking at everything. I put him in the chair, and he immediately hopped out. I picked him up and put him in the chair again. I took one step back and Dewey was gone.

'He's nervous. He hasn't been out of the library much,' I said as I watched Dewey sniff the photo backdrop.

'That's nothing,' Rick said as we watched Dewey dig his head under a pillow. 'One dog tried to eat my camera. Another dog actually ate my fake flowers.'

I picked Dewey up quickly, but my touch didn't calm him. He was still looking around, more nervous than interested. But this wasn't fear; it was confusion. 'He knows what's expected of him in the library, but he doesn't understand this place.'

'Take your time.'

A thought. 'May I show Dewey the camera?'

'If you think it will help.'

Dewey posed for photographs at the library all the time, but those were personal cameras. Rick's camera was a large, boxy, professional model. Dewey had never seen one of those before, but he was a fast learner.

'It's a camera, Dewey. Camera. We're here to get your picture taken.'

Dewey sniffed the lens. He leaned back and looked at it, then sniffed it again. I could feel him getting less tense, and I knew he understood.

I pointed. 'Chair. Sit in the chair.'

I put him down. He sniffed up and down every leg, and twice on the seat. Then he jumped into the chair and stared right at the camera. Rick hurried over and snapped six photos.

'I can't believe it,' he said as Dewey climbed down off the chair.

I didn't want to tell Rick, but this happened all the time. Dewey and I had a means of communicating even I didn't understand. He always seemed to know what I wanted, but unfortunately, that didn't mean he was always going to obey.

I didn't even have to say *brush* or *bath*; all I had to do was think about them and Dewey disappeared.

But since his escape, Dewey not only anticipated what I wanted, he did it. Not when a brushing or a bath was involved, of course, but for library business. That was one reason he was so willing to have his photograph taken. He wanted to do what was best for the library.

'He knows it's for the library,' I told Rick, but I could tell he wasn't buying it. Why, after all, would a cat care about a library? And how could he connect a library with a photo studio a block away? But it was the truth and I knew it.

I picked Dewey up and petted his favourite spot, the top of his head between the ears. 'He knows what a camera is.'

'Has he ever posed before?'

'At least two or three times a week. For visitors. He loves it.'

'That doesn't sound like a cat.'

I wanted to tell him Dewey wasn't just any cat, but Rick had been taking pet photographs for the past week. He'd probably heard it a hundred times already.

And yet, if you see Dewey's official photograph, which Rick shot that day, you can tell immediately he's not just another cat. He's beautiful, yes, but more than that, he's relaxed. He has no fear of the camera, no confusion about what's going on. His eyes are wide and clear. His fur is perfectly groomed. He doesn't look like a kitten, but he doesn't look like a grown cat, either. His posture is remarkably straight, his head cocked, his eyes staring calmly into the camera. I smile every time I see that photo because he looks so serious. He looks like he's trying to be strong and handsome but can't quite pull it off because he's so darn cute.

A few days after receiving the finished photographs, I noticed the local Shopko, a large general merchandise chain, was holding a pet photo contest to raise money for charity. You paid a dollar to vote, and the money was used to fight muscular dystrophy. This was typical of Spencer. There was always a fundraiser, and it was always supported by local citizens. We don't have a ton of money in Spencer, but if someone needs a hand, we're happy to provide it. That's civic pride.

On a whim, I entered Dewey in the contest. The photo was for library promotion purposes, after all, and wasn't this a perfect opportunity to promote this special aspect of the library? A few weeks later, Shopko strung a dozen photos, all of cats and dogs, on a wire in the front of the store. The town voted, and Dewey won by a landslide. He got more than 80 per cent of the votes, seven times as many as the runner-up.

Dewey trounced the competition because the town had adopted him. Not just the regular library patrons, I realised for the first time, but the whole town. While I wasn't watching, while I was preoccupied with school and remodelling and Jodi, Dewey was quietly working his magic. The stories, not just about his rescue but about his life and relationships, were seeping down into the cracks and sprouting new life. He wasn't just the library's cat, not any more. He was Spencer's cat. He was our inspiration, our friend, our survivor. He was one of us. And at the same time, he was ours.

Was he a mascot? No. Did he make a difference in the way the town thought about itself? Absolutely. Not to everyone, of course, but to enough. Dewey reminded us, once again, that we were a different kind of town. We cared. We valued the small things. We understood life wasn't about quantity but quality. Dewey was one more reason to love this hardy little town on the Iowa plains. The love of Spencer, the love of Dewey, it was all intermingled in the public mind.

CHAPTER 8

I CAN SEE now, in hindsight, that Dewey's escape was a turning point, a last fling at the end of youth. After that, he was content with his lot in life: to be the cat in residence at the Spencer Public Library, a friend, a confidant, and a goodwill ambassador to all. He greeted people with new enthusiasm. He perfected the fine art of lounging in the middle of adult non-fiction, where he could be seen from the whole library, but where there was plenty of room for people to walk without stepping on him. If he was in a contemplative mood, he would lie on his stomach with his head up and his front paws crossed casually in front. We called this his Buddha pose. Dewey could zone out in that pose for an hour like a fat little man at peace with the world. His other favourite position was to sprawl out full on his back, wide open, his paws sticking out in four directions. He went completely slack, letting it all hang out.

It's amazing how, when you stop running and start sprawling, the world comes to you. Or if not the world, then at least Iowa. Soon after the Shopko contest, Dewey was the subject of Chuck Offenburger's Iowa Boy column in the *Des Moines Register*.

When I read the article, I thought, 'Wow, Dewey's really made it.' It was one thing for a town to adopt a cat. It was even better for a region to adopt that cat, as north-west Iowa had with Dewey. The library received visitors every day from small towns and farms in surrounding counties. Summer residents of the Iowa lake country drove down to meet him, then spread the word to their neighbours and guests, who would drive down the following week. He appeared frequently in the newspapers of nearby towns. But the *Des Moines Register*! That was the daily newspaper in the state capital, which had a population of almost 500,000. The *Des Moines Register* was read all over the state. More than half a million people were probably reading about Dewey right now.

After Iowa Boy, Dewey started making regular appearances on our local television newscasts, which originated out of Sioux City, Iowa, and Sioux Falls, South Dakota. Soon he began appearing on stations in other nearby cities and states. Every segment started the same way, with a voice-over: *The Spencer Library wasn't expecting anything more in their drop box than books on a freezing January morning* . . . No matter how they framed it, the picture was the same. A poor feeble kitten, almost frozen to death, begging for help. The story of Dewey's arrival at the library was irresistible.

But so was his personality. Most news crews weren't used to filming cats but Dewey always gave them what they wanted. He jumped over the camera for a flying action shot. He walked between two displays to show his dexterity. He ran and jumped off the end of a shelf. He played with a child. He played with his red yarn. He sat quietly on top of the computer and stared into the camera, the model of decorum. He wasn't showing off. Posing for the camera was part of Dewey's job as publicity director for the library, so he did it. Enthusiastically.

Dewey's appearance on *Living in Iowa*, an Iowa Public Television series that focuses on issues, events and people in the state of Iowa, was typical. The *Living in Iowa* crew met me at the library at seven thirty in the morning. Dewey was ready. He waved. He rolled. He jumped between the shelves. He walked up and put his nose on the camera. He stuck right by the side of the host, a beautiful young woman, winning her over.

'Can I hold him?' she asked.

I showed her the Dewey Carry—over the left shoulder, with his behind in the crook of your arm, head over your back. If you wanted to hold him for any length of time, you had to use the Dewey Carry. The host stroked his back. Dewey lay his head on her shoulder and cuddled against her neck. 'He's doing it! He's really doing it! I can feel him purring.' She smiled at her cameraman and whispered, 'Are you getting this?'

I was tempted to tell her, 'Of course he's doing it. He does it for everyone,' but why spoil her excitement?

Dewey's episode aired a few months later. It was called 'A Tale of Two Kitties.' (Yes, it's a pun on Charles Dickens.) The other kitty was Tom, who lived in Kibby's Hardware in Conrad, Iowa, a small town in the middle of the state. Like Dewey, Tom was found on the coldest night of the year. Store owner Ralph Kibby took the frozen stray to the vet's office. 'They gave him sixty dollars' worth of shots,' he said on the program, 'and said, if he's still alive in the morning, he may have a chance.' As I watched the show, I realised why the host was so happy that morning. There were at least thirty seconds of footage of Dewey lying on her shoulder; the best she could get from Tom was a sniff of her finger.

Dewey's breakthrough came when the library received a package containing twenty copies of the June/July 1990 issue of *Country*, a national magazine with a circulation of more than five million. It wasn't unusual for us to receive magazines from publishers hoping to drum up library subscriptions, but twenty copies? I had never read *Country*. I decided to flip through it. Right there, starting on page fifty-seven, was a two-page, full-colour article about Dewey Readmore Books of the Spencer Public Library, complete with photographs sent in by a local woman I didn't even know but whose daughter frequented the library. Clearly she had been going home and telling her mother about the Dew.

It was just a small article, but its impact was extraordinary. For years, visitors told me how much it inspired them. Writers, calling for information for other articles about Dewey, often cited it. More than a decade later, I opened the mail to find a perfectly preserved copy of the article, neatly torn out of the magazine near the fold. The woman wanted me to know how much Dewey's story meant to her.

In Spencer, people who had forgotten about Dewey, or who had never shown any interest in him, took notice. Even the crowd at Sister's Café perked up. The worst of the farm crisis had passed, and our leaders were looking for a way to attract new business. Dewey was getting the kind of national exposure they could only dream of, and of course, that energy and excitement was rubbing off on the town. Sure, nobody has ever built a factory because of a cat, but nobody has ever built a factory in a town they'd never heard of, either. Once again, Dewey was doing his part, not just in Spencer, this time, but out there in the larger world, beyond the cornfields of Iowa.

The biggest change, though, was pride. Dewey's friends were proud of him, and everyone was proud to have him in town. One man, back for his twentieth high school reunion, stopped by the library to flip through newspapers from that year. Dewey, of course, won him over immediately. But once he heard about Dewey's friends and saw the articles about him, he became truly impressed. He wrote later to thank us and say he'd been telling everyone in New York about his wonderful hometown and its beloved library cat.

He wasn't the only one. We had three or four people a week coming into the library to show Dewey off. 'We're here to see the famous cat,' an older man would say, approaching the desk.

'He's sleeping in the back. I'll go get him.'

'Thanks,' he said, motioning to a younger woman with a little blonde-haired girl hiding behind her leg. 'I wanted my granddaughter Lydia to meet him. She's from Kentucky.'

When Lydia saw Dewey, she smiled and looked up at her grandfather as if for permission. 'Go ahead, sweetie. Dewey won't bite.' The girl tentatively stretched out her hand to Dewey; two minutes later, she was stretched out on the floor, petting him.

'See?' her grandfather said to the little girl's mother. 'I told you it was worth the trip.' I suppose he could have meant Dewey or the library, but I suspect he was referring to something more.

Later, while the mother was petting Dewey with her daughter, the grandfather came up to me and said, 'Thanks so much for adopting Dewey.' Thirty minutes later, as they were leaving, I heard the young woman tell the older man, 'You were right, Dad. That was great. I wish we had come by sooner.'

'Don't worry, Mommy,' the little girl said. 'We'll see him next year, too.'

Pride. Confidence. Assurance that this cat, this library, this experience, maybe even this town, really was special. Dewey wasn't any more beautiful or friendly after the *Country* article; in fact, fame never changed him. All Dewey ever wanted was a warm place to nap, a fresh can of food, and love and attention from every person who ever stepped foot in the Spencer Public Library. But at the same time, Dewey *had* changed, because now people looked at him differently.

The proof? Before the *Country* article, nobody took the

blame for shoving poor Dewey into our book return. Everybody knew the story, but nobody confessed. After Dewey hit the media, eleven different people came up to me confidentially and swore that they had shoved Dewey down that hole. They weren't taking blame; they were taking credit. 'I always knew it would turn out well,' they said.

Eleven people! Can you believe it? That must have been one wild, cat-saving alley party.

I'm not naive. I know not everyone in Spencer embraced Dewey. For instance, that woman still wrote regular letters threatening to bring her cow downtown if the city didn't stop the injustice, the horror, of a cat living in a public building. She was the most vocal, but she certainly wasn't the only person who didn't understand the Dewey phenomenon.

'What's so special about that cat?' they would say over a cup of coffee at Sister's Café. 'He never leaves the library. He sleeps a lot. He doesn't *do* anything.'

By which they meant Dewey didn't create jobs. Dewey was appearing regularly in magazines, newspapers and on the radio around the country, but he wasn't improving our municipal parks. He wasn't paving roads. He wasn't out recruiting new businesses. The worst of the farm crisis had passed; spirits were rising; it was time for Spencer to spread its wings and attract new employers to our plucky Midwest town fairly far off the beaten track

THAT YEAR, 1994, the Spencer Public Library entered the modern era. Out went the antiquated book-management system, with its cards, stamps, catalogue drawers, checkout bins, late notice slips, complex filing systems and, of course, dozens and dozens of boxes. In came a fully automated system complete with eight computers. The bins for the cards, where Dewey loved to lounge in the afternoon, were replaced with a circulation computer. Kim's daisy-wheel typewriter, which Dewey had loved as a kitten, fell silent and motionless. We threw a party, pulled all the drawers out of our card catalogues, dumped thousands of cards on the floor, then turned on the one public-access computer that would replace them.

After the technology update of 1994, people began using the library differently. Patron visits to the Spencer Library rose between 1994 and 2006, but only a third as many books were checked out. In 1987, when Dewey arrived, it was common for the book drop to overflow with books. We haven't had a full drop box in a decade. Our most popular items for checkout are classic movies on DVD and video games. We have nineteen computers for public use, sixteen with internet access. Even though we're small, we are tenth in the number of computers available to patrons in the entire Iowa library system.

A librarian clerk's job used to involve filing and answering reference questions. Now it's understanding computers and inputting data. To keep track of usage, the clerk working the circulation desk used to make a hash mark on a piece of paper every time a patron entered the library. You can imagine how accurate that system was, especially when the library was busy and the clerk was answering reference questions. Now we have an electronic clicker that records every person who comes through the door. The checkout system tells us exactly how many books, games and movies come and go and tracks which items are the most popular and which haven't been touched in years.

And yet, for all that, the Spencer Public Library remains essentially the same. The carpet is different. The back window, which looked out on the alley, has been plastered over and covered with bookshelves. There's less wood, fewer drawers, and more electronics. But there are still children's groups laughing and listening to stories. Middle school students killing time. Older people thumbing through the newspaper. Businessmen reading magazines. This library is still a relaxed, and relaxing, place. We may not be the soothingly silent book depository of yesteryear, but we serve the community better than ever. The number of people entering the Spencer Public Library keeps rising. Does it matter if they are checking out books, renting movies, playing video games, or visiting a cat?

Dewey loved the new library. Sure, he lost a few boxes, but there are always boxes in a library that orders books on an almost daily basis. Computers may seem cold compared to the old hands-on system of wood, paper and ink, but to Dewey they were warm. Literally. He loved to sit on them and bask in the heat of their exhaust. I took a picture of him up there, which became the image on our new computerised checkout cards. The company that made the cards loved it. Every time I went to a library convention, I would see Dewey emblazoned on a huge banner above their booth.

Almost as good, at least from Dewey's perspective, were the new sensor posts beside the front door, which beeped if you tried to leave without checking out your library materials. Dewey's new favourite position was just inside the left post. He sat by that post for the first hour of every day, starting promptly at two minutes to nine. With Dewey and the posts crowding the entrance way, there was almost no space for patrons to walk. Before, it was difficult to ignore Dewey when he was in front door greeting mode; with the new sensors, it was impossible.

CHAPTER 9

THE COMPUTERS weren't the only change in Dewey's life. Crystal, Dewey's friend from the special education class, graduated and began a life I can't imagine, but one I pray was happy. The little girl who had been afraid of Dewey overcame her fear of cats. The other children her age, the ones Dewey had spent Story Hour with that first year, were growing up, too. He had been in the library six years, and it was inevitable that many of the children he had known were moving away or moving on.

Jean Hollis Clark, my assistant director, left for a new job. Eventually she was replaced by Kay Larson, whom I had known for years. I hired Kay because she was good with computers, and we needed someone who could keep up with new technology. I also knew she was a cat person. She thought Dewey was smart and beautiful, but she didn't think he was anything that special.

Despite the changes, Dewey's life stayed essentially the same. Children grew up, but there were always new ones turning four. Staffers moved on, but even on our skimpy budget we managed new hires. Dewey may never again have had a friend like Crystal, but he still met the special education class at the door every week. He even developed relationships with patrons like Mark Carey, who owned the electronics store on the corner. Dewey knew Mark wasn't a cat lover, and he took fiendish delight in suddenly jumping onto the table and scaring the bejeebers out of him. Mark took delight in kicking Dewey out of whatever chair he was lounging in, even if there was nobody else in the library.

One morning, I noticed a businessman sitting at a table, reading the *Wall Street Journal*. It looked like he had stopped in to kill time before a meeting, so I wasn't expecting to see a fluffy orange tail sticking out at his side. I looked closer and saw that Dewey had plopped down on one page of his newspaper. 'Oh, Dewey,' I thought, 'you're pushing it now.' Then I realised the man was holding the newspaper with his right hand while petting Dewey with his left. One of them was purring; the other was smiling. That's when I knew Dewey and the town had fallen into a comfort zone, that the general outline of our lives had been set, at least for the next few years.

Maybe that's why I was so surprised when I arrived at the library one morning to find Dewey pacing. He was never agitated like that; even my presence didn't calm him. When I opened the door, he ran a few steps, then stopped, waiting for me to follow. He kept pacing back and forth, crying for me. Dewey never cried unless he was in pain, but I knew Dewey. He wasn't in pain. He was waiting for me in the children's library. The poor cat was in knots.

'I'm sorry, Dewey. I don't understand what you're trying to tell me.'

When the staff arrived, I told them to keep an eye on

Dewey. If he was still acting strange in a few hours, I decided to take him to see Dr Esterly. I knew he would love that.

Two minutes after the library opened, Jackie Shugars came back to my office. 'You're not going to believe this, Vicki, but Dewey just peed on the cards.'

I jumped up. 'It can't be!'

The library automation wasn't yet complete. To check out a book, we still stamped two cards. One went home with you in the book; the other went into a big bin with hundreds of other cards. When you returned the book, we pulled that card and put the book back on the shelf. Actually there were two bins, one on each side of the front desk. Sure enough, Dewey had peed in the front right corner of one of them.

I wasn't mad at Dewey. I was worried about him. This was completely out of character. But I didn't have long to think the situation through before one of our regular patrons came up and whispered in my ear, 'You better get down here, Vicki. There's a bat in the children's department.'

Sure enough, there was the bat, hanging by his heels behind a ceiling beam. And there was Dewey at *my* heel.

Have you ever been lectured by a cat? It's not a pleasant experience. Especially when the cat is right. And especially when a bat is involved. I hate bats. I couldn't stand the thought of having one in the library, and I couldn't imagine being trapped all night with that thing flying all over the place. Poor Dewey.

'Don't worry, Dewey. Bats sleep during the day. He won't hurt anybody.'

Dewey didn't look convinced, but I couldn't worry about that now. I didn't want to scare the patrons, especially the children, so I quietly called the city hall janitor and told him, 'Get down to the library right away. And bring your ladder.'

He climbed up for a look. 'It's a bat, all right.' The ordeal was over in a matter of seconds. Thank goodness. Now I had to sort out the mess in the cards. I pulled out about twenty cards. Underneath them was a big pile of bat guano. Dewey hadn't just been trying to get my attention; he'd been using his scent glands to cover the stench of the intruder.

The next morning, Dewey started what I referred to as his sentry phase. Each morning, he sniffed three heating vents: the one in my office, the one by the front door, and the one by the children's library. He sniffed each one again after lunch. He knew those vents led somewhere and that therefore they were access points. He had taken it upon himself to use his powerful nose to protect us, to be our proverbial canary in the coal mine.

I suppose there could be something funny about such a vigilant cat but I found it very endearing. At one point in his life, Dewey wasn't content until he expanded his world to the street outside the library. Now that his story had gone all over the country, he wanted nothing more than to hunker down in the library and protect his friends.

Dewey's fame continued to grow. He was featured in all the cat magazines—if the magazine had *cat* in the title, Dewey was probably in it. He even appeared in *Your Cat*, a leading publication of the British feline press. Marti Attoun, a young freelance writer, travelled to Spencer with a photographer. His article appeared in *American Profile*, a weekend insert featured in more than a thousand newspapers. Then, in the summer of 1996, a documentary film-maker from Boston turned up, camera in tow, ready to put Dewey in his first movie.

Gary Roma was travelling the country, from the East Coast to North Dakota, to create a documentary about library cats. He arrived expecting the kind of footage he'd shot at other libraries: cats darting apprehensively behind bookshelves, walking away, sleeping, and doing everything possible to avoid looking into the camera. Dewey was exactly the opposite. He didn't ham it up, but he went about all his usual activities, and he performed them on command. Gary arrived early in the morning to catch Dewey waiting for me at the front door. He shot Dewey sitting by the sensor posts greeting patrons; lying in his Buddha pose; playing with his favourite toys, Marty Mouse and the red yarn; sitting on a patron's shoulder in the Dewey Carry; and sleeping in a box.

About six months after filming, in the winter of 1997, we

threw a party for the inaugural showing of *Puss in Books*. The library was packed. The film started with a distant shot of Dewey sitting on the floor of the Spencer library, waving his tail slowly back and forth. As the camera zoomed in and followed him under a table, across some shelves and, finally, to his favourite cart for a ride, you heard my voice telling Dewey's story.

By this time, I was used to strange calls about Dewey. The library was getting a couple of requests a week for interviews, and articles about our famous cat were turning up in our mail on an almost weekly basis. Dewey's official photograph, the one taken by Rick Krebsbach just after Jodi left Spencer, had appeared in magazines, newsletters, books and newspapers from Minneapolis, Minnesota, to Jerusalem, Israel. It even appeared in a cat calendar; Dewey was Mr January.

On the afternoon of 7 June 1999, I received a phone call from a Dewey fan. 'Vicki, turn on the radio. You're not going to believe this.'

I turned it on to hear 'And now you know . . . the rest of the story.'

Anyone raised on radio knows that sign-off. Paul Harvey's *The Rest of the Story* is one of the most popular programs in the history of radio. Each broadcast relates a minor, but telling, incident in the life of a well-known person. The gimmick is that you don't know whom Paul Harvey is talking about until his famous closing.

Now Paul Harvey was telling the story of a cat who inspired a town and became famous around the world . . . and it all started in a library book drop on a cold January morning in a small Iowa town. And now you know . . .

Who cares if nobody from Paul Harvey's staff called to check the facts? Who cares if they didn't know 10 per cent of the rest of the story, the part that made Dewey so special? I sat down at the end of the broadcast and thought, 'That's it. Dewey's really made it now.'

For years I had gone to the newspaper and the radio station to pass on Dewey news. With Paul Harvey, I decided to hold back. It wasn't that there weren't plenty of Dewey fans.

Patrons asked every day for the latest bit of Dewey news. Children ran into the library, eager and smiling, looking for their friend. But good news about Dewey no longer seemed to impress the rest of the town. In fact, I was beginning to worry it was pushing some people away. Dewey, I suspected, might be a little overexposed.

But only in Spencer. The rest of the world still couldn't get enough. I was working in my office one morning when Kay called me to the front desk. Standing there was a family of four, two young parents and their children.

'This nice family,' Kay said, with barely disguised amazement, 'is from Rhode Island. They've come to meet Dewey.'

The father extended his hand. 'We were in Minneapolis, so we decided to rent a car and drive down. The kids just love Dewey.'

Was this man crazy? Minneapolis was four and half hours away. 'Wonderful,' I said, shaking their hands. 'How did you find out about Dewey?'

'We read about him in *Cats* magazine."

'Okay,' I said, because I couldn't think of anything else. 'Let's go meet him.'

Dewey was, thank goodness, as eager to please as always. He played with the children. He posed for photographs. I showed the little girl the Dewey Carry, and she walked him all around the library on her left shoulder (always the left). I don't know if it was worth the nine-hour round trip, but the family left happy.

It happened again. And again. And again. And again. They came from Utah, Washington, Mississippi, California, Maine, and every other corner of the map. Older couples, younger couples, families. Many were travelling cross-country and drove 100 even 200 miles out of their way to stop in Spencer for the day.

What were these pilgrims expecting to find? A wonderful cat, of course, but there are wonderful cats sitting homeless in every shelter in America. Why come all this way? Was it love, peace, comfort, acceptance, a reminder of the simple joys of life? Did they just want to spend time with a star?

Whatever they were after, Dewey delivered. The magazine articles and newscasts touched people. We received letters all the time. His visitors, all of them, left smitten. I know this not only because they told me or because I saw their eyes and their smiles but because they went home and told people the story. They showed them the pictures. At first they sent letters to friends and relatives. Later, when the technology caught on, they sent emails. Dewey's face, his personality, his story, it all magnified. He received letters from Taiwan, Holland, South Africa, Norway, Australia. A ripple started in a little town in north-west Iowa and somehow the human network carried it all over the world.

Whenever I think of Dewey's popularity, I think of Jack Manders. Jack is now retired, but when Dewey arrived he was a middle school teacher and the president of our library board. A few years later, when his daughter was accepted at Hope College in Holland, Michigan, Jack found himself attending a reception for the parents of incoming freshmen. As he stood there, in a sophisticated Michigan nightspot, slowly sipping a martini, he fell into conversation with a couple from New York City. Eventually they asked where he was from.

'A small town in Iowa you've never heard of.'

'Oh. Is it near Spencer?'

'Actually,' he told them with surprise, 'it is Spencer.'

The couple perked up. 'Do you ever go to the library?'

'All the time. In fact, I'm on the board.'

The charming, well-dressed woman turned to her husband and, with an almost girlish giggle, exclaimed, 'It's Dewey's daddy!'

This is not to say everyone knew Dewey. No matter how famous and popular Dewey became, there was always someone with no idea the Spencer Public Library had a cat. A family would drive from Nebraska to see Dewey. They would bring gifts, spend two hours playing with him, taking pictures, talking with the staff. Ten minutes after they left, someone would come up to the desk, obviously worried, and whisper, 'I don't want to alarm you, but I just saw a cat in the building.'

'Yes,' we would whisper back. 'He lives here. He's the world's most famous library cat.'

The visitors who truly touched me, though, the ones I remember clearly, were the young parents from Texas and their six-year-old daughter. As soon as they entered the library, it was clear this was a special trip for her. Was she sick? Was she dealing with a trauma? I don't know why, but I had the feeling the parents offered her one wish, and this was it. The girl wanted to meet Dewey. And, I noticed, she had brought a present.

'It's a toy mouse,' her father told me. He was smiling, but I could tell he was intensely worried. This was no ordinary spur-of-the-moment visit.

As I smiled back at him, only one thought was going through my mind: 'I hope that toy mouse has catnip in it.' Dewey would regularly go through periods where he wanted nothing to do with any toy that didn't contain catnip. Unfortunately, this was one of those times.

All I said was, 'I'll go get Dewey.'

Dewey was asleep in his new fake fur–lined bed, which we kept outside my office door in front of a heating unit. As I woke him up I tried a little mental telepathy: 'Please, Dewey, please. This one's important.' He was so tired, he barely opened his eyes.

The little girl was hesitant at first, as many children are, so the mother petted Dewey first. Dewey lay there like a sack of potatoes. The girl eventually reached out to pet him, and Dewey woke up enough to lean into her hand. The father sat down and put both Dewey and the girl on his lap. Dewey immediately snuggled up against her.

They sat like that for a minute or two. Finally, the girl showed him the present she had brought, with its carefully tied ribbon and bow. Dewey perked up, but I could tell he was still tired. He would have preferred to snooze in the girl's lap all morning. 'Come on, Dewey,' I thought. 'Snap out of it.' The girl unwrapped the gift, and sure enough, it was a plain toy mouse, no catnip in sight. My heart sank. This was going to be a disaster.

The girl dangled the mouse in front of Dewey's sleepy eyes to get his attention. Then she delicately tossed it a few feet away. As soon as it hit the ground, Dewey jumped on it. He chased that toy; he threw it in the air; he batted it with his paws. The girl giggled with delight. Dewey never played with it again, but while that little girl was here, he gave that mouse every ounce of energy he had. And the little girl just beamed. She had come hundreds of miles to see a cat, and she was not disappointed. Why did I ever worry about Dewey? He always came through.

CHAPTER 10

SPENCER WAS thriving. In the late 1990s, the YMCA completed a $2-million renovation. The Spencer Regional Hospital expanded twice. Thanks to $170,000 in donations and 250 volunteers, the modest new playground planned for East Lynch Park turned into a 30,000-square-foot mega-playground called the Miracle on South Fourth Street.

We also have the Clay County Fair, one of the best county fairs in the United States and a tradition for almost a hundred years. Clay County has fewer than 20,000 residents, but the fair attracts more than 300,000 people for nine days of rides, contests, food and fun. We have a full-size track for races and tractor pulls, a separate ring for horses, and long metal barns for everything from chickens to llamas. There are hay wagons to take you from the parking lot (a grass field) to the front gate. We've even installed a sky bucket system to carry people from one end of the fair to the other. There's a year-round sign about ten miles south of Spencer, on the main road (and only road if you're driving more than a few miles), that counts down the weeks to the fair. It's painted on a brick building built on the highest hill in the area.

In the late 1990s, our city planner, Kirby Schmidt, spent

two years researching our downtown strip. Kirby was one of the native sons who almost left Spencer during the crisis of the 1980s. His brother left for the East Coast, his sister for the West Coast. Kirby and his young family decided to stick it out. The economy turned; Kirby got a job with the city. A few years later, I gave him the key to the library, and he started coming in at six every morning to search through microfiche files, old newspapers and local histories. Dewey mostly slept through these early visits; in the mornings, he only had eyes for me.

In 1999, Grand Avenue between Third Street and Eighth Street was placed on the National Register of Historic Places. The area was cited as a remarkable example of Prairie Deco and one of the few surviving comprehensive models of Depression-era urban planning. It usually took two or three applications to make the Registry, but thanks to Kirby Schmidt, Grand Avenue made it by unanimous vote on the first application. Around the same time, Kirby's sister moved her family back to Spencer from Seattle. She wanted to raise her kids the old-fashioned way: in Iowa.

That's another of Spencer's unique and valuable assets: its people. We are good, solid, hardworking mid-westerners. We are proud but humble. We don't brag. We believe your worth is measured by the respect of your neighbours, and there is no place we'd rather be than with those neighbours, right here in Spencer, Iowa. We are woven not just into this land, which our families have worked for generations, but to one another. And a bright shining thread, popping up in a hundred places in that tapestry, is Dewey.

Dewey wasn't special because he *did* something extra-ordinary but because he *was* extraordinary. He was like one of those seemingly ordinary people who, once you get to know them, stand out from the crowd. They are the ones who never miss a day of work, who never complain, who never ask for more than their share. They are those rare librarians, car salesmen and waitresses who provide excellent service on principle, who go beyond the job because they have a passion for the job. They know what they are meant to do in life, and they do it exceptionally well. Some win awards; some make a lot of money; most are taken for granted. Dewey came from humble beginnings (an Iowa alley); he survived tragedy (a freezing drop box); he found his place (a small-town library). Maybe that's the answer. He found his place. His passion, his purpose, was to make that place, no matter how small and out of the way it may have seemed, a better place for everyone.

I don't want to take anything away from the cat who falls out of the Winnebago, then spends five months trudging home through snowdrifts and scorching heat. That cat is an inspiration: never give up, always remember the importance of home. In his quiet way, Dewey taught those lessons, too. He never gave up during his long night in the box, and he was devoted to the library that became his home. Dewey didn't do one heroic thing; he did something heroic every day. He spent his time changing lives right here in Spencer, Iowa, one lap at a time.

Dewey won hearts, day by day, one person at a time. He never left anyone out or took anyone for granted. If you were receptive, he was there for you. If you weren't receptive, he worked to bring you around, a friend to anyone and everyone. There are dozens of library cats in the United States, but none come close to accomplishing what Dewey accomplished. He wasn't just another cat for people to pet and smile about. Every regular user of the library, *every single one*, felt they had a unique relationship with Dewey. He made everyone feel special.

Sharon often brought her daughter Emmy, who had Down's syndrome, to see Dewey, especially on Sundays, when it was her turn to feed him. Every Saturday night, Emmy asked her, 'Is tomorrow a Dewey day?' The first thing Emmy did every 'Dewey day' was search for Dewey. When he was younger, he would usually be waiting by the door, but as he aged, Emmy often found him lying in the sun by a window. She would pick him up and bring him to Mommy so they could pet him together. 'Hi, Dewey. I love you,' Emmy would say in a soft, kind voice, the way her own mother talked to her. For Emmy, that was the voice of love. Sharon was always afraid Emmy would pet him too hard, but Emmy and Dewey were friends, and she understood him as well as any of us. She was always wonderfully gentle.

Yvonne Berry, a single woman in her late thirties, came to the library three or four times a week. Every time, Dewey sought her out and spent fifteen minutes on her lap. Then he tried to coax her to open the bathroom door so he could play with the water. It was their ritual. But on the day Yvonne had to put her own cat to sleep, Dewey sat with her for more than two hours. He didn't know what had happened, but he knew something was wrong. Years later, when she told me that story, I could tell it was still important to her.

The century was turning, changing over, and Dewey was mellowing. He spent more time in his cat bed, and strenuous play was replaced by quiet book cart rides with Joy. Instead of jumping onto the cart, he would meow for Joy to pick him up so he could ride at the front of the cart like the captain of a ship. He stopped jumping to the ceiling lights, more out of boredom, I believe, than physical necessity. He couldn't abide rough handling, but he loved a gentle touch, like that of the homeless man who became one of his best friends. It is difficult to be invisible in a town like Spencer, but this man came close. He simply appeared at the library every day, unshaven, uncombed and unwashed. He never said a word to anyone. He never looked at anyone. He wanted only Dewey. He would pick Dewey up and drape him over his shoulder; Dewey would lie there, purring, for twenty minutes, while the man unburdened himself of secrets.

Dewey was stiffening up, and he could no longer tolerate the small knocks and bruises. He never lashed out at children, and he rarely ran from them. He simply began to scoot away and hide when certain children came looking for him, avoiding a situation before it began.

Babies were a different story. One day I watched Dewey plop himself down a few feet from an infant girl who was on the floor in a baby carrier. I had often seen Dewey interact with infants, so I wasn't apprehensive. But babies are delicate, and new moms even more so. Especially this one. Dewey just sat with a bored expression. Then, when he thought I wasn't looking, he squirmed an inch closer. A minute later, he did it again. Then again. Slowly, inch by inch, he crept closer, until finally he was pressed right up against the carrier. He popped his head over the edge, as if to confirm the child was inside, then settled down with his head on his paws. The infant reached her little hand over the edge and snatched his ear. Dewey adjusted his head so she could get a better grip. She laughed, kicking her legs and squeezing his ear. Dewey sat quietly, a contented look on his face.

In 2002, we hired a new assistant children's librarian, Donna Stanford. Donna had been around the world as a Peace Corps recruiter and she had recently returned to north-west Iowa to care for her mother, who was suffering from Alzheimer's. Donna was quiet and conscientious, which I thought at first was the reason Dewey spent a few hours every day with her over in the children's section.

It took me a long time to realise that Donna didn't know anyone in town besides her mother, and that even a place like Spencer—or maybe especially a close-knit place like Spencer—could seem cold and intimidating to an outsider. The only local resident who reached out to Donna was Dewey, who would ride on her shoulder while she rolled around in her office chair, shelving books. When he tired of that, he would climb down onto her lap so Donna could pet him. Sometimes she read him children's books. I caught them by surprise one day, Dewey resting with his eyes closed, Donna deep in thought. I could tell she was startled.

'Don't worry,' I said. 'It is part of your job description to hold the kitty.'

Then there was Jodi's boyfriend, Scott. Poor Scott was thrown right into the fire on his first trip to Spencer: my parent's fiftieth wedding anniversary. And this wasn't just a family party. The event was held at the Spencer Convention Centre, which had a seating capacity of 450 people. All their lives, Mom and Dad had treated the whole world as their family.

As soon as she left home, my relationship with Jodi improved dramatically. We were great friends, we realised, and terrible room-mates.

That night, after the party, Jodi and I took Scott to the library to meet Dewey. That's when I knew this relationship was serious; Jodi had never introduced Dewey to one of her boyfriends before, and none of her other boyfriends, as far as I knew, had ever been interested in meeting him. Dewey was, of course, overjoyed to see Jodi. She was for ever his love. Scott gave the two of them time together, then gently picked Dewey up and petted him. He walked him around the empty library in the Dewey Carry. He pulled out his camera and took a snapshot for his mother. She had heard the Dewey stories, and she was a big fan. My heart warmed to see the two of them together. Scott was so loving and tender.

It also never crossed my mind, at this point, to think of Dewey as the library's cat. Dewey was my cat. I was the person he came to for love. I was the person he came to for comfort. And I went to him for love and comfort, too. He wasn't a substitute husband or a substitute child. I wasn't lonely; I had plenty of friends. I wasn't unfulfilled; I loved my job. I wasn't looking for someone special. It wasn't even that I saw him every day. We lived apart. We could spend whole days in the library together and hardly see each other. But even when I didn't see him, I knew he was there.

Dewey was more special to me than any animal I had ever known. He was more special to me than I ever believed an animal could be. However, that didn't change a fundamental truth. He was my cat, but he belonged in the library. Dewey's place was with the public.

WE RECEIVED the email from Japan in early 2003. Actually, the email came from Washington, DC on behalf of people in Tokyo. Tomoko Kawasumi represented Japanese Public Television, which wanted to film Dewey. The company was making a documentary to introduce some new high-definition technology, and they wanted as wide an audience as possible. They decided first on a documentary about animals, then narrowed the focus to cats. They discovered Dewey through a feature in the Japanese magazine *Nekobiyori*. Would we mind if a film crew came to Spencer for a day?

That's funny, we had no idea Dewey had appeared in a Japanese magazine.

A few months later, in May, six people from Tokyo arrived at the Spencer Public Library. The crew had one day to film, so they asked me to arrive at the library before seven. It was a miserably rainy morning. The interpreter, the only woman in the group, asked me to open the first set of doors so they could set up their cameras in the lobby. As they were carting equipment, around the corner came Dewey. He was half asleep, stretching his back legs as cats often do when they first wake up. When he saw me, he trotted over and gave me a wave.

Once the crew set up the cameras, the interpreter said, 'We'd like him to wave again.'

I tried to explain, as best I could, that Dewey only waved once, when he saw me first thing in the morning. The director, Mr Hoshi, wouldn't hear of it. He was not only used to giving orders but to having them obeyed. He wanted that wave.

So I went back to my car and approached the library again, pretending I hadn't been in that morning. Dewey just stared at me.

I entered the library, turned on the lights, turned off the lights, went back to the car, waited five minutes, and approached the library again. Mr Hoshi thought this might fool Dewey into thinking it was the next day.

It didn't.

We tried for an hour to get footage of Dewey waving. Finally I said, 'Look, the poor cat has been sitting there this whole time, waiting for his food. I have to feed him.' Mr Hoshi agreed. Dewey ate a leisurely breakfast. By the time he was finished, the camera crew was set up inside.

Dewey was almost fifteen years old and he was slowing down, but he hadn't lost his enthusiasm for strangers. Especially strangers with cameras. He approached each member of the crew and greeted him with a rub on the leg. They were petting him, horsing around, and one cameraman lay down on the floor for a Dewey eye–view. The interpreter politely asked me to put Dewey on a bookshelf. He sat there and let them film. He jumped from shelf to shelf. Then she said,

'Have him walk down the shelf between the books and jump off the end.'

I thought, 'Wait a second. He's a cat, not a trained animal in the circus, and that's a pretty specific request. I hope you didn't come all this way expecting a show because there's no way he's going to walk that shelf, slalom between the display books and jump off at command.'

I trudged down to the far end of the shelf and called, 'Come here, Dewey. Come here.' Dewey walked down the shelf, slalomed between the books, and jumped down to my feet.

For five hours, Mr Hoshi gave orders and Dewey complied. He sat on a computer. He sat on a table. He sat on the floor with his feet crossed and stared into the camera. He rode on his favourite book cart with his feet hanging down through the openings in the metal grill, completely relaxed. No time to dally; move, move, move. A three-year-old girl and her mother agreed to appear in the film, so I put Dewey on the glider chair with them. The girl was nervous, grabbing and pulling at Dewey. Dewey didn't mind. He sat through the whole five-minute ordeal and never forgot to stare sweetly at the camera.

I had been telling the interpreter all morning that people came from all over the United States to visit Dewey, but I don't think Mr Hoshi believed me. Then, just after lunch, in walked a family from New Hampshire. Talk about timing! The family was at a wedding in Des Moines and decided to rent a car and drive up to see Dewey. Need I remind you that's a three-and-a-half-hour drive?

Mr Hoshi was all over the visitors. He interviewed them extensively. He took footage of them shooting their own footage of Dewey with their camcorder. I taught the girl, who was five or six, the Dewey Carry, and how to gently rock back and forth until he put his head down on her back and closed his eyes. The family stayed an hour; the Japanese crew left soon after. As soon as they were gone, Dewey fell asleep and was out for the rest of the day.

We received two copies of the DVD. After sixteen years, I was reluctant to talk about Dewey too much, but this seemed special. I called the newspaper. The electronics store on the corner loaned us a giant projection television, and we packed the library. By this time, Dewey had been on the radio in Canada and New Zealand. He had appeared in newspapers and magazines in dozens of countries. His photograph had been all over the world. But this was different. This was worldwide television!

I had sneaked a peak at the video, so I was a little nervous. The documentary turned out to be an alphabetic trip through the world of cats. There were twenty-six featured cats, one for each letter of the alphabet. Yes, our alphabet, even though the documentary was in Japanese. Most of the footage was of Japanese people and their pets.

When we hit the letter *W*, a cry went up around the room, no doubt waking the snoozers. There was our Dewey, along with the words *Working Cat* in English and Japanese. There I was, walking up to the library in the rain, while the announcer said something in Japanese. We understood only three words: 'America, Iowa-shun, Spencer.' Another loud cheer. A few seconds later we heard: 'Dewey a-Deedmore Booksa.'

And there was Dewey, sitting at the front door (I have to admit, a wave would have been nice), followed by Dewey sitting on a bookshelf, Dewey walking through two bookshelves, Dewey sitting, and sitting, and sitting and being petted by a little boy under a table and . . . sitting. One and a half minutes, and it was over. No little girl with Dewey on her lap. No riding the shoulder. No book cart. No family from New Hampshire. They didn't even use the shot of Dewey walking on top of the bookshelf, slaloming between the books, and jumping off the end. They came halfway around the world for a minute and a half of sitting.

Silence. Stunned silence. And then a huge burst of cheering. Our Dewey was an international star. Here was the proof. So what if we didn't have a clue what the announcer was saying? So what if Dewey's portion lasted barely longer than a typical commercial break? There was our library. There was our librarian. There was our Dewey. And the announcer definitely said, 'America, Iowa-shun, Spencer.'

The town of Spencer has never forgotten that Japanese documentary. Even today, when locals talk about Dewey, the conversation always comes around to, 'And those Japanese people came here, to Spencer, to film him.' What more needs to be said?

Spencer residents aren't the only ones who remember that documentary. After it aired, we received several letters from Japan and forty requests for Dewey postcards. Our library Website tallies the origin of visitors, and every month since the summer of 2004, Japan has been the second most popular country of origin, after the United States—more than 150,000 visitors in three years. Somehow, I don't think they're interested in checking out books.

CHAPTER 11

I HAD BEEN mentally preparing for Dewey's death since he was fourteen years old. By the time he was seventeen, I had nearly stopped thinking about it. I accepted it not so much as inevitable but as another milestone down the road. Since I didn't know the location of the marker, or what it would look like when we got there, why spend time worrying about it? That is to say, I enjoyed our days together, and during our evenings apart I looked no further than the next morning.

I realised Dewey was losing his hearing when one day someone said *bath* and he didn't run. He still ran when I *thought* bath, but not at the word. So I started to watch him more closely. Sure enough, he had stopped running away every time a truck rumbled by in the alley behind the library. The sound of the back door opening used to send him sprinting to sniff the incoming boxes; now, he wasn't moving at all. He wasn't jumping at sudden loud noises, such as someone setting down a large reference volume too fast, and he wasn't coming as often when patrons called.

Dewey still greeted everyone at the front door. He still searched out laps, but on his own terms. He had arthritis in his back left hip, and jostling him in the wrong place or picking him up the wrong way would cause him to limp away in pain. More and more, in the late morning and afternoon, he sat on the circulation desk, where he was protected by staff. He was supremely confident in his beauty and popularity; he knew patrons would come to him. He looked so regal, a lion surveying his kingdom.

The staff started quietly suggesting that patrons be gentle with Dewey, more aware of his comfort. Joy, who spent the most time out front with the patrons, became very protective of him. 'These days,' she would tell the patrons, 'Dewey prefers a gentle pat on the head.'

Even the elementary school children understood Dewey was an old man now, and they were sensitive to his needs. This was his second generation of Spencer children, the children of the children Dewey had got to know as a kitten, so the parents made sure their kids were well behaved. When the children touched him gently, Dewey would lie against their legs or, if they were sitting on the floor, on their laps. But he was more cautious than he used to be, and loud noise or rough petting often drove him away.

After years of trial and error, we had finally found our finicky cat an acceptable cat bed. It was small, with white fake fur sides and an electric warmer in the bottom. We kept it in front of the wall heater outside my office door. Dewey loved nothing more than lounging in his bed, in the safety of the staff area, with the heating pad turned all the way up. In the winter, when the wall heater was on, he got so warm, he had to throw himself over the side and roll around on the floor. His fur was so hot, you couldn't even touch it. He would lie on his back for ten minutes with all his legs spread out, venting heat. If a cat could pant, Dewey would have been panting. As soon as he was cool, he climbed back into his bed and started the process all over again.

Heat wasn't Dewey's only indulgence. I may have been a sucker for Dewey's whims, but now our assistant children's librarian, Donna, was spoiling him even more than I did. If Dewey didn't eat his food right away, she heated it in the microwave for him. If he still didn't eat it, she threw it out and opened another can. Despite our best efforts, though, Dewey was thinning down, so at his next check-up, Dr Franck prescribed a series of medicines to fatten him up. Dewey had outlasted his old nemesis, Dr Esterly, who retired at the end of 2002 and donated his practice to a non-profit animal advocacy group.

Along with the pills, Dr Franck gave me a pill shooter which, theoretically, shot the pills far enough down Dewey's throat that he couldn't spit them out. But Dewey was smart. He took his pill so calmly, I thought, 'Good, we made it. That was easy.' That's when he snuck behind a shelf somewhere and coughed it back up. I found little white pills all over the library.

I didn't force Dewey's medicine on him. He was eighteen; if he didn't want medicine, he didn't have to take it. Instead, I bought him a container of yoghurt and started giving him a lick every day. That opened the floodgates. Kay started giving him bites of cold cuts out of her sandwiches. Joy started sharing her ham sandwich, and pretty soon Dewey was following her to the kitchen whenever he saw her walk through the door with a bag in her hand. One day, Sharon left a sandwich unwrapped on her desk. When she came back a minute later, the top slice of bread had been carefully turned over and placed to the side. The bottom slice of bread was sitting exactly where it had been, untouched. But all the meat was gone.

After Thanksgiving of 2005, we discovered Dewey loved turkey, so the staff loaded up on holiday scraps. We tried to freeze them, but he could always tell when the turkey wasn't fresh. Dewey never lost his keen sense of smell. That's one reason I scoffed when Sharon offered Dewey a bite of garlic chicken, her favourite microwavable lunch. I told her, 'No way Dewey is going to eat garlic.'

He ate every bite. I thought, 'If we can fatten Dewey up on human food, why not? Isn't that better than a pill?'

Dewey's fur had lost much of its lustre. It was no longer radiant orange, but a dull copper. It was also increasingly matted, so much so, I couldn't keep up with a simple brushing. I took Dewey to Dr Franck, who explained that as cats aged, the barbs on their tongues wore down. Even if they licked themselves regularly, they couldn't do an efficient job grooming because there was nothing to separate the fur. Tangles and mats were just another symptom of old age.

Dewey's health was a concern. The staff didn't talk about it, but I know they were worried. They were afraid they would come in one morning and find Dewey dead on the floor. It wasn't his death that worried some of them, I realised, but the thought of having to deal with it themselves. Or even worse, having to make a decision in a health crisis. I couldn't promise the staff nothing would happen if I was away, but I told them, 'I know this cat. I know when he is healthy, a little sick, and really sick. If he's really sick, trust me, he's going to the vet. I'll do whatever it takes.'

Besides, Dewey wasn't sick. He still jumped up and down from the circulation desk, so I knew his arthritis wasn't too bad. His digestion was better than ever. And he still loved the company of patrons. But it took patience to care for an elderly cat, and frankly, some of the staff didn't think that was their job. Slowly, as Dewey aged, his support peeled away: first those in town with different agendas; then some of the fence-sitters; then a few patrons who only wanted an attractive, active cat; and finally the staff members who didn't want the burden of geriatric care.

That doesn't mean I wasn't blindsided by the October 2006 library board meeting. I was expecting a typical discussion of the state of the library, but the meeting soon turned into a referendum on Dewey. A patron had mentioned he wasn't looking well. Perhaps, the board suggested, we should get him some medical help?

'At his recent check-up,' I told them, 'Dr Franck discovered hyperthyroidism. It's just another symptom of age, like his arthritis, his dry skin, and the black age spots on his lips and gums. Dr Frank prescribed a medication that, thank goodness, doesn't have to be taken orally. I rub it in his ear. Dewey has really perked up. And don't worry,' I reminded them, 'we're paying for the medicine with donations and my own money. Not a single penny of city money is ever spent on Dewey's care.'

'Will this medicine help his fur?'

'Dullness isn't a disease, it's a function of age, like grey hair on a human.' They should understand. There wasn't a head in the room without a few grey hairs.

'But he doesn't look good.'

They kept coming back to that. Dewey didn't look good. Dewey was hurting the image of the library. I knew they meant well, that they were interested in finding the best solution for everyone, but I couldn't understand their thinking.

'Why don't you take Dewey home to live with you? I know he visits you on holidays.'

I had thought of that but dismissed it long ago. Dewey could never be happy living at my house. I was gone too much, between work and meetings. He hated to be alone. He was a public cat. He needed people around him, he needed the library around him, to be happy.

'We've had complaints, Vicki, don't you understand? Our job is to speak for the citizens of this town.'

The board seemed ready to say the town didn't want Dewey any more. I knew that was ridiculous because I saw the community's love for Dewey every day. I had no doubt the board had received a few complaints, but there had always been complaints. Now, with Dewey not looking his best, the voices were louder. But that didn't mean the town had turned on Dewey. One thing I'd learned over the years was that the people who loved Dewey, who really wanted and needed him, weren't the ones with the loudest voices. They were often the ones with no voices at all.

And even if what the board thought was true, even if the majority of the town had turned its back on Dewey, didn't we nonetheless have the duty to stand by him? Even if five people cared, wasn't that enough? Even if nobody cared, the fact remained that Dewey needed us. We couldn't just toss him out because looking at him, older and weaker, no longer made us proud.

There was another message from the board, too, and it came through loud and clear: Dewey is not your cat. He's the town's cat. We speak for the town, so it's our decision. We know what's best.

'I know I am close to Dewey,' I told the board. 'Maybe you think I love Dewey too much. Maybe you think my love clouds my judgment. But trust me. I'll know when it's time. I've had animals all my life. I've put them down. It's hard, but I can do it. The very last thing I want, the very last thing, is for Dewey to suffer.'

IN SEPTEMBER 2006, just a few weeks before the board meeting, a program at the library brought in almost a hundred people. I figured Dewey would hide in the staff area, but there he was, mingling as always. He was like a shadow moving among the guests, often unnoticed but somehow there at the end of a patron's hand each time someone reached to pet him. There was a rhythm to his interactions that seemed the most natural and beautiful thing in the world.

After the program, Dewey climbed into his bed above Kay's desk, clearly exhausted. Kay came over and gave him a gentle scratch on the chin. I knew that touch, that quiet look. It was a thank you, the one you give an old friend or a spouse after you've watched them across a crowded room and realised how wonderful they are, and how lucky you are to have them in your life.

Two months later, in early November, Dewey's gait became a bit unsteady. He started peeing excessively, sometimes on the paper outside his litter box, which he had never done before. But he wasn't hiding. He was still jumping up and down from the circulation desk. He still interacted with patrons. He didn't seem to be in pain. I called Dr Franck and she advised me not to bring him in but to watch him closely.

One morning near the end of the month, Dewey wasn't waving. All those years, and I could count on one hand the number of times Dewey wasn't waving when I arrived in the morning. Instead, he was standing at the front door, just waiting for me. I ushered him to the litter box and gave him his can of cat food. He ate a few bites, then walked with me on our morning rounds. I was busy preparing for a trip to Florida—my brother Mike's daughter Natalie was getting married and the whole family was going to be there—so I left Dewey with the staff for the rest of the morning. As always, he came in while I was working, to sniff my office vent to make sure I was safe. The older he got, the more he protected the ones he loved.

At nine-thirty, I went out for Dewey's breakfast of the moment, a bacon, egg and cheese biscuit. When I returned, Dewey didn't come running. I figured the deaf old boy didn't hear the door. I found him sleeping on a chair by the circulation desk, so I slung the bag a few times, floating the smell of eggs his way. He flew out of that chair and into my office. I put the egg-and-cheese mush on a paper plate, and he ate three or four bites before curling up on my lap.

At ten thirty, Dewey attended Story Hour. As usual, he greeted every child. An eight-year-old girl was sitting on the floor with her legs crossed. Dewey curled up on her legs and went to sleep. She petted him, the other children took turns petting him, everyone was happy. After Story Hour, Dewey crawled into his fur-lined bed in front of the heater, which was running full blast, and that's where he was when I left the library at noon.

Ten minutes after I got home, the phone rang. It was Jann, one of our clerks. 'Dewey's acting funny.'

'What do you mean, funny?'

'He's crying and walking funny. And he's trying to hide in the cupboards.'

'I'll be right down.'

Dewey was hiding under a chair. I picked him up and he was shaking like the morning I found him. His eyes were big, and I could tell he was in pain. I called the veterinary office. Dr Franck was out, but her husband, Dr Beall, was in. He said, 'Come right down.' I wrapped Dewey in his towel. It was a cold day, end of November. Dewey snuggled against me immediately.

By the time we arrived at the vet's office, Dewey was

down on the floor of my car by the heater, shaking with fear. I cradled him in my arms and held him against my chest. Dr Beall took Dewey into the back room. 'He needs an X-ray.'

Ten minutes later, he was back with the results. There was a large tumour in Dewey's stomach, and it was pushing on his kidneys and intestines. That's why he had been peeing more, and it probably accounted for his peeing outside the litter box.

'It wasn't there in September,' Dr Beall said, 'which means it's probably an aggressive cancer. But we'd have to do invasive tests to find out for sure.'

We stood silently, looking at Dewey.

'Is he in pain?'

'Yes, I suspect he is. The mass is growing very fast, so it will only get worse.'

'Is there anything you can give him for the pain?'

'No, not really.'

I was holding Dewey in my arms, cradling him like a baby. He hadn't let me carry him that way in sixteen years. Now he wasn't even fighting it. He was just looking at me.

'Do you think he's in constant pain?'

'I can't imagine that he's not.'

The conversation was crushing me, flattening me out, making me feel drawn, deflated, tired. I couldn't believe what I was hearing. Somehow, I had believed Dewey was going to live for ever.

I called the library staff and told them Dewey wasn't coming home. Kay was out of town. Joy was off duty. They reached her at Sears, but too late. Several others came down to say their goodbyes. Instead of going to Dewey, though, Sharon walked right up and hugged me. Thank you, Sharon, I needed that. Then I hugged Donna and thanked her for loving Dewey so much. Donna was the last to say her goodbyes.

Someone said, 'I don't know if I want to be here when they put him to sleep.'

'That's fine,' I said. 'I'd rather be alone with him.'

Dr Beall took Dewey into the back room to insert the IV, then brought him back in a fresh blanket and put him in my arms. I talked to Dewey for a few minutes. I told him how much I loved him, how much he meant to me, how much I didn't want him to suffer. I explained what was happening and why. I rewrapped his blanket to make sure he was comfortable. What more could I offer him than comfort? I cradled him in my arms and rocked back and forth from foot to foot, a habit started when he was a kitten. Dr Beall gave him the first shot, followed closely by the second.

He said, 'I'll check for a heartbeat.'

I said, 'You don't need to. I can see it in his eyes.'

Dewey was gone.

CHAPTER 12

I WAS IN Florida for eight days. I didn't read the newspaper. I didn't watch television. I didn't take any phone calls. It was the best possible time to be away because Dewey's death was hard. Very hard. I broke down on the flight from Omaha and cried all the way to Houston. In Florida, I thought often of Dewey, alone, quietly, but also surrounded by the family that had always sustained me.

I had no idea how far word of Dewey's death had spread. The next morning, while I sat crying on an aeroplane to Houston, the local radio station devoted their morning show to memories of Dewey. The *Sioux City Journal* ran a lengthy story and obituary. I don't know if that was the source, but the AP wire picked up the story and sent it around the world. Within hours, news of Dewey's death appeared on the CBS afternoon newsbreak and on MSNBC. The library started getting calls. If I had been in the library, I would have been stuck answering questions from reporters for days, but nobody else on staff felt comfortable speaking to the media. The library secretary, Kim, gave a brief statement, which ended up in what I now think of as Dewey's public obituary, but that was all. It was enough. Over the next few days, that obituary ran in more than 270 newspapers.

The response from individuals touched by Dewey was equally overwhelming. People in town received calls from friends and relatives all over the country who'd read about Dewey's death in the local newspaper or heard it on a local radio show. One local couple was out of the country and learned the news from a friend in San Francisco, who read about his passing in the *San Francisco Chronicle*. Admirers set up a vigil in the library. Local businesses sent flowers and gifts. Sharon and Tony's daughter, Emmy, gave me a picture she had drawn of Dewey. It was two green circles in the middle of the page with lines sticking out in all directions. It was beautiful, and Emmy beamed as I taped it to my office door. That picture was the perfect way for both of us to remember him.

Gary Roma, director of the documentary about library cats, wrote me a long letter. It said, in part: 'I don't know if I ever told you, but of all the many library cats I've met across the country, Dewey Readmore Books was my favourite. His beauty, charm and playfulness were unique.'

Tomoko from Japanese Public Television wrote to tell us Dewey's death had been announced in Japan, and that many were sad to hear he was gone.

Marti Attoun, who wrote the article for *American Profile*, wrote to say the Dewey story was still her favourite. It had been years, and Marti was now a contributing editor. It seemed so unlikely, given the hundreds of stories she had written, that Marti would remember a cat, much less still think of him fondly. But that was Dewey. He touched people so deeply.

By the time I returned to my office, there were letters and cards stacked four feet high on my desk. I had more than 600 emails about Dewey waiting in my inbox. Many were from people who met him only once but never forgot him. Hundreds of others were from people who never met him. In the month after his death, I received more than a thousand emails about Dewey from all around the world. Our Website, www.spencerlibrary.com, went from 25,000 hits a month to

189,922 in December, and the traffic didn't let up for most of the next year.

Many people in town wanted us to hold a memorial service. I didn't want a memorial service, nobody on staff did, but we had to do something. So, on a cold Saturday in the middle of December, Dewey's admirers gathered at the library to remember one last time, at least officially, the friend who had had such an impact on their lives. The staff tried to keep it light—I told the story of the bat, Audrey told the story of the lights, Joy remembered the cart rides, Sharon told how Dewey stole the meat out of her sandwich—but despite our best efforts, tears were shed. Two women cried the whole time.

Crews from several local televisions stations were filming the event. It was a nice thought, but the cameras seemed out of place. These were private thoughts among friends; we didn't want to share our words with the world. We also realised, as we stood there together, that words couldn't describe our feelings for Dewey. There was no easy way to say how special he was. We were here; the cameras were here; the world stood still around us. That said more than any words. Finally, a local schoolteacher said, 'People say what's the big deal, he was just a cat. But that's where they're wrong. Dewey was so much more.' Everyone knew exactly what she meant.

My moments with Dewey were more intimate. The staff had cleaned out his bowls and donated his food while I was away, but I had to give away his toys. I had to clean out his shelf: the Vaseline for his hairballs, the brush, the red skein of yarn he had played with all his life. I had to park my car and walk to the library every morning without Dewey waving at me from the front door. When the staff returned to the library after visiting Dewey for the last time, the space heater he had lain in front of every day wasn't working. Dewey had been lying in front of it that very morning, and it had been working fine. It was as if his death has taken away its reason to heat. Can a malfunctioning piece of equipment break your heart? It was six weeks before I could even think about having that heater repaired.

I had Dewey cremated with one of his favourite toys, Marty Mouse, so he wouldn't be alone. The crematorium offered a mahogany box and bronze plaque, no charge, but it didn't seem right to display him. Dewey came back to his library in a plain plastic container inside a blue velvet bag. I put the container on a shelf in my office and went back to work.

A week after his memorial service, I came out of my office half an hour before the library opened, long before any patrons arrived, and told Kay, 'It's time.'

It was another brutally cold Iowa morning in December. Just like the first morning, and so many in between. It was close to the shortest day of the year and the sun wasn't yet up. The sky was still deep blue, almost purple, and there was no traffic on the roads. The only sound was the cold wind that had come all the way from the Canadian plains, whipping down the streets and out over the barren cornfields.

We moved some rocks in the little garden out front of the library, looking for a place where the ground wasn't completely frozen. But the whole earth was frosted, and it took a while for Kay to dig the hole. The sun was peaking over the buildings on the far side of the parking lot by the time I placed the remains of my friend in the ground and said simply, 'You're always with us, Dewey. This is your home.' Then Kay dropped in the first shovelful of dirt, burying Dewey's ashes for ever outside the window of the children's library. As Kay moved the stones back over Dewey's final resting place, I looked up and saw the rest of the library staff in the window, silently watching us.

EPILOGUE

NOT MUCH has changed in north-west Iowa since Dewey died. The library rolls on, cat-free for the first time since Ronald Reagan was president. After Dewey's death, we had almost a hundred offers for new cats but there was no enthusiasm to take one. The library board wisely put a two-year moratorium on cats in the library. They needed time, they said, to think through the issues. I had done all the thinking I needed. You can't bring back the past.

But Dewey's memory will live on, I feel confident of that. Maybe at the library, where his portrait hangs beside the front door above a bronze plaque that tells his story, a gift from one of Dewey's many friends. Maybe in the children who knew him, who will talk about him in decades to come with their own children and grandchildren. Maybe in this book. After all, that's why I'm writing it. For Dewey.

Back in 2000, when Grand Avenue made the National Registry, Spencer commissioned a public art installation to serve as both a statement about our values and an entry point to our historic downtown. Two Chicago-area ceramic tile mosaic artists, Nina Smoot-Cain and John Pitman Weber, spent a year in the area, talking with us, studying our history, and observing our way of life. The result is a mosaic sculpture called *The Gathering: Of Time, of Land, of Many Hands.*

The Gathering is composed of four decorative pillars and three pictorial walls. The south wall is called 'The Story of the Land'. The north wall is 'The Story of Outdoor Recreation'. The west wall is 'The Story of Spencer'. It shows three generations gathering at grandma's house; the town battling the fire; and a woman making a pot, a metaphor for shaping the future. Just slightly to the left of centre, in the upper half of the scene, is an orange cat, sitting on the open pages of a book. The image is based on artwork submitted by a child.

The story of Spencer. Dewey is a part of it, then, now, and for ever. He will live longest, I know, in the collective memory of a town that never forgets where it's been, even as it looks ahead for where it's going.

A year after Dewey's death, my health finally caught up with me. It was time, I knew, to move on with my life. The library was different without Dewey, and I didn't want my days to end that way: empty, quiet, occasionally lonely. When I saw the book cart go past, the one Dewey used to ride on, it broke my heart. I missed him so much, and not just once in a while, but every day. I decided to retire. It was time. More than 125 people attended my retirement party, including many from out of town whom I hadn't spoken with in years. Like Dewey, I was lucky. I got to leave on my own terms.

Find your place. Be happy with what you have. Treat everyone well. Live a good life. It isn't about material things; it's about love. And you can never anticipate love. In life, the most important thing is having someone there to scoop you up, to hold you tight, and to tell you everything is all right.

For years, I thought I had done that for Dewey. I thought that was my story to tell. And I had done that. When Dewey was hurt, cold and crying, I was there. I held him. I made sure everything was all right.

But that's only a sliver of the truth. The real truth is that for all those years, on the hard days, the good days, and all the unremembered days that make up the pages of the real book of our lives, Dewey was holding me.

He's still holding me now. So thank you, Dewey. Thank you. Wherever you are.

VICKI MYRON

with BRET WITTER

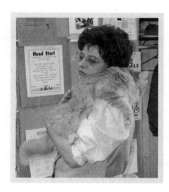

Vicki Myron grew up on a farm in northwest Iowa. She first trained as a psychologist, but at the age of twenty-eight she found herself divorced, raising a six-year-old daughter alone, and looking for a new job. She first worked at the Spencer Public Library as assistant director, and in 1987 took over as director. She had begun working towards a master's degree in librarianship, and was remodelling the library, when Dewey arrived in the night-drop box. She says, 'When everything in my life was so complex, my relationship with Dewey was so simple, so natural.' She has served on the Executive Board of the Iowa Library Association and on statewide advisory panels, and is now retired.

Bret Witter is a ghostwriter who was formerly Editorial Director of HCI, the publisher of the Chicken Soup for the Soul series. Vicki Myron says gratefully that Bret 'found my voice'. He lives in Louisville, Kentucky.

CHILD OF THE REVOLUTION

Growing up in Castro's Cuba

LUIS M. GARCIA

‘You can hear Fidel's voice wherever you go, booming out of television sets or from the radio. This time, Fidel is talking about wanting to build a new man—*un hombre nuevo*—which makes me think he must have some ingenious socialist plan to build human robots. But what he is really talking about is me, and my brother and all my friends. He wants to educate us to become the new men of tomorrow: hardworking, not interested in material things, and ready to fight the imperialists of the world. ’

1

DON'T LOOK BACK . . .

DON'T LOOK back. Whatever you do, don't look back. Because even at the last minute, even as you walk up the stairs into the plane, if you look back just once— just once!—and they see you looking back, they will *know* you don't want to leave Cuba and then they will bring you down those steps, *chico*, and they will keep you in Cuba. Your parents will go, but you will stay. You will *never* see them again. So, pay attention: whatever you do, *¡no mires para atrás!* Don't look back!

I am sitting on one of the stone benches that ring the promenade around the Parque Cárdenas, which used to be the municipal pride of Banes *antes del Triunfo* but now looks a little unloved. I am listening to one of my best friends, Pepito. He is older than I am, not by much, true, but somehow he seems to know so much more than I do. And he is the one who is explaining to me why, now that my family is finally being allowed to leave Cuba—nearly three years after we applied, Pepito, nearly three years!—why I cannot, under any circumstances, even hint that I may not want to leave with them. Look back, he repeats, and they will keep you here. These are words that instil absolute fear in my twelve-year-old heart.

Pepito and I are talking just hours after the news arrived at home. I don't know who brought it, but I heard my mother say something about the police. Whoever it was, they came knocking on our door with *el telegrama* while my brother and I were at school. This telegram, this magical, mythical telegram, contains the news we have been desperately waiting for since mid 1968—permission from Fidel Castro to leave Cuba. At least I think it's from Fidel. Everything in Cuba is decided by Fidel, according to my father, so I can just imagine *El Máximo Líder*, as he is always called in the newspaper and on radio, sitting there in his palace in Havana, going through piles of applications from people begging for permission to leave his workers' paradise. Fidel sits there and with a deep sigh signs our permission slip. Let them pack their meagre belongings and leave. Good riddance, I can hear him say, chewing on those fat cigars he still smoked back then. Good riddance ...

Everyone who applies to leave Cuba waits—sometimes for three years, sometimes for five years, sometimes for ever— for Fidel to finally agree to let you leave. And during that time, from the moment you apply to leave to the moment when *el telegrama* arrives, you become a *gusano*, or parasite. A counter-revolutionary who is made to pay in all sorts of subtle and not-so-subtle ways for the audacity of asking permission to leave. Of course, I know that once you are given permission to leave, you are not coming back. Fidel said so himself; if you leave Cuba, you are a traitor and you are never coming back. Never.

As soon as we applied for permission, my father was sent to the labour camps where all *gusanos* get sent, to cut sugar cane for the Revolution, and for a long time we only got to see him once every forty-five days when he was given a five-day pass. But I am sure someone there, the camp commander or someone in authority, has broken the news to him that *el telegrama* has arrived. I picture my father acting normally, as if nothing has happened, just in case the guards think he is too happy about leaving Cuba and decide to keep him back for another few months. But inside, I know he is jumping for joy.

My mother is jumping for joy inside, too, I figure, although you can't tell for sure. Her eyes are red from crying and I know there will be more tears, many more to come over the next two or three days before we finally leave Banes. Who wants to leave their family behind? She worries about her sisters and her brothers who are staying in Cuba. They are in enough trouble as it is for being related to *gusanos* ...

Everyone in our street seems to know about the telegram. Our neighbours next door. The Tavera sisters across the road, who are really like family. Everyone has heard about *el telegrama de los García*. I know that some of the neighbours will pop by later in the day, when it gets dark, to say congratulations in hushed, counter-revolutionary tones and wish us luck, but others, like the woman who is the boss of the neighbourhood Committee for the Defence of the Revolution—the one we call *La Compañera*—will be watching and muttering curses under their breath. Good riddance.

As I sit talking to Pepito, it hits me that this may be one of the last times I will see my friends, the park at the end of the street where we live, the neighbours, the basketball courts across the park ... So much for celebrating. But I can't look back. I know that much. Besides, there is so much to do. Now the telegram has arrived, we have just three days to finalise the documents we need to fly out, pack our stuff, and leave Banes for Havana where, God and Fidel willing, we will board the plane for Madrid. Not that there is much to pack. My mother told my eleven-year-old brother and me that the instructions from the police were clear: we are allowed to take just the one suitcase per person. No more. That's the rule. It's the paperwork that will take all that time. And saying goodbye, of course.

The first to arrive the very next day are the police—the *milicianos*. When you apply for permission to leave Cuba— when you fill in the application form that will change your life for ever—you get a visit from the police. Sometimes accompanied by someone from the Committee for the Defence of the Revolution, they set about taking written stock of everything in the house. A stocktake for *gusanos*.

They note down every single thing in your house—the number and style of plates, the number of cups and saucers in the pantry, the television set in the lounge room (we should be so lucky!), the ironing board, your jewellery, if you have any. Everything, regardless of monetary or sentimental value. It's all noted down in great detail because these goods no longer belong to you. They are the property of the People. They belong to the Revolution. You can use them between now and the day you get the telegram, but you cannot sell them or barter them or do anything with them. Because when the telegram arrives, the police will come again with their clipboards and pencils and make sure every single item listed on their forms remains behind in Cuba. It's the property of the People. If anything is missing, who knows what will happen?

So, the *milicianos* have come to complete their task. There are two of them—the more senior one, whose name is Morgado, is known to my parents. This is Banes, after all, a small, unpretentious town where everyone knows everyone else. The *milicianos* are polite and, I sense, a little confused, but painfully efficient when it comes to the paperwork. I am sure their instructions are clear—make life hell for these ungrateful *gusanos*. Make them pay. But this is Banes, so instead they don't say much, politely ticking away at their list of possessions, plate by plate, while my mother watches anxiously.

Since applying to leave Cuba, we have been extra careful with the plates and the glasses and the big American-made radio in the dining room. When a plate smashed in the kitchen many months ago, my mother picked up the pieces, carefully wrapped them up in newspaper and put the package at the back of the cupboard for safe keeping. Same with glasses. Same with everything. Now, I see her unwrap the yellowing pages of the papers, one by one, showing the broken china to these two policemen, making sure they know it's all there. I think she cries as she does this. I know she is dead scared that one of the *milicianos* will pause and then place a cross instead of a tick on his list. Just like that. A cross instead of a tick, and then we will have to stay in Cuba.

2

IN A TIME OF REVOLUTION

LEAVING CUBA seems like a totally crazy, totally foreign idea to my parents on this warm Friday, 10 July 1959, as my mother, lying back on an operating bed at the Hospital Civil de Banes, legs up in stirrups, face contorted by pain, pushes and yells and pushes some more to get me out of her womb and into the world. It's been a long labour—nearly twenty-four hours—and she is exhausted, but she keeps pushing, holding on to the midwife, imploring her doctor, Edmundo Prieto, to put an end to the pain, *¡por favor!* Instead, he whispers soothing words of encouragement: One more push, the doctor says. Almost there, *señora* ...

My father is not in the delivery room. Cuban men don't attend the birth of a child because, well—do I need to tell you that this is women's work? No, no, like most men of his generation, he has been waiting outside, smoking cigarette after cigarette, not knowing what is going on inside but silently praying to the patron saint of Cuba, the Virgen de la Caridad del Cobre, that everything works out all right, because when you are in trouble in Cuba, or even when you are just worried about something, you always pray to the Virgen de la Caridad del Cobre.

Eventually, the nurses will come out into the corridor and tell my father that everything is fine and then they will let him come into the room to have a look at his tired but beaming wife and his newborn son, and he will shake hands with Dr Prieto and, as is customary, invite the doctor to join him and his friends for a few celebratory drinks. In fact, my father's friends have started celebrating already, down at Bar Feria, a small bar in Bayamo Street that is just a few minutes' walk from the modest but promising haberdashery shop my parents own in the main street of Banes. They will celebrate until the late, late hours, drinking dark rum, top shelf, of course, for this is a special occasion. Later on, as the huge American jukebox in the corner keeps being fed coins so it can keep playing those syrupy Vicentico Valdez *boleros* that are all the rage in Cuba, there will be plenty of Cristal and Hatuey beers and everyone will be smoking big, fat Partagas cigars that have been purchased by my proud father to mark the birth of his first boy. After all, there is much to celebrate in Banes, and not just the arrival of a son.

It has been six months since President Fulgencio Batista fled Havana, unceremoniously chased out by a few hundred bearded guerrillas who had spent the previous three years fighting high up in the Sierra Maestra mountains, in the far eastern region of the country. Around midnight on New Year's Eve 1958, Batista packed up his family, his closest friends and suitcases said to be bulging with cash, and went into exile, to the delight of most Cubans. Within hours the *barbudos*, as the rebels are known, took over the island, captivating an entire nation—and quite a few on the outside—with their unkempt beards, olive green fatigues and prominent crucifixes hanging around their necks.

This revolution, the latest in a long list of often futile rebellions and uprisings going back over a century, is led by a young lawyer called Fidel Castro, the son of a Spanish-born landowner in Oriente province. He is known by everyone as Fidel because when you know someone well in Cuba, you always use their first name, and he is now running things in Havana, not from the Presidential Palace where all previous presidents and dictators have settled, but from his new headquarters in, of all places, the American-owned Havana Hilton Hotel, which has been renamed, with much fanfare, the *Habana Libre*—the Free Havana.

The winds of change are certainly picking up strength by July: over the past six months, the casinos in Havana have been taken over by the new revolutionary government and their American owners of dubious reputation have fled back to Miami or Las Vegas. Rents have been cut in half and electricity and telephone charges will also be reduced significantly. What's more, it seems the big, foreign-owned utilities are happy to go along with the *barbudos*, at least for now. In a show of goodwill to the new governing class, they have offered to pay their taxes in full—and in advance. Meanwhile, former Batista supporters, now stripped of their uniforms and their power, are being tried by military tribunals in spectacles that are televised live every night from the largest sports stadium in Havana, where thousands of audience members stamp their feet and yell out, *Paredón, paredón*—To the firing squad—even before the military judges have decided whether the accused is guilty or not.

Fidel himself, always wearing green fatigues, appears at the televised trials every now and then, sometimes even questioning the accused. As the crowds chant Fidel!, Fidel!, Fidel!, he promises that the trials will continue until all the criminals of the Batista regime are brought to justice, regardless of criticism from lawyers and human rights activists in the United States and Europe. Fidel has kept his promise made in the Sierra Maestra and seized large landholdings, including those owned by American companies, divided them up and is handing over small parcels of land—precious, fertile Cuban land—to *campesinos* who appear on television wearing big hats, missing teeth and crying in gratitude. Everyone expects Fidel to keep another of his key promises: to hold free and fair elections within eighteen months.

And here in Banes, a small sugar town some fifteen hours by road from Havana, there is plenty of support for the *barbudos*. Not from everyone, though: the town is home to dozens of American families, who are getting nervous about some of the anti-American pronouncements coming from the new leadership. There are some Cuban families, too, rich and well-known families like the Diaz Balarts and the Cárdenas, who are quietly packing up their bags for the short plane flight across to Miami. But most people think Fidel is on the right track, including my normally apolitical parents. They are pretty hopeful, like most other Cubans, that things are about to get better.

One way or another, every family in Cuba has been touched by the fighting of the past few years. My father's brother-in-law, my uncle Luis Felipe, had been working with the underground trade unions in the area, distributing anti-Batista pamphlets. On my mother's side, the involvement is just as personal: her oldest brother, my uncle Victor, made the trek up to the Sierra Maestra to join the *barbudos* about two years ago. Neither my mother nor her sisters knew for sure whether he was dead or alive until he, too, came down from the mountains as a liberator six months ago. After so many sleepless nights, his return was greeted by the family with great joy and much relief.

My uncle Tony, who works for an American mining company in the nearby town of Nicaro, also distributed anti-Batista propaganda. But my mother worried most about her youngest brother, my uncle Papi, who is barely out of his teens. He became involved in local demonstrations against Batista and came close to being sent to jail, where he would have been tortured and almost certainly murdered, according to my mother. It was a period of such anguish that, even when she talks about it nearly fifty years later, she becomes visibly upset. *Terrible*, she says, it was a terrible time.

My parents have been married for just twelve months, after what my mother's sisters describe as a whirlwind romance. The wedding was large and generous, at least by Banes standards. Since neither of my parents is a regular church-goer, the ceremony took place not in the local Catholic church but in the big old house that belongs to my mother's family, in the grandly named Presidente Zayas Avenue, which in reality is not much of an avenue but a very ordinary, unpaved road that turns into a river of mud every time it rains heavily. It's a timber house with a corrugated iron roof, where my mother and her sisters and her brothers grew up, where her father died a slow, terrible death from cancer long before I was born, where her mother, whom I never met either, died in agony soon after being diagnosed with severe pancreas problems. It's the type of house where the walls are scarred by family history and the rooms inhabited by far, far too many family ghosts. But on the day my parents marry, it is a happy house.

More than sixty relatives, neighbours and friends turn up to the wedding celebrations, the women wearing their brightest and finest dresses and the men in immaculate white linen suits and those thin ties that are so fashionable at this time, to toast the wedding of Gisela and Luis. The wedding even makes it into the local paper, *El Pueblo*, a brief item in the social pages. The celebration must have cost a bit of money, but no one seems to mind. Everyone is having far too good a time. There is plenty of beer and rum and tables groan under the weight of roast pork and *congrí*, a dish made from rice and black beans, and *yuca* and *malanga*—tubers and plantain—and a big wedding cake. When you look at the large, black and white photographs that are taken, you can see all my uncles and my aunts, on both sides of the family, and some of my cousins and my mother's friends, and everyone is enjoying themselves.

Since they married, my parents have been renting a semi-detached house in Flor Crombet Street, just a block from the Parque Cárdenas, one of two main parks in the town. The building is one big long timber house owned by a woman called Celestina, a widow of independent financial means who has wisely decided to divide the large property into three self-contained houses and rent two of them out.

On the other side of Celestina, in a smaller house, live the Castros, who are described by everyone in the street as quiet, hardworking and polite, but with whom we don't socialise at all. It never occurs to me that it's because they are black. We just don't.

The one-bedroom house in Flor Crombet Street is not a place for a growing family by any means. This is a temporary house for a young couple who dream of doing well in their small business. They are modest dreams. Already, my parents have started looking at empty blocks of land in town, including a block just next door to the family house on Presidente Zayas Avenue, but buying the land—it will be expensive—and then building a new house on the site will have to wait because now, in July 1959, my parents have other priorities, like a new son.

My father also has plans for the *Retacería García*, as their shop is called: he wants to expand the inventory and employ a couple of extra assistants. My mother is more cautious, thinking it best to consolidate first before expanding further. Like most girls of her generation, she never progressed past primary school—that was reserved for the boys—but when it comes to business, she is as sharp as a tack. Everyone in the family knows that. It's a trait most García women seem to have, and one their husbands tend to lack. Besides, she tells my father, there is just too much going on in Cuba at the moment. Let's wait. Let's not tempt fate.

In July 1959 my parents' shop is modest but still manages to make enough money for my parents to have hired two employees. It's in the perfect spot, in the same block on General Marrero Street as other, larger department stores and next to a bank branch, so passing trade is not a problem. And like most other shopkeepers in town, my parents are happy to give credit, which means they have built up a loyal clientele, not just in town but in the surrounding sugar cane plantations and farmhouses, where there are lots of peasants—*guajiros*—with large families. It's good times in the *Retacería García* and good times in Banes.

But that is the type of town Banes has always been. Prosperous. At least that's one version of the history of Banes. It's the version I will hear some years later, when I am older. It will be told to me in hushed, conspiratorial tones by my mother's aunts, elderly women with white hair and wrinkled skin who smell of Spanish gardenia perfume. They are always talking about how things used to be before the Revolution—*antes del Triunfo*—much to the dismay of the rest of the family, who keep telling them to please, please, keep your voice down and stop all this crazy talk. *Dios santo*, do you want us all to end up in jail?

In the version told by my mother's aunts, Banes started as a small, poor fishing village known as La Ensanada, where a local family who were descendants of earlier French migrants, the Dumois, started growing big, sweet bananas for export to Europe. The banana plantations would be the start of modern Banes, attracting workers from the surrounding areas, small businesses and a modest amount of prosperity. It didn't last long. In the late 1890s, the town was razed to the ground by Cuban independence rebels fighting the Spaniards. Then, at the end of that century, the Spanish American War would see the once-great Spanish empire resoundingly defeated in Cuba by a newly emerging, powerful world player: the United States. Spain was forced to cede the ever-loyal Island of Cuba, as the colony was known, to the Americans. The Americans in turn stayed in Cuba as an occupying power until 1902, when the new Republic of Cuba was born, independent but closely watched from Washington.

It was at about that time that the United Fruit Company arrived in the Banes area, attracted by cheap land and easy access to the Bahia de Nipe, the largest bay in the country, and changed the place for ever. Or at least until January 1959, when everything in Banes, and everything in Cuba, changed again. The United Fruit Company—which would become known to everyone in Banes simply as *La Compañía*—bought huge tracts of land in the district and started to grow sugar cane, lots of sugar cane, which was then cut by local Cubans during the harvesting months and sent for processing to two large sugar mills in the district. It was a hugely profitable enterprise. My mother's aunts tell me that this was the beginning of a golden age for Banes because *La Compañía* started building whole neighbourhoods for the American supervisors and their families, building new schools, new roads, new parks and public buildings. The Americans put Banes on the map, my mother's aunts say, their eyes lighting up with nostalgic excitement. It became the most American town in Cuba.

It meant that Banes was really divided in two: the American part of Banes, on one side of the River Banes, and on the other side the Cuban part of Banes, linked by a modest bridge. The American part of Banes was owned by *La Compañía*, and it had its own stores that were near-exact replicas of American shops, and its own schools and clubs, which were open only to those Cubans who were either well-off and could afford to buy their way in, or who worked for the United Fruit Company. The streets in the American part are wide and have large shady trees planted along the sidewalks, and the houses have lush tropical gardens at the front and big, leafy backyards. They have large, cool, enclosed verandas, timber floors and ceiling fans. Even mosquito nets.

Then there is the Cuban part of town, where we live. This part is older, the houses are smaller, very few have gardens at the front, and the streets don't have too many trees planted along the kerb. This part of Banes, the Cuban part, is where the main shops are and the church and the cinemas and the town hall, a three-storey wedding cake of a building that is known to all in Banes by the much more fancy name of *El Palacio Municipal*. It's a different world, the Cuban side of Banes. Unlike the American side, which is quiet and green and tidy and odourless, on the Cuban side someone is always yelling at the top of their voice, calling their kids to dinner or gossiping with neighbours or at the corner store, and there are gangs of school children riding their bicycles along the footpaths or playing *pelota*—the Cuban version of baseball— right in the middle of the street. And there is the smell of food, Cuban food, with plenty of garlic and onions and a tomato *sofrito* which you make with fresh tomatoes and a little lemon or lime juice, and there is always music blaring from a radio somewhere, a sweet *mambo* that makes you feel happy and makes you want to dance, right there and then, which is the only way to dance a Cuban *mambo*—in the middle of a Cuban street, on the Cuban side of Banes.

Almost all of the Americans who live in Banes at the beginning of 1959 are leaving. By the time I am born, American-owned companies like the telephone company and the railways have been confiscated by the revolutionary government, as have the foreign-owned sugar plantations and the sugar mills, like those owned by *La Compañía*. Then Fidel starts taking over the large sugar plantations owned not by rich Americans but by rich Cubans, like the plantation that is owned by his own family, which upsets his mother Lina no end; or the plantation that is managed by my grandfather, my father's father, who arrived in Cuba from Spain with nothing and then slowly built up his family and his home and did well enough to buy a house in the bigger city of Holguin and to send his children to school.

When Fidel takes over the large landholdings, the Americans in Banes pack up their bags and leave. My mother's aunts tell me later that it was a sad time because while some Americans were too shy to mix much with Cubans, or at least the Cubans on the Cuban side of town, others were well known and well liked, and they cried when they had to leave Banes and return home to Florida or Georgia or South Carolina, or wherever it is the United Fruit Company sent them to next. I can tell that the version of Banes' history as told by my mother's aunts is a nostalgic and golden retelling, embroidered by old women who may or may not be close to senility. I can also tell, even at my age, that this is a very subversive version of the history of Banes, especially the bits about the United Fruit Company, because this version of history is very different to the version I hear at school.

In the revolutionary version, which is the only version of history we get taught at school, the Spaniards arrived in the area and proceeded to wipe out the native population through maltreatment and disease. In the official version, during the Cuban War of Independence from Spain, the residents of Banes and the surrounding districts were caught in the middle of some quite ferocious battles between the colonial army and the heroic Cuban rebels, Cuban rebels always being heroic. And the eventual arrival of the United Fruit Company was bad news for Banes. The locals had no choice but to work and live in a company town where the Americans and the upper crust of Banes society—who mostly worked for *La Compañía*—led charmed lives in big, rambling timber houses in protected neighbourhoods complete with green lawns, exclusive country clubs and private beaches. Ordinary Cubans were not welcomed, except as domestic help. Meanwhile, the bulk of the population—the poor Cubans—had to work hard to make ends meet cutting sugar cane during harvesting time, but then going hungry for the rest of the year, unless they had a job as a servant to the rich Americans. And when Cubans became too rebellious, the Americans went and brought cheap labour over from the islands near Cuba, from Haiti and Jamaica, which explains why sometimes in Banes, if you pay close attention, you can hear groups of black women standing on a corner talking about God knows what in a strange language, which is probably a version of French or even a version of English, but one that seems foreign to me.

In the years to come, I will sit at school listening to my teachers tell us how lucky we are to live here in Banes, to live here in Cuba, because now, Fidel has sent the United Fruit Company and its wealthy, rapacious owners back to the United States, the sugar cane plantations have been 'nationalised', the sugar mills have had their names changed from Preston and Boston to Guatemala and Nicaragua and they now refine and ship Cuban sugar—the best in the world, says my father—to our new communist friends in Eastern Europe, countries with strange-sounding names and exotic histories that are always referred to in the newspaper as 'fraternal' and 'peace-loving'. And the big houses where the Americans and their Cuban lackeys used to live now belong to the People, and the private clubs and the private beaches are open to all Cubans, regardless of whether they are rich or poor, black or white, without them having to ask permission from their American masters.

That much I have been told.

3

¡VIVA CUBA SOCIALISTA!

JUST SIXTEEN months after my birth, my parents go back to hospital and leave me at home with my mother's best friend, Aunt Hilda. A few days later they come back home bringing with them their new baby. Another boy, whom they name José Antonio and who is supposed to be the spitting image of my father. My parents are over the moon with their new, enlarged family, but it doesn't last long—within three months, they leave home again. My brother is seriously sick. So sick, they need to rush him by ambulance to Holguin, a bigger city a couple of hours away with a much larger and better equipped hospital.

A very sick boy, everyone says when they talk about my baby brother, shaking their heads at the unfairness of it all, and while I am far too young to understand what's going on, when I ask about it years later it becomes painfully clear that these are the hardest days my mother and my father have had to endure—not knowing, my mother tells me, whether her second-born would make it through those first few difficult months. Your brother, he was this close to death, my mother says, and she brings her index finger and her thumb really close together so that there is just a very thin space in between.

They are long, long days, with my mother spending almost all her time at the hospital, sitting there by the tiny cot where my brother labours to breathe, hoping that all will be well. My aunt Mirta, who is my mother's youngest sister, is there too, and the rest of the family come and go. In the meantime I am in Banes, staying now with my father's only sister, my aunt Ana. It will be days before I see my parents again, but when they come back to Banes to check how things are going at the shop, everyone can tell they are totally exhausted, all the stuffing knocked out of them, all their optimism gone, and at night they go to bed without saying much. In the dark, inside his head, I can imagine my father doing something he rarely does—praying. He is pleading with God, the God he rarely talks to, to let his baby son live.

I don't know how many nights my father prayed to the God he doesn't believe in all that much, but the same God was probably listening because eventually, after more than two months, my parents are back in Banes, carrying their baby boy. He is still weak and very skinny and very pale and not totally out of trouble, but alive and getting bigger and a little stronger every day, and it could be because my father talked to God, or it could be because that is what fate had decided for him from the very beginning anyway, or it could be that the doctors in Holguin are really good.

While my parents have been busy doing whatever it takes to keep my baby brother alive, the rest of Banes and the rest of Cuba have been changing faster than anyone would have imagined in January 1959. Because all of a sudden, Cuba has turned away from the United States, the country that has been both its closest neighbour and its interfering protector, and embraced powerful new friends from the other side of the world: the Russians.

If I were older I would understand exactly what's going on. I'd understand why every time you turn on the television, there is a Russian arriving in Havana. You can see it in the old newsreels: Fidel wearing a funny fur hat and hugging Nikita Khrushchev, and shaking hands with Yuri Gagarin, who is Russian and handsome and has blonde hair and blue eyes, unlike most Cubans, and who is the first man to travel into space.

I am too young to understand what has been going on but Cuba has now become the epicentre of the Cold War. The large American companies that used to do a lot of business in Cuba, like the banks and the mining companies and even the United Fruit Company, have all been taken over by the Revolution— they belong to the People now. The Americans, who are not very happy about this, have decided to stop buying Cuban sugar and when Fidel tells them he doesn't care, they decide to break off diplomatic relations with Cuba.

It isn't long before the shortages start, which means the shops are now half empty and you have to queue to buy food or a shirt or a pair of trousers. There are queues even outside my parents' shop, which is a novelty at first. And before you know it, Fidel announces that rationing will be introduced in Cuba, but only for a year, he says, blaming the Americans for this although at the same time he says we don't need the Americans any more because now we have good friends in Moscow who will buy all of our precious sugar at very, very favourable prices. He is speaking in front of what looks like a million people in the big square in Havana that is now known as the Plaza de la Revolución. Standing behind a lectern that is covered with microphones, waving his arms about, pointing his right index finger in defiance at the sky, Fidel says there will be no bourgeois elections in Cuba any more because in Cuba we now have true democracy. We have a socialist Revolution, which makes the crowd go wild, applauding and chanting and yelling out, Fidel!, Fidel!, Fidel! Long live socialism, everyone is yelling: *¡Viva Cuba Socialista!*

Back home in Banes my mother doesn't understand what it all means, this socialism everyone is talking about. My father does: he says we are becoming a communist country, which is not good at all. The Americans will not be happy to have communism on their doorstep, my father says. He can tell there will be trouble ahead.

GENERAL MARRERO Street stretches from one end of Banes to the other. It's the street where all the main shops are, including my parents' haberdashery. It's not a big shop, but it's always done well, my mother says. Now, three years after *el Triunfo*, the shelves are looking empty and people aren't coming in as often as they did because there is nothing much to buy. Everything is in short supply. My father says it's because the Americans left and we don't talk to them any more, and our best new friends, the Russians, well, they may have sent that Yuri Gagarin into space and they may be paying lots of money for Cuban sugar and sending their technicians to Havana to help out, but they know nothing about shops.

It's not just my parents' shop that is looking deserted. A couple of doors down from the shop there is a bank. My father says this used to be a very busy bank, but now there is not much point in banking because the new Cuban *pesos* the Revolution has exchanged for the old capitalist *pesos* are not worth much. You can't change them for American dollars, which are now illegal anyway, although I know that my parents keep American dollars hidden in a small cigar box at home. Like everyone else in Banes, except no one ever talks about it. Even if you have one hundred of the revolutionary *pesos* you still won't be able to buy much because there is nothing to spend the money on.

A few doors further down on the other side of my parents' shop is the pharmacy owned by my father's best friend, Enriquito Martínez and his wife Armentina, who is close to my mother. I should say that *used* to be owned by Enriquito because the pharmacy now belongs to the People since Enriquito and his entire family packed up and left for Miami. At home, where no one else can hear, my father keeps talking about just how clever Enriquito was. He was one of the first to see right through the *barbudos*, my father says. He knew pretty early on that Fidel was a communist, despite the endless denials, he says.

Near the pharmacy is another shop that now belongs to the People: a branch of the department store chain El Encanto, which my mother says used to be the most expensive and best stocked in all of Banes, with the finest clothes, the latest electrical goods from *El Norte*, as everyone calls the United States, and the most delicate fabrics. It was really for the rich. Even today, with its shelves depleted, the place looks forbiddingly luxurious—the glass and chrome cabinets still sparkle and the black and white tiles on the floor are so polished you can see your reflection bounce back.

Now that we are no longer capitalists but socialists, like they say on the radio, the Revolution has started to take over all the big shops, like El Encanto, on the orders of Fidel, who said on television that in Cuba the exploitation of the masses is over, which means that all the big stores that were owned by rich Cubans now belong to the People. My parents aren't too worried about this because their shop is only a small shop and there is nothing much to sell in the shop and not too many customers.

Still, the Revolution is working in very strange ways because one morning my father arrives at the *Retacería García* to find two *milicianos* waiting. They have guns and they look very serious as they tell my father that his shop is under investigation because he exploits workers and, *compañero* (which is what everyone now calls everyone else in socialist Cuba), you must hand over your keys and go home while we check what's going on.

For the next few days my parents wait at home, not knowing what is going on at the shop. They go to the only lawyer they know in Banes, but the lawyer shakes his head and says there is not much he or anyone can do. Just wait, everyone says. But my father doesn't want to wait and someone suggests that perhaps, just perhaps, his mother, my grandmother Fulgencia, may be able to do something.

My grandmother, a formidable Spaniard, is a close friend of another formidable Spaniard in the district who happens to be the mother of a man called Sergio del Valle, a *barbudo* who is now a high ranking member of the Revolutionary Government and who is close to Fidel. And because this is Cuba, everyone knows for sure that while Sergio may be very busy helping Fidel with the Revolution and everything, he will still have time to listen to his mother. So my grandmother talks to Sergio's mother and Sergio's mother probably rings Sergio in his Havana office and has a talk to him about my parents' shop and probably tells him, too, before she hangs up, to eat, because he looks so skinny on television, and then, next thing we know, the *milicianos* who asked my father for the keys knock on the door at home and hand the keys back to my father, who is beside himself with relief. So is my mother, who says, *Gracias a Dios, Gracias a Dios*, thinking that God has given her back her shop, when in fact she should be thanking my grandmother Fulgencia and my grandmother's friend, Sergio's mother.

4

MISSILES IN PARADISE

MY MOTHER says we are off to the beach. On doctor's orders. My brother has been so ill for so long that the doctor has recommended, with typically Cuban certainty, that what my brother needs—what we all need—is to spend some time by the seaside, taking in the fresh air and enjoying the hot, Caribbean sun. So, we are off to Playa de Morales, which is only about fourteen kilometres away from Banes but seems much further.

One of my father's friends who used to be well off before the Revolution—*estaba muy bien*, is how my father puts it— but who is now in the same situation as everybody else, has lent his Morales beach house to my father for three months. It's not a flash house. It's a timber house with a very basic kitchen, very basic furniture and an outside latrine. There is no electricity in Morales, so we make do with a couple of large Chinese-made kerosene lamps and some candles. It's a little more primitive than what we are used to at home in Banes, but the house is right on the beach, in a fairly isolated part of Morales, and the sun shines every morning when we wake up, and the water is always blue and clear and magically warm.

There is a house next door, owned by another of my father's friends, Felelo and his family, and they have a boy about my age who becomes my instant best friend. But apart from us and Felelo and his family there is almost no one here, and we can sit outside by the water and look into the horizon and see nothing much most days. It's paradise and from what my mother says, it's doing a world of wonders for my brother's health.

Sure, things are getting tougher. It's true that since last year when those Yankee-backed invaders failed in their attempt to land at the Bay of Pigs—which in revolutionary Cuba is called by the much more heroic name of Playa de Girón—the Revolutionary Government has become even less tolerant of anyone who may have fancy ideas about elections. Nowadays, you watch what you say, which means it's almost always better not to say anything that might be misunderstood by your family or your neighbours as being somehow against the Revolution, let alone critical of *El Maxímo Líder*. But right now, all this business is far, far away from our little paradise here in Morales. Or so we think.

Every morning my father leaves for Banes, catching a ride with our neighbour, so he can open up the shop. Then, in the afternoon, he comes back from work. It only takes him about half an hour because it isn't that far and because the number of privately owned cars on the road is rapidly diminishing. There is no petrol around and no spare parts from the United States to keep the cars going the way they are supposed to. Instead, the roads are full of military trucks and jeeps, always rushing somewhere in the service of the People.

Finding food is a problem, but then again, this is always a problem in Cuba now. My father brings food from Banes, whatever he can find, and there is always someone coming around offering to sell something, or to exchange it for something else. But this is done on the quiet because, as we all know, there is no such thing as a black market in Cuba. Yet when you least expect it, someone knocks on your door, trying to exchange some plantains for a pair of trousers. Pork meat is a problem, though. Cubans love pork. It's the national dish, which may be why it is strictly controlled by the government. The theory is that no one in egalitarian, socialist Cuba should eat more pork than their neighbours, so the government controls supply and demand. It means you have to be careful when someone knocks on your door and offers to sell you a chunk of pork, because if you get caught selling or buying meat on the black market—if you get caught in possession of half a cow, say, or with half a well-fed pig in the boot of your car—you are in big, big trouble. You can go to prison. Every child in Cuba knows this. You get caught with meat, you can kiss your family goodbye and go straight to prison.

Today someone knocked on the door at Morales and offered to sell us pork. And not just anyone, but a *miliciano* who lives near Morales and is supposed to be one of the big military bosses in this area. My father knows him well enough to invite him in but not well enough to trust him when the *miliciano* says he has some pork left over and is happy to sell it. It's quite an offer. Meat! Tempting, but in the end caution wins the day and my father tells him, *Muchas gracias, compañero, pero no necesitamos carne.* Thanks but no, we do not need any meat, he lies. In Cuba, he says later, when the *miliciano* leaves, it pays to be careful. My mother nods in agreement.

Now, at night, my father is sitting on the narrow veranda at the front of the house, facing the beach, which is all dark, though you can hear the slow rhythm of the tropical waves, a sound that makes me want to go to sleep right there and then. My father sits there smoking one of his cigars and talking to our neighbour Felelo. My father says, You won't believe what happened today—that *miliciano* from up the road came to sell us meat. Can you believe that?

Felelo says, Did you buy any?

My father says, You've got to be joking. You think I am stupid? I knew it was a trap ...

No, *chico*, no, says Felelo, sounding incredulous. You turned down meat? Pork? *Estas loco* ...You are crazy, man. It's okay. I buy meat from him all the time. He is a communist but he is all right.

And that is how Cuba is divided now—there are the communists, and there are the communists who are all right. The ones who are all right are the ones whose job it is to protect the Revolution from the Americans, but who also come knocking on your door offering to sell you contraband pork.

I know my father could kick himself because, let's face it, a nice bit of *lechón*, at the beach, with a cold beer, well, is there anything more Cuban than that? Everyone is quiet on the veranda and you can tell they are all thinking about the pork and hoping that, having been politely but revolutionarily turned away by my suspicious father, the *miliciano* will nevertheless come back at some stage in the next few days, offering to sell us more pork.

I don't know this now but within days, our paradise will be no more. One night my father arrives home from Banes pretty excited. The Americans, he says, are ready to invade Cuba. It's everywhere on the television, in the paper and on the radio— Fidel says he knows for sure that the Yankee imperialists are readying to invade Cuba, and that brave, revolutionary Cubans will fight to the last drop of blood to defend their country. My mother looks out to sea to see if she can spot the American invaders, but there is nothing on the horizon. Some days later, everything becomes clearer—the Americans have gone to the United Nations and said that the Soviet Union, our new best friends, are building missile bases in Cuba, just one hundred miles from the United States. Missiles? In Cuba? Incredible.

True or not, my mother has gone into panic mode. She is sure the Americans will invade and she is sure that this means bad news for everyone because there will be war, she knows it, and she hates war, and she worries about my father being called up and her brothers, too, to fight the Americans. So in her own way she starts getting ready for war, putting away tins of Romanian processed meat (the type she tries to disguise

with some garlic and a bit of cumin, if she can find some somewhere) and some black beans and a few candles.

Days later again, my father arrives with big news from
Banes: an American spy plane has been shot down right in the
middle of town. Well, on the outskirts, really, but everyone in
Banes swears it's right in the middle of town. Like everyone
else, he first heard the buzzing plane really close to the shop
rooftops, then the distant gunfire, and then he watched as the
plane came down and he closed the shop and, like everyone
else, rushed on foot to see what had happened and whether this
was, after all, the much-heralded invasion by the Americans
which, he secretly hoped in his heart, would solve everything.
In truth, my father will admit many years later, he didn't get to
see all that much because by the time half the town arrived
to witness this piece of Cold War history—the only instance of
combat during the confrontation that would become known as
the Cuban Missile Crisis—Cuban *milicianos* and the Soviet
technicians with their loud shirts and short-cropped military
hairstyles had cordoned off much of the area, to keep curious
onlookers away.

We listen in disbelief, except for my mother, who thinks
the world is about to end and that we are going to get caught
in the middle of a war with the Americans, stuck in this
remote beach house, cut off from what is going on in the rest
of the country, and away from her beloved family. My father
tries to reassure her. Everything will be all right. But everything is not all right. As the Cuban Missile Crisis escalates, it
becomes quite clear that my mother is right, at least about us
being stuck in Morales. My father arrives home one afternoon with news that all the roads around Banes have been
closed off by the military, including the only road in and out
of Morales. He has locked up the shop in Banes for good,
and from now on we are staying put here, waiting anxiously
to see what happens.

By now, Morales has become a military camp of sorts. The
beachfront has been taken over by *milicianos* in their trucks
and jeeps, and we have been told to stay in the house, which
means we can't go exploring in the bush or along the beach
without my mother rushing out and yelling at us to get back

in here, do you want to get killed and give me a heart attack? There are five, six, probably a dozen huge, grey American ships anchored just off the coast. The ships look really close, as if you could almost swim to them, and they look threatening. At least one of the American ships is an aircraft carrier because from the shore, you can see planes take off, flying over the other ships and then disappearing out to sea until they look like tiny dots in the blue sky.

Over the next couple of days, all we know is that we have been told to stay put. And then, in the middle of what historians will later describe as the closest and most dangerous encounter of the Cold War, just as my mother's carefully rationed kitty is starting to run out, our old *miliciano* friend comes back knocking on the door, offering us some pork. It's a miracle, says my mother, who is really not very religious but can tell a miracle when she sees one. This time there is no hesitation on my parents' part. They buy the pork, thinking that if we are soon going to be at war with the Americans, then we might as well have some pork for dinner.

Maybe it was something to do with the pork, but now we have another visitor. My aunt Mirta arrives from her home in the nearby town of San Germán, where she and her husband have what was, *antes del Triunfo*, a large and growing department store. My aunt, like the rest of the family, has been frantic, having had no news from us for days. So, my aunt says, speaking really quickly like Cubans do when they are excited, she has been doing all she can to try and get to Morales and bring us back to Banes, so that if there is an invasion, well, at least we will all be close by.

Somehow, my aunt has managed to borrow a car in San Germán, get some rationed petrol and drive straight to Morales where she has done the impossible and broken through the military cordon that surrounds the area. If anyone in our family could do it, it is my aunt Mirta. As my mother says, she could sell refrigerators in the Arctic. And now, here she is on our doorstep in one of her colourful dresses and her American-style sunglasses, and everyone is hugging as if we haven't seen each other for years. My mother packs as quickly as she can, throwing our belongings into suitcases and bags. We jump in the car and drive out to the road that will, all things being equal, take us back home.

It's only when we hit the first of several military roadblocks that my mother admits to having packed up the leftover pork. She confesses later that she could imagine the *milicianos* stopping the car, inspecting the boot and finding the two or three kilos of contraband pork, a counter-revolutionary act so perverse, so anti-socialist, that she and her entire family will be banished for ever to some prison at the other end of the island. And yet it seems the option of stopping the car somewhere out of sight, opening the boot and throwing away the incriminating pork is not considered seriously either by my parents or by my aunt Mirta, confirming yet again that when it comes to the country of my birth, it's folly to stand between a Cuban and a pork cutlet.

Somehow my aunt Mirta manages, with some help from my father, to assure the *milicianos* along the way that we are, indeed, a family that got stuck in Morales and just wants to go home and help defend the Revolution. Until we arrive at the last checkpoint, at the very entrance to Banes, where we are promptly taken into custody and told to drive to the local police station. No one can hear it, but my poor mother's heart is racing at a hundred miles an hour, for sure.

God probably understands all about pork cutlets because the *milicianos* who have taken us to the police station haven't searched the car yet and as we enter the station my father immediately recognises one of his friends behind the station counter. His name is Hugo and he just happens to be in charge today and he asks my father what is going on. We explain and Hugo tells my father, *Mi socio*, don't worry about it, go home and make sure the family is looked after. I will sort this out. My father will be for ever grateful.

Years later, trying to recall the details of those momentous days back in October 1962 when the world came close to nuclear war, I ask my mother what she was thinking when she wrapped up the pork and dumped it in the boot of the car. What was I thinking? she says incredulously. We had *pork*, she says emphasising the word. What were we supposed to do? Leave behind good Cuban pork? No way!

5

GOOD LITTLE COMMUNISTS

As I WALK into the classroom for my first day at the Jose Antonio Saco primary school, I am welcomed by my teacher, Flor, who will in fact be my teacher throughout my primary school years. Like all good teachers, she will teach and nurture me and decades later she will still be remembered fondly. Even her name—which translates as Flower—makes an immediate impact on an impressionable child.

Flor is short, her skin is the colour of creamy milk chocolate; she is softly spoken, and she wears small metal-rimmed glasses that give her an air of absolute mastery in all things scholastic.

It doesn't take me long to discover that despite my initial reservations, I am going to enjoy school. We sit at our uncomfortable wooden desks learning to recite an alphabet where the F is for Fidel, the R for rifle and the Y for Yankees. Learning about Fidel and rifles and why we should hate the Americans can sometimes take up a fair amount of the school day, even in primary school. As we get older, more and more time is taken out for what my parents describe with growing alarm as indoctrination.

Some days we attend commemorations held outside the Communist Party headquarters, a big old house right in the main street. Until a couple of years ago the house belonged to the Gonzalez family, regular friends of my parents, who were well known all over Banes. When they left for the United States the house and everything in it was taken over by the People, like all the other houses vacated by *gusanos*. *La Casa del Partido*, as everyone calls it, is just a couple of doors down from my school so it's easy for us to march in from the playground up the street to attend protest meetings or to commemorate some revolutionary anniversary, or to swear loyalty to the Revolution: *Patria o Muerte*.

¡Venceremos! Fatherland or Death. We shall win! Which is how all speeches end in Cuba now.

Attending these *actos revolucionarios*, as they are called, means we get to stand in the sun listening to speeches until one of the older students is asked to step forward and, with great ceremony, raise the Cuban flag while we sing the national anthem and the 'Internationale', which is the best part of the whole thing, not only because I enjoy singing the 'Internationale' but because it means the ceremony is over and we get to move into the shade. My friends and I enjoy these *actos revolucionarios* because it means missing mathematics, which I hate anyway, or science, and all this talk about revolutionary heroes, about Lenin and Marx, makes us feel very grown up. It makes us feel like good communists, just as Fidel says we should. We like the marching, and the fact that we get shown how to assemble Russian machine guns and that we get to salute the flag and swear to give our lives, if necessary, on behalf of the Revolution.

I am not sure, however, whether my teacher Flor is all that keen on this revolutionary stuff. She looks thoroughly bored by the whole thing. My parents aren't too keen on this revolutionary stuff either, which is bad news for me because there is nothing I want more right now than to put my hand up in class and ask Flor if I can become a Communist Pioneer—a *pionero*—which is what all good revolutionary children want to become. When you become a *pionero* you get to go on excursions and wear a blue and white *pañueleta* scarf around your neck to show the world you are proud to be a good little communist. You also get to go on trips to other towns and to the beach, and sometimes they teach you how to fire a rifle, shooting in the distance at cardboard figures that are always dressed like bloodthirsty American soldiers who want to destroy the Revolution. If you are a really good *pionero*, you even get to meet visiting Communist Pioneers from the Soviet Union, and if you are a really, really good revolutionary pioneer you may even get to visit Russia or one of the fraternal countries in Eastern Europe, and there is no bigger prize in Cuba than getting a trip overseas, anywhere overseas, even if it is to the Soviet Union. Or Romania.

But despite all this, my parents refuse to let me join the *pioneros*. They say it's just a way of indoctrinating children. It's a problem, though, because many of my friends are proud *pioneros* and I am not, which can only mean one thing: my parents are not good revolutionaries. They are suspect. And I am scared they may get into trouble, that the police will come home, or worse, that the woman who runs the Committee for the Defence of the Revolution in our neighbourhood will knock on the door and ask my father why he never puts his name down for voluntary work, why he doesn't attend political meetings, why there is no picture of Fidel anywhere in our house. Can you explain, *compañero*, why your son is not a *pionero*?

So one day I arrive home wearing my scarf, beaming proudly, because not only have I become a good revolutionary but now my parents are safe, and no one is going to come and question them.

My excitement doesn't last long. My father looks at me in disbelief and says, No son of mine is going to be a communist.

Next morning as I explain to my teacher that my father has asked me to return the *pañueleta*, I imagine that our whole world is about to collapse around us, that we are doomed, because we are all suspect.

6

A CARNIVAL AND A FUNERAL

DON'T ASK ME how this came about but my father arrived home to tell us that he has been made the supply chief of the carnival. Talk about a surprise.

Every year, towns and cities up and down the island, no matter how small, how poor or how far from Havana, hold their own street carnival, and Banes is no different. Mind you, the Banes carnival is nowhere near as glamorous or as well known as the Havana carnival, which has a huge parade through the main streets of the capital and is televised across the country. Still, for the next two weeks the town goes berserk. It's really the ultimate Cuban party, which means that everyone goes to work or school during the daytime but as soon as the sun sets you come out again, dressed in your Sunday best, to join in the fun. The main streets are closed off to traffic for the duration, and for weeks beforehand dozens of temporary stalls are built along the streets to sell beer, rum and food—and no rationing. It all sounds to me a little too capitalist, but no one is complaining. Even Fidel says Cubans should enjoy the carnival.

Almost every night there is music, too, especially on the Saturday nights, with loudspeakers blaring cha-cha-chas and *rumbas* and *guagancos*, and orchestras and singers from all over Cuba, even from as far as Havana, make their way to Banes so they can play live atop a temporary bandstand set up in the Parque Domínguez, just across from the church. The bandstand is decorated with palm trees, paper garlands and revolutionary slogans encouraging Banes to work harder to make Cuba even more of a socialist paradise. It's strange to see the slogans up there talking about revolutionary sacrifice while everyone is having a great time down on the dance floor, but that's the way things are in Cuba.

It's even stranger to think that my father, who never puts his name down for voluntary work and who hasn't joined and is unlikely to ever join the Communist Party, or so he says, has been made supply chief of the carnival—the best carnival time job of all, except maybe for being Queen of the Carnival. But that job only goes to pretty teenage girls who are chosen by someone somewhere in the local Communist Party, not just for her beauty but also for her revolutionary fervour. Most of the time, the Queen of the Carnival turns out to be related to someone in the Party but I am sure that is just coincidence. Still, the Queen of the Carnival only gets to swan around town with a cardboard tiara and ride on a truck as part of the procession, which takes place on the first Saturday night of the carnival. On the other hand, my father gets to organise the stalls, organise the supply of food and alcohol, collect and bank all the takings at the end of the day and make sure that everything runs smoothly.

What's more, he gets to meet and take care of all the celebrities who come to town to perform. This year the star attraction, the act everyone in Banes wants to see, is a duo called Clara y Mario. Clara y Mario are glamorous and good-looking and are probably the most popular singing duo in Cuba right now, always performing on television and radio. They are the most famous people to come to Banes for a long time, and so everyone is pretty excited about it. And now, my father is going to meet Clara y Mario, believe it or not, and make sure they have everything they need while staying at the Hotel Bani right on General Marrero Street.

My mother and all her friends want to know what Clara y Mario are really like. My father, who is taking his job seriously, is happy to impart the occasional bit of celebrity gossip but then he says he is very busy with all this organising and, really, he has to get back to checking that no one has their fingers in the till and making sure none of the stalls runs out of beer because, well, things can get nasty when you run out of beer right after listening to one of those heartbreaking Clara y Mario *boleros*, you know ...

For the next two weeks I feel as if I am the most popular kid at school because everyone knows that my father is a big boss at the carnival headquarters, which also means we get to eat nice food at home as he controls all the extra supplies coming in for carnival time, and we get to stock up on beer and the occasional bottle of rum because, after all, that is what is expected when you are a big boss of the carnival. I am proud of my father because I can see he is enjoying the job, too, despite the responsibility and despite the fact that he arrives home in the very early hours of the morning, sometimes at 4:00am, with all this money he has collected from the stalls and for which he has to account, and he sits there making sure the numbers add up and then places the notes neatly in piles which he puts inside empty cigar boxes.

My mother worries about my father coming home so late with all that money because she knows that when carnival comes around, there is always trouble. The next day at school we always hear stories about a man who was drunk and discovered his wife kissing some other man who was also drunk, and then someone produced a big knife and threatened to kill the wife and her lover, and half of Banes as well, but in the end no one got killed because a *miliciano* arrived just in time and fired his revolutionary pistol in the air.

MY MOTHER'S grandmother has died. She was 108, which my aunt Nidia says could have made her the oldest person in Banes, although no one knows for sure. She is not really my grandmother but we still call her Abuela because that is what everyone calls her and, besides, I never met my mother's mother, my real *abuela*, who died before I was even born.

Abuela lived with my aunt Nidia in the family home in Presidente Zayas Avenue, where she was always surrounded by noisy relatives and gossiping neighbours. To be honest, I found Abuela a little scary. Sitting in her rocking chair on the front veranda, she looked as old and small and wrinkled as you can expect to be when you are 108. Whenever my brother and I visited, which was two or three times a week, my mother insisted we give Abuela a kiss on her cheeks, which was not something I looked forward to. It was like kissing parched paper—rough, wrinkly—and she smelled faintly of stale cologne, and when we kissed her she would say something about how grown up we looked, and then, without fail, she'd stick her dentures out at me, which really, really scared me. I think she did it deliberately too, because she would then give me a little hint of a smile.

I can tell that while everyone is sad about Abuela's death, there is also relief. All my aunts and uncles and even the neighbours say the same thing: Abuela had a long life, but it was a hard life, a poor woman's life, a life of looking after children and then her grandchildren and even the great-grandchildren. Now, they say, she can finally rest in peace.

This is my first funeral. My mother says funerals are not for children because funerals are too sad and they give you nightmares, but she relents and agrees that my brother and I, along with our older cousins, can say farewell to Abuela at the funeral parlour, provided we change into what she calls respectable clothes, and provided we behave when we get there.

It's quite an event, but then again, Cuban funerals always are. For three nights Abuela has been here in the funeral home in a black, shiny coffin with gold-coloured handles. The coffin is at the end of the long room, at about waist level if you are a grown-up, surrounded by a sea of wreaths which give the room the kind of funny smell that sticks to your clothes for days. They say it's the smell of the flowers, but even I know it's really the smell of death.

My father takes my brother and me closer to the coffin, and then he lifts each of us in turn so we can see inside. When I look in, it seems to me as if Abuela is not dead at all but just having a siesta, except her face seems too white and she is not playing around with her dentures. I can now understand what my mother meant about nightmares. As I lean forward to give her a farewell kiss on her cheek, I hang on to my father really tightly because I am afraid of falling right into the coffin, right next to my dead *abuela*.

It's peak viewing time and as I look around the room, I imagine Abuela must have had lots of friends because the room is pretty full.

There is no music, but the whole thing is like one big party, with cigars and coffee. The thing about Cuban funerals is that when you turn up, regardless of the time, someone will inevitably make coffee and come around with a big tray loaded with tiny china cups of *café cubano*, so dark and sweet you can feel your teeth crumble when you drink it. Right behind the coffee comes someone offering cigars to the men, who never say no because in Cuba you never say no to a cigar, even if you don't light it up but just put it in your shirt pocket for later.

The other thing about Cuban funerals is that there is no excuse for not turning up because the funeral home stays open around the clock as a sign of respect, and family members take turns to stay the night. My mother takes her turn and so do all my aunts and uncles and even more distant relatives who have come to Banes so they can farewell Abuela. I can't understand why they do this, why they can't go to sleep and then come back the next morning, but one of my cousins says that it's to make sure the dead are not left alone as they get ready to go to Heaven.

7

ALL IN THE FAMILY

IT'S CHRISTMAS EVE—*Nochebuena*—and there must be at least fifty people at the old family house in Presidente Zayas Avenue. The place is bursting at the seams, there are so many people in here. All of my uncles and my aunts and their children and even some of the neighbours. There is music in the background, but no one is dancing yet. That will come later, after dinner. Everyone seems to be too busy talking all at once, which is the Cuban way, and talking as loudly as they can, which is also the Cuban way, because that is the only way to be heard.

My mother and my aunts have managed to find enough tables and chairs for almost every adult to be able to sit down for dinner. My cousin Tonito and I, who are older, get to sit down. As I sit here, I think how I have never seen so much food or so many people looking and sounding so happy.

I don't know how my mother and my aunts managed to do it because, as I have said, there is not much food anywhere in the shops any more, not even if it's your turn to buy groceries at the *bodega*, but they have come up with quite a feast. There is plenty of *congrí*, which one of my aunts made with rice and black beans and even bits of pork belly; and there is *yuca*, a tuber that you boil until it's tender and then immediately smother in a *mojito* made with lots of garlic, oil and lemon juice; and there is even a giant salad of lettuce, red tomatoes and big green tomatoes, which taste really tart but which my mother says have many more vitamins than ripe tomatoes. And because this is Cuba and because this is *Nochebuena*, there is also pork. A whole pig, in fact, that has been roasted slowly in a pit through the day and which has now been cut into large chunks and placed on big platters that get passed around so everyone can have not just some of the moist meat but also some of the crackling, because it's not a Cuban feast unless you have some *pellejito*.

Later, there will be dessert, probably *casquitos de guayaba*, which my mother makes using the pulp of the guava fruit and about twenty tonnes of sweet Cuban sugar, so much, in fact, that you can feel your teeth dancing. There will be some white-coloured cheese imported from Bulgaria that goes just right with the guava, and Polish apples and pears cut into small pieces so that everyone can have a taste since these are fruits we very rarely see in Cuba, and some grapes, which are also rare and therefore strictly rationed. All this will be followed by Spanish nougat—*turrón*—which is without doubt the high-light of my *Nochebuena*.

My father and my uncles, meanwhile, have collected enough beer and Cuban rum over the past few weeks to last a month, or at least to last through *Nochebuena*; you can easily tell that most of the men have been drinking for some hours already—while roasting the pig in the pit—because they are all happier and louder than normal.

It's been a long day for the males in the García household, especially for my father, who has become the family expert at what has to be the most symbolically *macho* chore of the day— and the most gruesome. He has become the pig slaughterer.

Children are never allowed to watch this ritual, of course, but now that I am older I am determined to see what happens, so I find a hiding place right under the stairs at the back of the house, which is raised high from the ground. I know that if I am discovered down here by my mother or one of my aunts, they will send me out to play on the street with the other chil-dren. So I lie on my stomach, watching through the timber slats as my father and my uncles put the finishing touches to a huge pit they have dug in the ground, where a fire has started to take and where, later on, the pig will be roasted, in the tra-ditional Cuban way. But now, it's *la hora de matar el puerco*. Time to kill the pig.

My father moves to the corner of the yard where the pig is tied to a post with a long piece of rope. It's a massive pig and a happy one, always eating scraps and making noises that make you think he doesn't have much to worry about, at least for now. But as soon as my father gets closer, the pig goes quiet, looks up from the mud that has been building up in that corner of the yard and starts to back up against the fence. I am sure he knows he is about to be killed because suddenly, with a loud grunting noise that scares me rigid, the big pig tries to get away, running between my father's legs, which is futile because the pig is tied to the rope. It cannot escape.

It is only now that I realise my father is carrying a huge, shiny knife that he has kept half hidden by his side. Then he stands behind the pig, which is squealing really loudly now, holds the animal by the neck and with one swift move, so quick I almost miss it, he lifts the pig up by its front legs and plunges the knife right into the pig's lower chest. Straight into the heart, I assume. It's then that the pig gives the loudest squeal of all, an angry squeal, the squeal of death. I am sure it can be heard across half of Banes. It's the scariest sound I have ever heard.

Everything is quiet for a second, but my father keeps holding the pig because he has done this before, at other *Nochebuenas*, and he knows that any moment now the pig will try to run away again in a last desperate attempt to stay alive. My father holds the animal really close to his chest and all I can see is a long stream of blood coming out of the pig's neck; one of my uncles collects the blood in a big pan to make *morcilla* sausages later on.

It's the same pig we will eat later tonight, after it has been gutted, then shaved with boiling water and a knife, and then rubbed all over with plenty of salt and juice from bitter oranges. It will take hours before it's cooked and before the rest of the family arrives, wearing their best clothes, ready to eat, drink and celebrate another *Nochebuena*.

In our family, *Nochebuena* has always been a big deal but I guess that is the case for most other Cuban families. It's not that we are deeply religious or anything like that—far from it—but on 24 December just about every member of the family and a few distant relatives and the occasional neighbour will turn up as if by magic at the house in Presidente Zayas Avenue to celebrate Christmas Eve. As they sit at the long table that is really several long tables put together, there is always talk about past *Nochebuenas* and I realise that everyone seems to remember the *Nochebuena* of 24 December 1959 as among the best, coming just months after I was born and a year almost to the day after the *barbudos* deposed Batista.

MY AUNT Mirta and her husband, my uncle Rodolfo are coming to live in Banes. I don't realise this at the time but their decision to move to Banes is both an uncharacteristic admission of defeat and the start of a process that will eventually tear my mother's close-knit family apart. But for now, all I can think of is how great it is that Mirta and Rodolfo are moving here, because of all my aunts and uncles they are the most fun. Until recently they owned a big store in San Germán, a town not far from Banes, where they used to sell just about everything imaginable, from sofa suites and modern American washing machines, to fancy leather shoes you put on to go out dancing. It was the biggest shop in the town and for my parents, whose shop was much smaller, it was something to aim for.

But now, Mirta and Rodolfo don't own the shop any more because all the big shops in Cuba belong to the People. They work there but they don't own the place—they don't even manage the shop, as the Revolution has appointed to the position of administrator a woman who used to be one of the employees (and not a very good one, my mother adds with disdain); 'administrator' is the title they give the new bosses. You can tell just by looking at them that it has been a big blow to Mirta and Rodolfo. My happy aunt is not as happy as she used to be, and my laid-back uncle seems much more distant than I can ever recall. There is an air about them of absolute defeat which even a boy can recognise. All that hard work for nothing, is what they say.

The house my aunt and uncle have managed to find in Banes is a big, almost-new timber house on the outskirts, near the main road that takes you out of the town on the way to Holguin. Inside, the house is full of light with plenty of space and lots of rooms. Outside, there is a huge yard, the biggest I have ever seen, with enough room for a chook pen and even a corner to raise a little pig or two, says my uncle, smacking his lips in anticipation of the feast that he is sure will come. Compared to our house, it's a palace.

Every Sunday night without fail, we meet at my aunt's new place for dinner. Sometimes after dinner, we go to the sitting room and wait expectantly for my uncle to take out his American slide projector.

There, reflected on the white wall, are images of a recent past that now seems almost prehistoric—pictures of my uncle and aunt looking younger, standing outside the San Germán shop and smiling for the camera with a sense of optimism and satisfaction that seems to burn through the slide itself. There are pictures of my parents, my father still sporting his Errol Flynn moustache that, he says jokingly, used to drive the girls crazy. There are pictures of other family members on my mother's side, and one where everyone is looking happy and well dressed, sitting at a long table somewhere drinking Hatuey beers, ready to get stuck into the roasted suckling pig that sits on a huge platter in the middle of the table, right there, so colourful it feels as if you could just stretch your arm and touch it.

But despite the slide nights, I can tell that our Sunday dinners are becoming more and more serious as the months progress. After dinner, as my aunt and my mother start taking the plates to the kitchen to do the washing up, my uncle Rodolfo and my father sit around the big old table talking about how things are getting worse and how there is no hope in sight that Fidel will see the error of his communist ways and turn back the clock, which I figure means returning the shop to my uncle so he is happy again. When they get talking about these things, they tell me to go and play outside with my brother because these are discussions for grown-ups only. *Vete, vete a jugar,* they say. Go out and play, and I do as I am told but, of course, I think I know what's going on. I can tell by the way they speak almost in a whisper, scared that someone will overhear their conversation. I can tell what they are planning. I can tell that my uncle wants to leave Cuba, that he and my aunt are ready to apply for permission to go to New York, and he wants my parents and my brother and me to follow them.

8

RATIONING TALES

THE MOST important book in all of Cuba, the book you must guard with your very life, is *la libreta*—the ration book that every Cuban family needs to be able to buy food. It's something you learn from a very early age—you take care of *la libreta*, which is inevitably accompanied by *la jaba*, an all-purpose shopping bag my mother has made from old canvas that reeks of optimism and unfulfilled promise. You never know when you will need your *jaba*, to buy whatever is available, so it comes with you all the time.

My parents say rationing is not something they ever thought they would see in Cuba but they were wrong because now almost everything is rationed. That is the way it has been since 1962 when Fidel announced that rationing would be introduced, but only for a year, because the Americans don't want to sell Cuba anything any more, which means the shelves are empty in the shops. He says rationing is the only way the Revolution can ensure everyone has exactly the same amount of food to eat, which is the socialist way. I cannot understand why Fidel doesn't just buy more food from our Russian friends but I guess they have rationing of their own.

If the topic comes up at school, the teachers tell us that the *libreta* is the price we pay for being independent and anti-imperialist and, besides, it means everyone has enough food not to go hungry. I am not so sure about this and I wonder whether Fidel has his own *libreta* and whether he has to queue like my mother does so she can buy half a pound of black beans. But I keep these thoughts to myself. It's not something you say out loud and, anyway, we all know that Fidel is busy, day in and day out, defending the Revolution so it would be quite unpatriotic of me even to think about such things.

In fact there are two ration books in Cuba: one is for food, which is the one with the most pages, and the other one is for non-food items like clothes and shoes and bedsheets or towels. The *libreta* for food is the one you must take real care of because if you lose it or someone steals it, you are in big trouble. Just getting a new *libreta* from the central planning office can take weeks, and during that time you have to rely on your family or neighbours to get something to eat, and of course they never have enough. No one in Banes ever has enough, or at least no one I know, rationing or not.

In a move that would later strike me as Orwellian if only Fidel had not banned George Orwell's books for being counter-revolutionary, officially the ration book is not called a *Libreta de Racionamiento*, it's called a *Libreta de Abastecimientos* which, roughly translated means a 'supply book', hinting at an abundance which, even a child can tell you, most certainly is not there.

With the *libreta* a family like ours can buy a set amount of food which the government says is enough to keep us Cubans healthy and well-fed and alert should those Americans attempt to invade us. It means that every month, each person in our house is entitled to three pounds of rice, one and a half pounds of black beans, four ounces of ground coffee, three pounds of meat from the butcher, one toilet roll, one-quarter of a tube of toothpaste and, if you are old enough, two packets of cigarettes. Of course, you soon discover there is no guarantee that any of these goods will be in the shops, but if they are then that's what our family is entitled to, and that is what we get. If you eat all the food at once, then you are in trouble because you won't get any more until next month.

To make sure there are no anti-revolutionary acts like hoarding or pushing prices up, every family is allocated a *bodega*—a grocery store—where you must go once every fortnight to get your food. Same with the butcher shop and the bakery. You can't just buy stuff anywhere. And despite having an allocated shop and an allocated day to go and buy your allocated goods, often you still have to queue. The queue I am in now is long. There must be at least twenty people ahead of me, almost all of them women because this is Cuba and even in revolutionary Cuba queuing for food is regarded as women's work. So, here they are, revolutionary Cuban women in flimsy housecoats, in floral dresses that have seen much, much better days, some with their hair in rollers, the rollers covered with a *pañueleta*, a brightly coloured head scarf that has become a very Cuban fashion accessory now that no one can buy hair spray.

Everyone starts off in good humour, which is the Cuban way to cope with queues. But as the waiting drags on and on and on and the sun starts to really bite into your skin and make you sweat until you glisten, the jokes and the laughing give way to a resigned silence. Do you think that inside their heads they may be thinking counter-revolutionary thoughts? Like, when is this business of the *libretas* and the queues going to finish? Are you wondering whether all those *dirigentes*, those leaders of the Revolution who are always on television telling Cubans to work harder at building a socialist state, are also queueing right now? You'd better keep these thoughts in your head because they are dangerous.

Sometimes you don't need the *libreta* to buy things. Sometimes shops receive additional goods and they are allowed to sell them freely, or *por la libre*, although the prices are still controlled by the government. It doesn't happen all that often, but whenever there is food being sold without rationing, the queues that form outside are even longer than the ones that form when something arrives at the *bodega* for sale with *la libreta*. Sometimes it doesn't matter what's for sale *por la libre*—you see a queue and you just jump on the end, *jaba* at the ready, to buy whatever is on offer. You do this because you can never be sure when food will be on sale again, and because if you have a surplus, you can always exchange whatever it is with other members of the extended family or with your neighbours. If you don't smoke, you get your packets of cigarettes and then exchange them with someone you know who does smoke but who doesn't need as much oil as you or who doesn't like chickpeas. True socialism, no? But you still have to queue.

Most of the time, what is sold *por la libre* is food that somehow isn't rationed, probably because it is food most

Cubans don't like much or know nothing about, like funny-smelling sardines from Yugoslavia. Or ham from Russia that comes in small tins. *Antes del Triunfo*, my mother says, sounding surprisingly and dangerously subversive, Russian pressed ham was the sort of food we Cubans wouldn't even give to pigs ... *Ni a los puercos*.

Near our house there is a fish shop run by Jamaicans who speak Spanish with a funny accent. Every second day or so they get fish in, which I cannot quite understand because Banes is so close to the sea and you would think you could sell fish every day, but no one says anything because at least fish is not rationed. You don't need *la libreta*.

Today, as we queue for fish, the sun is hotting up and everyone is sweating and getting more and more impatient. My brother and I don't mind fish but often, by the time it's your turn in the queue, all that is left are fish heads. They are large and ugly and menacing but my father claims the fish heads are good because they are the tastiest and most nutritious part of the fish. Tonight my father makes fish soup for dinner.

My father likes to cook occasionally, which is something of a rarity for Cuban men of his generation. Like my mother, he says cooking was a lot easier and a lot more flavoursome back in the old days because you could buy proper meat and proper fish if you had the money, and you could pop down to the *bodega* any time and come back with herbs and spices and some pork fat to give the food some additional flavour. They paint a picture of abundance that seems to me totally unrealistic. I think they are exaggerating because they want me to believe that, despite what I get told at school, not everything was bad in the days before Fidel.

WE ARE GOING to Havana to say goodbye to my uncle Rodolfo, my aunt Mirta and my cousin Carrie, who is not even three. More than a year after applying, they have been given permission to leave Cuba, flying straight from Havana to the United States in flights that my uncle says are known in Miami as freedom flights—*el puente de la libertad*—but not in Cuba, where they are just a plane-load of *gusanos*. It's the only way to leave Cuba and you have to wait and wait and cross your fingers that there is no problem in the meantime.

I am sure I am going to miss my aunt and my uncle, especially my aunt Mirta, who can be so much fun with the way she talks really fast and how she manages to find presents for my brother and me even when there is nothing much to buy in the shops. But right now none of that is important to me because all I can think about is going to Havana; for a boy from Banes, that is quite a treat. Before we leave, my father sits my brother and me down and tells us, in the stern, low voice he reserves for serious occasions, that for the sake of our uncle and aunt, we have to behave when we get to Havana. Do you understand? he asks. You have to behave and that means you don't tell anyone that your aunt and uncle and cousin are leaving for *El Norte*.

I can't understand why this is such a big deal, but I don't care. It's a small price to pay, it seems to me, to be able to go to Havana.

Havana is huge compared to Banes and you can tell this as soon as the bus leaves the countryside behind and enters the city. And the closer we get to the centre, the taller the buildings become and the more people I see walking and queuing.

There are not too many queues where we are staying, though. Our home away from home is an apartment in Miramar, which I find out later is the most exclusive neighbourhood in all of Cuba. It was exclusive *antes del Triunfo* because this is where all the rich people built their mansions, not far from the beach, along wide, tree-lined streets that are called avenues and that look nothing like the streets and avenues of Banes. Most of the rich people left for *El Norte* a long time ago and their big houses and apartments now belong to the People—or to ambassadors and technicians from fraternal countries such as Russia and Poland, who seem to be everywhere when we go out later to walk the streets and enjoy the cool breeze that comes from the Straits of Florida.

The houses that now belong to the People really belong to people like my uncle Victor, my mother's oldest brother, who was a *barbudo* fighting in the Sierra Maestra with Fidel and who is now a senior officer in the army. Now we are in his apartment and, let me tell you, it is huge. It's like something straight out of a movie, with big windows, a balcony, lots of furniture, a big fridge and even a television. It's so close to the beach you can hear the sound of the waves. The whole building is like this: downstairs, I discover, there are other families whose fathers are also defending the Revolution and their apartments are also huge, and most of the fathers who defend the Revolution have a car parked outside, or an army jeep with a driver comes in the morning and picks them up to take them to work.

My aunt and my two cousins, who are much younger than me, are great fun to be with and they make us feel welcome from the moment we arrive, showing us the rooms where we will sleep, my mother, brother and I on one huge, very comfortable bed; and my aunt Mirta, my uncle Rodolfo and my cousin Carrie in another room. It's like we are on holidays in the best place we have ever been to.

Before we go anywhere, my mother reminds us not to tell anyone that we are here to say goodbye to my aunt and uncle and cousin who are leaving for the United States. Don't tell anyone because if you do, then your uncle Victor can get into trouble. Pretend you are on holidays, she insists. I am happy to pretend. I keep thinking that it's a good thing all those rich *gusanos* left and these houses have been given over to 'certain people', as my uncle Rodolfo says, gesturing to us by placing two fingers on his shoulder as if he is in the army. He winks and we know exactly what he means ...

In Havana, like in Banes, everyone has to queue outside the shops or at the bus stop, but not if you live in a big apartment in Miramar. At my uncle's house there is a woman who comes every couple of days to clean the house and she has no problem buying things. A big, black woman with a big smile, she makes a note of everything we need in the apartment and then goes out to a special shop for people who are protecting the Revolution, and she comes back with huge bags full of things we don't get to see too often, if ever, in Banes. Like chicken legs and steaks and plantain and rice, and it's like paradise, says my mother, who can't believe her eyes.

Today we are going to the zoo because everyone in Banes

said you have to go to the zoo in Havana because it is a great place for children. It's my first visit to a zoo anywhere. It's the first time I see lions and elephants in real life and it's fun getting a running commentary from my uncle Rodolfo as we move from one cage to another, because he seems to have a joke about every animal.

At the end of the day, as dusk starts to fall, we wait outside the zoo gates with lots of other people for the bus that will take us back to Miramar. There is a long queue but by now we are used to queues. Eventually we catch the bus and walk all the way to the back to take the only seats that are empty. The bus is packed, like all buses are in Cuba, but everyone is in good spirits because everyone has had a great time at the zoo. There is an elderly lady sitting in the seat next to where I am standing and she starts talking to my brother and me, asking us where we are from. We tell her we are from Banes, which is in Oriente province, and she tells us how polite we seem to be and did we enjoy seeing the lions and the giraffe, which we did, and then she asks, What are you doing in Havana? And because I have had a great day at the zoo and I feel comfortable and happy, I point to where my mother is sitting and I say to the old lady, We are here to say goodbye to our uncle and our aunt; they are going to the United States. Then I realise that this is not what I am supposed to say, that I have been warned not to even mention *El Norte*.

The back of the bus falls silent. No one says anything. I look at my mother, who is pretending not to notice. I can see that my uncle Rodolfo is quiet too, and no one says anything at all for the next twenty minutes, until we get to our stop in Miramar and file out.

The next day my uncle Tony arrives to pick us up. He has an important position in the revolutionary government too, although I don't think he is as important as my uncle Victor because he lives in a smaller apartment and he doesn't have a woman who comes to clean and who brings special food from the special shop. But my uncle Tony must still be pretty important because, unlike any other Cuban I know, he is allowed to travel overseas, heading delegations to fraternal countries and sometimes even to capitalist countries in

Europe. What's more, my uncle Tony has a car. It's a small Russian car given to him by the government because he is a good revolutionary and an important man and I decide right there and then that that is what I want to be when I grow up—a good revolutionary who is allowed to travel overseas representing Cuba and who is given a Lada.

My uncle Tony says he is taking us on a tour of Havana so my mother and brother and me and my aunt Mirta and my cousin all pile into the small car, which smells brand new.

We enjoy being driven around Havana, especially since there are few other cars on its streets. My uncle Tony tells me with a conspiratorial wink that Fidel has a house right here in Miramar too, but that in reality no one knows for sure where he stays on any given night because he likes to move around all the time, from house to house and apartment to apartment, to make sure he fools those Americans who want to kill him. As we pass yet another big billboard telling Cubans to become even better revolutionaries, I look out the window and wonder what the people we see on the streets are thinking, standing in long lines waiting for buses that never come.

The highlight of the day comes when uncle Tony takes us all to Coppelia, the huge new ice cream place which has become the most popular place in all of revolutionary Havana. And every child knows, of course, that the Coppelia serves more than one hundred different flavours of ice cream, and that you don't need *la libreta*!

Of course, you have to queue—and it's a really long queue—so we stand in line for what seems like hours. If I wasn't living in Cuba, I would probably have spent my waiting time trying to make up my mind which of the more than one hundred flavours of ice cream I was going to order when I finally got to the long counter at the front. But I know that when it's our turn to order, there won't be one hundred flavours to pick from. Or even fifty. Or even twenty. You get promised one hundred or more flavours of ice cream but you know, from the start, that there will only be two or three to choose from. If you are lucky. In this case we are not lucky and we never expected to be. All of us walk out of the Coppelia, licking strawberry flavoured ice creams which, of course, was the only flavour left.

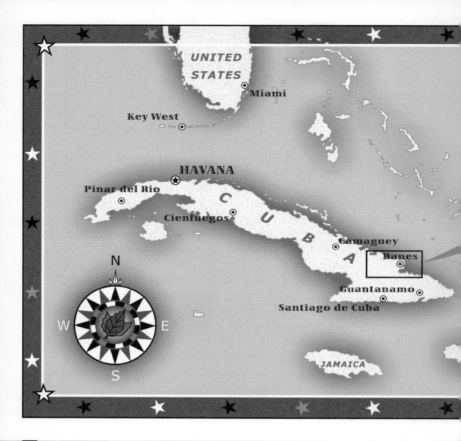

1

AREA ENLARGED

1 When Fidel Castro and his *barbudos* entered Havana in January 1959, a majority of Cubans were supportive of change, including my parents, who watched with amazement and a little apprehension from their hometown of Banes, some fifteen hours away from the capital by road.

2 My parents getting married on 20 July 1958, at the old family house on Presidente Zayas Avenue. They are surrounded by family and friends—and full of optimism about the future.

1 Me as a baby, with my parents, in Cuba some time in late 1959 or very early 1960. Back then, the mere thought of one day having to leave Cuba for good would have seemed totally crazy.

2 This photograph must have been taken some time in late 1959 because that's me wearing a *miliciano* uniform my aunt Mirta made for me. Like almost everyone else in Cuba at the time, the normally apolitical Garcias were optimistic about the new regime. Little did we know …

3 July 1960: this is my first birthday in our house in Banes. They were happy times. From left: my uncle Papi (my mother's youngest brother); my aunt Mirta, who is carrying my cousin Tonito; my uncle Rodolfo (Aunt Mirta's husband); my father, with his Errol Flynn moustache that, he claims, used to 'drive the girls crazy!'; and my mother, already pregnant with my brother, holding me.

4   That's my brother (with the open
    book), our cousin Carrie and me. My
    mother insisted on getting shirts made
    exactly the same for her boys. In this
    case, she must have managed to find
    enough pre-revolutionary material to
    get a skirt made for my cousin, too.

5   This is me, probably aged eight or
    nine. Back then, getting your photo-
    graph taken in Cuba was quite a big
    deal as cameras became rare—and
    finding a roll of film for sale
    anywhere a minor miracle.

6   The Garcia boys on our brand new
    bicycles in downtown Banes. I don't
    have a date for the photograph but it
    must have been taken on the Day of
    the Feast of the Three Kings—*el Dia
    de los Reyes*—before 1969 when
    Fidel Castro abolished Christmas
    and *el Dia de los Reyes*.

1 A view of the Parque Cardenas, which was at the end of our street. This is where all the neighbourhood kids would congregate to discuss important issues, such as why Fidel had cancelled Christmas.

2 The Teatro Hernandez cinema. Almost every night, my brother and I would join the other kids in the neighbourhood at the Hernandez, hoping that the film on show was an escapist, capitalist, all-colour Western European one—anything other than a long, dreary, patriotic black-and-white Russian film.

3 This is the Masonic Centre—La Logia—in the street where we lived. This is where the Committee for the Defence of the Revolution ordered my mother, and all the other women in the neighbourhood, to spend their evenings picking out the best beans for export to the Soviet bloc.

4 From the very beginning, Fidel Castro used televised mass meetings in Havana to explain his version of what was happening in Cuba and, indeed, around the world. He would often speak for five and six hours straight, which amazed a boy of my age. How did he do it without notes? And without a toilet break?

5 Castro's revolutionary victory over the Batista dictatorship in Cuba is heralded on the cover of the January 1959 edition of *Time* magazine.

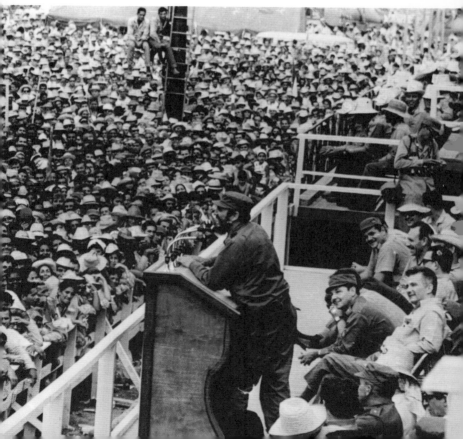

9

OPIUM OF THE MASSES

MY PARENTS are not what you'd call devout Catholics. As my father likes to point out, he and my mother didn't even get married in church! Mind you, as soon as my brother and I were born, they rushed to the Catholic church in Banes to have us both baptised. Like most Cubans do. I figure it's like a form of insurance. You know, just in case … The reason this is on my mind now is because my parents, who don't go to church, who don't pray at night and who don't even say grace when we sit down to dinner, and never will, have decided that it's the right time for my brother and me to start attending Sunday mass. This is not what I call good news.

But you don't go to mass, I say to my mother, trying to explain to her as best I can just how hypocritical her stance seems to be. Like every other school child in Cuba, I *know* that religion is bad. I know that Karl Marx called it the Opium of the Masses, a capitalist tool designed to keep the poor in their place. That's what Marx said anyway.

I also know that priests are parasites, thieves and fascists, which is why Fidel had them all shipped back to Spain as soon as he could. It's why the Revolution closed all Catholic schools, the Catholic radio stations and the Catholic newspapers. And instead of spending time on our knees praying for the resurrection of Jesus Christ, good revolutionaries now spend what used to be Holy Week celebrating the Great Anti-Imperialist Victory of Playa de Girón, which is what Cubans call the Bay of Pigs, the site where hundreds of Cuban exiles landed in 1961 to try to topple Fidel. Of course, my text-books don't call them exiles. They are called mercenaries, paid and trained by the Americans, and so lacking in true revolutionary courage that Fidel had no trouble capturing them within a couple of days of the landing. Then they were paraded in front of the television cameras for all Cubans to see what a mercenary looked like, before being sent to prison until the United States agreed to take them back in exchange for medicines.

Before my mother got this crazy idea about church, my brother and I used to get up early on Sundays, have breakfast, dress and then join every other child in the neighbourhood for the matinee at the cinema that happens to be—can you believe this—just across the plaza from the church. On Sundays the cinema shows cartoons—*los muñequitos*—and old American black and white serials like *Tarzan*, *Dick Tracy* and *The Shadow*, all dubbed into Spanish. And yes, you guessed right, the *muñequitos* and the old serials are shown at exactly the same time as Sunday mass. One of my aunts says this is deliberate, to discourage children from going to church. She says that in some other towns they have started staging puppet shows and giving away sweets and soft drinks to children just outside the church, right when mass is supposed to start. No such luck in Banes.

Still, much as I try to negotiate with my mother so we can skip mass and join our friends at the cinema instead, the response is always the same: *No, señor*. Never mind that going to church in Banes on a Sunday is either for losers or for *gusanos*, which is kind of the same thing when you think about it. Real revolutionaries don't pray; they volunteer to cut sugar cane on Sundays. Never mind that sometimes, when it is quiet inside the church—say, when everyone is supposed to be praying—you can hear the soundtrack of whatever old serial is being shown at the cinema on the other side of the square. Still, I must admit that it's very quiet and peaceful in here during mass, almost like the perfect place for a siesta. It's nothing like outside, where it is noisy and where the sun shines and the sky is so blue and so bright that I swear your eyes hurt just from looking at it.

After a time I begin to think that the smell of the incense is hypnotising me, just like Marx said it would, because slowly I start getting caught up in all this church business. So when Father Emerio suggests that my brother and I might want to become altar boys—*monaguillos*—we immediately say yes.

As the Sundays roll on, I start to enjoy coming to mass, although of course there is no way I am going to let my mother know this, let alone my school friends. I start to understand a little bit more about the Pope and all the saints and what all the prayers mean and why we have to kneel and praise the Lord. To be truthful, I am still coming to terms with the idea of God being three people at once because it makes no sense to me at all, but I no longer mind having to sit here in my *monaguillos* robes listening to Father Emerio reading in his deep voice from the Book of Matthew or the Book of John—how can you tell which is which anyway? From where I sit at the altar, I can smell the beeswax candles as they slowly melt, and hear the small choir as they sing another one of those hymns that ends up stuck in your brain for hours. And you know, they sing some of the hymns with a hint of Cuban rhythm, which is funny because you can't help but tap your feet, right here in church.

TWO OF MY best friends live just a few doors down from our house: Raulito and Fidelito. They are about the same age as my brother and me, we go to the same school, we go to the movies together, and we spend a lot of time playing together. We like their parents too. Their father knows a lot about history and geography and he has lots of carpentry tools that he uses to make toys and all sorts of wooden gadgets for his sons, while their mother is always calm and her hair is always perfect. They have a television set that works and also, believe it or not, an American car that is probably about ten years old, though it doesn't get driven all that much because petrol is rationed. And the parents never, ever fight, at least not while I am there. They seem to be the perfect family.

When I get home from school today and tell my mother I am going to Raulito's house, she says, No, not today, and I can tell something is wrong. It doesn't take long for the news to get around: Raul, the father, has disappeared. He has been gone for two or three days, and no one has heard from him, which means only one thing—he has left the country illegally. The story we hear from our neighbours is that Raul and a handful of other men from Banes spent the past few weeks secretly building a raft of some sort somewhere near the coast, stowing provisions and waiting for the right moment to put out to sea and row all the way to Florida. I know this happens because we are always hearing stories about someone somewhere who had had enough of Fidel and packed the entre family onto some rickety raft they built in secret and attempted to make it across the water. Some make it; everyone in Banes knows someone who has managed to get to the other side alive and well, if a little sunburnt. And those lucky enough to make it to *El Norte*, well, they are received with open arms by the Americans, according to one of my mother's friends. They are given piles of extra ham and cheese without having to queue, they get tender steaks for dinner every night, and a colour television set (yes, colour!), a new house with air conditioning and a pool, a new car and all the hair spray they want. They are the lucky ones.

But most of the stories we hear are of people who don't make it. Everyone knows of someone who knows someone who either drowned on the crossing because of bad weather, or who got eaten by sharks. Or they got caught by the Cuban coast guard and sent back home and straight to prison because it's illegal to leave Cuba. It's bad enough being a *gusano*, but a *gusano* who tries to leave without permission and fails is the absolute worst, particularly in a small town like Banes. Still, the stories of people trying to leave Cuba this way get told and retold and embellished by everyone in town, including my father, who listens to the ever more daring descriptions with what I assume to be a mixture of admiration and fear. *Esa gente sí que tienen cojones*, he says. Those people really have balls. But I know there is no way in the world he would even consider taking his family out of Cuba that way. There is no way in the world my mother would agree anyway.

It will be days before my friends' family confirms, with a sense of relief but also apprehension, that Raul and the others were not eaten by sharks but did make it to Florida and that they are all fine. I am happy for my friends' father, who is now eating all that ham and cheese and driving a brand new car, but I can't help feeling sorry for Raulito and Fidelito because

I know they miss their father a lot and because I know, like everyone else in our neighbourhood knows, that life is about to become a lot tougher for them.

CHE IS DEAD. The news has just come in and it has come from *El Maxímo Líder*. That's how important the news must be. Ernesto Guevara has been killed, Fidel said on television and radio, adding that Che was murdered by the CIA somewhere in Bolivia, which I know is a poor country in South America. Che was killed while fighting the Americans and their lackeys in the Bolivian army, Fidel said, and now all of Cuba is in mourning for three days to honour the man who is to be known from now on as *El Guerrillero Heroico*, or The Heroic Guerrilla.

Like every school child in Cuba, I know who Che is because we have been taught that Che was the *comandante* in charge of the rebels during the great Battle of Santa Clara, which was the turning point in the fighting by the *barbudos* against Fulgencio Batista back in 1958. I also know that later, *despues del Triunfo*, Fidel made Che a senior minister in charge of industry in the new Revolutionary Government and even sent him to Russia to get some ideas about how to run a good communist economy. Even now, you sometimes come across Cuban revolutionary *pesos* signed by Che when he was also head of the central bank back in the early days. Then, in October 1965, Fidel said on television that Che had left Cuba for good and moved to Africa looking for *nuevos campos de batallas*—new battlefields against the imperialists. No one has heard anything about Che since then, so you can see why some people are a little surprised by Fidel's announcement that Che has been killed in battle. Not in Africa but in Bolivia.

At the end of the three-day mourning period, Fidel gives another big speech. There are about a million people in the Plaza de la Revolución, the big square in Havana where all the major rallies against the Americans are held, and all the Cuban flags are at half mast. To one side of Fidel up on the podium there is a huge photograph of Che, as tall as a ten-storey apartment block, looking heroic and revolutionary.

The family of another of my neighbourhood friends have

their own theories about the death of Che—they have told him that they think Fidel is to blame. They think that Che was sent to South America by Fidel to get rid of him because he was becoming too much trouble for Fidel and for Fidel's brother Raul. So they sent him away to a place where the CIA could get at him and kill him. I know my friend's family are not communists—I think they may be *gusanos*—but I don't know where they get these crazy, counter-revolutionary ideas from. When I tell my father what I have been told he says, to my surprise, that he also thinks Fidel had something to do with Che's death. He says a lot of people in Cuba think the same way.

The thing about Che dying is that now there is nothing on television, on the radio or at the cinema but stories about Che. Even at school we have assemblies and meetings where we spend almost all day talking about Che and what a great example he is to Cuban children. At the end of all these meetings, right after we stand up to sing the national anthem—and sometimes, too, the 'Internationale'—we now say in a loud voice, *¡Seremos como el Che!* We will be like Che! Which means we will be true revolutionaries, not interested in money or material things, ready to fight the imperialists anywhere in the world. I have no problem being like Che because I know he was a revolutionary hero and it all sounds like dangerous fun, but I wish we didn't have to spend our time talking about Che so we could get back to normal, seeing movies at the cinema and listening to music on the radio again.

IN THE CINEMA newsreel there is footage of Fidel in his green uniform, which is all he ever seems to wear, holding two pineapples. But these are not ordinary pineapples. They are as big as oversized watermelons and Fidel is saying that these are the type of pineapples revolutionary scientists have developed in Cuba using the latest socialist technology. They are huge pineapples and they are supposed to be tastier and meatier and a lot more juicy than ordinary, capitalist pineapples.

As he speaks, Fidel is surrounded by the scientists in white coats and by the farmers who have come up with what I am sure are the biggest pineapples in the entire world. He says the pineapples are only in the development stage but soon enough they will be growing all over Cuba so that every family in the country can eat as much pineapple as they want. There will be so many giant pineapples we will export them all over the world.

I think it's great that Cuba now has the world's biggest and best pineapples, because this will show those Yankees what we revolutionary Cubans can do by working hard. We are good at coming up with great ideas like this, we Cubans. Mind you, I know this isn't going to impress my father. It seems as if there is nothing Fidel can do that will impress him nowadays. And I know that when I tell my mother, she will say something like, We haven't seen normal sized pineapples in the shops since 1960, which is true, of course, but does she have to be so counter-revolutionary? My father then says, I hope this giant pineapple is not like the giant strawberries Fidel was talking about last year.

Now, that comes as a shock. Giant strawberries? This is something entirely new to me. I know that when Fidel gave a speech to the Federation of Cuban Women he promised them giant cows that would provide so much milk everyone in Cuba would be drinking milk at breakfast, lunch and even dinner. In fact, there would be so much milk from the giant cows we would be selling milk to the Americans! I can just picture those embarrassed Americans having to drink Cuban milk! And yes, I know that Fidel also said Cuba would soon be producing more brie cheese and better quality brie cheese than the Europeans, but I had never, ever heard about the giant tropical strawberries.

IN BANES, no one talks about the past. Or at least not in a good way. In public, everyone talks about how bad things were *antes del Triunfo*, before Fidel came down from the mountains with his beard and his guns and kicked out Batista and his corrupt politicians, the American Mafia and the rich landowners who exploited the poor workers. We get those stories all the time at school and on television and in the papers because that is the history of Cuba. It will be many years before I recognise that this is a heavily edited version of the history of Cuba, but even at my age I suspect there must be another side to the story because I have heard my mother's aunts, who are so old they all have white hair, talk about the good old days in Banes. That's what they say—the good old days in Banes.

One of my mother's aunts, Juana, who is short and wiry and always smoking and coughing, usually at the same time, tells me that there was a time when there was plenty of money to go around in the town and lots of places in which to spend all that money. It was a time, she says with a wink, when everyone in Banes was a supporter of Batista because, after all, Batista was a Banes boy. Which is news to me.

If you ask her, Aunt Juana will tell you that Batista was born just outside the town in 1901, and that his parents were very poor and of mixed race—they had some white, some black and even some Chinese blood, which meant that he was a *mulato*. And a clever one, too, she says, raising one of her eyebrows. He left Banes in 1921 to join the army and within a few years he had been promoted to a military stenographer with the rank of sergeant. He was attached to the Army Supreme Command, which wasn't bad for a poor kid from a small town in a corner of Oriente province.

Batista was popular and crafty and ambitious, and in 1933 he became involved in a rebellion that was to topple the dictator of the day, Gerardo Machado. A year later, Batista was at it again. He led what became known as the Revolution of the Sergeants, a revolt against the temporary government that had proved to be highly inefficient and unpopular. From that moment on, Batista, who had been promoted to head of the army, became a major political figure in Cuba. Because he was from peasant stock one of his many nicknames was *El Guajirito de Banes*, the Little Peasant Boy from Banes, which wasn't meant to be much of a compliment. If you believe Aunt Juana, many people in Banes were very happy to be supporters of his—*batistianos*—even though, she says, Batista was no saint—*no era un santo*—and imprisoned and tortured anyone who opposed him.

When he was the strongman of Cuba, Batista would regularly visit Banes. Wearing an immaculate suit, his friends and supporters trailing behind him, he would shower everyone with money, says Aunt Juana. It wasn't his money, of course, but government money which in effect was the same thing. He would visit his old home town and make speeches and have a big dinner with the most important people in town at the old Club Banes. Every time Batista visited he left money behind to build something new, like a hospital, or to pave some streets. But now, says Aunt Juana, no one in Banes admits to ever having been a *batistiano*. Now no one talks about Batista in public, except to say what a tyrant he was.

Then again, no one in Banes talks about the times Fidel also used to visit the town. *El Maxímo Líder* was born only about one hundred kilometres away in an area called Biran, where his father owned a huge sugar cane plantation. Fidel even married a Banes girl he had met at university, Mirta Diaz Balart, whose family was one of the best known and most powerful in town—they worked for the United Fruit Company and, needless to say, were prominent supporters of Batista. The young couple married in the local church, the same church where my brother and I attend mass, and Aunt Juana tells me it was quite a wedding, with lots of rich people attending and half the town coming out to see the newly-weds. It was big news in the local paper, too, and everyone talked about the wedding for many days. Fidel and Mirta had a baby, Fidelito, but it wasn't long before the marriage collapsed and Mirta and her family left for Miami. Nowadays, of course, no one talks about it, not in the papers, nor on television or radio, and certainly not on the streets of Banes. Strange town.

MY UNCLE Tony, my mother's brother who took us around Havana in his Lada when we visited there, is in Banes. He comes to Banes a couple of times a year to see his sisters and, especially, to see my cousin Tonito, his son from his first marriage.

My uncle Tony is tall, handsome and, as far as I can see, the most worldly of all my uncles. Unlike my parents, he reads lots of books and he enjoys talking about things that don't normally get talked about around our dinner table, like history, which is, you may have gathered, my favourite subject at school. The other thing that sets my uncle Tony apart from the rest of the family—and in fact from most other Cubans—is that he gets to travel overseas, without having to wait years for Fidel's permission. I never know exactly what his job title is or what the job entails, but without fail my uncle goes away every year to fraternal countries in Eastern Europe and even to friendly capitalist countries like Spain and France. I think he has even been to Italy, and you don't get more exotic than Italy when you come from Banes.

My uncle is the one member of the family everyone seems to turn to when they need help, because he knows exactly what to do and whom to talk to to get things sorted out. He is the Mister Fix-it, and I can tell that my mother and all my aunts worship the ground he walks on. When he visits he never talks about politics, even though I assume he is a member of the Communist Party, as those really important jobs are normally open only to members of the Party. I think the fact that he doesn't talk about politics is one of the reasons my father gets along so well with him, even though my father is not a communist. Or even a half-decent socialist.

Every time my uncle comes to Banes, he bring presents. This time my uncle Tony has brought chocolates from somewhere in Hungary, some chewing gum and a book for me from Spain. Even the smallest present from overseas feels like a window opening onto the outside, a window that exposes an impressionable child to a very different and unattainable world.

Even better than all that, my uncle has brought my brother and me a pullover each from Europe. These are not ordinary socialist pullovers, either. They are soft to touch and they seem like the most sophisticated and luxurious clothing we have ever come across, which they probably are. There is just one problem—they are woollen pullovers, which means we are wearing them now in the middle of a Cuban summer and as soon as we put them on, we start to sweat and get itchy and uncomfortable. But they look so good, so foreign, that I don't care.

My uncle Tony has also brought some presents for my teenage cousin July. It's a Beatles record and my cousin couldn't be happier. I don't know much about The Beatles because as far as I can recall I have never heard their music or even their name on the radio. But my cousin obviously has because she is thrilled.

It's not difficult to see why: the music is catchy and exotic. And you can dance to this music, which is more than I can say for those protest songs and *Nueva Trova* music they play on the radio almost all the time now. Instead of *guarachas* and *boleros* and *rumbas*, all you get on radio are protest songs. All of my friends and I, sophisticated critics that we are, agree that protest songs may be revolutionary but they are also boring, and who in their right mind wants to dance to a song about some poor *campesino* family in Guatemala that is being exploited, maimed or murdered by bloodthirsty Yankees?

A friend of my cousin says The Beatles are banned from Cuban radio because they are considered a bad influence on teenagers, who will be seduced into capitalism and decadence by 'I Want to Hold Your Hand' and 'Love Me Do'. Instead of volunteering to cut sugar cane or attending meetings to discuss Marx, young Cubans who listen to The Beatles will be corrupted and spend their time sitting around doing nothing, letting their hair grow long and reading subversive, capitalist books. All of which will make me wonder, years later, what was my uncle Tony thinking? What was he trying to say when he brought back the Beatles record for my cousin July?

10

IN EVERY BARRIO, REVOLUTION

EVERY NEIGHBOURHOOD in Cuba, whether you live in a big city like Havana or a small, forgotten town like Banes, has its own Committee for the Defence of the Revolution, known to everyone as the CDR or *el Comite*. Or sometimes *los chivatos*, which is Cuban slang for someone who snitches. A dobber. Of course, you never call them that in public unless you are dumb or looking for trouble and, to be honest, there are plenty of other ways to get into trouble in Cuba without having to bother the hardworking revolutionaries of the local CDR.

In our neighbourhood, like in all others, *el Comite* rules supreme. They were originally set up in 1960 to defend the Revolution. Neighbours would join to help patrol the local streets at night, keeping an eye on anyone stupid enough to attempt to plant a bomb or paint anti-Castro slogans on the walls, which happened every now and then in the first year or so after *el Triunfo*. Then the CDRs were used to organise whole streets of volunteers to go and cut sugar cane on Sundays, or to join huge marches to protest against those Yankees who wanted to kill Fidel with exploding cigars. But in time, *el Comite* has become much more than that, as every Cuban knows.

Nothing gets done without *el Comite* having a say. For instance, if you want to complain about dogs barking late into the night, you go to *el Comite*. If you want someone to come and help you paint your house, you go and talk to *el Comite*, or if you are having problems at home with your kids, well, you go to *el Comite* too, and someone there will sit you down in a hard, straight-backed wooden chair and give you a little explanation about why you should obey your mother and work hard and study hard and learn how to use a rifle so you can defend the Revolution. If you want to travel to Havana it's wise to check with *el Comite* first since you will need permission to take time off work and to get a bus ticket. Need to vaccinate your baby? The CDR will arrange it for you. Same if you are thinking of changing jobs which, in reality, is almost impossible in Cuba.

A lot of the time you don't have to tell *el Comite* anything—they know even before you do. That's how good they are. They come to your house and ask you why you had so many visitors last night, and what they were doing until so late. They knock on your door and ask you to turn the music down because, *compañero*, we are all going to cut sugar cane tomorrow morning on the dot of five—you are coming, aren't you? And the CDR people always know all the gossip in the neighbourhood—who is sleeping with whom, which marriage is on the rocks, who is having an abortion. It's that kind of organisation and, not surprisingly, it tends to attract and nurture the nosiest people in every neighbourhood.

It's the same if you want to snitch on your neighbours—or on your parents. You go to the woman from *el Comite* and tell her that your parents are saying things they shouldn't about Fidel, and then she will do *her* revolutionary duty and tell the police and then, before you know it, there is a *miliciano* on the doorstep asking questions, which is never a good thing.

In our neighbourhood the CDR is headed by a woman who lives a few houses up from us, just around the corner. I don't really know—no one does—how she was selected or by whom, but naturally she is *de los duros*—a hardline communist— which may explain why we refer to her as *La Compañera*. My mother says that before her elevation, *La Compañera* was someone with whom you exchanged polite, neighbourly conversation every now and then, but no more. Since *el Triunfo*, though, she has become a very important person in our little corner of the world.

She always wears her militia uniform and she loves to gossip with the neighbours, or at least those neighbours she considers ideologically committed. It's not that she is rude to my parents, nothing like that, but you know she is keeping an eye on us. Which scares me, because I know very well that my parents are not good revolutionaries. You see, my father never puts his name down for volunteer work in the sugar cane fields, saying he works hard enough through the week without having to give up his Sundays as well. Besides, he says, half the time is spent not cutting sugar cane at all but listening to speeches by some local Communist Party leader about how terrific things are in Cuba—*¡vamos bien!*—and how much, much better they could be if only everyone worked a little bit harder and the Americans stopped planning to invade the island.

The truth is, though, that if you want to get anywhere in Cuba you need to do volunteer work, because whether you do or not is the type of detail that goes straight into your personal files: the *expediente laboral* if you are a working-age adult, or the *expediente escolar* if, like me, you are at school. Everything you do and everything you say goes into your personal files, including anything you may have said that someone may have misinterpreted as being disloyal to the Revolution, which is why my mother always tells us to be careful about what we say: *Ten cuidado con lo que dices, niño.*

Even school children understand how important the *expediente* is because it is used time and again to decide your future, like whether you are going to go to university or not when you finish school. A revolutionary *expediente* is essential if you want to join the Communist Youth Union, known as La Juventud, which is the first step to becoming a real communist, a member of the Communist Party, which in turn is the first step to gaining access to special shops in Havana where, I have it on good authority, you can buy ham and cheese and chewing gum and other stuff that you can never find in the local *bodega*, no matter how long or how often you queue.

The worst thing about the *expediente* is that you never really know what it says because you never get to see it, even if you ask politely. You know they have written things about you in the file but you don't ever find out what. You just hope it's all good. If it's all bad, you will eventually find out.

THERE ARE two cinemas in Banes: the Hernández, which is just at the end of our street, and at the other end of town, diagonally across from the Catholic church, the Heredia, where they show the Sunday matinées I no longer get to see because I am in church. We go to the Hernández almost every night because it's the closest. We don't have a television set so it's the next best alternative. Besides, it's cheap and is one of the few things in Cuba that isn't rationed, so you can go as many times as you want. Movies change every night, except for really popular films like *Fantomas*, which are shown two or even three nights in a row, but never longer than three nights because by then just about everyone in town would have seen it.

Fantomas is big in Cuba, and not just with children my age. It's weird, of course, because nothing could be further from the reality of revolutionary Cuba than these French films starring French actor Jean Marais. He plays Fandor, a sophisticated jewel thief who spends his time stealing from fashionable apartments in Paris, and attending lavish parties in elegant palaces somewhere in the countryside. Up there on the screen the women all look like magazine models and they wear shiny, expensive clothes and huge diamonds made for stealing. They are always jumping in and out of those long limousines that no boy in this cinema—no boy in Banes—is ever likely to see in real life. I think that's why the cinema is always full when *Fantomas* films are shown. It's funny of course, because they are not very revolutionary films at all.

The more popular the film, the longer it will run, which is another way of saying that Russian movies—of which there are lots—never get shown a second night. As far as I can see, using all the critical faculties of a pre-pubescent boy in unsophisticated Banes, the problem with the Soviet films is that they are set in a world where everyone is poor or hungry and very unhappy. They are what my aunt Nidia would call depressing—*deprimente*—or dreary. Unlike *Fantomas*.

It's strange what makes it onto the screen. Fidel says capitalists are bad and decadent and want to destroy the Revolution, but it seems that many of the films we see at night are from capitalist countries, including old American films that have been pirated, dubbed and, in theory at least, carefully vetted for subliminal anti-revolutionary messages. Even more weird is the number of films we see from capitalist countries in Europe: comedies from England like *Doctor in Clover* and *Morecambe and Wise*, soapy Spanish musicals and melodramas, and French action films with Jean Paul Belmondo, in which men with guns are always driving fast cars and kissing beautiful French women on the lips. There is nothing very revolutionary about these films, you can tell, and yet they have been approved as suitable. It's only years later that I realise how peculiar it is that the Spanish films that get the okay from the anti-communist censors in 1960s Spain are the same films that get the go-ahead from communist censors in 1960s Cuba.

THERE ARE not too many books in our house. My parents are not great readers, which my mother says is the result of her never having gone to secondary school—few girls of her age and class would have done so in a town like Banes when she was growing up. Not that there is a shortage of books in revolutionary Cuba. It's just that the choice is a little limited.

I walk into *La Marquesita*, which is the biggest of the stationery and book shops in Banes, and you can see that there are plenty of books on the shelves. Most of them have been written by Fidel or about Fidel, or are about how bad things were before Fidel. For just a few cents you can buy books about Che, *El Guerrillero Heroico*, as he has become universally known since his death in Bolivia, and books by Che, including his thoughts on guerrilla warfare, which we must all study at school but which everyone agrees is the dullest book of the lot.

Then there are books about the Glorious October Revolution, and plenty of Russian biographies of Vladimir Ilych Lenin, which you can buy for next to nothing. They are not fancy books—the covers are dull and the pages inside are badly glued together, so that they come apart almost as soon as you walk out of the shop. This is not a bad thing since by the time you get home with your Russian tome of Lenin's *What Is to Be Done* you can just make a hole through the loose pages and pin them up next to the toilet bowl for when you run out of toilet paper. I know, I know: it's not a very revolutionary thing to do but, believe me, even communists need toilet paper.

I have found that the best place for books in Banes is the municipal library, not far from our house. I feel right at home in there, sitting at one of the long tables in the middle of the room. The lights are bright and it's so quiet it is almost un-Cuban, and the lady behind the counter looks stern at first but later she smiles at me every time I walk in, as if secretly welcoming another convert into her little world of reading.

And once you make friends with the librarian, she will always alert you when new books arrive from Havana, especially books from overseas. It's in here that I discover the Tintin books, the fantastically rich and complex comics by the Belgian cartoonist Hergé, which the librarian says, in almost reverential tones, have been imported from Spain, as if explaining why the pages in these colourful books are so much thicker and more luxurious than the Russian-printed biographies of Lenin and Engels. And here I also discover *Huckleberry Finn*, published and printed in Spain although everyone knows it is an American story.

I soon realise that these Spanish-printed books are the jewels in the library's collection, speaking as they do of an impossibly distant world in which the pages of books are very white, very shiny and smell and feel very expensive. That is why you can read these books in here for as long as you want—as I do—but you can't borrow many of them. I also realise in the way boys sometimes do that what makes the Tintin books so attractive to me is not just the quality of the paper and the colour of the illustrations and the fact that these books have travelled all the way from a distant country—a capitalist country, no less. It's the fact that if they have any political message to impart, it totally eludes me. They are just fun to read. In revolutionary Cuba, that is quite a rarity.

11

THE GREAT REVOLUTIONARY OFFENSIVE

YEARS LATER, when I am older and living outside Cuba, I realise that 1968 was what historians like to describe as a momentous year in the capitalist West—a year of student demonstrations across much of Western Europe and of upheaval in the United States as the Vietnam War escalated and so, too, the number of American casualties. There was change in the air even in Eastern Europe, with the Czech Communist Party moving towards what they called 'socialism with a human face', to the dismay of the hard old men in Moscow who promptly sent in tanks to quash what would become known as the Prague Spring. In Cuba, 1968 is also a memorable year, and not just for the García family.

On 13 March Fidel addresses students at Havana University, an address that is broadcast everywhere. You can hear his voice wherever you go in Banes, up and down the streets, booming out of television sets or from the radio. Whenever Fidel speaks, everyone else shuts up, and so far he has been speaking for hours. This time, Fidel is talking again about wanting to build a new man—*un hombre nuevo*—which still makes me think *El Maxímo Líder* must have some ingenious socialist plan to build human robots. But I know that what Fidel is really talking about is me, and my brother and all my friends in the neighbourhood. He wants to educate us—the future of Cuba, he says—to become the new men of tomorrow: hardworking, uncomplaining, not interested in money or material things, and ready to fight against the imperialists anywhere in the world. Heroic men, just like Che.

The more Fidel speaks, the more animated he seems to get and the clearer his message becomes: it's obvious that he is a very, very disappointed man. Fidel says Cubans are far too undisciplined, too unproductive, too busy spending money on rum and beer, listening to *boleros* and *rumbas* all day. Too much time dancing in the streets. Is this any way to build socialism? We are so unproductive, he says, we are now being left behind by our communist brothers and sisters in Eastern Europe. But that is about to change.

It doesn't take long to discover what Fidel has in mind. It's called the Great Revolutionary Offensive—*la Ofensiva Revolucionaria*.

Now, Fidel says if we all work harder, he will abolish money some time in the future because money is bad. Boys with long hair are bad, too, and so is tight, provocative clothing like miniskirts, because they only encourage young Cubans to become lazy and decadent. Dancing to foreign music and reading capitalist books and magazines that find their way into Cuba are also bad because these books and magazines spread dangerous imperialist thoughts. From now on, everyone has to become true revolutionaries. What's more, if you don't agree or if you refuse to become a better revolutionary, then the police will come to your house, tell you to pack up your things and send you to cut sugar cane in the countryside until you see the error of your ways and start behaving like a socialist. It's called rectification, which sounds like very serious business to me.

Now Fidel is saying he is worried about bars. He says that nearly ten years after *el Triunfo*, there are still 955 bars in Havana owned by bartenders who are capitalists at heart and who just want to make money selling alcohol to people who should be cutting sugar cane instead. Bar owners don't believe in socialism, he says. This has got to stop. Everyone in the audience is now applauding and shouting, Fidel!, Fidel! probably because they think the speech is over, but Fidel doesn't stop there.

He is also worried about people who own hot food stands, known as *timbiriches* in Cuba. Fidel says an investigation by the Revolution has found that 95.1 per cent of people who own these *timbiriches* are *gusanos*. I am amazed Fidel knows so much about hot food stands but that is the way it is with Fidel: he knows lots about everything. He asks the audience: Are we going to construct socialism or are we going to construct hot food stands? And the audience yells out: Socialism! Socialism! Socialism! And that's when Fidel decides, right there and then, that all bars and all *timbiriches* and all private shops will be closed down. It's at that moment that Fidel decides that the Revolution will eliminate all private trade.

I have no idea what Fidel's announcement will mean for my parents and their shop. I know they are not very good revolutionaries at home, and I know they have probably thought about leaving Cuba, and I know they sometimes say capitalist things, but it's not as if they are out in the street looking for trouble or attacking the Revolution.

On the radio over the next few days, all the talk is about this Great Revolutionary Offensive, and how we must all be vigilant against people who may be a danger to the Revolution, even here in Banes where everyone knows everyone else. If we see any trouble-makers, we must report them at once to the Committee for the Defence of the Revolution.

My friend, who seems to know everything that's going on, says his mother told him that her cousin who lives in Havana told her that police had conducted major raids, or *redadas*, on famous people, including well-known writers whose names mean nothing to me, and singers. Even some television presenters, believe it or not, were taken away because they were too *efeminado*, which is the polite term Cubans use when they don't want to say *maricones*, which is what everyone else calls homosexuals. If you are an *efeminado*, my friend says, then watch out because sooner or later they will find you, cut your long hair and take away all your hippie music and force you to walk like a real man.

WHEN I GET back from school today, my father is home instead of being at work in the shop, and I can tell from the moment I walk in through the door that he is not in a good mood. He is talking to himself, saying things like, *¿Quien lo hiba a pensar?*—Who would have thought it? He tells us that when he turned up at the shop this morning there were two *milicianos* at the front, one on each side of the door, carrying guns, and looking determined. When my father said, Good morning, what's going on here?, they called him *compañero*, which my father thinks is always a bad sign, and then they told him that on the orders of the Revolutionary Government they were taking over his shop. Not just his shop, really. Every privately owned shop across Banes and the whole of Cuba—the Revolution is taking over 55,000 small shops and bars and cafes that are still owned and run by their capitalist owners because this is all part of the Great Revolutionary Offensive.

Now Fidel's speech makes a lot more sense to me. Not to my father. He can't believe it. He says when the *milicianos* said, Hand over your keys, he could tell they were not joking, so he handed over the keys and asked them, What now?, and they looked at him and said, *Compañero*, go home and wait for further instructions.

If my father is incredulous, my mother is totally beaten. Humiliated. She has her own story to tell: when she turned up at the shop to see what was going on, because she could not believe what my father had just told her, the *milicianos* were still there but she was met by a woman called Albita, who used to work in the shop some years ago. Albita, who was wearing her olive green *miliciana* uniform, was standing by the door looking quite satisfied with herself. When my mother tried to enter the shop Albita stood in front of her, placed her hands on her ample hips and said, *Compañera*, this shop now belongs to the People and you—here she pointed at my mother—you will no longer be allowed to exploit your workers! *¡Se acabó la explotación!* Which would have been more than enough for my mother to burst into tears of frustration and anger but she didn't because she was not going to give Albita the satisfaction of seeing her cry. So she turned around and went back home, too.

Can you believe it? she asks my father. Can you believe that anyone would accuse *me*, who has worked so hard to build that shop up, of exploiting my employees? She sounds angry but you can tell she has given up.

There is no consolation in knowing that she is not the only shopkeeper to lose her shop. All the other small shops in Banes now belong to the People too. Like Bar Feria, where my father celebrated the birth of his first-born, and the paper shop La Marquesita where they sell books about Fidel, and the Isla de Cuba hardware store and the pastry shop next door and, of course, the hot food stand near the park. That is gone too. No more capitalism.

As far as my father is concerned, this is the last straw. He has had enough. For nearly ten years, he says, sounding more incredulous than upset, he has been hanging on, hoping that things would change. But he knows there will be no change. He is determined that we leave Cuba—which is easier said than done. My uncle Rodolfo and my aunt Mirta, who now live in New York, have been encouraging my parents to make the decision for months. We have saved up the money, they say, we will lend you what you need for the airfares. Start the paperwork!

All that time, my mother has resisted. She doesn't want to leave Cuba because she doesn't want to leave her brothers and her other sisters behind, probably for ever. She knows what happens when you apply to leave Cuba: we will officially become *gusanos* and my father will be sent away almost immediately to a labour camp somewhere far from Banes to cut sugar cane for the Revolution for at least two or three years, or until someone in Havana says to Fidel, *Comandante en Jefe*, you can let these people go now; they have paid their dues.

She knows she will be left alone at home with two children who can be quite a handful at the best of times. She knows it will become even more difficult to find food on her own. She knows she will miss my father. But now, the decision has been made for her, although it is a decision no one will know about for some time yet. She is still reluctant but she is giving in, bit by bit—taking the shop away from her, the shop she worked so hard to build up, and then, she says in disbelief, to be humiliated as she has been in her own shop, in her own town, *¡Dios mio!* This could well be the end of the revolutionary road for my normally non-political mother.

I know what my parents are talking about and I know they will argue about it in the months ahead because my mother will change her mind and then change it again, but I keep quiet because neither of them has even thought of asking me, let alone my brother, whether we want to leave Cuba. I am glad they don't ask because if they did, I would say no, I would tell them that I don't want to go to no stinking capitalist country, thank you, because I am happy where I am. I like my school and my house and my friends and I don't want to leave. I don't want other kids in school calling me a *gusano*. I want to be like everyone else.

MY FATHER no longer owns or works in what used to be his and my mother's shop but the Revolution has found him a new job: he has been made foreman at the biscuit and noodle factory in Banes. He thinks it's funny because while he is a very good shopkeeper, he has absolutely no experience in running a biscuit and noodle factory. But that's the way decisions are made in Cuba, he says: they take you out of a job you can do and put you in a job you have no idea about. And then Fidel complains about low productivity!

My brother and I are mighty pleased with the new job, though. It means that every day my father arrives home with a big brown paper bag full of biscuits. No queues and no *libreta*. My father is not alone in this. He tells my mother that half the biscuits and noodles that are produced at the factory every day simply disappear, which means the people working there must be taking a lot of biscuits and noodles home to their families. Cubans don't call it stealing. They call it *resolviendo*; it means something like 'making do'. And if you have ever had to queue for two or three hours in the sun, with no hat or umbrella to protect you, so you can buy whatever is on offer that day, then you'd understand exactly what *resolviendo* means too. That's what my father says.

Meanwhile, my mother has been ordered to return to the shop she used to own, where she must report for revolutionary duty carrying on as if nothing had happened. It's not something my very fatalistic mother is happy about, especially when she gets there and finds that Albita is now the new boss, *la Administradora*. This is what has happened to every one of the shops taken over during the Great Revolutionary Offensive: the owners now report to someone like Albita, who is wearing her *miliciana* outfit just to prove she really is the Boss and gets to tell my mother what to do.

There is just one small consolation as far as my mother is concerned. Within weeks the shop will close. There is nothing to sell so there are no customers coming in through the door. And even in socialist Cuba, it's not a good thing to have an empty shop with nothing to sell. So one morning when my mother arrives to report for her revolutionary duty, she is told the shop is now closed. They put a big lock on the door and post a *miliciano* at the front to make sure no one breaks in and steals the light fittings and the glass cabinets and the timber shelving. And just like that, *Retacería García* ceases to be.

RICHARD NIXON has been elected President of the United States, which means that he is automatically an enemy of the Revolution, like all other presidents of the United States. His name is everywhere, on radio and in the *Granma* newspaper where they have replaced the X in Nixon with a funny sign that I soon discover is a swastika.

According to *Granma*, which is the only daily newspaper in Cuba, Nixon wants to crush the Revolution and return Cuba to the days when it was an American colony. Nothing good can come from *El Norte*, if you believe *Granma*—the poor are always being exploited or starving to death. Not that we buy *Granma*, which describes itself under the big, red title as the Official Organ of the Communist Party. My father refuses to buy it because, he says, while it costs only a couple of cents, it's all rubbish. Propaganda!

Much as I enjoy reading, I suspect my father may be right: there are not a lot of pictures in *Granma*, no comics and no news about what Los Zafiros are up to, even though they are the most popular musical group in Cuba today and famous all over Eastern Europe. Instead, there are reports about how an electricity plant in the city of Cienfuegos has met its production target; about heroic Vietnamese peasants killing a truckload of Yankee soldiers with a few bamboo sticks; and about how thousands of poor people sleep on the streets of Washington while the rich spend millions of dollars on dog food. Every few days Fidel gives one of his four- or five-hour speeches and the following morning *Granma* publishes the entire transcript, which fills up most of the paper.

Sometimes my parents relent and buy a copy or two of *Granma*, but only when we run out of toilet paper. My father cuts the pages up into squares and sticks them on a nail by the toilet bowl.

We don't have a television set at home and my brother and I think this is the worst thing ever. My friend's mother got her television set because she is a good revolutionary. That is the only way to get a television set in Cuba, or a new radio or lounge chairs, or the most prized possession of all: a new Polish refrigerator. You can't buy these things—the Revolution gives them to you, thanks to Fidel, but only if you deserve them. If you become the most productive worker in the factory, or if you cut the most sugar cane in the district, or if you are the busiest nurse in the local hospital, then someone in the Communist Party nominates you as an exceptional worker and eventually you get your East German television set to take home, or even a holiday at Varadero beach.

I know my father gets all the news he needs at night, after dinner, when he turns on the radio very, very low and fiddles with the knobs until, as if by magic, he gets the Voice of America, which I am shocked to discover later is an American station! Even I know it's illegal to listen to American radio stations but it must be worth the trouble because my father says listening to the Voice of America is the only way to know what is really happening in Cuba.

Despite my mother's protests, my father has been listening to the Voice of America again, which says that Russian tanks have invaded Czechoslovakia and that the Czech people want to withdraw from the Warsaw Pact, which every school child in Cuba knows is the pact that protects the Soviet Union and the other fraternal countries of Eastern Europe from Richard Nixon. I know they are twisting the truth because their story is very different to the story we get to hear on Cuban radio, where Fidel explains what really happened. He says Czechoslovakia was being taken over by liberals and imperialists who are, as you know, the enemies of socialism. That is why the real communists in Prague asked the Soviet Union to come in with their tanks and help them protect socialism from the Americans. Fidel says the Cuban Revolution and the entire Cuban people—*el Pueblo entero*— is right behind the Soviet Union. Obviously, no one has bothered to ask my father.

12

A MILICIANO AT THE DOOR

A *MILICIANO* is at the door, which is never a good thing in Cuba. Both my parents know immediately what the visit is all about—the police are now aware we have decided to leave Cuba.

The essential first step once you decide to leave is to get a relative or a friend overseas willing to deposit money into your account in Cuba because you will need that money to secure plane tickets. You can't even start the paperwork officially unless you have the money for the airfares, and the tickets must be paid for with capitalist dollars rather than revolutionary Cuban *pesos*. So my aunt Mirta and my uncle

Rodolfo went to their bank in New York and deposited over US\$3,000—a fortune, says my father—into our family's bank account in Cuba. As soon as that happened, the bank told the police, which they are obliged to do, and that is why there is a *miliciano* standing at our front door.

Making the decision to leave Cuba has not been an easy one for my parents, especially for my mother, who is torn between wanting to get her sons out of Cuba and not wanting to leave behind the rest of her family. She also knows that applying to leave Cuba could compromise her brothers, especially my uncle Papi, who is moving fast up the Communist Party ladder in our province. So, she has been avoiding the inevitable, keeping quiet the news of our decision to leave, which has been quite a feat since my father has had to start organising the endless round of paperwork, and we have all had to have our photographs taken for our passports. But there is no hiding any more. Now, the police are here and my father is confirming that, yes, we have applied to leave Cuba. My uncles and aunts will find out soon enough and so, too, will my teachers, my friends at school, the neighbours, the Committee for the Defence of the Revolution, and the rest of Banes. We are now officially *gusanos*.

The *miliciano* at the door is polite but firm. He tells my parents that he and one of his colleagues will come back later to *pasar balance*: to take stock of everything we own, from the plates and glasses in the kitchen cabinets to the pillows in the bedrooms. Every single item is going to be noted down, a meticulous process that will take hours.

Then the policeman turns to my father and tells him that he should pack up his working clothes, his toothbrush, too, some food and work boots and present himself tomorrow morning, on the dot of four, when it is still dark, down at the Parque Cárdenas. As happens with anyone who applies to leave, what this means is that my father has now lost his job at the noodle and biscuit factory. From now on he will have to work in the countryside, along with hundreds of other *gusanos*, until Fidel decides my father has paid his debt to the Revolution and is free to depart.

I knew this moment was coming; it's what happened to my

friend Jorgito's father. One day he was at home, sitting on his veranda in one of those old-fashioned rocking chairs that Cubans like so much, and the next he was gone. Off to an *albergue*—a labour camp—somewhere in Oriente province. I knew this would happen to my father too, but still the news comes as a huge shock to all of us, especially my mother, whose face is now contorted in anguish as she tries, without success, to hold back her tears.

Later in the day, the police come knocking again, as promised, except they are accompanied by *La Compañera* from the Committee for the Defence of the Revolution, who can barely hide her excitement. I imagine she is thinking to herself, I was right, the Garcías were *gusanos* after all. As they move from room to room, making sure they don't miss anything that belongs to the People, I can see both my parents getting increasingly anxious. I know my father feels humiliated too, which is probably what this process is intended to achieve.

One thing is made absolutely clear to us: when the time comes to leave Cuba, we can take with us only one suitcase per person. No money, no jewellery, no valuables of any type. All that belongs to the Revolution now, and if we are caught taking valuables out then, well, we are in big trouble because they can turn us around right there at the airport, snatch our airplane tickets from our very hands and send us back to Banes.

Now, when the police finally leave and my father starts to pack up his *mochila*, his backpack, it hits me that we won't see him again for quite a while, that this is the new life we have to get accustomed to, at least for the next year if not longer. And I wonder how my father is going to cope in the countryside. He was born in the countryside and he is used to hard work, but it's still a long way from supervising other people making noodles and biscuits to having to get up at five every morning to go out and cut sugar cane under the hot Cuban sun all day long—and for no pay.

We have no idea where he is going or for how long, and we won't find out until he gets there. And when he gets to wherever he is taken, he will not be allowed to leave. He can write to us and we can go and visit him on some weekends, depending on how far he is taken, but he is not allowed to leave the labour camp, except once every forty-five days when he gets a five-day pass.

How will my mother and my brother and I cope without him at home? I know my mother is strong but I am still worried that without my father we won't have enough money to buy food when it's our turn at the *bodega*. I worry that we will starve to death. I worry that there won't be anyone at home big enough and strong enough to protect my mother and my brother and me. I feel like crying but I don't because I can still remember very clearly what my uncle Rogelio said to me last night when we visited to tell him and my aunt Adelina the news. He looked at me and said, using his serious tone of voice, Now your father is going away, you will have to look after your mother and your brother ... You are the man of the house now. And I stood there, looking at him and wanting to cry right there and then because, let me tell you, they were the scariest words I had ever heard.

MY AUNT NIDIA has decided she wants to leave Cuba too. She says she can't stand it any more and she wants to get out as soon as possible. This is not good news for my father. In fact, he thinks it is a disaster as my aunt Nidia will apply to leave Cuba with us, as part of our family group—*nucleo familiar*—and he is not happy. Not that he can do much about it, as my aunt Mirta and uncle Rodolfo in New York have already sent the money for the plane tickets for all five of us.

My father and my aunt don't get along. In truth, my aunt doesn't seem to get along with too many members of her extended family. She is in her late forties, and she was married once, but my mother says that did not last very long and ended in divorce, as everyone in the family kind of expected, apparently. Now, she lives in the old family house on Presidente Zayas Avenue, with my uncle Rogelio and my aunt Adelina and my cousin July but in truth she seems to spend a lot of time dressed up as if she is going to a party, visiting her many friends around Banes and gossiping about other people in the town.

I think my aunt is great fun because she is unpredictable,

doing things you would never expect her to do, like taking me out for ice cream but refusing to queue, instead walking right up to the counter and demanding to be served immediately because, *por favor, señor*, can't you see that this boy here is too small to be waiting for hours just so he can get an ice cream? Somehow, my aunt Nidia always gets away with it and then as we walk away from the ice cream place, she looks down at me and winks, and then takes out of her bag a pressed, white linen handkerchief that smells of expensive eau de cologne from *antes del Triunfo*, and wipes my chin clean.

My aunt sometimes scares me, too, because I have seen her get very angry and start shouting and threatening. She fights with my father, over even the smallest, silliest things, and she always ends the fight with a comment about how my mother made such a mistake marrying him, which of course only makes my father angrier. Then my aunt turns on her heels and walks away as if the whole thing was finished and she had been declared the winner.

So I can understand why my father isn't happy that my aunt Nidia is now part of our *nucleo familiar* because he knows that my aunt is not the type you would call discreet, which is what you must be when you officially become a *gusano*—you shut up because everything you say will be reported back to someone and that someone has the power to take away your passport or your permission papers, and keep you in Cuba. But this doesn't worry my aunt one bit. She still spends her time visiting her friends and gossiping, criticising the Revolution and even Fidel, which sends my mother into a state of panic because you just never know who might be listening. Are you crazy? my mother says to my aunt. How can you say those things? And in public! Don't you know that saying those things might mean we don't get permission to leave? Then my aunt turns on her heels and walks away as usual.

I know it won't take long before my father and my aunt clash again—and it's not something I look forward to since I can already tell that my totally unpredictable aunt Nidia is destined to do something silly or say something silly that will result in Fidel refusing to let us leave Cuba.

WE NOW KNOW where my father has been sent. He is at a labour camp in an area called La Gabina, which is near the town of Bayamo. It's so far from Banes and transport is so bad that he could just as easily be in Russia, according to my mother, who is not coping well with the fact that her husband has been taken away from her. My brother and I also miss him, and we keep asking my mother whether she has any idea when he is coming back home. She doesn't know but she says that as soon as we can, we will go and visit him and take him some extra clothes and some food because she has heard the food in the camps is *malísima*. Very bad.

We also know there are about 150 other *gusanos* with my father at La Gabina, and a handful of *milicianos* whose job is to make sure the *gusanos* work hard, stay out of trouble and pay their dues to the Revolution. This means getting up at the crack of dawn every morning, having a breakfast of black coffee and a chunk of bread, and then going out into the nearby cane fields to cut sugar cane until six in the evening, when they return to the camp for dinner, a shower if there is any water left, and bed. Next day it starts all over again.

Not having our father at home is tough. To make things worse, everyone knows that our father is not at home because he is one of those ungrateful Cubans who wants to leave for *El Norte* to eat lots of American ham and cheese in exchange for becoming a slave of capitalism.

While I can see that my mother misses my father, I can also see that she is trying to be strong and pretend that life goes on as normal, so she wakes us up in the morning, prepares some breakfast for us and sends us off to school, just like she always did. But she gets scared at night, which is why she has asked her best friend, Hilda, to come and stay with us. My brother and I think it's great because we love Hilda—unlike my mother, she doesn't make too much fuss if we don't finish all our dinner. With my mother, on the other hand, well, you must eat all of your food because she thinks my brother and I are too skinny and, let me tell you, no sons of hers are ever going to look as if they are so poor they don't have enough food at home. Eat! Eat! I don't think we are all that skinny but there is not much point arguing with a Cuban mother when it comes to food.

Because we now know where my father is, and because we now know that he won't be coming home for quite a while, my mother is making plans for her, Hilda, my brother and me to go and visit him on Sunday, the only day that he is allowed a visit from his family. It's going to be difficult getting to La Gabina because it's a long way away and no bus service takes you there. Don't ask me how, but my mother has found a way of getting us on a truck that leaves Banes at four in the morning and will take us to a town close to where the labour camp is. From there we will have to hitch a ride in another truck or a cart or whatever comes along until we get to the camp.

When we finally arrive at La Gabina, I think we are in the wrong place. In my mind I had visions of a concentration camp like the ones I have seen on old Russian films about the Second World War, with electric fences, high towers and guards in black uniforms holding on tight to menacing, hungry dogs. Instead, it's a pretty open camp, although there are still *milicianos* around and they *are* carrying guns. But this is Cuba, the sun is shining and warm, the sky is sparkling blue, like Cuban skies are supposed to be, so we just walk through the entrance as though we are going on a picnic, along with fifty or sixty other families who have also made the trek from God knows where, all carrying containers heavy with homemade food and *jabas* with extra clothes.

My brother and I quickly spot our father among the large group standing just inside the gates. We rush to him and give him a hug and kiss his face, which is now rough, sunburnt and spiky. It's good to see him, and we think my mother is going to be happy too, but instead she bursts into tears at the sight of just how skinny my father is. Where has her husband gone? He is turning into a skeleton, she says, and cries some more.

We spend the day with my father, who introduces us to other *gusanos* who have now become his friends before taking us on a tour of the camp. Not that there is much to see. In the middle, there is a huge open-air building with a thatched roof and dirt floor and what seems like hundreds of simple bunk beds with canvas mattresses. Underneath the beds, or next to them, there are wooden boxes or big bags in which the men keep all their belongings.

As my mother unpacks the food she has brought and starts to pack up dirty clothes to take home to wash, my father is telling us that the work is hard but you adjust to it, although I think he is just saying that so we can all feel better. But the food, he says, the food is bad. *Malísima*. It explains why he has lost so much weight—fifteen kilos, my father says.

Over the next twenty-four months or so, my father is moved even further away, to larger labour camps where there are lots more *gusanos*, more guards, tougher work and the same awful food. The only thing that doesn't seem to change, my father says with a wry smile, is the number of latrines. There are never enough. First, he is moved to a labour camp in an area known as Casimiro, which isn't too far from La Gabina but almost impossible for us to reach; and eventually to a camp called La Brasa, where the number of *gusanos* swelled to nearly 500 and where conditions were so primitive, especially when it rained, that my father still recoils in horror when he talks about it.

Our visit to La Gabina on this sunny Sunday is my first and only visit to my father in the countryside. My mother will visit again later but she will decide, wisely, that it's just too long and unpredictable a trip for her two boys, so we stay home, counting the days until my father gets his five-day pass and appears at the front door as if by magic, looking thin and tired but happy to be home again, at least for a couple of days.

IT'S 26 JULY, the day all of Cuba celebrates the Revolution. It's a public holiday, which is good, and it's the day that Fidel gives the most important speech of the year, which is not so good because it means the cinema is closed and there is nothing on television or the radio except Fidel. Since early in the morning *La Compañera* from the Committee for the Defence of the Revolution has been knocking on doors and stopping people in the street to remind them that *El Maxímo Líder* is speaking tonight: Make sure you tune in, all right? This time, I think Fidel speaks for six hours. It's a mystery to a boy my age how anyone can stand up at a lectern in front of hundreds of thousands of people and speak for six hours without notes and without taking a break to go to the toilet.

Tonight Fidel sounds even more serious than usual, talking about his new idea to fix the Cuban economy once and for all so that we won't have to queue any more for rice and beans and we won't have to carry the ration book and *la jaba*. Fidel says the 1969 sugar harvest is going to be the sugar harvest to end all sugar harvests—ten million tonnes of sugar will be harvested and shipped to the world. Then, when the money rolls in, we will watch in amazement as the empty shelves in the shops fill up again with all sorts of goods, including not very revolutionary luxuries like toilet paper and shampoo.

All I can think of is that now my parents have applied to leave Cuba, we are going to miss out on all the food and the clothes and the television sets and the washing machines and the Polish refrigerators that Fidel is going to hand out to Cubans on the back of the biggest sugar harvest in the history of the entire world. Trust my parents to pick this time to leave.

Later, much later, historians will say that this one announcement changed the course of the Revolution. For the next twelve months, the island is turned upside down and everyone, absolutely everyone, no matter how old or how young or how frail, is expected to do their bit so we can reach that magical target of ten million tonnes. The effort will result in the total collapse of what was left of the Cuban economy but we don't know this now. We still think everything will be just fine.

On television, at the cinema and in the paper—all they talk about is the ten million tonne sugar harvest: *la zafra de los diez millones*. At school the teachers ditch the regular lessons so they can spend time explaining why the ten million tonne harvest is so important for the Revolution. At the cinema they even have cartoons about the ten million tonne harvest. On the news there are lots of reports about Fidel travelling up and down the island inspecting ordinary Cubans doing their job and offering hints and advice on how to work faster and better, as only Fidel can do. Billboards on the main road outside Banes carry pictures of Fidel in a big hat and working clothes, cutting sugar cane.

The ten million tonnes are so important to the future of Cuba and the future of the Revolution that everyone is expected to do their part. That is why *Granma* has pictures of happy Cubans—people who normally work as doctors, nurses, teachers or mechanics—changing into denim trousers and long-sleeved denim shirts and walking off their job for two or three weeks so they, too, can go and cut sugar cane. There are also lots of pictures of ministers cutting sugar cane with Fidel and pictures of smiling foreigners cutting sugar cane—even important visitors like the Soviet Minister for Defence. There are pictures, too, of young people from Europe and even some from the United States who have come to Cuba to help.

The stories in the paper say that these young volunteers have come from across the world to help because, with the exception of the hated Richard Nixon, the people of the world are all right behind the Revolution. In the pictures in *Granma*, they all look very white and very determined and, to my initial surprise, most of the young men from Europe and from the United States have long hair, which is strange because I always thought this was a sign of capitalism and decadence.

And almost every night, instead of old movies, both television channels will switch to a special report from Fidel in the studio giving a daily account of the harvest. On my friend's socialist television set, you can see *El Comandante en Jefe* standing before a huge map of Cuba. In one hand he has a half-smoked cigar and in the other he has a long, thin pointer that he uses again and again, just like my teachers do at school, to show how the production targets are going in different provinces, municipalities and towns.

Perhaps I am under the influence of my parents' counter-revolutionary scepticism, but sometimes I don't quite understand how all the problems in Cuba will be solved just because we end up with double the amount of sugar that is normally harvested every year. But I keep these thoughts to myself because, let's face it, if Fidel says the harvest will be ten million tonnes then it is pretty much guaranteed that no one anywhere will contradict *El Máximo Líder* because he *knows* what he is talking about.

13

NO MORE CHRISTMAS FOR YOU

THERE ARE LOTS of good things about the ten million tonne sugar harvest, like the way we don't get to do much work at school because half the teachers are cutting sugar cane in the countryside and those who are left behind are so busy, all they do is keep an eye on classes that seem to get more and more rowdy by the day. But there are some bad things about *los diez millones* too, even though no one complains about them. Like the way they have cancelled a lot of television programs so we can watch Fidel's nightly progress reports instead, or the way the cinema is now closed on most weeknights so that the projectionist can do his bit by the Revolution and go and cut sugar cane. And now, Fidel has announced that Christmas is cancelled.

My friends and I can't understand it, but it's true. We saw it with our own eyes: Fidel gave a speech in Havana in which he announced that, because of the ten million tonne sugar harvest, we would have to make a small sacrifice and postpone the Christmas holidays. There will be no *Nochebuena* this year. Fidel says Cuba is not a religious country any more and what is the point of celebrating a religious festival that was imported from Europe generations ago? In Europe, it is cold and snowy in December and everyone needs to rest indoors, he says, but not here in tropical Cuba. Here, it is still hot in December and, besides, it's prime sugar harvesting time.

So, Fidel says, we have decided that Christmas will be postponed this year. We will have to save the pork meat for later, and the beans that Cubans use to make *congri*, and the Spanish nougat sweets, and the beer and the rum. Because we will now celebrate six months later—in July, when it's the middle of summer. He says July 26 will be the new day for Christmas, because in any case, that is the day that commemorates the start of the Revolution; the day in 1953 when Fidel and his brother Raul and a group of other young men attacked the Moncada barracks in Santiago de Cuba. It's already the most important day in the Cuban revolutionary calendar, and now it will be doubly important, Fidel says.

And what a celebration this will be, he tells the crowd. Because by July 1970, the ten million tonne harvest will be over and Cubans will have met their revolutionary targets, having squeezed every last pound of sugar from every last acre of sugar cane. Then we will really have something to celebrate, says Fidel to thunderous applause from the audience, which is obviously as confident of success as *El Maxímo Líder*.

Everyone on television seems to think it's a great idea to cancel Christmas to help the Revolution but I have my doubts because *Nochebuena* has always been a big family holiday for us, when all of my mother's brothers and sisters and their families and my cousins come to Banes for a big dinner and a big party. Not this year. And on New Year's Day, too. There is going to be no *Nochebuena* for anyone, and no Christmas trees either because, Fidel says, they are a silly, antiquated European custom that has no meaning in revolutionary Cuba, where we are all busy building socialism.

What worries me most is not the postponing of *Nochebuena* or the abolition of the Christmas tree but what happens to the Day of the Three Kings, on 6 January. Have I heard this right? Did *El Maxímo Líder* really say that the Revolution will also postpone the Day of the Three Kings? This is the day when children up and down the length of Cuba wake up as early as their parents will allow them and head straight for the Christmas tree, complete with fake snow and coloured lights, to see what toys the Three Wise Men have left for them. Now it looks as if *El Día de los Reyes* is being cancelled too. Perhaps I misheard?

I run out of the house and around the corner to see Pepitin, whose family used to own what my mother says was the best pastry shop in all of Banes but which nowadays is only open a couple of hours a day, selling a few biscuits and every now and then a sponge cake, which you are allowed to order with your ration book if there is a birthday in the family. Pepitin is as confused as we all are about *el Día de los Reyes* so we run out of his house and down the street again, this time heading towards the park where we are sure we will find some of the other neighbourhood kids hanging around.

They are there all right but no one seems to know for sure what all this means. It takes a while for everyone to calm down and in the end we agree that, yes, 6 January has been postponed too. Fidel said so. He said that children were the most important people in Cuba and also the luckiest because since the Revolution, every child in Cuba has access to free health care and free education, which is something *El Maxímo Líder* is always reminding us about. In the old days, before the Revolution, only rich children got toys on 6 January while poor children never got anything, Fidel says. Now, thanks to the Revolution, every day is a good day for Cuban children, so like the good revolutionaries that we are, we will have to wait six months—until 26 July!—to get our presents. Except it will no longer be called *el Día de los Reyes*, but *el Día del Niño*—Children's Day.

It seems like a small price to pay to defend the Revolution, but I am devastated. I suspect all my friends are too, but we don't say much about it. As I walk back home, I start thinking: what happens if, despite all the work, and despite cancelling *Nochebuena* and abolishing Christmas trees and postponing the Day of the Three Kings, we can't reach the ten million tonnes of sugar? I realise immediately that these are very counter-revolutionary thoughts, even for the son of *gusanos*. But I can't help myself, and I am surprised, really, that apart from my father, no one else seems to think that the *diez millones* may not come true. Fidel says *los diez millones van*—the ten million is a done deal—and everyone agrees. No one ever contradicts Fidel.

LA COMPAÑERA has come around to talk to my mother about doing some volunteer work. This doesn't really mean you are invited to volunteer but rather you are told to turn up and do your bit on behalf of the Revolution. In this case, *La Compañera* has told my mother that she is expected tonight and every night for the next few weeks to help sort coffee beans.

In the past, my mother would probably have made some excuse, but things are different now. When you apply to leave Cuba you need a lot of important people to give you the tick before you are allowed out—important people like the president of your local Committee for the Defence of the Revolution. So, this time around, there is no way my mother is going to refuse or arrive late.

The volunteered volunteers will do their bit for the Revolution just a few doors down from our house, on the other side of the street, at the Masonic Centre, a two-storey building that adults would probably describe as elegant, at least by Banes standards. It has shuttered windows upstairs, a covered veranda and columns at the entrance that look like the ones you see in gladiator movies, and the building is surrounded by a high iron fence. To my friends and me this is the most mysterious building in the street, if not in all of town, because no one lives there and you very rarely see anyone going in or out.

Now my mother has the chance to see for herself what goes on inside the Masonic Centre because *La Compañera* says that the Masons have volunteered the building for volunteer work—and I want to go with her and have a look too. She agrees that I can come with her, provided I help out sorting the coffee beans, which I am happy to do. But when we get there, right after dinner, I find that no one is going to be allowed inside the building. No, no, says *La Compañera*, standing right in front of the locked doors. We are all working out there, *compañeras*, where it is much cooler, she says, pointing to the long table set up on the veranda that faces the street. Now I am stuck here helping my mother. She and about two dozen other women from the street sit at the long table, going through huge mountains of unroasted coffee beans, picking out the ones that have gone off or look too ugly and setting them aside. Then they pour the good coffee beans into huge sacks which are taken away somewhere to be roasted and then sent off to one of the fraternal socialist countries in Eastern Europe.

My mother keeps shaking her head as she selects the beans because, she says later, while the Russians and the Albanians drink our good Cuban coffee, back here, she says, we are lucky to drink any coffee at all since coffee is strictly rationed. Still, there is a plus from all this coffee work for my mother and the other volunteered women: when they think that *La Compañera* isn't looking, I catch them hiding some of the good coffee beans in their apron pockets so they can take them home. I am sure *La Compañera* can see them, but she doesn't say anything. She probably has coffee beans in her pockets too.

WELL, MY FATHER was right. It's now official: we have failed to harvest ten million tonnes of sugar. *La zafra de los diez millones*, the harvest that was to deliver Cuba from poverty and scarcity for ever, isn't going to happen.

It's really bad news—you can tell just by looking at Fidel on the television screen. He looks tired and his uniform looks like it needs a good wash. He explains that, despite a great revolutionary effort, we have missed our goal by fifteen per cent. It is still a huge amount of sugar but way short of the target.

Halfway through his speech, Fidel tells the crowd below that he is so disappointed about the harvest that he is quite happy to resign as *Comandante en Jefe* if that is what the People want. But just as you would expect, the crowd starts yelling out, No! No! No! and then they start singing the national anthem and chanting, Fidel!, Fidel!, Fidel!, which means Fidel isn't going anywhere. When Fidel fails, everyone fails. It's what the Revolution is all about.

Not that anyone on television or in the papers thinks of it quite that way, of course. They say this is nonetheless a magnificent, revolutionary effort; a record *zafra* that only the Revolution could have delivered. The biggest sugar harvest in Cuban history! No one points out that, given the effort involved, this is nothing to sing and dance about, especially since all other aspects of the economy have come to a costly standstill while everyone has been cutting sugar cane. It's the lowest point in Fidel's revolutionary experiment thus far, historians outside Cuba will say later, but for now I just try to understand what it means. All I know is what they say in the paper: like good revolutionaries, we must turn failure into victory!

Besides, deep inside, I don't want to admit that my father, who is so cynical about anything to do with the Revolution, could have been so right in his prediction. But he is—and it's not the first time, either. I remember when Fidel announced another one of his big ideas to fix the Cuban economy, the *Cordón de la Habana*, which meant digging up all the gardens and parks and forests around Havana so that volunteer workers could grow a special type of coffee plant. The coffee plants would encircle the city and produce so much coffee, Cubans would be able to drink strong, sweet Cuban coffee around the clock—and still export plenty to the rest of the world. Back then, my father said it was a stupid idea because coffee only grows well at high altitude, up in the mountains, no matter what Fidel says. He was right—despite all that work, the coffee bushes refused to produce coffee.

Then, when Fidel announced the ten million tonne sugar harvest last year, I remember my father shaking his head and saying, He is crazy. It will never happen. When I asked him why not, he said that anyone who has ever been near a Cuban cane field would come to the same conclusion. And I know what I am talking about, he said with a sure tone, because I grew up on a sugar cane farm. All those people who stop working as nurses and teachers and in offices so they can cut sugar cane, well, he says, all they will do is get in the way of the real cane-cutters, the professional *macheteros*. You will see, he says to me …

What I can't understand now is if my father, a simple *guajiro* from Banes, knew from the very start that ten million tonnes was a crazy target, why didn't anyone in Havana tell Fidel? Why did they let *El Comandante en Jefe* make those promises in the first place? My father has an explanation for that too: he says Fidel doesn't listen to anyone. When he gets a big idea, no one can stop him. Well, this time at least, before he made any announcement, he should have driven to

Banes in his olive green jeep and talked to my *guajiro* father because my *guajiro* father was right. Dead right.

Everyone I come across at school, at the Parque Cárdenas, sitting near the steps on the corner, seems to be totally deflated and confused. After so much work and so many promises, we are back to square one. And when the new, revolutionary equivalent of *el Día de los Reyes* is finally here, we will probably end up getting no toys or only very crappy toys because now that there is no *zafra de los diez millones*, where is Fidel going to get the money to buy all those toys he promised to the children of the Revolution?

I should not have worried so much—there will still be Children's Day and this year it will be held in July as expected and, yes, we are all going to get toys. But first, we will have to queue to get them. That is where I am right now, queuing with my mother and my brother at the only toy shop left in Banes, near my parents' old shop, the one that no longer exists.

It's a long queue, like all queues in Cuba, and while we wait and wait and wait, my mother talks to some of the other mothers in the line, trying to make sense of the new rules for buying toys that have just been announced in the paper. You can buy toys only if you have children and you need your ration book because toys are strictly rationed too. Fidel says this is so each child can get toys for Children's Day: a basic toy—*juguete básico*—which is the biggest and most expensive you can spot when it is your turn at the counter, and one non-basic toy which is smaller and less popular.

Of course, all the really good basic toys disappear quickly, so that whoever is first in line will usually get the biggest prize—the one Chinese-made bicycle in the whole shop, complete with a fancy bell and plastic tassels hanging from the handlebar and even a basket for your school books. When it's our turn to choose, the selection is already a little limited.

I look around the half-empty shelves but there is not much of a choice, as I feared, until I see it, right there near the till: a yellow-coloured dumper truck with big rubber wheels. I can tell it's a good toy and not only because it says on the box that it is made in Japan. It feels solid and forbiddingly capitalist. There is only one problem, says my mother: batteries. She is right—it is a battery-powered truck and batteries are very hard to come by in Cuba. You never see them in the shops. There isn't even a space in the ration book for batteries, that's how rare they are. You know what will happen when the batteries that come in the box run out, don't you? I can hear my mother saying. I know, I reply, I know what will happen but I don't care because I want the yellow-coloured, Japanese-made, battery-powered dumper truck and nothing she says will dissuade me from choosing this as my basic toy.

Do I need to tell you my mother was right? The batteries in the box lasted a day even though I was careful not to waste them by playing with the truck too much. I swear. I never saw batteries in Cuba again. At least that wasn't a problem with my non-basic toy: a box of colouring pens made in Hungary.

I have no idea what toys the families who were at the very end of the queue managed to get because I am sure there wasn't much left by the time they made it to the counter. I know there were lots of not very happy children in Banes, and probably all over Cuba, and a lot of not very happy mothers and fathers who had to put up with their not very happy children. So many not happy families that Fidel announced that a new, much fairer system would be introduced next year: a lottery to be organised by the Committees for the Defence of the Revolution in each *barrio* to decide which lucky family in the neighbourhood would be first in the toy queue ... and get the best toys.

14

WE WANT TO BE LIKE CHE!

I AM NOW in secondary school—my last year of school in Cuba, as it will turn out. Going to secondary school means you get to make new friends and meet new teachers but, best of all, it means I am now old enough to take part in *escuela al campo*, which my mother says is a crazy new revolutionary experiment designed to indoctrinate—that's the word she uses!—children to hate their parents. I am sure she is exaggerating. It means that every year secondary schools close down for a fortnight and the whole school—teachers, students, blackboards, everything—is moved to the countryside, to a camp that is a cross between a military base and a summer holiday spot for inquisitive and overactive adolescents. I can't wait to pack my things. To my mother, however, it's nothing short of a tragedy. She is losing her son to the Revolution and she is beside herself.

As our school principal explains it, we will get some lessons but much of the day will be spent helping the Revolution by picking lemons. Lemons are important, the principal says, because the Revolution can then export juicy, tart Cuban lemons to our friends in Eastern Europe in exchange for things we need in Cuba, like harvesters and tractors and petrol. I think we need lemons in Cuba, too, as we never see them in the shops, but I decide there is no need to be a smarty-pants.

The camp we are going to is at Punta de Mulas, or Mules Point, which is not all that far from Banes, probably an hour or so by road. The morning we are to leave for the *escuela al campo* there are several Russian-made military trucks waiting to take us to the camp. Someone has removed the canvas tops so we can all stand on the back and wave goodbye to our families.

Like most of my fellow students, I have a *mochila* that is huge, packed with school books, bedsheets, clothes, a tin or two of food my mother has managed to find somewhere (I never ask where or how), an enamel plate and mug and a pair of boots for all the hard work ahead picking lemons. We are all so excited you can barely hear anything above the shouting and the laughing and the singing.

It's true that we will only be a few kilometres from home but for my mother and the other mothers standing at the edge of the park, waving and shouting at their kids to take care, it is like we are being sent to Jupiter. There are no buses from Banes to Punta de Mulas. In fact, there is barely any transport at all. The road is not much more than a dirt track in some parts, so visiting will be an absolute nightmare for our families.

As the trucks start pulling out I wave goodbye to my mother, who is now holding my brother's hand tightly. She is about to cry and I am embarrassed by her tears, thinking, Doesn't she know I am a big boy now?

As soon as we leave the park someone starts singing some revolutionary song and everyone joins in like the good little communists that we are. Before we know it, the trucks are out in the countryside, the road is bumpy and in the distance I can see row after row after row of lemon trees, heavy with small green and yellow Cuban lemons. It hits me that picking lemons for the Revolution is not going to be as much fun as most of us on the back of the truck expected.

When we finally arrive at the camp, we drive through two large gates and see a number of what look like long, squat military barracks joined to rooms that look like classrooms which are in turn joined to a central area which, I assume, is where the kitchen and the dining room are located. We are told to jump out of the trucks and line up so that we can be assigned to our brigades, which will become a kind of surrogate extended family for the next two weeks. Then we are shown to the barracks where we are assigned bunk beds. Some barracks are for boys while others are for girls, with teachers sleeping in the middle, supposedly to keep an eye on older students who may get a little adventurous when it comes to sleeping arrangements. This is not something that even crosses my mind initially but I know that some of the older boys at school have been talking about the endless opportunities ahead to spend time with the opposite sex. As I will discover, they are right.

Once we have been shown where the showers and the latrines are we have to line up again for the teachers to select the students who will be the brigade leaders, a job that will involve not just ensuring everyone behaves but that everyone works hard enough for the brigade to meet its production target. The brigade that meets its targets most consistently by picking the most lemons will be awarded a certificate, just like the certificates that are awarded on television by Fidel or Raul to the best workers to recognise their outstanding contribution to building socialism in the tropics. There are no other prizes, of course, because this is socialist Cuba and in socialist Cuba we are building the New Man and, just like Che, the New Man doesn't want or need material goods to be a good revolutionary.

To my surprise, I hear my name called out. I have been selected as leader of my brigade, a group of about ten students, some much older than I am but obviously way less committed to picking lemons for the Revolution. Being chosen a brigade leader is like getting a huge revolutionary star on your forehead. When I think about it later, I realise that I am more relieved than excited at my new-found important role as a *dirigente*. I was dead-set convinced I would not be chosen for such an important revolutionary job because, well, you know, my ungrateful parents want to leave Cuba and take me away with them. But for now, I am thrilled with my new promotion. I want to be a good Cuban, which means I want to be a good revolutionary, which means I want to be like Che!

Picking lemons for the Revolution seems easy at first but it gets harder and more tedious as the day progresses. The thorns of the lemon trees appear to have no problem piercing through the gloves we have been given, so that, before long, if you aren't careful, your hands end up a bloody mess. The long-sleeved shirts offer only limited protection against the sun, which is getting hotter and hotter by the minute as we pick lemon after lemon after lemon. We carry the big wooden boxes full of lemons to trucks parked along a central trail, and these trucks take the lemons to a warehouse somewhere for further distribution. At least I hope so. This being Cuba, there is a sneaking suspicion that those lemons we have just picked for our friends in Prague and Warsaw and Budapest may well end up staying in the warehouse until they rot because there are no spare parts to fix the trucks or because someone, somewhere, failed to fill in the necessary forms.

Some afternoons the teachers attempt to conduct regular classes, without much success, and then at about five or six o'clock we are allowed time to have a shower and change into clean clothes. Some afternoons we also march in military style or learn how to disassemble and clean rifles, how to load an ancient-looking machine gun and how to shoot at targets because, as we are told every day and reminded every night, we must be prepared to defend the Revolution *con nuestra propia sangre*—with our own blood.

We then have dinner in the large dining hall where we queue for our food and a glass of water. The food is plentiful but uniformly tasteless: there is nothing on offer for the whole fortnight but boiled rice and a kind of stew made from canned Russian sausages that are a funny pink colour and that pretty much taste like cardboard, and not very good cardboard at that. Then, after dinner, the camp comes alive. Almost every night there is a show put on by one of the brigades—each takes a turn to perform and while some try to take it all seriously and read revolutionary poems by the Chilean poet Pablo Neruda or sing revolutionary *campesino* songs written by Carlos Puebla, in the end, most nights, it's just good Cuban fun with good Cuban music. Then we are all sent to bed, the lights are turned off, and the barracks fall silent. At least that's the way it looks to me.

Some days later, after dinner, I talk to a boy in my brigade who is in second year and whose nickname is *El Sapo*—the toad—although I never call him that to his face because he is older and taller and stronger than I am, even if he is not all that bright. We are both in the kitchen, scrubbing huge black pots because tonight it's my brigade's turn to help with the washing up. *El Sapo* says that all the action happens right after dark, once the lights are out. I have no idea what kind of action he is talking about but I keep quiet because I don't want to sound ignorant.

When all of you are in bed asleep, says *El Sapo*, and when the teachers disappear from sight, *chico*, that is when things get hot out there. *Caliente*, he says and he winks. If you believe him, the teachers are always catching couples kissing behind the barracks and doing other things, he says mysteriously. I don't know whether I believe *El Sapo* or not. I decide it doesn't matter. I am too tired, anyway, and all I want to do is go to bed.

Sundays are the best days of all at Punta de Mulas. On Sundays we don't have to pick lemons; instead, we get to sleep in until eight, or even later if you don't mind missing breakfast and if you can sleep with all the noise from the other boys in the barracks. Sunday is the official visiting day and by the time we finish breakfast dozens of mothers and fathers and brothers and sisters have arrived at the gates in trucks that have been organised by the school from Banes.

On Sundays, without fail, my mother arrives because she misses her boy and because she worries, as I knew she would, that her boy is not eating enough. Look at you, she says while she hugs me, look at you! So skinny. She has with her a huge *jaba* full of food she has cooked at home, probably the result of exchanging one of her old dresses or a pair of leather shoes for some rice and flour and, most amazing of all, some pork fat for frying. *Manteca.*

I am happy to see my mother but I am also a little embarrassed by all the food she has brought, especially when I look around and see that not every mother has had quite the same level of success as mine in finding little treats for their boys and girls. In fact, I can see that some students don't have visitors at all, which makes me feel like a very spoilt child, very bourgeois even, which I know is not something Che would have approved of.

Once my mother leaves in the afternoon, I carefully pack up the goodies she has brought and put them under my bunk bed, covering them with one of the spare towels. Later, I will share some of the cake with my friends and they will share some of their stuff with me, but for now, I don't feel like company because I don't want any of my friends to know that I am homesick. So I sit on my own in a grassy area near the dining hall, doing nothing, just watching a big, bright Cuban sun slowly turn into a radiant pink and then explode into the colour of blood before it disappears beyond the horizon. When you leave Cuba, I can hear someone in my head saying, you will never see such a sunset again.

My mother even visits a couple of times during the week, hitching a ride with the mother of my friend Fidelito in her still-shiny American car. She doesn't tell me this, but once during my time in the *escuela al campo,* she walked all the way from Banes because there was no truck, no *carreta* and certainly no olive green army jeep to take her to the camp at Punta de Mulas. It must have taken her three or four hours, carrying the heavy *jaba* with the food she had prepared. But she never tells me this, not until many, many years later. When she does, I feel terrible.

SOMETHING is up, I am sure of it. We just had word that my father is coming back to Banes. He has been away for nearly three years, since the day after the police arrived at our place to confirm that we were now, officially, *gusanos*. Since then my father has spent time in labour camps all over Oriente province, but he has never been sent to a camp anywhere near Banes. Now, out of the blue, the news has arrived that he is being transferred to work just outside Banes and we couldn't be happier. My mother says the fact that my father is being sent to a camp on the outskirts of Banes can mean only one thing: *el telegrama*—that magical telegram that says, yes, you are now free to leave—cannot be all that far away.

Of course, he will still have to work hard during the day but at night he will be able to walk home and have dinner with us and sleep in his own bed. Not only is he going to be close to home but he will not have to cut any more sugar cane. Instead, the camp he is being sent to is a carpentry shop where they make useful things like windows and doors and huge yokes for the oxen that are still used in the Cuban country-side to till the earth. My father says that, compared to cutting sugar cane every day of the week and having to eat the worst food you can imagine, the new place is like a luxury hotel, even if the *milicianos* are in charge and they still carry guns. We just can't believe our luck.

It will be good to have my father home every night so we can get back to something that at least resembles normal life—like it used to be before we decided to seek permission to leave Cuba. Best of all, I want to see my father walk out onto the small front porch of our house on Flor Crombet Street every evening, sit in one of the rocking chairs that have seen better days and then light up the cigars he always keeps aside for after dinner, filling the air with blue smoke and the aroma of Cuba.

15

THE MAGICAL TELEGRAM

IT'S HERE. The telegram that says we can leave Cuba has arrived, and now we have just three days to pack up our things (it won't take long, says my mother), say goodbye to the family and friends and get our bus tickets to Havana. Most important of all, we need to ensure our paperwork is in order.

Our passports have been safely stored for three years, with their prized Spanish visas which take a whole page inside, complete with colourful stamps and seals and the extravagant signature of the Spanish consul in Havana. By contrast, the most important of all the papers we need to be allowed out of Cuba is a simple, one-page letter written in pencil, with at least a couple of spelling errors, from the commander of the labour camp where my father has spent the last few months. The letter, which is known as *la carta de la agricultura*, confirms that my father has worked long enough and hard enough to be allowed to leave. It's the sort of letter you guard as if it was the most treasured of possessions, which in a way it most certainly is. Without it, you are going nowhere.

The police have come and taken stock of all our goods, which now belong to the People. In reality, we don't have all that much that is valuable but that does not deter the very efficient *milicianos* from going through their checklist with great care, making sure every single plate and every single glass is accounted for.

Packing up isn't much of a problem. The instructions from the *milicianos* are clear: you can only take personal effects, like your clothes and your toothbrush and a towel. The rest stays behind because, *Compañero, esto es propiedad del Pueblo.* All this, comrade, belongs to the People now. I still can't imagine who would want my old shoes or the singlets that my mother has washed so many times the material has become as thin as the skin of an onion, but I am not about to argue. Soon we are standing outside the house, our suitcases packed and ready. It's only then that the finality of what has just happened starts to sink in.

We are to spend our last night in Banes at my aunt Adelina's house before catching the bus to Havana in the morning, but we can't leave until a senior Communist Party functionary arrives to officially 'seal' the house. As we stand outside, mingling with the more curious of our neighbours, the official sent by the Party will lock the door and then place a seal across it, declaring that no one can go in or out of the house without permission. I don't know whether there is someone in the local party whose job it is to seal the houses of *gusanos* but the official who comes to seal our house turns out to be my uncle Papi, my mother's youngest brother and without doubt the one she feels the closest to. Now here he is, a senior official in the local Communist Party, locking the front door and sealing our house.

He doesn't say much but it's quite clear to my parents that this wasn't his idea. One of his superiors must have ordered him, my father says later, and you can tell that my uncle feels as uncomfortable as my parents. My mother can't believe her eyes but she says nothing. When he is finished, my uncle Papi says, I will see you later, and then he goes back to work. We pick up our cases and walk down the street and then up the hill to my aunt Adelina's house, waving goodbye to people along the way. Some of them stop briefly to have a quick, furtive chat and wish us luck in Spain. *¡Que les vaya bien!* I hope it all goes well! Good luck!

Up until now, I thought that leaving Banes would be straightforward, at least for me. After all, we have been waiting for this moment for a long time and now, finally, we are on our way, although in Cuba you can never be sure because at any time someone, somewhere, may decide to keep you back for just a little while longer—or for ever, if they want to. My father, who has become quite a pessimist, keeps saying we must do everything right. By the book. No surprises, no jumping around with joy, no provocations of any type because we want to make sure we get on that Iberia plane in a few days' time.

I know that what is really worrying him is my aunt Nidia, my totally unpredictable, totally crazy aunt Nidia, who is leaving Cuba with us as part of our *nucleo familiar*. My mother, on the other hand, is too busy worrying about her other sister, the sister she is leaving behind, my aunt Adelina, and about her brothers, especially my uncle Papi. She doesn't say so but I know what she is thinking—that she is deserting her family.

We spend our last day in Banes saying goodbye to as many people as we can, mainly our family, and we do it quietly—no fanfare—because we don't want to tempt fate. My father is busy trying to secure five tickets on the daily bus that travels from Banes to Havana. My aunt Adelina and my uncle Rogelio are coming to Havana, strictly speaking not to farewell us, you understand, but because my uncle needs to see a specialist, or at least that is the excuse. My aunt Mary, who is heavily pregnant, is coming too with my cousin Karina, who is just six, and my cousin Carlitos, who is four, but my uncle Papi is staying in Banes, as we expected, because he is busy at work, though I can tell that even if he wasn't busy, it would not be wise for a senior official in the local Communist Party to travel to Havana to farewell his *gusano* sister. My mother would have convinced him not to, I am sure.

I find it hard to say goodbye to my friends in the neighbourhood. Not because I am getting teary or anything like that—no, no, Cuban men don't cry. It's hard because it all seems so ... final?

As I say goodbye to my friends, one by one, I make sure I write down their addresses and I promise to write, of course. I will write to tell them about Spain and bullfights and about the latest music and films in Spain and Europe, and about what things are like outside Cuba. I promise them that inside each envelope I will hide a tablet of chewing gum too, because you can't buy chewing gum in Cuba, no matter how good a revolutionary you are.

Despite my best efforts, I get a little teary after all, when our two neighbours from the big house right across the street, Fabiola and her sister Ibis, come to say goodbye later that evening. They must be close to fifty, and they have lived across from us for as long as anyone can remember, if not longer. They are both teachers and neither has ever married. To my brother and me, they are like family.

And so I hug Fabiola first and longest because she has always been my favourite but it is Ibis who surprises me most by giving me a goodbye kiss and a hug, and telling me that I should study hard and respect my parents and look after my brother and help them in our new life. Then she says, *No te olvides de tu patria*—Don't forget your homeland.

THE COACH TRIP between Banes and Havana can take anywhere between fifteen hours and for ever. This is not because of the traffic—there is almost none on the highway, only army trucks and jeeps. It all depends on the coach. Some of the coaches that travel long distances from Oriente province to Havana are new ones imported from one of the fraternal communist nations of Eastern Europe. They are big and shiny and noisy and I can picture in my mind one of these socialist coaches sliding elegantly along some super-modern road outside Prague or East Berlin. But here in tropical Cuba, the socialist coaches are always breaking down because of the heat, so that the fifteen-hour trip to Havana can turn into a 24-hour trip or even longer.

Luckily for us, we are travelling instead in an old American-made coach that has seen better days. Strangely, though, the old American coaches don't break down as often as the Eastern European ones. Just as well. I can see that my mother is becoming increasingly distraught as we say goodbye, first to Banes, then to the small villages that surround it, on a trip that we all know is definitively one way.

The coach normally stops along the way a few times to refuel and so the passengers can buy a sandwich for lunch, if they are lucky, and stretch their legs. Within a couple of hours of leaving Banes, the first big stop is at Holguin, which is the much bigger town where my father used to live and where several of his brothers still live. And sure enough, at the station we spot my uncle Gerardo, who is even taller and skinnier than my father, waving anxiously.

It's not a long stop so my uncle gives everyone a big hug and kisses my mother and tells my brother and me to be good boys because, after all, we are going on a plane and despite his age he has never been on one of those new jets. He hasn't even been outside Cuba! And don't forget to write, he says to me. Then he gives my father a bundle of his best cigars and says, It's not much, but here is a little something for you to remember your brothers back home, in Cuba.

My father shakes his head and says, No, no, how can I take your cigars? They are so hard to come by. But my uncle Gerardo insists and so my father takes them and I am sure that, no matter what he says, he is getting emotional.

THIS IS ONLY my third trip to Havana and, once again, as the Banes coach nears the big capital city I am overawed by the sheer size of the place. I look out of the window to see streets swarming with people, walking, or just chatting on corners, or standing in queues that are much longer than the ones in Banes, waiting outside *bodegas* and cinemas or at bus stops for buses that may or may not arrive. I sense that this is one of those indelible mental pictures I will take with me when we finally fly out on our way to Madrid—a whole city, a whole country of people standing in line, waiting, waiting, waiting ...

In Havana, we stay not at my uncle Victor's apartment in Miramar as we did on our first visit, but in a neighbourhood called Reparto Mañana. For reasons that are not clear to me, one of our relatives, Olmer, who is a university student, has the keys to this big, empty house that I am assuming must have belonged to some *gusano* at some stage but now belongs to the People—or at least to someone who has in turn loaned it to Olmer for a few days.

It's a good thing we are only expecting to stay in Havana for three or four nights because this is not much of a house, or so we discover as soon as we open the front door. There is very little inside: a couple of fold-out beds, three or four old wooden chairs, some plates and forks and an old table. In a corner there is a bench seat from an old American car and my father points it out to me and says, This is going to be your *special* bed! He stresses the word special to make it sound exciting, I am sure, but he can tell I am not too impressed. My mother isn't impressed either, although she doesn't say anything.

The place is depressing no matter how much my father tries to make it sound like an adventure, but we all know that it is the best we can do and it's only for a couple of nights. And thank you, thank you, Olmer, you are a great *muchacho*, letting us stay in this place, this empty place, when there is really no other place to stay in. Because, you know, *gusanos* can't just turn up at the Hotel Nacional or the Habana Libre Hotel and say, Good evening, sir, we are *gusanos* from Banes and we want to rent a room. Thank you, Olmer.

My uncle Tony is overseas as a member of a delegation to Moscow and in any case there is no way either of my parents would have asked him to let us stay in his apartment because it is tiny. My uncle Victor, who is a big shot in the Revolutionary Armed Forces, who has his own car and who lives in the large apartment in Miramar where the rich used to live *antes del Triunfo*, has made it known to my mother that he has no room at his place this time. We can't stay there, he told my mother, which she understands fully, because if anyone found out he had *gusanos* staying at his place, even family members, he would be in trouble. My father is angry because how can there be no room in such a big place, he wants to know, when we have to stay here in this place and my sons have to sleep on old car seats so they wake up in the morning with sore necks and flea bites on their arms?

We don't spend any time in the house during the day. As soon as it's daylight we get up, have something to eat from the box of food my mother brought on the bus all the way from Banes, and then we go out to visit my cousin Eddi. She is my father's niece, one of his favourites, and she and her husband Orlando have agreed to let us stay at their apartment during the day and even have lunch there if we want to. This is no small favour and my parents are grateful beyond words. They warn my brother and me to make sure we don't tell anyone we are *gusanos* about to leave Cuba for Spain. Using his stern voice, my father says, If anyone asks, we are cousins from Oriente province. Understood? Understood, we reply.

I don't mind lying this time, especially when my father explains that my cousin's husband is a captain in the Revolutionary Navy, which means he is almost certainly a member of the Communist Party. Someone on the way up. I can't figure out why Orlando has agreed to let us stay in his house, even if it is only during the daytime, given his position. If anyone found out, he too would have some explaining to do, just like my uncle Victor. And yet here we are, grateful *gusanos* from Banes, having lunch in his home as if it was the most normal thing in the world, which I guess it might be in some countries but not here in Cuba.

Every day Orlando comes home from work in his navy uniform, bringing with him plenty of food for everyone, making my mother very happy, as well as plenty of beer and rum, which makes my father very happy.

I know it hurts my mother that she is here in Havana, about to leave Cuba for ever, and she still has not been able to see my uncle Victor and say goodbye to her oldest brother. These are not happy days for my mother and sometimes I wonder whether at some stage she is going to say to my father, No, I am not going to Spain. I can't leave the rest of my family behind.

The day before we are due to depart for the airport, my mother gets an unexpected visitor. It's my uncle Victor. He has come to the empty house in Reparto Mañana to say goodbye. My uncle, whom we never see because he now rarely visits Banes, is tall, and even though he is older than my mother, he looks quite fit to me. My uncle has come on his own and to my surprise he is not wearing his army uniform. Instead, he is wearing civilian clothes and looks just like any other *Habanero*. He hasn't come in his government car either, taking the bus instead, which surprises me even more because everyone knows that the buses are always crowded and late.

Now that my uncle is here, my mother apologises for not being able to offer him anything to drink. The truth is, there isn't even a comfortable chair to sit on, so they just stand there in the middle of this empty living room in this empty house in Reparto Mañana and say goodbye. It's the last time my mother will see her brother and, as they hug each other before he departs, I can tell that she is trying desperately not to cry. Then my uncle is gone.

TODAY WE leave Cuba. That's the plan, anyway, but of course in Cuba nothing ever goes according to plan. The Iberia flight between Havana and Madrid leaves mid-morning but we have been told to be at the Jose Martí International Airport, which is just outside Havana, at six so we have plenty of time for the *papeleo*, the paperwork. We arrive at the airport on schedule, but it becomes clear as soon as we walk in that the airport is pretty empty and that there is not much to do but wait.

Getting to the airport itself has been touch and go because petrol is scarce, *compañero*, and tightly rationed, so taxis are nonexistent, which is why everyone queues for hours to get on a bus, hoping against all hope that the driver makes it to their destination without running out of petrol along the way, or the bus breaking down. Somehow, however, the ever-reliable Olmer has found someone to take us to the airport. It's a friend of a friend of a friend who owns an ancient American car and who has managed to save enough petrol coupons to be able to make a run to the airport and back— and who wants 100 Cuban *pesos* for the trip, which is a lot of money but which my father is happy to pay since, in truth, he has little choice.

The money is exchanged indirectly, under the table, because in socialist Cuba, you are not supposed to be paying people money like this for a taxi. So we are told that if the police stop the car and ask what is going on, we must say that we are related to the driver, which would be a plausible story until the taxi that isn't a taxi arrives and the driver steps out, and we see with our very own eyes that he is a short, black man.

He politely nods his head in acknowledgement and then helps us pack the car. Then my parents, my brother and I, my aunt Nidia and my aunt Mary and my cousins, all pile as best we can into the old Chevrolet. It's like being inside a can of sardines, says my aunt Mary.

We are all sitting on hard plastic chairs in the terminal while my father goes over to the big desk with a sign that says Immigration to start the *papeleo*. But instead of spending an hour going through the papers as I expected, my father is now walking back to us and I can see as he gets closer that something is definitely wrong. He looks pale. All I can think of is that my aunt Nidia has done something silly or said something critical of Fidel and we are now being kept back in Cuba for another two years as punishment, which means my father will have to go back to cutting sugar cane for the Revolution and I will have to go back to school.

When he finally reaches us, my father says quietly, We are not leaving today. We aren't? No, he says, the plane is full and there are no seats left. My mother doesn't understand and neither do I. How can the plane be full? It's a capitalist plane, not a Havana bus! We are not leaving today, my father repeats, we have to go back to Reparto Mañana and wait until the Iberia flight next Tuesday. So close and yet so far.

I can tell it's going to be a long few days. Now the flight has been postponed, we are back at Reparto Mañana where Olmer has kindly agreed to allow us to stay—For as long as you need to, he says, and my parents don't know how to thank him enough. The most obvious problem is food. My mother and my aunt Mary had brought food with them from Banes but that is almost all gone since we expected to be in Madrid by now. We know we will have plenty to eat at the house of my cousin Eddi and her navy captain husband, but my father is reluctant to keep knocking on their door every day because he doesn't want to do anything that might compromise our relatives.

For the next few days my father spends his time finalising the paperwork—the endless paperwork—that will eventually allow us to get on that elusive plane. We are so close … My father has to confirm flights again, ensure there are no other hiccups, that there are seats on the plane this time around. He visits the Spanish Embassy to make sure the visas are still all right and, most important of all, he goes methodically through every piece of paper necessary, to make sure it's all there because these are the very documents that will allow us to walk up the steps into the plane. He can't leave anything to chance.

You can tell it's a tough time for my father. He is more anxious than I have ever seen him before. Sometimes, at the end of a long day, I can see his hands shaking, and I can understand why. When you are a *gusano*, nothing is for sure. At any moment, without any warning, the police can turn up and tell us we are not going anywhere. They don't need much of an excuse to keep us here.

Meanwhile, my mother, my brother and my aunts play tourists in Havana, even though we soon discover there are no real tourists at all in Havana. Not since Fidel announced some years ago that, *antes del Triunfo*, Americans and Europeans came to Havana, not because it was a beautiful city, but because they wanted to exploit Cubans, take drugs, sleep with our women and spend their time in casinos owned by the Mafia. The Revolution put a stop to all that, closed the casinos, stopped building flashy capitalist hotels, closed the country clubs and the golf courses and turned all those tourist planes back.

Most of the visitors we see in Havana—at the Havana zoo, the Vedado neighbourhood or at the aquarium—come from fraternal countries like the Soviet Union, the German Democratic Republic or from Hungary. You can tell them from far away, my mother says, because they all look so *tosco*, by which she means they look nothing like Cubans: they are blonde, have pink skin and short, spiky haircuts like the haircuts you get in the army, wear loud shirts and carry bulky Praktica cameras around their necks. The women always wear sandals too, and if you look closely, you can tell that many of them don't shave under their arms, which is definitely not the way Cuban women would walk around in public, Revolution or no Revolution.

It seems my mother and my aunt Mary are slowly solving the food problem. Because there is nothing to cook with, my aunt has been down the road to a hardware shop and somehow managed to convince the shop assistant to sell her the only container they have in the shop: a large enamel chamber pot. This is what my mother and my aunt now use to fry green plantains in. It hasn't been used, my aunt Mary insists. Still, she can't convince my aunt Nidia, who simply refuses to eat anything from it, saying something about, How low have we sunk, *¡Dios Mio!*

We also eat spaghetti. Almost every day. But as my mother says, it's either spaghetti or we go hungry. To get the spaghetti, my mother and my aunt Mary go out every afternoon and queue outside one of a handful of take-away places the Revolution has opened across Havana in the past few months. Each serves just one dish: spaghetti, already cooked in a rich red sauce that is supposed to have tomatoes and meat in it but, when you look closely, seems to be just tomato.

The only other food that seems to be freely available all over Havana—and in plentiful supply—is *merluza*, or hake. Nothing else is available in the fish shops apart from hake. It's the way things work in Cuba: no one can explain why there is so much hake around but, equally, no one is complaining because you can buy as much as you want without needing to use your ration book. It makes a change from spaghetti.

16

ADIOS, CUBA

WE LEAVE the house at Reparto Mañana at five o'clock on the day we are about to leave Cuba—unless we get sent back from the airport again. You never know, says my aunt Nidia, which makes my father even more anxious than he already is. I know what he is going through because in the pit of my stomach I feel sick too, but I keep it to myself. I don't know what we will do if we get sent back from the airport. I think we have had enough of spaghetti and hake and wouldn't it be great to sleep on a real bed again and not on an old American car seat? My neck hurts and my arms and my stomach and my chest area are blotchy and itchy ...

We are picked up by the same driver who took us to the

airport last week. My father pays another 100 *pesos*, no complaints, and then we all do the sardine trick again and squash back into the taxi that isn't, and then we are on our way. No one says much during the trip but I can tell what everyone is thinking: is this it? Are we really leaving today?

Outside, it is still dark. We drive past darkened government buildings that are ten storeys high, some with huge posters of Fidel or Che looking defiant and heroic. There is a giant billboard on the route encouraging Cubans to become better revolutionaries, ready to fight against imperialism. *Patria o Muerte. ¡Venceremos!* says another one. Fatherland or Death. We shall win!

As we drive, I notice small groups of people, barely visible in the dark, standing in queues—even at this hour!—waiting for the bus that will take them to work. I roll down the window and stick my head out of the old car and I swear I can smell the sea in the air and hear the waves in the distance. I am sure I can taste the salt in the light dawn breeze, but maybe I'm imagining things.

You can tell it's going to be another warm, sunny day, this first day of March. It's spring in Havana, for sure, but all Cuban days seem to be warm and sunny. Or at least that is the way I will always remember them. It's probably just like any other start to the day in Havana, with people up there in the apartment blocks only now waking up, making themselves a *cafecito* for breakfast. Perhaps a chunk of bread dipped in a mixture of oil, salt and a crushed garlic clove before setting off to work. Another day in revolutionary Cuba. But not for us.

When we get to the airport, it is almost empty again. We are wearing our best (and only) travelling outfits—*el traje de salir de Cuba*. Both my brother and I are wearing suits made for us over a year ago by a tailor in Banes, a friend of my father's, from the only heavy material my mother could find, a thick, grey, woollen material, probably from East Germany, that makes my brother and me very uncomfortable because it's getting hotter all the time. It's itchy in this suit and we think we look stupid, but my mother insisted because she says you only leave Cuba once and we want to arrive in Madrid—will we ever arrive?—looking our best. You know, there is no point arguing with your mother when she is determined like that.

My father tells us to go and find seats, just like he did last week, and then he walks over to the Immigration desk. Surely they are not going to do this to him a second time? From where we are sitting I can tell my father is nervous because he is tapping his right foot and fidgeting. Oh God, that little voice is saying inside my head, let's get this over with. I don't know how long it takes but it feels like long, agonising hours before my father turns around and walks over to us and says, with just a hint of a smile, we have seats. At this stage these are the sweetest words in the entire language.

We say goodbye to my aunt Mary and my cousins for what we all think will be the last time ever. It involves much hugging, crying and promises to write and to phone, as soon as we get to Madrid. Then my aunt Nidia, my parents, and my brother and I walk to the end of a corridor where a *miliciano* politely opens the door and ushers us into another section of the airport. It is a kind of reverse customs post where, instead of inspecting the luggage of incoming visitors, uniformed immigration officers ask *gusanos* leaving the country to open up all their luggage so it can be inspected, piece by piece.

The immigration official inspecting our suitcases is polite but thorough, unpacking every single piece of clothing and then, with great care, feeling around the inside of the suitcases searching for I don't know what. Neither my mother nor my father nor my aunt Nidia say anything as the inspection continues, item by item. We stand there and wait until the clothes are bundled back inside and the cases locked again and set aside to be taken into the hold of the plane. We hope.

Then we go back to our seats and wait. There are other families like ours waiting too, and all the mothers must be like my mother because everyone is wearing their best we-are-leaving-Cuba outfits: men in suits that are too tight, women wearing dresses that are way out of date, young girls with pretty ribbons in their hair and boys like my brother and me, forced to wear hot, itchy suits made from what I am sure is material for Arctic blankets.

There are plenty of *milicianos* around, standing guard,

guns at the ready but looking bored. You can tell they are keeping an eye on our group in case we try to smuggle out precious gold or diamonds that were kept hidden from *antes del Triunfo* and which now belong to the People.

I am not sure how long we have been waiting because I have stopped asking my mother what time it is. Both she and my father are jumpy, especially my father, who is sweating a little, and looking uncomfortable in his suit. He wipes his forehead with a white cotton handkerchief that has been kept untouched, brand new, for this very occasion.

We sit there and look out the glass windows but there is not much action outside, either. On the tarmac I can count only a handful of planes, including a couple of propeller airplanes that belong to Cubana, the Cuban airline. My father says, quietly, that they are old Soviet planes given to Cuba as a gift by our fraternal cousins in Moscow. He then whispers, I bet those planes are so old and in such poor condition, they can't fly. Then, a little further out on the tarmac, I spot the plane we have been waiting for. It's a large jet with red stripes and that magic word: Iberia. It's our plane—the weekly Iberia flight that takes *gusanos* like us to Spain, and let me tell you, it is a beautiful sight. We are so close. I keep thinking, they are not going to turn us back again, are they?

While I am looking at the planes, a *miliciana* comes over to where my parents and my aunt Nidia are sitting and talks to them quietly. Next thing I know, my mother and my aunt are being led away by the uniformed policewoman and they disappear into a room off to one side. We don't know what's going on. It won't take long, the *miliciana* said, just come with us, please. But my mind is racing and that voice inside my head is saying, Something is wrong; you and your father and your brother will be allowed to leave Cuba but your mother will be kept behind. I can hear my father trying to reassure my brother and me, but I am still scared. Please, God, don't let them take my mother away. My father is cursing under his breath; he is adamant my aunt Nidia must have said something counter-revolutionary while in the toilet, probably when talking to another *gusano* in there, and doesn't she know that every room in this airport is bugged? Even the toilets!

We sit and wait for what seems like at least half an hour. It's the worst half-hour I think I am ever going to experience. Then, finally, I see my mother and my aunt reappear from the room waving at us, and it's the most comforting sight I can imagine. It's all right, my mother says when she returns to our seats, but I can tell it isn't. For reasons that will remain a myster, my mother and my aunt were picked out of the group of *gusanos* for a full body search, taken to a small room off one of the corridors and told to undress completely. Stark naked. Then, my mother whispers to my father, they were searched by two *milicianas*. They searched everywhere, my aunt Nidia says cryptically. *¡Nos revisaron todo!* my mother confirms, and I can tell she feels angry and violated and totally humiliated. It's not the way she wanted to leave her homeland.

WE WALK out onto the deserted tarmac in single file because that is what we have been told to do, except my brother and I are holding on to my mother's hands and every step we take towards the plane's step-ladder is a step that seems to take for ever. All I can think of is the advice my friend Pepito gave me back in Banes before we left: Don't look back. Whatever you do, don't look back, or they will think you don't want to leave Cuba and they will keep you here.

I keep repeating the message in my mind: Don't look back. Don't look back. But I do. I can't help myself. For just a micro-second I turn my head around and look back, because I am leaving Cuba for good, I am leaving behind the rest of my family and my home and my friends and everybody else, and how can I not look back just once? As I turn around, just for that brief moment, I realise that there is a part of me that doesn't want to go. Despite what my parents say, despite what they have told everyone, despite what I have been saying. I am scared. I know that I can stay if I want to. All I have to do is say so to the *milicianos* I can see at the bottom of the plane steps.

I keep walking, holding tight to my mother, sweating now because I am sure, that having disobeyed everyone and looked back, that just as I reach those steps, one of the *milicianos* will put his hand on my shoulders and say, That's all right, *compañerito*, I saw you looking back, which means you don't want to leave Cuba, and that is all right, you can stay ...

WE ARE FLYING high up above the clouds somewhere over the Atlantic Ocean. It's been at least three hours since the plane took off from Havana and I am sitting by the window, next to my mother and my aunt Nidia, while my father and my brother are just across the aisle. I can tell from here that my brother is thinking, like I am, that he has just left his friends behind in Banes and he is going to miss them a lot, no matter what our mother says.

My father, on the other hand, sits there enjoying his lobster and potato salad that came in a small side dish. When the air hostess asks him, What would you like to drink with your meal, sir?, he looks at her, smiles and replies, *Señorita, lo que tenga*. Whatever you've got, Miss, which is why she has brought over a whole bottle of wine, Spanish wine so red it is the colour of blood. My father tastes it with great care and declares it to be *muy bueno*—very good. Later, before they take away the trays and bring dessert, he will eat my portion of lobster and half of my brother's. It's been a while since he has eaten with so much satisfaction and when everything is cleared away he stretches back in the seat, which is too small for someone of his size, and for a moment there he looks like a very satisfied *gusano*.

All this is a world away from Havana. When we walked up the metal stairs into the belly of what seemed to me like the biggest plane in the world, I could tell most of the other *gusanos* had not been on a plane before either, because they kept saying things like, My God! This is a really big plane! Some women were sobbing and using their best we-are-leaving-Cuba handkerchiefs to wipe away the tears, but everyone else was respectfully quiet, which is highly unusual for Cubans at any time. It's as if no one wanted to say or do anything, that might have encouraged the *milicianos*, who were still guarding the bottom of the stairs, to come up and escort you back down. Back in Banes my friend Pepito swore to me that his mother has heard of *gusanos* being marched down the plane—even after they put their seat belts on!—because their papers were not in order or something equally serious. Sometimes they even turn the plane back!

So, we enter the plane and find our seats, strap our seat belts on as we are told to and then sit there sweating, because it's very hot. Finally, once the doors are locked, I take one final look through the small window but the airport terminal is too far away now for me to confirm whether my aunt Mary and my cousins are still there, standing in the hot, tropical sun, waving us goodbye. In case they are, I wave.

Now the plane is rushing down the runway so fast it is shaking inside, which is quite scary, especially when this is your first plane trip ever. As the plane gains altitude and all I can see of Cuba is a diminishing speck of land surrounded entirely by a brilliant blue sea, the little light above the seats goes 'ping', meaning you can undo your seat belt, stretch your legs or go to the bathroom.

Right on cue, as soon as the little light goes off, there is this great communal sigh of relief inside the plane and everyone on board, I swear, starts talking at once and waving their arms around and acting just like normal Cubans. *Por fin*, I can hear my father say to no one in particular. At last. And his face is the face of a man who can finally relax.

Later, the air hostesses come around with a tray of cigarettes. American cigarettes. I watch my father light up, take a deep puff, look at the cigarette in his hand—This is a Chesterfield, he says to my mother across the aisle—and then give a little smile because it has been a long time since he had a capitalist cigarette. Cuban socialist cigarettes have no filter and precious little tobacco inside their thin paper wrappers. I know what this means. It means that from now until the end of time my parents will compare everything to how it used to be in Cuba, for better or worse. After dinner, when they dim the lights and the plane goes quiet again, or as quiet as you can expect of a plane-load of Cubans, I look out the window and all I can see is darkness.

Soon, you can see Madrid if you look down through the window. At least I think it is Madrid. Thousands and thousands of little points of light blink on and off hypnotically.

As we get closer, the lights get brighter and within minutes the plane starts to descend. My ears pop (what's going on here?), and then we land on the tarmac with a huge thud that shakes everything and everyone inside the Iberia jet. Some of the *gusanos* on board clap when the plane touches down, or they make the sign of the cross as we are now, finally, on firm ground.

Like my parents, I am pretty excited to have landed in Madrid but I am as nervous as I think they must be about what awaits us in Spain. My parents know a handful of families who used to live in Banes and have since settled in Spain but we have no relatives here and no idea what Madrid is like, how to get around the city, let alone where to go to find work, which my father says will be his number one priority. In the longer-term, our plan is to apply to migrate to the United States and join my aunt and uncle in New York as soon as possible. It's what most Cubans do when they leave Cuba: they make their way to the United States, preferably to Miami, which is hot and steamy and bright, just like Cuba. Except they have air conditioning. In truth, we have no idea how long we will have to wait in Spain or how we will manage. We don't have any money with us, although we know my aunt Mirta in New York has cabled money to a family friend, Nora, who is from Banes and is now living in Madrid with her two daughters. They are supposed to be at the airport waiting for us.

As we get ushered into the terminal, we all notice just how cold it is. It's March. In fact, the coldest March for years, as we discover later, and the suits my mother had made for my brother and me, and which we hated so much because they were hot and itchy in Havana, are now useless against the cold. It must be quite a sight, this plane-load of Cuban *gusanos*, happy and sad at the same time for having left their homeland and now exposed to the brutally cold reality of what is supposed to be a European spring.

As my father collects our old suitcases so we can go through Customs and Immigration, we spot our friend Nora on the other side, waving at us. I swear I can almost hear my father relax. There is much hugging and welcoming and questions about Banes and, How are things in Cuba? *Malísimamente mal*. Really bad, is the obvious reply. And then she hands my father a big fat envelope full of big, colourful notes, thousands and thousands of Spanish *pesetas*, which makes me think— wrongly, as it turns out—that we must now be capitalist millionaires or at least members of what Fidel calls the bourgeoisie. Then, suitcases at the ready, we and the rest of the *gusanos* are directed to buses that wait outside, where it is really, really cold, for the trip into Madrid and, in particular, to the Migration Offices, where all Cubans must go to register on arrival and be provided with whatever assistance the Spanish government can offer.

It's warm inside the bus, which smells new and is shiny and nothing like those old American buses back in Cuba, and everyone talks at once, asking each other, Do you have anyone waiting for you here in Madrid? One woman keeps crying quietly because she already misses her family in Cuba, and I hope she stops soon because otherwise I am sure my mother will start crying too.

My eyes are glued to the big windows of the bus because I can't believe how many cars and buses there are on the road, even at this time of night. Haven't these people heard of petrol rationing? As we drive into the centre of the city there are even more cars and we go past fountains made of white marble that spout water jets high up into the sky, and there are enormous billboards with flashing lights. To my surprise, they are advertising soft drinks and refrigerators and banks and there is not a single revolutionary slogan to be seen. Then there are the shop windows all lit up and full of stuff. Toys, food, clothes. It looks decadent and rich and imperialist and nothing, I tell you, nothing at all like Cuba. My aunt Nidia keeps pointing, *Mira, mira eso* ... Look, look there, directing my eyes to another shop window full of stuff. I think there is just too much to take in in one go. I wonder if this is how the capitalists capture your mind and corrupt your heart, with all these glittering prizes that no self-respecting socialist would want.

When we get to the Migration Centre in General Sanjurjo Street in Madrid there are Spanish officials waiting to place big stamps on our passports, and others, Spaniards and

Cubans like us, who help you find accommodation for the night. The place is packed, as you would expect, and yes, we need to queue, although this time none of the *gusanos* seems to mind too much. My brother and I are dead tired and all I want is a bed. It's then that I see my parents rush to a tall, skinny man with glasses and what looks like a very expensive, very counter-revolutionary overcoat, who appears to have been waiting for us. I don't know who this man is but my parents obviously do and his presence there, of all places, appears to them as nothing short of a miracle. His name, I am about to discover, is Enriquito Martínez, and he owned the pharmacy just up the street from my parents' shop. He was one of my father's closest friends in Banes until he and his wife Armentina and his whole family left for the United States in 1960. They haven't seen each other for eleven years.

It's a miracle, my mother keeps saying—and she is right. Enriquito and his family now live in Madrid, where he has a prosperous export business, and he heard from mutual friends in the United States that we were on our way. Now he is here, waiting for us like a guardian angel, which makes me think that perhaps this is my reward for going to Sunday mass in Banes all that time rather than to the cinema. Enriquito is telling my parents that he has rented a room for us in a hotel for the next few days and tomorrow, he says to my father, we will look for an apartment. Everything is all right now, *chico*, you are in Madrid. The communists can't get you any more. Everything will be fine ...

While Enriquito the miracle-maker waits to take us to the hotel, my father queues to get his papers signed and finalised. And because he is Cuban and this is what happens when you are Cuban, he reaches the head of the queue and finds that the man who is at the desk sorting out the paperwork is someone he knows. His name is Francisco and he is from Holguin, the city where my father lived as a young man. Now my father is talking to Francisco as if they have known each other for ever, which they probably have, and then my father calls us all over, including my aunt Nidia, so we can say hello too.

All I want is to go to bed because now I am really tired but Francisco just keeps talking. Migrating to the United States won't be easy, he is telling my parents as he sorts out the paperwork. You know, there is a long wait, probably two years, because there is only a limited number of visas every year for Cubans. And it's not easy to find good jobs here in Spain when you are an exile, you know. If you want my advice, he says—not waiting to see whether we do, because he is Cuban and Cubans give you advice even when you don't ask for it—my advice is to go somewhere else instead of *El Norte*. Go to a place that needs migrants; a place with a great future, where they welcome you with open arms. If it wasn't for the fact that my wife is in Cuba and I am waiting to get permission for her to leave, I'd pack up my bags tomorrow, he adds.

What are you talking about? my father asks Francisco. What's this place?

Australia, *mi socio*, Francisco says. Go to Australia.

That's another story. Now, I just want to go to bed.

LUIS M. GARCIA

Luis Manuel Garcia was born in Banes, Cuba, in 1959. After going into exile in early 1971 and living in Madrid, Spain, for twelve months, the Garcias migrated to Australia. Luis was educated in south-western Sydney—where he learned English—and then went on to obtain an Arts degree from the University of Sydney, majoring in government and public administration. In 1981 he gained a journalism apprentice-ship with *The Australian Financial Review*, before moving to *The Sydney Morning Herald*, where he edited a number of sections across the paper and was once acting Chief of Staff. He has also spent time as a media adviser in state politics and as Chief of Staff to the former Leader of the Opposition in New South Wales (1998–2002). He is a Partner with the corporate communications firm Cannings and is the co-author of *Chika*, the biography of a New South Wales politician. Luis is married, with a daughter and a son. He continues to wait for a change of government in Cuba so that he may revisit the country of his birth.

COPYRIGHT AND PICTURE CREDITS